DIETRICH
&
RIEFENSTAHL

———

DIETRICH

&

RIEFENSTAHL

Hollywood, Berlin,
and a Century in Two Lives

Karin Wieland

Translated by Shelley Frisch

LIVERIGHT PUBLISHING CORPORATION

A DIVISION OF W. W. NORTON & COMPANY

NEW YORK · LONDON

The translation of this work was funded by Geisteswissenschaften International—
Translation Funding for Work in the Humanities and Social Sciences from Germany,
a joint initiative of the Fritz Thyssen Foundation, the German Federal Foreign Office,
the collecting society VG WORT, and the Börsenverein des Deutschen Buchhandels
(German Publishers & Booksellers Association).

Originally published in German as *Dietrich & Riefenstahl: Der Traum von der neuen Frau*

For information about permission to reproduce selections from this book,
write to Permissions, Liveright Publishing Corporation,
a division of W. W. Norton & Company, Inc.,
500 Fifth Avenue, New York, NY 10110

For information about special discounts for bulk purchases, please contact W. W. Norton
Special Sales at specialsales@wwnorton.com or 800-233-4830

Manufacturing by RR Donnelley Westford
Book design by Lisa Buckley
Production manager: Anna Oler

Library of Congress Cataloging-in-Publication Data
Wieland, Karin.
[Dietrich & Riefenstahl. English]
Dietrich & Riefenstahl : Hollywood, Berlin, and a century in two lives / Karin Wieland ;
translated by Shelley Frisch.
pages cm
Includes bibliographical references and index.
ISBN 978-0-87140-336-0 (hardcover)
1. Dietrich, Marlene. 2. Riefenstahl, Leni. 3. Motion picture actors and actresses—
Germany—Biography. 4. Women entertainers—Germany—Biography. 5. Women motion
picture producers and directors—Germany—Biography. I. Frisch, Shelley Laura, translator.
II. Title. III. Title: Dietrich and Riefenstahl.
PN2658.D5W5513 2015
791.4302'80922—dc23
[B]
2015026548

Liveright Publishing Corporation
500 Fifth Avenue, New York, N.Y. 10110
www.wwnorton.com

W. W. Norton & Company Ltd.
Castle House, 75/76 Wells Street, London W1T 3QT

1 2 3 4 5 6 7 8 9 0

For Andrea

CONTENTS

I YOUTH *(1901–1923)*
The Streets of Berlin • 3
Body, Art, and War • 10

II CARVING OUT A CAREER *(1923–1932)*
Early Sorrow • 53
Blue • 124

III SUCCESS *(1932–1939)*
Hollywood • 177
Berlin • 258

IV WAR *(1939–1945)*
The Amazon • 319
The Soldier • 347

V PROSECUTION *(1945–1954)*
The Witness • 379
The Accused • 411

VI NEW CHAPTER OF FAME *(1954–1976)*
The Icon • 431
Camp • 448

VII THE END GAME *(1976–2003)*
In the Mattress Crypt • 497
At the Bottom of the Sea • 511

Acknowledgments • 525
Notes • 527
Suggestions for Further Reading • 575
Credits • 577
Index • 579

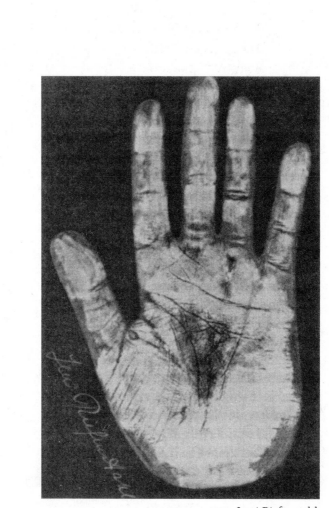

Leni Riefenstahl

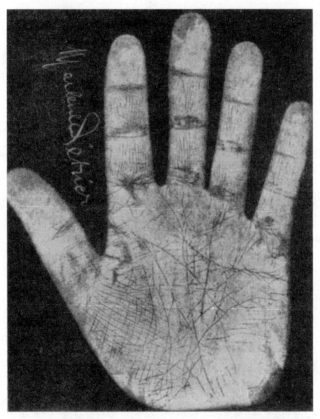

Marlene Dietrich

YOUTH

(1901–1923)

THE
STREETS
OF BERLIN

M arlene Dietrich would never forget the sounds of Schöneberg, Berlin, where she was born on December 27, 1901: soldiers marching in step, horses clip-clopping along, and trains whooshing by. Sedanstrasse, where she spent the first few years of her life, is situated on the so-called island, set off from the rest of the city by train tracks. The military had built barracks on the island, and since the time of the Franco-Prussian War, the railway was used to transport soldiers and weapons. Sedanstrasse was "a treeless part of Berlin,"[1] where the military dominated the lives of the civilian population. Marlene's father, Louis Erich Otto Dietrich, was a police lieutenant, his precinct located on the ground floor of the building where he lived with his family.

The Dietrichs were Calvinists who had been driven out of the Palatinate and settled in Brandenburg under the protection of Frederick the Great. Marlene's sister Elisabeth insisted, however, that they were actually Huguenots, who lived by the virtues of frugality,

hard work, and restraint.[2] These virtues do not seem to have been
very pronounced in her father, the son of a saddler who ran an inn
in the town of Angermünde, in the northeastern German district of
Uckermark. The Dietrichs eventually made their mark as town dignitaries. Their son Louis felt that he was destined for higher things
and sought to become an officer. He served with the Uhlans, a
cavalry regiment armed with lances, sabers, and pistols. In French
caricatures, the Uhlans were often portrayed as the quintessence
of Prussian militarism, with malevolent faces, glinting monocles,
and long lances. No officer by the name of Dietrich appears on
the ledgers of the Uhlan regiments in question, so Marlene's father
likely achieved no higher rank than a simple sergeant.[3] Even so,
he *felt* like an officer. He was elegant, generous, and popular, and
he enjoyed being seen in the company of lovely ladies and living
above his means. In the few photos of Dietrich that have been preserved, his penchant for posturing is striking: his proud, upright
stance emphasized his "lieutenant's waist," and his mustache
twirled upward. Born in 1867, he was one of the "Wilhelminians"
whose immediate ancestors had achieved it all, uniting the country
and defeating the French, but the men of his generation had no
prospect of earning fame on their own.

Louis did not remain in the military for long. In his early twenties, he switched over to police work, a career that offered the
potential of achieving esteem, security, and status, although little
in the way of advancement or pay. Berlin was divided up into individual precincts, and the official in charge of a given precinct had
to live there. The policeman was subject to a higher order. Even
after hours, he had to remain in uniform; access to taverns was
restricted; and membership in clubs was permitted only with the
consent of his superior. The policeman was an outsider, always on
duty. The only attractive part of the job was the prestige. Louis
lived beyond his means to conceal his material indigence. Marlene's

father did not tone down his brusque air of authority even within his family, where he was intent on displaying his strength, issuing orders, demanding obedience, and preserving his own power. It was abundantly evident in his appearance as well, notably in his wedding photo, taken in 1898, which displays his enduring love of uniforms and posing for the camera. The woman at his side looks tacked on, three of her fingers peeking eerily out of the crook of his left arm. He is paying no attention to her. Bare-headed and clad in his Sunday uniform, he stares straight ahead, while his bride, twenty-two-year-old Wilhelmina Elisabeth Josefine Felsing (who went by "Josefine"), peers at him timidly.

Like so many Berliners, the Felsings had moved there from elsewhere, in this case from Giessen. They had been clockmakers for generations. The shop they opened in 1820 was one of the best known businesses in old Berlin. The Felsings specialized in elegant clocks and proudly called themselves "Purveyors to Their Majesties the Emperor and Empress." In 1895, Josefine's father Albert Felsing donated a golden clock to the Kaiser Wilhelm Memorial Church. The family had a stylish residence in a building annex of Unter den Linden 20, which they owned. They were proud of their proximity to the royal castle and were not pleased to see their daughter marry a police lieutenant, which meant a drop in Josefine's social status. But Josefine was drawn in by Louis Dietrich's stylish appearance and fine-sounding words.

Louis and Josefine's first child, Elisabeth Ottilie, was born two years after the wedding, and their second, Marie Magdalene, followed in 1901. Josefine, now twenty-five years old, no longer saw her husband as much of a hero and went to great lengths to bring up the two girls in accordance with her ideals. She ran a tight ship in her household. Marie Magdalene smarted under this matriarchal rule. She and her sister differed in many ways: Elisabeth was the ugly duckling, shy and nervous, and Marie Magdalene the pretty child who was proud of her long hair. Elisabeth claimed that men went crazy for her sister when Marie Magdalene was only ten years old.

The everyday monotony in the police household was punctuated by several moves: in 1904, to nearby Kolonnenstrasse, and two years later to bustling Potsdamer Strasse. Elisabeth Ottilie wrote that she and her sister were afraid of these "passages." The girls must have sensed their mother's anxiety about further social decline. Louis's superiors gave him the poorest evaluations, and the change of apartment from the upper floor to the mezzanine took on a symbolic significance. Then Louis fell ill. "Once, my mother moved us to where my father was. She would walk us by the hospital, so my father could look down from his barred window and see us," Marie Magdalene would recall later.[4] On August 5, 1908, Police Lieutenant Louis Erich Otto Dietrich succumbed to his nervous disorder (which was likely syphilitic in origin) at the age of forty-one. The disgrace of the family's comedown was now compounded by the disgrace of this death. Josefine kept the cause of death from her children, no doubt fearing that their father's illness could have been transmitted to them.

Josefine, now listed as "Widow Dietrich" in the telephone book, moved the family to Tauentzienstrasse. As the daughter of a clockmaker, she was adamant about punctuality and discipline but lacked any interest in the pursuit of pleasure. She maintained strict control over her daughters' daily routine: she brought them to school at 8 a.m. and picked them up at 1 p.m. Half an hour was allotted for lunch, then the girls did an hour of homework. At 3 p.m., a "mademoiselle" or "miss" came to converse with them in their respective native languages. Sometimes they went for a walk in the park. Then there was another half-hour of homework. Seven-thirty was bedtime. Three times a week, they went to gymnastics, and twice a week to piano, guitar, and violin lessons. To avoid idleness or unnecessary reflection, Josefine forced her daughters to adhere to a daily routine of strictly regulated monotony.

o o o

Leni Riefenstahl was born in Wedding, a section of Berlin that reeked of confinement, adversity, and desolation, yet also came to be associated with modernity. Berlin attracted immigrants from the eastern provinces in search of employment. These immigrants would transform Berlin into a modern metropolis. Riefenstahl, a first-generation Berliner, was one of them. Her mother, Bertha Ida Scherlach, was the eighteenth child born to a carpenter in West Prussia in 1880. Leni's grandfather had set out for Berlin to seek his fortune but did not find work, and his children had to support the family. Riefenstahl claimed to have come from a solid middle-class household, but the few facts she revealed about her childhood and teenage years suggest that this was not the case. Her mother sewed blouses, and the rest of that branch of the family seems to have eked out a living by producing piecework at home. In one of her few written recollections about her relatives, she described the entire family sitting at a long wide table gluing cigarette papers.[5]

Leni's mother was a pretty, inquisitive young woman who dreamed of becoming an actress and using beauty and art as an escape route. But as a seamstress without formal training, she would need to rely on marriage to elevate her station in life. She met her future husband at a costume ball. Alfred Theodor Paul Riefenstahl was a plumber in Brandenburg and sought a wife who would help him manage his business. The young Miss Scherlach was an ambitious woman who shared his dream of upward mobility. They married on April 5, 1902. The wedding photograph was taken not in a studio, but in a banquet hall. The bride and groom are standing in front of a long table adorned with floral arrangements, with a kind of stage curtain in the background. The bride is wearing a high-necked white gown with a veil and train, which form an appealing contrast to her dark hair. In her left hand she clutches a bouquet of white roses, and her right hand is linked with her groom's. He was a tall, cheerful, robust man with blue eyes and blond hair. Riefenstahl was the kind of man who liked to break out in song and laugh loudly at his own jokes, although he could be roused to fury in an instant, as his daughter would discover. But in his black frock coat and white bow tie, he looked trustworthy and friendly on his wedding day. He posed bareheaded, his well-ironed top hat clamped under his left arm, with his bride standing bolt upright, looking proud and aloof.

Five months later, on August 22, Bertha gave birth to their daughter, Helene Amalia Bertha Riefenstahl. For the first years of Leni's life, the family lived in an apartment on Prinz-Eugen-Strasse in Wedding, a rather short street by Berlin standards, located near Leopoldplatz, around the corner from the crematorium. When Leni was three years old, her brother Heinz was born, and the family was complete. The Riefenstahls aspired to belong to the new middle class. Alfred's business was doing well. He was both a modernizer and a traditionalist, enthusiastic about progress in the technical and the economic realms but insistent on his special status as a craftsman, which set him above the rank and file of the labor force. Wedding was a case in point of both new industrial production and new social adversity. The factories of Osram, AEG, Rotaprint, Schering, and Schwartzkopff made this part of Berlin one of the key industrialized areas in the city. Multistory tenements sprang up to house the workers, many of whom were soon cheated of their hopes for a better life. They lost their jobs, turned to drink, and went to seed, and could be seen staggering through the streets of Berlin with nowhere to turn for help. The sight of this adversity right at Alfred's doorstep must have strengthened his resolve to achieve social distinction.

A photograph of his five-year-old daughter shows her standing in front of a tree in the woods and staring anxiously into the camera, her blonde hair adorned with a crooked white ribbon. One hand is holding a branch; the other is hidden behind her back. She is wearing a white jumper with dark ribbons at the neck and wrists, her underskirt peeking out. The girl looks tense and presses her lips together. Leni had yet to learn how to oblige other people. She shut herself up in her room to be alone with her dreams. During her very first visit to the theater, when she was four, Leni discovered that the world behind the curtain could be an enduring sanctuary. She was drawn to art at an early age. Her father was not pleased; he wanted a practical-minded girl who could buckle down and run a big household.

Leni used her body as a path to art and a means of escaping her father's pervasive power. An anxious girl by nature, she steeled her will and put her courage to the test. She played sports ambitiously and intensively. Training her body strengthened her in facing her father. First she joined a swim club, then a gymnastics club. Her father agreed to let her join the swim club, but was opposed to the gymnastics club. When he found out that she was doing gymnastics anyway, he punished her severely. It would become an enduring pattern of her life: Leni had to go behind her father's back to fulfill her wishes and thus herself.

Her ambitious physical training went hand in hand with her blissful relationship to nature. "I grew up as a 'child of nature,' amid trees and bushes, with plants and insects, shielded and sheltered," the girl from Wedding wrote about her happy childhood.[6] She regarded nature as a mirror of her soul, and worshipped it for the rest of her life. A photograph of the nine-year-old with her brother Heinz once again shows her dressed all in white, with sneakers and a tennis racket. Her brother, sporting a sailor suit, gazes jauntily into the camera, but his older sister appears reticent. Her dark eyes are sad, yet she radiates a strong physical presence, the ribbon now perched properly on her head.

BODY,
ART,
AND WAR

L eni's youth began with the revolution of 1918. At the age of sixteen, she dropped out of the exclusive private school she had been attending in the Tiergarten section of Berlin. (There she was very weak in history and singing, but at the top of her class in mathematics and gymnastics.) As she grew older, her father became more insistent that she live up to his expectations. He was moody, short-tempered, irascible—and petrified that his daughter would lose her virginity. He wanted to be informed about every step she took. Her mother stood by helplessly. She thought her husband was too strict, with both her children and herself. They were now living outside the city; Alfred had bought a house in Zeuthen. As a child, Leni had spent happy weekends here; she made her first attempts at swimming at Lake Zeuthen, and built up little retreats in trees, behind bushes, and in the reeds. But she was no longer a child, and nature was not enough to fulfill her. Leni experienced the dilemma of her parents' marriage up close:

the dreams of the little seamstress from West Prussia had not come true. Bertha did better her social situation, but she longed for the kind of success in beauty and art that the world of acting offered. Her husband, whose full focus was on his work and family, felt threatened by that world. He feared and fought the exaltation Bertha sought in art, and Leni bore the brunt of his ire.

As a girl from Wedding, where money and grammar were in short supply, as Joseph Roth quipped, Leni aspired to join those way on top someday.[1] But a house in Zeuthen was not in one of the elegant villa districts, such as Dahlem or Grunewald. Actually, her father had merely returned to where he had come from. He had turned his back on the city and brought his family to safety, as he saw it. Meanwhile, however, his daughter was testing out her effect on men and savoring their attentive glances. If she was out with her father, though, he barked: "Keep your eyes down; don't look at men like that"—and she obeyed.[2] When she walked through the streets alone, Leni waited for a man's gaze to rest on her shoulders, her legs, or her mouth, then lay in her bed at night replaying such moments. She thought about the city streets, where the stream of people never let up, and longed to be the center of attention in that life.

Leni began to defy her father. Every look that she returned violated his established rules. Her pride rebelled against walking next to him through the streets with her head lowered—yet she may have done it over and over anyway. But the more accustomed she grew to admiring sidelong glances from strange men, the more self-confident she became.

Her first stage was the city itself. After school, she would dash into the Tiergarten, pirouette on her roller skates, and await an audience. She was soon surrounded by admirers. The Berlin in which these little performances took place was the Berlin of the Great War, yet Riefenstahl never spoke about a wartime childhood with casualties, pain, and suffering.

Wilhelmine Berlin was developing a romantic rapture for steel, tracks, cables, high-speed elevated trains, and high-rise buildings. Wilhelm II had recognized the significance of technology and had arranged to improve the technical colleges and expand the engineering curriculum. Under his reign, Berlin became the model of the hectic city. Wide streets allowed traffic to come roaring through, and the Kaiser proclaimed "the century of the motor." Aristocratic ladies visiting Berlin rushed breathlessly across Potsdamer Platz and embraced one another with relief when they reached the other side. There was a big jumble of streetcars, newspaper vendors, handcarts, bicycles, and pedestrians pushing and shoving. Money was made and money was spent. Women wore plumed hats and laced-up bodices, and there was reveling on the streets and in dance halls. The city was amorphous, expansive, cosmopolitan, and ambitious. Berlin was intent on blotting out the impecunious past and flaunting the hypermodern present.

The desire for progress and prosperity trumped any interest in finding solutions to political problems. The Kaiser regarded prosperity as a new form of power. This attitude was frowned upon by the old aristocracy and the educated classes, but it appealed to the newly wealthy and those who aspired to wealth, like Alfred and Bertha Riefenstahl.

Leni's father liked to see himself as a foresighted businessman. In 1885, the first district heating system had been mounted in Beelitz, outside of Berlin, and since then, central heating and modern lavatories had been installed in new buildings. Alfred—who specialized in sales and installation of new technologies—earned good money, athough he was a long way from being solidly middle class, as his daughter later claimed. At the beginning of the twentieth century, a family with only two children was no longer out of the ordinary even in the working classes. Leni's brother Heinz was a quiet boy who hoped to become an interior designer, but his father wanted him to join the family business, as an engineer who would contribute to the modernization of Berlin.

The transformation of Berlin from a locus of imperial grandeur into a diverse collective was already underway before World War I. New social policies and functional design signaled a break with the nineteenth century. An unembellished coupling of form and function became the hallmark of a power-driven German industrial culture. In some sense, Alfred Riefenstahl regarded himself as an agent of modernist functionality; he looked to the future and was proud of his country's technological and economic capabilities. He and his wife felt that they were living in the right city at the right time. Berlin's lack of tradition was her chance to make a fresh start. Alfred applied his sound business sense and craftsmanship skills to improving his lot in life and partaking in the economic upswing. The Riefenstahls embodied the civic spirit of the new Berlin.

Although Alfred and Bertha signed their daughter up for piano lessons, their motive was less the love of music than a desire to enhance her prospects on the marriage market. Alfred's interest in art and culture did not extend beyond occasional visits to the theater. In his mind, actresses were women of loose morals. His wife, by contrast, felt that an actress ranked just below a countess, and supported her daughter's interest in acting. The new art of film acting was an especially fitting profession for dilettantes who believed in their artistic calling. Mother and daughter enjoyed learning all they could about movie stars. Leni began to entertain the idea of acting in a motion picture, and she responded to a small advertisement in the *B.Z. am Mittag* seeking twenty talented girls for film shoots at the Grimm-Reiter School of Dance on Kurfürstendamm 6. Helene Grimm-Reiter enjoyed a fine reputation as a trainer for stage and screen. Leni knew quite well that her father would never allow her to act in a movie, but her curiosity to find out whether she would be chosen won out over her fear of her father. One girl after another stepped forward, was given a brief glance by Frau Grimm-Reiter, and was told to leave her name and address. Leni was delighted to see Frau Grimm-Reiter put a check mark after her name. When she was about to head out, she peered through a crack in the door of a large room and saw young dancers rehearsing. The room reverberated with piano music and the teacher's commands. Leni wanted to be one of these girls, working hard to train her body to express grace and strength.

For the mother and her daughter, a bourgeois life meant showiness, beauty, and a carefree attitude, and they found all three of these characteristics in the cinema, which offered an escape from reality as a bonus. Leni learned to play the piano and draw, but her home life felt confining and gloomy. When she wrote about her youth in Zeuthen, the reader senses her unhappiness. Her father insisted that she become a typist in his company, although she felt the tug of an artist's calling.

Her mother agreed to let her sign up at the dance studio, and Leni was chosen for the film. They did not breathe a word of this news to her father. She rejoiced to herself yet did not dare to disobey her father, so had to turn down the film role. Even so, she stepped up her dance training: "No pain or effort was too great for me; I practiced outside of school for many hours a day, misusing every rail or banister for that purpose. On the streets I would do great leaps and prances, and barely noticed the way people stared at me, shaking their heads."[3] There was instruction in rhythmic gymnastics and dance exercises, interval training, fantasy dance, improvisation, diagrammatic representations of dance, and film studies. It was difficult at first, but her body was used to intensive training. Leni's transformation into a dancer took place behind her father's back, while the old world was falling apart. Triumph over pain and over her body was all that truly mattered.

Otto Dix had made Anita Berber the quintessence of the decadent 1920s when he painted her iconic portrait, and now it was

Anita Berber, of all people, who was clearing the way for Leni's first stage performance. Berber, who had also been a student of dance at Grimm-Reiter, was a rising star just after the revolution of 1918. Frau Grimm-Reiter was planning for her prominent pupil to perform, but Berber fell ill and had to cancel. The posters had been printed and the room rented. No one had any idea how to find someone to substitute for her. Then Leni admitted that she had been secretly observing Berber during rehearsals and had reenacted her dances in private. Why not let her stand in for Berber? Alfred was sent off to a hastily arranged card party, and his daughter hurried onstage. She later wrote that her performance was exuberant and the applause neverending. No one appeared to mind Berber's absence, we are told, and everyone now loved Leni Riefenstahl.[4]

The story did not end well. When her father got wind of what she had done, he sent her away to a girls' boarding school in the Harz Mountains, in the hope that Thale, the "pearl of the Harz," would cure her of any artistic ambitions. In Berlin, the name Thale still had the ring of high society; Thale was where ladies with nervous conditions were once sent.[5] Alfred wanted Leni to marry a rich man and forget about art. After a year in the Harz, she wrote her father a letter swearing off art and expressing her willingness to work at his company. However, she insisted on being allowed to continue taking dance classes—purely for fun. Alfred agreed, and welcomed his daughter to the Berlin office.

Women who worked as typists in Berlin may have dutifully rushed to work every morning, but many dreamed of becoming film stars when they went to the movies in the evening. They had a good grip on their modest lives; they were young, unmarried, and employed. They wore their hair short, smoked cigarettes dangling from cigarette holders in perfect form, and knew their way around men. Leni was not like this. She was also young, unmarried, and employed, but she worked in her father's office. Alfred appeared to be quite pleased that the repentant sinner had returned. In these troubled times, he wanted reassurance that his family was gathered around him. His wife kept house, and Leni and Heinz were right there with him at the company. He had prevailed: he had forbidden his son to work in interior design and had disabused his daughter of her nonsensical notions about dance. He was upholding the principles of a patriarch, even though that was no longer the modern thing to do. Now more than ever, he was intent on maintaining his professional pride, and he regarded his family's participation in the business as an expression of firmly ingrained class consciousness.

But he was sadly mistaken. Leni was hoodwinking her father. She had no intention of giving up art and her idolization of other performers. Quite the opposite: she aspired to be an idol herself, and she was leading a double life. She spent many hours a day on stenography, bookkeeping, and typing, and devoted three days a week to art. Her cheeks shed their chubbiness and her features were now marked by defiance and denial. She took up sports again and signed up at a tennis club. Her father had agreed to this activity because tennis was regarded as the sport of the wealthy, and he hoped she would meet a rich man there. Every day, father and daughter took the train to the city. She had long ago stopped trying to strike up a conversation with her father because he would shut down on the spot, and he had no interest in her plans for the future anyway. Day after day, they sat across from each other in the compartment in silence. The father read the newspaper, and his daughter parked herself in the corner and dreamed. Alfred sensed her growing discontentment. He was exasperated to realize that she was no longer finding fulfillment in her family, their work together in the office, and life in the country. Leni had discovered the city for herself. Berlin knocked you down or lifted you up; this was where you would sink or swim. An ambitious girl and the hectic pace of the city were a good fit. It was not a moral clash that stood between the father and his daughter; it was the attitude toward life of two different generations. Leni had come to realize from her father that times had changed. She was the new type, and her father "the fossil, the man who had outlived his day, the man from a sinking epoch who refused to believe that the tide of the earth had turned."[6] He embraced new technology, but his lifestyle and family values remained firmly patriarchal.

Leni had grown up with the pride of modern Wilhelmine Germany, but also with the slogans of the *Wandervogel* movement, a youth organization that emphasized hiking, camping, and the spirit of adventure. The previous century had offered a well-ordered world. Age and time had had different dimensions. Being young was equated with a lack of dependability and respectability. All gestures that might have suggested the curiosity or exuberance of youth were avoided, and people as young as forty took pleasure in stylizing themselves as venerable old ladies and gentlemen. By contrast, the new generation now claimed that just as the century was young, so were the people in it. Those in the Youth Movement demonstrated their lack of affiliation with the world of their parents. Girls wore their dresses loose instead of tightly laced, and boys preferred open-necked shirts (known as *Schillerkragen*) to confining starched ones. Both boys and girls opted for sandals. The vitality of the young body was contrasted with bourgeois life paralyzed by convention. Air, light, and sun liberated young people from the historical deadwood of past eras. The Youth Movement strongly emphasized comradeship. Mastery over one's own body held out the promise of courage, strength, and stamina. Personal experience took the place of reason. To be was to do.[7]

Leni did not belong to the *Wandervogel* movement; she was too young to join. But like the two friends Walter and Ulrich in Robert Musil's novel *The Man Without Qualities*, she had "just been in time to catch a glimmer of it." This movement did not draw in the masses; it grew no larger than several thousand. Even so, young people were swayed by it: "Something at that time passed through the thicket of beliefs, as when many trees bend before one wind—a sectarian and reformist spirit, the blissful better self arising and setting forth, a little renascence and reformation such as only the best epochs know; and entering into the world in those days, even in coming round the very first corner one felt the breath of the spirit on one's cheeks."[8] It was the spirit of vitality, of nature, and of community. All this, along with praise of technology, pleasure in objectivity, a will to succeed, and pride in the virtues of crafts-manship, formed the backdrop to Riefenstahl's youth. She, too, felt a breath of this spirit on her cheeks. The wordless art of the dance was her first bond with the trends of the era. The pioneers of mod-ern dance celebrated their first successes in Berlin.[9] The American Isadora Duncan was the first to appear onstage barefoot and in see-through Grecian tunics in Berlin.[10] Her admirers were at a loss for words, never having seen anything of the kind; her critics quipped that she was seeking her *soul* with her *sole*. Lovers of classical ballet felt as though they had been duped and turned their backs on her. In their way of thinking, Duncan's dances were pure dilettantism. German *Lebensreformer* (back-to-nature advocates) and followers of the Youth Movement, however, saw that she was one of them. This impression was confirmed several times over, by everything from her loose garments to her sandals to her reading of Nietzsche. The Germans found a dance concept of this kind, with its blend of Nietzsche, critique of civilization, feminism, nature worship, and spiritualism, irresistibly appealing. Duncan, who embraced the role of the anti-bourgeois, drew in young women from good fam-ilies who now wanted to learn dance-based gymnastics instead of ballet. In 1904, she opened a school in a villa in Grunewald to train the dancers of the future. "My body is the temple of my art," was her motto.

Riefenstahl cited two names in connection with her career as a dancer: Anita Berber, whose risqué behavior and lust for life had made her a role model for girls from good middle-class families, and Mary Wigman, whose school in Dresden she attended in 1923. Wigman, from Hanover, had been one of the first dance students of Émile Jaques-Dalcroze, who gave lessons in his *méthode rhythmique* in Hellerau, known as the "garden city." His maxim to his dancers was, "Now say it with your body." People needed to find their way back to a harmony of mind and body, he explained, a harmony that had fallen by the wayside in the course of civilization. Hellerau was a laboratory for modernity. Kafka, Le Corbusier, Poelzig, Diaghilev, and Rilke visited Hellerau on several occasions. Wigman lived there with Ada Bruhn, who would later marry the architect Ludwig Mies van der Rohe, and with Erna Hoffmann, who would marry the psychiatrist Hans Prinzhorn. Every person was artistically gifted, every person could be cured of the harm wrought by civilization, and every person could become someone other than who he or she was. Experimentation trumped tradition. This unbridled dilettantism and belief in the life-altering power of art made prewar Germany a field of experimentation for the new century.

Wigman found the perfect way to express the prevailing sentiments in the period immediately following the war, when people were fluctuating between euphoria and depression. In both ecstatic theater and expressive dance, the body was made to speak. She dispensed not only with music, but also with classical ballet costumes. The focus was on the self, barefoot. Wigman danced with such energy that the floor shook. She gave her dances abstract names that underscored the metaphysical background of her art. She preached a virtually cultic approach to one's own body, and she choreographed sacral themes and staged archaic rituals. Wigman made dance an art of the chosen few, an approach that appealed to Riefenstahl. Wigman was a modern artist; while pursuing her calling, she did not neglect the professional aspect. In 1920, she opened her own school in Dresden. In describing her pupils, she commented:

I also believe that there is quite a bit of justified egoism in all these young women, an egoism that starts by having them seek out themselves before taking on their surroundings and the world at large. Seeking themselves, feeling themselves, experiencing themselves. Dance is an expression of a higher vitality, a declaration of belief in the present without any intellectual digressions. Unimpeded by the past, and as yet to form any notion of the future, the young generation of women lives in the present and expresses this belief in dance.[11]

Many people had trouble grasping the notion of an explicitly unsentimental and energetic dance performed by a woman, but young women were enthralled and quite a few wanted to become artists in order to break with authority and tradition once and for all. The question of whether they were actually talented was of secondary importance. Riefenstahl was one of these young women.

She had stubbornly refused to comply with her father's vision for her future. She was neither looking for a suitable husband nor was she hoping to wind up as a junior director at her father's company. Her eventual departure to Dresden was preceded by grueling years marked by relentless quarrels that were followed by reconciliations. Alfred could not bear the thought of men paying to watch his daughter's body on stage. Indifferent to art, he regarded dance as no more than a display of erotic allure. And there were plenty of stories going around about expensive presents being exchanged for sexual favors in the dressing room. For a master craftsman, having a daughter become an artist signaled a betrayal of his professional honor. He told his daughter that if he were to read her name on an advertising pillar, he would spit in front of it. A study of the upward mobility patterns of daughters of skilled workers in the Weimar Republic concluded: "of the 61 visual artists and artisans, 3 are daughters of master craftsmen or 4.9 hundredths among 96 actresses and women singers, we have only 3 daughters of master craftsmen, that is, 3.1 hundredths of the total number."[12] Leni Riefenstahl was one of them. At some point, her father capitulated to the will of his daughter. Alfred admitted defeat and declared his willingness to finance "top-notch training" for her.

She received instruction in classical ballet from a once-famous Russian principal dancer and spent time at her dance studio. Leni was actually too old to have success in such a strenuous profession, but she was never put off by obstacles of this kind, either as a young or as an old woman. She wanted to show the whole world what she was made of. "I practiced until I was sometimes ready to black out from exhaustion, but time and again, I was able to overcome my weakness through sheer force of will," she said.[13] Her mornings were reserved for toe dancing, and in the afternoons she practiced expressive dance. A photograph from this period shows her in a tutu with bulging thighs. She is smiling uncertainly into the camera, but it is easy to tell that she is enjoying the display of her body. She had yet to decide between the enchanting artificiality of the ballerina and the dead seriousness of the expressive dancer. Ballet is concentrated lightness; expressive dance is pure energy. The ballerina is pure nineteenth century, and represents the ideal of the woman as a creature who serves only the beautiful. A ballerina dances the steps that the choreographer has arranged for her and masks her effort with a smile. An expressive dancer, by contrast, is the harbinger of the twentieth century, proclaiming the end of sentimental emotion and mawkish beauty. She creates her choreography on her own and obeys only the voice within her. It is not technical brilliance that is in the foreground; only the expression counts. Sigmund Freud was putting the history of the woman down on paper, while at the same time the expressive dancer ventured to put her innermost feelings on display onstage and avow them to everyone in the audience. The form her art took was hers alone. She had parted ways with her male creator and brought herself forth as an artist. It was through her body rather than in words that she pointed the way into the creative unconscious.

In 1922, Riefenstahl turned twenty. She was yearning for the event that would finally bring her into adulthood. The thought of the "not yet" preyed on her mind. She had *not yet* lost her virginity, and she had *not yet* achieved her breakthrough as an artist. Her adolescence had coincided with a grand historical event from which she was now profiting: The lost war had paved her way to her career. In the newly established Weimar Republic, women were put on an equal footing with men. Even as a child, she had not wanted to defer to her father's authority. She mobilized her body against her father's all-pervading power. Defiantly and mutely, she subjugated her body to her will. She played sports and grew strong. At home, she shut herself in her room and abandoned herself to her dreams. Expressive dance was the culmination of her desires: Her body gave expression to the messages within her, and she came under the sway of a new order that was no longer her father's. Riefenstahl's struggle with her father's authority corresponded with the end of monarchic rule. The stage was empty. The Kaiser had fled to Holland and kept busy by chopping down trees there; his anachronistic court vanished into thin air. Berlin became the epitome of itself: a city of the traditionless masses.

The soldiers returning home had entered the city through the Brandenburg Gate, which was bedecked for the occasion. For them, Berlin was the embodiment of what they had fought for. Nowhere was their futile battle for national greatness clearer than at the sight of the undamaged city. Berlin, the city of the vanquished—and a city of women—had remained intact. The beaten-down man and the New Woman came face to face. In 1918, the German man was a symbol of history and the German woman a symbol of society. Politicians did not trust this city of Berlin, which had thrown itself headlong into the arms of women and society. The first German republic was proclaimed in Weimar, not in Berlin. By choosing the

city of classical writers, the elite of the period between the two
world wars were once again counting on the decisive force and
power of the word. But things had changed. The new physicality
was a child of the war. In the legendary 1920s, the word was mistrusted and the body celebrated.[14] The new faces and bodies were
a reflection of a society that played the great equalizer. They were
slick, unembellished, well trained, and matter-of-fact. The world of
the aristocracy had gone under; the new societal dynamics not only
changed ballroom dancing, but also rendered ballet meaningless.
Harmony and serenity were passé; the new era called for expression
and strength. Many people—primarily young women—embarked
on a quest for a new (body) language that "lies dormant" within
every individual, as Mary Wigman claimed. Those who wanted to
keep up with the times engaged in rhythmic gymnastics or tried
out expressive dance. Young women could not wait to sign up
for gymnastics and dance schools, which sprang up everywhere.
Dance, a perpetual present, was well suited to Berlin, which was
an unending work in progress and constantly reinventing itself.
"Modern art reflected the experience of crises that traditional art
could not address. It expressed modernity in modern terms—and
modern liberations as well."[15]

For Alfred and Bertha Riefenstahl, the lack of tradition in Berlin
offered an opportunity to move up the social ladder. In a sense,
their daughter was continuing along this path, because her success
as an artist hinged on the end of traditional art. A period of experimentation was underway. All those who were inclined to express
what was on their minds with no holds barred were welcome to
join in. Young girls with no more than a smidgen of talent felt
called upon to demonstrate their dancing ability in public. By 1920,
Mary Wigman was noting with alarm: "Dilettantism grew, as one
might expect, because up to that point, there were no yardsticks
and directions to assess minor and major talents. Everyone had
to figure it out on her own, in anxious isolation, worrying about

her share of fame."[16] The audience got used to applauding sketchy presentations. Self-designated dance masters opened schools that enjoyed healthy enrollments.

In 1923, Leni's father allowed her to apply to Wigman's school in Dresden, which was housed in a villa with an enormous garden.[17] The rehearsal spaces had the size and functional look of a factory—empty rooms flooded with light and walls painted in multicolored glossy varnish. The instruments were set up in a corner, and there were chairs for people who stopped in. Wigman's own living space, which was also in the villa, was similarly simple, functional, colorful, and sparsely furnished. And then there was Wigman herself, enveloped in cigarette smoke, clad in extravagant garb, in front of the red or gold studio walls and focused intensely on her students' presentations.

Photographs of the school's daily routine show young barefoot women in light clothing performing all kinds of acrobatic routines in the garden. They are studying and encouraging one another, giving rounds of applause. The atmosphere is upbeat and casual, yet focused. By contrast, the ensuing recitals had the young girls playing priestesses clad in black, looking somber and trance-like. The Wigman school was a tight-knit community, with Wigman's charismatic personality its undisputed center. She taught her students that dance arose from the unconscious.[18] She gave her dancers the freedom to do as they wished, provided that their movements were well founded and well motivated. Wigman was also devoted to caring for the girls entrusted to her. "I see her before me cooking thick soups in enormous pots to feed her lean and hungry pupils," the writer Vicki Baum recalled.[19] Wigman attended to their every need, helping them out with issues ranging from lovesickness to homesickness.

Riefenstahl joined the master class: "The very next day I was allowed to audition for Frau Wigman and was accepted into her master class, where I took lessons along with Palucca, Yvonne

Georgi and Vera Skoronel."[20] Nevertheless, she did not enjoy her time in Dresden. She was bothered by Wigman's ascetic style and did not want to dispense with music. Moreover, she was lonely and assailed by doubts about her talent, which was no wonder in view of the aptitude of her fellow students. In secret, she rehearsed the dances she liked in a room she rented for this express purpose. In so doing, she was replicating her standard pattern: She had to keep her talent to herself, work herself hard in solitude, prepare to embark on her victory lap and dazzle the world with her art.

Riefenstahl felt unmoored. If she did not find confirmation for her exceptional qualities, she took to her heels. She left the disciplined community of women and returned to Berlin. There is not a single reference to Riefenstahl in Wigman's letters, essays, or notes. And she does not appear in Wigman's ample photo albums of important performances and family photos of former students. She is nowhere to be found among the young women with their serious expressions and matching hairdos, a group that included enormously successful dancers such as Gret Palucca, Vera Skoronel, and Yvonne Georgi. Riefenstahl's memoirs give oddly brief mention to her training in the famous Dresden villa. Years of quarreling with her father lay behind her, and now that he was finally financing dance school and she was in a class with the up-and-coming bright lights of German expressive dance, she took off again after a scant few months. Her terse explanation was that she felt out of place there. She provided far more detailed information about any crazy admirer who came along than about her encounter with the dance greats of her era. Riefenstahl wanted to convey the impression that she was an artist who had nothing left to learn. Her fellow students were surely not lacking in artistic self-assurance. Palucca, Berthe Trümpy, and Skoronel—to name just a few—did not remain tied to their teacher's apron strings but instead pursued independent careers. Riefenstahl's claim that she was unable to develop as an artist in Dresden is belied by Wigman's avowal that every student was fostered in her individual form of expression and did not have to limit herself to imitation. Considering the noble intentions of this teacher, it was no easy matter for Leni to part ways with these talented students. There were often heated disputes, but Riefenstahl kept her distance from them. She simply stole off from the illustrious flock and continued her training "more intensely than ever" in Berlin. She claimed never to have missed any performances by Wigman or Valeska Gert and called the two dancers her "goddesses."[21] Quite apart from the fact that the difference between the two artists could not have been greater, we wonder why she did not stay with her goddess Wigman. These inconsistencies strongly suggest that she left Dresden out of fear that she was not the best among the talented dancers in her class.

Even as a young woman, Riefenstahl could not stand to be compared. She regarded herself as the measure of all things and sidestepped any competition or evaluations. The few months in Dresden were the first and last time she ever joined a community of women. As a supposed student of Wigman's, she had an easier time presenting herself as a promising artist. When she returned to Berlin, though, she faced stiff competition. Countless students of dance were competing for a place onstage: "The many would-be dancers, who had left their run-of-the-mill families in an appalling manner, thought that their running around barefoot was modern dance, and infested the concert halls and theaters. . . . Sporting events, the *Freiluftbewegung* [open air movement], nudism, hiking clubs, gymnastics: all these purely practical activities had now culminated in modern dance, that is, in the landscape of art."[22] At this time of galloping inflation, in which a million reichsmarks in the morning might not be worth anything at all by the afternoon, a quick triumph was what mattered. Nowhere was this more evident than on the stage. Furthermore, going onstage was a way to earn money. Now that marriage had gone out of fashion as a way to gain financial security and many fathers had lost their assets, daughters needed a source of income. Sebastian Haffner ascribed a key significance to the year 1923 in the history of the Germans, calling it "that extraordinary year" in which the Germans developed "the cool madness, the arrogant, unscrupulous, blind resolve to achieve the impossible." Inflation changed the country and the people: the young and alert did well, but those who were old and out of touch had few prospects of succeeding. "Amid all the misery, despair, and poverty there was an air of light-headed youthfulness, licentiousness, and carnival. Now, for once, the young had money and the old did not."[23] A "new realism" was holding sway in the arenas of love and money. Riefenstahl profited from this new realism. Not only did she lose her virginity in 1923, but she also enjoyed her first self-organized appearance on stage. For Riefenstahl, 1923 was the year that put an end to the tormenting "not yet."

As usual, she went about things single-mindedly. To showcase her talent as a dancer and launch her fame, she needed public appearances. The course of action was relatively straightforward and well established: One rented a hall, printed posters, charged admission, got onstage, and claimed to be revealing one's innermost experiences to the audience. Then one hoped for positive reviews and many guest performances. But it took money to get to this point. Riefenstahl toyed with the idea of asking her father for help, but at the same time she was resolved to reel in a financially solvent admirer for her enterprise. There was no lack of men—rich, famous, and influential—to fall for her charms. When she placed second in a beauty contest, she received piles of cards from interested gentlemen. She plucked out the two that seemed most promising: F. W. Koebner, editor-in-chief of the magazine *Die Dame*, and Karl Vollmoeller, a playwright known for his "harem" on Pariser Platz. Both wanted to support her, and both made their sexual interest in her abundantly clear. She described these encounters in detail in order to underscore the temptation to which she was subjected. She remained steadfast, straitlaced, and strong-minded.

With both men, she emphasized that her artistic talent would lead her to success even without their patronage. She wanted neither money nor sex from these men. For years, she had had a crush on Otto Froitzheim, a professional tennis player who was the lover of the actress Pola Negri. In the 1910s, when he was very successful on the court, tennis was considered a frivolous pastime.[24] Riefenstahl arranged to meet Froitzheim, hoping that a relationship with him would give a boost to her career. He was a man about town with contacts in the world of film, and he had an apartment in an upscale part of the city. At the age of twenty-one, Riefenstahl had had quite enough of her father's strict supervision, and losing her virginity would take her one step closer to liberation. She rang Froitzheim's doorbell wearing black silk underwear under a coat trimmed with fake ermine. They chatted, then danced, then slept together. She later described her first sexual experience as a near-rape that left her feeling humiliated and disillusioned. But she had cleared the first hurdle: She was now a young woman with a lover.

By happy coincidence, she met a young banker from Innsbruck while vacationing on the Baltic Sea. He was watching her practice her dances on the beach, then he came up and spoke to her. "He complimented me on my improvised beach dancing and, during our very first conversation, he said, 'If you like, I can sign you up for several dance recitals at the Innsbruck City Theater.' 'Are you the manager or director of this theater?' I asked. He smiled. 'I'm not,' he said, 'but I have the money to rent the theater, and I'm convinced that you will have great success.'"[25] At times of inflation, it was relatively easy for a foreigner to be wealthy in Germany. Of course, this man was thinking not about art, but about the woman he had met. She rejected the marriage proposal he made at the end of the vacation. Harry Sokal, as the young man was named, would become one of Riefenstahl's key financiers, as would Adolf Hitler. Sokal had come to Germany from Romania as a child and had spent his youth in Berlin. He served at the front for two years, then went into banking when the war ended. When he met Riefen-stahl, he was setting up a foreign exchange department at a bank in Innsbruck.

Sokal was a tall, thin-faced, handsome man who wore his dark hair slicked back. Constantly on the prowl for amorous escapades, he became aware of Riefenstahl during a vacation in Warnemünde. He was captivated by her flowing movements and her wish to appear onstage. "If this dance were to express only a fraction of her charm, graceful movements, and beauty, she would be a great success, and in a matter of seconds, my mind was made up: I would take charge of her debut."[26] Sokal described Riefenstahl as a self-assured, radiantly beautiful young woman who enjoyed the effect she had on men, and he hoped to win her over by financing her first dance performance. Undaunted by the huge sums of money the performance would require, Sokal paid for the hall and the publicity for the event, which took place on October 23, 1923, in Munich. The hall was only one-third full, but Riefenstahl deemed her "Dances of Eros," which were inspired by her experience with Froitzheim, a resounding success.

While Riefenstahl denied having had an amorous relationship with Sokal at that time, he wrote that they spent their last night of their vacation in Warnemünde together. He was aware that love was not her highest priority. "She belonged far too much to her art, and above all to herself."[27] The performance in Munich was Riefenstahl's dress rehearsal for Berlin. Anyone who wanted to make something of herself had to survive the "trial by fire" of appearing before a sophisticated audience in Berlin. In Riefenstahl's eyes, however, the target audience in Berlin consisted of a single individual: her father. Her performance in Blüthner Hall had the sole purpose of convinc-ing him that she was a gifted artist. Finally, her father was willing to believe in her. She triumphed over him onstage.

o   o   o

Marie Magdalene Dietrich's mother did not remain a widow for long. Her second marriage was more to the liking of her extended family. Like Josefine's first husband, Eduard von Losch wore a uniform, but he was a high-ranking army officer and came from a noble family. Von Losch was seven years younger than her deceased husband, who had been a friend of his. Josefine remained true to her belief in the old system of the class society and retained her predilection for military-style masculinity. Von Losch was a stocky man with a handlebar mustache who liked to boast about his experiences in the war. He had spent time in China, and the two Dietrich girls hung on his every word about this foreign world. Unfortunately, there was a stigma attached to their mother's second marriage as well. This time the problem lay in her upward social mobility. The von Loschs were not thrilled with the prospect of their Eduard marrying a middle-class widow. Von Losch's mother kept her distance from her new daughter-in-law. Still, Josefine preferred disparaging looks from her new extended family to her former status as the widow of a second-rate police officer.

Two years before World War I broke out, Dietrich was given a gold-embossed diary bound in red leather. In the turbulent years that followed, she would confide her secrets to this diary, but her change of father went unmentioned; she was utterly preoccupied with herself. The pretty girl sought to be the center of attention without her mother catching on to her ambitions. Josefine's second marriage had not softened her; she was now bent on making her daughters live up to her new name, which for her meant teaching the children discipline. This discipline was relentless, strict, somber, and matter-of-fact. The daughter of a clockmaker with the soul of a sergeant was utterly humorless. Dietrich's cousin Hasso Conrad Felsing claimed that even his Aunt Josefine's normal conversational tone was imperious, and she would not tolerate any backtalk. Dietrich found an outlet from her mother's overbearing presence in ice skating when the city lake froze over. If she fell down, she was quickly surrounded by a group of boys scrambling to help her back up, and she responded to their overtures with either haughty or coquettishly bashful looks. Unfortunately for her, she was usually chaperoned by her older sister. Since Elisabeth was not a good ice skater, Dietrich had no trouble gliding away from her. But when it was time to go home, the younger girl could be found sitting on a bench unfastening her skates, her feet numb from the skating and the cold, tentatively making contact with the ground.

Their mother placed great value on leading a life that befitted their social status. Her first marriage had been a disappointment in that regard—and in so many others. Those dark days now seemed to be over; she had now joined the nobility with her new last name, "von Losch," while her children retained the Dietrich name. Eduard von Losch never lost sight of the privilege of his birth and, like her husband, Josefine was firmly convinced of the inherent superiority and leadership authority of Prussian officers. However, although she was regarded as a parvenu in her husband's circles, she resisted the temptation to compensate for her disadvantaged background as a middle-class widow by indulging in a lavish life-style or surrounding herself with luxury. In Dietrich's new home, there was an emphasis on the military values of duty, honor, and discipline: "[My mother] was like a kindly general. She followed the rules she laid down. She set a good example to prove that it was possible. No pride in success, no pats on the shoulder; the only goal was humble submission to duty."[28]

The daily pressures eased up when her parents were expecting guests. The big living room cabinets were opened up, and out came the spotless white porcelain dinnerware, the tightly woven linen tablecloths, green glassware, filigreed champagne glasses, and squat port wine goblets. The festive sight of the beautifully set table lifted Dietrich's spirits. Shortly before the guests arrived, she would lie in her bed with her heart pounding, picturing the guests entering the house through the hall with the chandelier, telephone, and potted palm, and her mother playing a quiet Chopin waltz, "her fingernails touching on the keys with a delicate little click." The piano music "belonged to a house full of flowers, my mother's perfume, her evening gown, her beautiful hairdo, the smell of my father's cigarette coming through the open door of the library where he strode back and forth on the thick rug and listened to my mother playing the piano. Everything was ready for the guests."[29]

The wife was the representative of beauty; a family's social success could be gauged by her appearance and her involvement in the arts. The husband was proud of his cultivated wife, and everyone envied him. That was the ideal for a family at the end of the nineteenth century, and Dietrich continued to cling to this ideal well into her old age. The family in which she grew up largely ignored the sweeping changes in twentieth-century society. Dietrich was raised for a world that was coming apart. This world was embodied by the only true lady in the family: her grandmother. Elisabeth Felsing, who was born in Dresden in 1855, was the third wife of Albert Felsing, a merchant. After he died in 1901, she carried on the business for several years before handing it over to her son Willibald. Her granddaughter considered her the most beautiful woman in the world.

Elisabeth Felsing brought glamour and sparkle into Dietrich's life. Her grandmother gave her cake, chocolate, and other delicacies and regaled her with stories about her childhood. She and her husband had enjoyed going to the Kaiserhof, one of the first luxury hotels in Berlin, where scarred officers, Jewish bankers, Russian ladies, and rich American women had their rendezvous. She read the Paris fashion magazines and delighted in objects that her daughter Josefine considered useless. "She awakened in me the longing for beautiful things, for paintings, for Fabergé boxes, horses, carriages, for the warm, soft roseate pearls set off against the white skin of her neck and the rubies that sparkled on her hands," her granddaughter recalled.[30] She impressed upon Dietrich that a lady never loses her poise; she simply disregards anything that is not to her liking. A lady is witty and alluring in a playful, lighthearted manner.

Dietrich also learned from her grandmother that the father and grandfather of the current Kaiser were buried in the same year. On an ice-cold day in March, Wilhelm I died at the age of ninety, and with his death, the connection to the eighteenth century was severed. Wilhelm I had met Talleyrand and entered Paris after the victory over Napoleon. His wife still had memories of Goethe and had witnessed the barricades in 1848. Her son, the new Kaiser Friedrich, had been crown prince for thirty years. When he ascended the throne, he was already at the brink of death. The days of his reign were days of his slow dying. Kaiser Friedrich left behind a son, the future Wilhelm II. Elisabeth Felsing had viewed Wilhelm II's accession to the throne with suspicion. The young Kaiser was too brash for her liking, and she had nothing but contempt for his bigoted wife and her sanctimonious smiles. This imperial couple lacked any sense of style.

Felsing impressed upon her granddaughter that times had changed, and it was now important for a girl to study hard in school. Unfortunately, Dietrich found school gloomy and oppressive.

Early in the winter mornings, I would squeeze my eyes tightly and tiny tears transformed the pale street lamps into long, thin, glittering beams of light. I played this game every morning, and my tears would flow easily. I didn't actually have to cry at all; the wind and the cold accomplished the same trick just as well. I knew all the closed shutters of the stores, all the jutting stones that I could jump over— on one leg, with my legs together or crossed—or slide on if it had snowed during the night. My feelings were just

as familiar: the certainty of having lost my precious freedom, fear of the teachers and their punishments, fear of
loneliness.[31]

Many of the teachers were reserve officers who liked to think of
their classrooms as army barracks. Dietrich was appalled by the
constraints and bleakness of the school.

As she grew up, she became increasingly alienated from her
family, and at the age of eleven she came up with a new name for
herself: Marlene. Back then, no one was named Marlene; she coined
it herself. She evidently wanted to get away from the biblical theme
(and she surmised that the only reason she was not named Maria
rather than Marie was because many maids had that name). Entries
in her notebooks show how much of her school time she devoted
to practicing her new signature. In changing her name, she nul-
lified the first decision her parents had made about her. Marlene
Dietrich was now embarking on the life she would be plotting out
for herself.

o o o

In the first days of World War I, during the summer of 1914, the
whole country was in a state of euphoria. The prominent men who
volunteered for military service included the poet Richard Dehmel;
the famous Reinhardt actor Alexander Moissi; and Otto Braun, the
son of Lily Braun, a socialist leader in the feminist movement. Lines
of young men eager to enlist formed in front of the barracks, where
there were reports of wild carousing, theft, and destruction. In
restaurants and cafés, bands played music to bring out the patriotic
spirit. There were endless refrains of "The Watch on the Rhine" and
"Hail to Thee in the Victor's Wreath," and schoolchildren belted out
"Hold Firm in the Roaring Storm!"

Dietrich must have had mixed feelings about the singing soldiers. Accustomed to military etiquette at an early age, she surely

found it odd to see a war being celebrated like a party. In school, the students were now being ushered off to the auditorium to hear "thunderous speeches." Young teachers were rushing into the classroom and proudly announcing that they would be following the call of the Fatherland. In no time at all, a good half of the Prussian elementary school teachers were off at war, replaced by elderly instructors who were often in poor physical health.[32] The war also became part of the curriculum: The outbreak and course of the war were studied over and over again; there were lessons in "war poetry" and "war geography," and the study of natural history featured discussions about war technology. Instructional time was devoted to knitting wristlets for the soldiers. "We sat in the classroom, dimly lit by the daylight, and knitted to warm the soldiers digging trenches far from home. They had us knit to make us feel useful, in order to fill the gaping void caused by the war."[33] The diary entries show a girl who feels as patriotic as her parents. In her memoirs, she was intent on proving her early love of France, but her diaries give no evidence of this love. As a daughter of an officer, her sympathy went to her nation, not to its enemies.

Detlev Peukert has identified a series of generations shaped by the war; his chronological scheme places Dietrich (along with such notables as Theodor W. Adorno, Heinrich Himmler, and others born in the first years of the twentieth century) squarely in the "superfluous generation."[34] The "superfluous generation" experienced war as youngsters, and it was a fixed coordinate in their lives. Sebastian Haffner, who was born in 1907, described how the war robbed children of their youthful innocence and manipulated their understanding of history and politics. "I, a seven-year-old boy, who a short while ago hardly knew what war meant, let alone 'ultimatum,' 'mobilization,' and 'cavalry reserve,' soon knew, as if I had always known, the 'hows' and 'whens' and 'wherefores' of the war, and I even knew the 'why.' I knew the war was due to France's lust for revenge, England's commercial envy, and Russia's barbarism, I could speak these words quite glibly."[35] Children avidly followed the headlines of special editions and got to know the map of Europe as they marked the victories and defeats.

All at once, the reports of victory stopped pouring in, and the days of canceling school to celebrate these victories came to an end. Since Kaiser Wilhelm II had left Berlin at the onset of the war, his name was rarely mentioned. But in Dietrich's home, the Kaiser was still held in high esteem, and the very idea that the Germans might lose this war was preposterous. On October 9, 1914, her uncle Willibald earned the Iron Cross; just three months later, on December 4, her uncle Otto was shot in the back of the neck.

Death had found its way into the family. The grief of the adults plunged Dietrich even deeper into her childhood isolation. She later recalled: "Children are condemned in advance to silence and solitude. They are not allowed to say that their own fears draw them close to those who suffer at the front every day and live in fear of ambush and mutilation."[36] The children did not understand the change of mood. The enthusiasm for the war had come to an abrupt end. Suddenly, no one wanted to spend time looking at photo albums of the glorious victories in 1870 or delight in jokes about the British.

By about 1916, there was no longer an authority to ensure that provisions reached the populace on a reliable basis. The downturn in production and the dramatic expansion of black market sales prompted by the war reduced the food supply. "Morning, noon, and night we ate turnips. Turnip marmalade, turnip cakes, turnip soup, the roots and leafy tops of turnips were cooked in a thousand different ways. . . . Nobody complained over these meager meals, the children even less than the grown-ups. At noon and in the evening there were potatoes, and in the afternoon too, if I was hungry. Potatoes, the true joy of childhood! There they lay, white, tender, and mealy."[37] Dietrich turned pale and gaunt. When she went to visit her beloved grandmother, her mother would pinch her cheeks to give them some color and make her look healthy. Josefine made sure to keep family life going at a calm and orderly pace on the surface, but even she could not shield the children from being gripped by uncertainty. Dietrich appears to have been relieved that her mother insisted on maintaining strict rules. "These rules were so inviolable that they seemed to be familiar and friendly. Lasting, unalterable, irrefutable, more protective than threatening, they were not subject to any mood or whim."[38] These rules gave structure and consistency to her life. Dietrich would invoke these "war rules" at times of crisis throughout her life.

Whenever the doorbell rang, her mother ran to find out if there was bad news from the front. Late in the afternoon, she took her younger daughter by the hand and strode to the town hall, where the lists of the men reported missing in action were posted. Dietrich's mother would slow down and squeeze her daughter's hand as she approached the lists. The girl was breathless with anxiety, her heart pounding in her chest. "She would never let go of my hand, when she stopped there, only her head moving from top to bottom as she scanned the names. I would watch her and try to guess when she would take the two steps sideward and, with her head held high, tackle the next list."[39] Her mother's eyes were seeking the name she was loath to find: Eduard von Losch. "Two more lists, hope, don't forsake me, 'his' name won't be on them; I don't want that to happen. . . . Now the last ones. . . . Her finger follows the black letters behind the glass pane smeared by countless fingers. The pressure of her hand lets up; she bows her head; her eyes are moist, but they are shining with a relief and joy only I can see."[40]

But one day there was news that Lieutenant von Losch had been wounded. "My mother received a *laissez-passer* from general headquarters so that she could get to the Russian front and 'give strength back to her husband,' as the telegram read. My father was seriously wounded and not transportable. By the time my mother came back, he had already succumbed to his wounds. Now a widow's cowl and veil, which hid her face, were added to her black dress."[41] Eduard von Losch had been injured outside of Kieselin in Galicia on June 20, 1916, and died of blood poisoning on July 16. His corpse was transported to Dessau and buried at the Memorial Cemetery for Fallen Soldiers. Dietrich had lost her father for the second time, and a black band was placed over her left sleeve. Her clothing had to be black or dark blue, and white cuffs and collars were the only decoration permitted.

The winter following the death of her father, and then of her uncle Max, was the start of the second phase of the war for Berliners. It was bitterly cold, and the city was suffering from an extreme shortage of fuel along with a dire shortage of food. Josefine moved to Dessau with her two daughters, and Dietrich sought companionship on the streets of this new city, as well as a respite from her mother's grief.

> February 4, 1917 I had a big fight with mommy. When she said if I *went out* with all those schoolboys, I must be *boy crazy*. First of all, I don't "hang around with boys," and, second, having a friendship with boys I know—you don't have to fall in love just like that—is far from being *boy crazy*. . . . She said, "If you get boy crazy, you will be sent to boarding school." Whew! I find that all so stupid and made up and I think "What a boring life!" Talking to a schoolboy on the skating rink makes you "boy crazy." No, no. That's too much for me.[42]

Josefine continued to be spurned by her deceased husband's family. On Eduard von Losch's obituary, the name of his mother had been listed—but not that of his widow. She was too old to marry again, and besides, there was a dearth of men in wartime. Josefine felt that she had been robbed of her happiness, and all her hopes now rested on her children. Elisabeth was the dutiful daughter, and

Marlene the rebel. Their mother made them wear their hair braided with a black band as a sign of mourning. One photograph from this period, which was probably taken in Josefine's living room, shows Dietrich sitting among her relatives. The many women are seated, and the few men are standing. All are wearing high-necked dark clothing and looking solemn. Dietrich appears deeply unhappy in this cold, severe group. She recalled later in life, "I dreamed of an armistice and peace, and I also dreamed of the warm, unkempt, fragrant sweep of hair that fell into my face and on my neck."[43] Dietrich had had quite enough of bowing to her mother's dictates; she wanted to seduce men, and the decorum befitting the family's station in life was a matter of indifference to her.

Josefine was in an unenviable spot, as the family was already up in arms about her younger daughter's unseemly conduct. Eventually she and her children moved back to Berlin, but the uproar continued unabated. By 1914, Dietrich was confiding to her diary that she had no intention of going to high school; she was on the quest for glory and adventure. She spent her money on autograph cards, acted in plays at school, and pinned up her hair. And she discovered the movies.

Josefine felt nothing but disdain for the cinema, which, she was convinced, appealed to people's basest instincts. Doctors and psychologists fretted about the spread of the "movie plague." They feared the power and influence of the images, that they would lead young girls astray. Nevertheless, the impact of film continued to grow. Shortly before World War I, respected theater actors began to accept movie roles, and movies were reviewed in the arts sections of newspapers.

Dietrich adored the actress Henny Porten, whom screenwriter Willy Haas called the "most German of all German film stars." Heavy breathing, dramatic gestures, and a quivering bosom were part of her standard melodramatic repertoire. To Josefine's horror, her daughter devoted all of her time to thinking about Porten, who played morally upstanding women abandoned by disreputable men and ostracized by society. The young Dietrich's role model was an actress who did not embody the spirit of the modern woman. Porten's style was premodern, oriented to nineteenth-century emotive visual modes of expression. And the type of woman she gravitated to portraying—pure, honest, natural, and morally impeccable—could scarcely be called modern. Why was Dietrich so drawn to this paragon of virtue? It is tempting to surmise that Porten's screen image suggested the mother figure she had always wanted: a woman of honor, like Josefine, yet soft and yielding. In the films shot during the war, Dietrich probably envisioned her own future, namely a destiny that in some way had to do with ill-fated love. Porten played women who faced difficult odds but remained pure and displayed greatness. The heroines in Porten films have melodious names: Adelina von Gentz, Viktoria von Katzenstein-Dernburg, Ruth von Erlenkamp, and Stella von Eschen. Dietrich's taste in the arts was fairly conventional, and she was oblivious to avant-garde movements. Henny Porten never let her down; she could be counted on to play conventional roles.

In the final two years of the war, school was canceled more and more often. The children skipped class because they had to stand in line for food, or were simply too weak from malnutrition to attend. Schools became central collection spots for a wide range of items, from forage to gold to groceries. Homework was a thing of the past; there were no notebooks, and it was simply too cold to buckle down and work in unheated apartments. During the last few months of the war, everyone lived in fear of what lay ahead. Dietrich would harbor feelings of betrayal for the rest of her life.

> We had been told we'd have a peaceful childhood, school,
> holidays, and picnics, long vacations with a hammock,
> beach, pail, shovel and a starfish to take home. We had
> been promised plans, plans to be forged, carried out,

realized, dreams to be dreamed and made to come true. A secure future—and it was up to us to take advantage of it. And now? No more plans, no secure future, and no knowledge that could be useful for the war.[44]

Dietrich felt as though the war would never end. Film offered her a retreat from the present and a semblance of hope for the future. By the last winter of the war, everybody went on foot: the bustling countess, the giggling streetwalker, and the weary soldier. Dietrich noticed that there were barely any well-dressed women to be seen. The faces around her looked numb and grave, with puffy faces and red eyes. She was living in a world of grieving women, and she longed for pleasure and charming men. Then a soldier entered into this world in the form of her cousin Hans, who kissed her. "The iron cross on his chest got caught in my dress and pulled a thread that stretched between us while the soldier stared at me."[45] The whole house roared with his laughter and booming voice. The girl closed the window so she would not have to hear him. His hulking body, which had survived the war intact, frightened her. Dietrich portrayed the scenes with her cousin Hans as her first encounter with a man who saw her as a woman, and as an intrusion on her regulated life. What he left behind did not begin to resemble the Prussian officer's daughter's vision of a brave man: The whole apartment was full of ashtrays overflowing with cigarette butts, and a tub in the laundry room contained two field gray shirts soaking in milky water. Were these the accoutrements of a well-fortified German man?

The Felsings, the Dietrichs, and the von Loschs were nationalistic adherents to the monarchy who found no fault with the imperial regime. Josefine, who felt increasingly committed to Wilhelmine values, passed them on to her daughters. Sedan Day, which commemorated the defeat of the French in the Franco-Prussian War, and the Kaiser's birthday appear to have been major events in the lives of the von Losch family. Like every other child in Berlin, Dietrich hoped to catch a glimpse of the Kaiser and his sons. However, Wilhelm II's popularity was on the decline. As the commander in chief of the German armed forces, he rarely put in an appearance in Berlin once the war began. The fact that he spent almost all his time at military headquarters was a mere formality. The military leaders may have let him speak, but they did not take him seriously. Respect for General Field Marshal von Hindenburg grew while the Kaiser receded into the background. The latter's end was wretched, devoid of any honor or dignity: From the remote railway station in Spa, Wilhelm II and his imperial train left for Holland on the night of November 9.

Capitulation and revolution wrenched Dietrich out of her dream world.

> Berlin, 9 November 1918 Why must I experience these terrible times? I did so want a golden youth and now it turned out like this! I am sorry about the Kaiser and all the others. They say bad things will happen tonight. The mob was after people with carriages. We had some ladies invited for tea but none of them could get through to our house. Only Countess Gersdorff did. On Kurfürstendamm, her husband got his epaulets torn off by armed soldiers, and everywhere one looks, there are red flags. What does the nation want? They have what they wanted, haven't they? Oh, if I were a little bit happy, things wouldn't be so difficult to bear. Maybe soon a time will come when I will be able to tell about happiness again—only happiness.[46]

The chaos on the streets made her feel vulnerable and in need of defining her place in society. Dietrich belonged to the world of ladies, and her heart went out to the Kaiser. The people with the red flags were ordinary; she was not.

The weather was rainy and gloomy in November 1918, and the mood was morose. Dietrich had borne witness to the drama of social degradation even before the defeat in war and the ensuing inflation. Her father had been no more than a minor official, yet he retained a great sense of importance. She had developed a keen sense of class distinctions early in life and mastered the fine art of keeping up appearances. Her whole life up to this point had been a social seesaw. The only fixed coordinate between life as a policeman's orphan and an officer's stepdaughter was pride in Prussia. Josefine and her daughters used this pride to gloss over the comedown and highlight the ascent.

When Dietrich had just turned twenty, she witnessed the collapse of the order to which she felt she belonged. She watched the Hohenzollerns and their military power founder. Officers ventured out of the house disguised as civilians. The military virtues and deeds of dead fathers no longer counted. Revolution and republic brought to Josefine and her daughters the death of their social positions. Dietrich fought off the phantom pain of all that she had lost by fictionalizing it. Her diary, her later interviews, and her written recollections convey the impression that she regarded her father as the epitome of Prussian manliness: "My father: tall, imposing stature, smell of leather, shiny boots, a riding crop, horses."[47] Her mother was locked in an ongoing struggle with the vagaries of history in her multiple roles as daughter, wife, mother, and—eventually—widow, while her father was unshakably bound up with power, victory, and death. Her father was swallowed up by history, and Dietrich regarded herself as his successor.[48]

The atmosphere at home was more somber than ever now that peacetime had arrived. Josefine was always in a foul mood, and Elisabeth was busily cramming for her final exams. Dietrich spent hours in front of shop windows staring at silk dresses and dreaming of being loved. After her grandmother died in the year following the revolution of 1918, the situation with her mother grew even more fraught. Josefine tormented the two girls; as far as she was concerned, they could do no right. She felt that she had gotten a raw deal in life, and she was despondent and quarrelsome. Dietrich, in turn, developed into a wayward daughter who threatened to introduce additional chaos into the family. The clearly contentious issue between the mother and the daughter was sex. In the social system of the Prussian Wilhelmine upper class, women who acted on their passion were ostracized. Josefine felt compelled to stick to these moral principles as a way of keeping her head held high in the face of the family's degradation. Sexuality and eroticism jeopardized the order she represented. She believed that enforcing strict standards was acting on behalf of the dead fathers. But the law of the fathers no longer applied.

> September 17, 1919 . . . Saturdays and Sundays I kiss enough for the whole week. I really should be very ashamed. All those who know me confirm this if I ask them what they think of me: I am all right for kissing and having fun, but to marry—God forbid! . . . I allow myself to be kissed so easily. Of course, I can't expect respect. I can't help it. It is not my fault if my romantic nature has no limits. Who knows where I will end up. Hopefully, somebody will come, have the kindness to marry me soon. There is a film in town called *Demi-Vierges*. They say it is a typical case of young ladies from the so-called upper class who-mature-sooner, want to experience the tickling thrill of erotic adventures. . . . Playing with fire, until one day they get burned, then laugh. This describes me exactly. Till now I still have had the strength to say No as it got to the very moment. . . . It would be so beautiful to just let go and love. But, of course, that can't be.[49]

Robert Musil noted that as a result of the war, "Woman is tired of being the ideal of the man who no longer has sufficient energy to idealize, and she has taken over the task of thinking herself through as her own ideal image."[50] The German men had lost their enemy and their leader when the war came to an end. To maintain their inner balance, these defeated men started a revolution, which did not, however, extend to those for whom the war was already over—the New Women. Pola Negri reported on the evening of November 8 that she was celebrating the premiere of her movie *Carmen*. Her lamé dress was as big a success as her acting skills. Everyone was having a grand time when volleys of gunfire suddenly rang out in the distance. She turned to Ernst Lubitsch in alarm to ask what was going on, and he whispered to her that that was utterly irrelevant, and she ought to focus on the movie.

This anecdote from revolutionary Berlin reflected a changed world. While the men in worn-out uniforms were on the hunt for an enemy in the magnificent buildings abandoned by their Kaiser, the New Woman was watching herself on the screen. The revolution represented the soldiers' attempt to wrest some last shred of meaning from the national delusions of grandeur to which they had succumbed. Meanwhile, General Erich Ludendorff, one of the parties responsible for having launched this war, was at a Berlin boarding house preparing to flee. Ludendorff, wearing dark glasses and carrying a forged passport, looked like a character in a bad movie as he made his getaway to Scandinavia. The political and military illusions of men had fallen apart; the artificially created illusion would become the hallmark of the dawning republican era. Women in the 1920s mastered the art of donning a deceptive sheen. Dietrich would be one of them.

The military brass no longer set the pace in Berlin, and the young soldiers coming back home in their discolored uniforms and worn-out field coats and shoes were unshaven and weary. Destitute passersby had no choice but to ignore the begging war veterans on the street, and they had no desire to be reminded of the war. Josefine forbade anyone to speak about the war in her presence.

Dietrich was finished with school and had to contemplate what lay ahead. Up to now she had not shown signs of any particular talent. Her greatest wish was to appear on stage, but she had to keep that wish from her mother. Acting was considered a seedy business, and having an actress for a daughter would have been a devastating comedown. As a girl from a good family, Dietrich had taken ballet lessons before the war; her ballet slippers are still part of her estate today. They were very fine, expensive-looking slippers, made in England, dusky pink silk with leather soles. These lightweight shoes show clear signs of use; she must have practiced quite a bit. There is a photograph showing her doing ballet exercises on a rooftop in Berlin. One of her shoulders is bare, and she is forcing a smile and looking quite stilted. Dietrich knew that the time had passed for girls to dance ballet. Her diary contains an entry dated May 1918, in which she wrote that she had given up ballet, but she would continue to go to the "barefoot class." Like so many other young women, she was drawn to rhythmic gymnastics and expressive dance. She loved music even more than dance. Her mother bought her an expensive violin in the hope that her artistic talent and the violin would take precedence over her interest in young men. But Dietrich wanted both. When her mother sent her to Mittenwald in Bavaria in 1920 to improve her skills on the violin, she promptly fell in love again, and when her mother realized what was going on, she brought her daughter home.

Josefine von Losch had had quite enough of her daughter's antics. She pondered long-term solutions and decided to send her wayward daughter to boarding school. She had threatened to do so on many occasions in the past but now she intended to act, and Dietrich was shipped off to Weimar for training as an artist.

Josefine hoped that placing her with the strict headmistress, Frau Arnoldi, might be the beginning.

"The boarding school was cold and forbidding, the streets were unfamiliar, and the air smelled different from my big hometown; no mother, no one I knew, no sanctuary I could flee to, no place for me to weep in secret, no warmth," Dietrich later wrote about her time in Weimar.[51] And in this case her recollections tallied with her diary entries as a young girl. In Frau Arnoldi's boarding school, the girls slept six to a room. What cadet school was for Prussian boys, the boarding school was for Prussian girls. Dietrich had come to a place in which rules and mores of a bygone era were taught. The young girl had no choice but to adjust to the routines and discipline at this institution. "You had to line up, go down the street two by two, lead the other pupils . . . and meet people who were free, shopping or gossiping on a street corner. You felt desperate, rejected, excluded."[52] Frau Arnoldi gave orders, expected obedience, and monitored everything they did. She was fastidious in all matters pertaining to cleanliness, punctuality, and morality. The minds and bodies of her pupils were subject to her command. Over and over again, the girls were told that the greatest possible disgrace was the loss of virginity. A respectable girl remained pure or wound up in the gutter. This type of education is sure to drive girls to furtive actions and foster a climate of hypocrisy. Dietrich described Weimar as a "prison."

She was torn between her own desires and her mother's expectations. Josefine dropped by every three weeks to size up the situation for herself. She regarded it as one of her most important tasks to wash her daughter's hair.

The idea that a mother would travel so far just to wash her daughter's hair might appear unusual, but my mother was very proud of my hair, and it meant a great deal to her that

it stayed beautiful. She had no confidence in me on this
matter. My hair always stayed elegant, and I'm sure that I
have my mother's help to thank for that. She dried it with
a towel, then made me sit down on a chair in the visitors'
room. My face was red from all the rubbing that went with
this treatment; my hair was still tousled and damp, and
tears ran down my cheeks, while I said goodbye to her.[53]

Whenever Josefine was there for a visit, Frau Arnoldi seized the
opportunity to sound off about Dietrich to her mother, casting
aspersions on the girl's character by letting on that Dietrich loved
to draw attention to herself and flirted in the concert hall. Dietrich
countered that it was not her fault that all the men stared at her,
but this defense did not get her very far. Her mother believed the
puritanical teacher and not her wanton daughter. Arnoldi was the
kind of headmistress who liked to exploit her power and she was
out to humiliate Dietrich, who feared and despised her. Arnoldi and
the mother formed an alliance. In their view, the daughter of an
officer was destined to carry on a culture centered on power, ascet-
icism, and militarism. Just because different values were now being
trumpeted did not mean they had to be adhered to.

Dietrich saw the matter differently. After losing two fathers and
enduring the war, she could not understand why she ought to forgo
happiness and stick to the rules. She had seen with her own eyes
how quickly everything could be over.

To inject a little sparkle into her small-town life, she put her
feminine wiles to the test with her violin teacher, Robert Reitz.
Reitz was the conductor at the opera and a welcome guest in the
artistic and intellectual circles of Weimar. Through him Dietrich
came in contact with the violinmaker Julius Levin, to whom she
poured her heart out in a series of letters.[54]

These letters paint a picture of her as a love-starved girl who
did not know where to turn; she was evidently unable to confide

in either her mother or her sister. Quite unexpectedly, her mother brought her back to Berlin. Supposedly Dietrich had no idea why, and her mother refused to answer her questions. According to Dietrich's daughter, Maria Riva, her mother had to leave Weimar because she had had an affair with Reitz. In Riva's description, losing her virginity was a humiliating experience for Dietrich. She went back to Berlin and her mother's control. She still had not made anything of herself, and she was no longer even a virgin. Her choice of music teacher shows that she had not given up hope of a career as a concert violinist: She received instruction from the renowned Professor Carl Flesch, who supposedly made her play eight hours of Bach a day. Eventually Dietrich came down with tendinitis. Her hand was put in a cast, and when the cast was removed, her doctors explained that this hand would always remain prone to injury. Mother and daughter would have to bury their dream of Dietrich's becoming a professional musician. This investment had been for naught. Dietrich would never celebrate triumphs in the great concert halls of the world, and the violin, wrapped in silk, lay unused in its black case.

CARVING
OUT
A CAREER

***

(1923–1932)

EARLY
SORROW

The Berlin to which Marlene Dietrich returned was bleak, gray, and desolate. Journalist Sebastian Haffner observed, "We had the great war game behind us and the shock of defeat, the disillusionment of the revolution that had followed, and now the daily spectacle of the failure of all the rules of life and the bankruptcy of age and experience."[1] Dietrich and her friends regarded life with weary skepticism. Ornaments were discarded, and every self-respecting shop had the marble of the Wilhelmine years torn down. Too much pomp was an unwelcome distraction. Dietrich quickly suppressed any memories of her father's fine-looking uniform; of Sedan Day, the annual celebration of German victory in the Franco-Prussian War; and of rides with her grandmother. She did not want to be one of those people who stood weeping under the portrait of the Kaiser, the way her mother and her mother's friends did. Her sister, who had now passed her teachers' examination, was constantly held up to her as a shining example. Dietrich was tired of being branded a failure and had no desire to face an unending barrage of questions about her future.

Calm had not been restored. There were frequent putsches from both the right and the left, and there were reports of political murders on an almost daily basis. Until 1923 inflation had obliterated only monetary assets, but after that, incomes were also affected by the devaluation. No longer could money be made by working. People had to come up with different ideas. Hyperinflation led to a complete collapse of the German economy. The events of 1922 and 1923 had effects of catastrophic proportions for Germans' savings. Even a substantial nest egg could disappear overnight, and class distinctions were leveled as a result. "The process throws people together whose material interests normally lie far apart. . . . An inflation cancels out distinctions between men which had seemed eternal and brings together in the same inflation crowd people who before would scarcely have nodded to each other in the street."[2] Gamblers and racketeers surged ahead and left the others behind. If people were handed money, they had to spend it as quickly as possible; it could be worthless the very next moment. The middle class could no longer maintain its standard of living. The usual night at the theater or birthday party could prove economically ruinous. It was the time in which the young Bertolt Brecht was enjoying success with *Drums in the Night*, Arnolt Bronnen with *Parricide*, and Fritz Lang with *Dr. Mabuse, the Gambler*. People had to be able to speculate, maneuver, hoodwink, and deceive in order to get by. Thomas Mann—reflecting on this situation—described his own children as "belonging by birth to the 'villa proletariat.'" They grew up enjoying the privileges of the upper middle class of yesteryear, but were now left "odd enough in it, with their worn and turned clothing and altered way of life."[3] Stefan Zweig described a very different facet of this "altered way of life" in Berlin in his autobiography, *The World of Yesterday*.

> Along the entire Kurfürstendamm powdered and rouged
> young men sauntered and they were not all professionals;
> every high school boy wanted to earn some money and in

the dimly lit bars one might see government officials and
men of the world of finance tenderly courting drunken
sailors without any shame. Even the Rome of Suetonius
had never known such orgies as the pervert balls of Berlin,
where hundreds of men costumed as women and hundreds
of women as men danced under the benevolent eyes of the
police. In the collapse of all values a kind of madness gained
hold particularly in the bourgeois circles which until then
had been unshakeable in their probity.[4]

Dietrich's snooty relatives felt that she was one of these amoral
women who had entered the netherworld of prostitution by seeking work in the theater. What else was she to do? She neither could
nor would stay at home with her mother, who never stopped nagging her. Money did not appear to be the major issue. The two were
quarreling about the harm to her reputation. Now that the dream
of a career as a concert violinist had fallen apart, Dietrich was facing a void. She had no interest in continuing her schooling, but she
did not find the prospect of sitting in an office or waiting on cus-
tomers in a store especially enticing either. Those careers were out
of the question for a beautiful young woman who had come close
to becoming a concert violinist. Dietrich wanted to carry on her
family's tradition of lavish living, but what could the daughter of a
Wilhelmine police officer do with her life? Her name was merely
Dietrich—lacking the noble "von"—so she was not an interesting
match for one of the many parvenus aiming for upward mobility.
No prince was going to come along and marry her, and the Kaiser would not be restoring the old order. She would be unable to
fulfill her mother's expectations, so she settled on acting, which
seemed liked an obvious choice since everyone was always praising her beauty, and besides, she knew quite a bit about the stars
and the cinema. She talked to quite a few girls about a career as an
actress, some of whom had found jobs in the theater or film. Most

of them were not even good-looking and had no training in music, nor had they even had the pleasure of taking ballet lessons. Dietrich would enjoy standing on stage and reciting Rilke verses and earning money for it. She was not interested in divulging anything about herself or expressing her innermost thoughts. She wanted to enjoy pretty things and make a good living while doing so. There was no talk of art.

Berlin was the stronghold of German-language theater. In 1905, Max Reinhardt of Vienna had taken over the Deutsches Theater, which was located near the Charité hospital, and developed it into a kind of theater conglomerate. By the time Dietrich signed up for the entrance exam at the Max Reinhardt School, the Kammerspiele and the Grosse Schauspielhaus (formerly the Zirkus Schumann, which had been rebuilt by Hans Poelzig in 1919) were also part of it. The most successful German-language actors belonged to this ensemble, and it was an unwritten law that the premiere of any important play would happen on one of these stages. The Reinhardt theaters were known for their excellent workshops and acting school. Josefine von Losch was aghast at her daughter's plan, but she simmered down when she heard the name Max Reinhardt. Dietrich continually assured her mother that she would not be engaging in honky-tonk entertainment, and that her goal was to become a serious actress.

The entrance exams took place throughout September, on the second floor of the building on Schumannstrasse. Dietrich waited in front of the testing room with the other candidates. She stole glances at the competition, relieved to see the nondescript-looking ones and fearful of competition with those having an air of self-assurance. Every now and then they heard an odd scream or an artificial laugh coming from the adjoining room. The candidates masked their nerves with arrogance. Finally, Dietrich's name was called. "A terribly large number of men sat in chairs and auditioned us for what seemed like hours on end."[5]

The New Woman of the Weimar Republic was under enormous competitive pressure, in particular when it came to the arts, where the training had yet to be regulated and the chance of success was slim. People figured they could get rich and famous overnight.[6] In the past, only ten or perhaps twenty candidates might have shown up; now hundreds were pushing their way to the stage. Dietrich found out just after her audition that she had been accepted to the school, but she wound up staying less than a year. In June 1922—after only four months of instruction—she dropped out, but continued to act in the theater. In the Deutsches Theater archives her name first appears in October 1922. Together with Grete Mosheim she appeared onstage in the Kammerspiele in a production of *Pandora's Box*. The cast included the celebrated actors Werner Krauss, Emil Jannings, and Gertrud Eysoldt. Dietrich had the minor role of Ludmilla Steinherz. She remained on the cast list for a month, then another actress took over her role. By the fall of 1922, she had continuous engagements at theaters in Berlin. She appeared in a production of *The Taming of the Shrew* with Elisabeth Bergner. Bergner was only three years older than Dietrich, but her reputation as a major talent preceded her and Dietrich was quite eager to work with her. The venue was the Grosses Schauspielhaus. Dietrich's role consisted of three sentences. During the rehearsals, there was a dispute with the leading man, who claimed no one could understand her. Bergner defended Dietrich to the director, which Dietrich continued to recall fondly well into her old age. Although the production was criticized for its "crudeness," Bergner became the actress to watch that year. It would take some time for Dietrich's name to appear in a review at all.

As an admirer of Rainer Maria Rilke, she knew about Eleonora Duse. For Duse, there was no difference between herself and the character she portrayed. She became herself by embodying the Other. This mystical approach was utterly alien to the experiences of the young Marlene Dietrich, who could not begin to identify with her roles; sometimes she did not even know quite what or whom she was playing. "In Wedekind's *Pandora's Box*, I was one of the 'silent observers.' Believe it or not, I knew nothing about the play, because I appeared only in the third act. To this day I don't know what it is about."[7] But novices coveted even roles like these, and Dietrich was able to become more than a mere extra in the theater. Again and again she managed to get roles, which was evidence of her assertiveness as she vied with all the other up-and-coming actresses for any bit part.

Dietrich was a theater actress of modest gifts whose stamina, appearance, and determination brought her minor roles. Her lack of conceit and abundance of discipline worked to her advantage, and she was undeterred in her quest to make a name for herself. With her fine sense of social distinctions, she found a place in the hierarchical world of the theater. She succeeded in becoming a "Reinhardt actor" with only a modicum of talent.

The young Dietrich was well-liked by her colleagues because she did not adopt the self-important attitudes that were typical in these circles: "I had no special talent and I knew it. Everyone knew it."[8] This unusual forthrightness put others at ease, yet she was able to make them believe that they might find it useful to know her. She acted as though she posed no threat to anyone's reputation, and in the process she outshone everyone. Her (seeming) lack of interest in her own advancement and her claim that she lacked talent only veiled her ambition. Dietrich worked hard during these years. She compensated for her lack of talent with indefatigable persistence. She criss-crossed the city to get to an odd assortment of theaters in order to recite peculiar lines, the context of which she often didn't quite grasp herself. "For instance, I played the role of a maid in the first act of one play, then took a subway or bus to another theater, where I was a matron in the second act of another play, and finished out the evening as a prostitute in the third act of a third play."[9] Times had changed. She did not sit in a horse-drawn carriage, the way she had with her grandmother, but instead used public transportation. Sometimes she did a favor for another actress by standing in for her, which no one appeared to notice, or she played several roles in a play within the space of a few days. She took what she could get. She watched her colleagues act, then struck up a conversation with them while they were applying their makeup in the dressing room. As the years went by, she became a sought-after actress for minor roles. "I usually spent more time getting prepared than I did acting,"[10] Dietrich made a virtue of necessity: If everybody was going to gossip about how pretty she was, she might as well make the most of her looks. Her dazzling appearance could mask her shortcomings as an actress. Fellow actor Bernhard Minetti had this to say about her: "Nice build. Untheatrical."[11] In addition to her evening performances and daytime rehearsals, Dietrich took singing lessons and learned to box. Boxing was well suited to these post-inflation years: it was about concentration, stamina, toughness, and winning.

When Dietrich started out at the Deutsches Theater, Max Reinhardt's days of glory were already behind him. Even during the war his plays had sold out, but that was changing. "There was revolution on the streets that led to the theaters," recalled Gusti Adler, Reinhardt's biographer. "Actors and audiences who had already walked for hours to get there often had to make their way across the Weidendamm Bridge or the jetty in a hail of bullets. . . . Only genuine drama could have risen above these difficulties, but the young writers did not live up to the challenge."[12] The dramas of the new generation of playwrights were, in Reinhardt's view, bogged down with too much political propaganda and abstract symbolism. Lotte Eisner recalled going to the theater quite often when she was a young woman—three times a week to Reinhardt's theater—but then Brecht came along. Dietrich started out at just this time.

She seems to have been largely unaware of the crisis, having been an avid theatergoer before the war. If she had inherited her beloved grandmother's estate, she would have been sitting in an orchestra seat in an elegant evening gown, not rushing from one stage to the next by subway to declaim this or that for paltry wages. Dietrich's career was a case in point of the downshift in the German bourgeoisie. The shift in the moneyed class's vested interests that was handed down through generations, the lowered status of the classic professions and of the military, and the accompanying rise in the status of technical expertise, coupled with inflation and a massive reduction in ownership of capital, had an impact on Reinhardt's audiences. Kurt Pinthus wrote about the 1923–1924 period: "The season began in the weeks of the most catastrophic inflation. When a theater director has to cope with the fact that the previous evening's revenue is worth only half that amount the very next day, there can be no thought of business as usual. The forcible stabilization then reduced the standard of living of all segments of the population to such a degree, while the ticket prices were kept at an excessive level compared with the prewar period and in comparison with other countries and with vaudeville shows and movies that going to the theater dropped off sharply."[13]

Herbert Ihering urged theater actors to recognize once and for all those for whom they were really performing. For Ihering—an adherent of Brecht's—the theater was failing to connect with its audiences: "It unfurls its ceremonious scope and the whole contrivance of the end to impatient audiences who get no further than the beginning." These audiences may have had the leisure time and money to go to the theater, but they could not make much sense out of what was set out before them.[14] In Ihering's estimation, the audience craved excitement and entertainment of the kind that boxing offered. The ideals of the educated middle class were a thing of the past. In contrast to her mother and most of their relatives, Dietrich was eager to take up the challenge. The revolution may have robbed her of her status in society, but the new republic offered young women new and unimagined opportunities. Dietrich had an utterly unsentimental energy that paid no heed to tradition, but only to her own advancement. She simply had to stand out in a milieu of ruthless competition, and the path she chose was to use scandalous props. As the daughter of an officer, she knew the importance of having just the right equipment. Early on, she began to assemble a set of items, most notably a monocle. In her memoirs, she wrote that the monocle was considered "the height of the 'macabre,'" and her mother had given her the monocle that had belonged to her father.[15]

Without a monocle, the face of a Wilhelmine gentleman was bare. Men who wore monocles were always among their kind; this peculiar masking of their faces signaled that they registered their surroundings in a manner that was reserved for them alone. Leaving off the monocle was the sign of a failure to see. When Dietrich went onstage "with my father's monocle tucked in my eye and my hair done up in hundreds of curls and wisps," she showed that she was initiated into the communication of gentlemen.[16] She used the former symbol of class superiority as an accessory for a femme fatale who knew the wishes and rules of men and would not let any gentleman play her for a fool.

Josefine von Losch made no mention of her younger daughter's machinations. "My mother had withdrawn into herself; she made no comments of any kind, nor did she mention my adventures in the 'world of film,' a phrase offensive to her ear. For her, film and the circus were one and the same thing."[17] In these years, Dietrich got to know her strengths and weaknesses, and put a great many professional touches on her showmanship.

It was only a matter of time before she would turn to show business. Blessed with long, beautiful legs, she got an engagement with the so-called Thielscher Girls. Guido Thielscher, who gave his group this name as an ironic allusion to the famous Tiller Girls, had been a local celebrity in Berlin before the war.[18] Dietrich and the other scantily clad "girls" kicked their legs or tap-danced. Joseph

Roth described them as "a transference of serious military drills for men into the feminine sphere. Their acts are a blend of militarism and eroticism."[19] On an artistic level these acts were nothing to speak of, but they gave Dietrich stage experience and show-business contacts. She was able to move up from the Thielscher Girls to an Erik Charell production, and thus join a new artistic milieu. Max Reinhardt, who had been unsuccessful at covering his costs in running the Grosses Schauspielhaus, had handed over the reins to Charell, a virtually unknown dancer. Charell's performances were a rousing success. He is said to have brought in up to one million reichsmarks per season. Charell produced popular entertainment on a tasteful level; there was no petit bourgeois sex in the style of the Thielscher Girls. He was a dapper dresser who put a premium on opulent stage sets. Dietrich had entered a shimmering sphere of sexual ambiguities. Charell's role models were not in historic Berlin, but in America. He successfully adopted the styles of George Gershwin and Florenz Ziegfeld. He worked with a highly profes-sional production team, and his performers were consistently more popular and gifted than those of other producers.

Charell's production for the 1926–1927 season was called *Von Mund zu Mund* ("From Mouth to Mouth"), and comprised two acts with four scenes each. It featured music by Friedrich Hollaender, Mischa Spoliansky, and George Gershwin, and included texts by Friedrich Hollaender and Erik Charell. The cast featured big names: Curt Bois, Wilhelm Bendow, Claire Waldoff, and Hans Wassmann. Josephine Baker's former partner, the American dancer Louis Douglas, was the choreographer. The plot of the revue was absurd and kitschy: Five children who have fallen asleep in the garden are dreaming about their future. In the second act, they are grown up and recount their dreams. Dietrich stood in for an actress who had fallen ill, playing the role of the emcee who hopes to star in a revue and spends every evening proving her skills on the stage. The emcee was not a major role, but Dietrich was now no longer one of the nameless "girls." The revue's advertising slogan proudly proclaimed: "Charell has the best performers."

The revue ran for six months to a full house. Dietrich's partner, Hubert von Meyerinck, wrote about her: "Your sensuous, exciting legs moved down the runway in jaded serenity. What you acted or did actually amounted to nothing, but this 'nothing' is what led to your fame. You made a style out of this 'nothing.'"[20] Von Meyerinck liked to give small, exquisite parties. The ladies wore evening gowns and the gentlemen tuxedos—although it could easily turn out that a gentleman was actually a lady, and vice versa. Dietrich liked being in these circles, which mimicked and mocked high society.

○ ○ ○

In May 1923, Dietrich married, and a year later she gave birth to a daughter. This would be her only marriage and her only child. Rudolf Emilian Sieber had an open face and a winning smile, and his broad shoulders seemed to offer protection and support. Germany was in a deep crisis at this time, and the Germans were experiencing a profound sense of instability. No one could claim to be safeguarded from the vicissitudes of life or to steer clear of the pervasive sense of danger. Dietrich fell in love during a period of inflation, and married during a period of hyperinflation. She was defying the widespread belief that nothing could endure. In her act of matrimony she was affirming the endurance of love and trust. When she met her future husband in late 1922, he had been in the city for just a short time. Sieber was Czech, from the border town of Aussig. After completing his military service, he moved to Berlin in early 1919 and took a production job at May-Film. The few official papers that have remained from his life give us an indication of what drew Dietrich and Sieber together: they were both displaced from another era. Sieber had a sumptuously decorated birth certificate, which attested to the pride of the prior Habsburg Empire. His father, Anton, and his godfather, Emilian, were Austro-Hungarian civil servants, one in Aussig and the other in Vienna. This birth certificate was issued for a life that Sieber would never lead. When he was born, people still believed in the security and stability of life in the monarchy. He went to war and left his home in peacetime, lived in Berlin and Paris for years, then died in Los Angeles. In a document dated March 1919, Sieber's profession was listed as "business academy graduate"; shortly thereafter, in Berlin, he turned to acting. However, the world would know him in only one role: as the official husband of Marlene Dietrich.

Still, for most of his life, this role was a sham. He remained loyal to his wife by refusing to provide the world any glimpses into their unusual marriage. Dietrich could not and would not deny that she loved him when she was a young woman: "He was nice, he was gentle; he gave me the feeling I could trust him, and this feeling was sustained during all the years of our marriage." Moreover, he was a man with connections to the film industry. Dietrich met Sieber when May-Film had him cast actresses in minor roles for the film *Tragedy of Love*. "Rudolf Sieber told us he was looking for 'demimonde ladies' of distinction. He decided that my friend Grete Mosheim looked 'too serious' for the role. I, however, was told to show up for work the very next day—that's how he thought of me."[21] Dietrich married the man who got her her first real film role. It is no wonder that her mother was not pleased, given her distaste for the world of cinema. Dietrich's mother most likely had no idea how to situate this kind of son-in-law in her hierarchical universe, to which he was an outsider. On May 17, 1923, Dietrich and Sieber were married at the Kaiser Wilhelm Memorial Church. The wedding photograph shows the young couple emerging from the church, with Dietrich, all in white, dashing on ahead, while Sieber, sporting a top hat and a white breast pocket handkerchief, lags slightly behind. Dietrich looks defiant, proud, and determined. She had gotten what she wanted.

This marriage made her a citizen of Czechoslovakia, and she was subject to the police department in charge of aliens and its bureaucratic requirements. Her new husband, whom everyone called "Rudi," wrote, "My stay in Berlin had to be reauthorized once a year. As a foreigner, I also had no right to get my own apartment, but instead had to live with my family as a tenant."[22] In 1924 Sieber submitted an application for Prussian citizenship, which was granted in 1926. As long as he was a Czech citizen, it applied to his whole family, including his daughter Maria.[23]

During the first few years of her marriage, Dietrich must often have felt lonely. The cover of Sieber's passport was falling apart, and many of its pages were full of notations in a variety of languages. The official stamps were from Italy, Austria, Spain, Denmark, Slovenia, Serbia, and Croatia. It is easy to imagine how this life from one residence permit to the next put the two of them to a difficult test. But Sieber had gained her trust. She did not have to put on an act for him. He got to know her as a flirtatious girl who did not hesitate to flaunt her charms. Sieber put up with it, and she was grateful to him. "He had no way of knowing that at home I was not the same girl as at the studio, the girl with the monocle in her eye playing the most depraved prostitute. Still, he did know that that was only a role, or else he wouldn't have courted me the way he did. He could see I was bluffing."[24]

Sieber must have been surprised to meet Dietrich's archconservative family. During their engagement, a chaperone prevented the young couple from meeting alone. Dietrich's uncle was the well-known German National member of the Reichstag, estate owner, and Privy Judicial Counselor Hermann Dietrich. He was a close friend of Alfred Hugenberg's, whose corporation also owned the Ufa Film Company, although it is difficult to determine whether this connection proved useful for her career. It appears unlikely, because Hermann Dietrich was too conservative to approve of his niece taking up acting. A photograph shows them spending time together at a summer resort. Hermann is lying on a lounge chair dressed in a suit, while Rudolf, Marlene, and her mother are posing in their bathing outfits in front of a canopied wicker beach chair.

On December 13, 1924, shortly before her twenty-third birthday, Dietrich became a mother. Photographs of her with her little daughter, Maria Elisabeth, show the fulfillment this child brought her. She looks tender and gentle, yet sad. There is also a remarkable series of photographs that Emil Orlik took of Dietrich not long before this.[25] We see her sitting in a dressing room in her lovely kimono, which was yellow, black, pink, and orange on the outside and bright blue on the reverse. The only way to wear this soft kimono, which was light as a feather, would be naked. In Orlik's pictures the kimono is open near the top, and we see a good deal of skin and cleavage, which Dietrich rarely showed. She is wearing elaborate makeup, with full lips and finely arched eyebrows. The actress Ressel Orla is leaning against her. Dietrich is clearly a woman who wants much more out of life. She is languorously sensual and beguilingly erotic.

This photograph must have been taken soon after her marriage, because she is still wearing her wedding ring. Two years later, she would take it off for good.[26] Sieber was not providing her what she had hoped for. Up to the time of her marriage, Dietrich had lived with her mother, who had experienced so much disappointment in life, and her dutiful sister. Her expectations for the man who would liberate her from the clutches of these two women were enormous. It is no wonder that Sieber did not fulfill them. Both were careful to uphold tradition and show their relatives that they were a good family, as is plain to see in the photographs taken every year during their vacation at the sea. In 1925, we see a happily smiling Dietrich in a stylish bathing suit with her daughter in a canopied wicker beach chair in Sylt; two years later comes a picture of the beach in Swinemünde in which Sieber looks self-conscious, with his arm draped around his wife's waist. He is proud of his lovely wife, while she is clearly straining to maintain a physical distance from him. And one year after that, all three are sitting together on a blanket amidst canopied wicker beach chairs and seem to be enjoying the sun and one another's company. To the outside world, the Siebers were a happy couple. The photographs of sand castles were pasted into the family album, but back home in Berlin, the two of them went their separate ways.

The reviews of the first movie in which Dietrich had a minor role found that the plot was shallow, but the film's technical refinement was dazzling. This kind of assessment would be repeated often in connection with her early productions. In *The Little Napoleon* Dietrich played a maid; the movie pandered to the public with pretty images, a modest degree of humor, and a sparkling portrayal of the military. *Tragedy of Love* was an improvement by comparison, and Kurt Tucholsky found parts of it captivating: "You can object to the genre, but if you don't, then it must be said that this is where the best German naturalist detective film has been created. Three men made it a success: Emil Jannings, Joe May, and Paul Leni."[27] Dietrich had found her way into a circle of true professionals. The memoirs of the set designer Erich Kettelhut give ample evidence of director and producer Joe May's astonishing speed, improvisational skills, and enthusiasm, but also of his jumpy disposition and quick temper. Sieber needed nerves of steel to work with this man. Dietrich played Lucy, the lover of an attorney. Her face looks plump and distorted in a set of grimaces, and her acting is painfully overwrought. Even her coquettish monocle did not help matters much.

Six months after the birth of her daughter, she played the role of Micheline, a fashionable prostitute known as a "cocotte," in the Ufa production of *Manon Lescaut*; Arthur Robison was the director and Theodor Sparkuhl the cinematographer. Hers was not a major role, but it was the second most important female role in the movie after the one played by Lya de Putti. *Manon Lescaut* was the last film de Putti made in Germany before going to Hollywood. The critics crowed that the historical film was not dead and praised the movie's splendid photography, picturesque scenes, and magnificent set designs. These so-called costume films enjoyed great popularity among Germans who were nostalgic for imperial pomp and circumstance.[28] This time, Dietrich's name appeared in the newspaper advertisements and reviews: "Playing alongside Putti, Marlene Dietrich, a strikingly talented young woman, has carried off her first major film role with great skill. We will want to keep an eye out for her, because she appears to be a star in the making."[29]

Alexander Korda, with whom she made her two next films, cared first and foremost about entertainment and lavish design.[30] In *Madame Doesn't Want Children*, Dietrich had a bit part in scene-stealing outfits. Sieber was the production manager. The film is notable because of its message and because its screenplay was written by Béla Balázs. Balázs was a Hungarian communist writer who had published an essay on "The Revolutionary Film" in communist party journal *Die Rote Fahne* in the fall of 1922, promoting the cause of proletarian, impassioned, and visionary cinema. *Madame Doesn't Want Children* was the diametric opposite. While this movie did not look kindly on bourgeois women who lived in the lap of luxury, it also poked fun at the New Woman on the quest for autonomy and pleasure. "This flimsy comedy with the flippant title ends with a paean to the blessing of children. It begins with a short skirt, extraordinarily low-cut blouses, and a sense of curiosity, but ends on a moralistic note, with childbirth."[31] The movie was shot in the record time of thirteen days because the Kordas were expected in Hollywood. The reviews were devastating; only the left-wing press saw it in a positive light, and it ran for months at movie theaters in Moscow.

The technical elements of Dietrich's earliest films were lauded, but the shallow plots, cheap effects, and kitsch came under critical fire. She did not have any other offers. She was hired because of her good looks. Louise Brooks, who was five years younger than

Dietrich, claimed that Dietrich had tried out for the role of Lulu in *Pandora's Box*, but director G. W. Pabst emphatically denied that later on, explaining that "Dietrich was too old and too obvious—one sexy look and the picture would become a burlesque." Brooks added, "She was the Dietrich of *I Kiss Your Hand, Madame*, a film in which, caparisoned variously in beads, brocade, ostrich feathers, chiffon ruffles, and white rabbit fur, she galloped from one lascivious stare to another."[32] Dietrich simply did not know any better—nor, apparently, did her husband. They offered slapstick, which could earn money but not fame. The world of film turned out to be a comedown for Dietrich, especially in light of the fact that she was originally aiming for a career as a classical artist. As a musician, she would have salvaged some remnant of nobility in her mother's eyes, because even in the Weimar Republic an artist was considered special. But as of now, she had become no more than a minor actress. On October 18, 1926, she wrote in her diary, "I play in the theater and in films and earn money. I have just reread this diary—oh god, where is all that wonderful exuberance, that being carried away by feelings? All gone!"[33]

Dietrich was in Vienna at the time, acting alongside Willi Forst in a movie called *Café Electric*, directed by Gustav Ucicky, son of the painter Gustav Klimt. This movie signaled a turning point in her career. *Café Electric* offered not only a heavy dose of morality, but also a realistic portrayal of the world of pimps, petty crooks, and floozies. It is a sad film in which Forst plays a pickpocket and Dietrich plays Erni, the daughter of a millionaire who has fallen for him. The relationship between the two is marked by violence and sexual subjection. The film runs counter to the spirit of the age: Marital fidelity is trumpeted as the highest value, while sexual freedom invariably leads to ruin. The Viennese newspapers praised her acting: "Marlene Dietrich's Erni, the daughter of a contractor, is simply a gem of the most impressive incarnation of a wretched girl whose upbringing is luxurious but far from good."[34] At this time, she struck up a friendship with fellow cast member Igo Sym and was fascinated by the way he played the "musical saw." When he left, he made her a gift of the instrument as a memento of their time together in Vienna. After Hitler's invasion of Poland, Sym, as a "citizen of the German Reich," helped set up the Polish theater. He promoted the Nazi propaganda film *Homecoming*, which was also directed by Ucicky. Once Sym's contacts to the Gestapo had been confirmed, he was liquidated by order of the Polish underground government in March 1941. When Dietrich returned to Europe in 1944, her suitcase contained the musical saw she would use from then on to entertain the American troops.

Dietrich proved to be an able match for Forst in her portrayal of the pampered yet neglected girl. Forst was an elegant bon vivant whose role of a lifetime is rightly considered to be *Bel Ami* (1939). He had come to Berlin back in 1925. When they were shooting the film *Café Electric*, he and Dietrich entered into an affair. Like Sieber, Forst radiated sunny optimism and had a compact, powerful physique. Forst's despairing letters to Dietrich spoke of his everlasting love for her. In the early 1930s, he wrote:

> I am right at the brink, tottering around in this city and not knowing what I'm doing here. . . . Darling, you must come to me soon, and you can never leave me alone again. I am boundlessly unhappy! This old Europe is cracking apart at the seams on the left and the right, and it affects everyone except me, because I have no feeling other than longing and no thought other than "you."[35]

His letters reveal a side of "Bel Ami" that differs substantially from the charming seducer. Forst was a harried, extremely unhappy man. He was always short of money, doubtful of his talent, and unsuited for any job other than acting. He hid his bitter melancholia under a sugarcoating of Viennese charm. Forst kept Dietrich up to date about the latest developments in the film industry; he admired her acting talent and tried to find suitable screenplays for her. We can only assume that the affair with Forst provided a substantial boost to further Dietrich's career in film. In his boundless infatuation, he also boosted her self-confidence about her acting skills. Forst was in a better position to support Dietrich than Sieber was; with Rudi, she produced nothing but flops. Dietrich appears to have helped Forst out financially on many occasions and suggested remedies for his hair loss, while he pined away for her, listening to her records, watching her movies, and wallowing in his suffering.

The only performance on a Berlin stage of lasting importance to Dietrich was at the Komödie Theater on Kurfürstendamm, a small neo-Rococo theater. She enjoyed the modern-minded, sophisticated audiences on the Kurfürstendamm. Dietrich had grown up in a part of Berlin that set great store by tradition, and time seemed to stand still. The Kurfürstendamm, by contrast, with its bars, movie theaters, and late-night revelers, was the embodiment of the big-city attitude toward life.

Dietrich was asked to try out at the Komödie, also run by Reinhardt, for a musical in a very new style. She would be accompanied on the piano by the composer of the revue, Mischa Spoliansky. Spoliansky, whom critics regarded as *the* composer on the Kurfürstendamm, went on to write the tune for her first hit, and the two of them would remain friends throughout their lives. Dietrich soon realized that she was now part of a Bohemian clique with a casual attitude toward marital fidelity. Their artistic inspiration came from the lyricist Marcellus Schiffer. He was a prematurely aged man who sported a monocle and knickerbockers, and took great pride in his erotic sketches. He had gone through a political phase but then discovered cabaret and targeted the snobbish, upper-class bourgeoisie, whose weaknesses he revealed bluntly and humorously with wicked charm.

The Schiffer and Spoliansky revue, which premiered in May

1928, was called *It's in the Air*. It was set in a department store. Dietrich's castmates were Margo Lion, Oskar Karlweis, Willy Prager, Hubert von Meyerinck, Otto Wallburg, and Ida Wüst. She found the rehearsals both exhausting and instructive, and gravitated to the star of the show, Margo Lion, Schiffer's lover and an unrivaled cabaret artist who satirized the era.[36] In addition to her professional elocution skills, Lion owed her success to her physical appearance: she was extraordinarily elegant and thin as a rail. Working with Lion brought Dietrich into the spotlight. Once the revue became a success, Dietrich was known throughout Berlin.

The reviews, which Schiffer neatly clipped and saved, confirm that *It's in the Air* was hailed in every major newspaper, and in many small ones, in Germany and abroad; it was called "a sterling achievement" (*Vorwärts*) that won over audiences with "wit rather than a big budget" (*Berliner Morgenzeitung*). Schiffer attacked the two tools of debasement: sex and money. *It's in the Air* was an elegant satire of the era. As a librettist, Schiffer did not overwhelm his audiences with ideology; this was quick-witted, amusing entertainment. The troupe played to a full house every evening for three months. On June 28, 1928, Lion and Schiffer were married. The wedding photograph that was printed in many newspapers was the best advertisement for their current production, since Lion also played a bride in the revue. But a duet by Lion and Dietrich also made headlines. In the "Sisters" scene, the two women, clad in black, sing this song:

> When the best girlfriend and the best girlfriend traipse
> through the streets, to go shopping, to go shopping, to
> shoot the breeze, the best girlfriend says to the best girl-
> friend: My best girlfriend! . . . Once there were gallants, but
> they dwindled away! Today, instead of gallants, there are
> girlfriends!

Then Oskar Karlweis comes up to the two women and asks, "How about we get along again?" and the women purr in response, "Oh yes, let's get along again."[37] They end the scene as a trio. Biographers can hardly resist the temptation to interpret the women's duet as an expression of sexual promiscuity, but Spoliansky intended it as a parody of the inseparable Dolly Sisters, who were quite successful at the time. With this text, Schiffer was making fun of the city's so-called high society and its many speculators and racketeers whose wealth had come from the war and inflation. In these circles, people enjoyed flouting social conventions and indulging in extramarital affairs, including same-sex affairs. The reviews emphasized Dietrich's acting prowess, youthful freshness, and lovely figure, while her sexual preferences went unmentioned. The sexual aspect was tacked on later by biographers, and may have arisen from the need to adhere as closely as possible to clichés about bisexual or lesbian woman of the 1920s. "Those twenties" came to be equated with sexual anarchy, also in reference to Dietrich.[38] Schiffer, himself a man without clearly discernible sexual preferences, was poking fun at modern liaisons with the now-standard bisexual backdrop. Pairing two such contrasting women for the duet heightened its appeal, with Lion embodying the parody of the modern androgynous creature (more intellectual than sensual, downright sarcastic, devoid of bosom and buttocks) while Dietrich evoked "old-fashioned sensuality . . . slim and cuddlesome, brimming with vigor and a zest for life."[39] Lion's odd appearance made Dietrich look positively radiant by contrast. Newspaper advertisements highlighted this study in contrasts, which became the hallmark of the revue, and created a media sensation. The *Berliner Börsen-Courier* reported, "These two very different women . . . are catapulting Berlin cabaret to international heights. We hear that even George Gershwin could not pass up the chance to see this revue."[40]

○   ○   ○

Dietrich and Lion captured the tone of Berlin: cheeky, tough, and right to the point. They shared a skeptical, saucy irony and a sad gaiety, the melancholy and aplomb of the city dweller. People who came to see Schiffer and Lion delighted in sexual ambiguity; the gay bars in Schöneberg were simply more amusing than the tea dances in Charlottenburg. After the performance, they headed to Eldorado on Motzstrasse, with a big hodgepodge of refined ladies, ambitious girls, pretty boys, transvestites, literati, financiers, and erotomaniacs. It was important to be on good terms with the owner, because not everyone was welcome here. If he did not like someone, he would come to the table himself and tell the guest that his order would be on the house, but he was not to return. An orchestra played dance music; the audience—which ranged from high-society Berlin couples to out-of-towners who had heard that Eldorado was the place to be—sat on either side on daises. The chubby bartender blew kisses, flirted with everyone, and could easily turn out to be a woman, while a lovely ballerina might unexpectedly turn out to have a male voice. Lion and Dietrich knew that they could not simply go home after their performance—they had to put in an appearance at Eldorado. This was where rumors flourished, and rumors made for the best publicity. Dietrich also socialized at the Silhouette, a small, disreputable bar on Gaisberg-strasse "with a nattily dressed black waiter and boys in women's clothing up at the bar. Everyone who was anyone could be seen here."[41] They sat together night after night in red booths, with the band playing "Just a Gigolo," and "I Kiss Your Hand, Madame." The atmosphere was less swanky and more intellectual at Schwan-necke, a wine bar near the Kaiser Wilhelm Memorial Church where established theater people and authors got together. The bar, harshly lit by bare lightbulbs, was generally overcrowded because there were only twenty tables. The proprietor was himself an actor at the Volksbühne. His famous, and not-so-famous, guests came late in the evening, usually after the performance. At Schwannecke, you could run into Carl Zuckmayer, Bertolt Brecht, Elisabeth Bergner, Conrad Veidt, Ernst Toller, Lion Feuchtwanger, Rosa Valetti, or Heinrich George. Schwannecke was the place to get roles, plan careers, and spark rumors. The cafés at the Kaiser Wilhelm Memorial Church, where Reinhardt's students gathered, were regarded as the waiting rooms of fame. But once someone had secured a place in the Schwannecke, one (almost) belonged. Erich Kästner found that in Berlin, the place at which an artist spent his time was the best gauge of his level of success. "When you hear: 'He doesn't go to the Romanische anymore. He now spends a lot of time at Schwannecke,' this implicitly signaled signed contracts, advancement, budget surpluses, imminent fame. The two places were no more than three minutes away from each other, but it takes some people decades to get from one to the other, and most never make it at all."[42] Dietrich, at any rate, *did* make it, once *It's in the Air* became a hit.

She was often away from home at night and had lovers, but she continued to live with her husband and child in a large apartment on Kaiserallee. The couple slept in separate rooms, Sieber in his study, and Dietrich in the master bedroom. When she was in Vienna, one of her colleagues took care of Maria. Tamara Matul was one of the many Russian women who had fled to Berlin with her parents and siblings before the revolution.[43] Her good looks and shapely legs landed her in show business, and she even had a small part in *It's In the Air*. Tamara was shy and lacked the skill to achieve stardom. Once she became Sieber's lover, she did everything in her power to please him: by day she was the devoted nanny, and by night the undemanding paramour. This arrangement worked out perfectly for Dietrich, who could pursue her relationships and maintain control over her husband's love life. Tamara was weak, vulnerable, and sweet, so Dietrich could rest assured that Sieber would not leave her for Tamara. Sieber was still struggling to get established in film and hoped that, with a bit of luck, his wife would be a success. She did not need to feign love or faithfulness, and she appreciated the fact that he let her do as she liked, but she literally paid the price by bringing home the money that guaranteed a good life for all of them. The two did not separate, and they raised their child together. They were a production team, with the product being Marlene Dietrich.

Dietrich was not one of those newcomers to the city who complained that Berlin was a locus of unhappiness or crowed about the city being so deliciously wicked. She was at home in Berlin, which Joseph Roth called a "young and unhappy city-in-waiting."[44] Unlike Paris or London, Berlin could boast of nothing but endlessly long streets and an array of train stations.

The Villa Felsing was located on Lichtensteinallee in the upscale Tiergarten section of Berlin. Dietrich's uncle Willibald was an attorney who had been awarded the Iron Cross during the war, as well as a successful businessman. He was quite fond of the cinema and liked to surround himself with actors and directors; he rented to Oskar Messter, a film tycoon, and he sometimes shared his villa on Lichtensteinallee with Conrad Veidt. Jolly Felsing, Uncle Willy's wife, was from Galicia. She was a beautiful woman, ten years younger than her husband. The cocktail parties at the Villa Felsing were the talk of the town. There was a Steinway grand piano in the parlor on which the Austrian tenor Richard Tauber was accompanied. Dietrich often came to the villa; she reveled in this mysterious, melancholy, yet oddly high-spirited atmosphere. As might be expected, Josefine von Losch did not want her daughter spending time there, but Dietrich paid no heed to her injunctions.

The social scene in Berlin had been transformed by war and inflation. Old and new money intermingled. Prosperous speculators enjoyed being seen in the company of destitute young women from noble families; Russian princesses waited on art dealers of the

European avant-garde; and conservative bankers furnished their homes in the Bauhaus style. The cocktail parties at the Villa Felsing brought together notables from the world of film—Conrad Veidt, Richard Tauber, Emil Jannings, Claire Waldoff, and Lil Dagover— with Wilhelminian Prussian princes Adalbert and Eitel Friedrich, influential businessman Alfred Hugenberg, and General Hindenburg. These parties were ideal for an ambitious young actress looking to make contacts. Dietrich's cousin, Hasso Felsing, vividly recalled Dietrich's presence at the social events in the villa.

Jolly Felsing was known for her extravagant taste, and pictures of her were featured in *Die Dame*, *Elegante Welt*, and other women's magazines. Eventually Willibald realized that his wife's lifestyle was not really cultivated; she simply liked spending money. The couple separated, and he died in 1934. She married twice more. Hasso heard that Dietrich had gone to America, but he would not see the movie that made her famous until after the war. Still, her husky voice resounded through the villa again and again. His mother spent whole days lying on the chaise longue in the big parlor and playing "Falling in Love Again" on the gramophone. The boy was surprised, because his cousin Marlene had never sung at the parties.

Dietrich earned good money, and her daughter recalled that plenty of it was spent: "As a very young child, I saw luxuries come and go, be replaced by more luxuries, without any fanfare or particular excitement. No 'Look everyone—I got it! The coat I have been saving for, the one I wanted for so long . . . It's mine! Isn't it wonderful? Let's celebrate!' My mother just appeared one day with a mink coat, threw it on a chair, from where it slipped to the floor, lying there forgotten while she strode off to the kitchen to cook dinner."[45] Dietrich was a woman with style, and what should a woman like her wear if not mink?

Kurt Bernhardt cast her opposite Fritz Kortner as a beautiful, mysterious creature named Stascha in *The Woman One Longs For*.

The filming was said to be fraught with tension, because Kortner aimed to be Dietrich's lover in real life as well. Stascha is an unhappy woman who makes her lover commit murders for her. This is not one of Dietrich's usual coquettish roles that had her rolling her eyes and striking poses. Her movements are those of a sleepwalker; she usually keeps her eyelids half closed; they open for only brief moments, with provocative languor. Dietrich slows the pace; her character is innocent and depraved at the same time, and seems to spend most of her time smoking. She now dispensed with her monocle and other cheap gags. In one scene, we see her sad, beautiful face arise from the smoke behind a frozen windowpane. Again and again we watch her apply her makeup. She does not have the trendy, doll-like, heart-shaped mouth; hers is big and sensual. Destruction and eroticism blend into one. Stascha demands sacrifices of men, whom she then sacrifices. Dietrich proved that she had mastered the game of devotion and delay. *The Woman One Longs For* was Dietrich's first movie to present her as a star, and she began to be known as "the German Garbo."[46]

Well aware of the limitations of her talent, she tried to find roles best suited to her. She started by playing lower-class, loose women, then unscrupulous women, and was eventually cast as the femme fatale. Strikingly often, the setting of these films was Paris, the subject was almost always love, and—oddly—they wound up perpetuating class distinctions. In the end, the aristocrats realize that they feel a need to stick with the principles of honor that befitted their station in life. These movies were set in the present, but they upheld the values of the past.

Dietrich made her way up in the business. She had experience in both theater and film, and she could sing and dance. Her work ethic was exemplary. True to her mother's teachings, she was punctual, friendly, well prepared, and uncomplaining. Although she was a wife and mother, she enjoyed making the rounds of the night spots, especially Schwannecke, Eldorado, or Eden. No matter how late she stayed out, Dietrich showed up on time at rehearsals or on the set, and everyone wondered how she managed to look so gorgeous early in the morning. At long last, she could be beautiful and seductive, and was even paid for the privilege. Her vibrantly colored clothes from this period were sophisticated and beautifully tailored. She enjoyed combining fashion that was considered typically feminine with traditional men's clothing. She would wear delicate lace cuffs and elegant kimonos, yet she also had bright blue sailor-style coarse linen trousers made to order. She had originally dreamed of performing in concert halls around the world, and now she was delighted to see her name on the cast list of a revue. But as a child of the war who had been raised in the Prussian spirit, she had learned above all how to get by. She persevered and grew progressively more successful in the business of fiction. She performed on small and large stages and acted in naïve, bawdy, and slick movies, yet no failures could keep her from forging ahead. She barely registered the political polarization of the Weimar Republic, agitprop theater, or the ideological messages of angry young writers. She now had to provide for a husband and a child, even though her marriage had failed to bring her happiness.

o o o

Leni Riefenstahl's luck as an acclaimed dancer held out all of six months.

> In these six months, my feet danced across the great
> stages, at home and abroad . . . more than seventy dance
> recitals. . . . Every hour and every thought was about
> dance, every day filled with tough practice that went on for
> many hours, rehearsing new dances, and designing new
> costumes. Everything I saw in these six months, paintings,

sculptures—everything I heard, music—for me, everything
had connections only to dance. I seemed destined by fate to
live my life exclusively in dance, today and for all time.[47]

Riefenstahl claimed that it had been Max Reinhardt who had
advanced her career; she liked to explain that her old admirer Vollmoeller had brought Reinhardt to one of her dance recitals, and
Reinhardt was so taken with her that he offered her a spot at his
theater right then and there. Moreover, she proudly pointed out
that she had been the first dancer to perform without an ensemble
"at the most famous theater in Germany." That is just as untrue as
the claim that she performed for six evenings and several matinees.
According to the archivist at the Deutsches Theater, Riefenstahl
had only two performances at the Deutsches Theater: on December
16, 1923, at noon and on December 20, 1923, at 8 p.m. Moreover,
she was not the first solo dancer to perform on Schumannstrasse.[48]
Her name does not appear in any of Reinhardt's writings.

    Riefenstahl choreographed her own dances. The back of the
stage was all black, and she used the music of famous composers,
such as Franz Schubert and Frédéric Chopin. She was barefoot and
wore loose garments; performing without toe shoes and a tutu was
a sign of commitment to an avant-garde aesthetic. She designed her
costumes herself, then her mother had them made. Once her father
was persuaded of Leni's talent, his wife could finally devote herself
to supporting their daughter, whom she accompanied, looked after,
and admired. Riefenstahl had prevailed: her career as an artist had
become a family affair, and would remain so. She surrounded herself with her family and her loyal admirers and brought her pianist,
Hermann Klamt, with her when she went on the road. Three years
earlier, Mary Wigman had had to bring in a new musical accom-
panist for every dance recital because she did not have sufficient
financial resources to add a pianist to her staff. Riefenstahl had
no such need to cut corners. She claimed to have taken in five

hundred to a thousand of the new, stable rentenmarks per performance, which enabled her to buy nice clothing and engage her own pianist. From this point on, she always found a way to amass substantial funding for her projects.

The beginning of Riefenstahl's career coincided with the period of hyperinflation. She was one of the young and nimble to emerge as victors in a time of upheaval and turmoil. She saw an opportunity for herself in the shifting function of culture that this period had triggered, with the help of Harry Sokal, who owed his fortune to inflation. Remarkably, she managed to sidestep the mass entertainment that came from America and never succumbed to the temptation to become a showgirl. Her artistic rise was a part of the history of the Weimar Republic that has yet to be told in full. The heyday of the avant-garde was over, and New Objectivity and neoclassicism were making their entrance.[49] This pan-European aesthetic *retour à l'ordre* was intensified in Germany by the above-mentioned political and economic upheavals in the wake of defeat, revolution, and inflation. For the impoverished middle class, buying a book or a ticket to the theater was no longer a top priority. Publishers and authors lamented a catastrophic decline in the level of public taste.[50] Riefenstahl's successes as a dancer need to be seen against this backdrop: She did not go in for the "grotesque dance" associated with Valeska Gert or the abstract style of Mary Wigman, but instead catered to an audience looking for middlebrow entertainment and wary of overly sophisticated art—in other words, an audience very much like herself.

Riefenstahl gravitated to a trivialized form of the avant-garde. Where there is an avant-garde, a rear guard cannot be far behind. She performed at a remove, and she did not get beyond the stage of feigned emotion.[51] Her dance was not innovative; she reworked experimental and modern forms of dance to craft a popular performance style. "She has the oriental physical pathos, the vibrant arabesque from Wigman, but with one major difference: for Wig-

man, dance is rhythmic thinking, abstraction, while Leni Riefenstahl always remains within the melodic structure."[52] Riefenstahl
was out for commercial success. Her advertising brochure bore the
title: "The Dancer Leni Riefenstahl. Excerpts from Press Reviews,"
and her portrait graced the cover. The brochure was printed in
Innsbruck, so presumably Sokal paid for this advertising material.
The reviews it contained were written in the period between October 1923 and April 1924. The critics rarely failed to point out her
beauty and youth, which seemed to be what drew them to the performances. In the words of one Swiss journalist: "She came, she
was seen, she conquered."[53]

Riefenstahl sought to reign triumphant. She adopted the dramatic solemnity of expressive dance, but applied it only to herself
as the embodiment of an artist. In doing so, she claimed to represent the spirit of a greater artistic totality. Her dancing was unper-
suasive because it lacked spiritual substance. Riefenstahl believed
that everything emanated from within herself, and the result was
hollow art. She was more interested in technique than in feeling,
and she was utterly unable to infuse her dance with emotion. She
figured that strenuous physical exertion could compensate for her
lack of inner conviction. "During the intermission, I would lie on
whatever couch I could find, bathed in sweat, incapable of saying
a single word. But my youth and the strenuous training made me
overcome any exhaustion." Art and pain went hand in hand. In
July 1923, she attended a summer dance course offered by the Jutta
Klamt School at Lake Constance. When she returned to Berlin,
she continued working with Klamt. In the mornings, she studied
classical ballet with Eugenia Eduardowa, and in the afternoons she
headed to Klamt's school of dance.[54] Klamt was one of the most
successful teachers of expressive dance in the twenties. She systematically appealed to women to awaken from their passivity. Klamt
immersed herself in modern aesthetics and claimed that her work
aimed at discovering spiritually inspired abstraction in dance.[55] She

would come to identify with National Socialism more closely than just about any other dancer. In her numerous writings, she consistently stressed an experience of wholeness and promised enhanced vitality to those who joined up with her. The recovery that she herself had experienced was of key importance to her artistic concept. The abstraction of dance, she explained, enables a dancer to liberate herself from an oppressive person or episode in her life. Dance enabled Riefenstahl to free herself from her father and become an artist. It brought her liberation and meaning, pathos and ecstasy.[56] Art, beauty, and strength would remain the core of all stages of Riefenstahl's career.

Before the war, both rhythmic gymnastics and expressive dance had been popular among well-bred young women. In the Weimar Republic, the social composition in the courses changed. The typical clientele for gymnastics now comprised saleswomen and female office workers aspiring to upward mobility. In a manner of speaking, Riefenstahl was one of them; she had exchanged her father's office for a dance studio. Rhythmic gymnastics held out the prospect of "perfecting the construction of the self" as well as "enhancing personality." Klamt and her husband were devotees of the Mazdaznan movement, which coupled ideas from the Far East with Western values and melded progressive performance concepts with critiques of civilization.[57] Mazdaznan invoked universally valid wisdom and modern scientific findings, amounting to a kind of health- and youth-based religion. This movement was popular among expressive dancers, artists, Bauhaus architects, and adherents of the back-to-nature movement; its followers claimed that Aryans were the chosen rulers, who had degenerated as a result of miscegenation, incorrect breathing, and poor diet. Youth, beauty, vigor, and good health were promised to anyone who lived according to Mazdaznan precepts. Klamt taught Mazdaznan thinking at her school.[58]

Riefenstahl focused on Klamt's pedagogical objectives: "Concentration on a goal—stamina—sensitivity—alertness—drive."[59] Riefenstahl never attained artistic freedom in any stage of her career until she had suffered severe physical torments and undergone a process of conversion and recovery. Her pain would bring her to a new artistic calling, which, in turn, would eventually culminate in pain once again. Throughout her life, she compensated for any misfortune in one branch of art by redoubling her efforts in the next branch. At the pinnacle of her career in dance, she was injured during a recital in Prague, "at a theater that could hold three thousand spectators. Anna Pavlova was the only other dancer who had ever performed here, and tonight the house was sold out to the last seat. My evening was a triumph, but perhaps my last. While making one of my artistic leaps my knee cracked, and I felt a pain so sharp that I could barely finish the dance."[60] Riefenstahl had to walk with a cane, and her future as a dancer was in doubt.

The man in her life was still Otto Froitzheim. He seemed to be taking their relationship quite seriously; he had already introduced her to his mother and pressured Riefenstahl to get engaged to him. She did not appreciate his treating her like his possession, but she could not bring herself to break things off. Riefenstahl relished the confirmation of her femininity and sexual attractiveness that came with this affair. Moreover, her lover was an international sports star who enjoyed great popularity in Germany as the top player on the German Davis Cup team.

Shortly after she came of age, Riefenstahl returned to the city and spent much of her time on Fasanenstrasse, just off Kurfürstendamm, at Klamt's studio. She was able to make the leap from Zeuthen, in Brandenburg, to the heart of the new Berlin, leaving her childhood home in Wedding far behind. As a native Berliner, she understood the significance of choosing just the right neighborhood. People hoping to be seen as modern opted for the New West over the eastern sections, which were mired in tradition. Up-and-coming young artists and the smart and trendy were moving west. Kurfürstendamm featured an array of luxury fashion stores with elegant window displays; there were also American-style bars, the first fast-food restaurants decorated with gleaming chrome, a great many movie theaters and neon signs, and a robust night life.

Riefenstahl steeled her body and her will and lived in conjunction with the new era. She was the very image of the New Woman: single, economically independent, tough, resilient, ambitious, and childless. She surrounded herself with people who supported and nurtured her ambitions, and avoided anyone or anything that might hold her back or keep her away from her art.

She also took boxing lessons with Sabri Mahir. Photographs clearly reveal the extent of her transformation from a somewhat pudgy, insecure girl to a slim, self-confident woman with a remarkably well-toned body in keeping with the ideal of beauty in her era. The vogue of the short straight line, emphasizing a woman's legs and negating the female form, had been superseded by a renewed emphasis on feminine curves on a slim, sporty body. The modern silhouette could no longer be attained by means of whalebone corsets and girdles; it had to be acquired by engaging in sports. "The modern dress is far too light, too thin, too distinct in its lines to allow for false pretences," *Vogue* magazine announced in 1928.[61] Whalebone corsets gave way to rippling muscles. The era of "sitting beauties" had passed; beauty was no longer a matter of couture, but a product of hard work. Rhythmic gymnastics and dance were strongly recommended to develop physical elasticity and give a graceful look to a slender body.

This message was no mere fashion dictate. The war had had a sobering influence on the relationship between the sexes. Ruffles were out; smooth lines were in. Seldom in history has the framework that politics and society set for men and women been as sharply demarcated and determinative as for those born between 1890 and 1910. This generation was defined by war and emancipation. For men, the war itself was the defining experience; for women, the sweeping changes—the right to an education and participation in politics through suffrage—came postwar. The war had left young men and women with a deep-seated mistrust of exuberance and passion. Love was objectivized to shield against disappointment. Physically fit young women were an expression of the new Germany. After war and hunger, women wanted to strengthen their bodies and test their limits in sports and in love in order to feel alive. The restrained quality of the young women in their practical clothing was an extension of the sobriety that characterized those years. A matter-of-fact self-confidence befitted the spirit of reportage and documentaries that left nothing to the imagination. The New Woman did not go in for illusions; she neither radiated an air of mystery nor demanded special treatment. The technologies of film and photography made these women into professional portrayers of themselves, who did not merely endure or long for a man's gaze, but instead self-assuredly required and requited it.

Lotte Jacobi's photographs taken in the late 1920s show us a different Leni Riefenstahl. Jacobi's studio was close to Riefenstahl's apartment. She sought to photograph the young and restless creative set. Her portraits have become icons of the 1920s: Lotte Lenya, the "Pirate Jenny" from *The Threepenny Opera*, beguiling with short hair and bangs, dark lipstick, a turtleneck sweater, and a cigarette; Egon Erwin Kisch, the "raging reporter," engrossed in a phone conversation; the siblings Erika and Klaus Mann, haughty and androgynous, in starched shirts and ties, a cigarette dangling from Klaus's lips, flaunting their twin-like resemblance. Jacobi's mother, Mia, was a master of advertising strategy and had good instincts for who might become famous. She considered Riefenstahl a prospect for the future. Riefenstahl sat for several photographs, but she would not agree to the exclusive contract she was offered.[62]

The Riefenstahl that Jacobi reveals is an oddly fragile-looking, mysterious woman. One photograph, which bears the title "Little

Sphinx," portrays the artist in profile, highlighting her delicately curved mouth, pointed nose, and one thick, expressive eyebrow over her dark eye. Her inscrutable gaze suggests a sphinx lying in wait for her victims.[63]

In the early summer of 1925, a few days after the tennis tournament in which her fiancé emerged victorious, Riefenstahl was waiting at the Nollendorfplatz subway station. Froitzheim had left town again, with her promise to marry him soon. Still, she was anything but a contented fiancée. During the tournament she had been a mere spectator, and in the celebrations that followed, she was reduced to the role of the woman at the victor's side. It had been painful for her to watch him revel in his success and his profession, while she sat next to him like a poor invalid. Standing by her famous man was not the role Riefenstahl had envisioned for herself, and she used this situation as a reason to split up with him. Froitzheim would not hear of it, and bombarded her with flowers and letters. "One day he stood outside my door," she later recalled, "asking if he could come in. Never would I have imagined that this man would fight so hard for me. I knew that if I let him enter, I would fall in with him again, but I still found it unspeakably hard not to open the door to him. . . . I bit my hand to stop my sobbing, but I stuck with my resolve. It was the most painful decision I had ever made. After his footsteps faded I wept until the morning."[64] That was the end of her first great love.

The pains in her knee did not let up, and dance recitals were out of the question. Her greatest fear was that her career as an artist would come to an end. She had no intention of returning to work at her father's office. She made an appointment with a very good doctor and hoped he would be able to help her. All previous consultations had culminated in advice to take it easy and get plenty of rest. But rest was exactly what she did not want. If she did not return to the stage, no photographer would continue to be interested in her.

Tired and demoralized, I stood waiting on the platform,
gritting my teeth as my knee began to throb again. My eyes
skimmed over the colors of the posters on the opposite wall
until all of a sudden they focused on one poster: a male figure clambering over a towering chimney. Underneath, the
poster said: "Mountain of Destiny—a Film about the Dolomites, by Dr. Arnold Fanck." Even though I had just been
haunted by thoughts about my future, I stared as if hypno-
tized at the picture, at those steep walls of rock, at the man
swinging from one wall to the next. The train arrived at last
and came to a halt between the poster and me. It was the
train that I had been waiting for so impatiently. When it left,
I could see the poster again. As if awakening from a trance, I
watched the train vanish into the tunnel of Kleiststrasse.[65]

She skipped the doctor's appointment, which had felt like her
last ray of hope just moments earlier, and went to the movies
instead. *Mountain of Destiny* was playing at the theater right across
the square.

The very first images fascinated me. Mountains and clouds,
alpine slopes and towering rock streamed past me. I was
experiencing a world that was alien to me, for I had never
seen such mountains. I knew them only from postcards,
where they looked lifeless and rigid. But here, on the screen,
they seemed alive, mysterious, and fascinating. Never could
I have imagined that mountains could be so beautiful. As
the film went on I became more and more captivated.[66]

She left the movie theater filled with a new sense of longing.
In her dreams, she saw herself heading across the mountains, and
resolved that she would not only get to know the mountains, but
would also meet the director of this film. There are two versions of

how she accomplished this, one from Riefenstahl herself, and the other from Luis Trenker. In her own account, she traveled to the Dolomites a few weeks after seeing Fanck's film, together with her brother Heinz, who supported her as she walked. They spent four weeks at the best hotel at the Karersee, where Empress Elisabeth of Austria, Karl May, Winston Churchill, and Agatha Christie also spent their vacations. Riefenstahl was hoping to meet Dr. Fanck there, or one of his actors, but her hopes were dashed. Still, she was enraptured by the alpine world, a world she had never seen, and felt as though she had been transported back to her childhood dreams. As always with Riefenstahl, the encounters that shaped her destiny did not occur until the last minute. Shortly before her departure, she met Trenker, who had played the lead role in *Mountain of Destiny*. In the hotel lobby, she had discovered a poster announcing that the film would be shown that evening. She later described her experience:

> I hobbled back to where the projector was set up and found, standing next to it, a man whom I recognized as the star of the movie. "Are you Herr Trenker?" I asked a bit shyly. His eyes glided over my elegant clothes, then he nodded and said, "That's me." My embarrassment vanished. My enthusiasm for the film, the mountains, and the actors just bubbled out of me. "I'm going to be in your next movie," I said with a tone of certainty, as though this was the most obvious thing in the world. Trenker looked bewildered, then began to laugh: "Can you climb mountains? An elegant lady like you shouldn't be traipsing around mountains." "I'll learn how. I will definitely learn how; I can do it if I make up my mind to." Again I felt a sharp pain in my knee, which tore me out of my euphoria and brought me back to earth. An ironic smile flitted across Trenker's face. Gesturing goodbye, he turned away.[67]

Once she returned to Berlin, she sent him a letter and asked him to forward it to Fanck. No reply was forthcoming.[68] In this version of the events, Trenker rebuffed her from the outset. Women— especially women from the city—had no place in his world. Trenker wrote in his autobiography that Fanck had hired him to distribute *Mountain of Destiny* in Italy. In order to find suitable contacts, he decided to show the movie in the big hotels. He and his piano player made the rounds of the luxury hotels on Trenker's motor- cycle, a copy of the film clamped under his arm, and wound up at Hotel Karersee. After the screening, a nervous man approached and asked if he could introduce Trenker to a lady who was eager to meet him. This man was Harry Sokal, Riefenstahl's admirer from the beach at the Baltic Sea, who had been underwriting her career to date. Riefenstahl, in turn, claimed that she had made it clear to Sokal even before she fell from the stage in Prague that she had no intention of becoming his lover, even though he continued to pursue her and shower her with gifts (such as fur coats) in the hope that he would be able to buy her affections. After a series of dramatic scenes, he finally promised to settle for her friendship.

Throughout her life, Riefenstahl endeavored to play down or deny the positive influence of Sokal's money on her career. She set great store by the version of her life story that had her art emerging victorious on its own, despite all odds, and skirted any mention of her large circle of male supporters. Sokal's account confirms Tren- ker's version. According to him, Leni, his former lover, lured him to Karersee to spend a few carefree days with him. They chanced upon the evening movie showing, and as they were coming out, she said, "I'd like to make movies like that too! I would like to get to know that man." They met Trenker that very same evening, and sat with him throughout the night. "And by dawn it was certain that we wanted to make a film together. A mountain film. With the same team that had made *Mountain of Destiny*, and was the best mountain film team of the time, and perhaps of all time. Arnold Fanck as the director and author, Sepp Allgeier and Hans Schneeberger at the camera, Trenker in the leading role—and two new additions: Leni Riefenstahl as the leading female role and H. R. Sokal (me) as the financier and producer."[69]

The fact that Sokal initially financed 25 percent of the production costs of Riefenstahl's first movie with Fanck, and that he did not stop these handouts until later, substantiates this account. There were simply too many of Riefenstahl's admirers involved in this film for his liking, and their jealousy made the shooting more difficult. Sokal did not reveal the extent of his own jealousy. In Trenker's version, once Sokal had announced to him at Hotel Karersee that a young lady simply had to meet him, Riefenstahl entered from the wings, dressed in white tulle. Sokal introduced the two of them, and Trenker dryly remarked that the name "Leni Riefenstahl" meant nothing to him. The young lady complimented him on the wonderful mountaineering scenes and confessed that she would love to climb one of the Dolomite towers herself, with him at her side. She conveniently ignored his objection that he had things to do in Bolzano and scheduled their meeting for the following morning. Unsettled by this much self-confidence from a woman, Trenker backed out. But she did not let up, and three days later she turned up at his office in Bolzano. "'I simply must be in your next movie!' 'Unfortunately, I'm not the director; you'll have to get in touch with Dr. Fanck. Are you an actress?' 'I'm a dancer.' With these words, she handed me a photograph. With her arms crossed in a devout pose and a gentle part down the middle of her hair, she looked like a Botticelli Madonna." She asked him for the director's address, and said as she left, "I'll see you again for the next film." Trenker, who figured he ought to warn Fanck, sent him Riefenstahl's picture and jotted on the back, "Very good-looking. Claims to be a dancer. Wants to play the lead role in your next film. You take it from here." Two weeks later, he got a reply from Fanck, calling him a numbskull who had no idea about women. "This young lady is the greatest dancer, and the most beautiful woman in Europe," his letter said. "Of course she will play the lead role in my next movie and will soon be the most famous woman in Germany."[70] Hidden between the lines are Trenker's feelings of rivalry toward this woman. He let no opportunity slip by to portray her as the sophisticated lady and himself as one of the simple mountain folk who were put off by her exalted airs. He failed to mention that he found Riefenstahl quite attractive and started a passionate affair with her that eventually left them as enemies.

Along with Fanck and Trenker, Riefenstahl was regarded as one of the most important exponents of the mountain film (which should not be confused with the sentimental film in a rural setting known as the *Heimatfilm*). The heyday of the mountain film began in 1924 and extended into 1940; only in Germany did it evolve into a genre of its own.[71] Siegfried Kracauer's pronouncement that the heroism of Fanck's protagonists was rooted "in a mentality kindred to Nazi spirit" found widespread acceptance.[72] Ever since, virtually all discussions of Fanck begin with Riefenstahl and end with *Triumph of the Will*, although there had not been any moral stigma attached to mountains before the 1920s, nor is there now.[73] At the beginning of the twentieth century, the mountains took on new interest for adventurers with the introduction of sophisticated Alpine technology and resources.[74] These adventurers were referred to as mountain vagabonds, and their heyday had arrived once the Great War came to an end.

Fanck, whom Riefenstahl eventually met at Rumpelmayer's pastry shop on Kurfürstendamm in Berlin, was these adventurers' role model. She must have been the first young woman to make an appointment with him to gush about his films. "I'm talking and talking, and Dr. Fanck is sitting there without saying a word, listening and stirring his tea. I don't have the slightest inkling of the impression my ecstatic words are making on him. Only once does he ask me a question: he wants to know how I spend my time. He knows nothing about my dancing; he has yet to hear of me."[75] As she was leaving, she promised to send him dance reviews. This meeting buoyed her spirits for days, although she had to admit to herself that not very much had come of it. "I didn't ask Dr. Fanck whether I could act for him, and he didn't bring up the subject either; he just listened and asked who in the world I was [yet] even so, a volcano erupted within me."[76] The shooting pains in her knee brought her back down to reality. She decided to take immediate action in order to be ready when and if Dr. Fanck contacted her. She had been putting off her knee surgery for months, but now she headed straight to the hospital to get her body in shape for the next stage of her career. The operation took place the very next day. "Although I was told that I would be in a cast for ten weeks, and that there was some danger that my knee could remain stiff, at this moment there was only one thing at stake, either-or. I have to get healthy, healthy in order to be able to go up into the mountains."[77] Three days later, Dr. Fanck showed up at her bedside. Instead of bringing roses, he brought a screenplay: "The Holy Mountain— Written for the Dancer Leni Riefenstahl." Thus began Riefenstahl's collaboration with a man she would come to loathe, but who was nonetheless her most important teacher.

Fanck, born in 1889, was the son of a wealthy businessman. He suffered from severe illnesses in his childhood, including tuberculosis and asthma. Any excitement would bring on spasms and difficulty breathing. He was educated at home, was not allowed to play outside, and lived in isolation inside his house. "Fear . . . was the gist of my childhood," he recalled in his memoir.[78] Then his father met a doctor who advised him to send young Arnold to Davos for boarding school, and his life changed. His medical ailments disappeared, and he was able to spend five hours a day romping outdoors. From then on, he wanted to live a life of sports, nature, discipline, and toughening up. This story of healing—from an ailing, effeminate, hysterical boy to a bold, healthy, strong man—gave rise to Fanck's lifelong obsession with the mountains. In conquering mountains, he conquered his fears. He studied geology, a branch of science that had been important for visual artists a hundred years earlier. Painters such as Caspar David Friedrich were influenced by drawings that geologists had brought back from their travels, and scientists in turn used artistic renderings to shed light on geological facts. Fanck's filmic images were modeled on Friedrich's paintings or drawings. One year before the war began, he shot his first ski film. Bernhard Gotthart, an innovative businessman from Freiburg who had founded Express-Film Company in 1910, sang the praises of Sepp Allgeier, an eighteen-year-old cameraman who could film on skis. Fanck and Riefenstahl would both go on to make many movies with Allgeier. Shooting *4628 Meter High on Skis: Climbing Monte Rosa* entailed a whole host of dangers.[79]

During the war, Fanck served in the counterintelligence corps and was assigned the task of producing exact replicas of photographs. He then incorporated this technique into his next ski film. *The Miracle of the Snowshoe* was shot without a script; the film is one long improvisation on the mountain. It is noteworthy for its combination of physicality, technology, and war, a first for Fanck. Riefenstahl would go on to combine these elements in her films. But the picture that ultimately drew Riefenstahl to Fanck was *Mountain of Destiny*, his first alpine film with a plot. *Mountain of Destiny* portrays the battle between two generations climbing a mountain. In his earlier ski films, Fanck had focused on landscape as a backdrop for athletic prowess, but in *Mountain of Destiny*, landscape becomes a peril, a facet of an overpowering nature. A mountaineering magazine wrote, "*Mountain of Destiny* is the first film in which the mountain has a role of its own and appears as a character; for the first time, the soul of the mountain speaks to us and makes ours resonate with it. In *Mountain of Destiny*, the mountain (as an entity that combines rock, air, cloud, storm, and tempest) comes alive."[80]

Luis Trenker had his onscreen debut in *Mountain of Destiny*. He was one of the young men who idolized Fanck. He had actually wanted to shoot a film himself, for which he had already written the screenplay and collected money. When Fanck came to Bolzano, he persuaded Trenker to transfer the approved subsidies to his project.[81] No distributor wanted to take on the film, so Fanck rented the Nollendorf Theater for four months, set up two projectors, hired cashiers and projectionists, and had the poster made that Riefenstahl would see at the subway station. The movie was sold out for months. Fanck later recalled: "When I saw Leni Riefenstahl, my first impression was: child of nature, not an actress. . . . I found the driving dramatic force for the plot: it struck me that the contrasts between nature and culture, skiing and dance, sea and mountains would yield suspense."[82]

Fanck took to the idea of making a film about an encounter between a bold mountain recluse and an impulsive, pretty, expressive dancer, and knew from the outset whom to cast in the lead roles: Luis Trenker and Leni Riefenstahl. Fanck actually preferred Riefenstahl's *lack* of acting skills. The body and its sportive energy were his primary concern; the ability to act was of lesser importance. Riefenstahl was hired with a star's salary of twenty thousand marks. Ufa, the motion picture production company, made a pianist available to her during the shooting and agreed to have a piano transported to the mountain huts. That was not bad for a beginner. Ufa had high hopes for this film, as reflected in its willingness to increase the production costs a great deal beyond the thirty-four thousand marks it had invested in *Mountain of Destiny*; five hundred thousand marks were budgeted for *The Holy Mountain*. The studio shots were filmed in Staaken, at the border of Berlin, and the location shots in the Swiss Alps, at the mountain resort of Lenzerheide. The filming took far more time than the three months that had been originally planned, and eventually stretched to eighteen months. The effort paid off handsomely.

The dramatically rendered scene at the Nollendorfplatz subway station became a turning point in Riefenstahl's life. She turned her back on the city and sought her destiny in nature. In Riefenstahl's portrayal of her life story, this subterranean train station would become a locus of transition: she was leaving the city that was compelling her to operate in functional terms. Riefenstahl went to the mountains, where camaraderie and closeness mattered more than functionality and detachment. She opted for personal interactions over impersonal roles. Elegance yielded to valor as she turned her back on urban niceties and sought freedom, beauty, and adventure in the mountains.

The screenplay of her first film seemed perfect for this new direction in her life. *The Holy Mountain* tells an unhappy love story among three people that culminates in the death of the two men; only the woman survives. Surprisingly, this movie, which Fanck dedicated to his friend who was killed in action, opens with Riefenstahl dancing in front of the raging and roiling sea in a short filmy garment. Her body is shot against the hard light, in contrast to the clouds, the waves, and the horizon. In this long opening sequence, Fanck was offering Riefenstahl once last chance at a major dance performance. These images reveal not only the woman's bond with the elemental force of the water, but also the way her dance emanates from joy in her body, which was something entirely new in his films. The men who would fall in love with this creature were friends: Vigo (played by Ernst Petersen, Fanck's nephew), and a character known only as The Friend (Trenker). We see the two of them sitting high up on a cliff, dreamily observing the mountains stretched out before them. This sequence introduces the major figures and their worlds: the woman and the sea, the friends and the mountains, the power of this male friendship, and the playfulness of the dancing woman (Diotima). Now the plot can begin. The friends go to Diotima's recital, where she dances "Dream Blossom," the choreography Riefenstahl is so proud of. Luxury hotel, big stage, elegant audience, garland of flowers, chauffeur, bevy of admirers—this is how Riefenstahl pictured the life of a successful artist, and Fanck was making it happen for her. In *The Holy Mountain*, Riefenstahl could play a dancer living life the way she had dreamed of. In the next act, we see The Friend coming down out of the ice while she jubilantly skips across blooming meadows and cuddles a lamb. Then she sits and stares awestruck at the towering mountain peaks. Eventually the two meet up. The Friend is sitting in front of the hut, contentedly puffing away on a pipe, as she sneaks up to him. When he sees her, his pipe nearly falls out of his mouth.

Diotima: Have you come from up there?
(Pause)
Diotima: It must be beautiful up there.
The Friend: Beautiful—hard—and dangerous!
Diotima: And what do you seek up there?
The Friend: Myself.
Diotima: And nothing else?
The Friend: And what do you seek up here—in nature?
Diotima: Beauty!

This dialogue cements their relationship. In the next scene, we see The Friend in his mother's living room. He wants to climb up to seek the most beautiful mountain to celebrate his and Diotima's engagement the following day. The sinister intertitle announces: "The sea and the stone can never be wed." When he comes back down, he happens to see his fiancée with a man who has his head in her lap, and she is caressing him. In order to wipe this image from his mind, he feels he has to experience something "completely wild." He decides to scale the perilous north face. Vigo goes along. Neither of them knows about the other's affection for Diotima. When a storm approaches, Vigo wants to turn back, but The Friend is hoping for death. With ice picks in hand, the snow-covered bodies face storm-lashed clouds and avalanches as they struggle up the mountain. The camera cuts away to Diotima in her luxurious hotel suite. She is preparing for her performance, full of foreboding about the impending disaster. Meanwhile, Vigo tries to bring his friend to his senses, but The Friend pulls his accordion out of his backpack and in the middle of the raging storm starts to play and sing wildly. Trenker's camera paints a ghastly picture of the depths of despair. "Do you have anything you're attached to down there with the rabble?" he asks Vigo. "A dancer . . . Diotima," is the bashful reply. The Friend pounces on Vigo with a cry of "It was you!" Vigo backs away and falls off the overhang into the abyss, but because he is hanging by his friend's rope, he does not plunge to his death. While these dramatic scenes are unfolding, Diotima is dancing. Her performance is interrupted by the mother's urgent message that her son and his friend have not come back. She asks whether anyone is willing to help, but her pleas fall on deaf ears. The dancer sets out alone on skis, at night, and fights her way to a hut, where she finds mountaineers who cut their reveling short and set out to save the friends. On the wuthering mountain, The Friend holds Vigo by the rope because he cannot fasten it to anything: there is nothing but glazed ice all around them. "Cut me loose! At least save yourself!" Vigo shouts to his friend. The intertitle reads: "Sacrifice his comrade—or himself along with him? The great question of the mountains." Throughout the night, The Friend holds Vigo, who has long since frozen to death. When the sun comes up, The Friend follows Vigo by plunging to his death. Diotima returns to the sea.

The hero of the movie is The Friend, who values loyalty above his own life. Riefenstahl plays Diotima, the alien element intruding on the men's close bond. The mountain engulfs both men, and the engagement of the man and the woman does not come about in this icy realm. Fanck did not grant Riefenstahl a view from above. A woman can follow a man as far as the hut, but then the world of men begins; there is no way onward for her. Her place is in the valley. In real life, Riefenstahl would not put up with this constraint indefinitely.

On December 17, 1926, the film premiered at the Ufa Palace. Riefenstahl started off the evening with dance. The *Berliner Morgenpost* published a scathing review of her performance: "Leni Riefenstahl had nothing to offer in the way of acting, nor did she look good. All her flitting about was sometimes hard to bear."[83] This review, and others in a similar vein, did not interfere with the box office triumph of *The Holy Mountain*, which is considered Fanck's first international success—and Riefenstahl's.

She had built up quite a network of lovers and admirers. Heinz von Jaworsky, ten years her junior and later her cameraman, was quite taken with her, and decades later still went into raptures when describing her: "Definitely a sexy woman, no doubt about it."[84] Fanck was not oblivious to her charms either. When she sobbed to him that her engagement was off and he gave her a comforting hug, Riefenstahl wrote, she sensed that his feelings for her were not merely "fatherly," as she had hoped. That is an odd thought, since Fanck was thirty-seven years old at the time—not an age at which a man has fatherly feelings for a woman in her mid-twenties. Although she rejected his advances, she stuck close to him. "I was unsettled . . . by the way Fanck grew more deeply in love with me day by day. He showered me with gifts, especially editions of Hölderlin and Nietzsche, woodcuts by Käthe Kollwitz, and graphics by contemporary artists such as Heinrich Zille and George Grosz."[85] Only on his bold mountain adventures and as the leader of a group of strong, brave men did Fanck appear not to have felt threatened in his manhood. Riefenstahl was the diametric opposite of the type of woman to whom he normally gravitated. Although she could put on a show of girlish innocence, she was actually a strong-minded woman who expected to be on a par with men. Because Fanck was fighting his own self-perceived effeminate nature, he must have been fascinated by a woman who posed such an unabashed challenge to men on their own turf.

The first serious complications arose when Fanck invited Riefenstahl and Trenker to Freiburg. Trenker was strikingly handsome; he was strong, amusing, and suntanned, and thus exactly the kind of man that appealed to Riefenstahl. Fanck invited his lead actress to pledge their friendship with champagne and drink to the success of the film. He would have been better off not having done so; the instant he left the room for a few moments, Leni and Luis fell into each other's arms. "It may have been the champagne, the delightful prospect of our upcoming work, or just the atmosphere of our being together, but all I know is that this was the first time that I ever lay in a man's arms under the spell of a happiness I had never known before." Fanck caught the two of them in the act. Riefenstahl's comment on this situation speaks volumes: "I pulled away from Trenker and was aghast at the idea that this incident might endanger our project. Would this destroy my dream of playing in *The Holy Mountain*?" Trenker left, and Fanck brought her back to the hotel. "No sooner were we alone than he broke down, sobbing and burying his face in his hands. From his incoherent, almost unintelligible words, I learned how deeply he cared for me, how much he had hoped for and dreamed about me, and how terribly wounded he had been by seeing Trenker and me embrace. I tried to comfort him while he caressed my hands, saying 'You— my Diotima.'"[86] This passage conveys the impression that the two of them were already rehearsing for *The Holy Mountain*, with its similar constellation of two men and one woman. Regardless of whether Fanck and Riefenstahl actually had an affair, their work together would not have come about without the sexual attraction he felt for her. The story of Arnold Fanck and Leni Riefenstahl is the story of a battle that was waged with every resource and on every level, a battle in which reality and fiction blended, and a battle that Riefenstahl would ultimately win.

Trenker never wrote a word about his affair with Riefenstahl, but in his memoir he seized every opportunity to malign her. In assessing the critics' response to *The Holy Mountain*, for example, Trenker wrote: "The press poured out praise and censure. Praise went to the magnificent way the mountain milieu was captured and to the movie's male actors, and censure went to the role of the dancing diva."[87]

The roundelay of her men extended beyond the two rivals Fanck and Trenker. Hans Schneeberger, a gifted cameraman, seemed to be interested in her as well. Riefenstahl's faithful companion, Harry Sokal, also got in on the act. She claimed to have been taken aback when she learned about Sokal's financial stake in the film, and she was convinced that he was out to use his position for the sole purpose of seeing her as often as possible. However, once it became apparent to Sokal, who would continue to invest in Fanck's and Riefenstahl's films, that all men were after Leni, he withdrew his financial support. "I noticed a suspicious gleam in the eyes of all three men [Trenker, Fanck, and Schneeberger] whenever they looked at their future leading lady or partner. And they looked at her incessantly." From then on, he declared that his only interest was in the film, not in the lady. "Riefenstahl needed all three men, Fanck even on two levels: as an author who wrote a starring role expressly for her, and as a director to present her well on screen. Trenker, who was already a star at the time, could reject the unknown novice as a partner, but could also be magnanimous enough to share the spotlight with her. And it was up to the cameraman to present her beauty in the proper light, in the truest sense of the term. . . . She still seemed to be looking at the three of them equally favorably, with a slightly more positive attitude toward Fanck, who was, of course, the most important one at the moment."[88] Riefenstahl's rejection of Sokal was a blow to his vanity. She had ditched him as a lover to replace him with the next man who might prove more useful to her career. He may have continued to emphasize how much he valued her as an artist, but at the same time he seized every opportunity to portray her as a schemer.

Riefenstahl filmed under difficult circumstances: The crew was small and the shooting extremely complex because of their dependence on the weather. Moreover, the director, lead actor, and producer were in love with her, and she was in no position to spoil things with any of them. It was a risky game: Her affairs could help step up her success, or they could spell the end of her work with Fanck. Fanck gave her access to the camera, let her select images, instructed her in the use of various focal distances, showed her the effect of color screens, and taught her how to work with lenses, all because he desired her as a woman and wanted to be close to her. In 1974, she said in an interview, "I soaked up Fanck's and his cameraman's experience until it became second nature."[89] The films she would make with Fanck in the years to come reflected the transformation of their productive yet explosive relationship as well as her evolving self-image as an artist.

In the latter half of the 1920s, Riefenstahl split her time between Berlin and the mountains.

> Yes, I love the mountains, love them passionately. I see
> them as symbols of struggle: the dangers, the resistance of
> the summits, I see the zealously repelling walls, the artful
> slyness of the snow cornices, all frozen over. I see the wild,
> romantic aspect of the green ravines, profuse with water,
> the magic of the calm cold mountain lakes, the great, great
> isolation, and the struggle, over and over again. That is
> strong, scintillating life, and life is beautiful.[90]

While shooting *The Holy Mountain*, Riefenstahl decided not to continue with dance and to pursue film instead. A cover picture in the magazine *Frau und Gegenwart* in 1927 reveals that in her role as a dance artist, she saw herself as a combination of femme fatale and priestess. This photo was a final reminiscence of a dream that had not come true but would never die. Shooting films with Fanck demanded all her time and energy. She accepted his offer to act in his next film as well, with Trenker and Schneeberger at her side. *The Great Leap* was a burlesque on skis. With two men courting her, Riefenstahl proved that she had learned to ski quite well. The interplay of camera and movement was the focal point of the film. In 1925, Fanck had published a groundbreaking new ski manual with photographs by Sepp Allgeier. *Miracle of the Snowshoe: A System for Skiing Correctly, and its Application to Alpine Cross-Country Skiing* contains little text but more than a thousand cinematic images. This book describes the Arlberg technique, which was developed by Hannes Schneider. This technique simplified skiing and was largely responsible for making it a sport for the masses.

Riefenstahl could finally savor the feeling of being desired by all the men on screen. Fanck's eroticism was limited to landscape and bodies; there is no trace of makeup, silk stockings, monocles, or cigarette holders in his films. He portrayed Riefenstahl as a woman who owes her attractiveness to her well-trained body and her joy in movement. It almost seems as though Fanck made the film expressly to call attention to Riefenstahl's erotic power and to humiliate Trenker and Schneeberger, his two competitors in real life. Trenker played Tony, the village fool. He pursues Gita, the goatherd (Riefenstahl). She is only using him, but he appears not to notice her indifference to him. And Schneeberger, as Michael Treuherz, gets to show off his muscular naked torso, yet his character is afraid of women and sex.[91] But no man can outshine Riefenstahl. To escape her bothersome admirers, she rolls up her sleeves, knuckles down, and scales steep rock faces. Fanck no longer casts her as a transcendent dancer, but instead as an appealing tomboy with supple feline movements. One titillating scene has her blissfully biting through a thick rope, wearing a diaphanous shirt that is soaked through, to help Schneeberger free himself. In *The Great Leap*, Riefenstahl projected a new image: she wears hoop earrings, short skirts, a fur vest that accentuates her curves, and dark eye makeup. She is lively, jaunty, and sexy. Once again, however, her acting talent was underwhelming. In *The Great Leap*, Fanck demanded extreme physical effort from his leading lady. Not only did she have to spend hours splashing about in ice-cold mountain brooks, but she also had to swim through a forty-degree lake clad in nothing but a coquettish little tunic. "We spent several days tumbling about in the mountain brooks of the Dolomites. Dr. Fanck has the wicked knack of finding the very coldest water, with the temperature hovering at about forty degrees. He even claims that this is still much too warm—and that we ought to be happy that it is not unmelted ice."[92] Fanck also sent her to work on her climbing skills with Schneeberger. As a former dancer, she had a highly developed sense of balance, and her dancing on pointe had given her strength in her toes. She enjoyed climbing, but she dreaded the barefoot training that made her feet bleed. She considered this torment unnecessary, but Fanck insisted on it. If she wanted to work with him, she would have to grit her teeth and do as she was asked.

It was an outsider, Schneeberger, who ultimately won Riefenstahl's heart. His colleagues described him as a very friendly, even childlike man. Schneeberger's story was similar to Fanck's. He had recovered from a severe hip ailment in the mountains. During the war, he had been a pilot decorated with the highest medal awarded for military valor. Before that he had studied architecture, like Trenker. Schneeberger, a short, venturesome man, was a superb athlete. When he skied, it looked as though his skis were dancing over the snow. Riefenstahl enjoyed the ways in which they complemented each other: "Although Schneeberger was seven years my senior, he liked being led: he was the passive partner, I the active one. Our life together was harmonious. We loved nature and sports, and above all our profession. We were not city people who liked parties or social obligations."[93] Trenker resigned himself to the situation and married in 1927, but Fanck continued to bombard Riefenstahl with love letters.

Upon her return to Berlin, she moved to a larger apartment in a new building at Hindenburgstrasse 97 in Wilmersdorf; her work on Fanck's films had earned her enough money to move from Fasanenstrasse. Her listing in the Berlin directory now read "Leni Riefenstahl, Actress." Her sixth-floor apartment came with a roof garden and a dance studio. Fanck bought her a grand piano for the studio. She entertained famous men in her new home; supposedly Erich Maria Remarque, Walter Ruttmann, and Ernst Lubitsch were guests there.

Although *The Great Leap* had been a success, no other offers were forthcoming.[94] She was difficult to cast because no other director made films like Fanck's. Riefenstahl could be effective only if the focus was on bodies and adventures; her acting skills were limited, and her tension was only magnified by the camera.

> People keep saying: Leni Riefenstahl is a mountain climber, not an actress. I suffer no end from this preconception. After all, I was a dancer, and have lived only for art—and now I'm thought to be nothing but a pure athlete? I love the mountains, and I love sports, but an artistic will to form burns within me most of all, and has to have an outlet, or else I cannot live. So now I am trying with all my might to fight this preconception. I've been battling in vain, week after week, month after month—rejections every which way—no one wants to believe in me.[95]

She wrote the director G. W. Pabst a card from her winter vacation in St. Moritz, in the hope that he would rescue her from this situation. If Fanck was the only director who would cast her in a movie, she would have to make sure that another director would join up with Fanck—someone who actually knew how to direct his actors.

Pabst had had his first success in 1924 with *The Joyless Street*, which made Greta Garbo famous. Perhaps Riefenstahl was hoping that he would bring about his next miracle with *her* and that she would emerge a star. In addition to Fanck, who was fanatical about achieving authenticity, she chose a director known for tormenting actors in order to achieve genuine emotional scenes. Riefenstahl's bold choice signaled her readiness at long last to be taken seriously as an actress.

The third member of this group was Harry Sokal, who now owned a production company on Friedrichstrasse. As a producer, he insisted that Riefenstahl be cast in the lead role even though she was supposedly a "box office handicap." *The Great Leap* was to blame. The movie was meant to be amusing, "but Leni, who doesn't have a spark of humor in her, was coy whenever she was supposed to be funny, and the film became a total loss for Ufa."[96] Pabst brought in his seasoned screenwriter, Ladislav Vajda, to coauthor the screenplay for *The White Hell of Piz Palü* with Fanck. It was quite a coup to sign on former fighter pilot Ernst Udet for this film. Udet, who would be known to later generations as the model for Carl Zuckmayer's *The Devil's General*, was a crowd pleaser. As many as fifty thousand spectators would come to his aerobatic displays. For some of his admirers he was a symbol of the brave German past, and for others, a modern hero of technology. And Riefenstahl had a man at her side who was already a star, which was sure to work to her benefit.

Two tragic love stories are interwoven in *Piz Palü*: At the beginning of the movie, we see a young couple (Dr. Johannes Krafft and his wife Maria) with an elderly mountain guide attempting to climb Piz Palü. Krafft turns a deaf ear to the guide's warnings. His wife, who has placed her trust in her husband, quickly falls into a crevasse, and the ice becomes her coffin. Many years after this dreadful event, a newlywed couple comes to spend a few days in the Diavolezza hut beneath Piz Palü; their arrival is the start of the actual plot of the movie.

As they are sitting in the hut, the door is flung open and a stranger enters. He sits down at the table with them. This stranger is Dr. Krafft, who had set out into the mountains with his wife all those years ago. Since her death, he has been wandering about restlessly. While he tells his story, the viewer sees images of the dead woman lying in her "grave of ice" alternating with close-ups of Maria Maioni (Riefenstahl), who is listening to him spellbound. With her full lips, bright eyes, and low-cut blouse, she seems to personify life itself. Krafft needs someone to accompany him when he ventures out to scale the north face, which has never been con-quered. Night falls, and the three are alone. Krafft tells Maria that she should lie down between them. At daybreak, when Krafft sets out, Hannes (Maria's husband) decides to go with him. He leaves Maria a letter that tells her he wants to show that he, too, is capa-ble. She wakes up, of course, and hurries behind them. Krafft wants to send her back, but he takes her along so as not to lose any time. He is intent on triumphing over the mountain. The three of them begin their climb, Krafft in front, Maria in the middle, and Hannes bringing up the rear. Then Hannes insists on going first, and Krafft lets him. Hannes stumbles and falls. When Krafft goes down to save him, he hands the rope over to Maria. The mountain begins to roar, and the temperature falls. The three are stranded on a ledge, and they cannot move forward or backward. Krafft's leg is broken, but he continues to brave the icy snowstorm, swinging a lamp in the darkness. He tenderly massages Maria's feet with snow. Hannes, who is insanely jealous and freezing cold, pounces on Krafft. There are enormously impressive images of the two half-frozen men staggering and fighting with each other in extreme slow motion in the raging storm. With Maria's help, Krafft is able to chain Hannes to the cliff. Udet, who reads about their plight in the newspaper, tries to save them. In a series of daredevil maneuvers, he flies quite close to the ledge on which the three are holding out, but he is unable to get to them. Krafft gives his jacket to Hannes and creeps behind an icy mountain ledge to die. Maria and Hannes are rescued once Udet spots them from the sky. He cannot land on the rocks, so he shows the mountain guide where they are located, and the mountain rescue service lowers them ropes to bring them to safety.

In *Piz Palü*, it is ice that dominates. Gustav Diessl gave one of his strongest performances in *Piz Palü*, playing Dr. Krafft as an introverted man determined not to surrender to his fate. Krafft may have an icy exterior, but he is a hotheaded man who has trouble reining in his ambition and his sexual desires. The movie suggests that women need to acknowledge the superiority of men. Fanck was wary of bold, intrepid, attractive women. He had fallen for Leni Riefenstahl and hoped she would become "a real woman" who accepts a man's natural dominance.

The role of Maria Maioni offered Riefenstahl a chance to show myriad facets of herself. Maria is alternately affectionate and imperious, loving and strong, but she is also despairing and feels that her life is over. Paul Falkenberg, a close associate of Pabst's, considered *Piz Palü* the only good film Riefenstahl ever made.[97] Maria is sporty, elegant, and matter-of-fact, a strong, self-confident woman who has nothing in common with the juvenile pathos of the dancer Diotima.

The movie took six months to shoot. Pabst's assistant director, Marc Sorkin, subsequently expressed his admiration for Riefenstahl's single-minded devotion to the project:

Most of the cast and the help came down with pneumonia. But Pabst and Fanck, they must have had a secret sadistic drive: and you can see that in the picture. . . . All night long we were drinking hot wine and punch, just to keep on breathing. That is why the film is so good: you can see all the harshness of the weather on the faces of the people. And I must say that Riefenstahl was wonderful; never mind what she did later—I know she became a Nazi and all—but in this picture she was driving herself as hard as anybody, and more. She worked day and night. Schneeberger was in love with her—and she with him, by the way—and they were a good team. She worked harder than anybody. Even Pabst had to admire her: he said, "It's terrible, what a woman!"[98]

Fanck never went easy on his crew or on himself. He sent his cameramen up to an altitude of 3,600 meters in temperatures of twenty degrees below zero to take pictures of icy rock faces. Richard Angst began to suffer from frostbite, and they had to turn back. Allgeier described working with Fanck as "flirting with death." For Fanck, flirting with death was the key to success, while Pabst focused on authenticity of feelings.[99] He studied his actors carefully, looking for signs of sexual jealousy and hatred.

This film focused squarely on sadism and professions of love on icy peaks. Pain was Riefenstahl's constant companion in film, as it had been in dance. In this movie, she would be hauled up along an ice wall with avalanches plunging down onto her. Fanck chose a wall on the Morteratsch Glacier that was nearly seventy feet high and had his crew spend days piling up chunks of ice and snow along its top rim. Riefenstahl was afraid of these shots, but Fanck assured her that she would be pulled no more than a few yards and then everything would be over. She had the ropes attached to her, was hoisted up, and was instantly subjected to a torrent of ice and snow.

Since my arms were bound up in ropes, I couldn't shield myself from the powdery snow. My ears, nose and mouth

were filled with snow and chunks of ice. I screamed at the
crew to lower me, but it was no use; despite what Fanck
had promised, they hoisted me all the way up the wall of
ice. Nor did they stop when I reached the sharp icy edge:
I was pulled over it, and I arrived at the top, in great pain,
and weeping with rage at my director's brutality. Fanck
responded with delight to the excellent footage.[100]

No matter how much she focused on her torments in later accounts
of this filming, what mattered most to her at the time was maintaining her place as the only woman up at the summit and not
being sent back down. Fanck could depend on her to test the limits
of her ability in her quest to please him.

Fanck got to know Riefenstahl quite well during the years they
worked together, and he knew with certainty that she would do
anything for success. Because her relationship with Schneeberger
was falling apart, Fanck saw cause for hope. Every night, Riefenstahl would find love letters and poems from Fanck hidden under
her pillow. She was in the unenviable position of being marooned
with Fanck and his men in a hut high up in the mountains and
hence unable to avoid him. Any candid statement of her feelings
for him as a man might jeopardize the entire film project. By this
point, she could hardly stand the sight of him. In her book *Struggle
in Snow and Ice* (1933), she wrote that alcohol was the only way to
endure shooting this movie. "I can tell you that I hated Fanck," she
confessed to Ray Müller decades later.[101] She could not afford to
act on this feeling as a young woman because Fanck was the only
person who wanted to put her in the limelight. Riefenstahl felt that
she was completely and utterly at Fanck's mercy, and she was well
aware of how much she could learn from him, so she stayed on.
Even off-camera, she had to bear up under the antics of the men.
One night, she woke everybody up with a scream: one of her fellow
mountaineers had put a dead calf wearing a nightcap into her bed.

The White Hell of Piz Palü, which cameraman Richard Angst called "the last great silent film in the world of film production as a whole," was a success. The premiere, at the Ufa Palace in Berlin, was greeted with cheers, and reviewers heaped praise on Riefenstahl's performance. "Leni Riefenstahl, whose acting was her best yet, blended feminine grace with a gamine-like courage and agility," the *B. Z. am Mittag* reported, and the *8 Uhr Abendblatt* in Berlin gave her similarly high praise: "Leni Riefenstahl, this woman with the lovely willful head of a young eagle, has major scenes that emphasize her physicality."[102] The *Berliner Morgenpost* was delighted by the images but muted in its praise of the actors, who seemed mere accessories for the scenery: "Leni Riefenstahl and Ernst Petersen . . . do not get in the way."[103] But the real surprise came from the United States. Fanck received a telegram from Douglas Fairbanks in Hollywood congratulating him on the movie and calling it one of the best he and Mary Pickford had ever seen.[104] *Piz Palü* was the first German film to be shown at the huge Roxy Theater in midtown Manhattan. This movie and Fritz Lang's *Woman in the Moon* were the big box-office hits of the 1929 film season.

Even so, Riefenstahl did not want to make any more mountain films, in part because her partner of about three years, Schneeberger, had left her for another woman. Schneeberger must have been her ideal companion; they shared a passion for mountain climbing, skiing, and camera technology. She indirectly blamed Udet for the breakup of her love affair. Of course, the notorious womanizer had tried his luck with her when they first got to know each other, but she had rebuffed him, with the explanation that she had been sharing "the happiness of a perfect love" with Schneeberger for the past three years. Udet then began to try to lure Schneeberger away from her. The two men had quite a bit in common; they had both been pilots in the First World War. Udet made arrangements to room with Schneeberger in St. Moritz. Riefenstahl stayed behind with the rest of the crew while Schneeberger had fun with the jovial war hero. At some point he apparently fell in love with one of the elegant ladies who always flocked around Udet. "Udet was a Bohemian—he has brought my friend into this life. And so I have lost him. I have lost my friend through Udet."[105] Schneeberger had no intention of coming back to Riefenstahl, who regarded this breakup as a dramatic defeat. "The pain crept into every cell of my body; it paralyzed me until I tried to break free with a terrible scream. Crying, shouting, biting my hands, I staggered from one room to the next. I took a letter opener and slashed my arms, legs, and hips. I didn't feel these physical pains; the mental ones burned like fire in hell."[106] She killed off her love for this man and focused more squarely on her career than ever before.

Riefenstahl was so stricken by this breakup not only because she had hoped for personal happiness with Schneeberger, but also because this relationship held out the promise of professional advancement. She wanted to get him a position as an assistant at Ufa so he could gain experience in studio work. Supposedly Schnee-berger had her to thank for becoming the assistant to the famous Günter Rittau. Rittau had filmed *Metropolis* together with Fritz Lang and was now under contract with a much sought-after direc-tor from Hollywood, who was preparing his next movie in Berlin. The director was Josef von Sternberg. Schneeberger left Fanck and Riefenstahl in order to shoot the sound film that everyone in Berlin was talking about—*The Blue Angel*—with the Hollywood director. In her memoirs, Riefenstahl included von Sternberg in the throng of her admirers. To take her mind off her heartache, she went to the movies quite often. She was fascinated by *The Docks of New York*. She wanted to meet the director, and managed to do so. He invited this young woman from Berlin, of whom he had never heard, to have lunch with him at the Hotel Bristol. She dressed up for the occasion, and over a meal of beef and savoy cabbage, she claimed to have learned all about his film project and search for a lead actress. The name "Marlene Dietrich" came up, and she recalled meeting a woman by that name at the Schwannecke artists' café. "I was struck by her deep, husky voice, which sounded a bit vulgar and suggestive. Maybe she was a little tipsy. I heard her saying loudly, 'Why does a woman always have to have beautiful breasts? They can sag a little, can't they?' Then she lifted her left breast slightly and enjoyed the startled faces of the young girls sitting around her."[107] It seemed apt to hire a whore for the role of a whore, she thought, and she advised von Sternberg to cast Dietrich in the role of Lola Lola. In Riefenstahl's account, he came over to her place for supper nearly every evening, and afterward they would head out to the set in Babelsberg. Von Sternberg would show her the dailies and ask what she thought of them. Although he was an attractive man, she spurned him as a lover, and he went home to his hotel alone every evening. Even so, they spent "poetic and entertaining hours" together.

Given the close spiritual affinity Riefenstahl felt she had with von Sternberg, she figured Dietrich was sure to be jealous of her; she even claimed that Dietrich threatened to kill herself. When Riefenstahl visited von Sternberg during his rehearsals in Babelsberg, she reported that Dietrich sat down on the barrel and "offered an unobstructed view of everything she ought to be hiding."[108] Von Sternberg, Riefenstahl claimed, furiously tried to bring her to her senses, whereupon Riefenstahl, a decorous young woman, decided it would be better to stop visiting the studio. Heightening the drama was the fact that the two women lived on the same block. Riefenstahl could see into Dietrich's windows from her roof garden, but the latter knew nothing about this neighbor and probably would not have cared.

Von Sternberg watched *Piz Palü* and asked Riefenstahl to go to Hollywood with him, but she still believed in her love for Schneeberger and did not want to leave Berlin. She also described the "stimulating evening" she supposedly spent with von Sternberg at the home of Erwin Piscator.[109] We are told that the famous director kneeled at her feet while she was spooning up caviar—which she was inordinately fond of—and implored her to come to the United States with him. "When I finally said farewell to von Sternberg—it was in January 1930—it still wasn't clear whether Marlene or I would be following him to Hollywood."[110] After the advance publication of the Riefenstahl memoirs in 1987 in *Bunte* magazine, Dietrich immediately leaped into action by writing a letter to the editor, declaring that if von Sternberg and Remarque (who, Riefenstahl had claimed, was her friend) were still alive, they would die laughing from Riefenstahl's descriptions.[111] Von Sternberg's autobiography mentions Riefenstahl only once, as one of the many visitors to Babelsberg. "And students of my work were present at all times, among them Leni Riefenstahl, the future director of the Nazi films *Triumph of the Will* and *Olympiade* (in which latter film the winners were not all of the master race)."[112] No talk of dreamy dinners, bouquets of lilies, avowals of love, savoy cabbage, or movie offers.

Like many other actresses in Berlin, Riefenstahl surely got her hopes up when she heard that an American director was looking for a leading lady. Von Sternberg could free her from the burden of the Fanck films at long last. His working method differed markedly from Fanck's; von Sternberg created a synthetic world in his films, using technology as a means of manipulation. She surely did not hesitate to ask Schneeberger to put in a good word for her with von Sternberg. It must have galled her that the man who had dared to leave her succeeded in attaining something she had dreamed of, namely shooting a film without Fanck. The critic Hans Feld claims that Riefenstahl bragged that she had the role of Lola Lola all sewn up. He was at Riefenstahl's apartment for dinner when she got a telephone call with the news that the role of Lola Lola had gone to Dietrich. She was so upset that she ditched both him and the goulash she had been warming up.[113]

Fanck was tantalized by the world "Above the Clouds" (his working title for *Avalanche*) and decided to film it. The movie's main character, who monitors a weather station, lives above the clouds. As always in Fanck's films, the male lead had to do battle with cold, isolation, hurt pride, heartache, disappointing friendships with other men, and the tempestuous harshness of nature. The shooting took place at Cabana Vallot, the highest shelter hut in Europe, beneath the summit of Mont Blanc at an altitude of 4,400 meters. The experienced trio of Angst, Allgeier, and Schneeberger was in charge of the camera work; Riefenstahl, Sepp Rist, Mathias Wieman, and Ernst Udet formed the cast. The soundtrack was by Paul Dessau. In no other Fanck film did Riefenstahl appear more modern and self-assured than in *Avalanche*. Since other film offers were not coming her way, she apparently tried to gain influence over the design of her next mountain film. She selected Rist to play the male lead. He was actually a police radio operator, and *Avalanche* was his first movie. Riefenstahl was taken with his striking facial features, angular head, and strong body (in one scene, we see his naked, muscular torso). His acting is immobile, introverted, and inert. In the past, it had been Riefenstahl's goal to follow the men onto the mountain and to be accepted as one of them, but this time she wanted to try out the role of a modern young lady. She cut her hair short and wore slacks, sweater vest, blouse, and bow tie. In this role, Riefenstahl embodied the New Woman enjoying après-ski. Wearing high-heeled shoes and a figure-hugging flounced dress, she hurried through the streets of the big city.

The film opens to the world above the clouds. Hannes, the weather station monitor, makes a fire in his hut, puffs away at his pipe over the sea of evening clouds, and uses the latest technology to stay in contact with the people in the valley via Morse code. Technology has taken over in Fanck's world, and Riefenstahl, alias Dr. Hella Armstrong, is the ruler over this technological realm. She and her father fly with Udet up to Mont Blanc to visit Hannes at the weather station. Hella sits right down at the microscope, and Hannes starts to wash the dishes. Her father turns to him and says:

"I've certainly brought up a lovely housewife for you. This is a girl who has only skiing and science in her head—nothing else." Hella: "You men could tidy up." The father: "At your command, Fräulein Doktor! Girls today are good for nothing." Hella: "Darning socks is not exactly my specialty." In *Piz Palü*, Maria Maioni may have acted like a housewife from the moment she entered the hut, but Dr. Hella Armstrong has no intention of doing so. She is interested in science and leaves the housekeeping to the men. Eventually she sets out with Hannes to a measuring station higher up on the mountain. Once they have reached the summit, the man looks down at the world below, lost in thought, and she looks up at him coquettishly. While the two of them are enjoying their respective views, Hella's father plummets to his death during a walk in the mountains. Alpine guides come to get her, and she descends the mountain with her father's corpse.

While she is in town consoling herself with Hannes's friend, a snowstorm with howling winds descends on the mountain. Hannes seeks refuge in his hut, which is already covered in snow. His frost-bitten hands make it impossible for him to strike a fire. The scene of him attempting in vain to strike a match shows that he is lost. These are impressive shots of him making his way on skis through the icy desert and trying to find a crack in the ice that is narrow enough to jump across. He eventually returns to the hut, where the door is open; everything is covered in ice and abandoned to the fury of the snowstorm. The freezing man desperately resorts to using his elbow to send an SOS message in Morse code. Hella, wearing a trenchcoat, receives the distress call. Udet eventually finds Hannes in the hut. Hella arrives, makes a fire, and lays her head in Hannes's lap.

This Fanck movie was also a success. In the words of one critic, "Leni Riefenstahl led the way. A sportive girl looking for like-minded people, she is also agreeably natural as an actress; the utterly unsentimental acerbity of her nature casts a strange spell, and what is more, one notices here too, in one scene, that Riefenstahl has the soul of a dancer."[114] Hans Feld declared that this film carved out "new cinematic terrain": "Fanck films are for everyone. They convey visual experiences, visual beauty. Their effects remain untouched by the conflicts of the day. They are not unpolitical, but rather apolitical—on a different level."[115] Once again, Fanck was making a movie about one woman and two men, but *Avalanche* still offered a great deal that was new. Technology took on key importance here as he featured an airplane, a telescope, a radio, a microscope, a telegram, and a Morse code machine. Fanck had technology win out against the forces of nature. The fact that a woman had mastered this technology was revolutionary for Fanck. Although the end of the movie shows the tender side of Hella Armstrong, there is no indication that she will cease her work with microscope or telescope in the future. However, the viewer cannot help being struck by the blatantly sexual staging. Fanck placed his leading lady in front of a big phallus-like device aimed directly at her lap; she sits in front of it with veiled eyes. Fanck, who had started bombarding Riefenstahl with lubricious letters once again during the shoot, used the technical device in *Avalanche* as a means of expressing his desire. Another love affair had a tangential role in the making of this film: Udet, who liked to bring his lover of the moment along with him while filming, had come with Marlene Dietrich's Aunt Jolly. It is not known whether Dietrich was aware of her aunt's whereabouts at this time.

Avalanche was Fanck's first sound film. It was shot as a silent film; the sounds, music, and voices were dubbed in afterwards. Riefenstahl realized she had to keep up with the times, and once she returned to Berlin after shooting the film in the mountains, she sought out a speech teacher. She had heard of actors' careers taking a nosedive because their voices were off, and she was determined not to let that happen to her. To ensure that she was equipped for the future, she took daily lessons from Herbert Kuchenbuch, the phonetics consultant for *Avalanche*, and was photographed for *Scherl's Magazin* during these lessons.[116] Lotte Jacobi shot five pictures of the teacher and his pupil. Riefenstahl, wearing a leotard and pumps, looks intently focused, as always. Still, the outcome of these lessons left something to be desired. Her high-pitched voice clashed with her exalted performance style.

She used the media to let her viewers know what she had gone through to make this movie.

> Oh, my dear colleagues over at the studio in Berlin, if you ever had to come in for close-ups the way I did up there! Whenever I was in the midst of this primitivity, which came up against the limits of human existence, and happened to picture the studio set-up down there, where you have your own hairdresser and sit in front of the mirror for hours until you're put together in a way that you can sort of believe will result in a beautiful close-up, I was often struck with horror at the thought of how I might look in *these* close-ups, where a soot-covered stool with a little pocket mirror on it and a comb in front of it were the only utensils on hand to prepare for a major international film.[117]

Filming began when the sun rose at 4 a.m. It was hard to get a decent night of sleep at these altitudes. Riefenstahl was never really warm because the hut had neither furnace nor stove, even though the temperature sometimes dropped down to five degrees. There was a constant sound of ice cracking, and the crevasses were so large that an entire cathedral could have fit inside them. Life was trying for her as the only woman in the group. "They all tried to outdo one another with obscene jokes. Some of them constructed blatant sexual symbols of ice and snow around the hut. Naturally, I was harassed."[118] Not that she wanted to share her position with any other woman; in fact, when a young actress showed up during the shooting of *Avalanche*, Riefenstahl demanded that the woman leave. She would not put up with competition, though she needn't have worried, because it would have been a rare actress indeed who would capitulate to Fanck's demands. When she was told to cross a ladder spanning a crevasse that was quite deep and fifty feet wide, the men took bets as to whether she would chicken out. She didn't.

In 1930, she went to Vorarlberg to shoot *The White Frenzy*, a ski comedy, with Fanck, Schneider, and Angst. Once again, Sokal was the producer. The plot of this movie was trivial, the humor vapid, and Riefenstahl's acting underwhelming. She played her standard role as a woman idolized by all men. This time, however, she was playing herself—she wore a sweater monogrammed with her own initials. Riefenstahl made skiing popular among women.[119] In 1930, the famous photographer Martin Munkacsi—who was also one of her lovers—had taken pictures of her skiing in a bathing suit to show how attractive this sport could be for a young woman, although there were rumors (which persist to this day) that she was using a body double.[120] The athletic Marta Feuchtwanger, wife of the writer Lion Feuchtwanger, who went skiing in St. Anton every year, reported that Riefenstahl would sit at Hannes Schneider's reserved table. The man who decided who could join this table was Walter Bernays, brother-in-law of Sigmund Freud and supporter of Schneider. The only criterion for inclusion was an ability to ski well. Feuchtwanger claimed that Riefenstahl did not live up to that standard, "but she always had to get the first prizes because that was publicity for the films."[121]

The many months under extreme conditions on the mountain made Riefenstahl strong, as is evident in a portrait of her painted by Eugen Spiro that was submitted to the contest "The Most Beautiful German Woman's Portrait of 1928," sponsored by Elida Cosmetics.[122] Spiro's portrait shows an unsmiling, energetic woman staring straight into the camera wearing a plain white sleeveless dress and a black belt, the simple cut of the dress accentuating her strong body. The only piece of jewelry she wears is a red beaded necklace. She has chin-length hair, a slender face, and striking dark eyes, and her hands are crossed in her lap. Riefenstahl comes across as a reserved yet resolute woman who has no need for decorative accessories and is fully aware of her own beauty, strength, and courage.[123]

For Fanck, Riefenstahl was both comrade and lover, not only in her role in *Piz Palü*, but also in her position on his team. Riefenstahl's fellow mountaineers were shaped by the experience of the war. Fanck had worked with counterintelligence then, and now felt the need to prove himself over and over again. After the war, he gathered together a group of young men who excelled as athletes and were utterly devoted to achieving visual precision and objectivity in their filming. Sepp Allgeier (born in 1895) was the first ski jumper who also knew how to work with the camera. He was an adventure seeker who was rooted to his homeland; before the war, he had filmed in the Arctic region of Spitsbergen, Norway. In 1913, he spent time in the Balkans, where he photographed the second Serbian-Turkish war, presumably on behalf of the Serbs. Allgeier served on the western front as a volunteer in the army, "where I was happy to swap my shotgun for a nicer 'weapon,' my camera, which was always primed to fire."[124] As a war correspondent, he took pictures of war graves before they were crushed by grenades; he also took photographs of soldiers to send home to their girlfriends. Allgeier survived heavy combat, his "faithful war camera" always at his side. After the war, Fanck trained him on how to use imagery in creating mountain films. Allgeier continued to film with Trenker, who was three years his senior, after Trenker stopped working with Fanck. Trenker, who had been awarded medals for bravery, had been a training officer in World War I for the high alpine troops. He later drew on the experiences and knowledge he gained during this time as a lifelong reservoir of stories to establish his career. The illustrated portion of *Struggle in the Mountains*, the book he published in 1931, suggests that Fanck reenacted scenes from Trenker's life during the war in cinematic form.[125] The images depict uniformed men deep down in crevasses, in ice tunnels, or at the entrance to a subterranean ice city. Schneeberger, who was also born in 1895, had been an officer decorated with a gold medal for valor. As a lieutenant with the Tyrolean infantry corps, he and his men held on to a position in the mountains until it was blown up by the dreaded Alpini, the elite mountain warfare soldiers of the Italian army. This experience formed the basis of his narrative chronicle, *The Exploding Mountain*, which was not published until 1941.[126] His fellow filmmakers noted that Schneeberger still looked at mountains from predominantly military perspectives. While filming on the mountain, he would spend the long evenings devoted to outdoor shots talking about his experiences as an officer in the Habsburg imperial infantry corps.[127] His close relationship with Ernst Udet (born in 1896) also stemmed from his connection to the war. For Schneeberger, Udet was the great hero of the Richthofen fighter squadron. Gustav Diessl (born in 1899) had also been in the mountain infantry. In 1930, he costarred in the Pabst film *Westfront 1918*, the first German movie about life at the front and in the trenches. Sepp Rist (born in 1900) was part of a submarine convoy fleet during the war. At the risk of their lives, these men had to guide departing ships through the minefield. And Hannes Schneider, a skiing ace born in 1890, trained a mountain regiment in World War I and goaded the soldiers over the mountains. A good skiing technique made the difference between life and death. Harry Sokal also spent two years at the front.

Riefenstahl's fellow mountaineers had been defeated as German or Austrian soldiers; their imperial structures disappeared and made way for a republic. However, the war had left an indelible mark on their minds and bodies. In a 1931 essay, Ernst Jünger declared that this experience altered people for life. "Victors are those who, like salamanders, have gone through the school of dan-

ger." It is not security, he argued, but danger that determines the
future order of life. He went on to explain that technical tools, such
as cameras and photographic lenses, ensure that man's new rela-
tion to danger is rendered visible. Man in the modern era is both
civilized and barbaric, and approaches the elemental with an acu-
ity of consciousness born of technology and death.[128] Jünger's brief
essay reads like a programmatic elucidation of Fanck's films. The
people Fanck chose for his movies sought out danger. The combination of the mastery of the body and the mastery of technical
apparatus is the absolutely modern element of his films, his production method, and his crew. The body, technology, and nature
are the guarantors of heroic experience. Riefenstahl was the first
woman to be placed at the side of these men. But not all of them
had come from the war; some were too young to have experienced
it, as she would have been, had she been born a boy. Riefenstahl's
childhood years had been war years, lacking any sense of security,
future, long-term prospects, or stability. The war was followed by
an unloved revolution, insurgencies, inflation, and economic hard-
ship, and this period instilled a manifest survival instinct and a
lust for adventure in many young people. They were on a quest
for something radically different. Hans Ertl (born in 1908), Albert
Benitz (1904), Walter Frentz (1907), and Richard Angst (1905)
would be Riefenstahl's young cameramen. They were children of
the war era, the way she was, and they called themselves "mountain
vagabonds." One of their few forms of entertainment was to watch
movies, sitting in the cheap seats. Love stories or gangster movies
left these men cold; they loved Fanck's mountain films, where they
could watch big strong men having adventures with skis and ropes
high up in the mountains, adventures that demanded nothing but
strength and courage.

Mountain vagabonds shied away from forming attachments
down in the valley; asked to choose because "living girls or dead
ice, dance or battle," they opted for the dead ice and the battle.

Getting involved with women, they felt, would diminish their passion and strength for mountain climbing. They were unconcerned with what would become of them, because times were hard and the future looked grim. Fanck could go on the assumption that his mountain vagabonds would pour their hearts and souls into their work. None of them had had any previous knowledge of photography or filmmaking, not even Angst, who would later become a noted cinematographer. Riefenstahl was the only woman in the group; she was surrounded by men who either had stories of their own to tell about the war or yearned for a great event on the war's scale. Riefenstahl had the sound of the war stories in her ear; she knew the fears, the energy, the desires, and the arrogance of these men. Over the course of the many months that she spent alone with them in their secluded location, she got to know them quite well, body and soul. She shared the danger with them all, and her bed with many of them. But beyond what she learned in these years about men, war memories, and danger, she also disciplined her body in snow and ice, and appreciated the value of technology for artistic expression. The work on the mountains transformed the young woman into both a creature of nature and a well-versed technological apprentice. Both of these changes would serve her well in the next stage of her career.

BLUE

I n 1931, Leni Riefenstahl began to feel as though time was running out on her. Her career as a dancer was clearly over, and she did not want the same to happen with her acting. She decided to make a movie herself. "I have studied the camera, I know about lenses, footage, and filters. I have edited films and have a sense of how new effects can be achieved. I'm wary about this, because I am an actress and don't want to split my energies. Still, I can't change the fact that I see everything with the eyes of a filmmaker. I would like to make pictures myself."[1]

Riefenstahl related two versions of how she was able to make this wish come true. According to the earlier one, which is far briefer and more matter-of-fact, she wrote a treatment for a cinematic fairy tale. Her friends liked what they read, but the film producers to whom she sent it deemed it boring. Determined not to give up, she put together her savings, had her ex-boyfriend Schneeberger agree to serve as cameraman without pay, and accepted the lead role in *The White Frenzy* in order to invest her earnings in a production of her own. She was short fifty thousand reichsmarks, but eventually Sokal agreed to help with the financing.

The later version was replete with accusations, aimed principally at Fanck. She felt that the filming of *The White Frenzy* was one long affront. Fanck, she claimed, was as sadistic as ever, and tormented her with a role that was far beneath her: "At almost every opportunity, the director asked me to cry out 'Oh, great!' I found it repugnant and I just couldn't get it across my lips. The result was tears and fights with Fanck, who enjoyed it."[2] Klaus Mann saw the movie and wrote in his diary on January 8, 1932: "With E., R., and Babs in 'White Frenzy' (Phöbus); astonishingly bad, and monotonous, snow and ski film with the insufferably rotten Leni Riefenstahl."[3] According to Riefenstahl's second version, she would be able to make her film only if she could stand up to Fanck and Sokal, who both took pleasure in humiliating her. She took on the director role out of financial necessity. It was only after she had pawned her jewelry and art and made the first screen tests that Sokal decided to finance the production and Fanck sent her an enthusiastic telegram. Her artistry had won over the two adversaries, and she could forge ahead.

The truth probably lies somewhere in between. The story about her financial difficulty served only as a pretext to downplay her ambition. It is hard to imagine that a person as egocentric as Leni Riefenstahl would consider entrusting her own screenplay to another director. And Sokal was closer to her than she was willing to admit. In 1932, they both lived at Hindenburgstrasse 97 in Wilmersdorf—on the same floor of the building. In Berlin, rumors swirled about their engagement, yet Sokal continued to deny that he had been one of her lovers.

> For me, her many love affairs and tragedies became a source
> of neverending amusement, as long as they didn't take place
> during my films. Sometimes they lasted only a matter of
> days, but during those days, Leni was totally engrossed in
> the partner in question, almost convinced that she loved
> him. Until the next one caught her eye and she loved him
> in turn. These partners were always the best in their field:

whether they were a producer, director, actor, skier, or
tennis player, they were unvaryingly the champions; her
nymphomania, if we are to call it that, had an elitist bent.[4]

Before the start of shooting, she founded her own production
company, L. R. Studio Films, Inc. Sokal oversaw the finances and
organization while the movie was being filmed. This solved many
problems. But Riefenstahl was a novice in the cutting room and
feared that her work lacked suspense. She asked Fanck if he was
willing to help her out, and handed over the print to him. They
agreed that he would have a look at it and that they would bring
it to the editing table together the following day. When she came
by the next morning, however, Fanck announced that he had re-
edited the film during the night, changing every scene in the process. Riefenstahl was convinced that he had ruined her movie. She
worked hard to salvage it, but her relationship with Fanck was over.
"I was no longer under his influence. My new, independent career
had begun."[5] It is unclear whether Fanck's fears of losing her really
did drive him to destroy the film, but Riefenstahl's subsequent version came with a major advantage: in this version, the film arose
solely from her own genius. His influence on her ended when he
destroyed her first film; according to this new legend, parting ways
with Fanck enabled her to emerge as a director.

In the literary estate of Béla Balázs, who worked with Riefenstahl on the screenplay for *The Blue Light*, as her movie came to be
called, there is a letter Leni Riefenstahl wrote to him from Moscow
in February 1932 that casts doubt on the second version of her
story. The letter clearly indicates that Fanck was involved in editing
the film, and Riefenstahl appreciated his work. She wrote that the
screening of the material she had edited had been "devastating,"
and that the film seemed "insanely boring and stiff, overstated and
unnatural." Fanck re-edited and thus saved the film, and Riefenstahl praised his work to Balázs.[6] Fanck contributed significantly to

the success of *The Blue Light*—a fact that Riefenstahl never admitted in public.[7] The dramatic end of the relationship between Riefenstahl and Fanck, as depicted in her memoirs, shows how much she feared Fanck's destructive energy. For her, it was a repetition of a similar situation ten years earlier. Back then, her father had wanted to forbid her to dance, and she had to go behind his back. Riefenstahl knew that there was only one solution for her to get away from Fanck: she had to be better than he was. In her mind, it was not a contradiction that she brought Fanck into the filmmaking process in order to achieve this goal. She had no qualms when it came to putting forward her art. The visual language of her movie had to differ markedly from Fanck's. She wanted to strike a new path in form and content.

Riefenstahl chose her cast and crew carefully for her ambitious project. True to her principles, she positioned herself as the only woman. She surrounded herself with men who had demonstrated their loyalty to her, had been her lovers, or had at least shown that they worshipped her, starting with her three cast-off paramours, Sokal (producer), Fanck (editor and adviser), and Schneeberger (camera). Walter Riml, whom she got to know and grew fond of during the filming of *The Great Leap* and *The White Frenzy*, was an excellent sportsman from the mountains. He was put in charge of the still photography, and he took the Junta photograph that has been reproduced countless times. Mathias Wieman, who had appeared in *Avalanche* with her, was the male lead. Heinz von Jaworsky served as both camera assistant and press secretary.[8]

A key member of the team whom Riefenstahl left unmentioned, presumably so that she could take all the credit for the film's success, was Carl Mayer. His work on the film is briefly mentioned in her book *Struggle in Snow and Ice* (1933), and then sixty years later in Ray Müller's film *The Wonderful, Horrible Life of Leni Riefenstahl*: "I met Carl Mayer, the well-known screenwriter, the best one, who had written the Murnau films, and Béla Balázs, who was then considered the best screenwriter, and they were so taken with the subject matter that they offered good advice, and Balázs even helped out without a fee."[9] In a letter to the film scholar Jürgen Kasten dated February 1994, she put forward a different version, stating that she would have *liked* to work with Carl Mayer, but Mayer was too busy and recommended Béla Balázs to her.[10] Perhaps this version was a reflection of her failing memory. In any event, it certainly appears as though Mayer helped shape her first film.

When Riefenstahl met Mayer, he had already made film history by cowriting the script for *The Cabinet of Doctor Caligari* with Hans Janowitz.[11] He had been working in the film business for more than twenty years and had written six screenplays for F. W. Murnau, including the classic *The Last Laugh*. Mayer worked with Paul Czinner and Elisabeth Bergner on the Schnitzler adaptation *Fräulein Else* and with Gerhard Lamprecht on *Emil and the Detectives*. They probably met during the filming of *Avalanche*. Mayer had also been involved with this screenplay.[12] Riefenstahl knew that Mayer was regarded as the best visual screenwriter in the business. "A script by Carl Mayer was already a film," was cameraman Karl Freund's oft-cited pronouncement. That must have made him interesting for her, as she was pursuing the goal of creating entirely new images for her first film. Riefenstahl was intent on making people believe that she had effortlessly achieved a masterpiece with *The Blue Light* as a director and screenwriter. She later made a point of concealing the fact that this success was not solely an outgrowth of her artistic genius. In the book she wrote in 1933, she was still recounting long nights of discussing the script with Mayer, but sixty years later, this collaboration was reduced to a couple of "good bits of advice," and in the intervening years, she never even mentioned him.

Mayer conveyed his stories through imagery. His scripts juxtapose technical directions with visual cues. In Joseph Roth's view, "These directions reveal the structure of the creative process: the poetic vision is transformed (consciously or unconsciously) into the cinematic way of seeing. Intuition has formed a bond with technology."[13] Along those same lines, Riefenstahl wrote:

> Images arose from my dreams. I made out the hazy shape
> of a young girl who lived in the mountains, a creature of
> nature. I saw her climbing, saw her in the moonlight; I
> watched her being chased and pelted with stones, and
> finally I dreamed of this girl falling away from a wall of rock
> and slowly plunging into the depths. These images seized
> hold of me and grew more vivid, and one day, I wrote
> everything down as an eighteen-page treatment.[14]

She put her faith in technology to render the poetic imagery she was after in visual terms rather than in dialogue. She mistrusted words, and *The Blue Light* has elements of a silent film. The main character, Junta, does say a few words in Italian, but her true medium is her body. The viewer's lasting impression of Junta centers on her haunted look and her fitful, tremulous movements. Mayer, a shy yet friendly man, had a penchant for imbuing outsiders with symbolic meaning, which may be why he was eager to craft the story of the beautiful Junta, who remains an outsider among the mountain people. It is also known that he had had enough of studio films and was interested in taking a different approach. Moreover, he was plagued with debt, and in need of a source of income. For Riefenstahl, who was determined to make a name for herself as an author and director, meeting him must have been a stroke of good luck. Mayer transformed trifles into art.

Balázs wrote the dialogue and helped Riefenstahl shoot the film when she was on camera. Like Mayer, he was a devotee of the silent film and reinforced Riefenstahl's resolve to shoot *The Blue Light* using its aesthetics. Born Herbert Bauer in 1884 in southern Hungary, he adopted the name Béla Balázs in 1913. In the same year, he converted from Judaism to Roman Catholicism. He later became a

member of the famous Sunday Circle in Budapest, along with Georg
Lukács, René Spitz, Karl Mannheim, and Arnold Hauser. They held
casual meetings in Balázs's apartment, where they enjoyed debates
that ran from Sunday at three in the afternoon until 3 a.m. the
next morning about Cézanne, the aesthetics of German roman-
ticism, or French poetry. During the Hungarian Soviet Republic,
Balázs became the acting director of the People's Commissariat for
Education, in charge of literature and art. During this turbulent
period, he met the future film producer Alexander Korda (Sándor
Korda), Ladislav Vajda (László Vajda, the co-screenwriter of the *Piz
Palü* film), and Michael Curtiz (Mihály Kertész), who later directed
Casablanca. When the Soviet Republic collapsed, Balázs fled to
Vienna. He wanted to be seen as an artist, and he parted ways with
Lukács.[15] Balázs believed that communism was the only path to
human spiritualization and sought spirituality in the taverns of the
Puszta, in the faces of the rebels, in the bosoms of the nursemaids,
and, when he worked with Riefenstahl, in the Sarntal peasants.[16]
In 1926, he moved to Berlin. He wanted to make films, express his
views, and earn money. Balázs wrote two books about film as the
beginning of a new age, both of which are considered important
even today.[17] With Korda he shot the film *Madame Doesn't Want
Children*, with Berthold Viertel and Margo Lion, *Adventures of a Ten
Mark Note*. By 1928, his work as a screenwriter had begun to stag-
nate. It is difficult to determine whether his lack of success resulted
from his political views or his mediocre screenplays. None of his
planned projects came to fruition.

Several factors seem to have prompted Balázs to work with
Riefenstahl. Both of them had yet to achieve a real breakthrough.
Like Balázs, Riefenstahl repeatedly criticized the "industry" before,
during, and after National Socialism. She declared that for her first
film, she wanted to steer clear of the industry, by which she meant
the major film companies, which were supposedly unwilling to
finance true works of art. Balázs and Riefenstahl joined forces

to display their artistry to the world and defy the movie-making establishment. Heinz von Jaworsky reported that Balázs had a strong political influence on Riefenstahl: "Riefenstahl held political views similar to those of Balázs, that is, left-wing."[18] She and Balázs regarded themselves as misunderstood geniuses whom the industry was holding back from realizing their ideas.

In the spring of 1931, they began working on Riefenstahl's screenplay, and it was completed in mid-June. Balázs visited her in St. Anton during the shooting of *The White Frenzy* to work with her on it. There has been speculation that the two of them were having a love affair, and he wanted to be close to her for that reason as well.[19] If we take her account at face value, the filming of *The Blue Light* proceeded flawlessly. The crew she put together proved to be a dedicated group. "We were like a family of eight. Everything was paid from a common kitty. Each of us tried to spend as little as possible so as to keep the kitty going as long as we could. If the soles of someone's boots got torn, or something similarly urgent was needed, the money came from this kitty."[20] The photographs Walter Riml took during the filming convey this sentiment. We see a group of young people looking cheerful and utterly devoted. They all had one goal in mind: to film this magnificent woman and artist. Riefenstahl needed to be surrounded by men who were loyal to or in love with her. She found the work on this film quite stressful, and often felt on the verge of a nervous breakdown. In times of crisis, however, she proved to have nerves of steel. At one point, the entire group was stopped at the border en route to Italy, and the customs officials demanded a large sum of money from them, which they did not have. She proceeded to send a telegram to Rome, to the personal attention of Benito Mussolini, whom she had never met, asking him to waive the customs duties. After six tense hours they learned that Il Duce had given them the green light, and the group was allowed to go through the Brenner Pass.[21]

The Blue Light tells the story of a man and woman traveling through a mountain village on their honeymoon. They stay in a room that is decorated with pictures of a beautiful, Madonna-like woman. When they ask who she is, the innkeeper brings a book, *La Historia de Junta*, which recounts her story. This is where the actual plot of the film begins. It takes place in 1866, which distinguishes it from Fanck's films. By setting the narrative in the nineteenth century, technology and modern comfort are essentially absent; only in the brief frame story at the beginning do the objects we associate with modern life appear: the honeymooning couple drives a car, and both wife and husband wear trenchcoats rather than traditional costumes. The two main characters in the movie, Vigo, a painter from Vienna, and Junta, who is from the mountains, are not clad in traditional garb either. They do not belong to the local community, which regards Junta as a witch because she is keeping a secret and will not reveal it to anyone else. She is the only one who knows how to gain access to a grotto in the mountain with crystals that glow when there is a full moon and emit a blue light. Magically attracted by the strange light, young men from the village try to follow her, and in doing so fall to their deaths. After every full moon, the corpse of a young man is carried into the village. Why can a woman scale the mountain, yet the young men plummet? The villagers conclude that something is amiss. Junta skulks through the streets like a hunted animal when she comes to offer the berries she plucks to the villagers. The sight of her arouses disgust or desire: contemptuous stares from old women and lascivious glances from young men. Junta wears her hair loose, walks barefoot, and is dressed like a ragamuffin; her shabby clothing reveals a good deal of skin. She is a wild, alluring creature who does not go to church and scratches and shouts when anyone comes too close. In one scene, Tonio, the son of the innkeeper, pulls her into a dark corner in an attempt to rape her, but she is able to escape. Riefenstahl remained true to her signature role; she is the woman between two men, although in *The Blue Light*, Junta is not interested in men. When Vigo saves her from the angry crowd of villagers that seems intent on lynching her, he wins over her trust. He visits her up on the mountain, where she lives with a shepherd boy and goats in a simple hut. Vigo leaves the village to be with Junta, while Tonio watches warily. Vigo speaks German, and Junta Italian; neither understands the other's language. Yet Vigo seems to be happy in this largely mute relationship; he stays close to the object of his desire, gazing at her with a somewhat moronic, leering grin. But Junta finds crystals more beguiling than sex. When the full moon returns, she sets out on the climb to her crystal grotto, with Vigo and Tonio behind. Tonio plunges to his death, but Vigo follows her inside and sees her sitting amid the glittering stones, which wield a strange power over her. Back in the hut, Vigo decides to tell her that he will go down into the valley and reveal the approach to the grotto to the townsfolk. Junta, who is indifferent to wealth, does not understand the implications of this action. The locals arrive with pickaxes and wheelbarrows to loot the grotto, and Vigo is celebrated. Suspecting the worst, Junta clambers back up to the grotto only to find it empty. The crystals are gone, and the beauty is destroyed. Junta loses the strength to live and falls to her death; Vigo finds her corpse. This brings the story in the book to an end, and the honeymooning couple gazes up at the full moon.

Vigo, representing the viewer's perspective, realizes from the start that he has come to a village in which something is awry. Before he meets Junta and their story begins, he arrives in a coach in which the coachman and the other passengers seem strangely lifeless. The door of the coach slams shut by itself, as if by magic, and the coach drives off. The innkeeper is suddenly standing next to Vigo, having appeared out of nowhere. He takes Vigo with him to the eerily silent, dark village. This beginning is reminiscent of Jonathan Harker's ride to the count's castle in Friedrich Wilhelm Murnau's *Nosferatu*, and since Mayer had worked with Murnau, this opening scene appears to be a deliberate nod to that film. Riefenstahl was also quite taken with Murnau's films, especially with his *Faust*. In contrast to Fanck, who favored a "stylized objectivity" achieved by accentuating contours, she worked with soft focus and filters, which yielded a painterly effect. Riefenstahl shot her films on location; her camera went inside alpine huts, farmhouses, and even the village church. For the first time she used a lighting truck for indoor shots. She was on the quest for faces of people who were not out for fame or wealth, and found "her" villagers in the remote Sarntal in southern Tyrol. If they rebuffed her attempts to photograph them, she would stay in town for a few days. After going to church on Sundays, the villagers sat together in the tavern over a glass of wine. She approached them, showed them photographs she had taken of them in secret, and ordered several additional pitchers of wine. The alcohol had the desired effect, and they agreed to serve as extras in the movie.

She set her film in the secluded world of Sarntal. Riefenstahl continued to be proud to the end of her life that she had found her way into the community and was able to film the locals even during a church service. The villagers were photographed with stark lateral lighting, which gave their faces a wrinkled, weatherbeaten, and gaunt cast. Junta, by contrast, the mysterious, seductive creature, was filmed in soft focus. Riefenstahl exploited the effects of light and shadow to make it difficult for viewers to distinguish between day and night, or fantasy and reality. She gave shape to her dream world by implementing technical innovations. "I contacted AGFA, hoping to find a film emulsion that is insensitive to certain colors but, when used with special filters, could produce color transformations and unreal visual effects. AGFA was quite cooperative; they did some experiments, and the result was 'R-material.' Later on it was used universally, especially in day-for-night shooting."[22] She was able to make the sun rise over the mountains like a mysteriously radiant full moon. The scenes in the village are often dark to draw attention to the menacing narrowness of the streets and the hostile severity of the faces. The viewer thinks it is night and fails to notice that it is actually daytime until Junta has left the village. By contrast, light streams up to Junta's mountain pasture, and the ominous darkness in the village gives way to blazing brightness.

In *The Blue Light*, Riefenstahl did not have to cope with snow and ice and could wear skimpy outfits, because the movie takes place in the summertime. She uses her body language to good effect in this movie when she slinks through the village crouched over and poised to attack, advances fitfully, or skips across the mountain pastures looking relaxed and graceful. In contrast to the people in the village, she moves about freely and exposes her physical allure to the gazes of others. The villagers are encased in traditional costumes that seem like protective armor, while Junta blithely reveals quite a bit of skin. Barefoot, nimble, and lithe, she clambers up the mountains, and no man can follow her. Junta is more animal than human, and she feels closest to her crystals. The cosmic energy of crystals complements Junta's sexual energy. Riefenstahl portrayed her as a footloose, wild woman whom men desire and women despise. Junta remains true to her ideals. Vigo is sadly mistaken in his belief that she will belong to him after the grotto is destroyed. Junta would rather die than live without beauty.

Riefenstahl made two movies in which she played the lead role: *The Blue Light* and *Lowlands*. In both films, her characters are a Gypsy-like amalgam of erotic fantasies and social ostracism. Junta, a woman of uncertain origins, does not belong to the village community and is free of its conventions. She drives decent men out of their minds. Junta desires not the man, but an image of herself, which she finds in the crystals glowing during a full moon. The blue light they emit is exceptionally beautiful, but cold. Junta is protected by a supernatural power and is the intermediary for a ritual that costs young men their lives. At the end of the film, Junta herself dies. The looting of the crystals has sealed her fate, and all she leaves behind is the legend of her life and her picture, rimmed by crystals.

Riefenstahl claimed that this movie foretold her ultimate fate "as if it were a premonition."[23] That is nonsense. *The Blue Light* was so important for her because she subsequently used it to verify what she was capable of without Hitler's patronage. She counted on its success to whitewash her reputation. In her capacity as a screen-writer and director, Riefenstahl shaped the image of male fantasies. It is the woman herself who sets the stage for her sacrifice in the film. This sacrifice enabled her to emerge as an artistic construct. This was ultimately Riefenstahl's most effective means to set herself apart from Fanck—by robbing him of his heroine.

Balázs's influence on Riefenstahl and her first film should not be underestimated. Her images of the *Volk*, which would continue to play a role in her collaboration with the National Socialists, were strongly influenced by the communist Balázs's sentimental visions. Before she met Balázs, she had not been so keen on fairy tales. Balázs was the one who had been fervently devoted to these stories since his childhood. In the People's Commissariat, he set up a unit for fairy tales. Riefenstahl responded well to the simple form of the fairy tale. The characters are clear-cut and the plot moves quickly. People in fairy tales do not grow through experience; they are iso-lated, yet connected to everything. Nothing has to be explained, and everything is sublimated to weightless images. Riefenstahl claimed that she was a medium for fairy tales, and that her mov-ies welled up unconsciously from deep within her. In making this argument, she was disclaiming any responsibility for their content.

The premiere for *The Blue Light*, which took place on March 24, 1932, at the Ufa Palace in Berlin, was staged as a major cinematic event. Riefenstahl, the coproducer, screenplay writer, director, and lead actress, envisioned it as a celebration of her breakthrough. Before the premiere she liked to claim that she was the first woman film director, thus conveniently overlooking the work of Olga Chekhova, Leontine Sagan, and Hanna Henning.

She wore a white, low-cut evening gown and was flanked by five men in tuxedos. Riefenstahl was ready to graduate from a mountaineer to a movie diva. Balázs did not attend; he had headed off to Moscow. She described her movie as a "sensation" and claimed that the critics at home and abroad were falling all over themselves with excitement. Like many of her accounts, this was half true at best. In the *Film-Kurier*, she was lauded as "a courageous woman in her work and her singleminded dedication."[24] The *Berliner Tagblatt*, however, deemed the movie a failure: "The characters of the legend are not fleshed out; they are ambiguous and blurry; they have too little contour and content, and hence the plot is wishy-washy."[25] Riefenstahl's mountain climbing, readers are told, was more impressive than her acting. The critics praised Riml's photography and Schneeberger's camera work, but Riefenstahl's directorial and acting skills were either disparaged or ignored.[26]

Riefenstahl continually drew attention to the silver medal that *The Blue Light* was awarded at the Biennale in Venice. In 1930, control of the Biennale had passed from the city of Venice to the national fascist government. For the eighteenth Biennale, in 1932, film artists were invited for the first time. The Esposizione Internazionale d'Arte Cinematografica was held at the Hotel Exelsior. From August 6 to August 21, 1932, the high dignitaries of the fascist state hobnobbed with film artists from around the world. Greta Garbo, Clark Gable, James Cagney, and Joan Crawford were among Mussolini's guests. Riefenstahl did not write anything about a trip to Venice, so it would appear that she did not attend. The movies were shown to large audiences; however, there *was* no competition held at the film Biennale in 1932, so exactly *which* silver medal *The Blue Light* might have been awarded remains Riefenstahl's secret.[27]

The Blue Light was certainly a remarkable movie that highlighted her talent, but she had not achieved a masterpiece. Sokal claimed

that her bitterness about the reception of this film, by Jewish critics in particular, turned her into an anti-Semite on the spot.[28] The
foreword Paul Ickes wrote for Riefenstahl's *Struggle in Snow and
Ice* reveals just how disappointed she was with these reactions.
The many conversations that critics had with her convinced him
that she was a great artist who had turned her back on the typical
machinations of the "industry":

> Surrounded by a male-oriented, liberalistic outlook on the
> film industry, Leni Riefenstahl did not meekly accede to
> the role division of the often unscrupulous supervisors of
> so-called German film. . . . As a woman, she showed the
> men who cared only about profit that a personal commit-
> ment is well worth the effort if there is an idea behind it.
> Her success proved her right, because material success
> is sure to follow sooner or later from a commitment to
> ideas. . . . But the same press that was under the spell of the
> profit-oriented economy and encroached on the spiritual
> revival of the people with this attitude withheld its alle-
> giance from the artist Leni Riefenstahl, because allegiance
> is contingent on understanding, and no understanding was
> possible here.[29]

Riefenstahl clung to this image of the highly gifted woman who
pursues her goals in a man's world and is thus unloved throughout
her life.

In May 1932, she traveled to icy Greenland to make the movie
S.O.S. Iceberg. This last film she would work on with Fanck in some
respects represented an exception to the movies they had made
together. Universal Pictures in the United States had asked Fanck
for a good screenplay. He sensed that the time was right to make
a dream of his come true: he wanted to outdo his standard mountain theme by shooting a feature film about nature set in Green-

land. Because Greenland was a country closed off to foreigners in order to protect the Eskimos, he persuaded Knud Rasmussen, the renowned polar explorer, to oversee the film. At the invitation of Carl Laemmle, the head of Universal Pictures, who was originally from Germany, Fanck traveled to America in April 1932. In honor of his German guest, Laemmle threw a party at which many Hollywood stars were present. Fanck had the honor of sitting next to Marlene Dietrich. She had just shot her second movie in the United States, but Fanck failed to appreciate this honor. Dietrich was supposedly too "painted" for his liking; in any case, he wrote that he had no idea what to talk about with this woman who was not interested in skiing or mountains. They had "absolutely nothing in common," and so he sat next to Dietrich "as awkward as a schoolboy."[30]

Universal insisted that Leni Riefenstahl had to act in this film because she had made such a good impression on Americans in *Piz Palü*. Fanck protested that Riefenstahl would have to play a pilot in the movie, and everyone knew she could not fly. He would rather cast Elly Beinhorn, a famous female pilot, in the role. Besides, no woman had ever taken part in an Arctic expedition. But Fanck made no headway with this argument; the Americans insisted on Riefenstahl. "It was only when our Leni came to me in tears in Berlin and begged me not to take away the ten thousand dollar fee she would get did I give in, to compensate for all the strains she had already endured in my films. This decision detracted from the film by introducing a false note—although just a minor one."[31] Most likely he could not stand the fact that he was not enough for the Americans on his own. Fanck and Riefenstahl had little choice but to grit their teeth and take another stab at working together. This film would bring in quite a bit of money, as well as the prospect of their making the leap to Hollywood.

Riefenstahl claimed that the deciding factor in accepting this offer was her wish to go on an expedition of this kind with her old friends. In fact, she had no option but to work with Fanck once again. However, she did manage to get Paul Kohner at Universal on her side. Fanck's literary estate contains a letter from Kohner to Fanck, dated May 21, 1932, in which he asks Fanck to give Riefenstahl a more substantial set of lines than just the occasional "Oh, fine!" in *The White Frenzy*.

Kohner would appear in Riefenstahl's life again. Carl Laemmle had brought him to the United States when Kohner was eighteen years old. At the age of twenty-two, he was named casting director and sent to Germany. Word quickly got around that Kohner was conducting a talent search in Europe. Riefenstahl may have read the article about him in the *Film-Kurier*, which said, "Kohner merits the attention and support of the German trade press, since he is one of the most zealous proponents of the European spirit in the American production center. Against all odds, he is paving the way for German literature and art to be considered by American film producers."[32] Between 1930 and 1933, Kohner was in charge of Universal's film production in Germany. To comply with German import regulations, German Universal produced low-budget films in Germany to offset the many films imported from the United States.[33] Kohner was thus a man of influence who could establish a connection between Berlin and Hollywood.

The meetings to plan for the elaborate expedition took place in Fanck's villa. His literary estate contains a personal photograph showing Fanck, Udet, Kohner, and Riefenstahl enjoying a glass of wine. They are sitting close together on the couch. Fanck is staring intently off to the left at Riefenstahl, who is seated between Udet and Kohner. Udet is gazing pensively at Fanck; Riefenstahl has turned to Kohner and is beaming at him, her dark eyes shining. Kohner appears to be smiling at her in response. This photograph seems to suggest that Fanck is worried that the flirtation between Riefenstahl and Kohner could blossom into an affair. In this gathering on the couch, her familiar position as the only woman among men was preserved, although the expedition itself would start with many female participants. Because they would be on location in this icy terrain for months, Fanck decided that the women could accompany their men. Together with the American affiliates, who would be filming a comedy with a different director at the same time, the number of participants grew to forty. Thousands upon thousands of pounds of food and supplies, four airplanes, two motorboats, and three polar bears were transported to Greenland; the preparations for the expedition posed quite a logical challenge. One of the men who had to solve this problem was the uncle of historian Eric Hobsbawm. Hobsbawm, who was living with his uncle Sidney in Berlin in the early 1930s, recalled these goings-on quite well later in life because this was his uncle's last job in Germany.[34]

Many newspapers carried reports about the bold venture. There were so many women in the group that the accompanying photographs failed to highlight Riefenstahl. One picture shows everyone standing at the railing shortly before the ship left the shore. Above their heads is a large banner that reads: "Universal-Fanck-Greenland-Filmexpedition Sponsored by Carl Laemmle 'It can be done.'"[35] However, it would prove difficult to live up to this watchword.

When their ship dropped them off in the ice after eleven days of travel and headed back to Europe, they began to see that this would be no ordinary filming. They were far away from civilization as they knew it, and they could not simply take off to a luxury hotel for a few days to rest up from the filming. They were stranded in inhospitable surroundings. The Eskimos were very friendly, but it was difficult to communicate with them. Their customs and ways of life were totally alien to both the Americans and the Europeans. There were neither huts nor houses, so the people who had come to make this movie pitched tents to be used for sleeping and eating, and also set up darkrooms, cages for the polar bears, and a kitchen. With the exception of a few Eskimo scenes, the filming had to be done entirely on ice floes and icebergs. Confronted with the bare, barren, and icy world of Greenland, the people on the expedition realized that Fanck was obsessed with his project and intended for his men to use the camera lens to look death in the eye.

While Fanck and Udet were looking around for suitable ice-bergs, Riefenstahl was getting herself a new lover: Hans Ertl, a mountain vagabond from Munich. He was considered one of the best ice climbers and a daredevil. "Of all the male members of the expedition, he was, without a doubt, the most attractive. . . . Once, when I wanted to paddle out with my boat all by myself, he came with me, in order, he said, to teach me the right way of paddling. A casual flirtation suddenly turned into passion. I forgot all my resolutions and was happy to be in love again."[36] Many years later Ertl enjoyed recalling this boat ride, during which he fondled Riefenstahl's breasts from behind while she paddled the boat. His predecessor, cameraman and photographer Walter Riml, advised Ertl not to delude himself: "For Leni, young sportsmen like us are like candy, good to nibble at as long as it's fun."[37] Ertl embodied the blend of adventurer, athlete, and technical artist that Riefenstahl found irresistible. Fanck seems to have been resigned to her fre-quent affairs and refrained from displays of anger. He also had bet-ter things to do, because the Arctic posed entirely new challenges for him. Here he could live out his somewhat sadistic ambition. He had Sepp Rist swim about twenty laps in a row in ice water when the temperature outside was well below freezing. Rist would drag himself out of the water and into his tent feeling "deathly weary." During this brief time, his clothing froze to the point of cracking as he undressed. In the pictures that show him stepping out of the icy water, Rist looks like the incarnation of pain. His work with Fanck left him with a case of rheumatism that lasted the rest of his life. Expedition member Ernst Sorge remarked about Riefen-stahl's insistent desire to seek the spotlight on the ice: "Our daring Leni had no mind to lag behind the men, and anyone had only to remark, 'I fancy that the water hereabouts is too cold to bathe,' for her to spring in courageously next moment, although the film did not exact it of her."[38]

Every day, Fanck used binoculars to seek out any iceberg that appeared safe for filming. The shooting dragged on for months, and the polar summer was coming to an end. By the afternoon, it was pitch black and ice cold. All night, there was a loud cracking of ice, which for the men brought back memories of the war because it sounded like "the continuous low roll and rumble of artillery fire on the western front."[39] Riefenstahl came down with a bad cold and a high fever. She lay trembling in her tent, racked with spasms. Once again, she had come to a point at which her body refused to cooperate, but there was no escaping this situation. Fanck ordered her to go on with the filming, even though it would have been an easy matter to have someone else stand in for her. She did as she was told, although she was writhing in unrelenting pain and feeling utterly miserable in this dark, icy world. She was about to film the scene with Udet in which she flies her plane into the wall of an iceberg; the plane bursts into flame, and she saves herself by jumping into the water. Because Riefenstahl did not know how to fly, Udet was concealed inside the plane to steer it and make sure that it caught fire. She closed her eyes during the filming, and when she opened them for a moment, she felt as though the iceberg were hurtling straight toward her with a boom. She plunged into the ice-cold water at lightning speed. After this test of endurance, she was allowed to go home to recuperate. The missing scenes could be reshot in the Swiss Alps. A Danish freighter brought her to Germany.

Politics had held little interest for Riefenstahl thus far, but that would change in February 1932. When she returned to Berlin after her cinematic tour with *The Blue Light*, she saw posters hanging everywhere with Adolf Hitler's picture announcing his upcoming political rally, and she decided to attend the event in the Sports Palace. It was her very first political event, and as it turned out, the exact right one for her purposes. She was seated too far away to see Hitler, but she still gained a vivid sense of how this man was able to transfix his audience. It cannot have been his physical appearance that drew Riefenstahl to Hitler, because he was certainly not the type of man she went for. She favored well-built men with broad shoulders, weatherbeaten faces, and prominent muscles. Hitler, by contrast, was pallid and flabby and always carried a whip, which made him look oddly effeminate. It would be difficult to picture him on skis or in swim trunks. But she, like so many others, was unable to resist his spell, and commented: "No doubt about it; I was afflicted."[40] After making plans to travel to Greenland for five months of filming, she became fixated on the idea of meeting Hitler in person before she left, and wrote him this letter.

Dear Herr Hitler,

Recently I attended a political rally for the first time in my life. You were giving a speech at the Sports Palace. I must confess that you and the enthusiasm of your audience impressed me. I would like to meet you in person. Unfortunately, in the next few days I have to leave Germany for several months to make a film in Greenland, so meeting you prior to my departure will scarcely be possible. I do not even know whether this letter will ever reach you. I would be very glad to receive an answer from you.

Cordially, Leni Riefenstahl[41]

One day before she was scheduled to head to Greenland, the "adjutant to the Führer" called her on the telephone and invited her to visit his boss. The problem was that Hitler was not in Berlin, but up in Horumersiel on the North Sea. Riefenstahl had to decide whether to head to Hamburg or to Wilhelmshaven the following morning. Universal was planning to use the train ride to Hamburg as an opportunity to publicize *S.O.S. Iceberg*. The movie's actors, director, and producer would be taking this trip together with journalists from Berlin, and interviews had been scheduled with the lead actors so as to make the film an event right from the start. The next morning, her fellow cast members waited for her in vain; she was on a train to Wilhelmshaven. Leni Riefenstahl had opted for the Führer.

For the particulars of her first personal encounter with Hitler, we have nothing to go on but her own descriptions. As she tells it, she was picked up at the train station by several men in a black Mercedes limousine. This royal treatment was sure to have flattered her. Hitler's adjutant, Wilhelm Brückner, was knowledgeable about movies because he had worked as a film recording technician in the early 1920s, and he started the conversation by praising Riefenstahl's artistry. He told her that he had taken a stroll on the beach with Hitler, and Hitler had told him that Riefenstahl's dance in *The Holy Mountain* was the most beautiful thing he had ever seen in a film. Later, Brückner was sorting the mail and happened to notice her letter. He brought the letter to Hitler, who read it and decided he wanted to meet Fräulein Riefenstahl. This flattering greeting made Riefenstahl realize that Hitler was an admirer of her art—and this did indeed prove to be the case. The Führer was dressed in a suit and, fortunately, looked "like a normal person."[42] Hitler and Riefenstahl took a walk along the beach, and he continued to heap compliments on her. He told her that he had seen all her films. "'The film,' he said, 'that made the strongest impression on me was *The Blue Light*, especially because it is unusual for a young woman to win out against the roadblocks and biases of the film industry.'"[43]

This was more than she had dared to dream: Hitler was a fan of hers, and an anti-capitalist feminist to boot. Riefenstahl now felt that "the ice was broken" and that they were in accord in their hatred of "the industry." Because Hitler felt that he was a man with a bright future who was against industries and for ideals, he made her an offer: "Once we come to power, you have to make my films."[44] She informs readers of her memoirs that she told Hitler she was the wrong person for that job, that she rejected his "racial prejudices" and did not want him to misunderstand her visit, because she had "no interest whatsoever in politics." If that was the case, it is hard to understand why she would visit him at all. Supposedly her statement made a very positive impression on him, and he replied that he wished the people around him would speak to him as bluntly as she did.[45]

During their walk on the beach, the Führer evidently took quite a shine to Fräulein Riefenstahl and invited her to spend the night, his reason being, we are told, that "I so rarely get the chance to speak to a genuine artist."[46] Now her scheduling was getting very tight, because the ship to Greenland would leave the following morning from Hamburg. Trifles like those were no problem as far as Hitler was concerned. "You will be there tomorrow morning. I will arrange for a plane," he declared, then raced off to a campaign rally.[47] Riefenstahl enjoyed a pleasant dinner with him and his myrmidons. Hitler declared that he was happy to have a woman join the group at long last. An evening stroll on the beach followed, and Hitler began to make advances to her. Riefenstahl's lack of response threw him for a moment, but he quickly rebounded and declared: "I cannot love a woman until I have completed my task."[48] She did not say whether she was impressed by this remark. They slept in separate beds, and the following morning, an airplane awaited her. He kissed her hand as she left, wished her a good journey, and asked her to get in touch with him when she returned from Greenland. After giving him a quick warning that there might be attempts on his life, she went off. We are told that he gazed after her for quite a while.

This was the beginning of a momentous friendship. Hitler courted her on whatever terms he was able; if he could not have her as a woman, he wanted at least to win her over as an artist. She, in turn, had found a kindred spirit who recognized true art when he saw it (in her dances and movies) and proved to be an ally in the battle against the industry. Riefenstahl was determined to portray her first encounter with Hitler in terms of following a voice inside her. In her memoirs, she claims she wanted to meet him because he had stepped up to put an end to unemployment. Her assertion that she skipped out on interviews with Berlin journalists in order to chat about reducing unemployment seems far-fetched at best. At that time, she had a ten-thousand-dollar contract in her pocket and was more focused on building her career than on the afflictions of others. Riefenstahl acted as though she did not really know what she was doing, but the timing of her first meeting with Hitler suggests a strategic move. By September 1930, the National Socialists could no longer be ignored. At the Reichstag elections, 6.4 million Germans cast their votes for them, making the NSDAP the second strongest party after the Social Democratic Party. Although Heinrich Brüning was the chancellor, Adolf Hitler was the chief political figure. Bookstores displayed Kurt Tucholsky's *Gripsholm Castle*, a bitter send-up of the Nazi movement, in their windows, and Fritz Lang's *M*, a film about a series of bloody murders, ran in movie theaters. In 1931, the SA (paramilitary wing of the Nazi party) in Berlin had bloody brawls with the communists in the Wedding district night after night. Everyone knew Hitler. By 1932, no one retained any faith in the Weimar Republic. On March 5, the presidency of eighty-four-year-old Paul von Hindenburg would come to an end. For his opponent, Hitler, it was a simple matter to distinguish himself as a champion of the young, dynamic Germany. "Old man . . . you must step aside," he proclaimed at the February 1932 rally in the Berlin Sports Palace. This was the rally that had "afflicted" Riefenstahl. Hitler was putting into words exactly what she was feeling; she, too, wanted people to step aside for her. Hitler traveled from one end of the country to the other, preaching renewal and change, sowing hatred and violence. Hindenburg wound up winning the first ballot; Hitler received 30 percent of the vote, in line with expectations. Because no absolute majority had been achieved, there needed to be a second ballot. In order to come across as young and dashing, the National Socialists came up with a highly inventive scheme: Hitler glided in from the skies by airplane on his first "Germany Flight," which bore the slogan "Hitler Over Germany!" On April 10, Hindenburg was confirmed as the president of the Reich, but Hitler's votes had gone up by nearly 7 percent. This was how the situation stood one month after the premiere of *The Blue Light*. Hitler and Riefenstahl were campaigning in Germany simultaneously: she wanted to sell her film, and he his politics. State elections were slated for April 24 in Anhalt, Prussia, Bavaria, and Württemberg, and city elections for Hamburg. The NSDAP made substantial gains in these elections as well.[49] By the spring of 1932, the National Socialists had entered the home stretch of their race to power. For Riefenstahl, Hitler was an option she planned to keep open. He was poised to achieve the breakthrough that she was still awaiting. He was enjoying success from voters that spring, while she had yet to become a sought-after artist. Riefenstahl took a two-pronged approach: she positioned herself as an artist with the Jew-hating Nazi leader while working for an American film company that belonged to a German Jew. To make matters even more inconsistent, her contractual partner, Universal, had in the previous year produced *All Quiet on the Western Front*, directed by Lewis Milestone, which was repugnant to the National Socialists. Joseph Goebbels, who was then Hitler's *gauleiter* (regional party leader) in Berlin, fought against this movie with every means he had available. *All Quiet on the Western Front* was banned in Germany; in the United States, it was awarded an Oscar. It is unlikely that Riefenstahl was unaware of this movie, especially because she liked to point out how well acquainted she was with Erich Maria Remarque. She had no qualms about flirting with the Jewish film producer one evening, then heading off to a merry gathering of the Nazi elite. Her meeting with Hitler also included his personal adjutant, Brückner; the future commander of the Leibstandarte SS *Adolf Hitler*, Sepp Dietrich; and the future Third Reich press chief, Dr. Otto Dietrich. In the spring of 1932, she hoped that either Hitler or Hollywood would finally make her a star.

In late September 1932, Riefenstahl arrived in Berlin. She headed first to the doctor, and then to Hitler. We know from Ernst Sorge that while in Greenland, she used her bouts of illness to study *Mein Kampf*:

> Leni Riefenstahl got a serious chill after this, and was ill for some long time. She moved from her tent to a little room in the house of the Overseer of the Colony, which she fixed up as comfortably as best she might. She had a small collection of books. . . . In addition, Adolf Hitler's *Mein Kampf* was never out of her hands. She studied it with the utmost interest, and openly declared herself fully to agree with its conclusions. She found a visible means of expressing her great admiration for Hitler by hanging up his picture, framed in sealskin, both in her tent and now in this new habitation.[50]

She must have learned from her parents, who had picked her up from the ship in Copenhagen, what had been going on in Germany in the interim. The summer of 1932 was a summer of violence. The paramilitary formations of the NSDAP bludgeoned and murdered their way through Germany. The Reichstag was dissolved; Chancellor Heinrich Brüning was no longer in office; and his successor, Franz von Papen, was weak and unpopular. The next reelections were slated for November 6. It was possible that Hitler would become the next chancellor. When Riefenstahl called him on the telephone, following up on her promise to contact him upon her return to Germany, his adjutant informed her that Hitler would be expecting her for tea at Hotel Kaiserhof. The Adolf Hitler that Riefenstahl got to know was determined to look respectable and trustworthy, as reflected in photographs of him in the early 1930s. His face may still have brought to mind a peddler hawking postcards, but he no longer posed for pictures wearing lederhosen and carrying a dog whip; instead, he was inclined to appear in a suit with a party badge.[51] Winifred Wagner and other prominent women gave him motherly advice and taught him manners, and his confidant, Ernst Hanfstaengl, taught him not to add sugar to his wine. Hitler now cultivated a lifestyle that was markedly different from his beer hall days. Back then, Riefenstahl surely would not have been interested in him. The man with whom she was associating spent money on bodyguards and chauffeured black Mercedes limousines and no longer stayed at rundown boarding houses, but rather at the luxurious Hotel Kaiserhof just across from the Reich chancellery. His relocation to the Kaiserhof marked a kind of ascent. All of Berlin knew that he was residing there. People took careful note of who was granted an audience. Everyone was abuzz over the party leaders' gigantic hotel bills, poked fun at Hitler's overindulgence in cake, and wondered where the National Socialists were getting all of that money. Riefenstahl rushed over to chat with Hitler about Greenland right in the middle of the election campaign. The very next day, an invitation followed to a soiree at the home of Joseph and Magda Goebbels. She found the wife pretty, but the husband coarse. The main topics of conversation were "the theater and other cultural events."[52] Hitler was there as well. He announced that he planned to stop by her place with his photographer, Heinrich Hoffmann. They sat together eating homemade cake in her attic apartment, and Hitler told Hoffmann to have a good look at the Riefenstahl photographs from *The Blue Light*, claiming that Hoffmann could learn a thing or two from them about composing pictures. Riefenstahl blushed at all this praise from the Führer.

In most instances we have to rely on Riefenstahl's accounts of events, but in this case there is a second version of Riefenstahl's visit to the Goebbels home. Ernst Hanfstaengl reported that one evening, Riefenstahl turned up at the Goebbels's dinner table. As an engaging and appealing woman, she had little difficulty persuading the Führer to visit her studio. Hitler accepted this invitation, as did Joseph and Magda Goebbels and Hanfstaengl, who were delighted that Hitler was showing interest in a woman. Ever since the recent suicide of his niece, Geli, Hitler's relationship to women had been making headlines. Geli Raubal, an attractive young woman, had been running Hitler's household for the past two years. The two often appeared in public together, and there were rumors of some sort of untoward relationship between them. Hanfstaengl recalled that Riefenstahl's apartment was "full of mirrors and trick interior decorator effects."[53] This was probably his discreet way of pointing out that Riefenstahl knew how to seduce men. While Hanfstaengl played the piano for Herr and Frau Goebbels, Hitler and his hostess were left to their own devices. Peering over at Hitler, Hanfstaengl noticed that Riefenstahl was using every trick of flirtation in the book while "I could see him ostentatiously studying the titles in the bookcases. Riefenstahl was certainly giving him the works."[54] The fact that Hanfstaengl and the Goebbels left Riefenstahl's studio before Hitler did not seem to have done the trick, however; Hitler remained loyal to his great love: Germany. There is no way of determining how accurate this account is, but Hitler's visit to Riefenstahl's studio does underscore their growing bond even before 1933. Most of her fellow artists had no idea how things would develop, but Riefenstahl stuck close to Hitler. She was a guest at the Goebbels home, chatted with Göring about his old war buddy Udet, and read the first edition of *Mein Kampf.* By the fall of 1932, she was confident that if Hitler emerged victorious, he would not forget her. Riefenstahl had taken the proper precautions. In January 1933, she went on a ski vacation to Davos, where she spent time with her handsome new Swiss lover, Walter Prager. Prager was eight years her junior and an outstanding athlete. She was waiting to finish filming *S.O.S. Iceberg*. She was eventually told to go to the Lake Bernina area, where Fanck, his people, and the film crew from Hollywood were awaiting her for the location shooting. This was Riefenstahl's first movie for the American market, and she was elated. In the spring of 1933, she returned to Berlin and prepared to shoot her next film—*Victory of Faith*—in late August. The film had been commissioned by Adolf Hitler.

o o o

On the morning of August 16, 1929, the American director Josef von Sternberg and his wife arrived at Bahnhof Zoo in Berlin. As always, this short man was clad in extravagant clothing. He loved wide-cut suits in soft, patterned fabrics. A walking stick, gloves, and elegant shoes completed his striking appearance. Von Sternberg had a full head of dark hair, and at times one lock curled onto his forehead. His sad, dark eyes lent his face the melancholy cast he aimed to achieve. He rarely smiled. Posing in the circle of his illustrious reception committee, he seemed more like the European ideal of the artist than a Hollywood director. One figure in the group towered over the others: the burly Emil Jannings, who graciously welcomed his director to Berlin. Jannings and von Sternberg had big plans. In the months ahead, they intended to make a sound film.

At four in the afternoon that same day, celebrities of the Berlin film world gathered at Hotel Esplanade for a welcome tea with the guests from America. Rumors had been swirling around the city for weeks as to who would be directing Jannings's sound film. Many names had cropped up, but now people knew it was von Sternberg. Although his name was relatively unfamiliar, his reputation for eccentricity had preceded him. Word also got around that Ufa was planning to invest huge sums of money in this project. For once, von Sternberg poured on the charm. After a few words of introduction in English, he switched to German, assuring the group that he was happy to be filming a movie "in the heart of Europe." He buttered up his hosts by declaring Germany a "film paradise." Then he came out with a statement that was calculated to cause a stir: "It's as if I died in Hollywood and woke up in heaven."[55]

He spent the next few days getting the lay of the land in this heaven. Von Sternberg was staying at a hotel on the Spree River, and here he found the leisure time to mull over the film he was planning. Berlin was quite a change from his hometown of Vienna. Although he had spent only a few short years in Vienna during his childhood, he had strong ties to the city and its culture. Vienna was compact, homogeneous, and tradition-bound, while Berlin was spread out, diverse, and bewildering.

All around the steel concourse of the Friedrichstrasse train station, neon signs wooed audiences to the local theaters. Only a few minutes away on foot was the Grosses Schauspielhaus, where sumptuously produced revues were enjoying great success. A couple of blocks farther down, Bertolt Brecht had created a theatrical sensation with *The Threepenny Opera*. However, the revenues of Berlin theaters were steadily declining in 1929, while movie palaces were springing up. With eight large movie theaters, the area around the Kaiser Wilhelm Memorial Church was no longer considered a quiet residential neighborhood; it was now an entertainment hub. But the attention of the American guest was drawn less to the outer trappings of the city than to its moral decline. He saw Berlin as a precarious and dangerous place. Venturing outdoors, he claimed, was "like shooting the rapids."[56] He was also taken aback by the gender-bending he saw all around him; many a woman with rouge, veil, and beauty spots turned out on closer inspection to be a man. Everyone was on display.

Von Sternberg was in an unenviable position in this chaotic city, unable to tell the difference between men and women, and baffled as to what he would be filming. His friend Jannings had called him, and he followed the call. Jannings was an international star and one of the first German actors to have gone to Hollywood. Perhaps he went because his father was an American, but it is more likely that the high pay (he was rumored to be getting $1,000 a day) was the lure. Jannings felt he needed to live in the lap of luxury. The ascent of the German cinema is intimately linked with his name. Ernst Lubitsch had been his director, as had Friedrich Wilhelm Murnau, for whom he played the lead role in *The Last Laugh* in 1924 and the role of Mephisto in *Faust* in 1926. Von Sternberg knew that Jannings liked to work with directors who cultivated their own styles and led their actors with a firm hand. He considered Jannings's acting brilliant but was unnerved by his tyrannical nature. Once they had finished making their final film, *The Last Command*, he thanked Jannings, then assured him that he would never make a movie with him again, even if he were the last living actor on earth. Jannings said a polite goodbye to his director. He made three more movies in Hollywood, then returned to Europe in 1929 after becoming the first person ever to win an Academy Award for Best Actor in a Leading Role for his performances in *The Last Command* and *The Way of All Flesh*. Although he was famous in America, he wanted to go back to Germany, presumably because his heavy German accent made him unsuitable for Hollywood roles in the new sound films. By making one of the first sound films at Ufa in Berlin, his risk of producing a flop would be minimized. The name Jannings guaranteed high art and box-office success.

One morning, Jannings came to von Sternberg's hotel in a state of great excitement and, "with a show of enviable enthusiasm," he handed von Sternberg a copy of Heinrich Mann's 1905 novel *Professor Unrat*. Von Sternberg read the book and thought something could be made of it. Seven days after von Sternberg's arrival—on August 23—Ufa bought the film rights to the novel. Mann received the exorbitant sum of 25,000 reichsmarks, with an additional 10,000 reichsmarks promised to him once the English-language version opened in the United States. Time was running short, because von Sternberg's vacation lasted only until December 31, 1929. Beyond this date, he would be able to work for Ufa only with Paramount's consent, and even then only until January 14, 1930. The first task at hand was to transform the novel into a screenplay.[57]

For *The Blue Angel*, as the movie was eventually called, four authors are named: Heinrich Mann, Karl Vollmoeller, Carl Zuckmayer, and Robert Liebmann. The competing claims about how the screenplay was written reveal a great deal about the male egos that the only important woman in the movie—Marlene Dietrich—would have to cope with. Von Sternberg asserted that he wrote the screenplay all by himself. Supposedly he met with Mann and asked whether Mann had anything against changes that might be made, but was given the green light. According to von Sternberg, Zuckmayer was listed only to avoid upsetting the Germans, since, von Sternberg claimed rather unconvincingly, he feared trouble if such radical changes to a German novel were made by an American. He respected Vollmoeller, but found him useful primarily as a "valuable guide to the Berlin of that day," and supposedly wanted to help Vollmoeller out by listing his name.[58] Von Sternberg confirmed Liebmann's role in making the film. Liebmann was the only professional screenwriter in the group, and also the only one who would stay above the fray in the wrangling about the screenplay. Vollmoeller's contribution was to pare down the script. He soberly noted that the main advantage of the sound film was to express silence, and steered the film from the background. Mann's memoirs were remarkably restrained in passages pertaining to *The Blue*

Angel. "A jumping jack with my head and the legs of an actress was in high demand. The film material by me brought fame to all three, the talent of the woman and her two charming limbs."[59] Perhaps he was miffed that the film had become more famous than his book.

Zuckmayer's contribution to the screenplay is not entirely clear even today, but in his autobiography he claimed sole credit for the setting and dialogues in *The Blue Angel*. In an article published in March 1930, he went into great detail about the difficult collaboration among the authors of the screenplay. Jannings, von Sternberg, Vollmoeller, Mann, and Zuckmayer, and producer Erich Pommer had their initial meeting in Berlin. A photograph of this meeting shows six vain, elderly gentlemen with striking faces and suits sitting on a sofa. It is evident that each of them is out to impress the others. According to Zuckmayer, their "show of politeness was duplicitous and highly suspect." They came to an agreement to focus on the fate of the teacher and to play down the issues surrounding his pupils. Zuckmayer was asked to come up with a first draft.[60] Eventually their work came to a happy end in an office on Kochstrasse in Berlin. When Zuckmayer was asked, "To what extent did you have a free hand in putting together the scenario?" he replied brusquely, "Only until von Sternberg took over the direction and contributed key ideas." Von Sternberg did not let anyone tell him what to do, and he alone determined the form the movie would take. No matter what anyone had written, he did whatever he liked with the screenplay.

While von Sternberg and his team were working on the script, Marlene Dietrich was rehearsing her next performance in the revue *Two Neckties*. The director was Robert Forster-Larrinaga, and Mischa Spoliansky composed the music. Dietrich was delighted about this revue, hoping that she would be able to follow up on the success of *It's in the Air*. She would soon be reaching the ripe old age of thirty and had not been willing or able to work in revues for a long time. She did manage to draw attention to herself as a "German Garbo," but she had yet to be acknowledged as a full-fledged actress with talent. She was not deluding herself; she knew that she had gotten most of her roles on account of her looks rather than her talent. Her personal life was similarly uninspiring: she had been married to the same man, Rudi Sieber, for six full years. She was well aware that he had no objections to her being the breadwinner. Sieber tried, but never made it into the big leagues. They continued to sleep in separate beds. He showed no inclination to get involved with any lovers other than Tamara Matul. Dietrich had no desire to change this state of affairs, because it also kept this illegitimate part of the family under control. She realized that she and Rudi had simply fallen out of love, but she had no intention of separating from her husband. She had a child and a sense of honor, so she would make the best of the situation, which was quite easy to do with Sieber.

When von Sternberg went to see *Two Neckties*, he actually intended to have a look at Rosa Valetti and Hans Albers, both of whom were in the cast and had already signed on for his movie, but as soon as he saw Marlene Dietrich, he lost any interest in everyone else. "She leaned against the wings with a cold disdain for the buffoonery, in sharp contrast to the effervescence of the others, who had been informed that I was to be treated to a sample of the greatness of the German stage. She had heard that I was in the audience, but as she did not consider herself involved, she was indifferent to my presence."[61] Many of the actresses in Berlin who were suggested to him for the role of Lola Lola had simply been too fat for his liking, but "Fräulein Dietrich" was voluptuous in all the right places. On the day after the show in Kreuzberg, von Sternberg complained that his crew had not pointed him in Marlene Dietrich's direction.[62] He was told that this lady was not actually an actress, but he was not put off and insisted that the Fräulein from Berlin be brought to his office.

Later that afternoon, Dietrich sat on his sofa looking bored.

She was dressed in a ladylike two-piece suit with matching gloves, hat, and fur. Once again she made no effort to hold his attention. "And that is what interested von Sternberg—the fact that I was not interested," she told Maximilian Schell when she was eighty years old.[63] She just sat there looking unperturbed and giving him flippant replies. When Jannings and Pommer arrived, she obediently followed their instructions. She knew what their awkward silence meant, and did not appear to have expected any other reception. But Sternberg did not give up so easily. The next day, he had a look at her last three movies. "In them she was an awkward, unattractive woman, left to her own devices, and presented in an embarrassing exhibition of drivel," he concluded harshly.[64]

Dietrich presented a challenge, and von Sternberg decided to take it on. He knew the film business inside and out and realized that for his first German sound film, he needed a discovery—ideally, of course, a woman. Von Sternberg was well aware that only a new and exciting woman could preclude the expected outcome of an "Emil Jannings sound film." That is precisely what he did not want. He intended to put his own stamp on the film and not be reduced to the role of facilitating Jannings's ambition. Dietrich was invited to Babelsberg for a screen test.

Also quite accidental was von Sternberg's discovery of Friedrich Hollaender, who went on to compose Lola Lola's world-famous songs. One cold September morning, Lucie Mannheim and Hollaender, who had worked in revues and composed music for a play by Else Lasker-Schüler together, had gone out to Babelsberg. Hollaender had no trouble recognizing von Sternberg. "He was wearing a bilious green winter coat, an elegantly gnarled walking stick, and a droopy mustache, which gave him a slightly coquettish hint of pessimism. He spoke a very American German, although he was born in Austria, and every now and then struggled to come up with a German word that he couldn't recall at the moment."[65] He used his walking stick to point to the piano and adjusted a chair for himself. The two of them got going, and von Sternberg listened attentively, then sent them off with a nonchalant "We'll call you." Mannheim would never see the man from America again, but he did hire Hollaender.

The other contenders tried to give their all, but not Dietrich; she barely moved a muscle. "All the actresses were falling all over themselves . . . to get the role. And there's that brash kid from the acting school sitting over there, saying she won't get the role anyway. That intrigued him, didn't it?"[66] She said she was not prepared. Von Sternberg sent her to the dressing room to change. She came back in a sparkling but unbecoming outfit. Von Sternberg asked her to sing one German and one English song. She had heard the hit "You're the Cream in My Coffee" a hundred times before, and now sang it for him. "She came to life and responded to my instructions with an ease that I had never before encountered. She seemed pleased at the trouble I took with her."[67] After this prelude, von Sternberg knew that Dietrich was willing to be transformed by him. She herself described this prelude as a humiliating process. "And they had sewn me into some sort of dress and frizzed my hair, and the air was full of smoke. And then von Sternberg told me I should go up there and sit down on the piano."[68]

The screen test displayed a pudgy Dietrich grimacing horribly while she sang. She fluttered her eyelashes, rolled her eyes, and tilted her head. She wore a peculiar-looking sequined dress, and her hairdo looked like a scrub brush. From one moment to the next, she could interrupt her affected recitation to bawl out the pianist like a streetwalker for the way he was playing. Her acting was skillful, although not everyone saw it that way the next morning. The nearly unanimous opinion was that Mannheim ought to get the role. But von Sternberg insisted on his discovery. Producer Pommer gave in, and Dietrich was cast in the lead role.

In October 1929, von Sternberg and his actors and screenwriters were busy with discussions, screen tests, and inspections of studio sets while the world outside was undergoing a sea change. Gustav Stresemann, foreign minister and cowinner of the Nobel Peace Prize, had died within hours of suffering a stroke on October 3. The manner of his death was utterly unlike that of Walter Rathenau, who had been shot in his car by young ultranationalists in June 1922, but the shock wave it triggered was of a similar order. In Stresemann's years as chancellor and then as foreign minister, the traditional patriotic, pacifist, and liberal values still applied; these were dispassionate but significant years for Germany. Hundreds of thousands of people walked behind his coffin on October 6 with the sinking feeling that the time of peace was drawing to an end. Just three weeks after Stresemann's death, the stock market crashed in New York. The day that came to be known as Black Thursday ushered in a worldwide economic crisis. Stocks plummeted and bankruptcies came with increasing frequency. Never before had statistics and numbers played such a key role in daily life. The growth of unemployment and equity prices, the number of bankruptcies and foreclosures, tax revenues, and debt levels were no longer relegated to the business section of the newspaper; these figures were featured in the lead stories and attested to the readers' everyday woes.

The lovely summer was followed by a raw and rainy fall in 1929. Sebastian Haffner recalled the oppressive atmosphere at this time: "Angry words on the poster columns; and on the streets for the first time, mud-brown uniforms and unpleasant physiognomies above them; the rat-tat-tat and piping of an unfamiliar, shrill, vulgar march music."[69] Black Thursday brought any last vestige of economic optimism to an abrupt end. The economic crisis gave rise to doubts about the equity of traditional policies and social conditions in a democratic society. Fears of a new period of inflation gripped the Germans, and fewer and fewer of them believed that a parliamentary democracy could cope with this crisis. Despite several notable cultural achievements of that year—Thomas Mann was awarded the Nobel Prize in Literature, and Alfred Döblin published *Berlin Alexanderplatz*—people began to wonder what would become of the Weimar Republic.

In these gloomy times, the sound film offered a new dimension to the cinema. For many years, Ufa had refused to take note of the development of talking pictures, but the great success of the American sound film *The Jazz Singer* made it clear that the days of the silent film were numbered. Now Ufa rushed to catch up, and its production director, Ernst Hugo Correll, announced that in 1929, 50 percent of the forthcoming movies would include sound. In order to implement this ambitious goal, Ufa invested in the biggest sound film recording studio in Europe. On April 25, the demolition of the old studios began, and many a monument to the silent film was destroyed in the name of looking to the future. One month before the world economic crisis hit, Correll proudly and optimistically opened his dream studios. The new layout reflected the sober functionality of the 1920s, a decade that was now coming to an end. The structure consisted of four film studios that formed a cross. At the intersection of these austere brick buildings was a square atrium leading to all four studios. The almost windowless exterior façades were wainscoted with red clinker bricks. The buildings were soundproof; neither the pattering of rain nor the racket of airplanes could be heard. There was much praise for Ufa's devotion to sound film, but it also came in for heavy criticism. Many movie theater owners could not afford the new systems; silent film musicians were no longer needed; and people who worked in live theater feared this talking competition. Sound film required both directors and script editors to rethink their tasks. They had to match sounds to plots and try out new forms of dialogue. The defenders of silent film aesthetics argued that the soul of the moving picture might be lost if words were interjected between images and viewers. But the actors themselves were most apprehensive about the new technology.

Even the great Jannings was afraid of his own voice and feared for the loss of his expressive power. By contrast, Dietrich's voice sounded calm, she was able to sing, and she had training in music. She was unperturbed by the presence of a microphone. She had always worked with her voice, and she now saw the perfect opportunity to put it to new use. And unlike Jannings, she had never been a silent film star and had no reputation to defend.[70]

Expectations for von Sternberg were running high. His studio was anticipating an artistic and economic success; Jannings, the temperamental international star, wanted to be presented onscreen as a brilliant sound film star, and liberal viewers were eager to see how Mann's novel would be adapted for the screen. All the excitement left von Sternberg cold. He explained matter-of-factly that sound film gave a director the opportunity to integrate noise, music, and words organically, and as a necessary component, into a plot whose visual sequences did not differ substantially from silent film.

Pommer, who had worked in Hollywood for two years, recognized the opportunities the sound film had to offer. The fact that he allowed von Sternberg to sign Dietrich over Jannings's opposition indicates the great trust he was placing in the man from America. Günther Rittau was the head cinematographer. His training was in photochemistry, and he had worked with developing special technology for documentary filmmaking. He had been responsible for the special effects in Fritz Lang's *The Nibelungs*. His assistant, Hans Schneeberger, was known as a daring maker of mountain films. After *The Blue Angel*, he would film *Avalanche* with Arnold Fanck and Leni Riefenstahl. Waldemar Jabs, who had worked on Max Reinhardt's stages for decades, was in charge of makeup. In *The Blue Angel*, Jabs demonstrated his minimalist art on Professor Raat's beard as it reflected the state of Raat's social decline. On set, Jabs ran into many actors he already knew from the theater. Eduard von Winterstein, who for years had given acting lessons at the Deutsches Theater and who may have been known to Dietrich from this period, played the school principal, and Kurt Gerron, who had last been seen as the police chief in the legendary production of *The Threepenny Opera*, played the head of the traveling troupe. Hollaender was the composer, and the best jazz band in Berlin, the Weintraub Syncopators, provided the music.[71]

Jannings planned to keep the spotlight squarely on himself and had no intention of stepping aside for Dietrich. He spent every day of shooting fighting for his special position. He arrived on the set at the dot of seven every morning. His transformation into Professor Raat began in front of his "sanctum," his three-way mirror. The process was more psychological than cosmetic, according to his makeup artist. Von Sternberg had to inquire about the state of Jannings's health at a quarter to nine; if he failed to execute this gesture of submission, Jannings would inform him that he needed to call an ambulance because he was deathly ill. If all went according to plan, von Sternberg would enter Jannings's dressing room only to have his friendly greeting received with a reproachful look.

Then Jannings lit a cigarette, exhaling the smoke as if his soul went with it, cleared his throat . . . and followed this by casually mentioning that I no longer loved him. I would counter this by assuring him of my undying affection and then ask him to show his love for me by assisting me to make a few more feet of film. Jannings would then extinguish the cigarette as if to grind me into ashes, and view me through the mirror with his limpid eyes filled with the usual self-induced torment, a prerequisite to winding himself up to be his masochistic self in order to be able to act, and would say, as if never before had me made so horrendous an accusation, "You did not lunch with me yesterday."[72]

Mealtime was sacred to Jannings. His favorite dish was a huge plateful of sausage. If we picture the short, trim von Sternberg with Jannings hulking over steaming hot sausages, we get an impression of the power struggle raging between the two. Von Sternberg tried to calm him down with all kinds of excuses, but Jannings would accuse him of showing preferential treatment to Fräulein Dietrich; he had heard that his rival had gotten up bright and early to prepare lunch for her director. Von Sternberg pointed out that as a married man, he ought to be aware of the difference between men and women. Diva Jannings countered that no woman could offer anything that he could not. Von Sternberg realized that he had no choice but to agree to eat lunch with him alone, but now he had to go to work with the other cast members, whereupon Jannings ripped off the beard that had taken hours to glue on. Von Sternberg used his powers of persuasion to get him to continue shooting the film. But Jannings would not hear of it; he again accused von Sternberg of wanting to eat with Dietrich. This was the cue for the final phase of the morning ritual. "He would hurl himself to the floor so that the whole room shook, weep, scream, and shout that his heart had stopped, and I would pick him up . . . then kiss him on the mouth, moist with tears and return him somehow to his mirrors."[73] Once this ritual had run its course, the filming could begin.

Dietrich, who recalled Jannings's shenanigans from when they filmed *Tragedy of Love* and considered him a psychopath, wisely stayed in the background.[74] She had waited for her big chance long enough, and now that it had been offered to her, she was determined to seize it. Her protestations that she was a silly goose with no talent rang hollow. She had every intention of taking Jannings down from his throne. Dietrich wanted to succeed Jannings as diva. She was an intelligent woman who knew that she would have to wage her battle guilefully and in secret, so for the time being she did not make any attempt to compete with Jannings, but instead was the picture of sweetness. She showed up on time for shooting every morning, with nary a complaint about lack of sleep or the demands of motherhood, and greeted everyone with a smile.

She no longer had to spread herself thin between dozens of roles, but instead could devote her energy to the role of Lola Lola. "I was always ready when I was called. I stood a bit off to the side so as not to get in the way of the other actors, but I paid attention to the slightest sign from Mr. von Sternberg ordering me onto the set."[75] He did not let her down, and she gave her all to becoming the person von Sternberg envisioned for her. He asked her to design her own costumes, although he himself envisioned Lola Lola bringing to mind the women painted and sketched by Félicien Rops and Toulouse-Lautrec. "I decked out my costumes with top hats and workers' caps, replaced the jewelry with ribbons, tassels, and braids, everything I thought was affordable for a B-Girl in a cheap waterfront saloon."[76] Von Sternberg made Dietrich his ally and involved her in the creation of Lola Lola, while involving himself in choosing Dietrich's own clothing, movements, and self-image. Von Sternberg had all the answers, and she liked that.

Dietrich wore the finest lingerie. Her panties were little works of art, made of soft, flowing pink silk chiffon topped with golden-brown lace. Lola Lola donned many layers of clothing, as though preparing for a striptease. Dietrich's chaotic dressing room had boas, scarves, skirts, and panties scattered everywhere. Depending on the upcoming scene, she would quickly throw something on or take something off. She did not always keep her garters out of sight under her skirt, exposing her thighs for all the world to admire. When she sat on her barrel, her top hat askew on her curls, clutching one gartered leg perched on the knee of the other, singing while eying the audience coquettishly over her bare shoulder, she looked half naked. Her top hat was white; her panties—a key prop in her relationship with Professor Raat—were big and frilly. Lola

Lola went in for stork feathers on her dressing gown, and ostrich feathers embellished her slippers. She donned men's hats with her lingerie, which resulted in a peculiar fashion mix of seduction and severity. Dietrich was able to wear vulgar clothing without appearing vulgar. She imbued Lola Lola with a unique sense of dignity, undiminished by tasteless costumes and the speech patterns and body language of a B-girl, snapping her garters and making suggestive cracks.

Von Sternberg was crazy about her Berlin diction. The Berlin style of speech was considered coarse, and it was invariably associated with snippy repartee. The main feature of this diction was "a crass egotism, a naïve, utterly sincere sense of superiority."[77] Von Sternberg emboldened Dietrich to speak in a way that she had never dared to before. In the film we hear how brilliantly she succeeded, above all in her songs, which are just as much a part of Lola Lola's adornment as her garters.

Lola Lola is not a lady or a femme fatale; she is a sassy, savvy, honky-tonk B-girl. The transformation into Lola Lola must have been eerie for Dietrich, because right in front of the camera, she was turning into the woman that her mother had always feared might be hidden inside her daughter.

Dietrich was fascinated by the magical effect of cameras and lighting. She followed every detail of von Sternberg's working method and learned a great deal from him about the miraculous effects that could be coaxed from a camera. He allowed her to join him at the editing table. She was determined to master the art of film.

It must have made Jannings livid to read all the high praise of Dietrich in the press, such as this comment in the *Film-Kurier*: "Marlene Dietrich's voice is as supple as her body. Just as she does on the stage, she starts softly, then sharpens up somewhat into the call of the triumphant woman that no man can resist."[78] Jannings was painfully aware that von Sternberg was one of these men.

Jannings had to pretend to fall in love with Lola Lola in front of the camera, while von Sternberg actually did fall for Dietrich when the cameras were turned off. Both of them were married. As a woman approaching the age of thirty with a husband and a lover, Dietrich was no longer driven by the need to satisfy her curiosity for adventure. She knew what she was doing when she got involved with von Sternberg; she was not giving in to a whim. He gave her the feeling he would never let her down. He knew the answers to everything, encouraged her to be independent, and guided her. She had never met a man like him before. She liked his extravagant style of dress and behavior, and admired his divine and demonic power, which enabled her to become the woman she had never dared to be. This deliberately conspicuous man was her savior, a kind of sorcerer who had come to "Pygmalionize" her. Von Sternberg was not interested in the sweet coquetry of a young girl; he wanted a woman who had experienced passion and remorse. He relished the feeling of being the only one who knew how beautiful Dietrich really was. "Never before had I met so beautiful a woman who had been so thoroughly discounted and undervalued," he wrote many years later.[79] "Eroticism has next to no conscience and makes hasty decisions," he wrote in August 1969, just a few months before his death.[80] He left his wife, Riza, who had come to Berlin with him, after meeting Dietrich.[81] No other woman could stand up to her; "her personality was one of extreme sophistication and of an almost childlike simplicity."[82]

Maria Riva provided glimpses into von Sternberg's visits to Kaiserallee. "When a stocky little man with a big droopy mustache and the saddest eyes I had ever seen appeared, I was rather disappointed. Except for a long camel-hair coat, spats and elegant walking cane, he didn't look so important at all. His voice was wonderful, though. Deep and soft—like silky velvet."[83] Because her family was the center of her life, Dietrich simply made her lover part of her family. When von Sternberg and Dietrich saw each other on the set, she had to follow his instructions and they were surrounded by observers. When they got together in Dietrich's apartment, she mothered her lover in front of her husband. They appear to have had their romantic trysts in hotel rooms, perhaps posing as transients under assumed names.

The closer they grew, the more prominent the role of Lola Lola became. Zuckmayer recalled von Sternberg altering Dietrich's role according to his directorial concept. Von Sternberg was the one to set the title of the movie and to change the name of Rosa Fröhlich in the novel to Lola Lola for the film, citing Wedekind's "Lulu" as a model. Jannings felt as though something was going on behind his back. During the shooting, he sensed that von Sternberg and Dietrich had already agreed on the shots. Everyone else on the crew also noticed the balance shifting in favor of Dietrich as the filming progressed. A woman named Resi was assigned to be her personal dressing-room attendant. Joe Pasternak, the young and highly successful production director at German Universal, requested an appointment with Dietrich. Pasternak, who wanted to make her an offer for Hollywood, knew that von Sternberg kept Dietrich under lock and key but decided to try his luck. She let him in, and when he looked at her, he broke out in a sweat. All she had on was a negligee, and she agreed to give due consideration to an offer from Universal. Dietrich was growing into her new role, on screen and off.

On January 22, 1930, filming of *The Blue Angel* was completed, and on February 11, von Sternberg left the city, heading to Hollywood. In his suitcase, he had a song that Hollaender had composed for Dietrich. Von Sternberg was keeping it from the public for now because he wanted it to become Dietrich's first Hollywood hit. Two days after von Sternberg left, *Tempo* magazine reported that Dietrich would be following him to Hollywood. Sidney Kent, a manager at Paramount, had come to Berlin to find new faces. He watched a private showing of *The Blue Angel* and liked what he saw. Readers of *Tempo* were informed that "according to Marlene Dietrich's contract, she will be spending only six months a year in Hollywood."[84] She told the journalists at the *Film-Kurier* that she had hesitated quite a while before accepting the offer, because although it signified a great professional opportunity, it also meant she would be separated from her child. Then she added, "As soon as I said yes, I got right in touch with the *Bremen* and talked to von Sternberg, who was delighted to learn of my acceptance."[85]

All those unspeakably boring afternoons conversing with French and English tutors proved to be an unexpected boon to her career, because the offer from Paramount was evidently an outcome of the successful American version of *The Blue Angel*. Jannings received far more money for his role than Dietrich did, but he was painfully aware that the shifting of the film's title from that of the novel (*Professor Unrat*) to *The Blue Angel* reflected the fact that even before the movie was released, Dietrich was the center of attention.

In the film, high-school teacher Raat is feared by the pupils and disliked by the townspeople. He is an eccentric tyrant who lives alone with his bird and his books. When he discovers that his pupils have a flirtatious postcard of the singer Lola Lola, he decides to pay her a visit and give her a piece of his mind. Disoriented, he wanders around the harbor until he winds up at the Blue Angel nightclub. There a new world opens up to him, a world he does not understand and cannot decipher. Lola Lola turns out to be a lovely, self-assured young woman who unhesitatingly allows him into her dressing room and thus into her life. He now spends every evening with her, feeling important and privileged. Raat is socially inept, especially around women. He feels drawn to the strange performing troupe with whom Lola Lola travels, although it does not live up to any of his strict standards. The performers soon get used to him; after all, he is treating them to champagne and seems to adore Lola Lola. He is turning into a suitor without even realizing it. Lola Lola, for whom he represents a change of pace, enjoys dazzling him with her body, her voice, and her intimate accessories. Raat enters into an erotic relationship with the singer and undergoes a complete transformation in his late-blooming sensuality. He eventually marries Lola Lola, which makes the townspeople despise him. He goes off with Lola's troupe, but many years later the troupe returns to the Blue Angel. Raat has deteriorated markedly; he is now an old, unkempt, ludicrous man playing a clown on the stage. His wife is still beautiful; she defends him the way she would a child, and assumes the traditionally masculine role of protecting him.

The enterprising director announces him as Professor Raat, and the locals turn out to see what has become of him. Raat has to mount the stage in a clown costume, submit to having eggs cracked on his head, and crow like a rooster. The height of his humiliation is reached when he realizes that Lola Lola is cheating on him. He tries to strangle her, but is subdued; then, like a wounded animal, he creeps back to his old school and dies, slumped over his desk.

The movie takes place from the years 1925 to 1929; the novel had been published back in 1905. In the novel, Professor Immanuel Raat remains in the city and wreaks revenge on the supposedly upstanding citizens in his city who drove him from his post. While Mann's novel showed how an erotic encounter utterly transforms a representative of Wilhelmine culture, von Sternberg was barely interested in German history and utterly indifferent to social criticism. Well into the 1960s, von Sternberg's critics on the left took issue with his having used this German setting without commenting on the situation in Germany. "I must be forgiven if I state once more that most of the story of the film and its details existed only in my imagination, that I knew very little about Germany before I began it, that then I had not yet seen anyone resembling a Nazi, and that the entire stimulation to make the film came from a book that was written by Heinrich Mann in the good old days before

1905."[86] Professor Raat scurries through the narrow streets in his wide, cape-like overcoat the way Dr. Caligari had many years earlier. The architecture in this movie, which was one of the first major sound films, recalls expressionist silent films. Von Sternberg used sound to intensify the images, but objects were all he needed to create a milieu or set a tone.[87] Lola Lola and Raat are worlds apart not only in their clothing, behavior, and gender, but above all in the way they sound. He speaks a punctilious German, and she a sloppy Berlin dialect. His world is filled with quiet and books. The only sounds come from his pet bird and the glockenspiel of the town hall clock playing a tune from *The Magic Flute*, which runs through the movie like an acoustic leitmotif. Apart from Raat, everyone—including Lola Lola herself—knows that she is no artist.

The Blue Angel premiered on April 1, 1930, at the Gloria Palace in Berlin. The government of the Social Democratic chancellor Hermann Müller had collapsed just days earlier. On March 30, Heinrich Brüning—a man who had nothing to offer the country but "poverty, the curtailment of liberty, and the assurance that there was no alternative," as Sebastian Haffner wrote—was appointed chancellor.[88] The end of the Weimar Republic was near. It is difficult to say whether Dietrich had any awareness of these developments. The previous months had been quite draining for her. She was continually assailed by doubts as to whether she had truly been qualified for the role. The period of waiting for the premiere was also a time of farewell to Berlin, Rudi, Maria, Willi Forst, friends, and her mother. The hardest part was leaving her child. Dietrich was unwilling to release anyone from her sphere of influence, least of all her daughter. "After long discussions, my husband and I finally decided that I would go to the United States alone. Our daughter would remain with him in Berlin until we could see what impression that strange country called America would make on me before we dared to 'transplant' our little Maria and her governess.

I was sent out on a reconnaissance mission."[89] She knew that she was expected in Hollywood. Von Sternberg was longing for the woman he loved and desired and for the actress he could mold as he wished. Dietrich was also flummoxed by the question of what to wear to the premiere. She wished "Jo" (as she called von Sternberg) were with her; he would know what would show her off to her best advantage.

Pencil drawings sketched on the night of the premiere show nervous policemen in their tall military hats, horse-drawn carriages stopping outside the theater, and people in festive garments charging into the brightly lit movie theater. Curious onlookers lined up out front. The high-priced tickets had been sold out for days. By 8 p.m., the lobby was full to overflowing. Many guests for the premiere had come in evening gowns, but there were also stylish cocktail dresses and simple dress suits. Dietrich had opted for ladylike fashion. If she was going to be playing such a crude woman onscreen, she would certainly want to shine as a sophisticated lady onstage. She wore a long, frilly white dress topped with a wide-collared white fur; white gloves; and a long, dark necklace. Her hair was parted and combed back. Everybody who was anybody in the world of Berlin cinema was in attendance, and the excitement ran high. An expectant silence filled the theater when the lights went down. Latecomers and noisy spectators were hissed at. Jannings made a point of standing at the buffet, sullenly sipping his coffee, while the movie was playing. Only at the final applause did he hurry onto the stage to join Dietrich. The two of them stood side by side, maintaining as much physical distance from each other as they could while holding hands. The rounds of applause were for both of them, but the triumph was for Dietrich alone. "Immediately following the premiere of the Jannings film *The Blue Angel*, Marlene Dietrich, Jannings's partner, headed for the train station to travel on to Bremerhaven and from there to New York and Hollywood. A group of close friends and family and two photographers escorted her. The artist showed no signs of cheerfulness. . . . What will the future bring? Anything noteworthy apart from dollars? Marlene Dietrich does not seem to be cherishing very great hopes."[90] She stood at the open window of the train in her white dress with one bouquet of lilacs and another of roses in her arms. She said goodbye to Berlin with an almost sheepish grin.

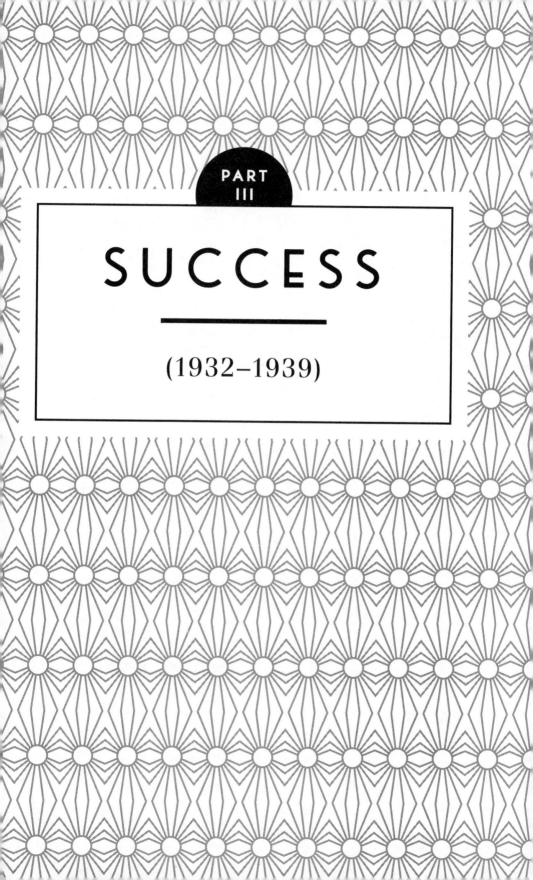

PART
III

SUCCESS

(1932–1939)

HOLLYWOOD

D
ietrich was sitting in her cabin, looking at the many bouquets of flowers from the premiere on the previous day and
wondering whether they would still be fresh when she got
to America. The *Bremen* had left Bremerhaven at 10 a.m. Resi, her
dressing-room attendant, grew seasick, and then, to make matters
worse, her dentures fell into the water. She staunchly refused to
walk on deck with Dietrich. Not that anyone was interested in the
actress—for most of the people on the ship, she was an attractive
woman unaccompanied by a man. The passenger list indicates that
she registered as "Marie Sieber-Dietrich, married, actress from Berlin," and gave her age as twenty-five, thus making herself three
years younger.[1] Marie Sieber-Dietrich and her housekeeper Theresia Kunzmann were traveling as first-class passengers. In a photograph of her first time crossing the Atlantic, Dietrich is seated on
her mountain of luggage, which consisted of several suitcases plus
an array of bags bound with cords and wicker baskets. (Later she
would always travel with monogrammed wardrobe trunks.) She is
gazing intently into the camera in a tense pose. The huge luxury
ship with eleven decks and four passenger classes frightened her.
She spent most of her time in her cabin. The ballroom, library,
swimming pool, and fashion salon on the ship held little interest

for her. After months of demanding work under intense strain, Dietrich was exhausted. Suddenly no one was telling her what to do. The applause when she was standing onstage at the Gloria Palace was still ringing in her ears. Berlin was already in her past, and Hollywood was not yet her future.

> "Frau Dietrich, you are wanted at the telephone!" With these words, the adorable little page interrupted my reveries while I was lying on a comfortable deck chair. For the first time in my life, I got to use my knowledge of American slang when I replied: "Quit your kidding!" which means something along the lines of: Don't make fun of me. "But madam, there is most certainly a telephone call for you!" . . . That was quite a sensation! Friends were calling me up to tell me about the great box office and critical success of my latest movie. I was beside myself with joy, because we had truly worked hard and were devoted body and soul. And the success was a fabulous reward, which greatly eased my understandable nervousness about my American debut and filled me with hope. Large numbers of radiograms came my way every day, as though it were necessary to keep my thoughts of Berlin alive.[2]

Telegrams, sea voyages, telephone calls, solitude, doubts, and waiting would be part of Dietrich's life from this point on. She would commute between Europe and America, at times with lovers at her side; she would visit her daughter Maria; and she would exchange letters and telegrams with her husband Rudi, but once the *Bremen* set sail on the morning of April 2, 1930, she would essentially always be alone to the end of her life. Now, too, she sat by herself in her cabin, hearing and reading about her triumph in faraway Berlin: "The event: Marlene Dietrich. Her singing and acting come across as almost detached, lethargic. But this sensual

lethargy is arousing. She is crude in an unforced manner. Everything is film, and nothing is theater. For the first time, the audience
could hear a woman's voice in a sound film with timbre, tone quality, and expression. Extraordinary."[3] Even Heinrich Mann chimed
in to the chorus of praise. Erich Pommer had brought a copy of *The
Blue Angel* to him in Nice, and there he saw it for the first time. In an
empty movie theater on the beach, he encountered the big-screen
versions of the characters he had created in his novel.

> Marlene Dietrich is the physical embodiment of Lola
> Lola. . . . When she sings the famous refrain *"Ich bin von
> Kopf bis Fuss auf Liebe eingestellt . . . "* [the English-language
> version of which is "Falling in Love Again"] for the final
> time in the movie, she brings the philosophy of the work
> to the fore with a terrifying intensity. She embodies carnal
> love through and through with her bare sensuality, and she
> sings of her own destiny and that of the broken man who
> drags himself through snow-covered streets to his final
> place of refuge. I don't think that an artist could possi-
> bly identify more strongly with the character the artist is
> portraying.[4]

Josef von Sternberg had already been informed about the positive
reception of the movie in Germany. It is difficult to say whether
he cared, because in his autobiography he claimed to be relieved
to have left Germany. "As the *Bremen* pushed itself away from the
shores of Germany I watched the receding decks and turned to my
assistant to say, 'I'm glad that's over. Let's hope that nobody follows
me.'"[5] He most certainly hoped that Dietrich *would* follow him.

Their next movie together was about the fate of a woman who
follows the man she loves. Intentionally or not, Dietrich had given
von Sternberg the book that would be adapted for her first American movie. In her usual considerate way, she gave him a basket

with some travel materials before he left for America, which contained the 1927 novel *Amy Jolly* by Benno Vigny. Her view of the book was not very positive; she told von Sternberg it was "weak lemonade."[6] But he saw it as a promising gambit to feature Dietrich as a foreigner in her first American movie. He wanted the plot to be short on dialogue and long on images, because he was horrified by her German accent and felt strongly that "an image that had no accent, German or otherwise, could not be subjected to a guttural pronunciation."[7]

Jo would not meet up with Dietrich until she arrived in Los Angeles; she would have to take her first steps into the New World on her own. An extended period of bad weather delayed the arrival of the *Bremen*, but on the morning of April 9, the ship finally approached the New York harbor. Off in the distance, the skyscrapers came into view; the ship headed for the mouth of the Hudson and at long last came to the North German Lloyd pier in Brooklyn. Dietrich waited in her cabin for someone to pick her up. She had chosen a gray outfit for the morning of her arrival, just as her grandmother would have done, figuring that she could not go wrong with that. There was a knock at the door, and a well-dressed gentleman entered, who introduced himself as Mr. Blumenthal of Paramount Pictures. He had come to escort her ashore. Blumenthal looked her up and down with a critical eye and informed her with a charming smile that she could not leave the ship looking the way she did. She failed to grasp what he was getting at. Her stockings did not have any holes, her skirt was not too short, and her jacket was spotless. Blumenthal told her bluntly that in this outfit, the Americans would think she was a lesbian. He advised her to leave the ship in a black dress and a mink coat.[8] Dietrich understood that it would be best to follow his advice. "As the ship moored and I stood in the morning sun in a black dress and a mink coat, I was both excited and fearful."[9] It dawned on her that a new chapter of her life was about to begin. However, there was no time to mull over this prospect. Blumenthal asked her to take a seat in the limousine that was waiting for her. They drove through long straight roads lined with high-rise buildings. He dropped her off at the elegant Hotel Ambassador, where the press conference would be taking place.

That evening, Dietrich had an appointment with Walter Wanger, the vice president of Paramount, who would be showing her around New York along with his wife. When she arrived at the reception desk at the appointed hour, she saw a handsome man standing there who looked to be in his mid-thirties. He came up to her with a smile and kissed her hand. "My wife's not feeling well," he told her, "so we'll have a tête-à-tête dinner."[10] Wanger was the great exception among the movie bigwigs. He spoke perfect German and French and was "college-educated, with excellent manners, liberal opinions, but evasive and 'diplomatic.'"[11] He brought Dietrich to a speakeasy, and she was fascinated to see how the guests reached under the table to pour themselves scotch or bourbon from the bottles they hid there. All of a sudden, Wanger whisked her onto the dance floor. She was so annoyed at his authoritarian behavior that she seized the first possible opportunity to make a quick exit. Her pride was wounded. Paramount had hired her as an actress, not an escort. When she got back to her hotel, she called Jo, who told her to leave New York the very next morning and not to talk to anyone. We may never know whether this account of her first night in New York is true, but it does say something about her feeling that Americans were phonies who put on a show of morality while reaching under the table for their whiskey; they masqueraded as gentlemen but left their wives at home and sought adventure elsewhere. The only person she could trust in this vast country was Josef von Sternberg.

Hollywood was almost three thousand miles from New York. The fastest train took two nights and three days. Dietrich and Resi had to change trains several times; as they ate their tasteless meals, they wondered what they were doing in this country. Every time Dietrich woke up from a nap and looked out the window to see the unvarying view, she felt as though they had made no headway at all. Endless fields of grain alternated with small towns boasting a movie theater, a gas station, and a drugstore. There was not a single human being as far as the eye could see. Finally von Sternberg appeared on the platform like a mirage. As usual, he was dressed to the nines. "Now all was well—as always with him, he had 'taken us over,'" she fondly recalled.[12]

Jo had told her that on his first visit to Hollywood he felt as though he was far from civilization. Hollywood was nothing but an empty village where the streets were lined with eucalyptus trees. Most of the studios were vacant. On occasion he would see a limousine bringing an actor to work. "I knew that there were famous stars in the community who lived in castles on the hills which surrounded their workshops. Hollywood Boulevard showed an occasional cowboy, but most of the time the sun shone on people who had migrated from Iowa, Kansas, and Minnesota."[13]

When Dietrich arrived in Los Angeles, she faced the traffic of a modern city with more than a million inhabitants roaring by. The warm climate, the lovely beaches, the scent of orange blossoms, and the vast expanse made this part of the world seem like paradise. Von Sternberg's welcome present was a Rolls Royce and a chauffeur; he had instructed her not to drive. Paramount's publicity photos show her next to this outsized Rolls Royce. She later noted on the back of one of these photos: "Wish I had it still." Dietrich met with photographers and costume designers. She was homesick for Berlin and longed to see her daughter, but she reveled in von Sternberg's unconditional love. His wife Riza filed a complaint against Dietrich, blaming Dietrich for her marital estrangement, but he refused to let anything distract him from his goal of making a motion picture that would live up to the high standards he had set for himself, bring in a great deal of money for Paramount, and make an utterly unknown German woman the new star of Hollywood. He chose two utterly dissimilar men to costar with her: Adolphe Menjou, a well-known silent film actor who had acted with Rudolph Valentino and Douglas Fairbanks, Sr., and Gary Cooper to play Menjou's rival.[14] Cooper's prior roles had portrayed him as the good, honest, handsome American cowboy. But von Sternberg had something else in mind for him.

The filming of *Morocco* began in July. Dietrich's very first shot seemed doomed to failure when she had trouble pronouncing the simple sentence: "I won't need any help." To make matters worse, she was surrounded by a crowd of inquisitive spectators. Somehow she managed to get through the day, but by the evening, in her dressing room, she was drowning in misery. She wanted to get back to Germany as fast as she could, and her director sensed that. "Von Sternberg was standing at my dressing room door; after knocking lightly, he came in. He cheered me up within twenty minutes. 'Never break off your contract, rule *numero uno*. Never give up, rule *numero due*. In other words, stay.' That's what he said to me."[15] As always, she followed his advice. On August 18, 1930, the shooting of *Morocco* was completed. Dietrich had come through just fine.

Before Dietrich appears onscreen as Amy Jolly in *Morocco*, a foghorn is heard. As she heads to the railing to watch the ship dock, her suitcase opens and dolls fall out. (One of those same dolls had been in the dressing room in *The Blue Angel*.) A man in a trenchcoat comes to her aid. He is not put off by her standoffish behavior, but seems to take an interest in the beautiful stranger. When he asks a ship's deck officer whether he knows this woman, the officer replies with a disparaging glance: "A vaudeville actress, probably. Oh, we carry them every day. We call them 'suicide passengers.' One way ticket. They never return." That is the scene that introduced Marlene Dietrich to the American public. Von Sternberg cleverly tied her situation in real life to that of the woman she was playing onscreen. But the first scene of the movie is Gary Cooper's. Cooper plays the foreign legionnaire Tom Brown, who is returning with his troops to the city of Mogador from battles in the desert. Lee Garmes, von Sternberg's cinematographer, captured this world as an impenetrable thicket of light and shadow, white garments and headgear against dark skin and uniforms. We meet up with him again in a kind of nightclub that is frequented by natives and foreigners. The gentlemen are wearing burnouses, tailcoats, or uniforms. The man from the ship is in this group as well. He is introduced as a wealthy Frenchman named La Bessière. While Brown finds a seat downstairs, La Bessière joins the table of an adjutant named Caesar and his wife up in the gallery. Madame Caesar, who is obviously bored, also seems to be one of Brown's playmates. We see the beautiful stranger from the ship in her dressing room, preparing for her performance. She is now wearing a men's dress shirt, enjoying a cigarette, fanning herself, humming a song, and admiring her reflection in her hand mirror. Then Dietrich emerges from behind the curtain and radiates indifference even to the hooting and the jeering of her disgruntled audience at the sight of her top hat and tails. Dietrich performs her song, "Quand l'amour meurt," in her inimitable way, neither melodious nor mellifluous, but triumphant. Brown sees her as a kindred spirit. With a somewhat military tip of his cap he salutes her, and she reciprocates with a tip of her top hat.[16] The women are annoyed by the intrusion of this strange rival in men's clothing. Dietrich plucks a flower from behind the ear of a woman who is giggling at her and asks whether she can keep it. When the woman consents, Amy Jolly kisses her on the mouth.[17] This oft-cited kiss is a deft display of Amy's superiority and seductive prowess. She takes the flower and throws it to Brown, who sticks it behind his ear as she prepares for her next number. While she is unreceptive to La Bessière's overtures, she gives her apartment key to Brown.

On her wall is a set of photographs that could just as easily have come from the life of Dietrich or Lola Lola as Amy Jolly, and on her bed is her collection of dolls. Nothing much happens beyond lingering gazes, a show of legs, kisses, lighting cigarettes, and blowing out matches lasciviously. Amy knows that you never ask why someone has become a Legionnaire, and Brown says he buried his past when he entered the Legion. Now it is her turn to confess: "There's a foreign legion of women, too, but we have no uniforms, no flags—and no medals when we are brave and no wound stripes when we are hurt."

Meanwhile, Adjutant Caesar has found out that his wife has been cheating on him with Tom, and sends him off on a suicide mission. Amy appears with La Bessière to say goodbye to him. She is elegantly dressed and evidently planning to marry La Bessière. Brown and his fellow legionnaires are accompanied by a crowd of women. "Who are these women?" Amy asks the man who has stayed with her. "I would call them the rear guard." She: "Those women must be mad." He: "I don't know. You see, they love their men."

On the evening of their engagement party, she hears the trumpets and drums of the returning legion. Out of her mind with excitement, she jumps up, her string of pearls rips apart, and she hurries out onto the street. She finds Brown in a bar having a good time with women, music, and liquor. When she discovers that he has carved her name and a heart in the table, she thinks she finally has proof of his love. The next morning, she comes to the edge of town with her fiancé. The two men and the woman say goodbye in a polite and distant manner. The wind is gusting; one step through the city gate and the desert begins. The Legionnaires report for duty, and the women with goats lug their belongings. Amy looks desperate. Legionnaire Brown turns to her with his charming smile and uses his fingers to indicate their familiar greeting; she returns the gesture. He marches off. Leaning on the gate, she watches the Legionnaires and their women. Amy goes back to the car, embraces La Bessière, gives him a kiss on the hand (as an expression of gratitude, not love), then strides through the gate, her clothes fluttering in the wind and her feet sinking into the sand up to her ankles. She sheds her elegant shoes, leaves them lying in the sand, and does not look back. The wind blows away any traces of her, and La Bessière and the movie audience stare into the void. In the end, all we hear is the whistling of the wind.

Brown, the rogue, stays true to his company, which is why he forsakes the love of the beautiful stranger. La Bessière, by contrast, vacillates between feelings and conventions. The special relationship between La Bessière and Amy is reflected in the similarity of their clothing, from their tailcoats to the light trenchcoats they both have on when they are looking for Brown.[18] Von Sternberg staged this film like a silent movie, but he advanced the plot adroitly by means of sounds and music. The trumpets and drums signal not only the arrival and departure of the Legion, but also Amy's fate.

On the evening of the premiere, in the famous Grauman's Chinese Theatre in Los Angeles, Dietrich got a preview of her impending fame. Banners bearing her name were hanging out in front, and the red carpet was rolled out. She was surprised and asked von Sternberg in a whisper whether this event would also be covered in the *Berliner Zeitung* back in Germany. All of Hollywood turned out on this evening: Charlie Chaplin; Adolphe Zukor, the president of Paramount Pictures; Douglas Fairbanks; Mary Pickford; and Irving Thalberg and his wife, Norma Shearer. Dietrich wore a black chiffon dress and a cape adorned with silver fox tails. She looked elegant and European—just the way her lover liked to see her.

Dietrich as Amy Jolly was neither the great sophisticate nor the emancipated flapper nor the bisexual temptress. Quite the opposite: Amy Jolly is a marked woman who wants to be saved by the love of a man. In forsaking herself in order to find herself, she realizes that her life as she knows it will cease to exist. The deck officer's prediction comes true: she will never return. She goes off barefoot into the desert. The ending of this movie is one of the most famous in the history of the cinema.

To Dietrich's astonished delight, her performance in *Morocco* pleased both viewers and critics. Sergei Eisenstein cabled von Sternberg: OF ALL YOUR GREAT WORKS, MOROCCO IS THE MOST BEAUTIFUL. ADMIRATION AND LOVE TO YOU AND MARLENE.[19] After this success, Paramount offered her a new contract: $125,000 per movie, with two movies a year. Paramount was hoping that Dietrich would be its answer to Greta Garbo. In Hollywood, she had to show that she was on par with Garbo's star quality, yet entirely different. She accomplished this by letting the public in on her life. Garbo did not grant interviews or give the public glimpses into her personal life. She never wrote memoirs or appeared on television. At the height of her fame, she would retire from the world of film and insist on staying out of sight and maintaining her silence. Dietrich, by contrast, kept her public informed about her affairs, her recipes, her parenting, and her furniture. She did not withdraw from the public eye until the final years of her life, at which point she—like Garbo—retreated into the anonymity of a big city. But in 1930 in Hollywood, Dietrich was anchored in the real world, with Garbo up in the sphere of the divine. Garbo's appeal came from her aloofness from the social realm, which is where Dietrich sparkled. Dietrich worked with her body; Garbo's face left her body behind. Dietrich always kept pace with the times, while Garbo radiated classic immutable beauty: "She is always herself, and carries without pretense, under her crown or her wide-brimmed hats, the same snowy solitary face."[20] The derisive pleasure and the self-mockery of a Dietrich were alien to her. But both of them were European women who played roles that were not intended for Americans.

In Berlin it would never have occurred to Dietrich to go on a diet, but in Hollywood she felt fat. Von Sternberg loved women "full of life, with thighs, breasts, and sex appeal," yet Dietrich wanted to be as slender as the American women.[21] She did not especially like the women in Hollywood, whom she described as bossy and grasping, but she was impressed by the looks and lifestyle of American women. Working women were not a rarity in the United States, for far longer than had been the case in Germany. Women were expected to look sophisticated and dress in the latest styles. In the 1930s, it became fashionable for women to polish their fingernails, go to the hairdresser, show off their figures, and wear sheer stockings and subtle makeup. Dietrich was drawn to the pragmatic modernity of America, which she found lacking in Europe.

A few weeks after the filming of *Morocco* wrapped up, the shooting began for *Dishonored*, her third movie with von Sternberg. Gary Cooper was the first choice for the male leading role, but he turned it down. He did not want to subject himself to von Sternberg's transformations one more time. Of course rumors were swirling about an affair between Dietrich and Cooper, but Dietrich later provided a matter-of-fact explanation for von Sternberg's jealousy: "You know, he couldn't stand it if I looked *up* at any man in a movie. . . . It would infuriate him—and Cooper was very tall—and you know, Jo was not."[22] Victor McLaglen, a British swashbuckler and former professional boxer, took the role instead. And it is easy to see that Dietrich was not pleased with her tough counterpart. There is no singing in this movie, but there are several awkward piano interludes by the leading actress.

In the opening scene, we see a pair of nice-looking women's legs up to the knee. They are standing in high-heeled shoes in the rain. The woman straightens out one of her stockings, then wheels around. The camera travels up to the face of Marlene Dietrich, which is alluringly concealed behind the veil of her little hat. She is a prostitute who is dressed like a lady as she waits for johns. The man she takes home with her is the head of the Austrian secret service. After she gives a sample of her patriotism, he tries to recruit her as a spy, attempting to sweeten the deal with the prospect of travel and beautiful clothing, but she cuts him off by saying, "What appeals to me is the chance to serve my country." He had not counted on a woman who sold her body being unwilling to sell out. X-27 (her spy name) is a widow named Kolverer whose husband died in the war. Her mission is to turn in two high-ranking officers who are suspected of working for the Russian enemy. She quickly hunts down the first of them, but she falls in love with the second one, Lieutenant Kranau. The initial showdown between the two takes place in her boudoir. He defends his actions by attacking her: "I'm a soldier, but you bring something into war that doesn't belong in it. You trick men into death with your body." He fails to grasp the fact that she also regards herself as a soldier who is trying to restore her lost honor by serving her country. After many adventures, they see each other once again at the Austrian headquarters. The Russian prisoners of war, including Kranau, are brought out. X-27, clad in a leather uniform, asks for permission to interrogate him. She enables him to escape and is court-martialed for her actions. The presiding judge asks her why she has betrayed her country for the sake of a passing affection. "Maybe I loved him" is her terse reply. The execution is set for the following morning. Her last wish is to die in the uniform in which she served her fellow countrymen, by which she means the suit with the fur trim. She saunters up to the site of her execution in a ladylike manner. Young men with rifles are awaiting her. She uses the sword of the captain in command as a mirror to freshen her lipstick. The young man who has been assigned the task of overseeing the execution shouts that he refuses to do so. She straightens her stockings while he delivers his passionate plea. Widow Kolverer evidently considers his behavior unseemly, and is shot instead by the lieutenant who is next in line. The lovely corpse lies in the courtyard, and the young soldiers march off. The old head of the secret service salutes X-27 as he leaves.

Dishonored is a flawed film that was slapped together far too hastily. Von Sternberg makes the viewer the accomplice of his longings as the camera rests on Dietrich's legs, breasts, hips, and ankles. A combination of a diet, sheer determination to succeed, homesickness, work, and love had made Dietrich lose quite a bit of weight, and she could now show off her figure in clingy outfits and uniforms. The theme of the movie is loyalty and betrayal. Kolverer no longer offers her body for money, but for her country. As a captain's widow, prostitute, spy, and traitor, she embodies both honor and dishonor. The focal point of the movie is Dietrich's body, and the plot a mere extension of her physicality. She remains true to herself, not pretending to be anything other than a woman who sells herself. The men need to don uniforms to carry out their treachery; she relies on intelligence and sex. Like *Morocco* before it, *Dishonored* portrays the self-destruction of a woman who falls victim to love. The film's flaws notwithstanding, the historian Carlo Ginzburg has called *Dishonored* the "most beautiful movie in the history of the cinema."[23]

And then Dietrich was back at Bahnhof Zoo in Berlin. Once the filming was complete, there was nothing to keep her in Hollywood. She longed to go home and be with her child, her friends, Rudi, and the city of Berlin. It was only when she got back that she realized how much had happened over the past few months. Only a year had passed since von Sternberg came into her life, yet everything had changed. She was famous. She was still self-conscious of what she thought of as her ducklike nose, but she was getting better at hiding these kinds of feelings. When she heard the familiar diction of Berlin, she realized how much she had missed all of this while she was under the palm trees. Dietrich was happy "to be in this Berlin, which I will never flush from my blood," as she confided to Franz Hessel.[24] Christmas was a few short weeks away, and she was looking forward to celebrating Maria's birthday with her. Of course she did not check into a hotel, but instead stayed at her old apartment on Kaiserallee. She knew that the love affair between Rudi and Tamara was still going on, and although she had no actual objections, she wanted to be the one to set the tone. The role she defended more than any other in her life was that of wife and mother. Her daughter needed a moment to grasp the fact that the slender woman who never stopped talking, filled the hall with her huge wardrobe trunks, and was constantly being called to the telephone was her own mother. Maria described her mother's return home in terms that suggested that her life was being taken over by a stranger.[25] That year the Christmas tree was gigantic, and Maria was given a gift of a grocery-store replica that would have been the envy of her friends, had she known any other children; instead, she had to play alone or with Tamara.[26]

Dietrich may have sensed that she had come home only to say goodbye. As Stephen Spender wrote, Germany had become so politicized that it was now divided against itself. "Berlin was the tension, the poverty, the anger, the prostitution, the hope and despair thrown out onto the streets. It was the blatant rich at the smart restaurants, the prostitutes in army top boots at corners, the grim, submerged-looking Communists in processions, and the violent youths who suddenly emerged from nowhere into the Wittenbergplatz and shouted: 'Deutschland Erwache!'"[27] Dietrich wanted to make as much of an impression on Berlin as possible in a short time. Quite likely she was hoping for a follow-up career in Europe. In March 1931, she made disc recordings at the Ultraphon studio. The songs she sang included "Peter," Hollaender's "Johnny wenn du Geburtstag hast," and the film hit "Leben ohne Liebe kannst du nicht"; her friend Mischa Spoliansky had written the music for this song, and he accompanied her on the piano at the studio as well. "Leben ohne Liebe kannst du nicht" was one of her mother's favorite songs, which indicates that this severe woman must have had a very sentimental side as well. Peter Kreuder conducted the orchestra. Back in February 1930, Dietrich had recorded all the songs from The Blue Angel, and the vocal numbers from Morocco were already for sale as records. Her records sold well and provided a solid source of revenue for the rest of her life. Dietrich's songs were sung and whistled by teenagers, housewives, attorneys, and factory workers, and appealed to people from every walk of life. The photographs from the recording studio show a self-assured, cheerful Dietrich wearing a two-piece men's suit with a tie, shirt, cuff links, and breast-pocket handkerchief.

She did not want to go back to America alone, so she took Maria with her. She was indifferent to what the Hollywood bosses might think when their femme fatale turned out to be a loving mother. The only one who mattered was Jo, and he liked Maria. The day before Dietrich left Berlin, her mother threw a party for her. Her friends and admirers gathered on Kaiserallee to say goodbye. They all waited for Dietrich to put in an appearance. Her cousin, Hasso Felsing, who was among the guests at this party, realized how quickly she had learned to act like a star. Dietrich could afford to keep the others waiting. Finally she turned up. Leaning against the doorway in a decorative pose, she declared to the group: "Darlings, here I am." Everyone erupted in cheers.

About a month later, on May 22, 1931, she sent a telegram from Los Angeles to Rudi Sieber at the Hotel Eden in Berlin: MY DEAR HOW DO YOU LIKE BERLIN WE ARE THINKING OF YOU LONGINGLY YOU ABSOLUTELY MUST VISIT US I HAVE TO FIND AN OPPORTUNITY THE CHILD IS TOO DIVINE TO ENJOY HER ALONE MILLION KISSES MUTTIKATER. Dietrich was "Mutti," and Maria was "Kater," so the family called them "Muttikater." She did not want to be without her child, and she did not care whether that was a smart move. When it came to family, she had no intention of adapting to American customs. "Paramount Studios had strictly forbidden any mention of my maternity. I wasn't willing to sub-mit to this regulation."[28] She had a transatlantic marriage, and she wanted her child to feel just as much at home in America as she did in Europe. Maybe she was hoping that Riza von Sternberg would finally let up on her if her rival's role as a mother was empha-sized. But maybe Dietrich also wanted to prevent Jo from becoming overly possessive by living with Maria. Von Sternberg could be the director and lover of the mother, acquaintance of the father, and friend of the daughter, but the family was and would remain Rudi, Marlene, and Maria.

While she was in Europe, von Sternberg picked out a new abode, a Spanish-style art deco villa on North Roxbury Drive, for the woman he adored. North Roxbury Drive was the "street of stars." The interior of the house was quite luxurious, with the standard Hollywood look featuring a great many mirrored walls. The front of this house seemed like a fortress. It was impossible to peer inside. The façade appeared to be hermetically sealed. Dashiell Hammett wrote that it was rumored in Hollywood that von Sternberg and Dietrich were "living in sin."[29] The two of them hid behind the forbidding walls of this fortress and were happy to leave the world outside.

For Dietrich, who was used to the exciting night life and cultural offerings in Berlin, Los Angeles had little to offer. Von Sternberg did not like to socialize and disparaged the "Coconut Grove culture" of Hollywood. In his view, *culture* was a dirty word in this town. He wanted Dietrich all for himself and did not allow anyone to take up direct contact with her. While he read scripts in the evening, she may have been wondering whether the delectable goulash was on that evening's menu at Mutzbauer. Maria had quickly grown accustomed to the warm climate, the wonderfully blue sky, the scent of jasmine, the villa, and the fabulous food. She was privately tutored and had a governess, and needed to be at her mother's beck and call. Several sequences of Dietrich's colorful home movies show the family life of this threesome on North Roxbury Drive. Dietrich and Maria are romping at the pool, and von Sternberg is posing with Maria in front of the camera, smiling more broadly than usual. In one set of pictures that von Sternberg took of the two of them at the pool, we see what appears to be a cheery six-year-old girl with her happy mother. Maria was not the only one in the family to have left Berlin; Rudi had gone as well. The last time they celebrated Christmas in their apartment was 1930. Never again would they live together as a family. Right after his wife and daughter left Germany, Rudi moved to Paris with his lover. When he returned to Berlin, he would stay at the Hotel Eden.

On November 7, 1931, Josefine sent a telegram to her daughter: RUDI ASKS FOR YOUR CONSENT SOON TO GIVE UP 54 HE SAYS SINCE IS NOT ENOUGH FOR DEFINITIVE RETURN MORE PRACTICAL HOTEL MONTHS FURNISHED PLACE OR HOTEL. Dietrich's reply to her husband shows that she considered this suggestion unreasonable: I DON'T UNDERSTAND WHY MUTTI DOESN'T TAKE OUR FLAT AND ACTS LIKE OWNER OF ALL OUR THINGS I HATE THE IDEA OF DESTROYING OUR HOME WOULD LIKE THAT EVERYTHING STAY AS IT IS UNTIL I COME BACK AND BUY OR RENT A HOUSE I DON'T INTEND TO LIVE THERE I JUST WANT IT AS A PLACE FOR OUR THINGS. . . . MILLION KISSES MUTTIKATER.[30] For her, there was still a "we," which no longer existed for Rudi. She wrote him that for her, closing down the apartment would spell the end of the home they had shared, but that did not seem to interest him, and he did not reply to this comment in his letters.

Sieber had found a job as production manager of the European branch of Paramount in Paris, most likely on von Sternberg's recommendation. The advantage of this was that he was on the scene for the synchronization of the Dietrich and von Sternberg movies. Sieber, who was fluent in French, enjoyed residing in Paris.[31] He could live with Tamara openly and dispense with all the sneaking around. This was probably also why he was so eager to get rid of the apartment in Berlin. Sieber had discovered his fondness for the good life. Even decades later, he still knew where to buy the best caviar and cognac in Paris. He was happy to give up Berlin, while Dietrich was homesick in her villa in Beverly Hills.

o   o   o

In the same year that Dietrich was born, seven-year-old Jonas Sternberg (Josef von Sternberg's birth name) crossed the Atlantic for the first time with his mother and his two siblings to live with his father, who had emigrated several years earlier. After three years the family returned to Vienna, where Jonas gravitated to the Prater, which featured a flea circus, performers of all kinds, women who were sawed in half, sword swallowers, and elephants on tightropes. Time and again, his movies would reenact scenes from the Prater. The boy developed a fine sense of the erotic enticements that surrounded him: he kept a close eye on the maids who were on the lookout for dashing officers and was left speechless at the sight of a girl sitting upside-down on the swing in some Vienna basement, showing the boys what was under her dress. When he was fourteen, he went back to New York, taking his memories of eroticism, performance art and artificiality, dark secrets, and mind-boggling spectacles with him to the New World. A year in high school brought his formal education to an end, after which time he found a job as an errand boy in a lace warehouse on Fifth Avenue and learned the differences between rose point and lace from Brussels, Chantilly, and Venice. These were his years as an apprentice in eroticism, because lace and women's skin went together. His coworkers entertained him with stories of brothels and the resultant quests for medical help. He left the apparel industry with quite a bit of knowledge about matters pertaining to lace and syphilis.

When his mother turned her back on the family, he also ran away from home. At the age of sixteen, he was alone and abandoned in the big city. He eked out a living with odd jobs and eventually wound up at the movie business. Jonas Sternberg began at the very bottom; he became a gofer for a man who cleaned and coated films in his basement. There followed jobs as projectionist, film repairer, and finally as personal assistant to a film producer. During the war, he made films for the U.S. Army that trained soldiers in the use of weapons, and when the war ended he continued to learn everything he could about film, working as an author, editor, and assistant to various directors. Eventually he was hired as an assistant director in Hollywood, and in the credits for the movie *By Divine Right*, his name was lengthened to Josef von Sternberg, much to his own surprise. In 1924, he directed his first movie, *Salvation Hunters*, for which he had also written the screenplay. Overnight, he was famous.

Photographs of von Sternberg and Dietrich together in Berlin show not two separate individuals, but a symbiosis. Although they are not touching, they appear to blend. Photographs, letters, telegrams, gifts from von Sternberg, and Dietrich's memoirs attest to their love. She later wrote:

> He didn't want me to talk about him. Well, since he's dead now, I'm free to do so. He created me. . . . The eye behind the camera, the eye that loves the creature whose image will be captured on the film, is the creator of the wondrous effect that emanates from this being and evokes praise and enthusiasm from moviegoers all over the world. All that is precisely calculated and not by chance. It is a combination of technical and psychological knowledge, and pure love.[32]

Von Sternberg sent her a monogrammed vanity case. He loved the way she transformed herself in front of the mirror, the eccentric finery, and the ways she augmented her beauty. In the photographs she handed out of herself in 1929 in Berlin, she had been made to look like a female impersonator. Aside from her daughter, her musical saw, and a few recordings, she did not seem to attach any lasting value to things. "As I came to know more about her I also became familiar with the conditions that had produced her, her family, and the circle around her. Her energy to survive and to rise above her environment must have been fantastic. She was subject to severe depressions, though these were balanced by periods of unbelievable vigor."[33]

Von Sternberg sensed that Dietrich was prepared to do anything, even transform herself into his work of art. "Josef von Sternberg was the only person I allowed to patronize, instruct, and control me."[34] He made her into the woman that he aimed to identify with. "I am Marlene," he declared, thus recalling Flaubert's equation of himself and the heroine of his novel.[35] On the photograph she sent him in May 1931, she wrote: "To my creator, from his creation." He sent her a photo of himself on which he wrote: "For Marlene— what am I, really, without you?"

In contrast to Flaubert, von Sternberg was dealing with a flesh-and-blood woman. MY DEAR I AM TERRIBLY LONELY AND DON'T KNOW HOW I WILL STAND THIS LONG TIME YOU ARE MY WHOLE WORLD AND ONLY YOUR TELEGRAMS GIVE ME STRENGTH TO BREATHE . . . MY LONGING IS END-LESS DON'T CRY AND DON'T STAY AWAY TOO LONG I ADORE YOU JO.[36] He was closest to her when they were making films together. During these periods, he was her creator and her lover all at the same time.

In August 1931, they began shooting *Shanghai Express*. The action begins at a train station in Beijing. Von Sternberg leads his audience right into an alien and bewildering world, just as he had done in *Morocco*. Dietrich's character casually steps out of a taxi, shows her ticket, and heads to the train, although her manner of dress is anything but casual. She is in black, but this black shim-mers in the sun and seems ablaze with color. She has wrapped a feather boa around her shoulders, and her hair is covered with a tight-fitting cap. She is a rare black bird amidst the brightly clad travelers. One of them claims that she has already wrecked the lives of a dozen men. She is met with mistrust and fear and winds up sharing her compartment with the only Chinese woman, Hui Fei, a reserved, stern-looking, allegedly disreputable woman. Shanghai Lily, as Dietrich is called, reacts to the contempt others show with a jaded, amused sense of irony, which she retains even when she runs into a former lover, Donald Harvey, a British officer and military doctor. "It took more than one man to change my name to Shanghai Lily," is her now-famous remark, delivered not as a confession but as a simple statement of fact. Harvey is offended, yet he must admit that she is more beautiful than ever.

A civil war is raging in China, and the train is taken over by rebels. When the passengers are summoned to the commander of the revolutionary army, they realize that he is one of their fellow passengers. Mister Chang has exchanged his white suit for a uniform. He needs a hostage, and to find the right one, he subjects the passengers to an interrogation. These seemingly honorable travelers all have something to hide. Under interrogation, Shanghai Lily states that she has been living in China for eight years. When Chang tries to seduce her, Harvey, who has overheard everything, breaks down the door and knocks Chang to the floor. After this proof of Harvey's love, Lily's irony turns dead serious. To protect Harvey, she is willing to sacrifice herself for him and become Chang's lover. In a final dramatic sequence of shots in the train, Dietrich shows what she has learned. During the night, she leaves her cabin wearing a black lace negligee adorned with feathers. The narrow corridor of the clattering train is her catwalk. The camera follows her until she gets to Harvey's door. Before she knocks, von Sternberg shows his lover in all her splendor. In this moment, she seems to belong to him alone. He desires her with his camera gaze. Love conquers all in *Shanghai Express*, and Donald Harvey and Shanghai Lily are reunited as a couple.

The exotic milieu that von Sternberg constructed in the California desert highlights Dietrich's beauty and distinctiveness. She glides through the movie like an aristocratic black swan. Dietrich knows how to show her feather boas, lace panties, veils, gloves, furs, and silk to their best advantage and comes off as one unending enticement, even though she reveals neither leg nor bosom. Shanghai Lily is a beautiful, cynical plaything who plays with the men—not the other way around. However, her lovely façade is the masquerade of a dead woman. In *Shanghai Express*, von Sternberg shows a new variant of the story of the demimondaine with a big heart.

The men of honor in uniform turn out to be con artists, cowards, or sadists. The supposedly disreputable woman, by contrast, proves to be big-hearted and brave. Dietrich remained true to the role of the brave adventuress and lover: Amy Jolly follows her lover into the desert, Marie Kolverer is shot for saving a man she may have loved, and Shanghai Lily is willing to sacrifice herself for a man who is oblivious to her love.

Shanghai Express was Dietrich's third Hollywood motion picture. Little by little, she was learning how the movie business worked. When she was filming, she was "like a soldier going into battle."[37] She was ready to leave for the studio before five in the morning, with her daughter Maria in tow. They drove through the cold streets of the desert town in silence. Dietrich always brought a large number of lemons with her to fight her queasiness. She made the driver stop several times along the way so that she could vomit at the side of the road. Once they had passed through the Paramount gate, the preparations for the shoot followed a prescribed path. Dietrich was the first to enter her dressing room, followed by Maria and a group of assistants. She switched on the lights, still silent and utterly focused on the transformation ahead. She took off her clothes, and Maria handed her the makeup smock. Dietrich tied the cloth belt tightly around her waist, then her men's oxfords were untied for her and she put on her open-back slippers. Maria placed "the green tin of Lucky Strikes with the gold Dunhill lighter by the large glass ashtray, next to the dish with the marabou powder puffs."[38] The coffee was served with cream in a Meissen cup. Dietrich's hair was styled and makeup applied to her weary face. Then she took a last puff of her cigarette before her lipstick was added. The hairpieces, which were perfectly coordinated to her hair color, were secured in place with the "Westmore twist—a sort of half-hitch with a straight hairpin that just missed penetrating the skull."[39] By this point she was presumably completely awake, just in time for the arrival of the wardrobe girls to put on the costume she needed for that day. Dietrich waited until everything was assembled. When she called out "Let's go!" the lights were turned off, the door was locked, and they went off to the set. She brought along five thermoses filled with homemade soups and German coffee. She was ready to work with her creator.[40]

Her costumes for *Shanghai Express* were more extravagant than for any of her previous movies. Travis Banton, her costume designer from Texas, created true masterpieces of visual eroticism for her.[41] Banton, who was always exquisitely dressed, had an athletic build and a peasant face. Once a year he made a shopping trip to Paris. He had the gloves, suitcases, and handbags for *Shanghai Express* fashioned by Hermès. His studio was furnished with a lavish array of antiques and paintings. Dietrich spent many hours there standing in front of the mirror. Every studio came equipped with a small room with a couch for the exhausted stars to take a rest, but Dietrich had the stamina and discipline to hold out without using it. Since she was always on a diet, there was no need for meal breaks.

When Dietrich arrived in Hollywood, there was a set of procedures in place designed to turn a roly-poly girl from Berlin into a Hollywood goddess. Hair dying; plastic surgery; calisthenics; employing cosmetic tricks such as "opening up" the eyes by shifting the eyebrows; and taking instruction in speech, dance, walking, and singing were standard practice for every woman who aspired to stardom. Dietrich's transformation was extraordinarily successful. She worked on her makeover with determination and discipline.

However, Hollywood also made demands that were not easy to live up to even for Dietrich, specifically those pertaining to manners and morality. Riza von Sternberg, who had no intention of resigning herself to the fact that her husband was in love with another actress, made Dietrich's life difficult. Riza knew, of course, that her accusation of Dietrich's immoral conduct was the best means to get her out of the way and to impede any future work with von Sternberg. A scandal could be deadly. Studio bosses were not pleased when their stars violated the stipulated moral principles. The so-called Hays Code specified how long a kiss could last, how long a skirt could be, and what expressions could be used.[42] The stars' personal lives were not spared from this puritanical zeal, and there were plenty of newspapers just waiting to exploit an affair and ruin a career. Dietrich was well aware of this. Shortly after her return from Europe, she sent a cable to Rudi in Paris:

SINCE YOUR PRESENCE HERE WOULD GREATLY HELP ME IN MATTERS
OF PUBLICITY WITH TRIAL OF FRAU STERNBERG AGAINST ME CABLE ME
EARLIEST TIME YOU ARE FREE THERE IF THEY DENY YOU VACATION I
DEMAND VACATION TIME FROM LASKY AS SOON AS I HAVE ASSIGNMENT
FROM YOU DON'T TELL ANYONE DETAILS ANSWER SOON YOUR MUTTI.[43]

He does not seem to have been very enthusiastic about the prospect of playing the role of the husband; her next cable made her seem peeved:

YOUR COMING EARLY AUGUST HAS LITTLE PURPOSE I AM WORKING
THEN AND THE PRESS SCANDAL IS OVER YOUR VISIT DELIGHTS US ANY
TIME BUT IF YOU WANT TO HELP ME YOU HAVE TO COME NOW ANSWER
IMMEDIATELY IF THAT IS POSSIBLE AND HOW MUCH MONEY YOU NEED
MILLION KISSES MUTTIKATER.[44]

Now Rudi seems to have noticed that the situation was dire. Marlene had already given him travel instructions in an earlier letter: "You fly to Cherbourg, take 4 days to cross the ocean, then 4 days by train, and you'll be with us."[45]

Dietrich waited for him in Pasadena, along with Maria and von Sternberg. Rudi must have been amazed at the villa, the pool, the blue sky, the Rolls Royce, and the sun that shone every day. A photograph shows the expanded nuclear family, Dietrich wearing a tie, hat, and sports jacket; Maria with her arms around her parents' shoulders; Rudi; and next to him von Sternberg, who has linked arms with Rudi. The men are wearing white suits, the child a white dress, and Dietrich a white skirt. They are gazing expectantly into their future. A few weeks later, Sieber returned to Europe. He had done his duty; everyone saw that Dietrich, true to her claim, really did have a husband.

In Hollywood, the story ran its course. Riza got a substantial settlement from the divorce, and Dietrich filmed her next movie with von Sternberg. Major advertising campaigns and two movies in three years made the pair well-known to the American moviegoer. She immersed herself in dubbing her films, with an eye to her career in Europe. Sieber at Paramount Studios in Paris helped her behind the scenes. On September 12, she sent him this transatlantic order: PLEASE IMMEDIATELY LISTEN TO FRENCH VERSION OF MOROCCO WITH MY EARS AND CABLE HOW YOU LIKED IT KISSES MUTTIKATER. She wanted him to tell her every detail of what was being said about her in Europe. However, Rudi did not write to her often. Her telegrams in the period before Christmas of 1931 grew briefer and briefer. Sometimes she sent him a million kisses, other times she wrote that she was working night and day, and still other times, she asked only why he was not replying, even though she was paying for the telegrams. She could travel to Europe and earn money, she wrote him, because her next shoot in Hollywood was not scheduled to begin until March. He did not reply. A few days later, she sent him a telegram with the message that she would not be coming to Paris, which meant that she had no source of income until mid-February. When her mother also asked her in early December to invest money in Berlin, she asked Rudi to take care of that.

A SUM LIKE THAT NOT EASY TO EARN NO ONE NOW INVESTS MONEY IN EUROPE
IF I DO THAN ONLY FOR MUTTI CERTAINLY NOT GOOD PLACE FOR MY MONEY.[46]
Until the next time she got paid, she borrowed money from von
Sternberg. He, in turn, had to sell securities in order to stay solvent.
When she had money, she spent it. Dietrich could not work with a
budget; Rudi saw to these unpleasant matters.

On October 9, *Morocco* premiered at the Gloria Palace in Berlin.
Her old friend, the screenwriter Walter Reisch, wrote to her: "My
dear and admired lady! . . . The press and intelligentsia really liked
your 'Morocco movie.' The masses were thrown off by the dialogue
and bold theme. . . . Incidentally, congratulations are in order for
you, now that you really don't have to live here. A beautiful woman
is out of place here these days. You belong in the land of the sun!"[47]
Dietrich was sure to have appreciated her friend's compliments, but
his description of the situation in Berlin sounded alarming: "The situation here is still so unsettled that it is almost pointless to draw up
a schedule for anything past five in the afternoon. Every half hour
brings a new change to the program. Exchange embargo, emergency decree, production cuts—catchwords that are governing the
moment."[48] The political situation had everyone on tenterhooks,
and the personal sphere diminished in importance. Young people
regarded uniforms as the promise of a better future. Assets kept
declining as unemployment rose; corruption and depravity continued under Brüning. The name "Hitler" came up with increasing
frequency. When Dietrich recalled the newspaper photographs of
this bumbling man in garish clothing with bulbous facial features
and a thick dog whip, she knew why Reisch said that a beautiful
woman was out of place in Berlin.

Should she go to Europe at all?

TELL ME DEAR WHETHER I OUGHT TO STAY HERE IN VIEW OF SITUATION
GERMANY . . . GET IDEA THAT VACATION BERLIN CANNOT BE ENJOYABLE
AND I COULD NOT TAKE RESPONSIBILITY FOR LOSS OF MONEY YOU

HAVE BETTER OVERVIEW OF SITUATION FROM THERE AND CAN GIVE
ADVICE KISSES MUTTIKATER.[49]

Sieber knew from Tamara, who visited her family in Berlin from time to time, how depressing the situation was there. She wrote, "It is quite miserable in Berlin . . . everyone has left and those who have stayed are in a bad mood. After Paris, Berlin is so dead. . . . There is nothing to do here (as far as business goes). No film. Everything dead. . . . It is very bad."[50] Sieber advised Dietrich not to come. He wanted to spare her this gloomy atmosphere in Berlin.

Some of the telegrams and letters that went back and forth between Paris and Los Angeles were about Dietrich's need to replenish her supply of stockings, gloves, literature, suntan lotion, medicine, and children's books. Sieber knew everything about her clothing preferences and measurements, right down to her lingerie, and he whizzed through Paris to locate the items she needed.

The United States was mired in an economic crisis and a crisis of confidence, which many regarded as an acute threat to their existence. After criss-crossing the country, Franklin D. Roosevelt, the Democratic candidate for president, reported that he had looked into the faces of thousands of Americans: "They have the frightened look of lost children." He promised people a return to normality with the campaign slogan: "Happy days are here again." Hollywood eagerly echoed this sentiment. In the presidential election year, and against the backdrop of the Great Depression, Dietrich and von Sternberg made a movie that differed strikingly from her others. *Blonde Venus* is set in the United States and highlights the atmosphere of this period in history. Dietrich plays the role of a mother.[51] A great many conflicts flared up in the ensuing months about the various screenplay versions, the director, the star, and the artistic direction of Paramount Studios. By the end of 1931, Paramount was experiencing serious difficulties in the turbulence of the Great Depression and could not afford a flop. The studio pinned its hopes on Dietrich and von Sternberg. Letters, telegrams, and telephone calls went back and forth between the film bosses, with frantic deliberations as to how one could bring about a success of the Dietrich and von Sternberg duo, and they ultimately came up with the idea of a story of a mother. B. P. Schulberg, the production chief at Paramount, liked the idea of presenting Dietrich as a loving mother, as he stated in a telegram to his colleague Emanuel Cohen:

> THIS STORY COMBINES EVERY ELEMENT OF DRAMATIC INTEREST THAT
> COULD POSSIBLY BE CROWDED INTO A DIETRICH SUBJECT GIVING HER A
> STRONG EMOTIONAL SYMPATHETIC ROLE THAT IS FAR REMOVED FROM
> ANYTHING SHE HAS YET DONE AND SHOULD THEREFORE BE WEL-
> COME RELIEF AT SAME TIME GIVING HER OPPORTUNITY TO SING DRESS
> SMARTLY AND BE GLITTERING STAGE PERSONALITY WITH WHICH SHE
> CAPTURED PUBLIC IN BOTH MOROCCO AND BLUE ANGEL.[52]

However, it was not easy to implement this plan. Power struggles within Paramount, strict censorship regulations, and profit seeking stood in the way of a unified approach. Schulberg himself had to leave in the course of the year, and von Sternberg also tried to walk away from Paramount before the shooting even began. He did not want to film the script that had been presented to him in revised form. Von Sternberg provided this terse summary of a war of nerves that dragged on for months: "Miss Dietrich also left, refusing to work with anyone else, and I was forced to return, as we were both under contract."[53]

On May 26, filming of *Blonde Venus* began at long last, with Dietrich playing a German woman named Helen who has married an American chemist, Edward Faraday. Faraday has lost his job in the Depression and is seriously ill as well. They live in New York with their five-year-old son, Johnny. Helen, a former cabaret singer, goes back to her profession against her husband's wishes. In her search for employment, she has to present herself in multiple guises and under several different names, and has to outshine innumerable competitors. Everyone is on the quest for a job. Von Sternberg again portrayed Dietrich as a nightclub singer. The men are after her, and she chooses the best of them, Nick Townsend (played by Cary Grant), to be a lover. He gives her money to finance a cure for her husband's medical condition. When her husband finds out about the affair, a battle for the child ensues. Helen flees, and Faraday has the police chase her around the country. The people Helen meets are tough and pitiless. While on the run through America, she goes to rack and ruin and winds up as a homeless boozer with tattered clothing and crude manners. Many Americans feared ending up that way. When she has hit rock bottom, she gives up. She stays behind at some godforsaken train station in shabby clothes, while her husband leaves with their son. After experiencing a meteoric rise as a singer in Paris, Helen returns to New York and asks her husband to take her back.

In 1932, when it had become clear that the big party in the United States was over, Dietrich's European approach to motherhood went quite well with the new domesticity. People no longer headed out to clubs, bars, or restaurants for entertainment, but instead discovered the joys of parlor games they could play at home. Puzzles, bridge, and checkers gained in popularity. Dietrich played the role of mother both lovingly and matter-of-factly. When Helen leaves for her first performance and gives Edward, who is standing around helplessly, quick instructions for making dinner and putting their son to bed while she is memorizing her role and packing her bags, she is portraying a situation that working mothers everywhere have faced. Dietrich's fierce commitment to motherhood is strikingly absent from the public's perception of her. She played Helen Faraday as a mother who has remained a desirable woman. At that time only she could do that. As a housewife, she wore white blouses, white aprons, and black skirts, but also form-fitting, fur-trimmed coats. As a singer and a lover, she is draped in flowing, seductive robes, or she makes her appearance in a white tailcoat and a top hat. Once again, Dietrich plays the woman who is passionately in love, but here the object of her love is neither the offended husband nor the debonair lover; it is her son. Posing as an androgynous femme fatale serves only to mask her disappointment in love. Besides a mother, wife, lover, and singer, Dietrich in this movie is also a German. She has to tell Johnny again and again how she and his father first met: "It was springtime in Germany . . ." In the evening, she sings him German songs, such as "Leise zieht durch mein Gemüt" and "Ein Männlein steht im Walde." In this movie, made in 1932, Germany is the country in which American men can fall in love with beautiful German nymphs on warm spring evenings and in which live famous researchers who can cure what ails you.

However, the news Dietrich was hearing from Berlin at the beginning of the new year did not bode well. The showing of *Dishonored* in Berlin had been disrupted. Walter Reisch did not ascribe much value to these actions.

> Wonderful Marlene! I have just come from your film X 27.
> Unfortunately—or should I say thank goodness—I did not
> get tickets for the premiere, because I would surely have
> had to tussle with a good many rowdies. To get right to the
> point: I find the movie splendid! The ruckus and scandals
> are surely the work of some rowdies who see any premiere
> around the Kaiser Wilhelm Memorial Church as an oppor-
> tunity to attract attention. . . . Apart from them, everyone
> is unanimous: Marlene's best performance as an actress.
> Von Sternberg's sparkling, lush, colorful, dramatic, stirring
> production. By the way, it has been sold out every time so
> far. . . . Moving on to another subject: many sincere thanks
> for your lovely letter; I was triply delighted by every single
> line, I am quite upset about your complaining that you

don't like it over there anymore! Your yearning for Europe is totally incomprehensible for us over here! Anyone here who knows about politics, economic and social collapse, etc. has no understanding whatsoever for a yearning for Europe.[54]

In the same month, Dietrich got a request from Rudi and Josefine to grant them power of attorney over her assets. They feared economic decline and wanted to ensure that they had enough to live on. The letters and telegrams that went back and forth over the next few months between Paris, Berlin, and Los Angeles show how woefully incapable each side was of understanding the other. In 1932, Dietrich had no secure source of income and was feeling uneasy among the sharks of Hollywood, although Rudi and Josefine figured she was rich and carefree. In November 1931, she had been nominated for an Academy Award as Best Actress for her role as Amy Jolly in *Morocco*, and von Sternberg had been nominated as Best Director. Neither had won. This would be Dietrich's only Oscar nomination.

Then a new crisis drove her to the brink of insanity. On March 1, the twenty-month-old baby of the aviator Charles Lindbergh was kidnapped from his parents' home. The Hollywood stars feared for the safety of their children. Dietrich received an extortion letter with a threat to kidnap Maria. She was partway through filming *Blonde Venus* and was utterly incapable of thinking clearly. Every morning she took Maria to the studio with her, and at night, Maria was protected by her mother's male friends. One night, Maria recalled, "I found von Sternberg on the floor by my bed, revolver ready, fast asleep. Another night, Chevalier, equally armed and ready, snoring musically.[55] When Rudi Sieber came, Dietrich arranged for him to be guarded by two FBI officers, and bars were installed on all the doors and windows of her house. She threatened to leave the United States, but that went against everyone else's interests. Von Sternberg wanted to keep Dietrich by his side, and Sieber was quite content to live in Paris without his wife. In the end, everything stayed as it was, and Dietrich remained in Hollywood. Where else could she go, anyway?

o o o

Paramount was considered *the* American film studio in Europe. European stars such as Emil Jannings, Ernst Lubitsch, Marlene Dietrich, Sergei Eisenstein, and Maurice Chevalier were under contract with Paramount. In her relationship with Chevalier, Dietrich tried to keep her memory of Europe alive and to fight off her homesickness. He was thirteen years older than Dietrich, had been a street urchin in Paris, then became a revue star after the war. His elegant clothing—suit, straw hat, and bow tie—was his trademark. Even in his love letters to Dietrich, he could not stop playing the charming Frenchman. Chevalier called Dietrich "*ma grande aimée, ma femme, ma grande.*" He gave no evidence of originality in his communication with her, but rather wallowed in platitudes about love. JE PENSE A TOI SANS CESSE ET TU ES ENCORE DANS MES BRAS.[56] By the fourth letter, this kind of talk had become wearying. Chevalier was too guileless to hold Dietrich's interest. It is easy to picture the two enjoying a good laugh about the Americans, singing together, or rhapsodizing about Paris. Chevalier met up with Sieber in Paris, and as usual, Sieber got along famously with his wife's lover. Their topic of conversation was, of course, Dietrich. These encounters with Forst, Chevalier, von Sternberg, and the rest kept Sieber well informed as to the state of Dietrich's relationships with her current lovers. Not only did he have a complete picture of her finances, but he also knew his way around her love life. He retained a vestige of power over her. Almost every second telegram—the longer she was away, the fewer letters they exchanged—contained his request for money. PLEASE MUTTI SEND MONEY I NEED IT MILLION KISSES FOREVER PAPA.[57]

In September, Dietrich repeatedly asked Rudi how the situation was in Germany, and whether he would advise her to come.

I UNDERSTAND YOU SO WELL BUT IF I SHALL ADVISE YOU SHOULDN'T GO TO GERMANY NOW POLITICAL SITUATION TERRIBLE NEW ELECTIONS DANGER OF CITIZEN WAR.[58] Her friends did not appear to be faring well, and she heard that Marcellus Schiffer had taken his own life. Margo Lion had left Berlin and moved to Paris.

Dietrich took Rudi's advice and stayed in Hollywood with Maria. *Blonde Venus* came to movie theaters in late September. The American critics felt that the time had come to lash out at von Sternberg and his star. "His latest movie, *The Blonde Venus*, is perhaps the worst ever made. In it all Sternberg's gifts have turned sour. The photography is definitely 'arty'—a nauseating blend of hazy light, soft focus, over-blacks and over-whites, with each shot so obviously 'composed' as to be painful."[59] None of the participants had really wanted to make this movie in the first place, and no one was surprised when it flopped. Dietrich and von Sternberg were no longer regarded as an artistic couple who stood for success. With all the external pressure they were facing, the intervals between their spats became briefer and briefer. He was considered difficult because he felt superior to everyone else, and she supposedly always obeyed him. They had to give careful thought to any future collaboration. Von Sternberg wrote matter-of-factly that after their fifth movie together, he had finally persuaded her to work with a different director.

Von Sternberg traveled to the West Indies to film a hurricane. He and Dietrich were taking a break from each other. Marlene asked Rudi how *Blonde Venus* was received in Berlin, and he told her that even in the third week it was still completely sold out. VENUS BERLIN BIG SUCCESS ALL CRITICS FANTASTIC FOR YOU ALSO MARVELOUS FOR JO.[60] However, this positive reception does not seem to have inspired her to continue making movies. In early December she asked Rudi impatiently when he would finally come to them, and she contemplated going back to Europe with him: HOPE TO GET AWAY WITHOUT MAKING PICTURE CABLE AT ONCE MILLION KISSES MUTTIKATER.[61]

The year 1933 began on a note of trouble. Dietrich did not show up for work, and Paramount sued her for breach of contract. She was finally pressured into meeting her new director. A photograph of Dietrich with Rouben Mamoulian shows how very different they were. He looked as though he cared only about philosophical issues, while she had donned a glamorous get-up to gain attention. However, the two of them got along. She liked the fact that he accepted her as she was. The film they would be working on together for Paramount had been adapted from Hermann Sudermann's novel *Song of Songs*. Dietrich recited her little piece about how she, like every German girl, loved and cherished this novel. A telegram from von Sternberg, who was back in Berlin in late January 1933, shows that she was quite happy to have gained Mamoulian as an admirer.

DEAREST JUST GOT YOUR FIRST LETTER THANKS A MILLION NOW YOUR TELE-
GRAMS FROM WHICH I GATHER THAT YOU ARE HAPPY AGAIN AND DELIGHTED
BECAUSE OF ROUBEN WHOSE ENTHUSIASM IS LIKE MINE BACK THEN . . . AM
DELIGHTED THAT YOU ARE NOT SUFFERING. . . .[62]

Nine days later Adolf Hitler became the chancellor of Germany, and the National Socialists felt as though they were "in a fairy tale," as Joseph Goebbels declared.[63] Dietrich's correspondence with both her American lover and her husband barely mentioned Hitler at first. Von Sternberg found Berlin unchanged in the three years that had passed since *The Blue Angel*. He stopped off there to have dinner with Alfred Hugenberg. When he went on to Vienna the next morning, the cab that drove him to the airport was delayed in front of the burning Reichstag. In Paris he met with Sieber, who telegraphed to Dietrich that he and von Sternberg talked over their problems, most likely in regard to her staying in the United States. (In February 1932, she had stated in an interview with an American newspaper that she was thinking of returning to Germany, but nothing came of that idea.) By the time von Sternberg was sitting in the taxi watching the Reichstag burn, he must have realized that the National Socialist takeover would also impinge on their plans,

but in late March, Rudi was still lighthearted: HAPPY NOTHING SERIOUS
HAPPENED ARE YOU WELL AGAIN . . . MILLION KISSES LOVE YOU PAPA.[64]

Dietrich was feeling lonely in Hollywood. Once she started
shooting the film with Mamoulian, she came to appreciate what
she had had with Jo.

> EVERYBODY EXCITED OVER MY SO CALLED ACTING HAVE NO DIFFICUL-
> TIES WHATSOEVER MAMOULIAN LOVES EVERYTHING I SAY AND DO
> TWO TAKES OF EACH SCENE THE LAST TIMES WITH JO SEEM TO BE A
> BAD DREAM ALTHOUGH THE INSPIRED ATMOSPHERE IS MISSING AND I
> SEE NOW MORE THAN EVER HOW FAR ABOVE EVERYBODY HE IS.[65]

Maria watched her mother memorizing her lines for the first time.
In von Sternberg's view, scripts existed only for the studio bosses.
Dietrich relied on his genius and knew that he would tell her in
good time what needed to be done. She did not consider Mamoulian a genius, so she learned her lines by heart.

Song of Songs was the movie in which Dietrich sang "Heidenröslein" and "Johnny." The song repertoire replicates the range of
her role. She begins as the innocent young woman from the country, falls in love with a young artist in Berlin, is paired off with a
sadistic baron in Pomerania, and eventually winds up as a cynical
sensualist. The filming was completed by early May, and Dietrich
had time off. She wanted to take Maria to Europe; the only question
was—Berlin or Paris? She knew from Sieber that her mother was
expecting her in Berlin. Josefine von Losch was not alarmed about
the political events. Like most Germans, she believed that this was
none of her concern. RADICAL UPHEAVALS NO MATTER TO US NEWSPAPER
REPORTS SURELY EXAGGERATE EVERYTHING ALL WELL HUGS MUTTI.[66] But
Sieber sounded a note of caution. He advised her to travel with a
French ship and to have a new American contract in her pocket
before setting foot on German soil. She was still quite popular in

Germany, and in April of the previous year, the premiere of *Shanghai Express* had sold out.

SHANGHAI EXPRESS GREATEST SUCCESS IN YEARS DAILY THREE SHOW-
INGS SOLD OUT SATURDAY FORCED TO TURN AWAY ATTENDEES WITH
TRAFFIC PATROL NIGHT PERFORMANCE.[67]

Dietrich wanted to leave the United States without delay, but where was she to go? Should she consider Berlin after all?

The letters and telegrams from the spring of 1933 convey the impression that Dietrich was on the run. Her options were unappealing: Germany had Hitler, and Paris the wife of Maurice Chevalier. Should she take a German or a French ship? Where should she disembark? What should she say, and in what language? On May 8, Rudi sent her a clear message:

SITUATION BERLIN TERRIBLE EVERYBODY ADVISES AGAINST YOU GOING
STOP EVEN EDI THE NAZI AFRAID OF MOB SCENES MOST BARS ARE
CLOSED STOP CINEMAS IMPOSSIBLE STREET EMPTY ALL JEWS FROM
PARAMOUNT BERLIN HAVE BEEN MOVED TO PARIS VIA VIENNA STOP I
EXPECT YOU WITH MUTTI CHERBOURG . . . LATER SWITZERLAND OR
TYROL GOT PHOTOS FANTASTIC WONDERFUL I WAIT FOR YOU LONGING
KISSES PAPA.[68]

Dietrich was seeking refuge with her husband. The telegrams she sent him while she traveled to Europe were filled with the feelings of loneliness she so dreaded, and her longing for him. By the time of her arrival in Cherbourg, she was at the end of her rope. Her child was seasick, and she had not slept for three nights.

The photograph of their arrival in Paris shows her making a regal entrance. Dietrich is shielding her eyes from the curious onlookers with dark sunglasses. The expression on her face reveals that she knows everyone's eyes are on her. She is flanked by Sieber and Marcel Boursier, who made the preparations for her stay. Maria is not in the picture. The men seem barely able to keep up with Dietrich. These are the most dynamic photographs of her. She had finally gotten away from Hollywood. The fact that she was wearing men's clothing—suit, shirt and tie, loose coat, and beret—created a sensation in Europe.[69]

Dietrich had her suits, tuxedos, slacks, and sports jackets made by traditional men's tailors. She loved this finely detailed and practical clothing, which showed her good posture to best advantage and had added subtle touches of femininity. Red wool slacks, buttoned on the side like sailor trousers, were tailored in a standard men's cut, but the waistband was lined with a floral strip. A piece of fabric with typewritten text sown into the slacks read: "Mr. Marlene Dietrich. Date: November 1932, Watson & Son Tailors, Hollywood, California." The fabric of her tuxedo is dark, thick, and heavy; only a woman with a commanding presence would not be overwhelmed by this massive piece of clothing. In addition to stylish camisoles and seductive lace panties, her collection of underwear also included monogrammed silk boxer shorts with an open fly.

Of course there was work awaiting her in Paris as well. She oversaw the dubbing of *Song of Songs* and in the process got to watch her husband at work. And how did Rudi cope with the delicate situation that his wife, daughter, and lover were all in Paris? His daughter recalled, "Like many ineffectual men, he was a tyrant in those categories in which he could get away with it. . . . Restaurants were his favorite arena to play Nero in, his famous wife, the type-cast Christian. With her he always chose a public place for his tantrums and toward people who couldn't talk back. Employees feared for their jobs, establishments the loss of Dietrich's patronage. Tami, I, and [the dog] Teddy just feared—period."[70] Her mother ignored these outbursts. This kind of behavior was ridiculous for someone like him at a place like Paramount, and Dietrich knew it. She felt that she owed it to Sieber to let him indulge in these scenes in her presence in exchange for his agreeing to play his role as the husband. She also paid for his cashmere jackets, Cartier cigarette lighters, and tweed suits. Dietrich's earnings enabled him to lead a life of luxury.

It took no more than a few short months after the National Socialists came to power for her sympathies to become clear to all. Her suite in the Hotel George V would become a familiar address for emigrants in the 1930s. Dietrich treated them to meals, gave them money, got them work, and paid for their travel to America. Janet Flanner remarked on her cordial reception by the Parisians: "She is the sweet pepper that brings crowds to the modest Hungarian restaurant on the Rue de Surène where she customarily dines; she is the bitters at fashionable cocktail parties only when she fails to appear. . . . She speaks excellent French, deports herself modestly. . . . Fräulein Dietrich is the first foreign female personality Paris society has fallen in love with in years."[71]

In September, Dietrich and Maria went back to America. Dietrich shuddered at the thought of the emptiness that awaited her there. Von Sternberg had rented an even more luxurious villa for her in an even wealthier neighborhood. He wanted only the best for her. In addition to the Rolls Royce, he gave her a sapphire ring, rhinestones, malachite, lapis lazuli, and a gold cigarette case with the inscription: "Marlene Dietrich / woman, mother, and actress like no other, Josef von Sternberg."

Her trip to Europe had been doubly fraught, with the new regime in Germany and the many quarrels she had had with von Sternberg. He was head over heels in love with her, and she could not muster up the courage to break off their relationship because nobody could put her in the limelight better than he. In May, von Sternberg had sent her a love telegram nearly every day. On May 10, he wrote: MY DEAR GODDESS EVERYTHING IS SO EMPTY AGAIN AND I AM BURNING UP WITH LONGING AND LOVE . . . ALL MY THOUGHTS AND DREAMS

ARE WITH YOU JO; a telegram sent the following week expressed similar sentiments: WOULD LOVE TO THROW AWAY THE WHOLE KIT AND CABOODLE AND FLY TO YOU . . . I MISS YOU WITH EVERY THOUGHT AND LOVE YOU MORE AND MORE EVERY SECOND YOU INCOMPARABLE WOMAN AND MOST BEAUTIFUL CREATION.[72] He knew that the woman he worshipped would be getting together with her husband and her lovers. Just hours after sending off a telegram to her, he fretted that she would not reply and posted declarations of love to her on ships and trains, recalling experiences they had shared and trying to make plans to see her again.

When the cameras were off, he was submissive to her, but when they were turned back on, he expected her to bow to his wishes. In his view, actors were living props and he could make them do whatever he had in mind, since it was the director who imbued the actors' work with meaning. Humiliation and praise were von Sternberg's educational tools, and he insisted on complete silence on the set.[73] He made everyone take off their wristwatches because the ticking disturbed him. Von Sternberg's tyranny was the perfect complement to Dietrich's mechanical working method. She did precisely what he asked of her. She did not ask a lot of questions; she obeyed. She needed his instructions and his eyes on her to be able to act; both reassured her. No matter what he demanded of her, she complied with his wishes. She did not tolerate complaints, least of all from herself, although von Sternberg had no compunction about going to extremes.

While they were shooting her next movie, *The Scarlet Empress*, she had to ring the cathedral bell to proclaim her victory. To simulate the ringing of the huge bell, the thick pull rope had been rigged on counterlevered pulleys and weighted with sandbags. A massive mahogany crucifix rimmed in steel was attached to the end of the rope to keep it hanging taut. As she pulled on the rope, stretching her entire body up high then bringing it down, all the way to her knees, the crucifix slammed against the inside of her thighs, and down her calves. Over and over she repeated this action, until she had executed the required eight strokes. She must have been pulling twenty pounds of dead weight with each motion, in full resplendent uniform complete with cavalry shako and dangling regimental sword.[74]

Von Sternberg made her repeat this scene fifty times, knowing full well that she would not complain. That was the power he still had over her. When her dressing room attendant and Maria helped her off with her costume, they saw that her inner thighs were bleeding. The sharp metal edges of the crucifix had lacerated her. Dietrich ordered them to shut the door, then she poured alcohol over the wounds. Maria, who was standing next to her, sensed the searing pain, but her mother did not even flinch. She was driven home, then she cooked Jo's favorite dinner and limped across the dining room to serve it to him. He spent the night there, and over breakfast she thanked him for helping her to play the scene just the way he wanted it. Von Sternberg asserted until the end of his life that "Miss Dietrich" was the best assistant he had ever had.

Ever since they made their first film together, she had been his pupil. Von Sternberg and Dietrich were highly professional, technophile perfectionists. They turned the production process into a complex, sensual, experimental arrangement. Decades later, when she recalled how he shone a light on her for the first time, she described a moment of pure eroticism: "Never will I forget the wonderful moment when I climbed up to the set, a dark and cave-like set where he stood in the dim light of a single bulb. Lonely? Not really. A strange mixture, which I would get to know. He sent away everyone who was standing near me, but he allowed me to stay while he set up the lighting for the scene. . . . The voice of the lord who created the visions of light and shadow and transformed the bleak, bare set into a painting suffused in a vibrant, magic light."[75] He never touched her while they were shooting, and always spoke to her in German. If other members of the crew wanted to com-

municate something to her, they had to come to him.[76] Dietrich
was keenly observant and unfailingly willing to carry out his
orders without a fuss. She showed him what could and could not
be depicted, and how a woman would act in a given situation. His
name and her look formed an everlasting merger.

In the summer of 1933, von Sternberg was nervously awaiting
her return to Hollywood. When it became clear that she would be
staying on longer, he asked if he could come to her.

MAY I JOIN YOU FOR A COUPLE OF WEEKS IT WOULD BE INEXPRESSIBLE
HAPPINESS FOR ME COULD BE IN PARIS IN TWO WEEKS OR ANYWHERE
IF YOU DON'T WANT IT I WILL DEFER TO YOU AND WORSHIP YOU FROM
AFAR BUT FOR ME IT WOULD BE THE FAIRY TALE I'VE LONGED FOR.[77]

Dietrich did not want to have him in Europe. She already had her
hands full with her husband, lover, daughter, mother, sister, and
nephews. Von Sternberg wooed her with a film project. Hadn't she
always wanted to play Catherine the Great? In mid-July, he was
overjoyed to be able to fulfill her wish. Both Dietrich and Paramount jumped at the prospect. He had succeeded in luring her
back to his set.

Right from the start, there was something immoderate and
imperious about *The Scarlet Empress*. Von Sternberg took charge
of nearly every aspect of this movie; he even composed and conducted parts of the soundtrack. He was not interested in documentary fidelity; the idea was to use a historical model as a springboard
for his artistic fantasy. The rooms in the Kremlin are gloomy and
cluttered with Byzantine ornaments, religious symbols, and hor-
rid figurines. The baroque opulence arouses claustrophobic fears.
These rooms are the stuff of nightmares. They do not have human
dimensions, but rather seem to be made for giants. Candles flicker
everywhere and cast eerie shadows onto the walls. The few lighthearted moments in the movie are set in Germany, Catherine's

birthplace. The child princess, Sophia Frederica, is played by Dietrich's daughter, Maria. In the opening scene, she is lying in bed under a portrait of Frederick the Great. Marlene Dietrich plays the fourteen-year-old princess and the adult Catherine. Not only was she too old for the role of the adolescent, but she was ill-suited to the role of an innocent girl. Princess Sophia's carefree youth comes to an end when the king decrees that she is to marry the Grand Duke of Russia. His envoy, Prince Alexei, escorts Sophia to the impenetrable world of the Kremlin. The tsarina, who speaks and acts like a fishwife, has Sophia checked right there and then to establish whether she is fertile. When Sophia meets her fiancé, she realizes why that is so important: Grand Duke Peter is out of his mind. He loves toy soldiers and executions. Sophia's husband-to-be is a savage simpleton. When she first lays eyes on her bridegroom, pure horror is written all over her face. Sophia's role is to mitigate the insanity that inbreeding has spread through the Russian dynasty. She is being set up to wed an idiot and become a "brood mare." Von Sternberg filmed the wedding ceremony without sound. Catherine is trapped in eerie splendor. The tsarina savors the wedding as a personal triumph, the bridegroom goes through the ceremony with a foolish grin on his face, and the bride is gripped with fear. Catherine's lovely, pale face is hidden behind a veil, and there is a candle in front of her mouth, flickering from her rapid breathing. In just a few more minutes, she will give her hand in marriage to Peter, thus sealing her fate. Catherine realizes what she needs to do when she discovers that the tsarina secretly has lovers brought to her, and soon thereafter, Catherine gets pregnant by a dapper officer and gives birth to the desired successor to the throne.

As the mother of the future tsar, she wields great power. Catherine conquers the army with sex. The officers are at her beck and call; she takes one after the other at random to be her lover. In the end, she wins out over Tsar Peter, who has established a reign of terror after his mother's death. Catherine leads the procession of the soldiers astride a white horse, wearing a white Cossack uniform. Tsar Peter is forcibly removed from office and killed. Tsarina Catherine the Great is exultant as she rings the bells, but her laughter twists her face into a grotesque grimace at the moment of her supreme triumph.

The Scarlet Empress tracks the transformation of a well-behaved young princess from the German countryside into a coldblooded, sex-crazed ruler of a world empire. The court of the Russian tsar was brimming over with debauchery, greed, cruelty, and perversion. Catherine becomes schooled in lies, humiliations, and scheming. Once she has freed herself from her romantic notions of love and Protestant values, she devotes herself to sexual pleasure, picking out her lovers from among the men in uniform. There is no lack of reinforcements; one man is as handsome as the next. Catherine's heart is cold; she has become utterly self-possessed and highhanded. The role of a woman who uses her intelligence and her sexual appeal to control men was tailor-made for Marlene Dietrich.

The costumes for this movie posed a special challenge for Travis Banton. The Catherine that von Sternberg was envisioning could not come across as a historical figure. The costumes had to highlight Dietrich's power, energy, and authority as she played the role of Catherine the Great. Von Sternberg used Catherine's clothing as an outward display of her inner transformation. When she was an innocent young girl, she favored flowing fabrics and frills, but as she sheds her illusions, she begins to wear dresses that hug her body and emphasize her curves. For her triumphal procession, Catherine dons a white uniform with close-fitting slacks; boots; saber; and a high, white fur hat. Sexual, military, and political power come together in her hands. Amy Jolly, X-27, Shanghai Lily, and Helen Faraday were willing to subjugate themselves for the sake of love, but loving Catherine requires submission and sacrifice on the part of men.

Even though this film has several fine scenes, it did not sit well with most critics. When *The Scarlet Empress* opened in May 1934, audiences were going for short, witty films with snappy dialogue. Andrew Sarris summarized the problematic mismatch as follows: "Sternberg was then considered slow, decadent, and self-indulgent, while gloriously ambiguous Marlene Dietrich was judged too rich for the people's blood—it was a time for bread, not cake."[78] *The Scarlet Empress* was most definitely cake.

Von Sternberg knew that their time together was coming to an end. His love of Dietrich was devouring him. As a kind of self-defense in the face of the growing crowd of her lovers, he had begun an affair of his own. Dietrich feared parting ways with him, yet she pressed ahead with doing so. At the same time, she was realizing that she would not be able to return to Europe. She was worried about her husband in Paris.

Dearest Papitsch,

I've finally gotten around to writing to you. Have my first free day—and even this chance is possible only because I have worked at night for the whole week. . . . I look sweet in the movie, very young—as I said, in the movie. In real life, I have the wrinkles on my cheeks that you already discovered once. I'm just getting old. What is Tami doing—is she putting eggs on her face, and who is laughing with her? The Arden mask she got me is quite lovely. Apart from that, there isn't much that can be done. I still need a good cream for the night. I long so terribly to see you and Tami. And you could be of such great help at work. . . . You would have a fabulous and interesting position here. Maybe you'll think it over after all and come here. I never suggested it to you before because of you, so as not to push you into an inadequate position, but now things are different. . . .

Please leave right away if danger is looming. Do me the

favor of buying big suitcases tomorrow so you can throw
everything into them and get out. You know that suitcases
are always in short supply at the last minute. And if you're
trying to take everything with you in a hurry, it can spoil
everything if you don't have suitcases. Please do it. Please,
Tami, help me make sure that he gets everything ready so
that he can leave Paris in a couple of hours if possible—
he'll always find ships. Your things can be packed quickly,
but his papers and books and other things take up a lot of
space. Please, please do it!

I've taken out accident insurance, 600 dollars a year,
premium of 25,000 dollars in case of death, 1,000 dollars
a month for 52 weeks if unable to work. I signed the life
insurance policy on Monday. 100,000 dollars payable to you
upon my death. 200,000 dollars if the death results from an
accident. (But I firmly believe that I will not die in bed.) . . .
I find that it is irresponsible not to be insured. This way our
child will have an inheritance and you will have no worries.
Darling, I miss you so much. Even though you sometimes
gripe, you are the best and truest. I love you, your Mutti.[79]

There was a new tone in this letter. She was feeling old. Almost
shyly, she was making an offer to her husband to work with her
and von Sternberg. This was a sensitive subject, because Sieber felt
inferior to von Sternberg. The passage about the suitcases always
being in short supply while ships are always available is symptom-
atic of Dietrich's life. After she left Berlin, she lived out of suitcases. Her innumerable suitcases, which were perennially en route
between Europe and America, encased her like protective armor.
She never attached much importance to houses, but suitcases were
quite another matter.

Despite her enduring feelings of unhappiness and melancholy,
Dietrich was voracious in her quest for love affairs. At a Harald

Kreutzberg dance performance in September 1932, she had met Mercedes de Acosta. De Acosta was trying her hand at screenwriting, and all of Hollywood was whispering about her relationship with Greta Garbo. But Garbo had gone off to Europe and had left the "White Prince," as de Acosta liked to call herself, alone in America. The initiative for the affair supposedly came from Dietrich, who is said to have positively besieged de Acosta.[80] On September 16, Dietrich and de Acosta spent their first night together, as we gather from a letter from de Acosta two months later: "On the 16th of this month it will be eight small weeks since that holy and flaming night that you gave yourself to me." De Acosta's letters show that she was an utterly unhappy, lonely woman desperate for attention. She was one of the many unsuccessful and penniless screenwriters in Hollywood. Time and again, Dietrich lent her large sums of money, for which she expressed her gratitude in florid prose: "Always I remember the beauty of your gesture in giving me this money."[81] Often she could pay back only a fraction of the money, or nothing at all. De Acosta advised Dietrich never to ask anyone for money. The rule of the film business was to appear indifferent and rich. De Acosta's letters to Dietrich were one long affirmation of her love, yet all she could come up with was hackneyed pathos. As for Dietrich, the idea of sharing a lover with Garbo might have been intriguing.[82] Supposedly the two of them never met, but their lives intersected again and again. Mamoulian shot his next film after *Song of Songs* with Garbo. In *Queen Christine*, Garbo was a Swedish queen, while Dietrich was playing Catherine the Great at virtually the same time. De Acosta's penchant for Hollywood gossip was her undoing. Dietrich felt betrayed by her and ended the relationship. Her farewell letter to de Acosta speaks volumes.

> In which manner Mr. von Sternberg treats me on the set
> is nobodys affair and to tell Twardowski about the signing
> or not signing up of an actor because I liked him is too

much. . . . I understand that you are alone and have the desire to talk to someone—please leave me out of these conversations. Excuse my English and the mistakes; I must go to the studio and am in a hurry. Marlene[83]

Dietrich then embarked on an affair with her colleague Brian Aherne, whom she had met during the filming of *Song of Songs*. Aherne was a British theater actor who had been working in Holly-wood since 1930. Perhaps she shifted her homesickness for Europe from France to England, and replaced Chevalier with Aherne. Aherne's letters provide a glimpse into the quintessential course of a love affair with Dietrich. At first he was overwhelmed by the fact that this beautiful woman had chosen him to be her lover and felt a bit haughty toward his predecessors. Aherne sent poetic let-ters embellished with quotations from Shakespeare. He liked to write while sitting in his dressing room at the theater waiting to go onstage. He was surrounded by things she had sent him: an ashtray, pajamas, a cigarette case, and even a hairbrush. There would appear to be a strategy at work here. She gave generous gifts to all her lovers. At first they were delighted, but when all that remained of the affair were the gifts themselves and Dietrich no longer showed her face, these objects of memory became a source of torment. Aherne was no exception. He started in on the usual litany of complaints about her failure to contact him, declaring that he was eager to follow her anywhere—if he only knew where she was. She did not reply. His notes to her took on a tone of despera-tion, and his only consolation lay in picturing the times they had spent together. When he spoke to her on the telephone, her voice was cold and unfeeling. He wrote: "Do you think, Dietrich, that you might manage one day to say something nice to me on the telephone?"[84] Jealousy and doubts welled up in him, even as he tried to convince himself that he ought to be happy about what he had shared with her. Aherne wrote letters of the sort Dietrich had read many times before. He was sitting in some hotel room feeling lonesome, tired, and unhappy, with only one wish, namely to take her in his arms and make love to her. Eventually he started to find his own letters and declarations of love tedious. In any case, Dietrich turned a deaf ear to his pleas, and Aherne despised himself for his love and desire. She covered up the fact that her love had faded by soothing him with a home-baked cake and shopping for him when he was shooting his next film in Hollywood, but she made herself scarce when he wanted to eat with her.

While Dietrich was in Europe, Aherne came over to shoot a film in Austria. He had accepted this offer only because they had made plans to meet in Munich or Salzburg. Now he was stuck in a remote Tyrolean village. The rain never let up, the food was inedible, the evening entertainment was limited to folk dancing, and he spent his nights freezing under a heavy blanket. Clinging to his faith in her, he sent her ardent love letters, and when she did not reply, he called her up and found out that she had gone to Salzburg. He felt betrayed. Shortly before he left Tyrol, she sent him a startling telegram stating that they would not be able to get together at all because she was on her way to Vienna, and on September 20, she would be heading back to the United States. "I have never in my whole life been so willfully hurt," he wrote.[85] Aherne was forced to realize that Dietrich had already plunged into her next love affair, and he had been shunted aside. She scanned his letters and telegrams only for compliments and declarations of love; nothing else interested her.

In late October 1933, Rudi Sieber supplied facts and figures to show her that it was not worth keeping the apartment in Berlin until the lease ran out in 1936. He wanted to close up the apartment once and for all and store their furniture with Josefine von Losch. Dietrich found it difficult to warm up to this idea. She was homesick: "I'm very unhappy, full of longing. . . . You have to come if I can't travel after this movie. Frankly, I'm horrified at the thought of packing up again and dragging the whole cavalcade across the ocean. We could get together in New York. . . . Or doesn't Tami feel like doing that? Kisses kisses kisses always, Your adoring Mutti."[86]

Although Dietrich was blessed with lovers, sunshine, and luxuries of every kind, she was unhappy. All the back and forth between Europe and America was taking a toll on her. A brittle, faded letter from Sieber to the state authority in Prague, dated November 30, 1933, indicates that the Siebers were attempting to apply for Czech citizenship. Sieber cited his merits on behalf of the country in World War I and asserted that he and his wife had taken on German citizenship against their will.

> My wife is acting in Hollywood under her stage name,
> Marlene Dietrich . . . and has not gone back to Berlin
> since March 31, 1930 apart from a brief vacation in 1931.
> Likewise, I have not been in Berlin at all since 1931, but
> instead have been steadily employed in Paris as an executive
> producer at Paramount and as of April 1931 I gave up my
> residency in Berlin permanently.

He affirmed that they intended to transfer their assets and settle down in the town of Aussig, although it may be hard to picture Dietrich leaving Hollywood to live there with her husband and their child. Once the fees were due and they were required to disclose their finances, the Siebers withdrew their application.[87] As is evident here and elsewhere, their lack of money was a central theme of their relationship. Even though they had given up their apartment in Berlin, two households still had to be maintained. Sieber hesitated to come to America because Tamara had only a Nansen passport that was issued to stateless individuals. The question was whether she would be able to get a visa for the United States. "Of course it would interest me to work with you in a position that is worthy of you, or of me as 'Herr Dietrich.' But how do we solve the problem of 'Tami'?"[88]

The last movie Dietrich made with von Sternberg was *The Devil is a Woman*. Von Sternberg gave her no directives, yet she put in a brilliant performance. She first appeared on screen as a veiled beauty in a horse-driven carriage on the occasion of the Carnival celebrations. Dietrich did not know what von Sternberg had in mind until she was already standing in the carriage. Balloons were covering her face. Then he shot at the balloons with an air gun. "When the scene began, I took aim and exploded the concealing balloons to reveal one of the most fearless and charming countenances in the history of films. Not a quiver of an eyelash, nor the slightest twitch in the wide gleaming smile was recorded by the camera at a time when anyone other than this extraordinary woman would have trembled in fear."[89] One last time, he would assert his power on the set over the woman he loved. He was quite sure that she would not bat an eyelash when he shot the pellets. As the daughter of a Prussian soldier, she was able to weather sadistic attacks of this kind. Right down to the end, she let him be her creator. Making up at home was just as much a part of this game as humiliation in front of everyone else. After his death, she admitted that she had suffered under him. "Before I finish this chapter, I would like still to mention what I feared most in him: his contempt. A shocking experience. Several times during the day, he would send me back to my dressing room so that I could cry in peace. After talking to me in German, he would turn to the technicians and say: 'Smoking break. Miss Dietrich is having one of her crying fits.'"[90] When he scorned her, she was seized with panic that he would send her back where he had found her. Dietrich believed that she could not act without the safeguard of von Sternberg's genius.

The movie was based on the book *La Femme et le pantin* (*The Woman and the Puppet*) by Pierre Louys; John Dos Passos helped develop the screenplay. Dietrich played Concha Perez, who, like Bizet's Carmen, works in a cigarette factory, where an older, high-ranking officer named Don Pasqual takes an interest in her. Concha is out to destroy him. He squanders his fortune on her and has to give up his military career, all for a woman who no longer even lets him kiss her and is openly cheating on him. *The Devil is a Woman* is set during Carnival. Confetti, masks, costumes, balls, and streamers form the background of the movie. Everyone is in high spirits, and everything seems permissible. But death can lurk behind any mask. The only one who seems to fear neither death nor devil is Concha. Dietrich pulls out all the stops: she sweet-talks, pouts, offends, beguiles, triumphs, lies, seduces, deceives, and savors the power of a woman. Draped in fine lace, caressed by light and shadows, she waits like a spider for men to enter her web. Her wide-brimmed hats and high mantillas make every man— even those in uniform or masks—appear small next to her. In this movie, Dietrich sings a seductive little song yet barely shows her legs, and seems to be brimming with energy. She often strikes her signature pose with arms akimbo, looking daggers at everybody and upstaging them all.

In April 1934, she wrote to her friend Max Kolpé in Paris that she fell quite ill after the filming of *Scarlet Empress* was completed:

> This movie was the hardest thing we ever made. I don't
> know if I'm any good—I don't think so. I'm not bad either,
> but insignificant, it seems to me. Sternberg was a pure
> genius once again. . . . Maybe because it's the spring over
> there, but all of a sudden I'm longing for Berlin. Here, in the
> everlasting summer, I really miss that. I think back to late
> afternoons in a car with the top down (down for the first
> time that season), heading along the Kurfürstendamm, and,
> for no apparent reason, a chuckle in my throat. Perhaps it
> was because we were young and at home. I am fighting so

hard against feeling dead here and against feeling dead in general, against the hollow feeling inside. I keep giving, and I get nothing in return. The child is all grown up now. Please do write to me Marlene.[91]

There she was, sitting in her villa in Hollywood with a swimming pool, everlasting sunshine, and a Rolls Royce, and she was longing for a spring drive on the Kurfürstendamm. She recalls the "chuckle in my throat" that welled up "for no apparent reason." That kind of thing had not happened for quite some time, because in Hollywood nothing comes about inadvertently. Once the final movie with Jo had been shot, Dietrich felt as though she had no home. She was feeling her youth slipping away at the age of thirty-three. She could not complain about a lack of lovers, but she *was* afraid of what the future held. And now she had to cope with the end of her work with Jo. The hollow feeling inside came back, a feeling that Jo had been able to assuage every now and then. To whom could she confide her doubts about her talent once Jo was gone? Dietrich was enough of a professional to know that their relationship had reached an impasse. As a lover, he became more and more draining, and in the film industry he was no longer considered a bigwig after a series of flops. The critics wrote that he had made her a "Paramount whore." She needed to leave him in order to advance her career, and he gave the artist Marlene Dietrich back to the larger world of film. Directors were already lining up to show the world what fabulous movies they could make with her. With *The Devil is a Woman*, von Sternberg was intent on paying a final tribute to the woman he loved and the artist he had created, and she declared that this was her favorite film. On May 3, 1935, their last motion picture together premiered in New York. From then on, their cinematic partnership was history.

Dietrich could always be sure of von Sternberg. Time and again he took her back, no matter whom she thought she loved at the time. Now that she was over thirty, she was forced to see love in a new light, not the way she had back in Berlin when she was in her twenties. Even a woman like Dietrich could not get around the fact that a list of things she had not achieved and might never achieve was taking clear shape. Von Sternberg, who loved her, had shielded her from ideas of this kind. When she was an old woman—long after von Sternberg had died—she took the blame upon herself for what had gone wrong. Von Sternberg would love Dietrich for the rest of his life. A smile still lit up his otherwise serious face when he saw Lola Lola on the screen during a 1961 interview. When Peter Bogdanovich met with von Sternberg in his later years, he sensed the latter's deep sorrow and pain about the love he had lost.[92] Von Sternberg was extremely reluctant to discuss his films with Bogdanovich because doing so touched on the most sensitive spot of his emotional life, namely his unrequited love for Dietrich. His movies were his way of wooing her. He offered her his artistic services, and demanded unconditional compliance in return. For him, training went hand in hand with discipline, and Dietrich, the daughter of a Prussian soldier, understood that. "It was not my beauty or charm that fascinated him, but rather my peculiar capacity for discipline, which is almost unheard of among actresses, that attracted him to me."[93] She would love him in her way, but he was head over heels in love with her. In 1935, he parted ways with his divine "Miss Dietrich."

Dietrich worked under subsequent directors with the disdain of someone who is accustomed to better. And once she was gone, von Sternberg was no longer capable of effecting transformations. They would both experience phantom pain for the rest of their lives.

o   o   o

"A slight man with one of those obligatory cashmere polo coats, complete with trailing belt. He was sharp, quick-witted, with a sense of humor and New York savvy."[94] This was Maria Riva's description of

Harry Edington, Dietrich's right-hand man. As her agent, he saw to all the details: the story, the director, the pay, the cameraman, the dressing room—and in a matter that had now become essential, he made sure that her partner was not too young. He dealt with her landladies and made it his business to find her good house-keepers, rooms in hotels, and secretaries. He took care of every matter, large and small, right down to which dresses, capes, and trousers would be arriving on which ship. He discreetly steered her away from movie magazines to which she would be better off not granting interviews and told her what fees were appropriate for what tasks. On top of that, he made every effort to ensure her well-being and sent her telegraphs with invitations to games of ten-nis or dinners. Edington, who also represented Greta Garbo, was regarded in Hollywood as one of the agents who had free access to the studio bosses. For Dietrich's next film, *Desire*, he negotiated a fee of two hundred thousand dollars. Frank Borzage was the direc-tor, and Ernst Lubitsch oversaw the artistic direction. By working with Lubitsch, Dietrich was in a sense returning to Berlin, yet at the same time the opportunity to work with Lubitsch meant that she had truly arrived in America. Lubitsch was born on Schönhauser Strasse in Berlin and began his career at the Deutsches Theater; now he was a Hollywood hot shot, and the Americans loved his sophisticated comedies.

In *Desire*, Dietrich played the jewel thief Madeleine de Beaupré, who steals a pearl necklace in Paris and plants it on an American auto mechanic, Tom Bradley, at the Spanish border. Bradley unwit-tingly brings the stolen goods through customs. To get the pearls back, Madeleine has to resort to all kinds of tricks, but love foils her plan when she falls for the American. The cunning jewel thief becomes an honest wife. Von Sternberg was sure to have sneered at this shallow story. Dietrich was not a sphinx, but a beautiful con artist whom love brings back onto the straight and narrow path of virtue. *Desire* is set in the glamorous world of luxury hotels, grand suites, and champagne glasses. Somehow one feels reminded of Dietrich's old silent films, although these could not begin to compete with *Desire* in décor, spirit, and humor. *Desire* is light and witty entertainment—nice to watch, but lacking in depth. As von Sternberg had predicted, the critics were pleased to find that at long last, Dietrich had departed drastically from her usual style. Her costumes were no longer supercilious, erotic, and fantasy-filled, as they had been in von Sternberg's films. Madeleine de Beaupré is an elegantly dressed woman who wears double-breasted jackets and white, medium-length skirts, yet she also dons extravagant hats and dazzling evening gowns.

The Wall Street Crash of 1929 had had a profound impact on the fashion industry. Couturiers clothed their famous clients free of charge in the hope of getting a publicity boost. These influential clients were not just aristocratic women and artists' muses; most of them were actresses. In 1934, Dietrich became known as "the most imitated woman in the world." Her function as a role model in the world of fashion has continued to this day. In 1935, she was one of the leading ladies in the film *The Fashion Side of Hollywood*. Now that she had been freed from von Sternberg's influence, she no longer had to traipse about on railway platforms in exotic countries wearing evening gowns, but could also appear in fashionable contemporary sports blouses and blazers. Dietrich was highly critical of her old roles and von Sternberg's way of portraying her at arm's length. "Mr. von Sternberg never let me play love scenes—not ordinary ones, I mean, with hugging and all that, because he hates ordinary love scenes."[95] Since he was no longer there, she re-established a bond with her audiences, as evidenced in the photographs that were now circulated about her personal life.

One famous series of photographs taken by Eugene Richee in 1935 provides an uncommonly candid view of Marlene Dietrich. Dressed in a buttoned-up white blouse, white shorts, and white high-heeled shoes, she is stretched out on a lounge chair at the pool.

Basking in the sun, her laugh showing her full red lips, she is the very picture of the attractive sporty woman. She had now become part of the Hollywood society that von Sternberg disdained. Dietrich no longer sat at home and cooked while Jo worked his way through stacks of screenplays; she put in a cheerful appearance at parties, ceremonies, and premieres. Photographers from the publicity department were always on hand. A letter from Willi Forst reveals that she started to drink at this time in order to fall asleep at night.[96] Although she was relieved about not having to work with Jo anymore, once they separated, she realized the extent to which he had smoothed things over for her.

Dietrich never felt truly comfortable in Hollywood, but in public she was able to act as though there was nothing more beautiful than life in America. In this respect, she had a special position among the Germans. By the mid- and late 1930s, and into the 1940s, many German artists such as Thomas Mann, Vicki Baum, Arnold Schönberg, Peter Lorre, Franz Wachsmann, and Friedrich Hollaender were living in California, having sought refuge from Hitler. The Americans took note of the Germans' presence in a friendly but indifferent manner, soon coming to refer to them as the "Beiunskis" because their demeanor, language, and art appeared to be guided by the phrase *bei uns* ("back where we come from"), which the Americans considered egocentric. These exiles were still quite proud of German tradition and German culture, and that was something that held little interest for the Americans, least of all for the Americans who wanted to live in Hollywood and earn their living by making films. This was a painful experience for many. Dietrich generally kept her distance from the tightly knit and narrow-minded exile circles in Hollywood, though from time to time, she dropped in on Salka Viertel's salon in Santa Monica. She knew that cultural or political arrogance would not bolster her career. She was an outsider among the outsiders. Dietrich was a German Protestant artist who happened to wind up in the United States in order to work there. Assimilation was not a problem for her. It was her profession to be an actress, and she could be seen in both good and bad movies. She did not actually enjoy life in Los Angeles. Although she got offers to work in Germany, she felt that the only decent option was to reject them. She had no intention of working with the National Socialists, and so she stayed in the desert, where a person could not put down roots.

Los Angeles is a city that has always attracted foreigners. Every resident is an emigrant from somewhere in the world, yet the diversity of backgrounds is undercut by the monotonous sameness of the living conditions. Southern California, with its mild climate, wide horizon, and virtually boundless spaces, developed into a mecca for talented architects, urban planners, and designers who came to make Los Angeles a city of the future. The city was largely spared from the economic depression and was the place in which the American dream was still center stage, unfazed by the woes everywhere else. The sun shone for everyone. Here there was the money, the optimism, and the space to build a new world. Wilshire Boulevard, which extended from the Pacific Ocean into the city, created a link between nature and culture. The stars cruised from their beach houses to the film studios in their sleek automobiles. This was the modernity that made southern California the envy of the world. One needed a car and a telephone to survive in this city. Anyone who was not mobile did not belong.[97] This was where the modern architectural designs were perfected for consumer-oriented modernity on the move. Supermarkets, motels, urban highways, gas stations, shopping centers, and drive-ins came to be defining features of the middle class throughout the world, with bank withdrawals, purchases, breakups, and hellos and goodbyes handled by rolling down car windows. Business and everyday transactions were conducted matter-of-factly and with impersonal friendliness. Everyone was on his or her own. Los Angeles was an avaricious city that was all about winners. The climate could drive you crazy, Hannah Arendt claimed, and even people who were reminded of Italy would be hard pressed to find the beautiful soul of this city. What mattered here were roles and earnings; everything else was relegated to the sidelines. Party lists were put together according to box-office success. All too easily, people were erased from these lists and waited for invitations in vain.

Eventually Dietrich came to accept the fact that she would have to remain in Hollywood and tried to make the best of it. She had been accustomed to spontaneous get-togethers back in Berlin, and she enjoyed going to the farmer's market that opened in Hollywood in 1934. It was laid out in the American colonial style, like a farm in the Midwest. There were stands that sold fruit, meat, vegetables, and fish, along with concession booths that had their own tables and chairs. Something was always going on here—people were shopping, haggling, talking, gossiping, drinking, and eating. She liked this rather European type of public space. A person could drop in on a casual basis and meet up with people without advanced planning or invitations. Dietrich also greatly enjoyed riding out to an amusement park in Ocean Park, Santa Monica, perhaps because all the hustle and bustle reminded her of her life in Berlin.[98]

In November 1932, Franklin Delano Roosevelt was elected the thirty-second president of the United States. His message of making the "forgotten man" the central theme of his campaign proved to be a winning strategy. For the past fifteen years, the country had undergone a process of profound change: The entry of the United States into World War I had made the country a world power overnight. For the first time in the history of this country, some two million young men were being sent to a continent far away to wage war. After the dreadful years of the war and the Great Depression, Americans in the early 1930s were receptive to a politician who gave them cause for optimism. Roosevelt's inaugural address found just the right words for the country's state of mind. "The only thing we have to fear is fear itself." This statement was the new credo that Americans had been waiting for.

In contrast to the grim, inscrutable dictators in Europe and the Soviet Union, Roosevelt made no secret of his love of life. The dictators stayed in the background for quite some time. America was preoccupied with its own issues. Roosevelt won the presidential election of 1936 by an overwhelming majority. This success certainly rested in large measure on his promise not to lead the United States into war. Americans did not want to be embroiled in the conflicts of others yet again. This was especially true of people in the film industry in Hollywood, who wanted to earn their money in peace. Adolph Zukor, head of Paramount Pictures, declared: "I don't think that Hollywood should deal with anything but entertainment. The newsreels take care of current events. To make films of political significance is a mistake. When they go to a theatre they want to forget."[99] In the 1930s, Hollywood was a world power. Nothing could make a bigger mockery of the dead seriousness of the dictators than the flippant refinement of Hollywood.

Dietrich chose to live in exile on her own. She remained in Hollywood. In letters, telephone calls, and telegrams, she kept up with what was going on in Berlin, Vienna, and Paris, but the extant correspondence barely mentioned the political situation. Personal issues and needs were front and center, as usual. She preferred to turn to her mother when she had medical questions. Dietrich suffered from the delusion that she was too fat, and her daughter too tall. There was no medical remedy for either of these conditions, but Josefine von Losch went ahead and asked Dr. Salomon in Berlin for advice, and telegraphed his reply to her daughter in Hollywood. Josefine was now so thrilled with her daughter's acting prowess that she even copied out movie reviews and dispensed advice. She asked: "How satisfied are you with your staff? Are class distinctions emphasized or is everything peaceful?"[100] Her tone was affectionate, and she often reminded Dietrich of little sayings and ditties from her childhood. Aunt Jolly, whom Josefine had never liked and who had now taken off with Ernst Udet, was making life difficult for her. She poured out her heart to her younger daughter about the hardships the merry widow was causing for her. Josefine devoted herself to firming up her daughter's reputation in Germany. SEND ME CABLE PROVING THAT YOU ARE NOT COMMITTED MENTAL INSTITUTION AS TRI-BUNE HEADLINE SCREAMS HAVE TO DENY IGNORE RUMORS WRONG ATTITUDE ABOUT TIME YOU TAKE MY ADVICE MUTTI.[101] There is no mention of her wanting to leave Germany and come to America. Quite the oppo-site: Josefine hoped that her daughter would return to Europe after parting with von Sternberg, whom the family liked to call "Etoile." In August 1935, she wrote her a letter in which she expressed regret about her daughter's decision to remain in America. She thought it was terrible to live only for money, devoid of any joy and pleasure, the way Dietrich was living.

> Everything that happened with Etoile, his hapless, divorced
> wife, everything? Everything took its toll in time and
> nerves. . . . Here it was said a thousand times that if Mar-
> lene Dietrich only didn't have that bizarre, eccentric Etoile
> anymore. . . . You are in any case to be pitied from the
> bottom of my soul. *'Landgraf werde hart.'* [Landgrave, grow
> hard.] I have a thousand worries that you will only be dis-
> appointed once again and you will eat up your disappoint-
> ments slowly like tasty tidbits instead of getting a whiff of
> them beforehand and avoiding them in the first place. Poor,
> dear Lena; it's too bad that there is an ocean between us.[102]

This letter reveals a side of Dietrich that she tried to conceal from the public. Her mother characterized her as someone with a pen-chant for suffering, someone who gobbles up disappointments like tasty tidbits and makes no attempt to steer clear of them. In November 1936, Dietrich was terrified at the thought that she might have gotten this penchant from her father. Her mother tried to calm her down and reassure her. She urged her daughter to leave aside her brooding once and for all and to enjoy life.

Rudolf Sieber continued to live in Paris, but visited his wife from time to time. On these occasions the whole family gathered in Coconut Grove. Dietrich, wearing a big hat, a well-chosen array of jewelry, and an elegant evening gown, was easy to identify as the most important person at the table. The others were mere accessories. Sieber looked startlingly young in his tuxedo and had his beautiful lover Tamara at his side, who followed everything that was going on around her with wide eyes. Maria sat between her parents. She was a bright, well-behaved girl, and spent a lot of evenings with her parents and their lovers in fine restaurants. To redress the gender imbalance, Fritz Lang or von Sternberg would be asked to join the group on occasion.

In January 1935, Dietrich welcomed Elisabeth Bergner to the United States. *Catherine the Great* and *The Scarlet Empress* coexisted peacefully. The friendship between Bergner and Dietrich served to boost the success of the films, then blossomed into a love affair. Dietrich was Bergner's "sweet lover" and "Circe." Bergner was spirited and tender, while Dietrich was cold and restrained. Their affair must have been passionate, though it was a well-kept secret. In April 1935, Bergner sent Dietrich this cable to Hollywood: I EAT YOU I SMELL YOU I GREASE YOU POWDER OIL RUB OINTMENT ON YOU AND WHAT I HAVE FORGOTTEN IS KNOWN TO ME ALONE LISL.[103]

After parting ways with von Sternberg, Dietrich proceeded to make money rather than art. The truly remarkable part of her next movie, *The Garden of Allah*, was the fact that she was able to earn two hundred thousand dollars and be filmed in Technicolor for the first time. The movie would not be a good one, but the large sum of money was enticing, and she had no real alternative. She devoted her energy not to her acting but to making herself look good. There was constant bickering about the lighting, the costumes, and her need for impeccable hairdos. Part of the movie was shot in the Yuma Desert, under trying conditions. Everyone was sweating, and toupées were slipping out of place, but Dietrich was "as dry as toast," as her daughter wrote.[104] The colors in the movie were beguiling, and the stills of Dietrich in a chiffon robe in the desert wind were seductive, but the movie itself was unbearable. "The great abstractions come whistling hoarsely out in Miss Dietrich's stylized, weary, and monotonous whisper, among the hideous Technicolor flowers, the yellow cratered desert like Gruyère cheese, the beige faces."[105] No sooner was the shooting over in July 1936 than Dietrich packed her bags and traveled to London for her next film. This time, she had been loaned to Alexander Korda for a movie that would pay her $450,000, a romantic drama set in the period of the Russian Revolution and directed by Jacques Feyder. As with every other director after von Sternberg, she had difficulty working with Feyder. Dietrich staunchly defended her vision of how she needed to appear. When things got especially bad, she whispered into the microphone, "Jo, where are you?" Feyder complained that everything had to be tailor-made to her specifications. The only reality that she was prepared to accept was a beautiful image of herself. If she had got it into her head that she wanted to wear an evening gown while working in the fields, the screenplay would simply have to be changed. *Knight Without Armour* is better than its reputation. Dietrich played Countess Alexandra as a proud and courageous woman. One morning she wakes up and rings for her servants, but none of them responds. Wearing a white chiffon coat, she comes upon rebelling peasants and servants in the park, destroying paintings and furniture and looting the castle. In the course of the plot, she has to struggle along between the lines of the White and Red armies. Both the Whites and the Reds have power-hungry and brutal men, but there are also sensitive and smart ones. The film was not successful, but Dietrich's fee was so substantial that its reception was not terribly important to her.

Her mother and sister kept her informed about her sustained popularity in Germany. *The Scarlet Empress* was the hit of the year in 1934 in Berlin; *The Devil is a Woman* was also shown and *Desire* ran in theaters until mid-January 1939. Dietrich's portrait was featured on magazine covers, and attempts to vilify her as a "non-German" failed at first.[106] Even propaganda minister Joseph Goebbels preferred Dietrich's femme fatale to the pasty faces of the new era. "Then with Hitler. 'Shanghai Express.' Marlene Dietrich is talented."[107] He regretted the fact that she was no longer working in Germany.[108] Horst Alexander von der Heyde, the production manager at Tobis Cinema, flew to London in 1936 at Christmastime to meet with Dietrich. Her mother had assured him that she would see him. He did not come empty-handed; he brought her a Christmas tree from Berlin and two official letters. The Reich Ministry of Public Enlightenment and Propaganda affirmed "that from this point on, publications by the German press that are detrimental to the reputation of Frau Dietrich will no longer be printed."[109] The propaganda ministry urged that negotiations with Dietrich be taken up for a movie in a German and English or French version. Dietrich was assured she would get every possible accommodation from the top German administrators for matters pertaining to direction, themes, screenplays, exchange rates, tax issues, acting fees, and personal amenities. Von der Heyde sat alone in his London hotel room under the Christmas tree from Berlin and waited in vain. Dietrich did not contact him.

She had found a new lover in London. Douglas Fairbanks, Jr., the twenty-six-year-old son of the great actor Douglas Fairbanks, was divorced from Joan Crawford. He was a rich American who was generous with his money. He made her a present of a gold cigarette case studded with diamonds and sapphires. Fairbanks was not as poetic as von Sternberg; the engraving he chose was a simple *Duschka* (darling).

On one of her many trips to Europe, Dietrich had bought a 16-millimeter camera and enjoyed making home movies or being filmed off the set. She often brought her camera to work and filmed the crew, but most of her pictures were of her family, friends, and colleagues. Of the twenty-eight minutes of Dietrich's home movie material that have been released, a good many are devoted to Fairbanks. Dietrich and Fairbanks did not act like two American film stars, but like a British upper-class couple. They liked to put in appearances at the race track. During a boat ride on the Thames, a beaming Douglas sat with a pensive Dietrich, and in a second boat sat an awkward Rudi Sieber, his daughter at his side. Dietrich, quite pale, with lips painted bright red and a high-necked pullover, looked like a lady. In a rare harmonious scene, we see Dietrich lying on a ship, the sleeping Douglas on her lap. She is dressed all in white, her outfit forming a nice contrast to the blue water, and she has placed a hand on his shoulder as though to protect him.

In the summer of 1937, Fairbanks traveled with her to Arlberg, Austria. Sieber and Tamara Matul came with them. A photograph shows Fairbanks standing in front of the train with a Tyrolean hat, with Dietrich, Sieber, and Matul approaching on the railway platform, all four dressed in the traditional garb of their travel destination. The women are wearing crocheted jackets that are fitted at the waist; Dietrich is in white, and Matul in black. Fairbanks took pictures of them in short lederhosen in front of their vacation cottage. He is lying in the grass, playing with a blade of grass between his lips, his white shirt unbuttoned. He is a handsome, strong, suntanned man with a distinctive face who looks like the embodiment of temptation. Dietrich is clearly impressed.

Just a few days after Fairbanks left Austria, Dietrich went to Venice to see von Sternberg. Since their split, he had sought solace in travel and collecting works of art. In 1935, the Los Angeles County

Museum dedicated an exhibit to his art collection, which included works by Egon Schiele, Vincent van Gogh, Aristide Maillol, Oskar Kokoschka, Karl Schmidt-Rottluff, Auguste Rodin, Rudolf Belling, Constantin Brancusi, Georg Kolbe, Alexander Archipenko, and Picasso's *La Gameuse* as the highlight. In the same year, von Sternberg had a house built. The architect was Richard Neutra, who was also born in Vienna. Neutra was regarded as the radical modernist. The house was a fortress of solitude. The structure was elegant and elongated, and the building was surrounded by a castle moat filled with water. The outer walls were covered with aluminum. The rooms were bathed in light, and in front of the house, an American flag waved in the desert wind. This is where von Sternberg safeguarded the treasures of his past and yearned for Dietrich. She did not like his new house. Avant-garde solitude was not her style. A single visit to inspect the place was quite enough for her. Von Sternberg did not hold out for long in San Fernando Valley.[110] He had intended to make this desert castle a refuge from Dietrich, but he was not far enough away from what he wanted to leave behind him.

So he set out on a trip around the world. While Dietrich was staying at Claridge's in London, enjoying her love affair with Fairbanks, she received cards full of longing from Jo in Asia. She got a postcard from the temple at Angkor Wat. In the jungles of Cambodia, he lit a candle for her. He visited the gods and wrote to his goddess. In the fall of 1936, he wrote her one of his last long love letters from the Great Wall of China. He had been to Korea, Japan, China, and Manchuria, yet the letter conveys the impression that all he had found anywhere was Marlene: "Shanghai Lily was often sitting next to me." He was still struggling with the end of their romance. "Every now and then, I'll let you know where I'm staying, so that you can send me a telegram every now and then. You still write lovely words, but unfortunately not only to me." He was uncertain about whether he would ever make another motion picture. "Get some nice work done and give me a treat—and if you often think of me, I'll know it, and the place in my heart where I have tucked you away will glow, Jo."[111] In the summer of 1937, he was in Europe preparing for a new movie. Dietrich had been filming *Angel* with Lubitsch in Hollywood until June and had no other contract lined up. In recent times, she may have paid too much attention to the fee she was offered and too little to the quality. Getting together with her creator, and in Venice at that, would draw the press's attention to her.

During September of 1937, von Sternberg's heart was not likely to have glowed very often. "A great deal happened to us in September—the Lido with the boats along the horizon in the evening like butterflies," Erich Maria Remarque wrote to Dietrich after the end of their love affair. She would be his "autumn love."[112] It was not the first time that their paths had crossed. In 1930 in Berlin, they had met in the bar of the Eden Hotel. Remarque recalled the vision of the young Dietrich in a light gray suit with her even shoulders, which he loved so dearly. Back then, in Berlin, he claims already to have known that she would be staying in his life. In the hotel bar, he ought to have risen from his chair, gone up to her, and said: "Come away with me—why stay here?"[113] But he backed away instead. For seven years, he sought refuge "in indifference and adventures, in ruination and dissipation, in the vapid freedom of the witless."[114] Venice brought them together again. We do not know whether Dietrich recalled this meeting in Berlin when she saw Remarque in Venice; she was probably just attracted to this elegant, good-looking, successful, and well-to-do man. Although Remarque was charming and amiable, she sensed his shy reserve and regarded it as a challenge to break through it. In her memoirs, she told of having met up with him again the following day on the beach with a volume of Rilke poems under her arm, which impressed him. He commented sarcastically: "I see you read good authors." She replied: "Shall I recite a few poems to you?"[115] Decades later, however, she described their encounter somewhat differently in a telephone conversation with her friend Johannes Mario Simmel: "On the way to the hotel, he said: 'By the way, just to clarify things right away so there are no silly discussions later: I am totally impotent . . . but, at your request, I can of course be quite an enchanting little lesbienne.' Marlene: 'God, was I relieved! God, did I love that man.'"[116] His impotence was only temporary, and she kept on loving him nevertheless.

Of all of Dietrich's many lovers, Remarque was most similar to her in nature. Remarque, a soldier and teacher from Osnabrück with a penchant for writing, had come to Berlin in 1925 as an editor of a sports newspaper. He was a dapper dresser, and his colleagues regarded him as a stuffed shirt. He had no political affiliations. In 1927, he wrote *All Quiet on the Western Front*, an antiwar novel that became the most successful German-language book of the twentieth century and brought him fame and fortune overnight. Regarded with hostility in Germany, he left the country and led a nomadic life that his newfound wealth made possible. Remarque became an art collector and a wine connoisseur, and lived in luxury hotels. As was the case with Dietrich, this early departure from Germany gave him a cosmopolitan outlook tinged with a vague sense of homesickness. Both had nagging doubts about their own talent and were tormented by thoughts of failing as artists. Remarque, like Dietrich, would not return to Germany. He bought himself a villa outside of Ascona in Switzerland, right on Lake Maggiore. In the 1930s, he spent lengthy periods of time in his lakeside house far away from people and cities with his dogs, his pictures, and his books. His neighbor, Emil Ludwig, commented that Remarque cultivated a life of solitude, enlivened by women and cocktails. He could spend his nights on bar stools for months on end, listening to other people's confessions, then head to a dive to pick up a streetwalker and bring her to his room. Remarque was considered an *homme à femmes*; he loved women, and they loved him. He tended to fall for slender, aloof, beautiful women like Dietrich.

In September 1937, Dietrich and Remarque became lovers in Venice. Since neither of them had to answer to anyone else, they spent the months up until her November 10 departure at Hotel Lancaster in Paris. Their romance centered on hotels. Remarque kept hoping that she would visit him at his house on the lake, which he talked up with such pride, but she never did.[117] Dietrich would never row across the lake with him, never drink an aperitif in the small bars he frequented, and never walk with the dogs. She was not interested in his garden or the village life in the south, and she had no intention of sharing his solitude. Anyone who wanted to be with her would have to adapt to her lifestyle. In her own capricious way, though, Dietrich loved this man with "his ever-skeptical eyes," and was touched by his vulnerability and almost pathological melancholia.

The letters that he wrote to her over the following months reveal how they fared during their first autumn in Paris. He spent the nights in his house in Porto Ronco longing for his lover.

> It is nighttime, and I'm writing for you to call from New
> York. The dogs are sleeping around me, and the gramo-
> phone is playing—records that I found—easy to love—I got
> you under my skin awake from a dream . . . but it's daytime
> where you are, the lights in the streets are just going on,
> you're standing in your room, someone will go out with you
> to eat, to go to the theater, and the evening gowns are lying
> on the bed and you don't know whether to wear the white
> one with the gold bodice by Schiaparelli or the black and
> gold one by Alix.

He delighted in picturing her trying on her clothes, imagining her transformation into a vision of beauty. He had studied her every detail in the weeks they had lived together and knew all her gestures and sounds. "But first your hair is combed with the black comb. Quickly, your head tilted to the side, and harshly torn through. Then the sigh, the gaze starting out somewhere and ending somewhere, the drifting smile directed at no one and everyone, the swift walk and the warm evening breeze on the wide Champs-Élysées."[118] Dietrich replied to his elaborate, handwritten letters with brief, infrequent telegrams, which confounded him because *he* was normally the one to make himself scarce. They rarely had time alone. Even when they were together, they were always surrounded by other people or hurrying off to meetings. Remarque longed for telephone calls so that he could hear her voice at night.

But Dietrich had other things on her mind. Back in Hollywood, her persistent fears that she had been shunted aside proved to be well founded. The Americans had seen quite enough of her and her European-inspired movies. Besides, she was not a young actress like Hedy Lamarr or Ingrid Bergman, who had now arrived in Hollywood. Harry Edington had told her back in August that he was not making much headway in his quest for a new contract. *Knight Without Armour* had been a flop. He implored her not to make any more movies in Europe for the time being: "It is my firm belief that you should not attempt any picture in Europe until after your citizenship is established here."[119] In March 1937, Dietrich had filed an application for American citizenship. Edington assured her that it would take no more than seventeen or eighteen months for the application to go through, and then she would be an American, which would greatly improve her position in the studios.

In Germany, the news that Dietrich sought to acquire American citizenship caused quite a stir, and officials felt compelled to issue a denial. Goebbels sent Heinz Hilpert to Paris. Hilpert had staged George Bernard Shaw's *Misalliance* during the 1929–1930 season, with Dietrich playing the part of Hypatia. Max Reinhardt had left Berlin for good in May 1933, and one year later, Hilpert had been appointed director of the Deutsches Theater and the Kammerspiele. In November 1937, Goebbels was counting on Dietrich's return to Berlin. "At our embassy in Paris, Marlene Dietrich issued a formal statement disparaging her slanderers and emphasized that she was, and would remain, a German. She will also be performing with Hilpert at the Deutsches Theater. I will now take her under my wing."[120] Once Hilpert had reported back to him, Goebbels thought Dietrich would be performing in Berlin.[121] She made no written mention of her encounter with Hilpert. In order to return to the United States, she needed to renew her German passport, which is why she was visiting the German embassy. She would not come back to Berlin until the end of the war, clad in an American uniform.

Remarque must have told Dietrich that his most recent novel, *Three Comrades*, had been bought by Metro-Goldwyn-Mayer the previous year.[122] F. Scott Fitzgerald wrote the screenplay, and shooting was set to begin in November 1937. She cabled Edington in October 1937 that she would do anything in her power to act in the film version of Remarque's last book. In December 1937 word got out that Paramount was giving Dietrich $250,000 in severance pay if she agreed not to make her next picture there. This was a tidy sum of money, but it was also a degrading situation for a woman who was used to success, because it meant that the studio was losing money on her movies. At roughly the same time, a group of independent film distributors took out an advertisement in the *Hollywood Reporter*, highlighted with a red border, that listed the actors they considered "box office poison." Dietrich was on this hit list, along with Mae West, Katharine Hepburn, Joan Crawford, and others. By the beginning of the following year, Remarque had become aware of the unpleasant position his lover was in. On January 9, 1938, he sent off one of his relatively rare telegrams, offering her the lead role in *Three Comrades*. Although another actress had already been cast in this role, he intended to offer his services as coauthor of the screenplay to MGM if Dietrich played the lead. BEGINNING NEW BOOK FOR YOU EXCLUSIVELY CABLE WHAT IS GOING ON AND

WHO SHOULD COME YOU OR I DON'T RUSH NEVER FEAR NEVER GET UPSET
WE'RE JUST STARTING AND EVERYONE WILL BE AMAZED.[123]

There is no record of her response to this offer, but Margaret
Sullavan did not hand over the star role, and Dietrich came away
empty-handed. The new book Remarque wanted to write exclusively for her would take several years to complete. But "Ravic," as
the main character would be named in the novel *Arch of Triumph*, is
mentioned in his letters as early as 1938. When Remarque realized
that he was unable to hold Dietrich's interest for long, he got the
idea of splitting himself into several male selves. Most of the time
he turned himself into either "Alfred," the innocent little boy who
loves Aunt Lena (Dietrich) passionately and writes her postcards
and letters in old-fashioned penmanship, or "Ravic," the valiant and
melancholy man who loves and supports Dietrich. With "Ravic,"
the war and the hardships of emigration enter into their correspondence. Although Remarque was not taken seriously by his left-
wing colleagues because of his lack of party affiliation, the National
Socialists regarded him as their enemy. In 1933, Remarque's books
were burned and banned. He abhorred the National Socialists
and tried to embody "the other Germany": cultivated, intellectual,
and cosmopolitan. At the beginning of the Nazi dictatorship, he
believed that he was keeping a safe distance, but by 1938 he realized that the threat was drawing closer and encroaching on his life.
His ex-wife, Jutta Zambona, panicked that she might be deported
to Germany, and he agreed to remarry her.[124]

In Remarque's dreamy letters to Dietrich, the word "war" started
to crop up more and more often. During a nighttime air-raid drill,
when all of Switzerland had gone dark, he turned on the gramophone and reveled in doom and gloom: "It is sending music into
the tubercular night, music of a different continent, of a different
star, weary music of ruination. When will the world break into
pieces?"[125] In a German magazine, he came across photographs of
her and gazed in bewilderment and dismay at the woman he loved,

posing for a picture eating breakfast at home, in an alien world. "Do people really believe what they're claiming," he asked her in a letter, "that you are going back to Germany and becoming an ornament for Ufa?"[126] When he read in the newspapers that Paramount would not be extending her contract, he assumed she would come back to Europe, and to him. WILL EXPECT YOU SOUTHAMPTON EAT AT HORCHES LONDON THEN WITH THE CAR NAPLES CAPRI AND BUDAPEST WAR OFF SPRING ON.[127]

But she did not come. He spent the spring alone in his house at the lake. In his letters to her in Hollywood, he mourned for a past that they had not shared. "Why was I not with you everywhere, at least in that radiant time when the world was nothing but a really fast car and glittering froth, laughter, and youth! . . . We would never have been sad. We would have laughed and not spoken, and sometimes we would have had hours when the weight of the world would have felt like gray fog."[128] This opportunity was gone. Remarque smelled the gunpowder and heard the muffled rumbling on the horizon. His diary entry on February 21, 1938, read: "Swimming in the afternoon. Washing hair, cleaning up—after Hitler speeches, misery of the times, and expectation of the bleakest future. In the evening a bottle of Wormser Liebfrauen Stiftswein, 1934. Necessary. The night with all the stars—over martyrs, idiots, imbeciles, fanatics, the wounded and the dead; over Spain, China, battlefields, concentration camps, sprouting fields of daffodils, criminals, crimes, and the twentieth century."[129] In early March, Hitler incorporated Austria into the German Reich. Salzburg and Vienna were in the hands of the enemy. The impending war dredged up Remarque's memories. "We all have so little warmth for ourselves in our hearts—we children of troubled times—so little faith in ourselves—far too much bravery and far too little hope. . . . Stupid little soldiers of life—children of troubled times—with a dream, sometimes, at night."[130]

On May 3, 1938 Dietrich arrived in Paris, where Remarque

was waiting for her. Their first weeks together appear to have gone
smoothly. She cooked mushroom soup, meatballs, scrambled eggs,
Serbian rice with meat, apricot dumplings, and crabs for her family
and for her lover in Sieber's apartment. Together with Max Kolpé,
they drank Pilsener in a little bar and touched on political issues
as they chatted. Even though Dietrich was there, Remarque kept
up his usual habits: he partied the nights away in fancy restaurants
and backstreet bars, drank too much, and surrounded himself with
prostitutes. After one of these nights, he wrote in his diary: "Letter from Marlene on the bed. Went over. Had waited. Was sweet.
Even so, went away again. My room. She came. Stayed. I stank
of liquor, garlic, and cigars."[131] Remarque was driven by feelings
of farewell: farewell to peace, to Europe, and to happiness. At the
same time, his lover was needling him incessantly. She was jealous
of Zambona, who was also in Paris, and who, in turn, was jealous
of her husband's lover. Dietrich reproached him for having gotten
married, and he countered that she had always had lovers on the
side. Remarque's diaries reveal a side of Dietrich that is at odds
with the image of a libertarian love life. When he told her that he
was off to meet up with his old girlfriend, Ruth Albu, she was not
above hiding his shoes so that he could not leave the house. The
worst part of life with Dietrich, he found, was the constant need to
interact with her family. Rudi, Tami, and Maria were omnipresent.
Remarque found Rudi in particular hard to take. In his view, Rudi
was "an exquisite study of a glutton who constantly takes offense
if anything is not right," a "mindless glutton."[132] Because he loved
Dietrich and her family was part of the package, he had no choice
but to live in close proximity to these people. "I'd be better off not
knowing the family," he concluded.[133] He nonetheless went along
with this group for a two-month vacation at a summer resort in
Cap d'Antibes.

　　Even at the Côte d'Azur, the ominous signs of the times could
not be missed: "Evenings, while we're swimming, three big gray

French war ships putting out to sea."[134] Befitting their social status, they stayed at the opulent Hotel du Cap-Eden-Roc. Dietrich was a regular guest at this hotel, which was run like a private club. The price of this exclusivity was immense. Dietrich paid for everybody, even though she had no source of income and no prospects lined up. She stayed in connecting suites with Remarque and her husband on the upper floor. Tamara Matul and Maria had separate accommodations. Dietrich and her entourage went on outings in the area and put in appearances in Cannes and Juan-les-Pins. On a photograph from one of these outings, we see a tanned Dietrich at a restaurant table with Sieber, Matul, and Remarque. Dietrich and Sieber are looking into the camera, while Remarque is shielding his face. He hated these kinds of public appearances with flashbulbs popping. They spent most of their time together at the sea. Remarque stood around in large white bathing trunks, wearing sunglasses that he would not take off when a camera was on him. He was perfectly coiffed, as always, puffing on a cigarette and looking like someone who was uncomfortable in his skin. His half-naked body seems oddly soft and ungainly. In a suit, he was a good-looking man, but in swim trunks he lost his virile elegance. His diary entries make it evident that the sea air and beach life did nothing to ameliorate his feeling of suffocation. Love in a family setting was unbearable for him, even at the Côte d'Azur. But when he finally had a chance to be alone with "the puma," as he called Dietrich, all was well again. For him, she was "nothing but seduction." Even so, he sensed that both he and she were feeling that their love affair was coming to an end. Remarque was not enough for Dietrich. In late August, she began an affair with a Canadian millionaire named Marion Barbara Carstairs, who went by the nickname Joe. Joe Carstairs's brawny female physique contrasted sharply with Remarque's feeble-looking male body. Everyone at the luxurious holiday resort bore witness to Dietrich's humiliation of Remarque. He would stand in front of her closed door, and everyone—including him—knew that she was with Joe. "The puma" hated reproaches and commitments. Sieber helped her carry out her betrayal of Remarque. In his role as the lifelong cuckold, he was content when it happened to someone else. As always, he was Dietrich's confidant, and he presumably offered Remarque wise words of comfort. But Remarque was clever. Although he was so deeply wounded by Dietrich's behavior that he stood in front of his mirror and wept, he presented a cheerful façade to her. That was the best way to handle it, because Dietrich did not appreciate displays of weakness.

This undignified charade was accompanied by a steadily growing fear of war. On July 4, 1938, two weeks before Remarque arrived in Cap d'Antibes, his German citizenship had been revoked. He regarded it as an honor to be expatriated by the Nazis. In mid-September, when they returned to Paris and learned from Dietrich's personal assistant, Resi, that draft notices had been sent out in Germany and it was rumored that the French were drafting the stateless, Dietrich changed the subject. She was distraught by the fact that Remarque had been in France for four months and had yet to receive his *carte d'identité*. "Sat at the radio until midnight. Ultimatum expired. Eleven dead. Czech government first demanded silence, then negotiations. Went out onto the street. Met Kolpé. Went to Le Jour. Then to Fouquet. Sat till two. Puma developed plans the whole evening. Wanted to go to Porto Ronco for me, get all of us onto a ship—go to the American embassy."[135]

No sooner had they arrived at the hotel than the subject of world politics was cast aside and the sexual hijinks started up again. Dietrich wanted to spend the night with Carstairs, but she was already asleep. Remarque was disgusted by her behavior, but she had a firm hold on him. She admitted to him that she never missed having men in her bed—only women. Even so, Dietrich asked him to buy her a wedding ring. Remarque agreed, and they headed off to Van Cleef & Arpels. He noted in his diary: "Slept with the puma.

During the night she clung to me through to the morning. Had taken off Jo's ring and watch band."[136]

Remarque knew that her soft side never lasted long. If her standoffishness got to be too much for him, he played the little boy "Alfred," which was sure to delight her. It took a fair amount of coaxing to get her to show affection. "In the morning, the tender puma, tender, intimate, without sex. Explained she loved me and would be unhappy in America. I said she would find someone for massages, hair combing, chatting, and sleeping next to her. Maybe it's true that for women tenderness is a more frequent need than sex. Certainly for Puma."[137] Remarque recalled that their love had once been more passionate than companionate, and he wondered what had happened to their desire.

When "the puma" finally boarded her ship in Le Havre on November 18, 1938, he returned to his house at the lake and devoted himself to his writing. By early December, he was working on the Ravic novel, the book designed for Dietrich. It did not take long after her departure for his longing and veneration to set in. On the last day of the year 1938, he wrote her a long love letter. Remarque began the new year with a feeling of restored youth. He was calm and happy, and he was able to work because she answered his letters with letters of her own. From Dietrich's correspondence with Sieber at this same time, we know that she complained if "Boni" (as she called Remarque) did not write or call her immediately. He was one of her links in Europe and needed to be at her beck and call around the clock, otherwise she would ask her husband to find out where her lover was. In February 1939, Remarque completed the first polished draft of his novel *Flotsam*, which bore the epigraph: "It takes a strong heart to live without roots." On March 18, he took the *Queen Mary* from Cherbourg to New York.

"Very early in the morning, at about five o'clock, the skyline of New York, gray and massive against the bright sky, surprising and

not surprising, often seen in photos, but magnificent, of course."[138]
His agent showed him the night life. He enjoyed seeing the lovely
shades of gray as the light played on the concrete buildings, and
admired the neon lights in the evenings, the skyscraper canyons,
and jazz music. When he got back to his hotel at four in the morning, there was a message from Puma, who scolded him for behavior
with journalists that was not to her liking. He knew that the best
way to win her over was to feign indifference and put her in the
position of courting him. Four days later, when he arrived in Los
Angeles, he found Dietrich in front of her house, looking bashful
and beautiful in a yellow outfit. She was excited to show him her
home and hoped that he would like it. "Pretty and atrocious, but
very comfortable and a great deal of effort went into setting it up
for me."[139] The quarreling started up a few days later. Dietrich was
still without a movie contract. She had expected Remarque to bring
her a text she could use for a movie. "Puma terribly disappointed
that I did a book about emigration and not Ravic. Finds the book
bad. Also disappointed that I didn't bring any material for a film.
Looks at the newspapers every day to see if we're in them. Guess
she expects it—and expects me to help her. But how? Material for
films? Where would I get that?"[140]

His hopes and dreams of love burst asunder in the cold light
of day with Dietrich, the fallen Hollywood star. When they were
invited to a film preview at Warner Brothers, she was worried about
whether Remarque would look good in photographs. "It makes me
a little sick, although I do understand it. I'm not a show dog."[141] At
the premiere, they ran into Thomas Mann, who could not stand
Remarque and was envious of the brisk sales of Remarque's books.
"Remarque and Dietrich, inferior," he noted that evening in his
diary.[142] Remarque did not like Hollywood. Dietrich was either
congested, jealous, ill-tempered, hostile, or temperamental. Love-
making was out of the question, and he generally slept alone. He
soon tired of rum cocktails and Hawaiian cuisine. The puma he

loved had nothing in common with the Dietrich who appeared in magazines or at public events. He had written her a fretful letter even before he came to America to ask what she really stood to gain from these characters in the movie magazines.

> OK, you may earn money there—but is that worth the
> effort? To throw away your life, which is getting more and
> more precious, piece by piece? It would be one thing if
> this were about achieving major goals—but in the age of
> Shirley Temple? . . . You can earn your living anywhere—
> so that Mr. Sieber feels a bit more secure with somewhat
> more money? Or your child? Your child will get by. There is
> enough for that purpose. Rudi could try to work for once.
> And you could finally start to live the way you deserve."[143]

His appeals did not get through to her. Remarque was baffled by his puma's desire to hold her own among the cretins of Hollywood and enjoy herself with people who were constantly striking a pose in the hope of being photographed. Remarque loathed the very things that made Dietrich's professional survival possible. By 1939 she could no longer delude herself. She had to face the fact that no one wanted to make a movie with her anymore. It was not that she cared about Hollywood, but she *did* need money.

On June 9, 1939, Dietrich swore an oath of allegiance to the American Constitution. She must have hoped that Edington was right in prophesying that she would be interesting to the studios once she had her American citizenship. She was in bad shape. Dissatisfied and distracted, she made a mountain out of every molehill. At times she was preoccupied with her daughter's weight, and at other times with some item in the newspaper. Everything else paled into insignificance as far as she was concerned, including her love for Remarque. Although he kept toying with the idea of leaving, he stayed. His trip was not a success. In June 1939, the two of them took a train to New York. Sieber, Maria, and von Sternberg were waiting for them there, and they all planned to cross the ocean to Europe together. But now that she was taking her first trip as an American citizen, Dietrich ran into difficulties with the Internal Revenue Service. Two officials showed up, demanding $240,000 in back taxes.[144] It turned out that as an American she could not be detained, but her husband could. In the end, she was able to settle this debt by handing over her jewels.

Remarque found Dietrich's moods hard to take. To calm his nerves, he got together with his friend Walter Feilchenfeldt, who was an art dealer in Zurich, and bought two Cézannes and a Daumier. Owning European art was his compensation for the shortcomings of living in America. In late July, the caravan moved on from Paris to Antibes. This time von Sternberg joined the group as well, which did not make things any easier. Von Sternberg was jealous of Remarque, even though he claimed to be in love with Dolly Mollinger. Pictures of von Sternberg from the summer of 1939 give new meaning to the phrase, "He looks like a shadow of his former self."

In Dietrich's home movies, this final summer at the Côte d'Azur before the war was captured in Technicolor. As usual, they spent their days together at the seaside. The sparkling light of the Mediterranean sun gave their bodies a brown cast; the sea was blue, and their clothing quite colorful. The Kennedys were there as well, and the young John F. Kennedy can be seen in a bathrobe with a predatory grin, baring his absolutely perfect teeth. Despite the sun and luxury, however, no one was really happy, with the threat of war looming.

Remarque was drinking and agonizing about frittering away his time, his love, and his life. Matul needed antidepressants to get through the day. Sieber was tormented by the fear that she would leave him. He confided to Remarque that she was planning to run off with a Russian man, and if she did, what would happen to him?

He was sure that Tamara was the only woman who would put up with him and this situation. Maria, who had been sent off to a Swiss boarding school, was no longer the bright-eyed, pretty child she had been. She had pubescent unhappiness written all over her face. And Remarque described Dietrich as distracted, exhausted, and melancholy. "Surrounded by my husband, my daughter, Erich Maria Remarque, Josef von Sternberg, and a group of friends, I would always wonder: 'To which world do I belong? Am I a bad star, a has-been star, or simply a zero?' 'Box office poison' was the judgment of those gentlemen in Hollywood. But I had the same feeling as at the beginning of my career: what if I were to be a disappointment?"[145]

It was in this mood that she received a call from Hollywood. Joe Pasternak, who had been so taken with her in Babelsberg, was now a Hollywood producer. He knew quite a bit about what the public wanted to see, yet he still chose good artists for his movies. Always open to new perspectives, Pasternak was willing to take a chance on offering a role to Dietrich, the "box office poison." She would be playing a bargirl in a Western. Pasternak figured people would enjoy that. Dietrich accepted the offer in spite of the ludicrous salary of $75,000. The summer in Cap d'Antibes came to an abrupt end. Von Sternberg was the first in the group to learn that war was just days away. Dietrich became quite agitated and immediately planned to leave. Remarque wrote this in his diary on August 16, 1939: "The small, brightly lit, bare train station in Antibes. The *train bleu*. The puma gets in. Rudi insulted her at the last minute by saying that in the future she ought to respect him more. The train started up—waving—and with that, the summer was over." Fifteen days later Hitler invaded Poland, and World War II began.

BERLIN

L eni Riefenstahl had to have known whom she was dealing
with. In May 1933, when she resumed her relationship with
Adolf Hitler, a great deal had come to pass in Germany. In
the first days of February, the Reichstag had been dissolved and
new parliamentary elections were slated for March 5. On February
27, the Reichstag was set ablaze. Arrests began in the early morning hours of February 28. Thousands of leftist party officials and
other individuals who were deemed unwanted were hauled into
cellars and prisons where they were beaten, tortured, and even
murdered. The next morning, this state of affairs was legalized.
An emergency decree "for the protection of people and state" sus-
pended civil liberties for an indefinite period of time: freedom of
speech, assembly, and the press, as well as the privacy that had
been guaranteed to postal, telegraphic, and telephonic communica-
tions. The constitutional state of the Weimar Republic was replaced
by an ongoing state of emergency under Nazi rule. Political scientist Ernst Fraenkel called this law "the constitutional charter of the
Third Reich."

For Riefenstahl, by contrast, the best time of her life began in
1933. Within the space of five years, she would be world famous
and finally attain the success for which she had yearned for so

long. She achieved this status by means of unwavering cooperation with the new Führer of the Germans. "Adolf Hitler had achieved his goal, but as Reich Chancellor he interested me far less than he had before the takeover," she later wrote in her memoir.[1] In Hitler's milieu, of which she was a part, everyone made a point of saying "takeover of power" rather than "seizure of power."[2] Her remark that he interested her less once he was chancellor is odd, since she had spent the previous year preparing for this very situation. She claimed to know nothing about National Socialist anti-Semitic policies until she came back from the mountains.

Riefenstahl had spent the previous five months abroad and could stay abreast of the political events in Germany by reading independent newspapers. Still, she pleaded ignorance about the boycott of Jewish businesses, quotas for Jewish students, destruction of the unions, burning of books, and the *Ermächtigungsgesetz* (enabling act), which gave the government the right to pass laws without parliamentary consent. Riefenstahl feigned astonishment at the changes: "Many great Jewish actors and actresses, such as Elisabeth Bergner, were no longer performing, and Max Reinhardt and Erich Pommer had also left Germany by this point. What terrible things must have happened there! I couldn't understand any of that. What was I to do? I hadn't heard anything from Hitler since December or, of course, from Goebbels, which I was happy about."[3]

She maintained that she now fared badly in Berlin. Because of her extended absence, she was unable to capitalize on the success of *The Blue Light*, and she was running low on money. She decided to get in touch with Harry Sokal, to whom she had "trustingly" left everything. But when she called him up, she found out that he had left, which was understandable, in her opinion, because "Sokal was half-Jewish."[4] She declared in frustration that he had not given her a penny of the profits from her "international triumph" and had even taken the original negative of the movie with him.

In the throes of a deep depression and out of money, Riefenstahl bided her time in Berlin until she got a call from the chancellery and learned that Hitler wished to meet with her the following day. Trembling from head to toe, she "didn't have the courage to say no."[5] When she headed to the chancellery on a warm and cloudness summer's day to pay Hitler a visit, she had on a simple white dress and light makeup, in deference to his taste. Hitler offered her artistic oversight of German filmmaking, but she turned him down, claiming that she lacked the ability to assume this task. Then he offered her the opportunity to make films for him. Again she demurred, this time on the grounds that she was an actress and wanted to achieve success in that arena.

Joseph Goebbels's diary reveals that Riefenstahl went to see him one week after the May 10 book burning. He noted in his diary: "Afternoon Leni Riefenstahl. She tells me about her plans. I suggest a Hitler film. She is keen on the idea." They got along so well that Leni Riefenstahl accompanied Goebbels and his wife to the opera that evening.[6]

A photograph of an opera evening five months later shows Riefenstahl next to Magda Goebbels in a box seat. The Italian ambassador to Germany, Vittorio Cerrutti, was keeping them company; Joseph Goebbels and his adjutant can be seen in the background. Riefenstahl looks relaxed and does not give the impression that she is unhappy in this group. To the end of her life, she vehemently denied having had any close collaboration with Goebbels, which she got away with in large part because the diaries cited here were not tracked down until 1992 in Moscow.[7]

Riefenstahl claimed that Goebbels never stopped besieging her during the spring of 1933. He called her up when she was on vacation, appeared at her door at night, and summoned her to his official residence on Pariser Platz in Berlin for private talks. Their meetings invariably ended with Goebbels trying to kiss her or fondle her breasts. When he realized that she would not be intimidated or yield to his advances, his desire flipped into hatred. Even before she shot her first film for the National Socialists, we are told, he was already her enemy.

Riefenstahl was determined to focus squarely on Hitler. From this point on, she believed that only the admiration and support of the omnipotent dictator would be suitable for her genius. But Goebbels evidently gave her quite a bit of help. She could heap blame on him and count on his inability to defend himself. She would later deny doing everything in her power to get into the social circles of Goebbels and Hitler so she could advance her career.

Goebbels got to know Riefenstahl on November 2, 1932, before his speech in the Sports Palace: "I meet Riefenstahl . . . very enjoyable, smart, and pleasant. . . . We chat for a long time. She is a very enthusiastic supporter of ours."[8] Two days later, she visited Goebbels and his wife at their home. "Late in the evening Leni Riefenst. at our house. She entertains us until four in the morning. A clever and amusing person. She is very pleasant. Magda likes her as well." From then on, Riefenstahl seems to have been a welcome guest at the Goebbels home. Two days later, she shared a sofa with Hohenzollern prince August Wilhelm and Hitler supporter Viktoria von Dirksen. In late November 1932, Riefenstahl displayed her talents. Together with Adolf Hitler, she was a guest at the Goebbels residence. "Evening Hitler at our house. Leni Riefenstahl too. It is very nice. Leni R. dances. Good and effective. A lithe gazelle."[9] Goebbels was well informed about Riefenstahl's love affairs. In her mountain films, which Hitler also found quite appealing, she played the sexually active woman who challenged the men.

On December 3, there was another big party at the Goebbels'. "Riefenstahl flirts with Göring. And Slezak entices her away from Hitler. A great show. Goes on until 4 in the morning."[10] Over the course of the next few days, she turned on the charm for Italo Balbo, a leading Italian fascist, and invited Ernst Hanfstaengl, Magda and Joseph Goebbels, photographer Heinrich Hoffmann, and Hitler to her home. Presumably this was the attempt to pair off Hitler and Riefenstahl that Hanfstaengl described. Her later claim that she had only minimal contact with Hitler is highly implausible in light of these casual get-togethers.[11] Riefenstahl actively sought out contact with Hitler by way of Goebbels and played up her feminine charms to capture the interest of both men.

o o o

Although the cinemas, theaters, and cafés were packed and every-thing appeared to be the same as ever, the world was beginning to fall apart. Sebastian Haffner wrote, "It was as if the ground on which one stood was continually trickling away from under one's feet."[12] But Riefenstahl herself was on firm ground. She does not appear to have noticed that there was only one political party left, that the red notices posted on advertising pillars announcing the latest executions were updated on a near-daily basis, and that many of her colleagues in the film industry were no longer around. She was caught up in the whirl of her new circles and no longer needed to beg Arnold Fanck for roles or cultivate contacts in the odious film business. At first she seems to have consulted with Goebbels on matters pertaining to film. Although she claimed otherwise, she was discussing a film project with him in November 1932. This film, *Madam Doctor*, would depict the life of a World War I female spy.[13]

On March 13 the Reich Ministry of Public Enlightenment and Propaganda was established, and Goebbels was appointed to head it. This ministry oversaw film as well as many branches of art and the media. Goebbels had been attempting for several years to exploit the film medium for the party. In the "Gau Berlin," of which he was in charge, the first party film division had been established in the fall of 1930. But short films, such as *With the Berlin SA to Nuremberg*, did not accomplish much. Now that he was finally in power he was eager for change. On March 28, 1933, at Hotel Kaiserhof, the film people were told what Goebbels expected of them and what they could expect from him. They were dumbfounded to learn that he did not want to support any "so-called National Socialist" films, and were equally surprised when he revealed the type of films he favored. No one would have imagined the titles he named. At the top of his list was Eisenstein's *Battleship Potemkin*, followed by a diverse group of movies that included 1928's *Love* (Edmund Goulding) with Greta Garbo, 1932's *The Rebel* (Kurt Bernhardt) with Luis Trenker, and Fritz Lang's 1924 *The Nibelungs*. The propaganda minister appreciated both Hollywood and the avant-garde.

He knew of Riefenstahl as a supporter of the party and as an actress. On December 1, 1929, after seeing *The White Hell of Piz Palü*, he wrote in his diary: "The beautiful Leni Riefenstahl is in it. A splendid child! Full of grace and elegance."[14] The two of them seem to have gotten along splendidly at first. They had a picnic with Hitler at the seaside resort of Heiligendamm and watched the latest Hans Albers movie together, and Goebbels was positively tickled by her sympathetic understanding of the Nazi soul. "She is the only one of all the stars who understands us," he wrote in his diary.[15] Riefenstahl was now a regular guest at the Goebbels' home and chatted with SA section commanders and film colleagues until all hours of the night. There were unforeseen difficulties with the subject matter of the film. "Evening Corell, Köhn, and Riefenstahl: Film Madam Doctor. I'm helping as much as I can. Now there are objections regarding foreign policy & R. W. [Reichswehr]."[16]

Riefenstahl claimed that Ufa wrote her a brief letter stating that her film project could not be completed because the Ministry of Defense had prohibited the production of spy films. The descriptions of Riefenstahl's meetings with Goebbels refute her claim that she had no social ties with him and provide insights into the events leading up to her first Reich party rally film. Her claim that Hitler forced her to make this film had no basis in fact; once her feature-film project had fallen apart, she was "thrilled" to be offered this opportunity, as Goebbels noted in his diary.[17]

In late August, Riefenstahl finally had it in black and white, and readers of the *Film-Kurier* learned what a coup she had scored:

> At the directive of the Reich Administration for Reich Propaganda, Department IV (Film), a film will be made of the party congress. Fräulein Leni Riefenstahl will be the artistic director, at the special request of the Führer, and supervision of this movie will be in the hands of the director of Central Department IV (Film) Party Member Arnold Raether. Party Member Eberhard Fangauf is the technical manager. Next week, Fräulein Riefenstahl will go to Nuremberg after a detailed consultation with Party Member Raether to lay the groundwork for this film.[18]

Victory of Faith was the first film Riefenstahl made for the National Socialists. The fact that many artists had left Germany, fearing for their lives, worked to the advantage of those who, like Riefenstahl, chose to offer their artistic services to the new rulers. There were now unprecedented opportunities for advancement, and Riefenstahl did not hesitate to take full advantage of the situation. Hitler needed no more than a couple of months to establish his dictatorship and get his adversaries out of the way. At the same time, Riefenstahl had become a favorite of the dictator's. She could finally heave a sigh of relief: Hitler had freed her from the constraints of the film industry and she could give free rein to her genius. However, she had not taken the party members' views into account. Up to this point, she had been dealing only with high-ranking National Socialist dignitaries and their adjutants. She often spent whole nights with them, feeling like a great artist. When she got together with Hitler for tea at the chancellery, she was always alone with him and she savored her proximity to power. But now she had to deal with a larger group of small-minded, overly ambitious party members as well. For these men, Riefenstahl was an outsider and a troublemaker. A set of correspondence provides insight into the kinds of attacks she faced. A mere three days after the official announcement of Riefenstahl's appointment, a confidential note called for a background check of her Aryan ancestry. "Herr Podehl, the dramatic adviser at Ufa, met with the film author Katscher, a Jew. Herr Katscher is married to an Aryan. Frau Katscher explained that Leni Riefenstahl was her cousin, and that Leni Riefenstahl was the only Jew among her blood relations. Leni Riefenstahl, she went on to say, has a Jewish mother, who is thought to be the only Jew in her extended family."[19] The next day, Riefenstahl received a letter requesting documentation about her mother and grandparents on both sides of her family "in order to verify your Aryan lineage." These investigations confirmed Riefenstahl's Aryan ancestry. Arnold Raether, the head of the film division, was immediately informed of this status, and on September 8, he sent a handwritten letter to a fellow party member, Hinkel.

Dear Party Member Hinkel,

Your letter in the matter of Riefenstahl was forwarded to me while I was on vacation. In Nuremberg, I had called Herr Hess's attention to things known to me as well, since he wanted to have the case investigated. I have received notification from Berlin that with regard to her ancestry nothing detrimental has turned up. Not that I can imagine that even a Jew would make up something of this sort. One thing is certain: until a year ago, Fräulein Riefenstahl knew nothing about National Socialism. Her landscape films—or rather, the films made by good cameramen—were also put together for the sole purpose of business.

Heil Hitler and yours sincerely, A. Raether[20]

Raether was one of the few people in the propaganda ministry who knew anything about film. He had studied business, then worked as a manager at Ufa. He joined the Nazi party in 1930. Raether was a former member of the Free Corps and a staunch National Socialist. He was responsible for *Hitler over Germany* (1932), *Hitler Youth in the Mountains* (1932), and other films in that vein. Goebbels was not particularly fond of this overblown party glorification, but he knew that Raether was a loyal party member and competent worker, and he assigned him many key functions, entrusting him with a seat on the Film Credit Bank's board of directors and putting him in charge of allocating loans for film projects. The recipient of this letter appears to be Hans Hinkel, who had been decorated with the prestigious Blood Order for participating in the 1923 putsch. In July 1933, he became a state commissioner in the Prussian Ministry of Culture and the Prussian regional director of the Combat League for German Culture. Riefenstahl worked directly with Raether and Eberhard Fangauf. Fangauf, who was born in 1895, volunteered for military service and was honorably discharged when he was severely injured in 1918. In April 1933, he joined the Goebbels ministry as a film consultant and was put in charge of organization and production management of government and party-run film propaganda. He would remain in this post until 1945.

Fangauf, Raether, and Hinkel, all confirmed National Socialists, were profiteers of the new system and disgruntled to learn that Riefenstahl had been commissioned to film the party congress. They did not want to yield any of their privilege and status, especially not to a woman. Riefenstahl, in turn, was buoyed by her own sense of importance as the artist who had been chosen by the Führer. Now that she had finally succeeded in finding a powerful patron and admirer, she had no intention of backing away. Raether, Fangauf, and Hinkel had not counted on a woman like Riefenstahl. She had already tackled more difficult situations. With Fanck, she had learned how to assert herself as the only woman among men.

A chilly reception awaited her when she went to see Fangauf in Nuremberg to discuss the film work. Fangau was disturbed by her presence in the place that was rightly his and refused to make film stock and cameramen available to her. Once again, Riefenstahl was able to turn a seemingly hopeless situation to good advantage. She signed cameramen on her own and sought to maintain her independence from the cumbersome party machine, which was hostile to art. Her former lover, Sepp Allgeier, joined her crew. As was so often the case, her erotic connection to this man enhanced their artistic collaboration. However, she had not enlisted his services for sentimental reasons. In 1932, Allgeier had worked as the cameraman in Trenker's feature film *The Rebel*, and Goebbels and Hitler loved this film. Allgeier joined the NSDAP in 1935. Riefenstahl's other cameramen were Franz Weihmayr and Walter Frentz. Frentz had been recommended by Albert Speer, whom Riefenstahl had met in Nuremberg. Because he was able to infuse Hitler's May Celebrations at Tempelhofer Feld with some degree of theatrical atmosphere, he had been sent to Nuremberg to reenact this feat there. Speer later recorded his impressions of Riefenstahl in his memoirs.

> During the preparations for the Party Rallies I met a woman who had impressed me even in my student days: Leni Riefenstahl, who had starred in or had directed well-known mountain and skiing movies. Hitler appointed her to make films of the rallies. As the only woman officially involved in the proceedings, she had frequent conflicts with the party organization, which was soon up in arms against her. The

Nazis were by tradition antifeminist and could hardly brook
this self-assured woman, the more so since she knew how
to bend this men's world to her purposes. Intrigues were
launched and slanderous stories carried to Hess, in order to
have her ousted.[21]

Riefenstahl thought of Speer as her friend. The tie that bound them
was their utter devotion to Hitler.

Frentz was similarly pleased to find a point of affinity with
Riefenstahl: "We had very much the same attitude toward film:
I hated wastefulness and so did she."[22] With Allgeier, Weihmayr,
and Frentz on Riefenstahl's side, she dared to defy small-minded
and spiteful party members. However, shooting on location turned
out to be more difficult than the crew had anticipated. No matter
where they set up their equipment, they were thrown out by SA or
SS men. Eventually Riefenstahl was summoned to Hitler's deputy,
Rudolf Hess, who confronted her with an SA man's claim that she
had made disrespectful statements about Hitler. As we know from
Raether's letter to Hinkel, he had advised Hess that Riefenstahl was
a shady person. Hess was a man known for his modesty in everything except his love of Hitler. In all probability he was jealous
of this young woman and daunted by her beauty and talent. But
Riefenstahl did not get distracted. She went back to her filming,
confident in her mandate and her skill.

The *Volk* that Hitler was addressing as chancellor had yet to
evolve into the *Volk* he envisioned. Once the democratic structures
had been done away with, he was planning for an inner reedu-
cation of the German people. Hitler wanted to reorient the Germans to become a *Volk* that would go off to war for him and attain
supremacy in the world, and he envisioned the film of the party
congress serving to propagate this vision. As a lover of movies and
an aficionado of Riefenstahl's films, he knew that she was predestined for this kind of work. Her art had never been based in reality.

Movies had been made of the Nuremberg party rallies in 1927 and 1929. The focus of the 1927 film was the party itself, specifically the men from the SA, whose merry camp life was shown in great detail right down to their odd rituals. In the movie that was made two years later, Hitler was still far from his later role as savior. Such a depiction was no longer considered appropriate. In September 1933, he wanted to be portrayed on film as the Führer of the Germans.[23] Riefenstahl admired Hitler. She knew nothing of all the scheming that had plagued the party—or at least she had no desire to know. She focused squarely on Adolf Hitler. He could rest assured that she would make him the centerpiece of the film.

Beyond her burning ambition, her boundless admiration of Hitler, and her talent, Riefenstahl was able to develop a plan with military precision. Her orders had to be obeyed; everyone and everything had to submit to her will. Three days before the rally began, she arrived in Nuremberg. A film journal reported on her preparations for the shooting:

> The city was already festively decorated. With the aid of a city map that highlighted the scheduled events and in particular the parades and processions, the filming strategy was plotted out. The car with Leni Riefenstahl and her crew raced from one place to another, again and again; the camera placements were selected, the possible time schedules planned and altered. And then came the four big days themselves: an enormous amount of work from early in the morning until late at night, with new arrangements and split-second decisions necessitated again and again, which required an overview of the whole situation and great powers of concentration.[24]

Fanck had taught her how to lay claim to uncharted territory. Her work in the mountains had also taught her the importance of waiting for just the right moment. Still, everything had to move very quickly in Nuremberg. She needed cameramen she could rely on. Every detail was planned out, yet was subject to spontaneous change if an enticing opportunity arose. "The sheer abundance of events threatened to overwhelm us all the time," she wrote. "The mass of material being presented to us could have kept a hundred crew members busy. That was the only possible way for us to capture the key moments on celluloid."[25] Her cameramen had to be on site for all the important speeches and events, but they could neither be noticeable nor disturb the events with their equipment. The final day of shooting in the Luitpoldhain municipal park would pose a particular challenge in this regard. The cameramen would follow the rally from the scaffolding and also stand among the SA men as they filmed so that every last spot in the huge complex was covered. Everything was worked out to the last detail to bring together a film of lasting historical import.

Victory of Faith begins without people. After catching a glimpse of the clouds, we see a city from above in the morning light. The city awakens, an old city with densely clustered buildings, crooked alleyways, and a great many church towers. The camera comes back down to earth, and the following shots look as though they were taken from a moving car. Fountains, clocks, statues of saints and kings go by, accompanied by a music track. Suddenly, people appear: young men are building bleachers in front of a church; the mood is elated. Carpenters hoist a small swastika banner, which flutters gaily in the wind—the first indication of what lies ahead. Not a word has been uttered. Then a sea of swastika banners comes into view. Scenes of urban traffic with backlit passersby, legs cut off, and a muddle of bodies and automobiles recall the aesthetic of the previous decade.

In the following shot, we see formations of SA men marching into the city. Boots in lockstep, singing, old and young men in rank and file—that is the new aesthetic. The SA arrives on foot, on horseback, in carriages, or by car, and is hailed as it marches through the villages. The onlookers stand at attention and give the Hitler salute. Several times, Riefenstahl also shows children with their arms raised in the air. Cheerful party officials emerge from trains and limousines in uniform, though a few are in civilian dress. An airplane lands. Hitler appears in a trench coat, a dismissive look on his face. Voices can now be heard for the first time: the spectators are roaring "*Heil!*" Hitler has a magnetic effect, and everyone streams toward him. The camera shows him from behind, standing in the car as it moves past the rapturous crowd. At this moment, the viewer can almost share Hitler's perspective. The city is full of life. People are now climbing all over the fountains that were still empty in the earlier morning shots. The storefronts are decorated with swastika banners, their own ornamentation blocked from view. Bells are ringing. There are unintentionally funny scenes, such as when Hitler fidgets with his hair or when he is flummoxed by two children handing him a bouquet of flowers, and so passes it along to Hess, who is seated next to him.

Hess opens the Reich party congress. The people jump up from their seats, laughing and shouting "*Heil,*" barely able to grasp the fact that Hitler is among them. Riefenstahl shows a heterogeneous, enthusiastic crowd. There are close-ups of elegantly dressed women, but at the stadium ceremonies we see only determined, angular faces of young men. Röhm, the head of the SA, displaying his facial wound from World War I like a mark of honor, is clearly Hitler's right-hand man. He reports that one hundred thousand SA, SS, and Stahlhelm troops have lined up. When Hitler speaks of the "young German freedom movement," he is referring to his own party. In long sequences, Riefenstahl shows marching SA men, then the SS, who appear in the film for the first time. Hitler is clearly the master of the German people's emotions. He radiates equanimity while unleashing frenzied fervor in the crowds. The film closes with fluttering swastika banners and the anthem of the Nazi party, the Horst Wessel Song.

Hitler was the first politican who sought to be portrayed in a full-length film. The earlier films of party rallies ran only thirty minutes; Riefenstahl's film would be twice as long. She regarded herself as an artist, not as a filmmaker with a party badge. Her goal was not merely to edit footage, but to find a rhythm and a cinematic language for this massive political event in the new Germany. Together with her cutting-room assistant, Erna Peters, she headed back to Bergmannstrasse in the Kreuzberg section of Berlin, where the Tesch printing laboratory was located, to edit the film. The work took longer than expected, and she excused herself in the pages of the *Film-Kurier* for the weeks of waiting. It required great effort to "create a flow for events that were repeated again and again, escalate the action, find transitions, in a word, to give rhythmic form to this great film of the movement."[26]

Riefenstahl's decision to present the material without voiceovers and out of chronological order gave her more latitude to diverge from the sequence of events at the rally. Apart from the music track, she used only original sounds, thus rendering the film an acoustic acclamation for Hitler. The shouts of *Sieg Heil* roar, boom, and break forth again and again, while the ardent crowd stands with right arms outstretched at eye level, palms open in the Hitler salute. On July 13, 1933, this salute had been made mandatory. Riefenstahl's first film for the National Socialists served as instruction in the proper ways to act in this new era. It is unlikely that even a single German was unacquainted with the need for a *Sieg Heil* accompanied by a Hitler salute. The film demonstrates impressively how many people on the streets of Nuremberg adhered to this ritual of compliance and subjugation. *Victory of Faith* would be shown in villages as well as big cities; the idea was to reach as many Germans as possible. Many of them now got to see something about which they had heard or read but had not witnessed up close. "The movie shows the Germans' dedication to the idea of National Socialism," according to a review in *Die Filmwoche*.[27] *Victory of Faith* is a kind of object lesson in how a National Socialist needs to behave.

On December 1, 1933, the premiere took place in the Ufa Palace in Berlin. Just three months earlier, Riefenstahl had stood on the stage here after the premiere of *S.O.S. Iceberg*. The time between the filming in Nuremberg and the premiere in Berlin had been brief. "One simple telephone call to Hitler got her the use of his big tri-motor airplane, along with a personal pilot, Captain Bauer. We can imagine the effect of this unexpected arrival on the eye-witnesses, when the big silver bird landed in Tempelhof and the triumph of Leni when she stepped out, with a smile on her lips and accompanied by a handsome blond lad!"[28] *S.O.S. Iceberg* was well received by the critics, but they panned her acting: "Leni Riefen-stahl, whose acting is just as rudimentary as it has been for years, plays a stereotypical feminine adjunct in monumental mountain films and thus runs the risk of being typecast in these outdated kinds of movies."[29] Not even Joseph Goebbels had liked her in this movie: "Film *S.O.S. Iceberg*. Magnificent nature scenes. Plot quite anemic. Leni Riefenstahl seems awfully conventional. She was not effective here."[30]

Her success with *Victory of Faith* more than compensated for this criticism. The premiere was splendidly orchestrated. Hitler, Goebbels, Röhm, and Hess were present, along with von Papen, von Neurath, and Frick, to celebrate her debut as a political film star. The curtain rose, and for a good hour, the audience of party members could bask in its own glory. "When the final sound faded away, the audience, which was visibly moved, rose to its feet spon-taneously to express its bond with the Führer and his movement by singing the National Socialist song of security and strength. Even then, there was no clapping, but rather reverent silence, followed by a burst of enthusiasm and resounding applause."[31] The audience roared its approval of Riefenstahl, and the Führer handed her a bouquet of flowers. The two of them were the stars of the evening. To celebrate the premiere of the film, Hitler threw a big party.

After 1945, Riefenstahl dissociated herself from *Victory of Faith*. Her only mention of it was to dismiss it as a mere "short film." For a long time this film was thought to be lost, and her statement could not be verified. She claimed that after telling Hitler about the impediments to her work in Nuremberg, Goebbels had been enraged and became her enemy on the spot. However, Goebbels's diaries reveal that he was a supporting and calming influence on her during the three months it took to make the movie.[32] On November 29, when she showed her film to an intimate group, he noted: "Dinner at Alfieri. . . . Hitler comes later. Film *Victory of Faith*. Marvelous SA symphony. Riefenstahl did a good job with it. . . . Hitler moved. This will be a huge success."[33]

With *Victory of Faith*, Riefenstahl cut her critics and enviers down to size. Hitler thought more highly of her and she stayed in close contact with Goebbels. She would have been ill-advised to have a falling-out with Goebbels, who, in turn, could not do without her because there were not too many talented directors remaining, now that most had fled the country. Her moment of triumph came through in the film's opening credits. Her name appeared in large and bold print; Raether's was small and thin. He had failed in his attempts to upstage her as artistic director. Now even mid-level party officials knew that Riefenstahl was a force to be reckoned with. In the 1990s, a copy of *Victory of Faith* surfaced in the State Film Archive of the GDR, and Riefenstahl faced a barrage of questions. She deflected director Ray Müller's question with the remark that she had a few scenes on hand and simply assembled them. In her eyes this was not a film at all; it was nothing but exposed film stock that satisfied the party members who had commissioned it. She was not prepared to take their satisfaction as praise, she insisted, because "Let's face it: they were happy with every newsreel. The main thing was to have swastika banners on view."[34] A statement of this kind makes it clear how superior she felt to the average party members. Riefenstahl savored the privileges of her insider status, no longer dependent on the evil "industry." As Hitler's darling, she did not have to worry about box office success. Riefenstahl could rest assured that her film would be shown nationwide, and everyone would see it.[35] She reported to the press that she was thrilled to have experienced the rally in Nuremberg. "What I saw in Nuremberg," she declared, "was one of the most impressive experiences of my life. All of it was so enthralling and grand that I would not be able to compare it to anything I have experienced in my previous work in the arts. I will never forget the processions of the hundreds of thousands of people [and] the cheers of the masses when the Führer and his closest associates appeared."[36]

Before setting off with Walter Prager on a ski trip to Davos, she met with Julius Streicher, editor of *Der Stürmer* and the *gauleiter* of Franconia. He was known as a fanatical anti-Semite and a corrupt businessman. This was the man to whom Riefenstahl chose to grant power of attorney just a few days after the premiere of *Victory of Faith*: "I hereby grant Herr Gauleiter Julius Streicher from Nuremberg, editor of *Der Stürmer*, power of attorney in matters concerning claims by the Jew Belà Balacs [sic] pertaining to me. Leni Riefenstahl."[37] This power of attorney was handwritten on Hotel Kaiserhof stationery. It is not known whether Balázs had taken legal action against Riefenstahl to get his payment.[38] In any case, Riefenstahl had no qualms about pitting her new friends against her old ones on both financial and artistic matters. She wholeheartedly supported and exploited the terrorist dimension of the *Volksgemeinschaft* (people's community).[39] If *The Blue Light* were to have a revival, she wanted to reap the fame all on her own.

The change of mood that emerged among the German people in the spring of 1934 set the stage for Riefenstahl's second party rally film, *Triumph of the Will*. After a year of National Socialist rule filled with celebrations and terror, the excitement curve had leveled off. It was not that the Germans missed their civil rights or opposed the National Socialist violence against the Jews, but rather they were frustrated that the miracles they were anticipating failed to materialize.[40] There were also National Socialists—the men in the SA—who were dissatisfied with what had been achieved. Their chief of staff, Ernst Röhm, was the only one in this group whom Hitler addressed with the familiar *du*. The SA men equated politics with brute force, which had enabled Hitler to become chancellor. Röhm was well aware of his special status and boasted that he was preserving the revolutionary legacy of the party. Röhm judged the world exclusively from the standpoint of the soldier. His goal was to make the SA the most powerful military organization in Germany and have the Reichswehr generals obey him. His vision was summed up in this statement: "The gray cliffs must be swallowed by the brown tide." The Reichswehr officers looked down on the proletarian SA men, who were neither disciplined nor schooled in the art of national defense. The Reichswehr may have been inferior to the paramilitary SA in terms of numbers, but its prestige was much higher. It enjoyed support from the nobility and the conservative middle class; it had weapons; and it established a connection to President Hindenburg, who had served as a commander in the Reichswehr. To secure total power in Germany for the long term, Hitler had to have the support of the Reichswehr. If Hindenburg died in the near future, he would be able to bury him only if the Reichswehr stood by him.[41] Even so, he could not afford to sever his ties to the SA, which was experiencing an enormous increase in membership. In the spring of 1934, Röhm had command over 4.5 million men. In the course of a single year, the number of SA men increased sixfold. In *Victory of Faith*, Riefenstahl showed that these young men were drawn to the SA by its military features: the uniforms, male bonding, banners, and marches. Röhm spoke more and more often about a "second revolution" that had yet to occur. Hitler could not allow this "revolution" to take place. His useful private army SA had become a growing destabilizing factor. To defuse the situation, Hitler arranged with Röhm to send the SA on vacation for the entire month of July 1934. In early June, Hindenburg had moved to his manor in East Prussia; evidently he was close to death. It was time to designate a successor. As usual, Hitler had been letting things slide and avoiding confrontations with the SA, but Hindenburg's imminent death forced him to take action. All SA leaders arrived at the town of Bad Wiessee in Bavaria on the morning of June 30 for a meeting with Hitler, who got with Goebbels there shortly after 6 a.m. The SA leaders were brought to Stadelheim Prison in Munich, and many were executed that same day in a purge that has come to be known as the Night of the Long Knives. In Röhm's case, Hitler waited until the following day. Two SS men brought a pistol into Röhm's cell in the expectation that he would take his own life, but when he did not do so, he was shot. Göring saw to the smooth liquidation of the death squads in Berlin. Among those murdered were Kurt von Schleicher, the former chancellor of Germany, and his wife, who were shot in their home. Other prominent victims included Edgar Jung, a consultant to Vice-Chancellor Franz von Papen; Gregor Strasser, the former national organization leader; and Erich Klausener, the head of the Catholic Action group. The SA was stripped of its power, and Hitler emerged victorious from this bloodbath.

Hitler asked Riefenstahl to make a film about the 1934 party congress, and she was offered every conceivable advantage, including distribution of the film by Ufa.

> The managing board hereby authorizes a distribution agreement with Leni Riefenstahl as a special agent of the NSDAP Reich leadership. . . . The artistic and technical direction of the film goes to Fräulein Riefenstahl, who was commissioned by the Führer to do so in the name of the NSDAP

Reich leadership in a letter dated April 19, 1934. According to a letter sent the same day, Fräulein Riefenstahl will have up to 300,000 reichsmarks at her disposal. The Führer has given his approval to having the film distributed by Ufa.[42]

She chose Walter Ruttmann, who had made the film *Berlin: Symphony of a Great City*, one of the most important cinematic expressions of New Objectivity, to be her codirector. His film was driven not by plot but by atmosphere, dynamics, and rhythm. Riefenstahl knew that this film of the party congress would also revolve around atmosphere and dynamics, and that Ruttmann was the right man for the job. Ruttmann and Riefenstahl shared an aversion to the motion-picture industry, which in their view only stood in the way of art. In the late 1920s, he had worked as Abel Gance's first assistant in Paris, and in 1932 had gone to Italy. To the surprise of his friends, he returned to National Socialist Germany in March 1933. Ruttmann was a friend of Philippe Soupault's and was held in high esteem by René Clair. James Joyce was said to have felt that only Eisenstein or Ruttmann would be capable of adapting his *Ulysses* for the big screen.

Riefenstahl was in a lesser league. In 1934 she was largely unknown outside of Germany, and within the country her name was associated with athletic prowess in mountain films and her close relationship with Hitler. Ruttmann does not appear to have thought much of her talent as a director, and he even coined a term specifically for *The Blue Light*: *beautise*, a portmanteau of foolishness (*bêtise*) and beauty (*beauté*). Still, he accepted her offer and was reported to have declared: "I am nothing but a whore; I have sold myself to Riefenstahl."[43]

It appears likely that he was dependent on Riefenstahl if he wanted to pursue his career in National Socialist Germany. And Riefenstahl would stop at nothing to recruit and retain other men of talent for her projects, as she had already shown with Béla Balázs

Marlene Dietrich at age five,
January 1, 1906.

Marlene Dietrich with Josef ("Jo") von Sternberg in Berlin, 1928.

Marlene Dietrich, actress Anna May Wong, and Leni Riefenstahl
at Berlin Ball, 1928.

Still from the film *The Blue Angel* (1929; director: Josef von Sternberg) with Marlene Dietrich and Rosa Valetti.

Marlene Dietrich poses with her husband, Rudolf Sieber, and their daughter, Maria, in Hollywood, 1931.

Leni Riefenstahl meeting with Adolf Hitler in 1934.

Leni Riefenstahl
photographed by
Martin Munkacsi
on a shoot that
also produced
Munkacsi's cover
for *Time* in 1936.

Opening of the 1936 Olympic Games by Adolf Hitler at the Berlin Olympic Stadium. On the balcony, from left: Werner von Blomberg, Rudolf Hess, William Frick, Count Henry de Baillet-Latour, Adolf Hitler, unknown, Theodor Lewald, Joseph Goebbels, Hermann Göring, Leni Riefenstahl.

Leni Riefenstahl at the camera, 1930s.

Marlene Dietrich, 1942.

Marlene Dietrich with French actor Jean Gabin at the restaurant and nightclub Ciro's, Los Angeles, California, November 15, 1941.

Marlene Dietrich greets veterans on the *Monticello* after the ship docked in New York City on July 20, 1945.

Leni Riefenstahl and her lawyer before the district court in Munich, November 25, 1949.

Leni Riefenstahl, at the age of seventy-six, on a submarine adventure in the Caribbean Sea to make a series of photographs, August 2, 1979.

and Carl Mayer, and would do so again with Ruttmann. Riefenstahl was well aware of what a talented artist she was placing under her command by hiring Ruttmann. She was superior to him solely on the basis of her good relationship with Goebbels and Hitler, even though not a single one of her cinematic achievements measured up to Ruttmann's. Her awareness of this inequality doomed their collaboration to failure from the start; as always, she strove to outshine everyone else.

In October 1933, Ruttmann applied for admission to the Reich Film Department. On June 1, 1934, his application was granted and he could start in on his work. According to Riefenstahl's version, she thought of Ruttmann because she had no intention of making a second party rally film by herself. It is odd that she still consulted with Goebbels about her new film. She was involved in two projects at once, traveling to Spain with a small team (Hans Schneeberger, Sepp Rist, and Heinrich George) to make the feature film *Lowlands* while Ruttmann laid the groundwork for the party rally film in Germany. We can only imagine her feelings of omnipotence as she played the beautiful, passionate Marta in Spain and everyone awaited her orders in her Führer-appointed role of director back in Germany.

While Riefenstahl was having one nervous breakdown after another in Spain as a result of countless delays in filming, Ruttmann traveled through Germany with Sepp Allgeier. The *Film-Kurier* introduced Ruttman as the scriptwriter for the party rally film who worked with Riefenstahl on the artistic presentation. He filmed German landscapes, workers, peasants, SA men, and labor service men, as well as the Feldherrnhalle in Munich, the Landsberg Prison in Bavaria, and a memorial to Albert Leo Schlageter, a hero to the Nazis who had been executed in 1923. Ruttman envisioned movement and "productive people" as the foreground of the movie—not Hitler.

When Riefenstahl had a look at his footage in Berlin, she was shocked. "What I saw on the screen was, to put it mildly, unusable. It was a jumble of shots of newspapers fluttering along the street, their front pages tracing the rise of the Nazi Party. How could Ruttmann present work like this! I was absolutely miserable."[44] She decided to dispense with him and the footage he had shot. Now she supposedly had no choice but to bite the bullet and make the movie herself.[45] Ruttmann switched over to the Ufa commercial division, and Riefenstahl would go down in history as the creator of the second party congress film, as she had intended all along.[46]

Enterprising as ever, she wrote a book about the making of the film. *Behind the Scenes of the Reich Party Rally Film* was published in December 1935 by Eher-Verlag in Munich, the central publishing company of the NSDAP. After 1945, she claimed that Ernst Jäger had written it and that she had not even read it in advance of the filming, which does not sound credible coming from a woman with her control mania and business acumen.[47] She names Sepp Allgeier as the head cameraman; Walter Ruttmann is not mentioned at all.

Before the shooting began, she was a bundle of nerves. "Discussed party congress film with L. Riefenstahl," Goebbels noted disapprovingly in his diary on August 28, 1934. "This will not amount to much. She is too tense." However, her tension must have subsided by the time she arrived in Nuremberg. Riefenstahl relaxed in the circle of her crew, which included many people she had worked with before. Guzzi and Otto Lantschner and Walter Prager were signed on as her assistant directors, and Sepp Allgeier, Walter Frentz, Franz Weihmayr, and Walter Riml as her cameramen. Hans Schneeberger's wife, Gisela, would be in charge of the publicity stills. One week before the party congress opened, Riefenstahl and her key crew members traveled to Nuremberg. She wanted to personally oversee the preparations for this film, which would "convey a stylized reality in documentary form for centuries to come."[48] Extensive arrangements were required. She spent several days roaming through the city in her long white coat with her aides, examining, approving, or rejecting camera positions. She knew the strengths and weaknesses of her men; she divided up and assigned the tasks. "One is good at pictorial images, another at exhilarating motion. One can capture inner life on film, another sees only the outer forms. Many different capacities have to be allotted appropriately."[49] Allgeier, the lead cameraman, was quick on his feet, a wizard of lighting, an athletic ski jumper, and tough as nails.[50] Allgeier and his colleagues clung to monuments, gables, façades of houses, church steeples, or fire escapes to shoot this film. Lifts were installed on statues and flagpoles, and in one building, a twenty-meter-long track was installed on the second floor so that a dolly could travel back and forth with a camera capturing the marching troops on film.

The crew stayed at a villa on Schlageterplatz.

> Within 24 hours, this house, which had previously been vacant, was newly furnished throughout, and then Leni Riefenstahl could move in with her large staff. The mezzanine had a big reception room and several offices, and upstairs, on the second floor, there was a big conference room, which was also used as a breakfast room. The other rooms served as quarters for Leni Riefenstahl's entire technical team, including cameramen, assistant cameramen, sound engineers, lighting technicians, and so forth, for a total of about 120 men. All of them had to sleep here for the duration of the party rally so that they would be on call at all times.[51]

Makeshift darkrooms were set up in the cellar. Riefenstahl had a telephone switchboard, office and work rooms, and a conference hall. Eight to ten men slept in each room. Riefenstahl was familiar with this kind of camp life from her work on mountains.

The members of the film crew dressed as SA men so that they would fit into the picture. Perfectly camouflaged, they could operate within in the crowd. Riefenstahl herself wanted to remain recognizable. Wearing a trench coat–style elegant white coat with a white peaked cap, she could be made out even in all the hubbub. In the published photographs of the filming process, she assumed multiple roles. In one, she had a motherly chat with a Hitler Youth member; in another, she lay on the pavement with her cameramen to try out different camera angles. In yet another photograph, she is sitting among her cameramen, looking regal in a ladylike white outfit complete with white hat and white gloves. She is not wearing a party badge, but she is clearly in a key position.

Even today, Riefenstahl's films foster the illusion that these party congresses were highly disciplined events riding on a wave of enthusiasm. This was decidedly not the case.[52] In 1934, half a million people were expected in Nuremberg. The political leaders, who numbered 180,000, were the largest group. The rest comprised 88,000 SA men, 12,000 SS men, 60,000 Hitler Youth, 50,000 Labor Service men, 120,000 party members, and 9,000 SS functionaries and special police.[53] Nuremberg's 400,000 residents had to cope with the onslaught of hundreds of thousands of people, which also included spectators who often came in for just a day. In order to portray the *Volksgemeinschaft* and cover the immense costs of all the fanfare, there needed to be a large turnout of paying participants and spectators. The men who marched in *Triumph of the Will* had paid a rally fee, and those cheering them on from the sidelines had bought admission tickets.[54] The status reports of the Nuremberg vice squad indicate what sorts of entertainment the participants sought out after the rally. One hundred SS men were assigned to keeping their fellow party members from heading to brothels. Their efforts were likely in vain. The number of prostitutes was rising every year, a great deal of alcohol was consumed, and drunken political leaders staggering down the street were now part of the urban landscape. Albert Speer reported that even the party elites who were privileged to sleep under the same roof as their

Führer in the Hotel Deutscher Hof carried on like this. The *gau-leiter* went on drunken rampages. As Speer saw it, "only in alcohol could these fellows resurrect their old revolutionary élan."[55] Hitler did not need to worry about Riefenstahl and Speer, however. His architect went to every Wagner opera, and his director devoted her efforts to portraying him and his party rally exactly as he wished.

There were daily briefings in the villa. Every evening at about nine o'clock, Riefenstahl climbed onto a chair, called the group to order with a bottle of beer, and shouted: "The gentlemen whose names I now announce have to be ready to leave at 6:30."[56] Each cameraman was assigned the use of a car. White and red slips of paper on the car windows indicated to the security forces that these vehicles had clearance to enter the grounds. The management directed the vehicles to the cameramen's locations. These sessions often ran until two in the morning. Breakfast was served in the dark at 5 a.m. Military order prevailed in the villa. On a huge chalkboard, the boss noted down the final instructions for her crew. During the day, the cameramen were on their own. No retakes were possible; the shots needed to be perfect the first time around. The hunt for images was carried out on the streets and from an airplane.

"On September 5, 1934, 20 years after the outbreak of the World War, 16 years after Germany's Suffering, 19 months after the beginning of the German Rebirth, Adolf Hitler again flew to Nuremberg to review the assembly of his faithful followers." This opening crawl is all that remains of Ruttmann's prologue. The film begins above the clouds with an airplane approaching the city of Nuremberg. The shadow of the fuselage glides over the medieval walls of the city. The viewer cannot see who is in the airplane, but it can only be Hitler. This opening scene is remarkable because the images formed by the clouds evoke not only an enormous realm of fantasy as defined by the history of Western imagery, but also recent German history. The World War I combat pilots ranked among the unforgotten heroes of the Germans. All alone in the skies, their sole mission was to kill the enemy. As they fired, they were like gods bringing death to the people below.

Hitler's arrival is eagerly awaited. Riefenstahl shows us crowds going wild at the sight of him, in much the same way as she had in *Victory of Faith*. Even before a single word is uttered, we hear the roar of *Heils*. In Riefenstahl's films, the crowds remain mute apart from formulaic acclamations. Standing in an open Mercedes, Hitler celebrates his entry into the medieval city. The fixed black formation of the SS men shields him from any intrusiveness from the crowd. The camera casts what seems like a loving eye on every detail lingering almost tenderly on boots, belts, black uniforms, and helmets. Hitler is tacitly present throughout the film, as sequences shot from multiple perspectives and with a movable camera convey the impression that everyone in Nuremberg is constantly on the lookout for a glimpse of the Führer.

On the rally's opening day, Riefenstahl shows the men awakening in their tents. A merry chaos ensues. Young men splash water at one another, wash their backs, line up to get their food, and roughhouse. These scenes of exuberant masculinity make it perfectly clear that Hitler and Riefenstahl needed the collective energies of hundreds of thousands to create the image they were after. Rudolf Hess opened the party congress, directing his special greetings to the foreign diplomats, who had turned out in large numbers, and to the men of the Reichswehr. Riefenstahl edited the subsequent speeches by the leading party members to ensure that each one appeared briefly on the screen. To limit the amount of time spent on speeches, she included footage of each speaker with a statement she regarded as typical for him. Even her artistry could do nothing to improve the puffy, vacuous, disagreeable, sweaty, and unsightly faces of these men. During the labor service roll call on the rally grounds, she highlighted a series of clear, proud, fanatical faces that were welcomed by their various regions with the question, "Comrade, where do you come from?" Riefenstahl's men had installed wooden tracks on the field on which they now rode back and forth to get direct shots of people's heads. Hitler greeted the men in the labor service who were taking part in a party rally for the first time. To William Shirer, they seemed like a "highly trained, semi-military group of fanatical Nazi youths."[57] Their roll call was followed by a commemoration of the casualties in World War I, during which Riefenstahl displayed Hitler's face against the sky.

The atmosphere at the evening SA gathering is almost eerie, with open fires burning, swastika banners fluttering, and smoke rising. The men are heard singing. The new SA chief of staff, Viktor Lutze, disrupts this elaborately staged setting when he begins to speak in his shrill voice. The crowd starts shouting: "We want to see our chief of staff!" In these scenes, Riefenstahl was making a direct reference to recent history. This evening assembly is the only part of the film that is not listed in the official program. Going into this much detail was the director's decision. She presented Lutze, Röhm's successor, as a popular, well-respected chief of staff. Long shots of fireworks symbolize the explosion of the SA men's feelings, followed by images of interlocked male bodies seeking physical closeness to their chief of staff.

The next day, Baldur von Schirach reports to his Führer that sixty thousand Hitler Youth have arrived. He calls on them to endure sacrifices and steel themselves. While he speaks, the camera scans the rows of the listeners. These cross-cutting sequences were one of Riefenstahl's key stylistic devices to show Hitler in constant interaction with his audience. "The Hitler Youths are generally filmed at a different time in a different place—but the editing sequence suggests that they are hanging on to the 'Führer''s every word. The technique of contriving fictitious encounters on the editing table is both simple and effective."[58] Riefenstahl shows

us handsome, sincere-looking faces of young men that her cameramen culled with telephoto lenses.

Aside from the black bronze eagle on the speakers' platform,
three large swastika flags hoisted on steel poles over a hundred
feet high are the only decoration at the tribute to the dead in the
Luitpoldarena. Hitler strides down the center aisle through the line
of the 120,000 men, followed by Himmler and Lutze. They are
the only ones in motion; the masses are frozen in place. In these
scenes, the lift mounted on the flagpole is visible. Nobody besides
Riefenstahl and the men she appointed have access to this aerial
view. Hitler enters the atrium of the memorial, pauses in front of
the wreath and the "blood flag" from the failed 1923 putsch, and
honors the casualties of the Nazi movement and the war.[59] Mussolini had figured out how to use the casualties of world war as his
political capital. The "aristocracy of the trenches," the dead and the
living, were united in comradeship. The fascists would ensure that
their comrades had not died in vain. Mussolini had hit a nerve with
this ploy more than a decade earlier, and now Hitler was copying
it, with Riefenstahl supplying the requisite images. The death ritual
at the party rally was not backward-looking, however, but rather
future-oriented. Hitler would demand proof of loyalty to the death
from the men lined up there.

Then all the marching began. A never-ending stream of male
bodies poured through the narrow streets of Nuremberg like mol-
ten lava. SA, SS, the Stahlhelm paramilitary organization, and the
labor service men filed past Hitler. One of his secretaries found
out how he managed to keep his arm outstretched for hours at a
time: "At teatime one day, he said . . . that daily exercises with an
expander enabled him to accomplish this, but that a strong will
was needed as well. He added that he tried to look at every man
who marched past in the eye to give him the feeling that he was
singling him out."[60] Riefenstahl's shots reflect this attentiveness.
Hitler saw the individuals only as a part of a series, but for each of

these men, this parade signified a very personal recognition as a National Socialist.

In *Triumph of the Will*, the words of their Führer seem to be inscribed on the men's bodies. The masses are either feverishly active or rooted to the spot, reminiscent of the characters in Riefenstahl's mountain films, with some intrepid climbers scaling the cliffs and others winding up as frozen bodies in the ice. Hitler captured the masses with his gaze and his words, Riefenstahl with her cinematic direction and montage. After 1945 Riefenstahl categorized *Triumph of the Will* as a documentary, but prior to that time, she called it an "artistically constructed film" in order to distinguish it from mere newsreels.

She and her crew needed two weeks to sift through the footage at her film laboratory, Geyer, in the Neukölln section of Berlin. One workroom was adorned with a larger-than-life portrait of Hitler, and the vestibule displayed pictures of NSDAP leaders. She had the latest technology at her fingertips. According to Steven Bach, no director in Germany—and perhaps anywhere in the world—had ever enjoyed these kinds of working conditions.[61] However, she kept falling into a state of exhaustion and being assailed by doubts.

For Riefenstahl, art and utter devotion, both mental and physical, went hand in hand. In 1934, she strove to be better than in 1933. If this film won over the top brass, a place at the top would be hers. On October 17, 1934, Goebbels noted in his diary, "Leni Riefenstahl talks about the party rally film. It will be good." In the fall, she visited Hitler at his mountainside retreat in Obersalzberg to fill him in on the progress of her work. In December he came in person to visit the cutting room, which indicated to the Germans that she was still in his good graces.

Quite a bit had changed since the 1933 party rally. On October 14, 1933, Hitler had proclaimed that Germany would be pulling out of the League of Nations, which was tantamount to pulling out of the league of civilized countries. Abroad, the word "war" came up more and more frequently in connection with Germany. The photographs Erich Salomon took of the conferences of European politicians in the late 1920s and early 1930s in Geneva, London, and Paris show well-dressed men sitting together in beautifully appointed salons and deliberating the state of the world. There is no hint of the fanatical pathos that the National Socialists brought into politics. The Germans, by contrast, considered it a sign of national strength for their chancellor to show up in his bizarre swastika uniform.

Triumph of the Will was conceived of as a lasting document, and it certainly became one. Riefenstahl's images continue to have a powerful impact to this day. Excerpts and stills from *Triumph of the Will* are shown again and again to illustrate the relationship between Hitler and the Germans. No distinction is drawn between intention and impact: the film conveys the National Socialist experience. Riefenstahl documented Hitler's wish as reality. Her film displayed the body of the masses. These masses then see themselves onscreen as a powerful historical force. In this sense, the films of Riefenstahl are an important part of a self-referential system that is still evident today. In *Triumph of the Will*, a single individual—Adolf Hitler—stands apart from all the others. He alone enjoyed the privilege of not mingling in the social sphere. Riefenstahl molded these images of the great loner into the enduring images of Hitler.

On November 22, 1934, she showed the first segments of her film. Goebbels wrote in his diary, "Afternoon with Leni Riefenstahl; splendid shots of the party rally film. Leni is quite adept. Imagine if she were a man!" And five months later, he remarked, "Afternoon Nuremberg film. A magnificent show. Somewhat long-winded only in the last part. But otherwise a stirring display. Leni's masterpiece." Two days later, she met with Goebbels again and talked about the film. Her appearance must have alarmed him, because he noted, "She simply has to take a vacation."

On the evening of March 28, Riefenstahl, sitting next to her

mother in box seats with her eyes shut, re-experienced her "sleepless nights and the grueling efforts at finding transitions from one
sequence to the next."[62] For the premiere at the Ufa Palace in Berlin,
she wore a black evening gown from the famed Schulze-Bibernell
fashion salon that showed off her slim figure and red curls. When
she heard the long applause at the end of the film, she knew that
she had made it. "While the film was still running . . . the viewers
rose from their seats, and, gripped by the intensity of this experience, sang the Horst Wessel Song. Then the lights went up, and the
man who would resurrect the nation, who was being glorified in
this film stood at the balustrade of his box seat. It was as though
a spell hung over the crowd, a spell that resolved into enthusiastic
shouts, enthusiastic *Sieg Heils*. The Führer handed the creator of
this cinematic work, Leni Riefenstahl, a big bouquet of lilacs with
a gilt-edged bow."[63]

In the photograph of the two of them, she is staring deep into
Hitler's eyes and seems as though she is in a trance. Suddenly she
fainted dead away and lay on the floor while the steps of Hitler and
his escorts faded away outside. A doctor on call gave her an injec-
tion. Carl Zuckmayer claimed that she had actually hoped to fall
into Hitler's arms, but her plan misfired, so she landed at his feet
and he had to climb over her.[64]

However, Riefenstahl recovered and basked in the glory of her
triumph. The Germans faithfully queued up in front of movie theaters and did not undermine the predetermined success of the Riefenstahl film. On Sunday afternoons, there were even showings
for children.

Once her film had gotten off to a successful start, Riefenstahl
and several of her crew members went off to Davos to relax in the
mountains, and on May 1—while she was still there—she learned
that *Triumph of the Will* had been awarded the National Film Prize.
As soon as she heard the happy news, she hastened to send off
a grateful telegram to Hitler: DEEPLY MOVED AND DELIGHTED I HAVE

JUST HEARD THE ANNOUNCEMENT OF THE FILM PRIZE ON THE RADIO THIS GREAT DISTINCTION WILL GIVE ME STRENGTH TO CREATE MORE FOR YOU MY FÜHRER AND FOR YOUR GREAT ACHIEVEMENTS YOUR LENI RIEFENSTAHL.[65] She accepted the prize from Goebbels on June 25, by which point they were already in negotiations for her next film, *Olympia*.

But before starting in on a new project, she had to go to Nuremberg one more time. Evidently the military felt that it had been misrepresented in *Triumph of the Will*. The closing day of the rally, during which the Reichswehr had put its strength on display, had been rainy. Riefenstahl was dissatisfied with the footage and cut most of it out, which caused problems with Hitler when the generals complained to him. She therefore decided to film the military maneuvers of the Wehrmacht at the "Rally of Freedom" in 1935. The result was the twenty-eight-minute short film *Day of Freedom—Our Wehrmacht—Nuremberg 1935*. [66] In March 1935, Hitler reintroduced compulsory military service in Germany. Accordingly, Riefenstahl's new film was closely tied to current political developments. Hans Ertl reported that Riefenstahl looked fabulous and was full of plans. As always when she undertook major film projects, she sought out colleagues and friends for her crew. The men gathered in Riefenstahl's penthouse on Hindenburgstrasse to plan out the project. New to the group was Willy Zielke, a former teacher at the State Academy for Photography in Munich, whose latest documentary film, *The Steel Animal*, had impressed them all.[67]

Ertl divided the world into artists (by which he meant himself, his close associates, and Riefenstahl) and party bigwigs who knew nothing about art. "The real connoisseur and artist did not have an easy time of it then provided that his art was not an end in itself and had no primitive, propagandistic value. Even a Leni Riefenstahl had to contend with scathing criticism and intrigues, although she was quite adept at combining art and propaganda in her party rally films."[68] But he left no doubt that she was adept at using Hitler's admiration for her to push through her own interests. In early September, Riefenstahl and Ertl traveled to Nuremberg together. This time, the cameramen did not appear in quasi-military uniforms, but rather as camera sharpshooters. Their disheveled hair, relaxed suede jackets, and long corduroy pants marked Riefenstahl's men as the artistic fringe of the party rally. She deftly distributed her men throughout the premises to have them "'partake in the combat' as roving reporters and camera shooters—they went around with their 'celluloid ammunition' and long, telephoto lenses that looked like gun barrels shooting, right alongside the young maneuver soldiers."[69] According to Ertl, the days in Nuremberg were both a challenge and a sport. He depicted his boss and her crew as a close-knit group that carried out its mission with a high degree of professionalism. Riefenstahl's cameramen had to be bold, well-trained, and daring. During World War II, many of these men went on to make war films.

o   o   o

Day of Freedom—Our Wehrmacht is an alarming film. It shows an army gearing up for war. The sounds of military technology combine with bellowed *Sieg Heils* to form a deafening soundscape. Peter Kreuder, a talented composer who had also produced the sound effects for Zielke's *Steel Animal*, was in charge of the music. In this film one could hear what lay ahead: state-of-the-art military technology and German soldier songs.[70] There were demonstrations of motorcycle militias, anti-aircraft guns, armored cars, reconnaissance aircraft, bombers and tactical aircraft, cavalry, and machine guns. These miracles of technology were operated by serious-looking young soldiers and observed with evident excitement by heavyset older men in swastika uniforms up at the podium. On December 29, the *Filmwelt* carried an advertisement with a shot of Riefenstahl in profile, looking up at Hitler and his young soldiers.

The caption under the picture indicates that she was in charge of this German Wehrmacht film, which *Völkischer Beobachter* hailed as "the first cinematic monument to the German military."[71]

William E. Dodd, who was serving as the United States Ambassador to Germany at this time, was dismayed by the film:

> [T]his evening my wife and I went to the great movie theater, the Ufa Palace, to see the widely advertised Unser [sic] Wehrmacht (Our Defense Power) film. For an hour a huge audience watched and applauded the scenes: vast army fields with tanks and machine guns operating and soldiers falling to the ground, all shooting and some killed great parades of heavy trucks and big cannon [sic]; air attacks with hundreds of flying machines dropping bombs on a city. At strategic moments Hitler, Goering and even Goebbels appeared on the scene indicating their approval of all that was going on. The audience applauded many times. I could hardly endure the scene and what seemed to me the brutal performances.[72]

The movies that Hitler commissioned from Riefenstahl's production company made her a wealthy woman. Even though she spent long hours behind the camera and in the film laboratory, she made sure not to neglect her public image. Sporty, independent, successful, childless, talented, unmarried, with short hair—and short on charm—she became a prominent figure in National Socialist Germany. In the mid-1930s, Nazi Germany developed into a modern feudal system. Nothing was more coveted than personal access to Adolf Hitler. Riefenstahl was skilled at deflecting rumors about a love affair between her and Hitler; she neither denied nor confirmed them. She was called "the Reich's glacial crevasse" behind her back, which referred not only to her past work in mountain films, but also to her cold-blooded, calculating work method. Everyone knew that the Führer adored her and that she cherished him. She left everything else to the imagination, and thus built up an aura of power. No one knew for sure how much influence she wielded.

People wondered why the Führer was so adamant about placing her in charge of major film assignments. "She raves about Hitler, calls *Mein Kampf* a revelation; during a film expedition to Greenland, she had Hitler's picture hanging in her tent. She is part of the innermost circle, uses the informal *du* with both Hitler and Göring, yet explains that Hitler stands high above any personal relationship," Konrad Heiden wrote in his 1936 biography of Hitler.[73] Hitler gravitated to *Flietscherln*, somewhat coarse young women, yet he also liked to surround himself with admiring society ladies. Riefenstahl offered him both. She savored the role of the well-bred daughter who became the great artist and cosmopolitan lady, racing through Berlin in her silver-gray Mercedes coupe that Hitler had given her as a present, ordering the latest styles in the fashion boutiques. However, she was also a woman who fell in love again and again, and had many affairs. Riefenstahl was an attractive woman who made the most of her feminine wiles. As an artist she gave Hitler the feeling that he was an important patron of the arts, which in turn gave her—along with all kinds of material advantages—the feeling of towering above everyone else with her genius. In the official portrayals, she was celebrated as a woman who bravely took on the honorable commissions of the Führer and was extolled for her utter dedication, ceaseless drive, boundless energy, and iron will. Riefenstahl's name was now known beyond the borders of Germany. *Time* magazine, which featured her on the cover on February 17, 1936, reported that Hitler regarded her as the epitome of a German woman, as evidenced by her health, energy, youth, love of sports, ambition, and beauty.[74] Riefenstahl became an important representative of National Socialist Germany and had no trouble leaving the country. She gave lectures in

England, shot a film in Spain, took a vacation in Switzerland, and visited Italy. During her trips abroad, she could hear an array of opposing views and observe Germany from the outside. However, she did not make comparisons.

In early March 1936, there were rumors in Berlin that Hitler was planning a foreign policy coup. He convened the Reichstag on March 7. The evening before, eager officials gathered in the Kaiserhof, and their Führer did not let them down. He explained that Germany no longer felt bound by the Locarno Pact, and that as of that day, the German government would be restoring unrestricted and absolute sovereignty of the Reich in the demilitarized zone of the Rhineland. The six hundred delegates leaped up and extended their arms in a Nazi salute. Hitler felt that he was well on his way to predominance in Europe. On the domestic front, he had secured absolute power within three years. No one could stand in his way; his adversaries had been disposed of; and the majority of Germans believed in the mission of their Führer.

Hitler's juggling of war and peace formed the backdrop for the 1936 Summer Olympic Games in Berlin. The Olympics had been assigned to Berlin back in 1931, and Hitler pledged that no part of these arrangements would change under National Socialist rule. Even though there were protests, the International Olympic Committee stuck with its decision to hold the Olympics in Germany, but they called on Hitler to embrace the Olympic ideal.[75] Hitler paid lip service to it because the Games would offer him a unique opportunity to present the "new Germany" to the world at large. He would spare no expense or effort. The best means of disseminating images of a modern, peace-loving Germany was film. He entrusted Riefenstahl with the task of presenting the best side of National Socialism to the world. Despite all evidence to the contrary, Riefenstahl stuck to her version of the facts: that she was commissioned to film the Olympic Games by Dr. Carl Diem, the Secretary General of the Organizing Committee of the Berlin Olympic Games. She also claimed to have financed this mammoth enterprise independently of Hitler. As usual, Goebbels figured as her dark adversary, but the accusations she leveled at him were nothing but smokescreens to distract from her own privileges and entanglements. The records show that both parts of the *Olympia* film were financed by the German Reich at the express wish of Joseph Goebbels. In August 1935, she told him about her preliminary work. He noted admiringly: "She is a clever one!"[76] Three days later, Goebbels came to meet with Hitler. One of the outcomes of their discussion was a decision to authorize one and a half million reichsmarks for the *Olympia* film.[77] In early October Goebbels talked to Riefenstahl again about the Olympia film, and he stated unequivocally that she was "a woman who knows what she wants."[78] Eight days after this evening they had spent together: "Contract with Leni Riefenstahl regarding Olympia film approved."[79] This course of events tallies with the records stating that on October 16, 1935, Riefenstahl was offered a contract to make a film of the Olympic Summer Games for a fee of 250,000 reichsmarks. Olympia Film Inc. was a shell corporation of the propaganda ministry, founded on December 9, 1935; the partners were Leni Riefenstahl and her brother, Heinz.

The year 1936 got off to a good start for Riefenstahl. On January 26, she was received by Mussolini in Rome. Il Duce's interest in this director of the Reich party rally films stemmed from his recently developed secret admiration of the Führer. He was impressed by the fact that Hitler had left the League of Nations and announced that there would be compulsory military service. Mussolini began to suspect that he had underestimated this strange German and might be well advised to have Riefenstahl make a film for him as well. He suggested filming the drainage of the Pontine Marshes. She turned down this idea, explaining that the production of the Olympic Games documentary would keep her busy for a good two years. Six months after this meeting, the Italian film institute Luce awarded Riefenstahl the grand prize for *Triumph of the Will.* At a ceremony in the Italian embassy, Ambassador Bernardo Attolico presented her with the Coppa Mussolini. In attendance were Joseph Goebbels; Oswald Lehnich, the president of the Reich Film Chamber; Ulrich von Hassell, the German ambassador to Italy; and Countess Edda Mussolini Ciano, daughter of Il Duce and wife of the foreign minister, and hence an influential woman in Italy. There is a photograph showing the countess congratulating Riefenstahl. Both women are in elegant evening gowns, and they are smiling joyfully at each other. The men in tailcoats gathered around them look delighted. This was a prize among friends.

The preparations for the Olympic Games were guided by the motto, "Olympia—a National Duty." For the National Socialists, this duty included the enhancement of their image in the international community. They wanted to demonstrate that their opponents were liars. Anti-Semitic posters and signs were taken down, but the daily terror against the Jews went on unabated. For many Berliners, the Olympic Games amounted to a kind of "pseudo-freedom": the guests from abroad in the city made it possible for them to forget the fanatical pathos of the National Socialists for a few days. With any luck, they could listen to American jazz pianists in the bars and buy the *Times* or the *Neue Zürcher Zeitung* at the newsstands.

Riefenstahl knew that the whole world would be her audience. Earlier films of the Olympic Games had been of poor quality. Even in 1932 in Los Angeles, filming took place, but no actual film resulted from it. Riefenstahl thus once again faced the challenge of transforming an event that so far had not been discovered by the cinema into a cinematic work of art. She was certainly spurred on by the knowledge that this film could make her famous beyond the borders of Germany. Kings, princes, and other notables had confirmed that they would be coming. They were curious about the new Germany.

Riefenstahl's productions in National Socialism could not have come about without patronage at the highest level, yet they were so powerful artistically because she worked with a group of cameramen who regarded themselves primarily as artists and not as National Socialists. Walter Frentz was appointed head cinematographer; he was also in charge of capturing the sailing and the rowing regatta events on film. To bring on Hans Ertl, Riefenstahl had to entice him away from Arnold Fanck. She was able to offer him quite a bit more money, and he signed on. Hans Scheib, who had been a highly skilled cinematographer in the Marlene Dietrich film *The Woman One Longs For*, became Riefenstahl's expert on telescopic shots. Her camera team also included Willy Hameister, the cinematographer for *The Cabinet of Dr. Caligari* (1919).

Once she had put together her crew, she was constantly on the move: in the Olympic village, on the Reich athletic field, and in Grünau or Kiel, where preparations were underway for the sailing regatta. She was generally accompanied by members of her crew. They discussed camera placements, experimented with footage, and tested the equipment on site.[80] She surrounded herself with innovative and ambitious men who were absolutely loyal to her and carried out her orders. She had a combination of talented young people and skilled experts. Nearly all of them were avid sportsmen. "I spent many months doing nothing but experiments. I began to study one type of sport after the other systematically. . . . I doggedly went from sports field to sports field, studied where the most enthralling and dramatic competitive moments of each sport and the greatest beauty and grace took place, and determined the best way to capture these moments on camera."[81]

To film the stadium from the aerial perspective, they sent up a balloon equipped with a handheld camera every morning. They placed a newspaper advertisement asking for it to be returned at the end of each day so they could evaluate the results. Small cameras were mounted on boat seats, on flying spearheads, on the saddles of the cavalrymen, and on oar blades. In the Olympic stadium, pits were dug for the cameramen so that they could come quite near to the competitors. Riefenstahl wanted to go right onto the scene with her camera and film what a spectator would not be able to see even up close. She needed "sweating" images that would convey the excitement, the effort, and the fever of the athletic competitions. She had to respect the fact that the Olympic Games were not a party rally and comply with regulations that forbade her from interfering with the athletes. She took many of the shots during training sessions, or reshot footage after the official competitions. A system had to be developed to classify and review the film footage immediately. The Geyer printing laboratory guaranteed that the footage would be ready by the next day. A copy machine was developed for the express purpose of processing the immense quantities of film at top speed. Each roll of film was labeled with the name of the cameraman, the date, and the type of sport. Two supervisors assessed the quality of the images and wrote up reports that were passed along to the cameramen to keep them informed about their daily output. Ten assistants organized the footage according to time and subject matter.

The film crew's base camp was Ruhwald Castle, a nineteenth-century, thirty-room villa with a park in the vicinity of the Reich Sports Field. Riefenstahl and her 180 crew members lived there under one roof for the whole month of July and the first half of August. A work schedule on which everything was planned down to the last minute determined the sequence of events. The day in Ruhwald Castle began at six in the morning with a meeting in which Riefenstahl assigned tasks to each individual crew member for that day. In the evening, they met again to plan the following day. Riefenstahl seems to have been the only one who was not worn out after a sixteen-hour workday. She responded to complaints by reminding them that they could sleep once the Games were over.

The weather was cold and rainy. The weary cameramen worked

around the clock; they were hollered at by the marshals in the stadium, and at times they were booed by the audience or thrown out by the security guards. A major source of interference for the cameramen, in turn, seems to have been Riefenstahl herself. Even during the most exciting competitions, she was running from one camera to the next and giving important stage directions with sweeping gestures. To make matters worse, her personal photographer, Rolf Lantin, was following her to shoot publicity pictures. The party officials, who had to sit with the spectators and lacked any important role, were annoyed at how Riefenstahl was crafting an image of herself as the great director. Ertl suspected that it was Riefenstahl's foes in the party who started chanting "Leni, Leni, let's see you!" to make her look ridiculous. Narcissistic as she was, she waved delightedly to the crowds, and was promptly booed. At several points she came close to suffering one of her nervous breakdowns. During the filming, Riefenstahl would go from displaying remarkable energy and steely resolve to losing her temper over petty matters and revealing her frayed nerves. Her crew was used to her breakdowns, and their deep respect for her artistic ability was undiminished. She was able to snap out of her bad moods, halt her torrent of tears, and show that she was a tough director. She made no concessions in her quest for the best camera angles. A *New York Times* reporter complained bitterly about the way Riefenstahl took charge of everything. Any cameraman who stood on a spot that she did not approve of would get a pink slip from one of her attendants, which said: "Remove yourself from where you are now—Riefenstahl." If people disregarded her instructions, she threatened to have them removed from the premises.[82]

Often even Riefenstahl's own crew members were thrown by her behavior, but they stuck by her. They knew full well that her adversaries from the Reich Film Chamber were just waiting for her to fail, in which case the *hetaera* (courtesan), as they referred to her, would lose her power. Her crew was not about to let this happen. These party members were no match for the bond Riefenstahl had formed with her men.

In the stadium, pits were dug and steel towers erected to give the cameramen perfect vantage points. Riefenstahl did not care in the slightest whether that would bother the guests of honor. Frictions arose between the propaganda minister and the director. Goebbels, who was otherwise quite satisfied with the way the Olympic Games were going, noted in his diary on August 6: "I bawl out Riefenstahl, who is acting unspeakably. A hysterical woman. Clearly not a man!"

In the *Olympia* film, Riefenstahl added a human component to Hitler's portrait. In the party rally films, she had portrayed him as a Führer who stood apart from all others, but in *Olympia* she played up his affable side. He watched the events through his binoculars, chatted with his neighbors about the competitions, fretted about major decisions, and grinned when the Germans won. Although it was somewhat odd for the German chancellor to show up in uniform at a peaceful event designed to promote understanding among nations, in the *Olympia* film Hitler played the dictator who knew how to behave himself. He let the athletes shine and happily assumed the role of spectator. *Der Film* reported, "We have never seen Adolf Hitler looking so human, warm, and up close in any newsreel. A deep immersion in the noble games is the mark of the true Führer, who can bring enthusiasm and a sense of humor to these 'non-political' matters."[83] Riefenstahl's imagery conveyed the message that the world ought to trust this man.

Complex logistics were required to get all the cameramen sufficient film stock. Two cars went back and forth constantly to bring negative stock to the shooting locations, and two trucks had been converted into darkrooms in order to transport the exposed film from the Olympic stadium to the Geyer laboratory in Neukölln. By the time the group gathered for the evening meetings to plot out the following day, Riefenstahl had already viewed the footage and made up her mind about the coming day's work. She devoted five minutes to each crew member. Each photographer's work was marked with a number; once she reviewed the footage, she knew who had taken the good and the bad shots.

The fact that she fell in love in the stadium heightened her desire to make this film a perfect success. Her passion for the American decathlete Glenn Morris was proof positive of her love for athletes, whose beauty and strength she sought to immortalize in her film. When she met him for the first time, we are told, she was thunderstruck. He had won a gold medal, and the stadium was darkened for the awards ceremony. "When Glenn Morris came down the stairs," she later recalled, "he headed straight to me. I held out my hand and congratulated him. Then he grabbed me in his arms, ripped off my blouse, and kissed my breasts, right in the middle of the stadium, in front of a hundred thousand spectators."[84] Not wanting to complicate the situation, she then avoided him. Morris returned to the United States and tried his hand at acting in a 1938 flop, *Tarzan's Revenge* (he played the lead role), but his onscreen role of a lifetime was in the *Olympia* film. He eventually became an insurance agent.

The closing ceremonies took place on August 16. The National Socialists had offered the world a refined, well-orchestrated exhibition; Hitler had received royalty at his table; Goebbels and Göring had hosted lavish parties. The National Socialists had put on a show for the Olympic Games, but they had no intention of changing. Thomas Wolfe described the situation in his 1940 novel *You Can't Go Home Again*:

> The sheer pageantry of the occasion was overwhelming, so much so that he began to feel oppressed by it. There seemed to be something ominous about it. One sensed a stupendous concentration of effort, a tremendous drawing together

and ordering in the vast collective power of the whole land.
And the thing that made it seem ominous was that it so evidently went beyond what the games themselves demanded.
The games were overshadowed, and were no longer merely
sporting competitions to which other nations had sent their
chosen teams. They became, day after day, an orderly and
overwhelming demonstration in which the whole of Germany had become schooled and disciplined. It was as if the
games had been chosen as a symbol of the new collective
might, a means of showing to the world in concrete terms
what this new power had come to be.[85]

Riefenstahl's film helped shape this symbolic complex.

She spent the period from October to mid-December archiving
the material.[86] She was eager to revel in her success even before the
film was complete. On September 16, 1936, she wrote a letter on
her personal stationery to Paul Kohner at Metro-Goldwyn-Mayer
Studios in Los Angeles:

Dear Mr. Kohner,

I am also convinced that the Olympia film will enjoy colossal success throughout the world. It has never been possible
to make such a magnificent sports film with these kinds
of resources and artists. As you have already read in the
reports, this will of course not become a documentary, but
instead a timeless, artistic film that is a hymn to the beauty
of the human body, and its dramatic elements are competition and record-setting. Because the American Olympic
champions, such as Morris, Meadows, Carpenter, Towns,
Owens, and many others, have made themselves available
for an incredible number of special shots and close-ups and
we were thus able to obtain unprecedented footage, particu-

larly of the Americans, I think that this film will be of great
interest to America. . . . The ultimate decision regarding
who gets the film lies with Herr Reich Minister Goebbels.
Olympia Film Inc., of which I am the business manager,
has had an enormous number of inquiries and offers for the
Olympia film from all over the world. . . . If an American
company of the size of Metro-Goldwyn-Mayer makes a very
good offer for foreign distribution to Olympiafilm GmbH,
it is conceivable that it will be able to acquire the film for
foreign distribution. If you really are quite interested, I
would suggest that you make offers to my company as soon
as possible, because in the space of the coming four weeks
it will be decided whether Tobis will be getting the film for
foreign distribution as well. . . .

With best regards,
Leni Riefenstahl

Kohner wrote to his boss, Ben Goetz, on September 30:

In view of my previous connections with her (having
made some pictures with her in Europe) she offers Metro
an opportunity for the foreign distribution rights of the
picture in all countries of the world outside Germany. In
view of the unquestionable importance of this picture, for
the completion and perfection of which neither time nor
money is being spared, I thought that possibly Metro might
be interested in it. In this case it will be necessary for me to
cable Miss Riefenstahl. Details of the negotiations could, I
presume, be handled by Metro's representative in Germany,
but it is essential at the present moment that I advise Miss
Riefenstahl in principle whether or not Metro is interested.
Paul Kohner

And he replied to Leni Riefenstahl as follows:

Dear Leni Riefenstahl,

Many thanks for your letter of September 16. I just wanted
to let you know that I have passed along your proposition
to Metro's head office in New York and as soon as I have an
offer, I will get in touch with you right away. Until then I
remain with best regards

Sincerely yours, Paul Kohner.[87]

This correspondence clearly shows the influence Riefenstahl
wielded. In a somewhat condescending tone, she was deigning to
offer Hollywood her film. Kohner, who had experienced the enthusiasm for National Socialism up close and worked in Vienna, Paris,
Rome, and London until 1935, knew who was making him this
offer. He would have known Riefenstahl's film of the party rally, and
met the ambitious Riefenstahl out at Fanck's home in Grunewald.
We know that he learned everything he could about her because
in his literary estate there is a collection of newspaper clippings
about Riefenstahl's prominent role in National Socialist Germany.
Kohner was Jewish, and in the following years he would devote
himself tirelessly to securing sponsorships and affidavits to save as
many persecuted people as possible. Even so, he did not dissuade
his boss from entering into negotiations with Joseph Goebbels. By
the time Riefenstahl paid a visit to Hollywood in 1938, the situation had changed.

In early January 1937, she decided to make two films out of the
Olympic footage. In mid-January she moved to the film laboratory in Neukölln and began to edit it. Her work was part logistics
and part intuition. The logistics of the hunt for images had been
successfully concluded, and it was time for intuition to take over.

Michel Delahaye asked her in an interview for *Cahiers du Cinéma* whether she set down her ideas in writing before the filming began. She replied that she did not need even one page of a script for either *Triumph of the Will* or the *Olympia* films. "It was purely intuitive."[88] Like Albert Speer, she used a combination of cold methodology and organizational mania. She identified completely with the planning and execution of a project, and regarded her subsequent work in the cutting room as the actual creative process. Riefenstahl withdrew from the outside world for nearly two years to edit the *Olympia* films. She did not come home until five in the morning. No one could help her to find the proper rhythm for the images. The slightest deviation could mean the loss of the desired effect. People who saw her at this time described her as a ghost. She edited and assembled the film alone. She stated in an interview in *Cahiers du Cinéma* that this was how she achieved the special character of her films. There is a photograph of Riefenstahl in the cutting room in a white lab coat with many filmstrips around her neck. With the same enraptured gaze as her cinematic counterpart, Junta, when staring at the mysterious glowing crystals, Riefenstahl's eyes are trained on the images, oblivious to the outside world, in a state of ecstatic devotion to the artistic process that is her calling in life. However, this art exacted its price. Riefenstahl made endless demands. Her disputes with Goebbels centered on a report from the supervisory board of the Reich Ministry of Public Enlightenment and Propaganda on October 16, 1936, which alleged that the financial management of *Olympia* did not meet the requirements of proper accounting. The Film Credit Bank planned to launch a full evaluation of this project. She fought that with everything in her power, arguing that she did not have to answer to anyone besides Hitler, and obstinately applied for a budget increase of five hundred thousand reichsmarks. When Goebbels turned her down, she went to see him. After her visit, Goebbels noted in his diary: "Fräulein Riefenstahl is turning on the hysteria for me. It's impossible to work with these wild women. Now she wants ½ million more for her film, and to make two films out of it, even though things are more rotten over there than ever. I stay cool. She weeps. That is a woman's ultimate weapon. But it doesn't work on me anymore. She ought to be working and keeping things in order."[89] In the end, Riefenstahl got her money from Hitler.

In addition to coping with these disputes, she had to finish her work on *Olympia*. The dubbing posed a special challenge. Herbert Windt had written most of the film score, which was played by the Berlin Symphony Orchestra. Once Riefenstahl was finished editing the film, she got together with Windt and told him precisely what effect she intended to achieve with the music. Every sound had to match the image on the screen down to the last second. Even the composer worked with a stopwatch. This was the first time Riefenstahl was using announcers. Two radio sports reporters were charged with this task.[90]

Hitler decided to put an end to all the talk about Riefenstahl's and Goebbels's quarreling and arranged for a visit to Riefenstahl's new house in Dahlem. At roughly the same time that Hitler settled on the idea of building the Berghof, it also occurred to Riefenstahl that she had always wanted a house in the country. Now she could build the house that her father had never been able to afford. The ground floor had an expansive living area with a sunroom, kitchen, and pantry, and a work area with an anteroom, workroom, photo laboratory, screening room, and vault. Upstairs was the bedroom, along with a spacious dressing room, two bathrooms, several guest rooms, and a large massage room. The detached garage had an adjoining living room and bedroom as well. Riefenstahl had built herself a house that was tailored to her personal and professional needs. A family was not in her plans.

A reconciliation visit took place at her home in the summer of 1937; Goebbels and Hitler were joined by Heinz Riefenstahl and his wife, Inge. A photographer took a picture of the group for the press. The men wear civilian clothing, and Hitler tries to look easygoing—Goebbels fails utterly in this regard. The hostess has on a white dress and is smiling bashfully. "With Führer at Riefenstahl's for lunch. She's built a very nice little house. We talk for a long time. She is so effusive."[91] Riefenstahl was not just sitting at the cutting table in Neukölln and drinking coffee with Goebbels and Hitler in Dahlem; she also took trips abroad to rub shoulders with the international gilded youth of the 1930s. When Erich Maria Remarque was in St. Moritz for two months in the spring of 1937, he avoided the ski slopes, but spent his evenings at the hotel bar where he saw Riefenstahl in the company of a long list of luminaries.[92] Remarque's lover, Margot von Opel, was a close friend of Riefenstahl's. They spent several weeks together on the island of Sylt before the outbreak of the war. In 1940, von Opel would be living in New York with her new lover, the Swiss writer Annemarie Schwarzenbach, a close friend of Erika Mann, Thomas Mann's eldest daughter. Riefenstahl clearly kept in contact with the emigrants in the art world.

o o o

In July 1937, she left her editing room yet again to attend the International Exposition in Paris and introduce her films in person. The art that the dictators displayed in Paris staged totalitarian power as public and populist theater. Albert Speer was honored for his pavilion, and Riefenstahl for three films: the *Olympia* teaser film, *The Blue Light*, and *Triumph of the Will*.

On the trip back to Berlin from Paris, she was invited to visit Hitler at Berghof, his residence in the Bavarian Alps. This was a privilege that was extended to only a select few. He wanted to meet with her in an intimate setting and hear about her impressions from Paris. A black limousine picked her up in Berchtesgaden. An adjutant greeted her and brought her into the empty entrance hall. As she stood there alone, she saw that a film was running and recognized Marlene Dietrich on the screen. Then Hitler came to get her.

Hitler congratulated her on her successes, and they chatted while strolling outdoors. There may not have been any new agreements or promises made during this get-together, but the very fact that it took place at all was an unequivocal message: Leni Riefenstahl enjoyed the Führer's protection.

o   o   o

On March 11, 1938, German troops crossed the border into Austria. Two days later, the "annexation" of Austria to the German Reich was announced. When Riefenstahl found out that these political developments would likely postpone the premiere of her film until the fall, she sprang into action by taking the next train to see Hitler in Innsbruck. When she voiced her concerns to him, he initially reminded her that politics now had to take precedence over films. But then Riefenstahl thought of a date that would draw a great deal of attention to the film and connect it to the political situation: April 20, Hitler's birthday. As was so often the case, she found a way to turn a seeming minus into a plus for herself.

On April 20, 1938, the Ufa Palace was decorated with huge red swastika flags and white Olympic flags. Riefenstahl drove up in her Mercedes limousine. Clad in a white kimono-like dress, she strode through the line of men in their black uniforms. The premiere of the *Olympia* film served as the highlight and finale of the festivities for Hitler's forty-ninth birthday. Riefenstahl could not have dreamed of a more sumptuous venue for her film. About two thousand guests were expected. Every one of the party leaders was in attendance, as were many members of the diplomatic corps, *gauleiters*, Olympic champions, film stars, and high-ranking members of the International Olympic Committee. Riefenstahl sat with her parents and her brother, Heinz, in box seats next to the Führer. She stood out in her Asian-inspired evening gown. After the first break,

Hitler turned to her and shook her hand. The applause went on for several minutes. The Greek ambassador gave her an olive branch from the sacred grove on Mount Olympus on behalf of the crown prince of Greece. There she stood with the Führer, her face aglow with pleasure, clutching her olive branch. Her efforts had paid off; he liked the film. And if he liked it, its success was guaranteed. At the end of the second part, Hitler handed her a bouquet of white lilacs (representing Olympia) and red roses (for the swastika), and the audience went wild. Then Goebbels hosted a reception at the propaganda ministry.[93] Riefenstahl had demonstrated to the world what National Socialist Germany was able to achieve. To assure her international success, she issued several versions of the film, in German, English, and French, and thus sought outreach to an audience that was not especially fond of watching Hitler. With *Olympia*, Riefenstahl had succeeded in making an overtly political motion picture that is still considered one of the finest sports films ever made. *Olympia* set new benchmarks for cinematic sports coverage.

Festival of Nations, as part one was called, opens with a prologue that establishes a connection between ancient Greece and National Socialist Germany. Riefenstahl used this introduction to make it clear that the audience would not be seeing a newsreel; this was a work of art. The camera meanders over deserted temple ruins, smoke rising, and clouds passing. The image of Myron's *Discobulus* statue dissolves into a flesh-and-blood athlete. A lone torchbearer runs along the sea, on his way to Berlin.

The Olympic stadium, seen from an aerial perspective, resembles an ancient coliseum yet highlights the technological progress of the twentieth century. The action clearly takes place in the present, complete with rounds of *Heil Hitler* accompanied by Hitler salutes. It is as though the director wanted viewers to awaken from the dream into which the prologue had transported them. The film started with the statue of the discus thrower evolving into a human being, and the competition itself begins with the discus throwing event. The camera shows us the feet in motion, the concentration, and the athletes' utter devotion before, during, and after the throw. Footage of the competitions is interspersed with shots panning up to the scoreboard, the Olympic flame, Hitler, or the spectators, who take on the role of commentators with their gestures, facial expressions, and shouts, as we see Germans, Japanese, and Italians worrying about, rooting for, or rejoicing with their athletes.

The spectators, who have turned out in large numbers, are elegantly dressed and international. A Wehrmacht officer settles in happily next to an English gentleman. Together, they chuckle over a false start, groan when the baton is dropped during a relay race, and form groups to cheer on the athletes. During the men's 110-meter hurdles, the bodies seem to fly synchronously over the hurdles. Often, the pace of the filming varies during a competition, and one can study the athletes' technique, muscle tension, and strength giving out in slow motion. Riefenstahl shows the joy of the winner, but also displays the effort and exhaustion that accompany this victory. The images of the runners lurching to the finish line, their faces contorted with pain, are tantamount to an autobiographical reminiscence of the film's director. She knows what it means to triumph over the body. The men's pole vault goes on for five hours. Japanese and American competitors fight the battle for medals until nightfall. The athletes are photographed against the backdrop of the twilight sky as they push off their poles and soar through the air.

Festival of Beauty, the second *Olympia* film, opens with shots of the Olympic Village. In the morning fog, a group of runners approaches, their bodies reflected in the lake as they complete their morning training session. These elated men head into the sauna, crowding together on the benches and massaging each other's sweaty bodies, then jump into the lake. The naked men sitting together on the landing stage in the early morning form a tightly knit group. It is evident that the female bodies in artistic gymnastics held little interest for the director. The shots of divers flying through the air like birds make it hard to tell whether they are moving toward the sky—and out of the water—or the other way around, and show the directorial mark of the former dancer. At the editing table, she was able to fulfill the unfulfilled dream of every dancer: weightlessness in space.[94]

Riefenstahl perfected the blend of physicality and technology. Technology enabled her to pull away from reality and create images that suggest pure energy. The diver's body melts into the infinitude of the sky, then we see it shoot into the water. His body appears to be sheer force and motion juxtaposed with images of composure and serenity. We see happy bodies soaked with sweat. With perfect organization, artistic intuition, and technical proficiency, she was able to shoot a film that helped her rise to the position of exemplary artist in 1930s Germany.

On May 1, Goebbels awarded Riefenstahl the National Film Prize for 1937–1938 for the *Olympia* film. Then she went on tour. She had been radiantly happy since the triumphant premiere. She had finally made a film that was understood throughout the world and aroused interest everywhere. Over the weeks that followed, she showed her film in Brussels, Belgrade, Athens, Zurich, Rome, and Paris. The young German director was acclaimed by people of note. A photograph taken of her with the film director Sasha Guitry after the premiere in Paris shows a well-to-do gentleman in lively conversation with an elegant lady. Riefenstahl hoped that her appearance and demeanor would quell the rumors about the evil Nazis. Her visit shocked the German emigrants in Paris, who thought they had found a safe haven. Riefenstahl was advised not to attend the premiere because of feared protests by the emigrants, but she could not follow that advice. She slipped into the movie theater without revealing her identity, and supposedly she witnessed the French breaking into applause whenever Hitler appeared on the screen. She was eventually recognized by the crowd, which gave her an enthusiastic reception. The German magazine *Lichtbild-Bühne* carried this report from Paris: "The emigrants here were left speechless by this success. . . . This powerful document of history in the new Germany is tearing away at many a web of lies, and many foreigners will be seeing the Third Reich in a whole new light."[95]

There is no doubt that Riefenstahl was on the move as a cultural ambassador for Adolf Hitler. This artist confounded people's images of a National Socialist. She did not have a husband or children at her side, did not braid her hair, wore elegant evening gowns, and was not averse to having fun. In late July, another tour took her through Scandinavia. Her itinerary included Copenhagen, Stockholm, Oslo, and Helsinki. The artist was received by prime ministers and kings, and her premieres were attended by generals, diplomats, princes, and princesses. On August 26, she headed to the Venice Biennale, where *Olympia* was competing with Walt Disney's *Snow White and the Seven Dwarfs* and Marcel Carné's *Port of Shadows*. *Völkischer Beobachter* reported, "At the very beginning, the creator of the film, Leni Riefenstahl, who was in attendance and sitting in the first row of the balcony between Minister Alfieri and Count Volpi, was given a special hearty round of applause."[96] Everyone rose when she entered the room. She was awarded the Coppia Mussolini, and gave a radio interview that was broadcast throughout Italy. Riefenstahl looked dazzling. Her hair was upswept; she was wearing an eye-catching gown and long glittery earrings; her face was relaxed, and her fingernails red. During the summer months of 1938, she felt like an internationally acclaimed artist. She finally had the feeling that she was a star.

In order to keep her image as an actress alive, she arranged for *The Blue Light* to be brought back to movie theaters right after her European tour. However, the names Béla Balázs and Carl Mayer, and the financing by Harry Sokal, were kept from view.[97] Her name dominated the film posters.

This summer of triumphs also marked the beginning of Riefenstahl's comedown. Her art paled in comparison to politics. During the summer months, the Sudeten crisis was keeping Europe on tenterhooks, with people fearing that Hitler would initiate a military strike against Czechoslovakia. The coming weeks were spent in negotiations with England and threats against Czechoslovakia. On September 26, Hitler gave a speech in the Sports Palace. The whole world awaited this speech with bated breath; it was a matter of war or peace. He bellowed about getting his Sudetenland on October 1. Foreign observers noted that for the first time, he seemed to be losing his self-control. On the evening of September 27, when *The Blue Light* was rereleased, a motorized division rolled through Berlin, heading to the Czech border. People on their way home from work hurried to the subways and made a point of ignoring this military demonstration. The Munich Agreement, which was signed in the early morning hours of September 30, 1938, averted war for the time being.

One month later, Riefenstahl traveled to the United States on the German luxury liner *Europa*. *Triumph of the Will* had given her quite a reputation in this country, and the Americans were curious to find out more about the career of this unusual artist who bore no resemblance to their vision of a Nazi German. Riefenstahl and her seventeen monogrammed suitcases arrived in New York on November 4. She preferred to travel under the pseudonym "Lotte Richter," but she was quickly recognized on the ship. Riefenstahl was accompanied by Ernst Jäger, her personal adviser, and Werner Klingenberg, who had served on the preparatory commission for the 1936 Olympic Games and was now acting in the same capacity for the 1940 Games. Klingenberg, a fervent National Socialist, had lived in the United States and spoke fluent English. Now that Riefenstahl had achieved fame and fortune at home, she wanted to conquer the world, and in the world of the cinema that meant conquering the United States. Her suitcases contained several versions of her *Olympia* film. Jäger later insinuated that she was actually intending to spread propaganda for Hitler, but that is unlikely for such a self-centered individual. She was looking to boost her own fame. Whatever became of the others—and in this case Hitler was no exception—was of secondary importance to her. Her expectations were high, but she soon realized that not all Americans were on her side. The influential Anti-Nazi League sought to prevent her film from being shown in the United States. However, she also found influential supporters, such as Avery Brundage from the IOC, who was kindly disposed to National Socialist Germany. Before she could show her film to anyone, though, something happened that threatened to upend her further plans in America.

On November 9, the synagogues in Germany burned; Jewish businesses were set aflame; Jewish private residences were destroyed; and Jews were locked up, assaulted, and killed. Everyone urged Riefenstahl to head home. People tried to make her realize that no one in the United States had any interest in seeing her film now, let alone acquiring it. She could not accept that, and insisted that the news was fictitious. Riefenstahl refused to believe what she was reading in the American newspapers. She claimed not to have noticed any anti-Semitic sentiment in Germany before her departure. She bore the consequences of this willful ignorance when doors were slammed in her face. After flying high in Europe, she came crashing down in America. The negative headlines about the National Socialists dashed any hopes she had for success in the United States.

Determined as ever, she continued on to Hollywood and arrived on November 24. No red-carpet treatment awaited her, and the Garden of Allah, where rooms had been reserved for her, did not wish to have her as a guest. "American films are barred from Germany, so we have nothing to show Miss Riefenstahl," a studio executive informed her curtly.[98] The major studio bosses saw no need to get together with her. Parties that had been arranged for her were canceled, and she was ignored when she showed up at a gathering, even though she had packed her best designer clothes and sassy fur hat. Eventually there was a private showing of the film in the presence of Glenn Morris and Johnny Weissmuller, followed by articles in the *Los Angeles Times* and the *Hollywood Citizen News* that praised *Olympia*. These two reviews and a visit to Walt Disney were all she had to show for the weeks she spent in the United States.

Although Riefenstahl had ample opportunity to stay informed about the events in Germany, she chose to keep her eyes firmly shut and side unequivocally with the National Socialists. On January 15, 1939, she returned to Berlin from the New World. An entry in Goebbels's diary dated February 5, 1939, reveals her true feelings about her trip: "In the evening Leni Riefenstahl tells me about her trip to America. She gives me an exhaustive picture, which is far from gratifying. We have no say over there. The Jews are running things with terror and boycotts. But for how long?" Leni Riefenstahl must have been glad to be back in the familiar totalitarian terrain. Hitler was busily preparing for war, and she was planning her next motion picture. In a sense, they were both setting the stage for the roles of their lives: Hitler as the self-proclaimed greatest commander of all time, and Riefenstahl as the Amazon warrior Penthesilea.

On March 8, 1939, one week before German troops invaded Czechoslovakia, there was an initial meeting about the "Construction Project Leni Riefenstahl." In order to meet the requirements of the major tasks ahead, she would be getting her own studio lot. A plot of land near her villa was being sought for this purpose. Albert Speer was involved in the project and attended the meetings. The Party would cover the full costs. Riefenstahl could ask for whatever her heart desired: spacious, brightly lit workspaces; a film archive; a casino; a gymnasium; dubbing rooms; cutting rooms; projection rooms, all on a lot measuring 2,700 square feet. The prospect of a mini-Hollywood in Dahlem made it easy for Riefenstahl to put the ignominy in America out of her mind. In addition to working on this major project, she devoted herself to her dream role, Penthesilea. She lost no time in founding Leni Riefenstahl Film Inc., then hired her loyal crew members Walter Grosskopf and Walter Traut as officers in the company, practiced horseback riding, and engaged in "Amazon gymnastics" to tone her body.

When Riefenstahl went on vacation on August 30, bombers had been thundering over Berlin for a week. Two days earlier, a comprehensive system of food rationing had gone into effect for the population, and troops were heading east. All signs pointed to war. In this highly charged situation, Riefenstahl went off to the mountains so that she could relax before traveling to Libya for the film shoot. She most likely encountered military vehicles on the autobahn when she left Berlin and headed to Bolzano in her sports car. On August 31, she stood on a mountain top, "happy, and filled with dreams of the future," blissfully unaware that *Penthesilea* would be called off.[99] As of September 1, there was war.

WAR

—

(1939–1945)

THE
AMAZON

The morning of September 1, 1939, was gray and cloudy in
Berlin. Anti-aircraft cannons had been positioned in the
vicinity of the Kroll Opera House to safeguard Hitler during
his speech, which was set to begin at ten o'clock. He wore a gray
military uniform and looked fatigued and agitated. Leni Riefenstahl heard him announce that as of 5:45 a.m., the Germans had
been returning fire: "Once again, then, I have put on the coat that
was most sacred and dear to me. I will not take it off until victory
is achieved, or—I will not live to see this outcome!"[1] The radio was
reporting the rapid advance of the Germans into Poland. Riefenstahl now felt so close to Hitler that she incorporated his decision
to go to war into her own plans for the future.

Most people in Berlin did not experience major changes in their
everyday lives after the outbreak of the war. Attendance at opera
houses, theaters, soccer stadiums, and movie theaters held steady.
Income taxes went up drastically, food was rationed, and windows
were darkened at night, but people were confident that this war
would soon end in victory.

Riefenstahl regarded the war as a test of her loyalty to Hitler.

In view of her prominence, she could not go on as before. If Hitler went to war, she had to follow him. She knew full well that he would continue to support her after the war only if she had done her part to support the war effort. She frantically considered her options, which even included becoming a nurse, then concluded that film was her best vehicle.

In Riefenstahl's account, her staff urged her to set up a film group to provide media coverage of the war. She went to the Reich chancellery and presented her case to a high-ranking officer, and received authorization within twenty-four hours. A major in Grune-wald gave her and her men quick instructions in handling pistols and gas masks, and they slipped on their slate blue uniforms and headed off to the front lines. This account does not really clarify what she hoped to achieve by taking the trip. Riefenstahl scrapped her plans to film *Penthesilea* and followed Hitler to Poland. She was the only one of the artists in favor with the National Socialists who was so willing and eager to do so. Her eagerness is explained in part by the fact that Hitler had made provisions for his artists in the event of war. Toward the end of the summer of 1939, his military adjutant had requisitioned from the district defense offices the papers of the artists the Führer wanted to keep out of military service. The papers were simply torn up, so these men ceased to exist as far as the military registration office was concerned and thus could not be drafted. Singers and actors made up the largest group of exempted artists, but there were also architects and sculptors. There was certainly no expectation that Riefenstahl, as a woman, would be heading to Poland just a few days after the outbreak of the war. She could just as easily have stayed in her villa in Dahlem. Her trip to the front was important as a symbolic gesture. Riefenstahl was putting on a display of anticipatory obedience.

On the evening of September 3, Hitler had boarded an armored train at the Stettin station in Berlin. His destination was the war. His favorite director followed him in a matter of days. As usual, Riefenstahl was surrounded by her confidants, including her current lover, the sound engineer Hermann Storr, as well as Walter Traut, Otto and Guzzi Lantschner, Sepp Allgeier, and four other technicians. In putting together this film crew, Riefenstahl had provided for her emotional and sexual well-being, and set the course for her professional work. Her approach to the films she had made for the National Socialists so far indicated her extreme reluctance to devote her genius to the vile work of reporting from the front. Just a few years earlier, she had made disparaging remarks about this way of making a film, and regarded her own task as creating "artistically constructed" films. Particularly since the international success of the *Olympia* film, she was unlikely to have changed her mind.

Right from the start the Poles were fighting a losing battle, with Polish cavalry up against German tanks. In a mere two days, the invaders were able to destroy the Polish air force.[2] On September 6 the conquest of Krakow was reported, and two days later, the Wehrmacht got to the outskirts of Warsaw. The Polish government had already fled to Lublin. The Germans were confident that they had won the war.

When Riefenstahl headed to Poland, she and her men knew full well that they were entering a country that had already been attacked and defeated. She failed to mention that her mission there was to film for the Führer. A memorandum was issued by the Reich Ministry of Public Enlightenment and Propaganda on September 10, 1939, concerning the "Riefenstahl Special Film Unit."[3] On September 5, "the Führer issued an order to establish a 'Riefenstahl Special Film Unit' in the framework of the propaganda ministry." This was sent to the city of Opole on September 10 at seven o'clock. According to this memorandum, the propaganda ministry contributed the services of Stolze, a governing official and the SS-Hauptsturmbannführer who held the Nazi paramilitary rank of Truppführer (the rough equivalent of a sergeant first class); Stolze would also take care of all costs incurred. The Special Film Unit was also provided two fully fueled six-seater Wanderer trucks, plus drivers, a BMW motorcycle with a side car and a driver, and gas ration cards for seven hundred liters. Riefenstahl made available her film technicians, a sound film truck, uniform attire, gas masks, and pocket pistols (!). "All members of the Riefenstahl Special Film Unit hold identification cards of the RMfVuP Propaganda Assignment Post issued in their names."[4] The film footage was classified as strategically vital, and it was ordered to be sent to the propaganda ministry in Berlin in the quickest way possible.

The chief of staff of the Army Group South to which the Special Film Unit had to report was Erich von Manstein. His memoirs, which were published in 1976, include a description of Riefenstahl's visit.[5] Even after the more than thirty intervening years, the reader senses his astonishment about this encounter. One day, this well-known actress and director showed up with her cameramen and announced that they would be filming at the front by order of Hitler. She had come to Lubliniec, she told him, because she was "following the Führer's trail." According to Manstein, it was "ultimately quite abhorrent" to the soldiers there to have an assignment of this sort carried out by a woman. However, Riefenstahl had come on Hitler's orders, and there was nothing to be done. Her appearance startled them almost as much as the fact that she was there at all. A woman could not wear the "holy robe," so she had a uniform tailor-made for her. She looked

good and raffish, a bit like an elegant partisan who might have obtained her outfit on Rue de Rivoli in Paris. Her beautiful hair swirled around her interesting face with its close-set eyes like a blazing mane. She was wearing a kind of tunic over breeches and soft, high-top boots. A pistol hung from the leather belt around her hips, and her combat gear was supplemented by a knife stuck into her boot-top, Bavarian style.[6]

Von Manstein was bewildered by the appearance of this amateur Amazon showing up on Hitler's orders in the middle of a war. Riefenstahl seemed to be taking her assignment seriously: her uniform looked quite real, and she was armed. She had to be taken seriously even though her appearance struck the soldiers as ridiculous.[7] Because no high-ranking officer was able to dissuade Riefenstahl from going out to the front and because she and her men could not be allowed to do so on their own, General von Reichenau was entrusted with this delicate task. Von Reichenau and Riefenstahl had known and liked each other since the filming of *Day of Freedom*. Von Reichenau had a key role in this war. "With his panzers and motorized divisions, he was instructed to spearhead the attack through Silesia towards Warsaw. In the preliminary discussions Hitler had suggested that he 'look neither right nor left' but 'look only forwards towards his goal,'" Hitler's adjutant Nicolaus von Below recalled.[8] Riefenstahl traveled to Konskie with this important officer. Her memoirs make no mention of this fact.

General von Rundstedt's diary reveals that Konskie was seized during the night of September 7.[9] Two days later, the news arrived that Hitler would be coming to visit the army units there. Riefenstahl missed out on seeing him and wound up in the middle of combat. After spending the night in a tent in Konskie, she awoke to gunfire. She claimed that bullets ripped through her tent and commented, "I hadn't imagined it would be this dangerous."[10] Perhaps it was now dawning on her that it might be useful to show some interest in reality from time to time. Her men had talked over the situation with the soldiers and learned that on the day before their arrival, Polish civilians had maimed and killed four German soldiers and a high-ranking officer. Most likely hoping to be able to film some good scenes, she and her men made their way to the market square.

In the middle of the square, some Polish men were digging a pit, the grave for the dead German soldiers. Their faces revealed mortal fear. They understood no German and were terrified that they were digging their own graves. Then a German police officer appeared, stood at the edge of the grave, and ordered the soldiers to maintain calm and discipline. He gave a brief speech: "Soldiers, cruel as the deaths of our men may have been, we do not want to return tit for tat." Then he told the soldiers to send the Poles home and to bury the dead.[11]

When she witnessed the Poles being brutally kicked by the Germans in violation of their superior's orders, Riefenstahl claims to have shouted:

> "Didn't you hear what the officer told you? You claim to be German soldiers?" The angry men now faced me menacingly. One of them shouted, "Punch her in the mouth, get rid of that woman!" Another called out, "Shoot that woman down!" and aimed his rifle at me. . . . When the gun barrel was leveled at me, my crew jerked me aside. . . . Even before I knew what had happened, I reported to Reichenau to protest the undisciplined conduct of the soldiers. Only then did I learn of the terrible things that had happened. A shot fired by a Luftwaffe officer had started a panic that in turn had led to a senseless shooting spree. Soldiers had fired at the Poles who were running away; they assumed that some of them were the ones who had committed the massacre. More than thirty Poles fell victim to this senseless shooting.[12]

Reichenau promised to court-martial the perpetrators. "I was so upset by this experience that I asked the general to allow me to terminate my film reporting. He was very understanding. I wanted to get back to Berlin as soon as possible."[13] This was the extent of Riefenstahl's depiction of her work as war correspondent.

Once again, her unabashed profession of ignorance is nothing short of astonishing. When she decided to travel to Poland and shoot her film at the front, she must have been aware that she was with the aggressors. Hitler had invaded a country and was waging a ruthless war, so it ought to have come as no surprise to her that the Poles were putting up a fight against the brutal superior strength of the German soldiers.

Riefenstahl also chose not to mention that the murdered Polish civilians were Jews. Alexander B. Rossino described the situation her team encountered as follows: On September 12, the 8th Air Reconnaissance Unit entered Konskie and found four corpses of German soldiers. They reacted by taking an undetermined number of Jewish men between the ages of forty and fifty, bringing them to the local church graveyard, and ordering them to dig graves. While the Jews dug, they were kicked and beaten. When the local police commander came to the scene, he told the soldiers to allow the Jews, who believed that they were digging their own graves, to get out of the pit. The Jews tried to flee, with the soldiers beating them again and tearing at their clothes. Then the soldiers opened fire. Twenty-two Jews were shot dead.[14]

General von Manstein, who was apparently relieved to see Riefenstahl leave, commented, "There had already been shootings that involved civilians during the occupation of Konskie, and now, a flak officer's nervousness when a group gathered on the market square resulted in a gratuitous outbreak of panic and then a senseless shooting that claimed multiple victims. The film troop witnessed this regrettable scene and our visitor, who was thoroughly shaken, left the area."[15] After the war, Major General Rudolf Langhaeuser, the chief intelligence officer, verified that Riefenstahl had stormed into his office. "She had seen twenty-two Jews shot and could not continue work with her film unit. Langhaeuser made a report to the commander of the Southern Army, von Manstein, who ordered 'investigation and immediate action in all cases,' but the incidents continued to take place in the Southern Army area for another two months."[16]

Riefenstahl had unquestionably displayed courage in lodging her complaint. Still, once the war was over, she was determined to portray herself and the German military in a favorable light. By 1987, when she published her memoirs, she knew perfectly well what had happened in Poland during those days yet made no mention of the genocide. There are photographs of her standing behind the soldiers in her uniform in Konskie, her face frozen in horror and fear. There are tears in her eyes, and she seems to be struggling for breath. These photographs reveal a moment of truth in Riefenstahl's life, her world breaking apart as reality descended on her. The war was not a costume party. No one was paying any attention to her command, and there would be no lovely images for her to exploit.

She made her getaway to Danzig on a military aircraft. Hitler was staying at the Casino Hotel in the spa town of Sopot, outside of Danzig. Riefenstahl claims to have reported the events in Konskie to him. He already knew what had gone on, and supposedly told her that "such an offense had never occurred in the German army, and the guilty would be court-martialed."[17] But she had even more news to report about the highly principled Hitler. While she sat next to him, he received a telegram with an urgent request from the supreme army command to issue orders to launch an attack on Warsaw. She claimed that she witnessed Hitler angrily turn to the aide-de-camp who had come with the telegram and order him to report back to Warsaw that it was being offered another chance to capitulate, because it was madness to attack a city that still had women and children in it. The truth of the matter was that on September 22 and 25, Hitler had taken a plane from Danzig to the outskirts of Warsaw to see firsthand the effects of the bombardment he had personally ordered.

On September 27, the town major of Warsaw ceded the city to the Germans. Hitler, who was in Berlin by this time, traveled back to Warsaw, and Riefenstahl followed him there. She flew with Ernst

Udet, who was now the chief of technical development in the Luft-waffe, to take part in the victory procession, because victories—not wars—were what mattered to her.

There are several photographs of Riefenstahl looking quite jolly in her uniform and aviator hat on the dais with many members of the Wehrmacht. All eyes were trained on this woman in soldier's garb. But Riefenstahl was only an onlooker in Warsaw; Sepp All-geier and the Lantschner brothers, Guzzi and Otto, were doing the filming. She stood next to Allgeier and watched him work, then she returned to Berlin without any footage in her suitcase. Her men stayed in the war.

Walter Frentz had been appointed to serve at Führer headquar-ters back in the late summer of 1939, and would remain a close associate of Hitler's until May 1945. Allgeier was shooting films for the Wehrmacht, and Hans Ertl was accompanying Erwin Rommel to capture his North African campaign on camera while their boss, the Führer's star director, stayed in the background. War did not furnish the beautiful images she needed for her art. She got the feeling that her work for the Führer had come to an end. Her cam-eramen stayed in the war, where her talents were out of place. She eventually realized that Hitler had found his fulfillment in war. He had no more need for art; war was everything.

Just a few weeks earlier, Riefenstahl had still been preparing for her role as military queen of the Amazons. She had told everyone about the movie she projected as the culmination of her career: a cinematic enactment of Heinrich von Kleist's drama *Penthesilea*. Once she had achieved great success with *Olympia*, fulfillment of this dream seemed within her grasp. Luckily, she enjoyed the support of Marshal Italo Balbo, the fascist governor general of Libya; at the last Biennale, he had insisted on sitting next to her. She wanted to shoot the battle scenes between the Greeks and the Amazons in the Libyan Desert, and she was hoping to make the movie under the clear blue sky that she pictured for her *Penthesilea*.

Balbo was delighted with this idea; however, she was unable to persuade Goebbels of the worth of this project. Goebbels did admire the writings of Kleist, but he could no longer put up with Riefenstahl's effusiveness. He wrote in his diary: "[Hitler] is quite satisfied with the management of the press and radio. Only film is coming up short. He wants to finance L. Riefenstahl's *Penthesilea* movie himself. That is the right course. I cannot do it from my funds and I have no real faith in the project."[18] It is hard to blame him for his skepticism. Most of what we know about this film project consists of grand pronouncements and providential crooning about what she intended to achieve. Riefenstahl claimed that she owed her discovery of Penthesilea to the great Max Reinhardt; that when he saw her, Reinhardt called out: "That is my Penthesilea!"[19] In 1939, she asserted that all the artistic work in her past had been no more than a preliminary stage for her work on *Penthesilea*. *Penthesilea* was about love and war, violence and desire, law and passion, and men and women. Penthesilea was both goddess and human being. Although Riefenstahl had not displayed any special acting prowess in the past, now that she was nearing the age of forty she wanted to take on the role of a twenty-year-old Amazon queen. She worked out daily, took horseback riding lessons, and recited the lines from Kleist's play. Like Junta, Penthesilea is a character driven by passion, a woman Riefenstahl called an "unrestrained, uncontrolled, wild feline."[20] She meets Achilles, the man she loves, during a battle. When her love cannot be fulfilled, she goes into a frenzy and mauls him. Violence and desire merge into one.

After her return from the United States, Riefenstahl devoted her time to preparing for this movie. She hired Herbert Windt to compose the music and signed Maria Koppenhöfer and Elisabeth Flickenschildt to play the priestesses. Since there was no lack of money, as usual, she picked out Lippizaner stallions in Vienna. "There were already close to a hundred girls in training. Not girls, but real women, who would be believable warriors."[21] To write the screenplay, she went off to the island of Sylt with her mother, her secretary, and her girlfriend, Margot von Opel. There she read, rode on horseback by the sea, and worked on her script about the Amazon queen. She repeatedly claimed that she had been preparing for this role for years on end, but letters to the Kleist expert Minde-Pouet reveal that her preliminary work was in a sorry state. In a letter dated August 4, 1939, she thanked him for the literature and newspaper clippings that he has sent her about Kleist, and it becomes apparent that she was only now starting to look into Kleist's life. Riefenstahl, who claimed to have waited all her life to make a movie version of *Penthesilea*, had never even read the *Iliad*. "Besides riding horses, swimming, and throwing javelins, I am fervently reading the *Iliad* (you don't have to worry that I might be reading the thick Schliemann book; I'm just flipping through a few interesting pages)—I didn't know it yet and am utterly spellbound by this powerful literature."[22] Three days later she contacted him again, asking him to recommend a book about ancient equestrianism. This letter also reveals that she intended to bring Hitler into the project. She explained that she was looking for "books you personally consider the best. What I mean is books that tell the story of Kleist's life and works in the easiest, most human way. No scholarly and overly analytical treatises. I would like to give the book to the Führer that best reflects who Kleist was."[23] Riefenstahl concluded this letter with the astonishing message that she would now begin her work on the treatment. Since she was heading to the mountains three weeks later, this work cannot have gone on for long. Evidently she did not have a clue as to how she would realize her ambitious plans. Although she made her notes about *Penthesilea* available in the 1970s, even those papers do not reveal an overall concept. Penthesilea was closely intertwined with Riefenstahl's hybrid self-image. For the rest of her life, she would continue to insist that she and Penthesilea formed an indivisible entity: "If there is a transmigration of souls, then I must have lived her life at some previous time. Every word that she speaks is spoken from the very depth of my soul—at no time could I act differently from Penthesilea."[24] She knew quite well that this project was not fully formed, and once she returned from Poland she did not go back to it.

The beginning of the war signaled the end of her dream of working in Hollywood. And for Mussolini, the idea of filming the drainage of the Pontine Marshes was no longer appealing. So Riefenstahl decided to go back to an earlier idea she had never completed. The *Lowlands* project had been aborted in 1934, and now she hoped to resume work on it. One advantage of this project was that she would not have to win over Hitler because he thought highly of the opera by Eugen d'Albert. After the war, Riefenstahl would claim that she filmed *Lowlands* only in order to avoid being compelled to make war and propaganda films. She alleged that Goebbels told her that once the campaign in Poland was over, she would have to shoot a movie about the West Wall (the so-called Siegfried Line, a system of defensive positions in western Germany), but she refused to do so. That cannot be true, because the documentary film *West Wall* was completed in August 1939. At the time Riefenstahl claimed to have been asked, the film was already being shown in movie theaters. Moreover, she continued to produce films that disseminated unadulterated National Socialist ideology and maintained close contacts with high-ranking Nazis.

She retreated to the mountains with a man and a romantic film project. Harald Reinl, an exceptional skier with a law degree, became her coauthor and artistic assistant. Even during the war, she could afford to rent a mountain cabin near Kitzbühel to write the script for *Lowlands*. She cast Bernhard Minetti, Maria Koppenhöfer, Frida Richard, and Aribert Wäscher, and decided to direct the film and play its lead role as well. She wanted the world to applaud her acting skills at long last.

The weather was icy cold at the beginning of 1940. Berliners

were suffering from a shortage of coal, while the number of copies of *Mein Kampf* was approaching six million. (Germans were
also reading Margaret Mitchell's *Gone With the Wind* and Trygve
Gulbranssen's *Beyond Sing the Woods*.) In the spring, the German
Wehrmacht invaded Denmark, Norway, the Netherlands, Belgium,
and Luxembourg. Cold, calculating young generals ran a gigantic
war machinery that handed Hitler one victory after another. On
the morning of June 14, 1940, Paris fell to the Nazis, and German
troops captured the city. The days and nights may have been mild,
but the streets were empty. About twenty thousand uniformed
Nazis were said to be in Paris. Riefenstahl, who was preparing to
shoot her film, congratulated Hitler on his victory.

> With indescribable joy, deeply moved, and filled with pro-
> found gratitude, we share with you, my Führer, Germany's
> and your greatest victory, the entry of German troops into
> Paris. You are achieving deeds beyond the realm of the
> human imagination, deeds that are without parallel in the
> history of mankind; how can we thank you? Offering con-
> gratulations falls far too short in showing you the feelings
> that are stirring within me.
>
> Yours, Leni Riefenstahl.[25]

Later, she would explain that she sent the telegram to express her
joy about what appeared to be the imminent end of the war—but
that is not how her message comes across.

In August, the filming of *Lowlands* was slated to start in Spain.
Franco had won the civil war with the help of the Germans, and
Riefenstahl could feel assured of the support of the Spanish authorities. However, Italy's entry into the war thwarted her plans. Mussolini sent troops to the south of France and thus made shooting a
film in Spain out of the question. Because money was no object, she

promptly arranged to have her "Spanish" sets built at the foot of the
Karwendel range of the Alps near the town of Mittenwald. When
she arrived to inspect the sets, she realized that the buildings were
too far apart and could not accommodate the camera angles she
had in mind. By this point she had lost any sense of financial pro-
portion, so she simply had the sets torn down—to the tune of half
a million reichsmarks—and then rebuilt. At the same time, strict
rationing regulations for food, clothing, and fuel were in effect for
the general public. Riefenstahl was confident of support from the
very top; she could play by different rules and use as much as she
pleased. She squandered more money on *Lowlands* than on any
of her other films. A year and a half after filming began, five million reichsmarks had already been spent. On December 16, 1942,
Goebbels noted in his diary: "Leni Riefenstahl reports to me about
her *Lowlands* movie. A whole host of complications has evolved. A
total of more than five million has already been squandered, and
it will take one additional year to be finished."[26] What sort of a
film was this, if it neither supported the war effort nor provided
comic relief?

Marquis Don Sebastian (played by Bernhard Minetti) rules over
the village of Roccabruna with despotic power. He diverts the only
source of water in the area to support his prized bulls and leaves
the peasants without water. One day, the beautiful dancer, Marta
(Riefenstahl), comes to the village and all the men go crazy for
her. Don Sebastian takes her on as a lover. Marta wants to help
the villagers, but the marquis refuses to allow them access to the
water and hits his headstrong lover, who flees to the mountains and
meets a shepherd named Pedro. To pay off his debts, the marquis
marries the daughter of the rich mayor, but because he cannot let
go of Marta, he marries her off to Pedro. On their wedding night,
the marquis hastens to Marta and demands his right to her body.
Meanwhile, she has fallen in love with the shepherd. Pedro is the
virginal figure in this movie; he is chaste and naïve. The men battle

it out, and just as Pedro had strangled a wolf with his hands at the beginning of the film, he strangles the marquis and frees the village from its oppressor. The lovers move to the mountains and leave the lowlands behind them.

The similarities to *The Blue Light* are obvious. The good people live on the mountain in freedom and in harmony with nature, while greed and avarice prevail in the lowlands. Like Junta, Marta is a Gypsy-like figure. No one knows where she comes from. Marta is a wild, irrepressible woman and a child of nature all in one. Junta and Marta are fairy-tale figures. Although Marta is on the peasants' side, she has no ties to them. Riefenstahl, in her role as Marta, is once again an outsider with great sexual vigor. Her mode of expression is her beautiful body, which she puts on display in dance. While the men cast lewd glances at her, she is focused inward. Marta is an innocent soul, but she is not sexually innocent. Pedro and the marquis take turns carrying her off to their beds.

The characters lack any psychological depth. As always, images take precedence over words. Riefenstahl devoted all her efforts— as screenwriter, producer, director, and actress—to orchestrating a self-image she had been dreaming of all her life. She wanted to be both goddess and woman, and rule over men with her body and her artistry. Like Junta and Marta, Riefenstahl was subject to a higher power that protected and preserved her. Junta and Marta were roles with which she fully identified. In both cases, she cast herself as characters who, like herself, step outside reality.

A look at the genesis of the film and the historical circumstances under which it was produced reveals a delusional side of Riefenstahl. In the five years from 1933 to 1938, she made four films, of which two established her international fame. In the five years from 1940 to 1945, she was unable to complete *Lowlands*. Contrary to her own account, her failure had only peripherally to do with the war situation. As usual, she denied having been financed and supported by the National Socialists and tried to convey the impression that she had launched the project as an independent producer with Tobis as a distribution company. However, sources make it perfectly clear that this was not the case.

Since the war broke out, it had become harder for Riefenstahl to set up a meeting with Hitler. In the spring of 1941, when she was suffering from one of her bouts of severe abdominal pain, he paid her a visit and offered her the services of Dr. Morrell, his personal physician. He also chatted about the films they would work on together once the war was over. That was one of the last times they got together. There were no more teatimes in the chancellery or merry evenings over a glass of punch at the Goebbels'. With his special armored train, Hitler traveled through Germany behind closed curtains. He spent many months far away from Berlin in his "Wolfschanze" military headquarters in East Prussia. After Rudolf Hess flew off to Scotland in May 1941, Martin Bormann became the man at Hitler's side pulling the strings in the background. In the 1940s, Bormann was Hitler's almighty secretary. He was put in charge of managing Hitler's personal finances; even Eva Braun supposedly had to ask him for money. Albert Speer, who competed with him for the Führer's favor, wrote about Bormann: "Even among so many ruthless men, he stood out by his brutality and coarseness. He had no culture, which might have put some restraints on him, and in every case he carried out whatever Hitler had ordered or what he himself had gathered from Hitler's hints. A subordinate by nature, he treated his own subordinates as if he were dealing with cows and oxen. He was a peasant."[27]

Riefenstahl got along well with this brutal man, who utterly lacked any sense of art. Bernhard Minetti remarked: "She dealt only with Hitler's secretary, that is, she had direct access to him. She used this access to clever advantage; if she could not obtain something, she threatened to lodge a complaint. Then she would say: 'It will happen immediately' and it did."[28] In the summer of 1942, she wanted to shoot a film in Spain, but lacked the foreign currency. She had already received 320,000 pesetas, but insisted on being paid an additional 240,000 pesetas. Walter Funk, the Reich economics minister in charge of foreign currencies, had given priority to the wartime economy and denied the payment. He argued that transferring this sum of money would require "cutting back the purchase of urgently needed raw materials for the war in that same amount. This would weaken our defense capability, and I cannot assume responsibility for that under the current circumstances."[29] Riefenstahl called in Bormann, who invoked the name of the Führer. "As you know, Riefenstahl Film Inc. was established with the special support of the Führer; the costs of the Lowlands film, which has been in production for more than two years, are borne by funds I manage on behalf of the Führer. I have submitted the records to the Führer, and he has decided that if at all possible, the sum of foreign currency requested by Riefenstahl Film Inc. is to be made available."[30] Riefenstahl received her money.

Her repeated assertion that Lowlands was doomed to failure because all resources were used for the war was therefore ludicrous.[31] She faced difficulties with bad weather, locating a tamed wolf, booking a studio, preparing studio sets, financing the film, and signing theater actors and codirectors. She initially envisioned having G. W. Pabst, who had come back to Germany from Hollywood in 1939, as her codirector, no doubt expecting that partnering with him would be a boon to her acting career. Pabst's work in France and the United States would also lend an international flair to the film, and, by extension, to her. However, she saw no trace of his much-touted originality and so she tried out Arthur Maria Rabenalt, Arnold Fanck, and Mathias Wieman instead. But the greatest difficulties came from within her own body. The severe case of cystitis she had contracted in Greenland had developed into a chronic illness, and she suffered from abdominal pain. She needed painkillers and nutritional supplements to get out of bed and carry on with her work. At times she could not appear before the camera because her face was so contorted with pain that even veils and a soft focus could not mask her condition. Since she was nearly forty—at least fifteen years too old for the role of Marta—she had to look her best on the set, but she was in no condition to do so. Even Goebbels was worried about her state of health: "Frau Riefenstahl has become quite ill as a result of her work and the burden of responsibility, and I urgently advise her to go for a vacation before she takes on the additional work."[32] She took his advice, and spent longer and longer periods of time recuperating in the mountains.

On June 22, 1941, the German Wehrmacht invaded the Soviet Union. As of September 19, 1941, Jews were required to wear a yellow star on the left side of their chests. On December 7, 1941, the Japanese bombed Pearl Harbor, and the United States entered the war. Hitler assumed supreme command of the army. On January 20, 1942, the infamous Wannsee Conference was held. In early February 1943, the Battle of Stalingrad ended with the destruction of the German 6th Army. The mood in Germany was dark and depressed, especially in Berlin. The Germans began to fear for their future with their Führer. In the summer of 1943, Riefenstahl traveled to Spain to shoot her film. "Here we had real coffee, bananas, oranges, chocolate, simply everything the heart desired," she exulted. Riefenstahl was filming her bullfighting scenes with six hundred rented fighting bulls and was delighted to report that "the locals have a pro-German attitude."[33]

When she looked over her bank statements that summer, she had even more grounds to rejoice. On March 31, 1943, Riefenstahl Film Inc. charged 102,329,893 reichsmarks to the General Building Inspector, Main Office of Administration and Management. The expenses for four unfinished films—about the construction of the Reich chancellery, the construction of bunkers, and bomb damage, along with a filmstrip called *The Führer Builds His Reich Capital*— were estimated to exceed one million reichsmarks. As producer, Riefenstahl had stipulated that an additional 10 percent of the production costs would go directly to her. In the "Reich chancellery" file at the federal archives, there are payment orders to Riefenstahl Film Inc. that range between fifty thousand and one hundred thousand reichsmarks. Her production company had also billed for every bouquet of flowers. The records indicate that the idea for the film about the Reich chancellery had come about in 1940 at the request of Hitler, who made an initial sum of seven hundred thousand reichsmarks available to her.[34] Arnold Fanck, who had joined the NSDAP in April 1940, was in charge of the project. In his memoirs, he stated that the inspector general's office in Berlin had commissioned it, but he made no mention of all the benefits that had accrued to him personally from his work for the NSDAP.[35]

Fanck had to defer to Riefenstahl, but he earned an enormous amount of money, and he and his wife could live in a swanky villa at the Wannsee. Fanck would work on this film for three years. He filmed in Vienna, where Gobelin tapestries were being woven for the Reich chancellery; visited Carrara, where marble for the chancellery was quarried; and took photographs in the Munich Workshops for Arts and Crafts, where the furniture was made. In February 1943 the project was called off because of the bombing, and the film was never completed. However, they continued to submit bills, albeit for more modest sums.

Working with Hitler made Riefenstahl a wealthy woman. She never put a stop to their complicity, and it continued during the war years. For *Lowlands*, she even haggled with her star, Minetti, over his acting fee. In December 1941, she tried to make him understand that he could no longer count on a daily payment. Arrangements of this kind were standard for films produced by the "industry," she explained, but not for Riefenstahl Film Inc. She offered him a lump sum, which worked to her financial advantage. Many of the people who appeared in this film did not cost anything. Once again, she had brought in the Sarntal peasants. The filming was taking too long for the peasants, who had to get home and harvest their crops, so they shaved off their beards, figuring that they would no longer look presentable for the camera. This ploy backfired, however: the makeup artist pasted fake beards on their faces and the filming went on. Riefenstahl evidently could not imagine what it meant to delay the harvest in a period of food rationing.

Maxglan, a district of Salzburg, had been a traditional gathering place for Sinti and Roma people. Barbed wire was placed around the site, and the Roma and Sinti were brought from other regions in Austria to be transported to Poland. Riefenstahl, who was intent on using any available resources for her art, had no apparent qualms about selecting her extras from this camp. Survivors testified that it was the director herself who chose the extras. In addition, she had Roma and Sinti brought to Mittenwald from the "Gypsy camp" in Berlin-Marzahn. Because these inmates were forbidden to use public transportation, Riefenstahl's production company arranged a travel permit for them. For the interior shots, which began in the studios in Babelsberg in April 1942, she worked exclusively with Sinti and Roma from Marzahn. The camp in Marzahn had existed since the spring of 1936. On the occasion of the Olympic Games, the capital had been made "Gypsy-free." Hundreds of Roma and Sinti were brought to the outskirts of the city, into the concentration camp in Marzahn. Reimar Gilsenbach and Otto Rosenberg have analyzed Riefenstahl's use of the Roma and Sinti by examining a list of the extras from the camp in Marzahn who were subject to taxation.[36] Riefenstahl Film Inc. drew up a detailed list of the "social compensatory levies for the Gypsies in making the film *Lowlands*" beginning on April 27, 1942. The list contains the names of sixty-five Sinti and Roma from the camp in Marzahn, not including the children, who probably received no wages for their work. Gilsenbach used the stills from *Lowlands* to track the Gypsies from Marzahn down to the death ledgers of Auschwitz and identified twenty-nine former Riefenstahl extras among the deportees. The ledgers of the Auschwitz concentration camp administration, some of which have been preserved, made it possible to determine the prisoner numbers. In sixteen cases, their deaths were expressly noted. "The Gypsies, both adults and children, were our darlings. We saw nearly all of them after the war. The work with us was the most beautiful time of their lives, they told us."[37] That is the version provided by "Aunt Leni," as they called Riefenstahl. Undoubtedly the prisoners had hoped that Aunt Leni, who got along so well with Hitler, would put in a word with him on behalf of her new friends. However, once they had played the roles of Spanish peasants and maidservants, they were brought to the extermination camp. To find her way into the role of Gypsy Marta, Riefenstahl had requested Gypsies from the camp, dressed them as Mediterranean types, and instructed them to applaud her dancing. Then they had done their part. This is particularly horrifying in the case of the many gleeful-looking children in the film. In none of her other productions had Riefenstahl demonstrated more clearly that she had no qualms about victimizing people for her own ends.

It was the beginning of the end in Berlin, and Riefenstahl left town. Her villa was still intact, but she was not willing to face defeat. In November 1943, she turned her back on Berlin and would never return to her hometown for any extended period of time. A year and a half later—on March 1, 1945—the Berlin office of Riefenstahl Film Inc. on Harzer Strasse in Neukölln would be closed down. In the late fall of 1943, she moved to the vicinity of Kitzbühel with a great deal of film footage and several crew members. She had bought a house there. Haus Seebichl was a magnificent property with a large screening room, a sound mixing studio, several editing rooms, and ample living space for her crew. The Tyrol and Vorarlberg regions were still considered the "air-raid shelters of the Reich," and anyone who had made it here could be considered lucky.

In Kitzbühel, Riefenstahl was safe from air raids but she was plagued by severe abdominal pain, and her two visits to Dr. Morell in Salzburg brought no relief. She also suffered from heartache. During the filming she had met Peter Jacob, who was acting as a stand-in for Bernhard Minetti in a riding scene. Jacob was a first lieutenant with the mountain infantry, and had been awarded the Iron Cross in the French campaign. He was spending his vacation in Mittenwald when the two of them met in 1940. Jacob was seven years younger than Riefenstahl, a dashing daredevil well-versed in war and love. "Never had I known such passion, never had I been loved like this. This experience was so profound that it changed my life."[38] Jacob surprised her with his visits, humiliated her with his infidelity, and made her roller coaster between the depths of unhappiness and the heights of bliss. Riefenstahl had no peace of mind. She feared for his safety and went crazy with jealousy. She kept wondering whether he would survive the war. She was constantly tormented by the idea that he was cheating on her. When they were together, their happiness was short-lived.

On March 21, 1944, Riefenstahl married Jacob in Kitzbühel. This wartime marriage was ill-fated. Jacob was her Achilles. Her descriptions of their love sound as though she was playing the role of Penthesilea in real life, complete with the war as well as the love. Riefenstahl was a very famous woman known for her stern assertiveness. Jacob, by contrast, was one of the many officers who enjoyed passing the time between his deployments with beautiful women in fine hotels. Riefenstahl was barely recognizable in her weakness and vulnerability. Jacob defeated and wounded her. Even so, she loved him and believed that he belonged to her alone. Riefenstahl seemed to be losing her identity as she desperately clung to the idea of a future with Jacob now that a future with Hitler was no longer possible. Riefenstahl was ravaged by physical and emotional suffering, but she kept crawling back to Jacob. She proudly bore his name, and called herself Leni Riefenstahl-Jacob.

On June 6, 1944, the Allies landed in Normandy, and on August 25, Paris was retaken by the Allied troops. Even in the summer of 1944, a period that was marked by military catastrophes for the Germans, Riefenstahl was able to continue her work on *Low-lands*. Everyone scrambled to comply with her wishes. If it looked as though one of her demands could not be met, her crew would mention that Riefenstahl would bring up the subject with Bormann or Julius Schaub, Hitler's chief aide, and she got what she wanted.

On August 7, Hans Hinkel received an inquiry as to whether the Riefenstahl film ought to be "combed through"—that is, examined for men and objects that would be fit for use in combat. He sent a handwritten reply: "yes (in a nice way)."[39] For the fearsome Hinkel, that was a remarkably friendly directive, one that suggests he had been instructed to handle Riefenstahl with kid gloves. On August 11, Hinkel, whom Goebbels had appointed Reich Commissioner for Total Military Service, wrote a letter to Riefenstahl explaining that in his new capacity, he had to ensure that objects and people were being properly economized, and asked her to send him a list of her employees at her earliest convenience. Ten days later, she complied with his request, indicating that she could not do without most of her twenty crew members. As Minetti flippantly remarked, not even a cable carrier was deemed dispensable in this film. This self-serving gesture also saved her crew from having to join the military.

In the case of one cameraman, Willy Zielke, Riefenstahl had no interest in shielding him from military service. The relationship between these two is hard to fathom. According to one version, Zielke had fallen in love with Riefenstahl and later sought to take revenge on her by revealing her wheelings and dealings. Another version has Riefenstahl turning on the charm with Zielke to win him over as a member of her crew. This latter version is supported by the fact that she sold and published many of his photographs under her own name. There is no doubt that she had more to gain from their association than he did. In Zielke's account of the events, she recognized his artistic potential immediately after seeing *The*

Steel Animal and took advantage of his skills by bringing him on board and having him work for her. In May 1936, he signed a contract to work on *Olympia* and filmed the prologue at the Curonian Spit. After he submitted his footage and received his fee, he was taken into custody and brought to an asylum in Haar, on the outskirts of Munich, where he underwent forced sterilization.[40] His wife, Ilse, stated that Zielke's guardian claimed that Riefenstahl was granted all decision-making authority over his future. Riefenstahl insisted that she went to great lengths to get Zielke out of the institution and agreed to assume personal responsibility for him.[41] She conveniently ignored the issue of his forced sterilization. Zielke claimed that after his release, Riefenstahl invited him to Haus Seebichl, when she needed a cameraman for *Lowlands*. Despite the food shortage, there was always plenty of good food on hand at Riefenstahl's house. In her library, he discovered American illustrated books in which his photographs were published under her name. Riefenstahl also had a copy of *The Steel Animal*. He was afraid of this woman and her power. Ilse Zielke, who had followed her husband to Kitzbühel, confirmed these details in a letter to Riefenstahl's publisher in April 1988.[42] In a personal discussion between the two women, Riefenstahl insisted that Zielke was ill, and she had brought him into the project and asked him to work on her film purely out of pity because "people like that are often the ones who have a great imagination and some of that can be used."[43] At that moment, Ilse realized that Riefenstahl intended to use her husband to inspire her own artistic imagination. Because he was classified as insane, he did not have to be listed in the credits. Willy Zielke stood no chance of emerging as a threatening competitor.

One month before the end of the war—on April 8, 1945—Riefenstahl sent a telegram to the Reich Cultural Chamber in Berlin asking to be informed when Minetti, whom she had asked to come to Kitzbühel five days earlier, had left. The world was going up in flames, and all she could think of was *Lowlands*. Riefenstahl and many of her biographers have regarded this single-minded focus as a flight from the terrifying reality.[44] That may have been true to an extent, but the major driving force behind her actions lay elsewhere: Once Hitler was no longer in power, she would have to go back to hawking her projects to the industry. She could not imagine having to watch her costs in shooting a film. Riefenstahl tried to get whatever she could, right down to the last day.

She had lost the battle for her last feature film. In spite of all her efforts and all the generous support, *Lowlands* was a stillbirth. Minetti matter-of-factly pointed to the reason: Riefenstahl had the audacity to act even though she was not an actress. Behind the camera she was energetic and spirited, but on film she seemed tense and uncertain.

In the final months of the war, Riefenstahl and Albert Speer closed ranks. They did not dare to think in terms of defeat and seemed intent on reassuring each other that everything would be all right. "I would be so happy to see you again; why not come here for a little relaxation," she wrote to him. "A cute little attic room is always waiting for you."[45] Riefenstahl figured she would worry about curing her illness once peacetime had arrived. "An eerie creative urge is living inside me. No matter how many great and beautiful works of art I have yet to create—they are all dormant within me, waiting for the right time. Soon the great turning point in this war will be coming; I feel it." She was probably imagining that the latest weaponry would bring the war to a quick end.

On July 20, 1944, the day on which Claus Schenck Graf von Stauffenberg tried to kill Hitler, Riefenstahl was at her father's grave in Berlin. Alfred Riefenstahl had died of heart failure at the age of sixty-six. He had worked in the company he founded until his death. Since the beginning of the war, hundreds of thousands of Poles were in Germany as forced laborers. As the shortage of manpower continued to increase, the National Socialists brought Soviet prisoners of war to Germany as forced laborers. Beginning in 1942, they were subject to *Ostarbeitererlasse* (decrees on Eastern workers), which confined them to locked, fenced-in settlements and affirmed the racial superiority of the German workers. In February 1943, Riefenstahl's company had 115 Germans and 84 foreigners on the payroll. Thanks to the outstanding connections Leni Riefenstahl had maintained to Albert Speer, the Reich minister of armaments and war production, her father's company had secured assignments of strategic importance for the war effort. To a lesser extent, the company worked on projects involving heating for industrial purposes. "Most of the assignments entailed heating and sanitary provisions for living areas, mostly barracks for foreigners. . . . There is no denying that this business is important for the war." The report quoted here reflects the state of the company's assignments as of February 1943, with sales amounting to 1.4 million reichsmarks.[46] This report, dated February 22, 1943, was issued at the request of the military registration office in Wilmersdorf. Heinz Riefenstahl, chief engineer and technical director of the company, would be drafted unless there were compelling economic grounds to exempt him from military service. As a plant manager, he was classified as *uk* (*unabkömmlich*, indispensable) until February 1943. However, anonymous complaints about him had been trickling in for years. In early 1943 they grew more frequent, and once his explanations began to contradict one another, his *uk* status was rescinded.

Heinz was a good-looking man, and his sister loved him. In contrast to her, he had not been able to stand up to his father; he had become an engineer and taken over his father's business. Together with the architect Eckart Muthesius, he had spent time in India and installed an air conditioner in a maharaja's palace, and from then on he proudly called himself an air-conditioning specialist. That might sound intriguing and modern, but Heinz lived in the shadow of his sister. He enjoyed lavish living, charming women, and showing off with Leni. Of course he socialized with party members, and the Riefenstahl name opened every door to him.

Heinz was a golden boy of National Socialist society. This father of two children was divorced in 1942, and was now enjoying his freedom to the hilt. It did not occur to him to act any differently in times of war, and he had no intention of cutting back on his glamorous lifestyle, which aroused envy. Espionage and intrigue were pervasive in National Socialist society, and brought about his denunciation. Complaints were filed about Heinz's lax work day: he did not go to work in the morning until ten o'clock, then went home for lunch at two, took a nap, and did not come back to the office until four in the afternoon. One hour later, he called it a day. He liked to go to concerts conducted by Herbert von Karajan. He used his car for personal travel, which was explicitly prohibited. Even after the defeat in the Battle of Stalingrad, he threw loud parties. The language of his denunciators is studded with malice and hatred. In June 1943, Heinz was recruited for basic training. During the following months, his father made several attempts to get home leave for his son. The grounds cited were bomb damage; Heinz's key position as the chief engineer at the company, which was imperative for the war effort; and Alfred Riefenstahl's cardiac ailments. On May 12, 1944, Leni wrote to Speer on this matter. "Dear Mr. Speer, I am asking for your advice and assistance as to how I can help my brother, who has been serving as a soldier on the Eastern Front for a year, and now finds himself in an unbearable situation as a result of anonymous defamations." As a soldier, he was "treated disgracefully, through no fault of his own, apparently for the sole reason that he is my brother and bears my name."[47] She believed, both before and after 1945, that she and Heinz had been treated badly on purpose. Heinz was sent to the front even though he was already thirty-eight years old. Leni was convinced that her brother was suffering from a "curse."

The Riefenstahl siblings were well-known throughout Berlin. Leni considered her brother one of her closest friends. She had always tried to smooth his way for him so he would not have to worry. Heinz was a profiteer of the war. His war contracts and the many forced laborers made it possible for him to live in high style. He seemed to think that he was entitled to this life. In the end, neither his sister's influence nor his father's letters were enough to save him. Heinz was killed in Russia. The news of his death reached his sister in Kitzbühel after her return from her father's funeral. With the death of her brother, the war had closed in on Leni Riefenstahl after all.

THE
SOLDIER

When the German troops invaded Poland, Marlene Dietrich was preparing to play an American in the Californian desert. In September 1939, shooting began for the Western *Destry Rides Again*. Dietrich finished out the 1930s as she had begun the decade: as a cheap nightclub singer, but this time in an American town rather than a German one. Because she desperately needed money and work, she had accepted Pasternak's offer. She no longer had much to lose, and this role was essentially no different from the ones she had always played: a wanton woman with a heart of gold. Her old friend from Berlin, Friedrich Hollaender, wrote her songs together with Frank Loesser, and Pasternak chose Jimmy Stewart to play opposite her. Stewart, who was several years younger than Dietrich, was considered the epitome of the boring, stodgy American. Next to her, he came across as naïve and conventional. In a reversal of the Western cliché, Pasternak wanted to give the male lead feminine attributes, and the female lead masculine attributes. Dietrich plays Frenchy, a saloon singer who helps Kent, the owner of the saloon, rig poker games. When the sheriff wants to put a stop to the con games, he is shot by Kent and his cronies. The town drunk is appointed the new sheriff, but to everyone's surprise, he takes his job seriously and brings in the son of a friend to help him out. That friend is Tom Destry, played by Stewart. Destry does not carry a weapon, and he earns scorn and ridicule. In the end, he does have to shoot in order to defend himself against Kent. Frenchy, who has come to warn Destry, is killed in the crossfire. This was an American-style love story of a girl sacrificing herself for the hero, with Frenchy as the indisputable focal point of the saloon and Dietrich the star of the film. She keeps the boys on their toes with her sayings and songs, belting out "The Boys in the Back Room" while gamboling along the counter, as the whole saloon roars with pleasure.

In none of her films does Dietrich put her body to more aggressive use than in this Western. In one famous scene, she gets into a fight with a jealous wife. Dietrich is said to have insisted on playing this scene herself. The two actresses scratch, bite, shriek, and scuffle on the floor until Destry pours a bucket of water over them. The American press raved about this scene. Dietrich had shed her European grandeur at long last. Frenchy's clothing is quite simple: she wears low-cut, figure-hugging dresses with spaghetti straps. Underneath her skirts are several layers of delicate, pleated chiffon petticoats, which accentuate her every move. Dietrich rarely showed so much skin, and her upper arms are muscular. Her short, curly hair gives her face a sassy look. She is heavily made up and sways past the men with a coquettish smile on her lips. Although these men can confide in Frenchy, who is strong, self-confident, big-hearted, and willing to lend a sympathetic ear to all, she will never belong to any one of them; Frenchy belongs only to herself. A woman of this sort cannot survive, so she has to die at the end. The genre of the Western dictates that women are good, and only men can be evil. The saloon is the alluring alternative to the puritanical home front. The men are glad to escape the morally complex world of their wives. In saloons, everything is easy and carefree. Here they enjoy their drinking, gambling, singing, and fistfighting, and have fun with women like Frenchy. With *Destry Rides Again*, Dietrich had left the European setting.

She now had a passport and a movie to show that she was an American. Pasternak's plan worked: Americans liked *Destry Rides Again*. The film is considered a classic Western. "Boys in the Backroom" became one of Dietrich's most popular songs. In her old age, she recalled that it had been fun to make this movie, and her pleasure shows. She enjoyed working with Pasternak, who spread cheer to everyone.

Dietrich was in demand once again, although she could not help noticing that she had yet to achieve a major success. It was 1939, the year in which *Gone With the Wind* trumped every other movie. Perhaps it was some consolation for Dietrich that her great rival, Greta Garbo, also lost out to *Gone With the Wind*. Garbo's career suffered as well, and just as Dietrich had to fight her way back into the headlines, Garbo had to laugh to draw attention to herself.

In Dietrich's next film, *Seven Sinners*, her acting seems wooden and lifeless, which might be attributable to the fact that she once again had to play a nightclub singer who falls in love with the wrong man. Echoes of von Sternberg films blend with scenes from the previous Western. The idea was to produce a box-office hit. Dietrich plays the singer Bijou Blanche, who is on tour in the South Pacific. Wherever she turns up, the men go crazy for her. She falls in love with Dan Brent, a handsome naval officer who is supposed to marry the governor's daughter. Brent, played by John Wayne, prefers the less respectable woman, which lands him in trouble. When Bijou and Brent meet for the first time, Dietrich is slowly descending a staircase, dressed in her white naval uniform and singing a song (this scene recalls von Sternberg's *Blue Angel*). When she is brought to the harbor in a rickshaw, Shanghai Lily comes to mind. In both movies, the events play out in a scintillating alien world, but the most exotic creature of all is Dietrich in her various guises. Brent visits her in her dressing room on a sultry night, the way Tom Brown visited Amy Jolly in *Morocco*. Bijou assures her officer that she will never desert him, but in the end she steps aside and leaves him to the respectable governor's daughter. One of the sailors beats Bijou because he does not approve of her romantic entanglement with his boss. There was no surer sign that Dietrich was no longer the unapproachable woman who ruled her own destiny. The former femme fatale had hit bottom. She had to get beaten up by stupid sailors, and her only potential lovers were the ship's tipsy doctors. Von Sternberg's diva had become a floozy. The songs in this film are better than the film itself. The critics were hardly effusive, but a reasonable amount of praise was forthcoming.

The war in Europe was far away, but many Americans were worried that history would repeat itself: first, neutrality, then war. President Roosevelt's "fireside chat" of September 3, 1939, affirmed that America would remain neutral: "Let no man or woman thoughtlessly or falsely talk of America sending its armies to European fields."[1] But once the German troops had marched into Paris in June 1940, Roosevelt knew that he would soon have to take a stand. While the Germans occupied one country after another, Americans were embroiled in debates about military intervention, with the majority still against entering the war. American artists and intellectuals, many of whom had spent years living in Europe, were emphasizing again and again that what was happening in Europe mattered to America as well. On December 7, 1941, the Japanese attacked Pearl Harbor, and America entered the war. At long last, Churchill heard Roosevelt say what he had waited so long to hear: "We are all in the same boat now."

Two weeks later, Dietrich turned forty. The fact that she was working again did not blind her to the fact that her career had reached an impasse. Her glamorous femme fatale image seemed quite outdated. Now that women could be downright mean in "film noir," she came across as anything but. Moreover, she was broke and could not afford to pick and choose when she was offered a part. In 1941 she made a movie with René Clair, playing the role of Countess Claire Ledoux. *The Flame of New Orleans* shows that women in the New World are prudish, ugly, and gabby. Women from the Old World, by contrast, are erotic, sophisticated, and beautiful. Neither Dietrich nor Clair nor audiences liked *The Flame of New Orleans*. If we bear in mind that John Huston was shooting *The Maltese Falcon* at the same time, we can see what an artistic nosedive Dietrich's career had taken. In many portraits from this period she looks frozen in place, as though fearing that any motion she might make could break the spell of her beauty.

The war added to her worries about the future and her financial situation. As a German living in America, she was an ocean apart from her mother, sister, and extended family. Josefine von Losch kept her daughter up to date about life in Berlin when she could. On March 4, 1940, she wrote to Dietrich that *Shanghai Express* was playing there.[2]

Once the United States had entered the war, the mood in the country changed. Young men full of patriotic zeal enlisted in the army. Dietrich had an American passport and behaved like an American, yet she felt that as a native German, she shared in the responsibility for this war that the Germans had begun. In December 1941, the Hollywood Victory Committee was established. Actors and singers were called upon to use their talents to serve their country. Dietrich appealed to radio audiences to buy war bonds, and from January 1942 to September 1943, she traveled throughout the country to promote war bonds in bars, on street corners, in factories, and in cafés, often six to eight times in a single day. She felt like a traveling saleswoman. She spent her evenings in nightclubs, selling bonds there as well. Accustomed to these kinds of performances from her earlier days in Berlin revues, she struck the right tone and was responsible for collecting a million dollars for the war effort. "I go on tour to collect money for the bombs that fall on Berlin. That's where my mother lives, and I haven't heard a word from her since the beginning of the war."[3] She was grateful to the country that had accepted her as a citizen, and she dedicated herself to her new homeland and to the victory over Germany with single-minded determination. At the same time, the thought of how her mother would fare in Berlin with bombs falling preyed on her mind. On March 30, 1943, she sent a telegram to Kaiserallee via the Red Cross:

EVERYONE HEALTHY, HOPE THE SAME OF YOU. HAVE GREAT LONGING. PLEASE WRITE AS OFTEN AS POSSIBLE. WE ARE WORRIED. ALL OUR LOVE AND THOUGHTS. MARIE MAGDALENE SIEBER.[4]

She also pitched in at the Hollywood Canteen, which opened in October 1942. The canteen was a restaurant with a bar and dance floor for servicemen headed overseas. Not only was everything free for the soldiers, but Hollywood stars also cooked for them. With any luck, they could have their soup served by Rita Hayworth while Dietrich made them a hamburger in the kitchen. Dietrich was in her element. She was delighted to display her domestic prowess and her patriotic feelings. Anything was better than the film studio. Erich Maria Remarque had nothing but scorn and derision for her charitable, military, and patriotic pursuits:

Little film ninnies as captains, dopey housewives looking
self-important, giving orders, etc. Hundreds of different uniforms. Men in aprons instead of in the army, washing dishes
in the soldiers' canteens, feeling wonderfully patriotic.
Carnival of conceit. Our puma in the thick of it. Frustration
finds an outlet: WAAC and the WAVES—women's organizations in the army and navy, with a full military rank.[5]

At this time, Remarque had been living in the United States for close to three years. In August 1939, he was in the south of France with Dietrich's family and they set out for Paris with his Lancia. The streets were full of military vehicles. Paris was dark. The war was weighing heavily on them. While preparing to leave, he contacted the puma, who was on the *Queen Mary* between Europe and America and was gripped with fear about her husband and child. He knew that he could not tell her what Rudi had confided to him. There was supposedly a Russian man in Tamara's life who wanted to marry her and take her to Berlin with him. If that were to happen, Rudi had told him, he would not be coming to America. Remarque had no idea what would happen to Dietrich, who was already questioning where she truly belonged. And if Rudi were to remain in Europe, Dietrich would be unnerved. In all this chaos, Remarque acted as the intermediary, and ultimately everyone agreed to travel to Dietrich.

Remarque spent the last evening with her at his favorite restaurant, Fouquet's. He was feeling wistful and conflicted about being able to get away while others had to stay in Europe, yet he firmly believed that the puma needed him. One day after the British and French declared war on the Germans, the travelers arrived in New York on the *Bremen*. Thanks to Dietrich's connections, Tamara Matul could enter the country with her Nansen passport, a document issued to stateless refugees. Matul's passport had been issued in 1933 in Paris—this long, colorful stream of paper reflected the fact that she did not belong anywhere. Every time she crossed a border, a new piece of paper was added on. Matul had no national identity; there were only countries that tolerated her presence. The final piece was issued in New York in 1939. Sieber and Matul took up residence in New York, where Dietrich had arranged for a job offer for Rudi at Universal.

Remarque headed out to Los Angeles to be with Dietrich. When he got there, he realized that he had been fooling himself. She did not need him; in fact, he was clearly in her way. Dietrich was in the middle of filming *Destry Rides Again*. He was amazed to observe the transformation of the woman he loved into a coarse American saloon lady. At home she was fidgety and volatile, and unfair to him. She had evidently entered into an affair with her costar, Jimmy Stewart. She often went out alone in the evening and did not come home until dawn. Whenever her new lover failed to call her several times a day and send her flowers, she sulked, and took it out on Remarque. He was living with her and working on his next novel about emigration. Her moodiness made it hard for him to get work done, and the American authorities were also making life difficult for him. His Panamanian passport was not recognized, and his wife, Jutta Zambona, who also had a Panamanian passport, had been detained on Ellis Island. His immigration attorney informed him that Dietrich had attempted to use her influence in Washington to have Zambona's entry into the United States denied. He was dumbfounded.[6] Dietrich was sabotaging him because he had not gone through with a divorce, even though she was now utterly preoccupied with her Jimmy.

Remarque acted friendly and aloof because he knew that this was the only kind of behavior that had the desired effect. If she got the feeling that a lover was losing interest in her, she would try to win him back. She tried to seduce him on several occasions, but he had grown wary since hearing her tell Carl Zuckmayer on the telephone that she could feign pleasure in bed. Remarque had to admit to himself that their love affair was coming to an end. He abhorred film people with their lies and pompous posturing. His thoughts kept returning to his final days in Paris, where fear of the Germans dominated everything and everyone. In Los Angeles, by contrast, people seemed naïve, cheerful, and confident. Although Dietrich was a German, she acted the very same way. Remarque could not make peace with the fact that she had decided to be an American.

And Dietrich could not see why he was so intent on pining away for Europe instead of seizing the opportunities that America had to offer.

In order to take care of passport issues, Remarque traveled to Mexico with his wife in March 1940. His homesickness for Berlin was tempered by his longing for the puma. He sent her a post-card with a picture of a Mexican boat, which reminded him of the Spreewald nature reserve in Germany. Remarque felt the home-sickness for Europe that Dietrich had not indulged in for so long. Time and again, he wrote to her about romantic evenings they had shared in Paris hotel rooms, about the Nike in the Louvre, or about the chestnut trees in blossom on the Champs-Élysées. He wanted to cheer up his sad puma, but she was far too busy surviving in Hollywood to find the time to share in his sentimentality. Although he did not hear from her at all, she was at the airport when he came back from Mexico four weeks later with an American visa in his pocket.

The time for long love letters had passed. He sent her little greeting cards that seem almost sheepish, as though he were shyly reminding her of his existence. This tactic did no good, because she rarely paid heed to her old lovers. They continued their sham of a relationship for quite some time. Dietrich was shooting a film in the desert and sleeping on the set; he gadded about from one dinner party to the next with Werfel, Mahler, and Stravinsky. All he really wanted was to be with her, which was exactly why she avoided him. Von Sternberg, "with his everlasting affection for the puma," became a cautionary example to him.[7] While Dietrich was fighting for her career and embarking on one affair after another, Remarque was battling homesickness and his lover's indifference.

At some point he had had enough, and he moved out. Having escaped the war in Europe, he had no intention of spending any more of his time in sunny California agonizing over Dietrich's moods. He resignedly returned to his old ways, visiting brothels, having affairs, drinking and smoking to excess, and dreaming of Paris. Meanwhile, Berlin and London were being bombed.

Dietrich kept up her punishing work schedule and did not let up on Remarque, impatient for him to start "her novel." He wrote letters to her, but what she truly wanted was movie material. *Arch of Triumph*, a novel of love and emigration about Ravic, the clear-eyed romantic, and the amoral Joan Madou, would not be published until many years after their relationship had ended.

Their final split came in November 1940 after a party in Josef von Sternberg's villa. Dietrich accused Remarque of being drunk and impotent when she wanted to sleep with him; he retorted that this was the result of having to have discussions about condoms beforehand "with someone who lies in bed like a fish afterwards." She claimed he had called her a whore; he replied that whores give something for what they get.[8] Remarque went off to New York for several months, and when he returned in the spring, she tried to win him back. When she found out that he had taken up with her rival, Greta Garbo, she went on the warpath, claiming that Garbo had syphilis and breast cancer and that she, Dietrich, was the one who had loved him so deeply and done so much for him.[9] He reveled in the breakdown of the woman he had loved so much. Sex with Garbo was Remarque's revenge on the fickle puma.

In the summer of 1941, Dietrich met Jean Gabin, who was the diametric opposite of Remarque. Remarque was intent on looking suave and urbane, and did not like to be reminded of his petit bourgeois background in the small German city of Osnabrück. Gabin, by contrast, did not stand for some sort of vaguely defined cosmopolitanism; he was French through and through. He would not spend his nights on bar stools. The latest trends held no particular appeal for him, nor did nightlife and cultural events. At home he enjoyed a middle-class lifestyle, perhaps because he had grown up in the entertainment world as the son of cabaret singers. He was all too familiar with the life Dietrich portrayed onscreen. When he came to the United States in 1941, he was thirty-seven years old, and a star in his home country. His greatest films were *La grande illusion* (1937), *La bête humaine* (1938), and *Le jour se lève* (1939). His favorite directors were Jean Renoir and Marcel Carné. Gabin was the *bon mauvais garçon* who stood for the melancholy peculiar to those outside the city.

Gabin preferred refuge in America to a life in occupied France. Dietrich made him feel at home in his new surroundings by creating a little French oasis in Hollywood. "We furnished his house according to his taste, with all the French objects we were able to scrape together from farmer's markets and Beverly Hills shops," she wrote.[10] Gabin was wary of anything that was not French—apart from Dietrich herself. Dietrich, who spoke fluent French, tutored him in English and cooked French meals for his friends. For Renoir she made stuffed cabbage, and her pot au feu was legendary among the French in Hollywood. She now spent many evenings with Gabin and his friends at the kitchen table. Dietrich explained America to them, helped them navigate contracts and applications for driver's licenses, and dispensed advice to the lovelorn.

Dietrich confided in Sieber what she hoped to gain from loving Gabin: "I am clinging not only to him, but also to the chance to be a real woman at long last." All she truly wanted was to provide happiness, but she had never succeeded in doing so with a man. She did not want things with Gabin to end the way they had with all the others, and used her influence to get him a visa.[11]

Her love for Gabin brought Dietrich back to Europe. Remarque was ultimately too German for her, but Gabin was so French that, as a German-American, she could feel European. When they went out together, she liked to belt out the Marseillaise at the top of her lungs. Gabin found that idiotic and laughingly called her "ma Prussienne." She rented a little house for the two of them in which she played the French housewife. When he came home, she brought him his slippers and kissed and admired him. But she also mocked him gently by knocking on his forehead and declaring that what she loved about him was his absolutely empty head. During a period in which the world was falling apart, she found a brief haven of peace in her tranquil life with Gabin.

After the grueling yet glamorous years at the side of the darkly depressive Remarque, the stoic homebody Gabin was a welcome change of pace. He could be a great seducer if he was so inclined, and was utterly dependable. Dietrich described Gabin as the most sensitive man she knew. He was an intriguing combination: reliable yet daring, sensual yet faithful. Life in America, particularly in Hollywood, seemed to cast doubt on his identity as a Frenchman: "*J'avais l'impression de ne plus être ce que je souhaitais rester, c'est-à-dire un Français* (I had the impression that I was no longer what I wished to remain, that is to say, a Frenchman)."[12]

Home movies capture scenes from their love life. On horseback in the desert, they are dressed like cowboys. We see Gabin in a bathrobe smoking and smiling in a way that helps us understand why Dietrich has fallen for this man. The table is set for coffee, and the bicycle leaning up against the wall casts a shadow. She is sitting in the sun in front of the house having breakfast. Dietrich looks relaxed; her hair is tousled, and she is smiling at her lover and smoking. He is swimming laps, and a suntanned Dietrich watches him from the edge of the pool. These Brentwood images reflect their happiness. The sun is shining, the sky is unnaturally blue, and the war is far away.

Dietrich took every opportunity to be seen in public with her lover. Gabin, with his compact body, was a skilled dancer. There is a photograph of the two of them at a table in a nightclub. Gabin is wearing a tuxedo and bow tie. He is sitting close to her, his eyes gazing warily into the camera. Dietrich, in a strapless evening gown, looks delicate and luminous, and her face has a timeless, youthful quality. She was seriously considering marrying Gabin. She signed a letter to him in which she adopted his actual surname (Gabin was a stage name) as her own: "Marie Madeleine Moncorgé."[13]

In late February 1942, she was planning to take a trip and leave her canary with Remarque. Over vodka, she told him that she wanted to get a divorce. She seemed to have aged, yet was still on the quest for liberating love. The pinnacle of her yearning for lasting happiness was her suspicion that she was pregnant with Gabin's baby. Dietrich got caught up in the idea of this pregnancy and dreamed of beginning anew as a wife and mother at the age of forty.

From her vacation with Gabin in Mexico, she wrote to Sieber: "You close your eyes and know that life isn't really like this. It may be so for many women—but I always figure that it can never be that way for me. . . . I have been through the mill of responsibilities for so long that I can't get used to the idea of a man taking on all my burdens. Most of the time, I have been the one to take on the burdens of others."[14]

As might be expected, Maria had decided to become an actress, and she was now attending workshops. Her first performances showed that she had inherited her mother's talent. Maria adopted the stage name "Maria Manton" and married Dean Goodman, a comedian. Now Dietrich had to take care of both of them, even though she was facing financial difficulties of her own. She wrote to her husband in New York that she needed to borrow money to provide their child with the necessities: "I had to buy plates, silverware, pots, tablecloths, etc., etc., and everything costs a lot of money. Besides, I can't let my life insurance lapse—so I have no money. I'm trying to sell my jewelry, but that's not easy. I have to rush off to the studio."[15] Although she had been working hard for years, she was low on funding. In *Manpower*, she costarred with George Raft as Fay Duval, a nightclub hostess who has been released from prison and has not gotten any breaks in life; she plays her as a vulnerable woman with no illusions. Fay believes that all she is able to do is entice drunk men to keep spending money on drinks. During the shooting of her next film, *The Lady Is Willing*, Dietrich broke her ankle, but that did not slow her down. Her willpower and work ethic were admired far more than the film itself. *The Spoilers* (1942) takes place in a saloon once again, complete with a sheriff, a free-for-all, and an inane maid. The sight of Dietrich as Cherry Malotte, who works in the saloon, is almost frightening. She looks like an old lady who thinks she is still sexy. With her hair upswept and wearing a white blouse, she is subjected to insults and affronts to her dignity. She acts like a wind-up doll, bored stiff. She wrote to Sieber, "I think I ought to take a break from this business, which drives me to earn money; after all, I'm not going to keep the money anyway. If I were still happy in this work, I would still have something, at least, but this hasn't given me any pleasure for quite a long time; instead, every movie is a false hope that brings only pain."[16] Actually she could not do it anymore. "I am tired, in body and soul. I don't know how the movie turned out—and I don't really care."[17]

One year after the United States entered the war, Dietrich acted in a propaganda film. The impetus was the mobilization of the American economy for rearmament. A voiceover speaks with a triumphant undertone about the weapons from the arsenal of democracy that will engulf the totalitarian tyranny. The movie features two men and one woman. Dietrich plays Josie, a coal miner's daughter of Polish ancestry who wants to escape her father's world, which centers on filth, sweat, hunger, and strikes. *Pittsburgh* is interspersed with documentary shots of the German invasion of Poland. Josie finds her soulmate in a miner named Pittsburgh Markham, who eventually strikes it rich and casts her aside. Josie commits herself to Pittsburgh's friend Cash Evans, who has loved her for a long time. Pittsburgh loses everything, and it takes his working in Cash's steel mill to make him a good American again. The patriotic mission of the war brings the three friends together. Josie turns to her quarreling friends and exclaims, "This is no time to think about personal feelings and personal grievances. There is a greater, far more important emotion. The only emotion that should guide each and every one of us today: devotion to our country!" In *Pittsburgh*, Dietrich is the good, patriotic comrade-in-arms along with the men. The film was intended to demonstrate to Americans the need for civilian commitment for a just war. American moviegoers and critics did not seem to care for Dietrich in the role of upstanding patriot. *Pittsburgh* was not well received.

By contrast, Dietrich's dedication to the soldiers was greatly admired. She visited wounded men in military hospitals, handed out photographs of herself, and paid for lampshades to protect the eyes of the wounded. She made radio broadcasts of texts that the Office of War had put together for her. The American military officers were pleased with the results: "The impact of your appearances on the air has already shown tremendous results and bond sales are mounting steadily day by day. I wish I could tell you how gratifying it is to work with people whose keen interest and honest patriotism makes it possible to do the kind of job that you did."[18] Her former lover, Remarque, found these activities sickening. He despised the Nazis, but he preferred bellyaching and drinking to taking political action.

Gabin, who knew that he would have to remain in the United States if the Germans won the war, reacted the opposite way. He reported to the representative of the Free French Forces in New York and enlisted to fight on the side of de Gaulle for the duration of the war. In January 1944, he was ordered to embark from Norfolk, Virginia, where there was a key marine base. He had been appointed tank commander in the 2nd Free French Armored Division. Dietrich accompanied her lover to Norfolk. Like thousands of other couples, they spent their final evening together having dinner and going to the movies. His ship sailed at 2 a.m. Gabin went off to fight for his beloved France and left Dietrich behind. His home-sickness for France won out over his love for Dietrich. She had no idea if they would ever see each other again.

But Dietrich took control of her destiny. She reported to the American army and waited for her induction order from the United Service Organizations (USO), a civilian group that provided live entertainment for the U.S. troops. Once Gabin had left America, she could go as well. Before following her lover off to war, she costarred in *Kismet* to earn some money. *Kismet* was a Metro-Goldwyn-Mayer movie, and her director was William Dieterle. She had costarred in his first film, *Man by the Roadside*, in 1923, and had had her legs lacquered in gold for the role of Jamilla, queen of the harem. Now she would be closing the studio door. Without a word of fare-well, she was leaving thirteen years of her life behind her. It almost seems as though she was glad to escape the dream factory.

On June 29, she received a telegram in her New York hotel from Abe Lastfogel: DEAR MARLENE YOUR TELEGRAM WAS REALLY A TONIC THAT MAKES UP FOR ALL OF DISAPPOINTMENTS WE RECEIVE HERE IN OUR WORK FROM DAY TO DAY.[19] Lastfogel was the director of the USO. He expressed his delight at her generous offer to entertain the troops and hoped that Danny—the comedian Danny Thomas—would have time to serve as master of ceremonies for Dietrich. Day after day she headed to One Park Avenue, where Lastfogel evaluated shows and entertainers for domestic and foreign performances. Censorship was ubiquitous. Artists had to be politically trustworthy and the shows entertaining, but they had to stay on the level of good, clean fun. Dietrich had to swear that only the material that had been approved by the censors would be performed, and any deviation from the script would be reported.

The time for expecting to be treated like a film star was over. Both personally and professionally, she was serving the United States of America. From now on, different rules from those in Hollywood applied. In the smoke-filled waiting room at One Park Avenue in

New York, she would think of her mother on Kaiserallee in Berlin, who had insisted on maintaining wartime rules. As a child, she had regarded these rules as protective, a precious constant in a world that had come apart at the seams. She felt much the same way now that she was past the age of forty: "What a pleasant feeling it is to wait for orders."[20]

Dietrich had stored away her personal possessions in two places: on Landsberger Strasse in Berlin, where she kept whatever was left of her family life with Rudi and Maria, and in Los Angeles at a Bekins storage facility, where she had rented three units to preserve her memorabilia as a Hollywood movie star. Nothing was keeping her in the United States, and she was ready to leave. Of course she was thinking of the future, fully aware that she was venturing into unknown territory. It was one thing to perform in revues when you were in your mid-twenties, but quite another to stand onstage in front of thousands of men in your early forties. Danny Thomas taught her the tricks of the trade that a solo artist needs to survive.

Before she left, Dietrich was given a uniform and a military rank of captain.[21] She tried on her tailor-made USO uniform at Saks Fifth Avenue; she put on boots and applied red fingernail polish. Instead of the usual innumerable wardrobe trunks and hat boxes, she was traveling light this time, since she was allowed to take no more than fifty-five pounds. She complied with this order without a word of complaint, but made sure to include sequined evening gowns, crisply pressed uniforms, and her musical saw. On April 5, she and the musicians, comedians, and other performers in her show flew to Algiers by way of Greenland, the Azores, and Casablanca. Before departing from New York, the two women and three men in uniform in this troupe were photographed gazing cheerfully into the camera. Dietrich did not stand out from the rest; she was simply part of the team.

Typically the artists did not learn where they were headed until they were already on board, but Dietrich must have known her destination in advance, because Gabin was waiting for her in North Africa. In March he had sent her several telegrams to say that he would be there, and then, to his delight, she arrived. Several extant photographs convey a sense of their time in Algiers. One shows Gabin—quite elegant in his dark blue naval uniform with gold buttons—with his arm proudly around Dietrich; he seems to be telling the camera that no one has a lover like his. She is also in uniform, her forage cap perched jauntily on her blond curls. Both seem happy and relaxed, and it is hard to bear in mind they are not on vacation, but in a war. The other photographs confirm this insouciant impression. In one, they are strolling arm in arm under palm trees; in the downtown area of Algiers, she is sitting on a small wall wearing men's shoes and slacks and has rolled up her shirt sleeves. She is wearing no jewelry apart from a few gold bangles.

Dietrich had come only because of Gabin, but once she was there, she was there for everyone. She gave her first concert for GIs at the opera house in Algiers, looking like a vision in her tight sequined dress. They could not believe that this beautiful woman had turned her back on Hollywood and luxury to be with them. From the very first moment, Dietrich made them feel that they were her greatest audience ever. She kicked up her famous legs, played her musical saw, indulged in self-irony, and sang. "The Boys in the Backroom," "You Do Something to Me," "Taking a Chance on Love," "Annie Doesn't Live Here Anymore," and "You Go to My Head" would become her standard repertoire. They are sad yet witty songs, easy to sing or hum along to.

In spite of the story the pictures tell, things were not going well for Gabin and Dietrich. The letters he wrote to her over the coming weeks and months tell of his despairing wait for news. He launched into descriptions not of the war, but of his great love for Dietrich. His declarations of love were composed on sheets of translucent, yellowed stationery without letterhead. In the upper margin he made careful note of the date and time, then recorded his thoughts about his love and doubts in dark ink. He complained bitterly that she was withholding something from him. He found it harder and harder to believe that she loved him. Feeling that he was not being taken seriously, he turned to Sieber for help, but the latter was unable to intercede on his behalf. Gabin's letters to Dietrich went to her USO address in New York and were forwarded to her, so he had no idea where she was at any given time or whether his messages were getting through to her at all. When he met American soldiers, he would ask how she was faring. It was a mystery to him why she would put him in a spot like this. Like all her other lovers, he could not accept the fact that she no longer loved him. On May 17, his fortieth birthday, he was feeling melancholy; this was the third birthday he had had since he was together with her, but the first that he spent alone.

Dietrich flew from Algiers to Italy. On the night of July 9, 1943, the Allies had landed in Sicily, and Mussolini was overthrown in Rome on July 25. In Northern Italy the Germans established a puppet state, the Republic of Salò, under Mussolini's leadership. Dietrich and her troupe followed the Allied advance, and she emerged from her airplane in Bari wearing sunglasses and a warm jacket. There are pictures of her performance in the theater there. Everything looks improvised and almost shabby. Standing in front of a ragged curtain on the simple stage in her evening gown, she must have summoned up colossal energy to cope with these conditions. There were no props or lighting controls; everything had to come from within her. After the performance, she was invited to the officers' club. A laughing Dietrich, clad in a simple dress, was gliding across the dance floor with a high-ranking military officer. Although she was under a good deal of stress, she must have welcomed the admiration and love she found here. She often performed on a stage that had been specially constructed for her, or outdoors beside an army truck. Sometimes as many as twenty thousand GIs came to see her perform. When she was onstage, she saw masses of soldiers sitting on their helmets and waiting for her to speak to them. These men—all in uniform—only had eyes for the woman with the bare shoulders and the high-heeled shoes. Sometimes the soldiers were able to scrounge up some roses to decorate Dietrich's tent. When she moved on, she would make sure to take the flowers with her.

The war gave Dietrich a new mobility. No longer tied to studio work, she went from place to place with her evening gowns and uniforms in tow. The letters from her daughter, who had stayed behind in America, are surprisingly affectionate. Maria was unnerved by her mother's long absence, and when a week went by without news, she grew alarmed and contacted her father, who had no idea of his wife's whereabouts either. Maria tried to hearten her mother from afar, as in this excerpt from a letter she wrote her in May: "I saw your picture in *Vogue* in your uniform. You really look wonderful. You look like you did when you made your first pictures."[22]

However, Dietrich's performances were no easy task. Although she had never done anything *but* entertain her entire life, she felt overwhelmed. She had to stand in front of thousands of soldiers who kept shouting and whistling at her. She was unaccustomed to these kinds of audiences from her studio work, and they were not always welcoming. Danny Thomas taught her how to avoid getting fazed, how to make a joke work, and how to keep the audience in line. She entertained the soldiers with a few songs, a few witty remarks, and a few skits to make them laugh and cry and offer a refreshing pause from their daily reality.

After Bari, she continued on her way to Naples. Soldier Dietrich was helping to recapture the country from the Germans. Some houses were roofless; most were completely destroyed. There was rubble everywhere, and children played in the ruins. Wherever the Germans went, they left behind death and destruction.

On the Italian front, a total of twenty ethnic groups and nationalities were fighting the Germans. Dietrich occupied a unique position among them because she was a German fighting against the Germans. In Capua she sat in the courtyard of a castle, her sequined dress sparkling in the sunshine, surrounded by jolly GIs. Despite the adverse conditions, she managed to look glamorous. Her hair was beautifully coiffed, her makeup was impeccable, her nails were polished, and her clothes were a perfect fit. She and Irene, her fashion designer, had decided to go with sequined dresses because they did not need to be reironed before each performance. In Caserta she stood at the microphone with the soldiers at her feet. She scribbled on the back of a photograph, "No love, no nothing. . . . Sinatra never had an audience like that." Each of these men wanted to attract her attention. They figured that if Dietrich was there, things could not be too bad; if the situation were truly dangerous, she would not be authorized to come to them. She was well aware of their thinking. Of course she was afraid, but she could not show any signs of fear.

Since January 1944, the Allies had been fighting for access to Rome. In May they finally achieved the crucial breakthrough. The conquest of Rome went according to plan once the Anzio beachhead was established. Dietrich was on the scene in the decisive days. She was the first Allied entertainer in Anzio. Then, on June 6, when news arrived about the success of the Allies in Normandy, Dietrich had the honor of announcing it onstage. She shed tears of joy when sharing the news about the crucial blow to Germany. The soldiers were jubilant. Everyone knew that the end of Hitler had come. Just a few days later, the Americans entered Rome with a long parade of cars. The soldiers threw around chocolate and cigarettes, and proudly shouted, "We told you we'll do it!" The capital of Italian fascism had fallen. Dietrich later reported that the Romans could not believe their eyes when they saw her sitting in a jeep. "They must have thought Americans are wonderful. We bring them freedom, bread—even movie stars."[23]

On June 17, she landed back in New York. Every newspaper of

note ran a photograph of her emerging from the aircraft in an army flight suit with little luggage and many helmets, which were gifts from her soldiers. At the press conference, she was wearing army trousers, shirt, tie, boots, and a forage cap, and her fingernails were painted red. She lit her cigarettes not with matches, but with a GI lighter. Her responses were brief and matter-of-fact. She struck the journalists as serious and utterly transformed from the Dietrich they had known. She had turned military and put her femme fatale persona behind her. The diva was now a soldier. She reported about "the boys": "They are very much alive and alert. That is why I want to go back."[24]

Dietrich had come back to put together a new troupe. Her selection was limited, because not many artists were willing to be away from home for half a year. Charles de Gaulle visited New York on July 11, and Dietrich was invited to his reception at the Waldorf Astoria. The newspapers featured pictures of her chatting with Mayor LaGuardia. She was now a political figure fighting for a liberated Europe. Hollywood seemed far away.

When we see her looking relaxed and self-confident in the political arena, we find it hard to believe that she was having a difficult time with her lover at this time. In late June, Gabin was overjoyed to get a telegram from her and called her the love of his life. Five days later, his happiness had flipped into outright despair. He read in the newspaper that her latest romantic affair was with an air corps brigadier general she had met while on tour. Now he understood why he had heard from her so rarely. She no longer considered him important, and he wanted nothing more to do with her.

However, Gabin could not tear himself away altogether and soon wrote her a letter in English, begging to learn the truth. He felt betrayed and lost, and asked her to write him if she wanted to renew the promise of their love; if she did not, however, he would resign himself to the situation, and she would never hear from him again. Dietrich laid his fears to rest, and he made the mistake of continuing to confess that he admired her "like a fool."[25] She was increasingly peeved with his admiration and jealousy, and knew all too well how wrathful, aggressive, and possessive he could be.

Once the storm had subsided, she calmly went about her business in New York. She continued to prune her possessions and put her furniture and jewelry up for auction. Earning money was no easy matter during the war. Dietrich had to take care of the entire family, and complaints about payment of back taxes and a lack of money were ongoing in her letters to her financial adviser, who was often appalled by her lack of cooperation. She did not know how to handle money. Dietrich hated the idea of not being able to spend money left and right. She spent a sunny afternoon on a roof garden in Manhattan being interviewed for *Vogue* by Leo Lerman, who wanted to learn all about her role in the war. The first thing he noticed was that her eyebrows were no longer shaved off and traced on, but had grown in naturally. "And Dietrich is funny, with that baggy pants comedian funniness, that belly-laugh vigor which her friends adore, but which Hollywood hid behind six-inch eyelashes and a million-dollar languor."[26] She wore no makeup apart from lipstick, and of course she had on her GI shirt and trousers. She struck Lerman as very thoughtful. The conversation went on for fifteen hours, and she seemed pleased that Lerman wanted to know how she was faring in Europe. She provided a particularly impressive description of her visits to the front-line hospitals:

> There are those rows of beds. In them, boys are sleeping or unconscious. Next to each bed stands a pole, and on that pole hangs a jar—a jar of blood. The only movement in that whole place is the bubbling blood, the only sound in that whole place is the bubbling blood, a little wisp of a sound . . . the only color in that place is the color of blood. You stand there with actual life running from bottles into the boys. You see it running into them. You hear it."[27]

She was asked to visit the German soldiers in the military hospital. "'Please go over and talk to them. You can speak German.' And I'd go over to those blank faced, very young Nazis. They look me over and ask, 'Are you the real Marlene Dietrich?'"[28] The German soldiers knew her only from what their mothers had told them; in their stories, she was always the blue angel.

Dietrich was deeply impressed by the morale of the American soldiers and the incredible efficiency of the army. In any case, she wanted to get back to the war. "I won't sign any contracts here that would tie me down. I will not sit here working at my little job and let the war pass me by."[29]

Kismet opened on August 22, before she left New York. She cleverly managed to interweave stories about her work with the troops when asked about the movie. She told one journalist the story of a severely wounded soldier who had lost the will to live, but regained it when he was overcome with eagerness to see her golden legs in *Kismet*. Going to the movies was his first plan for the future. The doctors asked her to put on quite a lot of perfume before heading to the front-line hospitals; smelling perfume on a woman, they explained to her, could make the difference between life and death. The wounded men even asked her to kiss their bandages, and she did. Dietrich knew how to shape her public presence. She mastered all the roles, from the soldier to the patriot to the saint. On one of her last evenings in New York, she enjoyed herself at her favorite club, El Morocco—in uniform, of course.

When Dietrich left for her second USO tour in early September, she knew that Paris had been taken back. Her itinerary began in the northern American bases: Iceland, Greenland, and Labrador. In Iceland, she was photographed looking lost and freezing in a desolate landscape; behind her, in a nod to her homesickness, a handmade sign read: "Park Avenue." In another photograph, she was at the stove in an army shirt and apron, with military officers all around her. "Iceland—kitchen making potato pancakes," she jotted on the back. Dietrich made a point of eating her meals with the enlisted men as a way of showing that she was there on their behalf. She listened to their stories, laughed at their jokes, and gave them a feeling of importance. Her shows, jokes, and skits were also attuned to their taste.[30] In one important respect, however, she and "the boys" were quite different. For the soldiers, the end of the war meant that they could go home, but she would have to figure out just where "home" was.

Her relationship with Gabin was moving along as usual. He waited for signs of life from her and was beside himself with happiness if she wrote him a letter. In November 1944, he told her he was tired of being alone and spending the years without her. He would likely have been horrified to learn that Sieber was the first one to read his love letters, then tell her whether they contained something important beyond the fact that Gabin was sad. Rudi wrote to her, "I shall make copies of all of them to send them to you and shall keep the originals for future reference."[31] Sieber no longer kept a tally of her income and expenses, but he took a rather sadistic pleasure in passing judgment on the feelings of others, and archiving his wife's love letters.

In writing to her on the front, Sieber skirted around the subject of the war, concentrating instead on managing his wife's lovers and ensuring that she had a steady supply of makeup. In return he received a monthly check, which enabled him to lead a good life. Dietrich's business manager, Charlie Trezona, who was alarmed at her dwindling assets, wrote her a strongly worded letter in February 1945. He had contacted Rudi, who seemed to assume that Dietrich would provide for him and Tamara until the end of their lives. He told her, "Mr. Sieber seems very worried about the possibility of your not being able to keep up your insurance payments and the checks for him in maintenance." Trezona tried to impress upon Dietrich that things could not go on this way. If she chose not to shoot any films and instead entertain the troops, that was her prerogative, but she had to be able to afford it. Dietrich had always opted for spending her money rather than investing it. Now she had nothing left. Trezona saw only one solution to this problem: she had to shoot a film or do radio broadcasts. American newspapers were printing letters from soldiers that were full of praise for her courage and dedication. On the other hand, the rumor persisted that she wanted to stay in Europe. Trezona admonished her, "This is very bad and should be corrected by you unless it is true. Your return should be looked forward to by producers of films and radio shows and the anticipation of your return should always be built with the view in mind of getting the maximum earning power when you return."[32]

There she was in France, its fate hanging in the air, and she was dealing with the cold and with crab lice and needing to turn her thoughts to her next film role. Nothing was further from her mind than Hollywood. Then she heard from her friend Walter Reisch, who had immigrated to America and now wrote to her in English:

> It gives a strange feeling to hear you talking about the cold
> and the dampness and the dark, but it is not a feeling of pity
> or regret, it is a feeling of pride and respect for your bravery
> and selflessness with which you serve the cause. Somehow
> we always felt it was just a whim of yours when you said
> time and again you will be first one to be over there—Paris
> and further on—and then you really did it. Grand! It is
> sunny and warm here, and still there are many who would
> trade with you.[33]

She found it irritating that her American friends acted as though the war was already over and done with while she was still in the thick of it. During her stopover in New York, she received an inquiry from the American secret service OSS (Office of Strategic Services) requesting her help with radio programs to be broadcast in the

German transmission area.[34] Dietrich, the unforgotten Blue Angel, seemed predestined for this assignment, and she accepted it. The broadcasts were recorded in London. She sang songs in German and English, most often "Lili Marleen," the World War II soldiers' song, the text of which originated during World War I.[35] After the defeat at Stalingrad, Goebbels had banned it on the grounds that it would "undermine defense efforts." The Allied soldiers had also gotten to know this song on the army's radio station in North Africa. Dietrich added it to her repertoire in late 1943. She sang this song for two years, in Africa, Sicily, Italy, Alaska, Greenland, Iceland, Belgium, the Netherlands, Germany, and Czechoslovakia. Hemingway said about his friend Dietrich: "If she had nothing more than her voice, she could break your heart with it."[36] This was intentional on the part of the OSS. The idea was to make the Germans melancholy and have them recall a time in their country that offered more than marches and exhortations to hold out. Dietrich sang this song as a soldier, unsentimentally and matter-of-factly, to bring back the poetry that the Germans had lost.

In August 1939, she had left the Côte d'Azur on the luxury train known as the "Train Bleu"; little did she know that it would be five years before she set foot on French soil again. In late September 1944 Dietrich was back in Paris, staying in a suite at the Ritz. Everything was still there: the brass bed, the dove-gray wallpaper, the marble fireplace, and the large gray vanity with the mirror. The food was terrible, but no worse than the army food she was now used to. And the Ritz still had plenty of champagne.

Only VIPs could stay at the Ritz. Two such guests were Ernest Hemingway and his new lover, the reporter Mary Welsh. Hemingway affectionately referred to Dietrich as his "Kraut." He admired her beauty and intelligence and thought she had the best "gallows humor" in the world. Both of them enjoyed making detailed plans for her funeral, which he would end by saying, "There'll never be such a show. You're immortal, my Kraut."[37] She would often head

straight into his bathroom and have a seat at the edge of his bathtub
to watch him shave while serenading him. They started drinking
champagne in the morning. Hemingway valued her judgment, and
every once in a while he read her parts of his new manuscript at the
hotel bar. He expressed his admiration in an oddly worded message: "I was so proud of you in the Ritz and how you looked like a
combat soldier and walked like one and even smelled a little like
one."[38] Hemingway admired her Prussian nature, and she loved
the writer and hunter in him. Their friendship was based on their
mutual awareness of the other's vulnerability. When Welsh met
Dietrich for the first time, she described her as "sinuously beautiful
in her khaki uniform and the knitted khaki helmet liner she wore
askew on her head."[39] Welsh was struck by Dietrich's matter-of-
fact manner and characterized her as a businesswoman "concerned
with every detail of her program from transport to accommodations, to sizes of states and halls, to lighting and microphones."[40]

No sooner were the Germans driven out than the French couturiers began to design their next clothing line. A photograph shows
Dietrich in a simple uniform, with men's shoes and a big handbag,
in front of Elsa Schiaparelli's studio. There she bought the ginger-
red silk coat in which Lee Miller photographed her at the Ritz for
Vogue, sitting on the floor and looking out into the distance. Miller
commented, "It is all right for her to shop in Paris, although the
city is out of bounds—as she is in USO and has to dress up for the
boys."[41] She continued to perform in eastern France, Belgium, and
the Netherlands, but she was exhausted and riddled with anxiety:
"I'm afraid, period. A funny feeling. Fear of failing. Fear of having
to give up, of being unable to endure this way of living. And everybody will say, with a smile, 'Of course, of course, that was a silly
idea.' I can't confide my fear to anyone."[42]

Dietrich had now replaced her USO uniform with the standard-
issue "Eisenhower jacket," along with the mandatory trousers, hel-

met or cap, and heavy boots. The closer she came to Germany, the more secure she felt in her uniform. A series of photographs shows her standing next to General Patton in France. For Patton, the uniform was an indispensable part of a successful military campaign. He understood the critical importance of the theatrical element in battle and the disciplinary power of the uniform.[43] Patton gave Dietrich a small revolver to defend herself if captured by the enemy.

After heavy bombing, Aachen, the "city of churches and kings," was the first major German city to fall to the Allies. Dietrich was surprised to feel neither threatened nor fearful, and she was given a cordial reception: "We pushed into Germany, and much to our surprise, we did not feel the least bit threatened or fearful. The people on the street wanted only to embrace me; they asked me to put in a good word for them with the Americans. They couldn't have been friendlier."[44] She had returned to her homeland with the victors. She was torn: she was a part of the old Germany, and she belonged to the new America that would decide Germany's fate.

She spread out her sleeping bag in what remained of a bombed-out house; it was cold, rainy, and muddy. There was no roof, and rats scurried every which way: "Rats have icy paws. You're lying on the bare floor in your sleeping bag, the blanket pulled up to your chin, and these creatures run over your face, their paws cold as death; they scare the life out of you."[45] By Christmas 1944, it was clear that this would be the final Christmas of the war. The Battle of the Bulge was a failed offensive. Dietrich was feeling glum; she was turning forty-three and had no idea what direction her life would be taking, both personally and professionally.

Dietrich was starting to forget where she was performing at any given time. The long months of the disorienting life on the battlefields of Europe had worn her out. She still refused to adjust to the demands of the war and continued to regard her life as chaotic right through to the day the war was won. She and the boys awaited their instructions like good soldiers. They were the victors, but they felt hollow inside. She finally received the order to fly back to LaGuardia Airport, where everything had begun. When the plane landed in New York, it was raining, and no reception committee was on hand. They were frisked from head to toe; Dietrich's souvenirs from the war were confiscated, including the revolver General Patton had given her. Captain Dietrich returned unarmed to her suite at the St. Regis.

PROSECUTION

(1945–1954)

THE
WITNESS

D
ietrich spent the summer in New York after the Germans
were defeated, healing from an inflammation of the jaw
and the aftermath of the frostbite on her hands and feet.
Once the war was over, her life grew complicated all over again.
There were no more orders, performances, or audiences for her,
and she did not have enough money to cover the checks she was
writing. Her friends, who had envied her courage, were delighted
to see her but were not terribly interested in hearing war stories.
Since Dietrich had no desire to go back to Hollywood and had no
idea what she would do in New York, she went off to Paris, where
Gabin was waiting for her. He had not been demobilized until July
1945. After the long strain of the war he felt weary and drained,
and had no intention of joining the victory parade on the Champs-
Élysées; instead, he watched his comrades go by from his hotel
room window.

The tone of Dietrich's latest letter to Gabin was testy. She did not
appreciate having to account for her comings and goings. Dietrich
assured him that she was moving ahead with an amicable divorce
from Sieber, and informed him that when she reached Paris, she

would be heading on to Berlin to see her mother as soon as she could—but once that visit was over, she would belong to him completely. "If you are nice to me, I will stay with you the rest of my life," she wrote to him, and added that if he wanted to have a child, they ought to get married.[1]

However, her stay in Paris turned out to be a fiasco. Gabin's arrangements at the Hotel Claridge did not live up to her requirements. She felt that staying together in a single bedroom and a salon was out of the question. She stubbornly insisted on her privacy, and on having a room for herself. "How can I live during winter in two rooms and one bathroom making a film. Where one has to wait for the other in the morning!!"[2] She had spent months living under far more adverse conditions, so the problem appeared to be not the number of rooms, but Gabin himself. He started to insist on having a child, and she pointed out that people have children when they're young—as she had done.

In late September, she finally got her visa for Berlin. Her mother picked her up at the Tempelhof airport. Dietrich was returning to her hometown as an American, in military attire and with a forage cap on her head. Both mother and daughter were wearing ties. Photographs show Dietrich leaving the airport, arm in arm with her mother.

The Berlin that Dietrich had left fifteen years earlier no longer existed. She recognized quite a few things, yet everything had changed, as she wrote to Sieber in New York: "The Kaiser Wilhelm Memorial Church is destroyed, Bahnhof Zoo, Tauentzienstrasse, Joachimsthaler—everything reduced to rubble. . . . Pappilein—how sad the world is. Our building, number 54, is still standing, and even though the building is full of shell holes, there are red geraniums on our balcony. Number 133 has nothing but the outer walls; it's gutted, and the balcony is sagging. Mutti spent several days rummaging in the wreckage and on top of the debris was the bronze mask of my face, intact! Then she sat down and cried for quite a long time."[3] In an apparent attempt to shield herself from this shattered world, she sought refuge in work. Dietrich gave two performances a day at the American clubs, danced the nights away, and barely ate. After many long years at the Hollywood studios and on the stage of the international, glamorous world, Dietrich found herself confronted with the confinement and pettiness of familial woes. She was a guardian angel in American uniform, and her family looked to her for salvation. But because she had only a limited residence permit, she headed back to Paris in October.

During the war, she had begun an affair with an American general, James M. Gavin. Uncharacteristically romantic, she called this military man, who was six years her junior, athletic (his men called him "Slim Jim"), and brave, "Abelard." Gavin had had a storybook career, starting life as an orphan from Brooklyn and rising to become a highly decorated general.[4] A series of photographs captured an encounter between the two on a secluded road. Dietrich, wearing a skirt, nylons, and an Eisenhower jacket, is casting an adoring glance up at the tall Gavin. The combination of love, war, and death must have had an irresistible effect on her. Her relationship with him turned out to be extremely helpful in the postwar period. At her request, he had visited Josefine von Losch and brought her groceries.[5] On November 3, 1945, Dietrich's mother died at the age of sixty-eight. Once again, Dietrich asked Gavin, who was now the city commandant in Berlin, for his help. He defied his government's non-fraternization policy and entrusted Colonel Barry Oldfield with the task of burying Dietrich's mother. At night, American soldiers dug a grave for the Prussian officer's widow.[6] Dietrich arrived in Berlin on a military aircraft just in time. She sat and stared at the coffin. When the ceremony was over, she was led away, and did not turn around a single time.

Dietrich sought emotional support from Maria, who was touring through Germany with the USO at this time, although she did not have the glamorous receptions her mother had been accustomed to.

Now that peacetime had come, the theaters were only half-full and she did not have the feeling that she was accomplishing anything important. Maria sent affectionate telegrams, but she could not cancel her tour as her mother wanted her to do. Dietrich felt abandoned in her grief. It was only when she returned to Paris that the news really sank in. "Only then I realized that my mother had died. Even when I stood at the grave—even the second time before I left Berlin, I did not quite know."[7] She quickly made sure that her love affairs would not leave too much time on her hands for mourning. Gabin felt that it was high time for him to know where he stood. He kept his hopes up and sent her flowers while Gavin was visiting and distracting her. Dietrich tried to lean on her daughter to help her bring order to her head and heart, although Maria had plenty of problems of her own. She had lived with her husband, Dean Goodman, for only a few months after marrying him in 1943, and was now contemplating divorce, which pleased Dietrich, who hoped to have her daughter all to herself once again. Dietrich repeatedly appealed to Sieber to take charge of their daughter's divorce. She did not hesitate to suggest unsavory methods to achieve this goal: "Papi . . . we must with detectives or other way prove Goodman to be homosexual. . . . The best thing is to get some proof and then put the irons on him. . . . Goodman lived always with men. But he has to be confronted with proof."[8] Dietrich had no qualms about blackmailing her son-in-law with accusations of homosexuality. She was happy at the prospect that no man would stand between herself and Maria anymore. In the emotional chaos she was experiencing, she clung to her family. Rudi not only had to send her pills, shoes, cosmetics, food, and clothing, but also put up with her letters. When he read about how much she missed him, he knew full well that she did not mean him, but rather a fictitious someone who loved her, someone she could pine for who did not contradict her. Sieber met her professions of love with silence.

Once the war had ended and no longer dominated Dietrich's

state of mind, her life went awry. She missed the war and the way it had held sway over her. In comparison with the war, everything else had become trivial and inconsequential. Worries about her love for Gabin, and her career, had been put off until the war was over. The war had brought her sold-out concerts, banner headlines, and great admiration. But that phase now lay in the past. This was the second time Dietrich was coping with the end of a war. In 1918, she had been young and able to take advantage of the opportunity for a fresh start. In 1945, she was more than forty years old, and younger actresses were now determining what constituted a new beginning. Gabin pulled a few strings with his old contacts to get himself and Dietrich roles in a Marcel Carné and Jacques Prévert movie. Carné and Prévert were the great actors of French cinema, internationally acclaimed artists, but the whole slant of the project was not to Dietrich's liking. She found the script bland and the dialogues sophomoric. Unexpectedly, she had changed her mind about Hollywood: "Hollywood is decent compared to the business people here—the Jewish film producers are not back yet and the goys just don't understand how to make good pictures and treat artists."[9] The project was called off. Gabin already had a new offer on hand: "It is a sort of *Blue Angel* role in a bourgeois environment. She is a bourgeois too, no singer, I just mean the traits in her character. He kills her out of jealousy. Wonderful role."[10] She decided to wait and see what came of it. If it fell apart, she saw no reason to stay on. Dietrich was let down by Paris. Occupation and war had altered the city, and some felt that it would never go back to being the way it had once been. "Only when I walk up the Champs-Élysées and see the Arc is it still the same place and just as beautiful."[11] She was not spared the adversities of everyday postwar life, which she seems to have taken as a personal affront on the part of the French. Bread was being rationed, and apartments were unheated. Dietrich froze as well, because she could not afford the coal from the black market. The electricity did not always work, and she often spent long hours in the dark, unable to make coffee or dry her hair. "It looks as if we fought the war for nothing. The people have changed (or didn't they?) so terribly, they seem to think only of their little life and the great spirit that was there during the war has gone or maybe was never there in civilians." Her life as a soldier had had meaning; now she had to adapt to peacetime.

Her only friends were Max Kolpé, with whom she shared packets of soup in his hotel room, and Margo Lion, who had made a name for herself in France as a singer of Brecht's songs. But both of them were busy during the day, whereas she had nothing to do but to think dismal thoughts. "No fittings, no *Hütchen*, *Schühchen*, nothing to do." She even had wool sent to her from New York. Sitting in her room, she crocheted for her friends out of sheer boredom. "From my window I see the planes going off to the sea. I look after each of them and feel like the girl in a fairytale looking after the birds flying away for the winter."[12]

Gabin was looking forward to a quiet life after the war. He wanted to marry and start a family, and preferably move to the country. This new phase would spell the end of Dietrich's unsettled life, divided between two continents and various lovers. Gabin was offering Dietrich the life of a French wife. At his side, she could try to find inner peace. But Dietrich was terrified at the thought of the intimacy of a marriage.

She systematically destroyed her relationship with Gabin. She complained to her daughter, her husband, and her friends about Gabin, whom she labeled unsociable and pessimistic, and whipped herself into a frenzy of dislike. She had no intention of breaking up with Gavin, who called her every night. Readers of his letters to Dietrich get to know him as a reticent man, who, like most of her lovers, could not believe his good fortune. In his letters, which were written in blue ink on airmail stationery in a large, loopy handwriting, he kept telling her that she was a wonderful woman and a special person. Although he was divorced, he did not pester her with plans for the future. General Gavin was what was left of the war for Dietrich. Her affair with him was reminiscent of an exciting and upbeat time in her life. Moroever, Gavin offered her a welcome change of pace because he was "no actor, no writer or chi-chi." At some point, Gabin had had enough of her infidelity and started an affair with a young actress. He went out with her every evening while Dietrich supposedly stayed at home and read old books by Erich Kästner or poems by Rainer Maria Rilke. Shortly before Christmas in 1945, the situation escalated. During a dinner with friends, Gabin verbally attacked Dietrich, and she responded with physical force: "I gave him a smack in the face. He then hit me unmercifully and the women cried and it was all very embarrass-ing."[13] She was at her wit's end. Their discussions about children, marriage, movies, Hollywood, and life in the country were going around in circles.

Even as their love was fading, Dietrich and Gabin were still united in their feeling of having been let down now that there was peace. They had fought for freedom and democracy, but now had to accept the fact that the memory of their dedication had faded. The death of Dietrich's mother shortly after the end of the war had been her absolute emotional low point, and she began to have her doubts about Europe: "This Europe I loved so much has dwindled down to some vague form of memory like in a strong way I have for my mother. I still long for it, forgetting that I am here and then realizing that it has probably gone forever too."[14]

When she and Gabin pursued acting roles, they were frequently told that they had been away from the screen for too long. Their greatest fear was that being labeled prewar stars in a world that longed for the new and unscathed was tantamount to a death sen-tence. Gabin had grown stouter, his blond hair was streaked with gray, and his facial wrinkles were becoming more pronounced. People in France still associated Dietrich's name with *The Blue Angel*. In early 1946, Dietrich and Gabin had to decide whether to make *The Room Upstairs* (*Martin Roumagnac*). Their fame as a couple could work to the advantage of the movie, but by the same token, their performance together might provide an unwanted reminder of the prewar era. Neither could risk a stigma of this kind. "Only artistic success interesting. . . . Cannot afford mediocre film."[15]

They did go ahead with it, and the shooting with director Georges Lacombe began in the summer of 1946. Gabin played Martin Roumagnac, a mason and building contractor from the country who falls in love with the beautiful widow Blanche Ferrand (Dietrich) and builds her a villa. Blanche, who comes from a good family and has lived in Paris for quite some time, now earns her keep by having affairs with rich men. Everybody in the village knows this aside from Roumagnac. He truly loves Blanche, but in a jealous rage, he strangles her. A sensational trial follows, and he is acquitted. Once he learns that his jealousy was unwarranted, he is a broken man. In the end, he is killed by Blanche's fanatical admirer.

The Room Upstairs turned out to be the flop they had feared. Even today, this movie is (unjustly) considered a failure. The black-and-white images of the French countryside still bore the traces of the years of occupation and war. Some scenes might well give viewers the impression that they are watching not Martin Roumagnac and Blanche Ferrand, but Gabin and Dietrich themselves. In one dialogue, which takes place in their hotel room in Paris, Blanche says to Martin that he doesn't know what Paris is, and he replies by singing the praises of the country. Martin, the decent mason from the country, and Blanche, the duplicitous lady from the city, bear a striking resemblance to the down-home patriot Gabin and the former Hollywood star Dietrich. In another scene, Blanche is standing in front of Martin in her high-heeled shoes and casting him a signature Dietrich lascivious glance. This brief moment gives viewers a glimpse into a very private scene.

Dietrich was unable to give her performance a new twist. She appeared to be oddly out of step with the times. Her clothing, hats, facial expressions, and gestures seemed passé.

Their names were not enough to act as a box-office magnet; the planned breakthrough turned out to be a fiasco. Dietrich was devastated. She could not forgive either Gabin or France for the failure of this film, and she concluded that her future did not lie with either of them: "This is a terrible country—twenty years behind. No work on Saturdays (except studio), no work on Mondays, holidays all the time and no tempo—just eat eat eat. . . . I thought of staying in France but changed my mind and coming back. . . . "[16] She wanted to go back to America and earn money.

She urged her agent, Charles Feldman, to get her a role in a movie that Mitchell Leisen would be making for Paramount Studios. At first, the studio turned her down. DEAREST CHARLIE . . . PLEASE ARRANGE FOR EARRINGS WANT SO MUCH TO DO IT . . . WANT TO COME HOME TO MITCH AND YOU . . . PLEASE DO ALL YOU CAN FOR EARRINGS.[17] Feldman's negotiations were ultimately successful, and by June Dietrich knew that she would indeed be joining the cast of *Golden Earrings*.

A letter she wrote to her daughter while en route to the United States tells of her poor state of health. Bothered by the way her fellow passengers were looking at her, she stayed alone in her cabin until the afternoon. She launched into lengthy descriptions of the various powders and pills she took for her many aches and pains. Her freezing hands turned red, which unnerved her. She was suffering from insomnia. Not even sleeping pills could bring her the sleep she longed for. Dietrich was apprehensive about coming back to Hollywood. She had closed the studio door rather haughtily behind her just two years ago, and announced that she would find something better almost anywhere else. In Hollywood, everyone knew that the best years of her life lay behind her and she was coming only for the money. In order to be able to pay the hotel bill in Paris, she had had to sell furs. Dietrich prepared to conquer

America a second time in lamentable shape: she was an actress in her mid-forties with red hands, insomnia, and hemorrhoids, one who wore out her old dresses and felt forced to play an absurd role in a preposterous movie. But she did not let on to the outside world how this bothered her.

Her "repatriation," as she called it, was eased by dividing up the world into civilians and military personnel. She felt like a soldier and longed for the lost world of camaraderie. Standing alone at the side of the road in Paris, she had watched the victory parade go by. "Angel Child came back from Champs-Élysées where I watched all alone victory parade. Only a few MP represented us. My heart was heavy with memoirs and loneliness in rain."[18] Nobody wanted to hear what they had endured. But in contrast to her, the former soldiers knew where they belonged, even if they felt out of place in their marriages and families.

Dietrich's most pressing question remained: "Where should I live, and with whom?" In Paris and with Gabin she had not found an answer, and she would not find one right down to her final retreat from the world. She scraped along through the somber postwar period. Her name still cropped up in the gossip columns, such as in reports that she had been seen with Burt Lancaster and had had an affair with a high-ranking officer. Her daughter was now also her secretary. Her name no longer had enough appeal for big headlines. At times she claimed to love Hollywood, and at others she said she preferred filming in France. She did not hold out for long in either the United States or Europe. Her life in the postwar period was one long state of transit.

Feeling forlorn, she got in touch with Remarque again. He knew her; she did not have to pretend with him, and unlike Rudi, he answered letters. "I'm writing you because I suddenly have an acute longing—not the kind I usually have. Maybe I need liverwurst sandwiches, the solace of the afflicted—and emotional liverwurst sandwiches. . . . I am at loose ends and empty and aimless. . . . I have no one left. . . . I've rebelled and lashed out (not always with the fairest means) and have cut myself free, and now I sit in freedom, alone and abandoned."[19]

But Remarque had gotten over her. His life had moved forward happily—or so he claimed. Remarque was exasperated when he thought about what had become of his great love, Marlene Dietrich. The idiocy of Hollywood, with its trivial images and wretched transformations, had rendered her unrecognizable. He desperately sought any remaining element of the time they had shared, but even the memory of their love was "failed, forgotten, futile, finished."[20]

Remarque had worked on the book about Ravic for years. In 1941, as he was coming up with the title, he realized that this book was evolving into an emotion-packed autobiography of the past years. In August 1944, he completed the first draft, and in mid-September the advance publication began to run in *Collier's*. Dietrich must have been bitter to realize that he had reworked their love story into a literary success, yet her own role was restricted to that of a reader.[21]

Arch of Triumph was adapted for the screen by Lewis Milestone. The role of Joan Madoux, which Dietrich had awaited for years, went to Ingrid Bergman. Even so, Dietrich and Remarque remained quite close. He sent her the German version of "our book," as he called it, and asked to meet up with her. Neither of the two wanted to relinquish the intimacy and closeness they had experienced. They were often seen together in New York nightclubs, and for her birthday he gave her a gold cigarette lighter encrusted with small rubies representing the Arch of Triumph, in memory of the city of their love.

Dietrich kept Sieber up to date about her unhappiness with Gabin, but she rarely got answers to her letters and was deeply disappointed in his lack of interest in her life. She enumerated everything she had done for him and complained about his lack of gratitude. "As I have lost everything to the Germans and you have saved everything you could at least get me the things that belong to me."[22] Her letters to him in 1945 and 1946 were filled with requests for makeup and laments about her loneliness.

Dietrich's life was more unsettled than ever. She had no permanent residence, had clothing sent to her, and lived in a hotel. Meanwhile, her daughter was starting a family. One year after divorcing Dean Goodman in June 1946, Maria married the set designer William Riva. Riva was a good-looking man who was not fazed by his mother-in-law's fame. It looked as though Dietrich was finally resigned to the idea of her daughter's finding happiness. The press reported how delighted she was about the marriage of her daughter. By marrying for love, Maria had chosen a different path from that of her mother. Neither her mother nor her father attended Maria's wedding. For once, the two of them were on the same continent in 1947: Dietrich was in Paris, and Sieber in Locarno. Maria's wedding day was not upstaged by either parent.

Suddenly, Dietrich got an offer for a Billy Wilder movie in Hollywood. In 1926 Wilder had come to Berlin, where he eked out a living as a reporter, paid dance partner, and screenplay writer. He had worked on the early Dietrich movie *Madame Doesn't Want Children*, and he was a good friend of Max Kolpé and Walter Reisch's, who were also close friends of Dietrich's. Wilder managed to produce one high-quality box-office hit after another. In every one of his movies, he tested the threshold of what American audiences would accept, and *A Foreign Affair* was no exception. He set this love story in the ruins of Berlin. Wilder had been sent to Germany just after the end of the war by the Psychological Warfare Department, which sought to set up new film industry rules for the Germans to comply with on their path to democracy. After twelve years away, he was coming back to Berlin in the fall of 1945 bearing the rank of an American colonel. "I will never forget how the city looked back then. I came with a camera man, we flew over Berlin, and I saw the devastation. It looked like the end of the world. I later used the documentary material for my film *A Foreign Affair*."[23] Wilder, whose grandmother, mother, and stepfather had been murdered in Auschwitz, recommended converting the Germans to democracy not only with educational documentary films, but also by means of entertainment sprinkled with a dash of ideology. Washington was not thrilled with this recommendation, but when he was planning *A Foreign Affair* a year and a half later, he used it as his guiding principle. During his stay in Berlin, Wilder observed the devastated city with a professional eye. He decided that this "crazy, squalid, and starving city" was the ideal setting for a film. Wilder knew Berlin; he picked out the right corners and took photographs. He studied the Germans, "from the university professor who lost his home during the bombing of Berlin to the three-cigarette whores in the Femina Bar," to gather material for his movie.[24] In late May 1947, his screenplay was complete. He could not imagine anyone other than Dietrich in the role of Erika von Schluetow, the former mistress of a Nazi, for two reasons. First, Dietrich, who was herself from Berlin, would lend the movie a note of authenticity better than any other actress could; and second, she was the only German actress who could get away with playing this role. She had misgivings, and at first turned down Wilder's offer on the telephone, whereupon he paid her a visit in Berlin to try to win her over. The $110,000 fee and the opportunity to work with a renowned director appear to have been motive enough for her to rethink her initial response.

A Foreign Affair opens with the approach to Berlin of an airplane bearing a congressional delegation from the United States, which has come to find out what they can about the morale of the troops stationed there. Gazing down at the city from above, they cannot imagine that people could be living in these ruins. "Like pack rats been gnawing at a hunk of old mouldy Roquefort cheese," is one of the cynical comments. There is one woman in this upstanding group: Phoebe Frost, a congresswoman from Iowa. Jean Arthur played Frost as a prim and proper puritan from the New World, but we come to realize that under her steely exterior, she yearns for love. Frost distrusts the way in which Colonel Rufus J. Plummer, the pragmatic commander in chief in Berlin, is going about this assignment. During his tour through the city, he points to some boys playing baseball as evidence of his success in bringing democracy to the Germans. He advocates patience and forbearance with the Germans. He conceives of his task as restoring order and reviving the defeated people's will to live. Frost will have none of that. Her focus is the moral integrity of the boys. She heads off to explore Berlin on her own and winds up at an illegal nightclub called Lorelei, which features the seductive, inscrutable Erika von Schluetow. The American and Russian soldiers cheer for her in equal measure. Dietrich played von Schluetow as a world-wise, cynical representative of the Old World. Von Schluetow is well-versed in guilt and atonement, but her only goal is survival. She sings "Black Market," a song about venality that has people selling their "souls for Lucky Strikes." For the first time in her life, the congresswoman from Iowa is confronted with an utterly cynical state of mind. "I'm selling out, take all I've got—ambitions, convictions, the works. Why not? Enjoy these goods." Frost is disgusted. When she also finds out that von Schluetow was the lover of a high-ranking National Socialist and is being protected by an American officer, she knows what she has to do. She asks Captain John Pringle (played by John Lund) for help in exposing von Schluetow's lover. Wilder did not want Pringle to embody the American hero: "Yeah, I wanted him to be a grown-up man, with pros and cons, not goody-goody, and then not a guy who fucks everybody, but just a human being. With errors, with faults, with wonderful things."[25] What Frost doesn't know is that Pringle is the American officer she is looking for: *he* is Erika von Schluetow's lover. Consequently, he plays a double game; by making Frost fall in love with him, he tries to distract her from pursuing her investigation. Von Schluetow wins the first showdown. She carries on about her rival's lack of makeup and odd hairdo. American women may be good democrats, but they lack any kind of refinement. Von Schluetow instantly senses that Frost is insecure and vulnerable in her femininity, yet this is the woman that poses a danger to her. Pringle spends too much time with her, and eventually they show up at the Lorelei together. Frost's infatuation has made her morally corruptible, as is evident from her clothing. Instead of her uniform-like suit, she is now wearing an evening gown she bought at the black market. At this encounter, von Schluetow is wearing a dress that Dietrich had worn for her performances in the war. She is accompanied on the piano by Friedrich Hollaender, who had also written the songs for *The Blue Angel*. On this evening, Frost gets her second lesson in disillusionment. The song that von Schluetow sings is called "Illusions," about buying "lovely illusions . . . second-hand," that reach far but are "built on sand." Frost's ecstatic delight comes to an abrupt end when the police raid the Lorelei. It is von Schluetow who saves Frost from having to reveal her identity, but in doing so robs her of her illusions about the man she loves. In a matter-of-fact monologue, von Schluetow opens the eyes of the woman from Iowa: "Everything [is] caved in . . . My country, my possessions, my beliefs." However, she draws the line at relinquishing the man who protects her and gets her nylon stockings. As a German, she cannot afford the luxury of generosity. As an "old gambler" at the roulette table of love, she advises Frost to leave the table and end the game. The American woman, who has experienced neither war nor love, understands her. She is now one of the disillusioned and has lost her naïve innocence. At the end, Frost takes Pringle with her to the Unites States, where he belongs. Von Schluetow sings her final song in a low-cut floral dress. "Amidst the ruins of Berlin / Trees are in bloom as they have never been."

A *Foreign Affair* was Wilder's triumph over Hitler. Hitler was dead, but Wilder and Hollaender had survived. Hollaender found his place at the piano, just as he had fifteen years earlier, and the

Lorelei was a smoke-filled, cramped club, just as it had been in
The Blue Angel. Wilder's Berlin is a beaten-down city in which the
victors and the vanquished try to get something out of life after
so much has been withheld from them for so many years. Von
Schluetow speaks on behalf of the vanquished, who haven't been
able to sleep for fifteen years: "First it was Hitler screaming on the
radio, then the war of nerves, then the victory celebrations, then
the bombing." Pringle, speaking for the military, complains that
everyone has gone back to their daily routines and forgotten the
soldiers. Frost, who represents the victors, is overwhelmed by the
moral complexity of the situation. Her rigid moral values make it
impossible for her to grasp the psychological anxiety and disorien-
tation the victors and the conquered were facing. In real life, Dietrich was in all three positions: as an American citizen she was one
of the victors; as a Berliner she was one of the vanquished; and as
a combatant against the National Socialists she was one of the soldiers. *A Foreign Affair* was Dietrich's film, portraying her own history. Erika von Schluetow was a logical follow-up to the Lola Lola
role of fifteen years earlier. Von Schluetow moves with the times,
flirts with a Nazi, and extricates herself neatly from the situation
once his power had ebbed, returning to the stage of a disreputable
club and singing her sage songs.

Dietrich had returned to Berlin in the role of Erika von Schluetow. Surrounded by sets of her destroyed hometown at the film
studio in Hollywood, she played an artist who knew how to turn
the Nazi reign to good advantage. In this role, Hitler's most famous
opponent showed that the era of morally unequivocally positions
was over, which was precisely why this film was disliked. The critics were furious about not seeing any American heroes. Captain
Pringle thinks only of his own pleasure, not the dissemination of
democratic ideals. And Phoebe Frost may be proper, but her puritanical zeal comes across as neurotic. The unflappable character in
this trio is the ex-lover of a Nazi. *A Foreign Affair* was nominated

for two Oscars, but neither was for Best Actress. Hollywood shrank back from honoring Dietrich for her portrayal of Von Schluetow. In Germany, screening of the film was forbidden. The screening committee was not amused by what it saw.

Wilder considered *A Foreign Affair* one of his better films. Working with Dietrich went smoothly. It was apparent to him right from the start that he could not put anything over on Dietrich, who had been trained by von Sternberg. In order to avoid conflict on the set, he granted her the privilege of selecting her own lighting. Wilder was one of Dietrich's few good friends. There are very few directors that she enjoyed working with as much as she did with him. During the shooting, Dietrich lived at Wilder's house, and it is easy to picture these two scandalmongers having quite a lot of fun bad-mouthing the others in the evening.

Hollywood may have withheld the Oscar from Dietrich throughout her life, but the military did not forget her. In November 1947, just before shooting began for *A Foreign Affair*, she was awarded the Medal of Freedom at West Point. This was the American military's highest distinction for civilians, and Dietrich was the first woman ever to receive it.[26] For the awards ceremony, she wore a high-necked dark suit, tasteful earrings, red lipstick, and a small hat. With perfect posture and an impassive expression on her face in front of the colonel, she is the very picture of poise. Her telegram to Rudi read: LEAVING TRAIN NOW GOT MEDAL FREEDOM ALL LOVE.[27] Her French lover and wartime comrade sent her his congratulations: MY ANGEL BRAVO POUR MEDAILLE . . . PENSE A TOI TOUT MON COEUR JEAN.[28]

o o o

"10:28 a.m. Maria's boy born" is written in red in Rudi's daily planner. When Dietrich began in Hollywood, having children was considered a blow to a woman's career. Almost twenty years later, history was repeating itself. The press pegged her "the most beautiful grandmother in the world." For an actress, a description of that sort could be deadly, but Dietrich tried to ignore the gossip that ensued.

Her personal life changed with the birth of her grandson. It almost seems as though she and Rudi were rediscovering family life. But she had no intention of retiring. She believed that Roberto Rossellini was the director who would know how to give expression to her postwar enervation. During her stay in Paris, she had often spent time with him and with Anna Magnani. She had even translated the screenplay for Rossellini's film *Allemagne année zéro* into German and typed it up herself.[29] However, Rossellini did not offer her a role. His star was the young Ingetraud Hinze.

The fact was that Dietrich was remaining in America only because she did not want to be in Paris. Gabin had sent her a positively exuberant telegram as the new year approached with the message that the coming year would be *her* year; he would make her the happiest woman on earth. But no sooner had the year begun than he realized that she actually wanted to be rid of him. Dietrich's letters were matter-of-fact. She did not understand what all the fuss was about. The final quarrels were about Gabin's belongings in America, and the matter was left to her business manager, Charlie Trezona. Gabin wanted to have his refrigerator and Cadillac, which led to an extensive correspondence between a patient Trezona and an increasingly peeved Dietrich, who made her opinions known primarily by telegram. Trezona gently reminded her that Gabin's refrigerator and Cadillac were making quite a lot of work for him and costing her quite a bit of money that she did not have. The correspondence with Trezona provides insights into the dreary life of a woman who is at her wit's end. The complaints about tax liabilities, a lack of work, and dishonorable lovers ran on endlessly. Her movable possessions were spread among various warehouses; her valuable assets, such as furs, jewelry, and paintings, had to be insured and thus entailed expenses. The bills for her hotels, telephones, and flights were high, and Sieber and Matul also had to live from her assets. Gabin's Cadillac was eventually sent to France by ship; his agent sent a letter of thanks. Trezona commented that Dietrich agreed to send it out of love. The Cadillac would be the final token of that love.

Gabin left Dietrich, and on March 28, in Paris, he married Dominique Fournier, a fashion model. She was fifteen years younger than he and bore a startling resemblance to the young Dietrich. Gabin had known her for only two months. This utterly unexpected marriage followed on the heels of Dietrich's earlier public degradation as the "youngest grandmother"; now she was the abandoned older lover. *Marlene minus fifteen equals Dominique*, the newspapers reported. The photographs of the wedding ceremony show a beaming Gabin sitting next to a beautiful young woman. In November 1949, Dominique gave birth to the first of their three children. With this marriage, Dietrich was dead to Gabin. When they ran into each other on the street, he did not even look her way. He shielded his wife from her, not wanting to give Dietrich any more power over his life.

In June, she flew to Paris. In a letter to Maria, she wrote about how she was coping with her feelings. "I played gay and almost felt like it."[30] She sat at her old table at Fouquet's with Remarque and an acquaintance and suddenly thought: *Why isn't Jean here?* She found out that his baby would be born in October. "We joked that in France they now make Babies in much a shorter time than it usually takes, and said that it must have happened the first night he knew her and there one can not be quite sure one is the father." She was full of sorrow and hatred. Dietrich lost her authority to the women who supplanted her, and reacted by painting Dominique as a slut who had already aborted many children. Overcome with panic, she was afraid of going out; what if she ran into Gabin? "And shaking hands with him and his wife I cannot imagine and know that I am not good enough an actress for that." She felt just as bad as she had as a child when she had eaten unripe cherries. In this sad letter, she may have found the most loving parting words for her daughter: "Forgive me for not yet being my age and a wise old Grandmother. Kiss your two men for me and be happy Mami." It was only when she had lost Gabin forever that she realized he was probably the last great love of her life.

She still had Remarque. They were both just as lost after the war as they had been before, and she wrote to let him know how much she missed him.[31] Dietrich had been one of Remarque's last ties to the Old World. Once he was back in Europe, he realized that this situation had not changed in the slightest. In the summer of 1948, he wrote sadly to her from Porto Ronco about his first trip to Europe and declared that one should never come back.

Remarque was suffering from Ménière's disease, an inner ear disorder that affects balance and hearing, and Dietrich took care of him with homemade meals. Wilder called her a "Mother Teresa with better legs." Remarque diagnosed her symptoms as a refugee illness of the kind suffered by the characters in his novels. "You need a strong heart to live without roots," he had written in the epigraph to *Flotsam*.[32] No one knew that better than the two of them. Their reemerging feelings of love fluctuated between affection, temptation, disdain, and intimacy. Remarque's face was marked by leading too indulgent a life in restaurants, hotels, brothels, and dives. He envied the courage she had shown. Dietrich loved to feed him home-cooked meals and give him vitamin pills. What is more, she no longer tried to change him. He led an unsettled life, just as she did, and in contrast to Gabin, he understood her back-and-forth between the continents. However, they were both too restless and narcissistic to restart their romance for real.

o o o

Ernst Lubitsch, who had started life as a tailor's son on Schönhauser Allee in Berlin, died in November 1947, and a few months later was followed by Richard Tauber, the Austrian tenor with whom Dietrich had worked in *I Kiss Your Hand, Madame* back in 1929. She had been one of the few friends willing to help him out financially.[33] The voice she loved so much had stopped singing forever. The end of the war confronted Dietrich with the confined world in which she had grown up. Her relatives started showing up. She saw her sister, Elisabeth Will, on her second USO tour in Bergen-Belsen. Contrary to Dietrich's initial assumptions, Elisabeth had not been in a concentration camp; she and her husband had run the officers' movie theater. Her husband had now left her, and she was alone with her son. Elisabeth was a timid and anxious woman who lived in constant fear of doing something wrong. She hoped that Marlene would help her son get an apprenticeship as a cameraman in the United States, but her hopes were dashed. Dietrich did not want to be saddled with relatives. She supported her sister with care packages and kept in touch with her, but that was about all that could be expected of her.

The focal point of her family was now in New York. After Gabin left her, she went through quite a domestic phase. She gave Maria some free time by taking walks in the park with her grandson. She learned all about childhood diseases and became the perpetual know-it-all. Following *A Foreign Affair,* she was onscreen for all of two minutes in the forgettable movie *Jigsaw.* She was not missing the film business per se—only the money it brought in. Her agent, Charlie Feldman, was none too pleased with her behavior. She had finally taken his advice and returned to America, but she had become extremely demanding and hard to work with. She found fault with every script, seemingly oblivious to the fact that she was difficult to cast. Feldman had to move heaven and earth to come up with roles for her. When he found out she was telling everybody that she found her jobs all on her own, he was furious: "This is far from the truth. . . . The talks I have had in connection with your business matters, expenses, and other problems would fill a book."[34] He milked his connections and got her a role in Hitchcock's *Stage Fright*.

The filming in London went from late May until mid-September 1949. As usual, Dietrich stayed at Claridge's. She complained to Maria about the bad food. The film moved ahead slowly, although they even used Sundays for shooting. Working with the famous Hitchcock seems to have been quite a challenge for Dietrich. She wanted to have a say in everything, and was bossy on the set. Hitchcock, who knew whom he had signed on, gave her a free hand and valued her expertise: "Miss Dietrich is a professional. A professional actress, a professional cameraman, a professional dress designer."[35] In a nod to Dietrich's past, her character in *Stage Fright*, Charlotte Inwood, is a singer. Dietrich performs two songs, both of which became part of her standard repertoire for the next twenty years. One was Cole Porter's "The Laziest Gal in Town," which was relatively unknown before this movie; the other, Henri Salvador's "La Vie en Rose," had already been made world-famous by Edith Piaf. Piaf allowed her to sing it because the two of them were friends. Jane Wyman, who was much younger than Dietrich, was jealous of her. Every day when she saw the raw footage, she compared herself to Dietrich, and the following day she would come to the set looking more and more primped, which worked to the detriment of her role as an unattractive maid. Hitchcock blamed Wyman's vanity for dragging down the quality of the movie: "She couldn't accept the idea of her face being in character, while Dietrich looked so glamorous."[36] Dietrich's wardrobe, which—as her contract specified—was hers to keep after the film was shot, was designed by Christian Dior, so she flew to Paris from time to time to try on new designs. Dior, who was three years younger than Dietrich, had caused a sensation in 1947 with his New Look. Wide skirts, unpadded shoulders, narrow waists, gloves, hats, and handbags transformed yesterday's comrade in arms back into a woman of mystery. Dietrich would recall her grandmother Felsing, who had told her so much about the magic of femininity, and she now made a point of wearing Dior. A uniform was passé. She played Charlotte Inwood as a beautiful, elegant woman who, despite her success, hates her profession of singing and acting. However, she has no other choice, because performing is her life. Apart from Dietrich, the actors in the movie are all very British, including Michael Wilding, who played an inspector. Dietrich sought solace with him. Wilding was eleven years her junior; he was handsome and he admired her. His letters reveal that she told him about her financial, professional, and familial obligations. As usual, Wilding was willing to follow her anywhere, and she was always able to fend him off. He felt inferior to the world-famous Dietrich and her illustrious lovers, and apologized for his shortcomings. Eventually he could no longer endure the torment of her constant absences. In 1952, he married the nineteen-year-old Elizabeth Taylor. Dietrich wondered why he had not stayed with her.

Dietrich's losses in her love life were somewhat balanced out by the growth of her family. May 1950 marked the birth of Maria's second son, John Michael. Sieber and Dietrich were in New York at the time. They drank a champagne toast to the second grandchild, and Sieber proudly wrote to his parents in Berlin that he had become a grandfather again. The role of grandmother kept Dietrich busy. Alexander Liberman, with whom she formed a friendship in the 1950s, photographed her in this role.[37] She sat on the floor with John Michael, beaming with pride and opening up presents. The private Marlene—the grandmother—always remained the public Marlene—the star. With her perfectly made-up face concealed behind netting, she rollicked with her grandsons in the back seat of a New York taxi. She had eyes only for the camera. Liberman also photographed her while she was cooking. The femme fatale had been transformed into an elegant housewife wearing a white blouse and apron with a part in her hair, contentedly stirring food in big pots. Dietrich was often a guest at the home of Liberman and his wife, Tatjana. They played canasta, and Dietrich did the cooking. The screen goddess had the hands of a housewife. Dietrich masked her immoderate demands on life under a cloak of modesty.

She could now be heard on the radio quite often, and she devoted herself to charity work, hoping not to be forgotten altogether. A film project with Wilder did not materialize, and to judge from Wilder's letter to her, she must have been upset, even deeply distraught, by the collapse of this project: "We are still young, Marlene. There are a lot of pictures left for us to do. If it wasn't this one, there's going to be another one. You know how much I love and admire you. It aches me just as much as you that it's not going to be the next one."[38] Her current and discarded lovers complimented her appearance, and it was left to her agent to tell her the bitter truth. The heroic Dietrich who had fought against Hitler no longer drew audiences; they wanted to see young, fresh actresses who were unencumbered by the past, actresses like Elizabeth Taylor, Audrey Hepburn, and Marilyn Monroe.

When an offer came from film director Henry Koster to act in a movie with Jimmy Stewart, Feldman pressed her to accept it. He tried to make her understand that she was no longer in a position to choose her roles, whether she liked it or not. It must have been the money that clinched the deal. In October 1950, Dietrich flew to London to shoot her new movie, *No Highway in the Sky*. As in *Stage Fright*, she had a younger actress at her side, and once again she played a film star who wore clothing by Dior. Her former lover Stewart, who played an eccentric scientist, no longer thrilled her, and she thought that Koster, the Berliner who was three years younger, was awful.

> Old German jokes all day long, no one laughs, German
> accent in American English, systematically attack the other
> so that he has to defend himself instead of making sugges-

tions, vain. (*I am a great comedy director*—this line is funnier! It's easy to see that he knows only Hollywood jargon and not the language.) Maybe he's all right in Hollywood, where the zookeepers look out for him and watch the rushes and steer him, but here, all alone, he is dangerous.[39]

Dietrich considered it outrageous to have to work with a director like this, but the worst part was that he could not stop ribbing her about her age. "With me nothing but: Grandmoththththther (he has a strong lisp): can you make it with your 75 years, careful, don't fall, you know bones get brittle with your age, etc."[40] She was plagued by bouts of pain, hated this movie, and grew thinner and thinner, yet she knew that she had to hold out. All she really wanted was to go straight to New York to be with her grandchildren.

By Christmas, she was back home. Photographs show her in the Rivas' living room with Iva Patcevitch, the editor of *Vogue*. Everything looks quite dignified: the big Christmas tree, the presents, the children, and the radiantly beautiful Maria. Dietrich is with the gray-haired, elegant Patcevitch, the two of them looking like aristocratic grandparents. To see her sitting smugly on the sofa in her elegant clothing, it is hard to imagine that she had to endure being bossed around on the set.

Yul Brynner, an exotic-looking young man with a mysterious background, piqued her interest. Noël Coward had introduced the two of them. Dietrich spent the next few years floating on air whenever he was with her, or agonizing when he kept her waiting. Brynner was nearly twenty years her junior. As his son put it, "For the first time, Yul found himself making love to a woman whom he had admired since his childhood."[41] Born in Vladivostok, he lived in China and Paris before coming to the United States in 1940. He had worked as a trapeze artist in France, but by the time Dietrich met him, he was a Broadway sensation in the musical *The King and I*. After the performance and before going home to his wife, he found time to have affairs. Night after night, Dietrich waited for him. Even if he had no more than thirty minutes for her, she considered herself lucky. Brynner declared his love for her, but stopped short of planning for a future that would include her. She attributed this to her advanced age and accused him of looking to other women for the long term. When he left without making plans for the next time they would see each other, she was depressed for days on end. She could not grasp the idea that a man might actually turn down the chance to be with her. She vilified his wife, the way she did with every rival. In a draft of a letter to him that ran to twenty-two pages, she launched into endless detail about how his wife was a bad mother. She evidently wanted to gain complete control over him and insisted that he inform her about his comings and goings. When she did not know where he was, or he forgot to call, she sank into a deep depression. The proud Dietrich sat next to the telephone for hours, waiting for a call from Brynner, a bald-headed, mediocre musical star. If he promised to call, she would often stay at home the entire day and get other callers off the phone as quickly as she could. On one occasion, she suggested they meet at Maria's apartment. "The children won't be there and we could put the babies to bed like if they were ours."[42] Dietrich, who was nearing the age of fifty, was trying to play house with her young lover. Brynner wrote Dietrich short letters in large, loopy handwriting. We can only hope that he was more imaginative as a lover than as a letter writer, as his correspondence was full of the usual clichés about longing, desire, and kissing. The young man was flattered by her attention; for him, theirs was an amusing affair that appealed to his vanity. His wife was not the only woman with whom he was betraying Dietrich.

Her friends noted the change in her with a mixture of amazement and concern. Sieber spent countless hours on the phone with her listening to her unending aggravation with Brynner, and Leo Lerman called Brynner Marlene's nemesis. Lerman was certain that Brynner had no intention of marrying her. Dietrich's passion for Brynner took over her life. Her constant fear that he would stop loving her was evidence of her dread of growing old and lonely. Her greatest fear of all was the loss of her sexual attractiveness. In order to keep her affair as discreet as possible, she rented an apartment on Park Avenue. She furnished the bedroom like a brothel. Her friend Lerman remarked that it had a "cocotte kitsch touch." There were mirrors everywhere, and she had fluorescent tubes installed under the bed to create a kind of indirect lighting. This was her stage set for the great passion with the bald-headed, muscular, and presumably potent Yul Brynner, lived from one night of ardor to the next.

Friends had died, and former lovers had gone their separate ways: Gabin was now the head of a household, and von Sternberg, married for the third time, had also become a father again at the beginning of the year. Boni had discovered psychoanalysis and yoga; he drank less and spent more time thinking about himself. After a visit to her Park Avenue apartment, he wrote:

> An evening at Puma's. Gave me something to eat; she ate
> potatoes with butter. Glued to the TV set, staring at her Yul
> and her daughter. Everything's off; exaggerated; nothing
> goes together. The half-furnished apartment—too little light
> in the living room; the putrid blond and beige on the floors,
> walls, furniture; the many mirrors; all disconnected, Holly-
> wood elegance, the synthetic celebrity who is run-down and
> coming apart at the seams yet encased in a shell that is still
> lovely, the mixture of genuine and fake, unbearable, because
> she is certainly intelligent enough to tell the difference.[43]

As if her anguish with her young lover were not enough, she also had to spend several weeks dealing with Fritz Lang. In March 1951, the filming of *Rancho Notorious* began. This movie was in

some respects a remake of *Destry Rides Again*, this time in Technicolor. Lang had been a star in Berlin, the way Dietrich had become
a star in Hollywood. He was unable to recapture his great success
once he came to the United States, but he stayed in the movie business. In the mid-1930s, Dietrich and Lang had had a brief affair.
His telegrams to her suggest that he was a romantic, somewhat
awkward lover. The man who was considered impeccably precise and cold had a playful handwriting that looked like a young
girl's: instead of dotting his *i*'s, Lang added curlicues. He could not
come to terms with the fact that he was no more than a common
employee at MGM, and he was considered arrogant and conceited.
Dietrich did not really want to make this Western, but once again,
it was Feldman who insistently pointed out that it had taken quite
a bit of wangling to get her the part. Hemingway bolstered her spirits and wrote that even if she made Westerns in Technicolor, she
would still be his heroine.

The five weeks that Dietrich spent on the set with Lang, who
signed his telegrams to her as "THE MONSTER," made her hate him
for the rest of her life. "Fritz Lang was the director I detested
most," she wrote in 1984.[44] Her Prussian discipline was the only
thing preventing her from walking away from the shoot. When
Dietrich filmed a movie, von Sternberg was a constant presence
in her mind, and she stuck to what he had taught her. Lang and
von Sternberg, both filmmakers from Vienna, did not get along.
Each resented the other, and Dietrich felt the consequences: "He
despised my reverence for Josef von Sternberg, and tried to replace
this genius in my heart and in my body."[45] Lang's method was to
humiliate and torment her in front of the whole crew. He marked
the actors' positions on the floor with adhesive tape, based on the
length of his own stride. No matter how tall or short the actors
were, they had to work with these positions. He sometimes made
them repeat scenes a hundred times, shouting at them from start to

finish. According to Dietrich, Lang delighted in tormenting people. Sporting a monocle and with his hair neatly slicked back, he would arch his eyebrows as he coldly observed his actors' missteps. The film historian Lotte Eisner described his method as perfectionism, but for Dietrich, it was pure sadism. She later wrote, "I won't shed a tear for him. I haven't lost a thing; I felt no friendship for the man, so no tears."[46] Lang could not stop making snide references to her age, and he claimed that she blamed him for the fact that she was no longer young, yet continued to play the role of a desirable woman. "Now, Marlene resented going gracefully into a little, tiny bit older category; she became younger and younger until finally it was hopeless."[47] *Rancho Notorious*, "a story of hate, murder, and revenge," received very few positive reviews. After working together on this movie, Lang and Dietrich parted ways for good.[48]

Fortunately, Dietrich found unfailing appreciation from Ernest Hemingway. He adored her looks and loved her without ever having slept with her: "I never thought you were a goddess nor a whore nor a cinema star. . . . I love to see you in a good picture and I love worse than hell to hear you sing. But I love you best in that beat up uniform and nobody could take punishment like we could."[49] Once she had lost sight of Gavin, Hemingway was the only one with whom Dietrich could talk and laugh about the war. He enjoyed telling her: "You know sometimes I miss you when we can't kill krauts. . . . Heil Dietrich." They kept their secrets to themselves, and no one else had any business telling them how the war was. "Toi and moi have lived through about as bad times as there ever were," he wrote to her. "I don't mean just wars. Wars are spinach. Life in general is the tough part. In war all you have to do is not worry and know how to read a map and give co-ordinates."[50] To lift her spirits, he offered to write a story about her and thus immortalize both of them. A few months after he made this offer, she reminded him of it when she needed him to write something about her for *Life* magazine. Ernest Hemingway kept his promise and wrote one of the most beautiful statements in existence about Dietrich.

> She is brave, beautiful, loyal, kind and generous. She is never boring and is as lovely looking in the morning, in a GI shirt, pants and combat boots as she is at night or on the screen. She has an honesty and a comic and tragic sense of life that never let her be truly happy unless she loves. When she loves she can joke about it; but it is gallows humor. If she had nothing more than her voice she could break your heart with it. But she has that beautiful body and the time-less loveliness of her face. It makes no difference how she breaks your heart if she is there to mend it.[51]

Dietrich allowed very few people entrance into her New York apartment. One of them was Hildegard Knef, whom Dietrich regarded as a younger version of herself. When Knef performed in *Silk Stockings* in New York, Dietrich invited her over. The din-ing table was in the alcove of the small foyer, and the kitchen was tiny. Knef was struck by the fact that there was not a single mink coat hanging in the closet. Dietrich, who had cooked a meal for her, watched her guest eat while she puffed away at her cigarette, gazed at herself in one of the many mirrors on the wall, and gave brusque replies. "She never sleeps. . . . In the morning, before any-one else even dreams of opening his eyes, she's already read the papers and made soup, aired the rooms, cleaned the ashtrays, and told the maid which soap she should use for the doors and which for the bathtub—and on top of it she smokes like an industrial development area and has fittings and appointments the whole day long."[52] Knef described Dietrich with a mixture of admiration and bewilderment. People never knew where they stood with her. She hung up the telephone as soon as she had said her piece, spoke very softly, and never seemed tired or upset. Even her laughter was quiet. She remained aloof from nearly everyone but her close friends Wilder, Reisch, and Kolpé. When she did put in an appearance somewhere, everyone's eyes were upon her. "Eyes followed her, devoured her, bored into her, envied, wanted to take possession, break through the majestic aura, the uninterest in surroundings and interest caused. She hovered along on legs that appeared too long to fulfill any function other than decoration, straightening the knees at every step, striding widely; she walked the way she ate, or stirred sauces: with complete concentration."[53]

On a quick shopping spree through the sweltering streets of New York, they ran into Sieber, who was on his way to California. Evidently this father, mother, and child could not live in one town. Sieber felt uncomfortable being in such close proximity to his wife. She made herself the center of his life. He had to go with her to fashion boutiques, console her discarded lovers, send her clothing, and always come when she called him. The list of medications he took for his stomach problems grew longer and longer as the years went by. His partner Tamara Matul, who lived on an allowance of six dollars a week, was in bad shape, and he was apprehensive. In 1951, he attached a carefully clipped newspaper article, "New Hormone Used for Schizophrenia," to his appointment calendar. Matul, who had been a beauty in her younger years, was still wearing Dietrich's hand-me-down clothing and was expected to be grateful even though she detested these castoffs from her lover's wife. The job in Paris had not worked out. Every day, Sieber noted the exact amount of money he had spent, down to the last cent. He was still living off Dietrich. In January 1953, he put an end to this situation by dispensing with "Marlene Dietrich Inc." In May he underwent major abdominal surgery, and in June, he moved to San Fernando Valley, California. He continued to record every detail of how long he slept, what he spent, when the curtains were washed, and when and to whom telephone calls were made. There was one big change, however: his New York cocktail-party social life gave way to raising chickens. Sieber had borrowed money to buy a chicken farm. Every day he noted the number of eggs that were laid; each egg brought him one step closer to independence from Dietrich. On New Year's Eve 1953, he and Tamara were in bed by nine-thirty in the evening. At midnight, the telephone rang. It was Dietrich calling from Las Vegas. Four days earlier, she had turned fifty-two, and now, at the Sahara Hotel in Las Vegas, she had just started her second career. She would spend the next twenty years traveling the world as a singer. She had decided to carry on as a stage legend.

THE
ACCUSED

Austria was the last country to be liberated from National Socialism. The advance of the western Allies did not begin there until late April 1945. In Innsbruck, a surprisingly enthusiastic reception awaited the Americans: the streets were decorated in red, white, and blue, and the masses hailed their arrival. Leni Riefenstahl was on the run at this time. At some point in the previous few weeks, she had realized that things were not looking good. Although she continued to work on *Lowlands* around the clock, she was finding it more and more difficult to retreat into the world of art.

Albert Speer had taken Riefenstahl's mother along from Berlin on one of his trips to Obersalzberg, a Bavarian mountain retreat for the Nazi top brass. Bertha Riefenstahl had been living with her daughter since February. Wilma Schaub, the wife of Hitler's oldest adjutant, SS-Obergruppenführer Julius Schaub, had also fled to Kitzbühel. She had a direct telephone line to the Reich chancellery, and supplied Riefenstahl with food, medicine, and news. There were reports of superweapons, damage from bombs, and the punishments awaiting them if the Allies were actually to win. Frau

Schaub had arranged for the original negatives of the party rally films to be brought to safety with a car coming from the "Brown House" (national headquarters of the National Socialist Party) in Munich to Bolzano.[1] When the report of the capitulation of Hamburg leaked out, it was said that Hitler and Goebbels had committed suicide. Swastika flags and Hitler portraits had vanished. Riefenstahl made a quick exit and headed to Mayrhofen, a small village in Tyrol.

Confusion reigned in Tyrol. The German soldiers who had been defeated on the Italian front were trying to get to Germany, and the Italian forced laborers were rushing back home. No one cared about Riefenstahl. She took a room in a small hotel in the village, and it was there that she learned about the death of Hitler. "What we had been expecting for a long time had finally come to pass. I cannot describe what I felt at that moment. A chaos of emotions raged in me—I threw myself on my bed and wept throughout the night."[2] She was crying only for herself. Without her Führer, she would not be able to proceed with the projects she had described to Speer the previous year. Her ability to run things her way had come to an end.

Her depiction of the postwar era, which was unvarying over the course of decades, reveals Riefenstahl's shocking degree of egomania. Right down to the end of her long life, she never tired of claiming that she had been the victim of a grave injustice.[3] Since no one in Mayrhofen was willing to help her out, she started to make her way back to her mother, and she and other civilians were arrested by American soldiers and brought to a prisoners' camp. Because the camp was poorly guarded, she was able to escape, only to be recaptured. This pattern of capture and escape occurred a total of three times. Riefenstahl ignored the fact that arrests and identity checks of minions of the National Socialist regime were a routine matter at this time. She regarded her "captivities" as a personal affront.

Once she arrived in Seebichl, she found that her house had

been seized by the Americans. Still, the American officer who met her at the door was courteous, and he even spoke German.[4] The Americans were looking for what was left of Hitler and his inner circle. Riefenstahl was questioned by Captain Wallenberg and Captain Langendorf, who had trouble reconciling their image of the plucky, attractive actress of the mountain films with the ailing, despondent woman sitting across from them. Riefenstahl's greatest source of anguish was that she could not continue her work on *Lowlands*. She figured that the project had come to a halt, as had everything in Germany. Then she affirmed that she had never curried favor with high-ranking National Socialists. After all, she had already been somebody before 1933. Riefenstahl, who was regularly handed one hundred thousand reichsmarks from the Goebbels ministry, claimed that if she, like many other colleagues, had only been working for the money, she could have been a millionaire by now. She trumpeted her artistic independence: "Had I ever had the impression that my freedom as creative artist would be limited, I would have gone abroad. . . . This I have kept until the last day of my work." Many party members made life difficult for her, and she even thought they were out to kill her. She hated Goebbels, and she now described Bormann as "such a primitive man." Riefenstahl recommended that those who had once been in Hitler's inner circle commit suicide. "And I cannot grasp how any of the people who shared Hitler's political ideas have the courage to continue living. I would have committed suicide, had I felt that I shared the responsibility for these crimes." By contrast, she was patting herself on the back for having known Jews (von Sternberg) and supported them (Ernst Jäger's wife). She had been terribly upset about the pogroms in November 1938, and was only able to calm down when she was assured that the responsible parties would be punished. The American officers did not regard her as a fanatical National Socialist, and found her open and sincere. Perhaps, they concluded, she truly did not know what had been going on in Hitler's state. In their eyes, Riefenstahl's moral corruption was a typical product of National Socialism. Hitler had held his protective hand over her and ensured that she could go on living undisturbed in her dream world. "If her statements are sincere, she has never grasped, and still does not grasp, the fact that she, by dedicating her life to art, has given expression to a gruesome regime and contributed to its glorification."[5]

Riefenstahl's husband and mother were now staying at Hörlahof, then in possession of the Ribbentrop family. She was also brought there by the American soldiers. But the joy of their reunion was short-lived, because Riefenstahl was again arrested and interrogated. She was shown photographs of concentration camps, and she had to put up with painful questions. Because she had been neither a member of the party nor Hitler's lover, she did not understand what was wanted of her. Then, on June 3, she was released, surprisingly quickly. The Americans gave her a document stating that there were no charges against her. Riefenstahl went back to Kitzbühel and assumed that the issues about her dealings with Hitler had been resolved. She returned to her daily routine and planned to finish up her work on *Lowlands*. It did not even occur to her that people might not want to see her films anymore. Riefenstahl did not feel compelled to reflect or make a fresh start. She merely noted that the end of the war had disrupted her work, but she was unfazed, all set to pick up where she had left off. In early May the Allies negotiated a change in the occupying power in North Tyrol. The French, who were intent on being considered a great power, insisted on an active role in implementing peace and rebuilding Europe. The removal of the American troops in North Tyrol and Vorarlberg began on July 5 and was completed five days later. This changeover had repercussions for Riefenstahl's life. The Americans regarded the Austrians just like the Germans, as a defeated nation. The French, by contrast, described themselves as an occupying power in a friendly country, which is why they had plaques mounted at the national border that read *Ici L'Autriche, pays ami*. The French policy can be summarized with three *d*'s: disannexation, detoxification, and democratization. Austria would be separated from Germany (*désannexion*), National Socialist propaganda would be removed (*désintoxication*), and the Austrians would be provided democratic political and cultural ideas (*démocratisation*). It is easy to see that Riefenstahl and her art were not compatible with this endeavor. Her clearance certificate that had been issued by the Americans was declared invalid because the French rejected the denazification process conducted by the Americans on the grounds that it had been too perfunctory and superficial. She was arrested and interrogated all over again, this time by the French military, and was ordered to leave Tyrol. It should be noted that this order was not some malicious act directed at her personally. The "Ostmark" no longer existed; all "ethnic Germans" were now considered foreigners and had to leave the country as quickly as possible.[6] According to her descriptions, she was subjected to gratuitous harassment by the French. After a stay in the hospital of the Innsbruck Women's Prison, she claimed to have been so demoralized that she wanted to die. Eventually her expulsion was withdrawn, and she was allowed to return to Seebichl House.

There she had a visit from Budd Schulberg. Schulberg was part of the old Hollywood upper crust. His father, B. P. Schulberg, had been the production chief of Paramount Pictures; Budd grew up with silent-film stars and knew quite a lot about the business. He had been one of the initiators of a boycott against Riefenstahl when she visited Hollywood in 1938. After the end of World War II, he was looking around Europe for movies and movie stills that could be of use in the war-crimes trials in Nuremberg on behalf of the American government. *Triumph of the Will* had already been confiscated and put to good use: "Its first use there was as a psychological experiment to try to break through Hess's 'amnesia.'"[7] *Victory of Faith* and *Day of Freedom*, which they wanted to show in Nuremberg to serve as a "memory refresher," still needed to be located. Schulberg went in search of Leni Riefenstahl, hoping to find these films. Reading the secret service files in Salzburg, he saw a reference to her last known whereabouts: "Last seen in Salzburg with Hitler's entourage early '43." He was referred to a Mr. Kahn, a member of the Rainbow Division, which had occupied the area around Salzburg. Kahn had been the first to interrogate Riefenstahl. He reported that she was able to supply a great deal of information about Hitler and explained that he would have liked to keep her incarcerated even longer. Because she was a VIP, however, she was turned over to the Seventh Army, which soon classified her as denazified and released her. Schulberg's quest then led him to Kitzbühel, where he asked the French officer in command where he might find her. Major Guyonnet did not think much of Madame Riefenstahl, and called her "a third-rate movie actress." Although he had interrogated her, he did not come away with much information and sent her back home.

Eventually Schulberg made his way to Seebichl House, an impressively large, beautiful building with a view of the snow-capped peaks of the Kitzbühel Alps. A short, nervous, exaggeratedly polite man with a stiff smile opened the door. This man was Peter Jacob, Riefenstahl's husband. He assured Schulberg that Riefenstahl was delighted at the prospect of his visit and asked him to come into the study. Schulberg found himself in a luxurious, oak-paneled room with a great many bookcases. He noticed quite a few classics of German literature, biographies of artists, film books, and leather-bound screenplays of Riefenstahl's movies, with the exception of *Victory of Faith, Triumph of the Will,* and *Day of Freedom.* She kept him waiting for half an hour, then made an appearance. Riefenstahl was wearing yellow, velvety corduroy slacks and a golden-brown leather jacket, which went perfectly with her tanned face. "She held out her hand to me, prima-donna fashion, and smiled grandly. She reminded me of I don't know how many actresses of her age I had met before, fading beauties who try to compensate in grooming, make-up and animation for what they begin to lack in physical appeal." He noticed how nervous she was. She asked him why he wanted to speak to her, and hastily pulled a piece of paper out of her pants pocket and held it up to him. Here, she said, take a look for yourself. She had been cleared, and was above reproach. When he replied that he was not from the Counter Intelligence Corps, but from the National Film Archives, and was looking for her films, her face relaxed. Riefenstahl took his hand and pressed it with gratitude. She sent her husband to the kitchen to have the cook bring them tea and cake. She was overjoyed to learn that someone had come to her from Berlin on account of her films. She happily repeated the movie titles as he listed them, but when he got to *Triumph of the Will*, she clammed up. She pulled her hand away, and her eyes, which had looked at him warmly until then, took on a wary aspect. It was only when he assured her that *Triumph of the Will* was a great documentary film that she calmed down again. "'Exactly,' she said. 'That's the way I meant it. Not propaganda, but—well, after all, a party congress in Nuremberg was something important happening, whether you were for it or not.'" Then she sent her husband off to get the certificate of the prize she had been awarded by the French government in 1937 for *Triumph of the Will*. When Schulberg asked about the two other films of party rallies, she had no desire to elaborate. *Victory of Faith* was short and uninteresting, she stated, and *Day of Freedom* an insignificant and pathetic effort, a mere concession to the Wehrmacht. She was more interested in discussing the certificate from Paris that Jacob brought her. "In Paris I was given an ovation. They treated me marvelously in London too. That's the way art should be—international." Schulberg tried to get her to talk about Hitler and his crimes. She actually claimed that Hitler had a very artistic and sensitive nature, but must have had a demon hidden inside him that no one could see. Her relationship with him was purely artistic. She had not heard a thing about the concentration camps until the Americans interrogated her. Then she turned to the subject of Goebbels, and claimed that she had feared that he would have her brought to a concentration camp. "'But why should you be afraid of concentration camps?' I said. 'After all, you hadn't heard of them.' 'Oh, I knew there were some,' Leni said. 'But I had no idea what they were really like, how terrible they were.'" After she had again ordered tea from her husband, she asked in a saccharine tone if he knew whether her name was on the black list. He did not know, but he assumed so. Then she asked whether he believed that her new, absolutely unpolitical film was likely to be boycotted in America. Schulberg said yes, and she confessed to him that she no longer knew what to do. Then why not try her new movie in Germany? "'Oh, no,' she said, 'I was never a Nazi, but the concentration-camp Germans will be in power.'" When he left, she walked him out to the front of the house. Once again, she tried to persuade him to intercede on her behalf. When Schulberg replied that he would not be able to do anything for her, any last trace of friendliness vanished for a moment. Then she gave him an odd smile, the kind that made him wonder whether she had used this same smile when requesting a favor from Hitler. She asked Schulberg for a can of gas, but he replied that it was against the rules for him to do so. After this second rebuff, her face took on a hard, self-pitying aspect. "As I drove down the hill," Schulberg wrote at the conclusion of his essay, "I saw her walking slowly back into her big house, back to her well-trained Mr. Jacob, her well-trained servants, and the stubborn ghosts of the third Reich who insisted on being part of the family."[8]

In this piece, Schulberg captured Riefenstahl's forlornness and factitiousness. She loved to speak about her successes as a great artist, and still dreamed of glitzy premieres and bursts of applause. Twenty-six years after Schulberg's visit, she would still go into a rage if his name came up. "No, no, don't mention Schulberg. *Keine*

[sic] *Mensch—Schwein!*"⁹ In 1971, she told her interviewer, Gordon Hitchens, that if she had been free and not so poor, she would have sued Schulberg. She had an odd concept of the law. What could she possibly sue him for? Right down to the end of her very long life, Riefenstahl would balk at the idea that she was in no position to play the injured party and adjudge right and wrong. The world lay in ruins, and she still thought she had every right to be the center of attention.

For Janet Flanner, two sights in Germany provided dramatic proof that the Allies had won the war. One was the devastation evident in any German city, and the other was "the small tableau of the Nazi-filled prisoners' box, beneath the floodlights, in the war-crimes courtroom in Nuremberg."¹⁰ Riefenstahl, who knew most of the defendants personally, had only the vaguest notion of the proceedings. She was so caught up in thoughts of what would happen to her personally that she was "almost like a sleepwalker" and incapable of making out the realities of the courtroom.¹¹ She would not admit to herself that she—like these men in the dock in Nuremberg—was one of the losers. Riefenstahl regarded the end of National Socialism as the beginning of tyranny. On April 15, 1946, she was ordered to leave Austria.¹² Her husband, her mother, and three members of her crew went with her. Every *Reichsdeutscher*— she had not been singled out, contrary to her description of the incident—was allowed to carry along only 30 kilos of luggage in this deportation.¹³ They were free to move to a German city in the French zone. Riefenstahl chose Freiburg, where she was hoping for help from Dr. Fanck, but he wanted nothing to do with her.

They eventually found a place to stay in the small town of Breisach, and then in the Black Forest village of Königsfeld. Her plans for a comeback—she already had a young woman at her side whom she intended to train as a film editor—were thwarted by the confiscation of her bank assets and her film equipment, including the footage itself.

Riefenstahl's marriage was in bad shape as well. Jacob, who could no longer escape to the battlefield, had to stay with her. He was a soldier whose war had been lost. Riefenstahl was plagued by her usual stomach ailments and craved her fame, or at least the prospect of attaining it. The two of them often fought. The thought that she might never be able to shoot a film again was devastating. She had actually assumed that the French would consider themselves lucky to have her in their zone. She must have wondered why they were not making her any movie offers, or bringing her to Paris to exchange ideas with the top French filmmakers.

She was ill-tempered, and living in close quarters with her husband and mother only made matters worse. Apart from the years she spent with Schneeberger, Riefenstahl had never lived with a man for long. The way she saw it, the victors in the war were to blame for the catastrophic state of her husband and her marriage: "My illness and the repeated arrests put a strain on him, especially since after almost five years of at the front, he deserved a better life after the war."[14] This can only mean that a German victory would have been the fair outcome. By the time a year had passed since the end of the war, Riefenstahl knew that she would have to gather all her strength to get back on her feet. She decided to separate from Jacob, who was constantly cheating on her. She would get along better without him. Riefenstahl reduced her family to a minimum: she lived with her mother, whose absolute admiration and support she could count on. Marriage, by contrast, consumed her energy and thus inhibited artistic development. Her divorce was finalized in the summer of 1947.

For her first denazification hearing in July 1948, she wrote up a chronology of her life. A key strategy in getting herself exonerated of the charge of shooting movies with National Socialist ideology was emphasizing the international recognition these films had brought her. To substantiate this point, she attached press reviews from fascist Italy and Nazi-occupied France. In addition, she asked

many of her former crew members for affidavits. The overwhelming consensus was that she selected her crew solely on the basis of
their technical and artistic merits. Personal adjutants of Hitler also
affirmed that Riefenstahl had never been Hitler's lover. On November 9, 1948, the verdict was handed down: Riefenstahl was found
"not in violation of the law." The explanation for this decision was
a virtually verbatim restatement of Riefenstahl's own argument:
Riefenstahl, the daughter of a respectable family in Berlin who
overcame considerable obstacles to become an artist, denied any
connection to National Socialism. She had enjoyed international
renown even before 1933. When Hitler came to power, the film
industry was nationalized and fell under Goebbels's authority, and
her difficult struggle for artistic autonomy commenced. Because she
was treated so badly and her movies were not authorized (*Mademoiselle Docteur* was cited as an example), she even left the country
and went to Spain. Once she was back in Germany, she was forced
to make a documentary about the Nuremberg Rally in 1934. She
had repeated serious conflicts with Goebbels, who tried to compro-
mise her in public and to disparage her accomplishments. Contrary
to popular belief, Goebbels did not back her; he persecuted and
impeded her. The fact-finding commission determined "unequivocally" that Riefenstahl had nothing in common with either the
party's or Hitler's ideas.

> The assumption among the general public that Leni Riefen-
> stahl must be regarded as a beneficiary of the Third Reich
> because of her high income level and financial holdings
> is not correct. We do know that she made 7 films prior to
> 1933, she did not receive a penny from the propaganda
> ministry, and the last 2 films, including *Lowlands*, have yet
> to be completed because nearly all of her film products and
> materials have been seized and removed from her posses-
> sion. Frau Riefenstahl is a poor woman today. Her home in

Berlin is destroyed, as is the one in Kitzbühel, and the only
livable property has been impounded by the occupying
power, so she has no rental revenue.[15]

At the hearing on July 6, 1949, Riefenstahl essentially stuck to
her story from the previous year. Since the Goebbels diaries were
still undiscovered at this time (they were in storage in Moscow),
she could get away with outright lies. Riefenstahl claimed that she
had never been invited to the homes of Goebbels, Ribbentrop, Bormann or other high-ranking National Socialists. The formal decision
came down that there was no presumption of guilt in Riefenstahl's
case and that she was not a beneficiary of National Socialism. On
December 6, 1949, the Baden State Commission for Political Purgation ordered a new scrutiny of the case, and on December 16, Riefenstahl was classified as a *Mitläuferin* (usually translated as "fellow
traveler," it essentially means "active sympathizer"). However, the
statement justifying this classification reads more like a vindica-
tion. Several pages from the document classifying her as "not in
violation of the law" are quoted, and at the end, there is no more
than a brief mention of the fact that her non-member status in the
party, associations, and so forth was not a sufficient reason to dismiss her political liability. Riefenstahl's work on the party rally and
Olympic films, which were used for National Socialist propaganda,
sufficed to regard her as a *Mitläuferin*. She was not charged, nor
was she banned from her profession. There were no sanctions or
prohibitions.

After this decision, which enabled her to work again, she packed
up, left Königsfeld, and moved to Munich. She knew exactly what
to do: she would pick up where she had left off, which meant that
she would complete *Lowlands*. This restart to her career had only
one catch: *Lowlands* was still in the hands of the French. To play up
the artistic and political importance of the film, she later claimed

in her memoirs that bitter disputes had broken out among various political groups in Paris about whether to return the film.[16]

Many other artists hailed the heady combination of chaos and freedom they experienced after 1945, but not Leni Riefenstahl. She lacked their curiosity about the aesthetic trends from which Germany had been cut off for so long, and saw no need for a personal or professional reassessment or an artistic new beginning. Driven out of her paradise, she was offended that she was not being welcomed as a key figure in the artistic world. Once she had been officially denazified, she could litigate—the courtroom offered her a new stage for performances that would earn her press coverage. A suit she brought against the publisher, Olympiaverlag, inaugurated a virtual orgy of court cases—fifty in all. *Wochenend* magazine had published excerpts of the supposed diary of Eva Braun, and Luis Trenker, of all people, claimed that Braun had given him this diary. Riefenstahl appears in the diary as "the rival," and she is said to have danced in front of Hitler and received monetary gifts. In September 1948, Riefenstahl won her suit in the Munich district court. Photographs of the trial show her sitting among her lawyers, sometimes wiping away her tears or shouting indignantly, always sporting a jaunty hat and elegant suit with a white blouse in the style of Dior's New Look. She knew how to plant herself in the limelight. People rightly wondered how a lady like this could possibly qualify for legal aid, which was how she financed these cases. One year later Riefenstahl brought a private suit against the publisher Helmut Kindler. On May 1, 1949, *Revue* magazine, of which Kindler was the editor in chief, had published a long illustrated article bearing the title "The Uncompleted Film by Leni Riefenstahl. What will become of *Lowlands*?" The article claimed that shooting this film had already cost seven million marks, and that for Riefenstahl, money was no object. She had selected Gypsies in concentration camps who had been mistreated to act as extras. Riefenstahl was suing Kindler for libel and defamation. In this trial as well, she was granted legal aid.

The usual suspects were summoned as witnesses; they swore that the subject of concentration camps had never come up and that the atmosphere on the set was upbeat, even jolly. The court did not buy the witness's story cited in the *Revue* and determined that because the witness was herself a Gypsy, her "subjective feelings were tarnished."[17] An additional key exonerating witness for Riefenstahl was the former SS-Sturmbannführer who had overseen the construction of the Maxglan camp. He was listed as an "expert in matters pertaining to Gypsies." In his statement, which ran on for several pages, he pointed out that Gypsies were criminal and abhorrent. The camp had been set up because there had been many robberies in the area, and this was a way of keeping better watch over the Gypsies. In Maxglan, they lived in a supervised environment behind barbed wire. To pay for these costs, the Gypsies were lent out, in this case to Frau Riefenstahl, who pampered them so extremely that he had to remind her to comply with the rules.

Alfred Polgar, a prominent drama critic, fiction writer, and essayist, attended this trial, and reported that although the topic was a horrifying one ("concentration camp inmates as film extras"), the atmosphere in the courtroom was exuberant. Everyone—including the judge and the opposing counsel—was charming to Riefenstahl, and her "birdlike profile" lost a little of its sharpness. The spectators hung on every word of her reports about meetings with the Führer, who was so understanding, and Goebbels, who was evil. "But even in these buoyant moments, the coldness never left Frau Riefenstahl's eyes and expression. Earlier in her life, she had been heavily involved in movies about glaciers, and maybe the frostiness in her face was a holdover from that time."[18]

Riefenstahl did not deny that she had worked with Gypsies, "but she emphasized that these people had been happy to have escaped the concentration camp for a few weeks."[19] She insisted

that she had not brought the suit against Kindler of her own voli-
tion, but had been compelled to do so by the Allied authorities
and the denazification tribunal in order to respond to accusations
that had been made against her in court. There is no evidence
to back up this assertion. She used this propitious moment to
announce that her pockets were full of foreign film contracts. The
crowning achievement came when Riefenstahl's lawyer belted out
to the courtroom: "The nation can be proud of Leni Riefenstahl!"
In the end, Kindler was fined six hundred marks and Riefenstahl
emerged from this trial on stronger footing. She had been able to
foil an ethical publisher and opponent of the National Socialists
whose publications supported a new, democratic Germany.

In 1950, she bought a three-room apartment in Munich. Riefenstahl claimed to have gotten the money for it from Friedrich Mainz,
the former head of Tobis Cinema. This was not just any apartment
building. Ady Vogel, known as "the salt baron," was a friend of hers
and had the idea of building an apartment house that combined the
advantages of a hotel and a rental building. Concierge, chamber-
maids, telephone switchboard, restaurant, hairdresser, and cleaning
service were available to the residents. This luxurious lifestyle was
new in Germany. The stately and elegant staircase at Tengstrasse 20
in Schwabing revealed the kind of setting Riefenstahl considered
fitting for herself. Her new domicile was not some little hole in the
wall in shabby welfare housing at the edge of town; this was a lavish apartment building right in the center of Munich's arts district.
Her dark days appeared to be over. When Peter Viertel, son of the
screenwriter Salka Viertel, was stationed in Munich as an American
soldier, he observed Riefenstahl holding court with friends at the
elegant hotel bar of the Bayerischer Hof.[20] She also profited from
the currency reform and the establishment of the Federal Republic
of Germany. However, she was unable to gain a foothold in the film
business. This had nothing to do with a "work ban," as she maintained. People associated her name with Nazi propaganda films,

and no one was drawn to those kinds of movies now. She had never made sparkling entertainment films, and her tepid reputation as an actress did not inspire people to look forward to her return to the screen. Unlike Wilhelm Furtwängler, whose return to the conductor's stand was supported by renowned soloists and distinguished politicians from around the globe, and whose artistic reputation trumped any accusations of political and moral guilt, Riefenstahl lacked any political or artistic backing.

German film in the immediate postwar period was what Fritz Göttler has called a "transit space," wedged between the old and the new. The first postwar films—entertaining flashes in the pan and highbrow social-problem films—were produced almost entirely by people who had previously worked at Ufa. These films lacked boldness, dynamism, ambition, and self-confidence. Film production was now centered in Munich and Hamburg; Berlin had been relegated to the background. Riefenstahl picked Munich as her new base and met up again with Harry Sokal, who had returned to Germany from the United States. Her memoirs have only snide remarks about him, but her old cameraman, Heinz von Jaworsky, reported that in 1948 he ran into Riefenstahl and Sokal arm in arm, enjoying a friendly chat in a Munich film studio. Riefenstahl pictured them producing films together, but Sokal no longer had as much money as before the war and would be unable to finance the completion of *Lowlands*. She would have to seek new investors.

The postwar films made it painfully clear that the Germans were in no position to summon up any real interest in their current era. Filmmaking was taking a very different path in Italy. Defeated and deprived, Italy was still able to achieve international recognition with its cinematic art. Thanks to Luchino Visconti, Roberto Rossellini, and Vittorio De Sica, Rome was soon regarded as the center of European film. Riefenstahl was invited to Rome in 1950 and later recalled: "I was in a state of euphoria. The blue sky, the warm air, the laughing people helped me to forget the grayness that I had left behind in Germany. They had found an elegant apartment for me, and next to the flowers there was an envelope with a large sum of money in lira bills."[21] At long last, she was being treated as a diva and revered once again. In the evenings she was taken out and there was great interest in her ideas for future projects.

Riefenstahl kept up with the times as far as her appearance was concerned. She dyed her hair titian red and wore an eye-catching green raincoat. With big hoop earrings, short curly hair, and chic summer dresses, she hobnobbed with the likes of Gina Lollobrigida in Cinecittà. She was still strikingly attractive and left no stone unturned in her quest to regain a distinguished place in society.

She continued to regard her films as classic masterpieces. Since she had also filmed on location, she mingled with the neorealists, conveniently overlooking the fact that the Italian neorealist directors knew how to tell a good story and she did not. Simple, powerfully expressive images told the unrecorded story of mankind. Italian directors such as Rossellini and Visconti drew on the great artistic tradition of their country using "genetic material" adopted from Giotto's medieval frescoes and Renaissance painters, while Riefenstahl rambled about Dürer, Kollwitz, and Van Gogh. Italian filmmakers created a reality that was deeply rooted in the history and geography of their country. This distinctive symbiosis of everyday people and film made cinema the gauge of the cultural and social development of postwar Italy. Riefenstahl, like her former benefactor, Hitler, had only idealized images of people in her head. Whether she was in Sarntal, at the Nuremberg party rallies, or in the Maxglan camp, she looked for extras who could play the role of regular people. Riefenstahl's films show no trace of having discovered the realism that infused the Italian cinema with new images.

People with political clout interceded to get the *Lowlands* footage back to her. It was the same old story: her valuable, irreplaceable film had been damaged, or even destroyed, by idiots. She spent days and nights at the editing table wrestling to restore the film. *Lowlands* premiered on February 11, 1954. After many glamorous premieres at the Ufa Palace in Berlin, Riefenstahl was now consigned to the boondocks. The distributor Allianz-Verleih arranged for a showing in Stuttgart. Although some reviews were scathing, others offered words of praise. Still, the outcome was clear: the movie that had sapped so much of her strength was a flop. The style and subject matter of this melodrama set in an unreal nowhere were behind the times. Riefenstahl had the sinking feeling that she had been "miscast" and was unable to breathe life into the role of Marta.[22] No one accepted her as the young Gypsy—least of all herself. A curse seemed to hang over *Lowlands*. For the cinema, 1954 was the year of Fellini's *La Strada* and Visconti's *Senso*—not *Lowlands*. Riefenstahl withdrew the movie from theaters after only a few showings. She had spent nearly a decade working on a doomed project.

NEW
CHAPTER
OF FAME

(1954–1976)

THE
ICON

The loss of Riefenstahl's former status cut her to the quick, and she tried to blot out the gray postwar era by recalling better days gone by. She found solace in friends who were in the same boat and gathered them around her. Emmy Göring, the widow of Hermann Göring, lived just a few doors down the street. The two of them had a great deal in common; Göring had also been an actress, so they were colleagues of a sort. Riefenstahl and Göring felt like queens without a country. Driven out of their villas in Berlin, they had wound up in three-room apartments in the Schwabing section of Munich. The Haus Savoy restaurant was on the ground floor of Riefenstahl's apartment building. It was owned by the wife of Hermann Esser, one of Adolf Hitler's earliest supporters. He had gone into hiding in 1949 and was sentenced to five years in prison in 1950, but a mere two years later he was released. Rounding out this illustrious group was Max Amann, who had been Hitler's sergeant in World War I and the third person ever to join the Nazi party. He had also taken part in the 1923 putsch, served as the business manager of the NSDAP in its early phase, published *Mein Kampf*, and later served as president of the

Reich media chamber. SS-Obergruppenführer Amann was sentenced to ten years in a labor camp in 1948 as a *Hauptschuldiger* (major offender). He often stopped by the Savoy during his imprisonment in the Bavarian town of Eichstätt, which surprised the American secret policemen who reported on his whereabouts since they could not understand why he was permitted to leave the labor camp so often.[1]

On her journeys back and forth through Europe, Riefenstahl desperately looked for investors for her absurd film projects. Nothing came of *The Red Devils*, but she devised a plan for a movie about the effects of nuclear energy, to be called *Cobalt 60*. For a documentary film about Spain—*Sol y Sombra*—she went on an extended trip to get to know the country and its people. For yet another motion picture project (*Three Stars on the Cloak of the Madonna*), she offered the lead role to Anna Magnani, a role in which Magnani would play a mother who has converted to the Christian faith. Magnani politely declined. Riefenstahl pictured big names—Brigitte Bardot, Jean Marais, Vittorio De Sica, and Ruth Leuwerik—acting in her films, but is unclear whether any of these celebrities were actually interested in working with her.

Riefenstahl was usually accompanied by her ex-husband on her trips through Europe. Despite their divorce, the two of them traveled as a couple. She now wore makeup. One of the first major social events where she put in an appearance after the war was the 1955 film ball in Berlin. The belle of this ball was Romy Schneider, but people also took heed of Riefenstahl, who wore a glittering evening gown that showed ample cleavage. She enjoyed being photographed and still knew how to strike a girlish, coquettish pose. Still, all the low-cut gowns, flirtations, and screenplays in the world did nothing to help her find a producer.

Always on the lookout for gripping images and stories, Riefenstahl came across a book by Ernest Hemingway, who had been awarded the Nobel Prize in Literature in 1954, that fit the bill. She was spellbound by his *Green Hills of Africa* and finished reading it in a single night. Hemingway's book is a lyrical journal of his African safari, with its detailed descriptions of eating, sleeping, drinking, and, above all, hunting. Hemingway loved the wild beauty of Africa and the hunt. For him, killing animals was tantamount to a rebellion against death. *Green Hills of Africa* was not one of Hemingway's finest works; it is longwinded and chatty. Its true strength lies in the depiction of a yearning for a primitive world with clear laws in the midst of overwhelming nature. Hemingway describes proud and beautiful men who have no fear and are filled with grace.[2] Riefenstahl got caught up in this yearning and believed that she could become whole again in Africa.

She now came into some unexpected money by recouping a loan she had made before the war. With these fourteen thousand marks in hand, she could finance her trip. In April 1956, Riefenstahl traveled to Nairobi on her own initiative.

> I had always lived in the world of the mountains, the ice
> of Greenland, the lakes of Brandenburg, the metropolis of
> Berlin. Here, I instantly felt the start of something entirely
> different—a new life. Against the light, I saw black figures
> in light garments coming toward me, seeming to hover
> in the quivering sunlight, detached from the earth as in a
> mirage. Africa had embraced me—forever. It had sucked me
> into a vision of foreignness and freedom, and affected me
> like a drug with a narcotic effect that has yet to wear off,
> even today.[3]

In the course of her travels through East Africa, she was involved in a car accident that left her badly injured. She spent several weeks at a hospital in Nairobi. This accident boosted her will to survive. Physical suffering gave Riefenstahl the message that she had to conquer something. "It was a dramatic baptism by fire. But in spite of this serious accident, my resolve to find the genuine, pristine Africa strengthened."[4] In Africa, Riefenstahl encountered "the tallest, best-built, handsomest people" she had read about in Hemingway.[5] The Masai women threw stones at her when she attempted to establish contact with them. Riefenstahl knew how to woo them from her experience with the Sarntal peasants. Doubly determined to succeed, she returned to the Masai village every single day, sitting down and reading and making her presence known. Her bold and dogged persistence paid off once again: the women and children began approaching her, full of curiosity. Eventually she was able to visit them in their huts and even photograph them. "Thus began my great love for the tribes of Africa."[6]

When she returned to Germany, all she could think about was getting back to Africa as quickly as possible. Riefenstahl negotiated with every film company and met with one rejection after another. In the end she appealed to Walter Traut, who had worked with her on the mountain films and felt obliged to come up with something. In July 1956, he founded Stern Film, Inc. to make a movie called *Black Cargo*, for which Riefenstahl had signed on a dancer, Helge Pawlinin, and a screenwriter, Kurt Heuser, to collaborate on the script. Riefenstahl became Traut's partner and equal manager in the company. Traut would invest up to two hundred thousand marks of his own money, and Riefenstahl would contribute the screenplay and her preliminary work on the project. She flew to Nairobi with Pawlinin, and they headed for northern Kenya. Riefenstahl began her hunt for exotic, beautiful people and for tall, muscular men to play the roles of slaves. Once she arrived at the island of Lamu, however, she was disappointed to find only slender people, so she set off with an interpreter to seek the physiques she was after. In Sarntal, she had won over the uncommunicative peasants by treating them to wine. In Africa, she offered the chief money, sunglasses, cigarettes, and wristwatches in exchange for his men. The offer was accepted, and she was able to choose freely among the villagers. She looked over the men, and those who made the cut had to come along with her. These actors in the making, separated from their families and their village, were not entirely clear about what was happening to them; many were afraid that Riefenstahl herself was a slave trader and would carry them off with her. A great deal of effort went into filming a few scenes. Riefenstahl had not considered the possibility that these amateur actors might have an outlook on nature that differed from her own. They were terribly afraid of the water and did not want to get onto the barge that had been constructed expressly for the shooting. She was overwhelmed, and began filming haphazardly. Her only goal appears to have been to shoot as much footage as she could. Then she got a telegram from Walter Traut in Munich, letting her know that all the money had been spent. He begged her to come back to Munich. If she brought good shots with her, they would find investors.

Riefenstahl had been able to shoot films only under the luxurious conditions of National Socialism, when neither money nor time mattered. However, there was no longer a party apparatus at her side. Her cameramen were scattered to the winds, and there was no one to provide organization or funding. She also had no real insight into the conditions in Germany by this point. She was incorrigibly bound to an overly elaborate, inefficient, and inordinately expensive working method. Traut paid off the remaining debts, and for Riefenstahl, the subject of Africa was over and done with for the time being.

In 1962, she got back most of the footage that had been confiscated by the Austrian authorities, along with her film equipment and cutting table. She now regained possession of *Triumph of the Will*, *Avalanche*, and Zielke's *Steel Animal*, and wanted to begin distributing her films as soon as she could. She rented two basements near her apartment and converted them to cutting rooms. Fifteen years after the end of the war, Riefenstahl began building up an archive.[7] She was dissatisfied with the distribution of her films and the suits for her rights. Accustomed to ordering others around, she had trouble accepting the fact that no one was listening to her anymore. After plans for an English remake of *The Blue Light* came to naught and no prominent supporters of hers were left in Germany, she thought about returning to Africa. She gave an appealing fairy-tale account of her second trip to Sudan, in December 1962, which became the prelude to her postwar career as a photographer. She depicted herself as a Junta-like figure sitting in the plane to Nairobi. This time, the place in which she stumbled across the picture that would change her life was not a subway station in Berlin, but a hospital room in Nairobi. She claimed that after her accident, she happened to see an issue of *Stern* magazine with a photograph by the British photographer George Rodger of two naked, muscular black athletes, one sitting proudly atop the other's shoulders. Rodger had captured the stark moment of triumph. "This picture changed my life. . . . These unfamiliar Nuba took such complete possession of me that they induced me to do things I would otherwise not have done."[8] From this point on, she invested all her energy in looking for the tribe to which these men belonged. All she had to go on was the caption under the photograph: "The Nuba of Kordofan." No one knew how to get to them; little had been written about these people, and it appeared uncertain whether they even existed. Riefenstahl set out to find this mysterious tribe, hoping to be the first to uncover this treasure. That is Part One of the fairy tale we might call "How I Discovered the Nuba." The truth is that she had been looking for the Nuba for quite some time already. She conveniently neglected to mention that in the spring of 1951—three years *before* the Hemingway book was published and five years before her first trip to Africa—she had contacted Rodger and offered him $1,000 to tell her how to get to the Nuba.

Rodger, one of the three founders of the legendary Magnum Photos, was six years younger than Riefenstahl. He had been at fifty-one front lines of the war, and up until the day he came to

Bergen-Belsen, he thought that nothing could shock him anymore. He was the first to take pictures in Bergen-Belsen, and they became famous overnight when they were published in *Life* magazine. However, Rodger could not forgive himself for having injected an aesthetic component into these horrifying images. He hoped to clear his mind of these awful memories by taking an extended journey through Africa. Rodger wanted to go to the Nuba; very few scholars or travelers from the West had seen them. In 1951, his pictures appeared in *National Geographic*, and his book, *Le Village des Noubas*, was published in France.[9] Riefenstahl is sure to have read the *National Geographic* article, because she contacted Rodger that same year. It must have been an odd coincidence for Rodger that six years after he had taken his photographs in Bergen-Belsen, he was being contacted by Hitler's favorite director with a request that he do her a favor. Rodger replied to Riefenstahl, "Dear Madam, knowing your background and mine I don't really have anything to say to you at all."[10] Riefenstahl never mentioned this unequivocal rebuff.

Eleven years later, Riefenstahl traveled to Sudan with a scholarly expedition led by Oskar Luz from the German Nansen Society in Tübingen.[11] The scholars would be shooting a series of films about the Nuba tribe. Riefenstahl was the only woman in the group, and its oldest participant. Now Part Two of "How I Discovered the Nuba" began. The regions they passed through became less and less fit for human habitation. "Blocks of stone and ancient trees gave the landscape an almost mythical character. The valley narrowed down, the mountains seemed to converge, and the path grew rockier and rockier. We had been driving through this valley for hours—no water, no people, not even animals anywhere."[12] Suddenly they saw a naked girl sitting on a boulder. "We were surrounded by great silence; the sun was fading and the valley seemed virtually lifeless. Stones and roots blocked our way." Leni-as-Junta had reached her destination.

One or two thousand people were milling about in an open
area surrounded by many trees in the light of the setting
sun. Peculiarly painted and oddly adorned, they seemed
like creatures from another planet. Hundreds of spear tips
danced against the blood-red orb of the sun. In the middle
of the crowd, large and small circles had formed, and
pairs of wrestlers faced one another inside them. They drew
each other in, fought, danced, and were carried from the
ring as victors on the shoulders of others, just as I had seen
in Rodger's photograph. I was dazed, and didn't know what
to photograph first.[13]

Her message was clear: As an artist who was treated unjustly and
maliciously by the civilized world, she had come to find people
whose hearts were still pure. Once she had seen the picture of the
black athletes with their strong bodies, she knew that this paradise still existed. She overcame every obstacle and miraculously
found her way to the Nuba.

In fairy tales, portrayals of abuse, sin, and injustice function
only as a means toward presenting a naïve moral. Riefenstahl saw
her situation in the same terms: penned in, persecuted, and ignored
in Germany, she underwent all kinds of adventures and eventually
found people who loved her unconditionally and with whom she
was finally happy again. When she had to say goodbye to the Nuba
after seven weeks, she was stricken with grief.

o   o   o

Riefenstahl did not fly back to Germany, but instead parted from
the anthropologists and went back to the Nuba mountains on her
own. She not only took photographs but also recorded the local
music and language. No matter how strong her emotional ties to
the Nuba grew, she was not about to forget the business angle. Just
as more than thirty years earlier she had had no qualms about

filming the Sarntal peasants in church, she now plunged right into
the lives of Nuba men to photograph them during their ceremonial
wrestling matches. These photographic quests always centered on
wresting the moment of ecstasy from faces and bodies, whether
they be Sarntal peasants, Hitler Youth, Olympic athletes, or the
Nuba. She later claimed that the photographs she took during this
trip were solely for her private use.[14] However, a letter she wrote
to Theo von Hörmann reveals that her stay with the Nuba had
clear commercial aims. "Since November of last year I have been
living exclusively in the bush in the most remote parts of Sudan
and made several thousand color slides for lecture tours, because I
didn't get any money to make a movie. . . . Now I will be going to
the Masai to complete my series of photographs."[15] However, she
also wrote about the happiness she felt with the Nuba. "First I was
traveling with a group of German scholars, but have been alone for
the past few months. Sleeping outdoors, without a tent—or helpers
of any kind—so primitively that I didn't even have a mattress, a
head rest, a chair, or a table. All the same, I have felt happier than
in Europe because the primitive natives who have not yet had contact with civilization are simply better people—even though they
go around without any clothes on." The photographs from her first
extended stay in the Nuba Mountains show a relaxed, cheerful Riefenstahl. She enjoyed wearing becoming safari suits or short, colorful summer dresses. Although she was nearing the age of sixty,
she retained the radiance of a young woman, and she would claim
for the rest of her life that she had never been as carefree as she
was there.

In the 1960s, she traveled to Africa every other year on average,
stayed for several months, and came back from each trip with a big
haul of thousands of photographs. The descriptions and pictures
of her trips to Africa recall bits and pieces of her previous careers.
In Africa she worked under ideal conditions. The Nuba did not ask
for any pay for the photographs; they sang, danced, and fought for

free. She could amass vast quantities of material from which to pick and choose later on, as she had done in filming the party rallies and the Olympic games. Without a script or a producer to answer to, she could film and photograph however she pleased. She was still unabashed when aiming for a good picture. She forced her way between people who were fighting or dancing without a second thought. She even disrupted funerals or death watches with her flash photography. Riefenstahl justified her actions at one of these gatherings as follows: "It wasn't easy for me to take pictures on this solemn occasion, but I felt I simply had to capture this ritual of a fading mythical culture in pictures."[16] These pictures were her booty. She knew that the more sensational they were, the better they would help her rise to new glory. The Nuba never asked about her background, and she did not have to put up with any annoying questions about her relationship with Hitler or her art. She felt loved and admired without reservation.

Riefenstahl's new friends and objects were people without a history. The Nuba did not use writing or otherwise chronicle their actions. They lived their lives beyond the grasp of history, with fixed rituals and with nature. Riefenstahl, who was fleeing her own history and had always distrusted words, found her way back to the beginnings of her art while in Africa. When she was with the Nuba, she experienced dance as a force that knit together a community. The dance ceremony, she felt, served to render a sacred quality to the social sphere. She regarded the physical ecstasy, solemnity, and pairing rituals she saw there as signs of reestablishing life within the cult. There are shots of her trying to dance with the Nuba men. Her movements clearly recall her performances as an expressive dancer. But these shots also expose her outsider status in this community. Just as in the mountain and party rally movies, she laid claim to an elevated position here in Africa. Riefenstahl was the only white woman, the only woman who understood the technology, and the only one who regarded herself as an artist.

She had fallen out with her crew members during all her previous journeys, yet she did not want to travel alone, so she went
looking for an ideal traveling companion for her next expedition to
Sudan. This companion "had to have a stable character and be in
good health"; he also needed to be a good driver and mechanic, and
know the basics of filmmaking.[17] Horst Kettner, an auto mechanic,
was recommended to her. She took an instant liking to this somewhat shy, good-looking man. Kettner was twenty-seven years old
and had come to Germany from Czechoslovakia just two years earlier. Supposedly he had never heard of Riefenstahl. The old woman
and the young man traveled to Africa by ship and Land Rover.
However, Riefenstahl's fourth visit to "her" Nuba resulted in one
long disappointment. She had been quite keen to show Kettner
a Nuba wrestling match, but she discovered that the rituals had
changed. The wrestlers were not naked; they were wearing multicolored trousers, and some even had sunglasses on. "I was horrified, and Horst was disappointed. . . . We scrapped our plan to film
the festival; it would have been a waste of every meter of celluloid."[18]

Riefenstahl returned to her fairy-tale diction when recounting
the story of how her love of the Nuba of Mesakin came to an end:

> Oddly enough, the weather had also changed completely.
> Every time I had been to the Nuba Mountains in the past,
> the sky had always been blue, but this time, it was very
> different. . . . An even more peculiar change was that the
> clear vista we had always known in the Nuba Mountains
> was no longer there. The air was hazy, and we no longer
> experienced the marvelous sunsets. . . . Even the Nuba told
> us that they had never known such weather.[19]

The time had come for the old woman, at the young man's side, to
go back to Germany. The Nuba may have let her down, but Kettner
did not: "Horst had once again proved himself to an incredible

degree. Hard-working, calm, and sensitive, he was an ideal companion. No work was too much or too hard for him, and he found a solution for every technical problem."[20] Her love of the Nuba gave way to her love of Kettner. Choosing Kettner as her new romantic partner showed that Riefenstahl was firmly anchored to her past. Kettner was the age that Ertl, Allgeier, and all the other cameramen had been when she shot the mountain films with Fanck. Fanck always chose technically skilled, athletic young men in their late twenties for work on his films and trained them as cameramen. In this same vein, Riefenstahl trained Kettner to be *her* cameraman. Their professional and romantic partnership would last until her death.

Riefenstahl was not the kind of woman to give in to old age. She was proud to have a lover at her side who was forty years her junior. Over the course of the following years, she traveled to Africa several times with Kettner. The spell that the Nuba had cast on her seemed to be broken. Each visit brought new disappointment. Her erstwhile affection had tipped into annoyance: "After only a brief visit, our one desire was to leave as soon as possible. The worst part was that our time was so taken up by the Nuba, who were as dear and trusting as ever, that we didn't have a moment's rest. They surrounded us like a swarm of bees, and all their affection notwithstanding, it was exhausting."[21]

In 1964, some of her photographs from Africa had been featured in *Kristall* magazine, but they were largely ignored. Five years later, *Stern* magazine published a series of her Nuba photos.[22] This publication launched Riefenstahl's fourth career, as a photographer. Much has been written about why the Nuba photographs were so successful throughout the world. Some see this success as the triumph of Riefenstahl's genius, and others as the continued presence of National Socialist attitudes. There is some truth to both of these assertions. A distinction needs to be drawn between the reasons for the success of these images and Riefenstahl's reasons for hav-

ing taken them. As contradictory as it might sound, Riefenstahl's
success stemmed in part from the cultural revolt of 1968. The very
social movement that wanted to settle the score with National
Socialism helped make Riefenstahl's long-desired comeback a reality. Up until that time, no attention had been paid to the way the
Nuba pictures were presented.

The editor in chief of *Stern* magazine was Henri Nannen, whom
Riefenstahl knew well and who was regarded as one of the most
innovative editors in Germany. He wanted to bring a breath of fresh
air to the German press, and he was able to do so together with Rolf
Gillhausen, whom he hired as *Stern*'s art director in 1955. Gillhausen placed a Riefenstahl photograph on the cover and designed the
series of images that would go along with it. In retrospect it must be
said that no one was better suited to this task than Gillhausen. As
a photographer, he had seen quite a bit of the world and was especially fond of American editorial design. At *Stern*, he was in charge
not only of the look of the magazine but also of the overall concept
and the journalistic content. Gillhausen drew his inspiration from
Life magazine in the United States and *Paris Match* in France. His
motto was "Take the best picture and make it big." Series of photographs extending across two pages, clear composition, and new
typography were the hallmarks of his style, which often brought to
mind the German magazine *Twen*, designed by Willy Fleckhaus.[23]
The typography was plain, the colors tantalizing and glamorous.
It was in this style that the Nuba photographs were shown to the
German readership. Gillhausen's design incorporated Riefenstahl's
photographs into the aesthetic of pop culture. All at once, her art
was in keeping with the times. This was not the past weighing
heavily on the present; it was modern and light.

Riefenstahl's photographs served to illustrate the catchwords of
the era: nudity, critique of civilization, art, free sexuality, and feminism. The Nuba were naked, and they had no need for money or
consumerism to achieve happiness. Women were on an equal foot-

ing with men, and everyone was an artist. Riefenstahl described the Nuba as musically gifted, soulful hippies who spent their lives cheerfully playing the harp.

In 1973, the illustrated volume *The Last of the Nuba* was published by List Verlag in Munich. With this book, which was translated into many different languages, Riefenstahl achieved her international breakthrough. She was celebrated as a great artist and researcher. It was as though the Nuba had not even existed before her discovery of them. Her publisher claimed that since the 1930s, not a single white person had undertaken any serious study of the Nuba.

One year before the book was published, Riefenstahl had turned seventy. At the Olympic Games in Munich, she was seen in the bleachers taking photographs with her telephoto lens, capturing the events for the *Sunday Times* of London. At the same time, her *Olympia* movies were being shown at the ARRI Cinema in Munich, with long lines forming to get in. When she was asked whether the images from 1936, with all their pathos, still made an impact, she replied: "And how! I'm surprised myself that this movie is still successful after thirty-six years—abroad as well. In England and America, people stand up and applaud after the showing. Some people are even moved to tears. But what's wrong with that?"[24] Film critics and reporters were beating a path to her doorstep; everyone wanted to meet and interview her.

Riefenstahl sought to capitalize on the market potential of this newfound popularity by getting her next Nuba book out as quickly as she could. In the quest for cultures that were as yet unspoiled by civilization, she and Kettner came upon the Nuba tribe of Kau during their Africa expedition in the latter part of 1974. As always, she had a voracious appetite for images. Each new expedition grew more elaborate and technically sophisticated. Now that her first Nuba book had been an extraordinary success, the pressure was on. She knew exactly what kinds of pictures she would have to bring home to delight her readers. To persuade the Nuba to cooperate with her, she carried documentation from the Sudanese government in which they were requested to support the work of Riefenstahl, who was a "friend of the country." She also handed out flashlights, batteries, candy, and pearls as gifts. She had no time to win over the Nubas' trust. She had never been bothered by tourists in her previous visits, but this time around they were everywhere. The success of her illustrated volume had had the unintended consequence of bringing out adventurous amateur photographers who hoped to reenact her triumph.

Her firm resolve got her the results she wanted this time as well. She was on the scene with her camera when young men fought with sticks and knives and when girls got tattooed; she even muscled her way into an event known as a "love fest." Riefenstahl regarded herself as the documentarian of a disappearing world. She went to "unimaginable lengths" to get pictures, "perhaps at the last possible moment, of these fascinating, unique South East Nuba as documents for posterity."[25] Her efforts paid off. *Stern*, which had acquired the initial rights to the German publication of the photos, published a twenty-page photo section designed by Gillhausen. "Leni Riefenstahl has photographed something no white person has ever seen—THE FESTIVAL OF KNIVES AND LOVE. The Nuba live to fight, to love—and to paint and decorate their bodies."[26] The reader is dazzled by the color contrast in these images: the dull brown of the earth, the gleaming black of the bodies, the brilliant blue of the sky, and the bright red of blood. Her second illustrated volume, *People of Kau*, surpassed all expectations. It sold to great acclaim around the globe. For the first time ever, she attended the Frankfurt Book Fair and introduced her book there. Riefenstahl had come through with the pictures people had expected of her. The photographs of strong men engaged in bloody battles with knives and love dances of long-legged girls seem a fitting follow-up to the draft of the screenplay she had written for her *Penthesilea* project. The passionate fights, ecstatic dance, and sexual love born of battle she had sought in the Libyan Desert were found in the Sudanese savanna.

The pictures Riefenstahl brought from Africa were criticized for their exhibitionism, their distorted image of the Nuba, and the dubious methods she had used to attain them.[27] Still and all, they mesmerized readers. Riefenstahl used her new platforms of radio, television, and print media to talk up her version of the unpolitical artist. Many Germans who had lived through the National Socialist era were gratified by Riefenstahl's comeback. If Hitler's favorite movie director could now be mentioned in the same breath as Francis Ford Coppola and Mick Jagger, the Third Reich must not have been all bad. For young Germans who knew National Socialism only from history class, Riefenstahl was an alluring figure. She had passed the age of seventy, yet she was an energetic, good-looking woman. With her dyed blonde hair, light makeup, high spirits, and colorful clothing, she came across as a cosmopolitan woman. She was rarely photographed without a camera in hand, and she was childless. Riefenstahl seemed to be the embodiment of the modern woman who confidently defined herself by her profession and her gender. Her defenders argued that if she had been a staunch National Socialist, she would surely not have spent months living with a primitive black tribe. This image of a modern, unconventional, professional woman appealed to American feminists. Her movies were shown at feminist film festivals, and she was hailed as a maverick whose achievements had brought her triumph in a patriarchal world.[28] Riefenstahl, as one of the first female directors of the twentieth century, and probably the most successful one, was far too good a catch for feminists to pass up on merely political grounds.

Susan Sontag was the only critic to throw cold water on this blaze of enthusiasm. In her essay on "Fascinating Fascism," published in February 1975, she did not deny Riefenstahl's artistic achievements but simply stated that the Nuba photographs were a direct outgrowth of the aesthetic of her films from the Nazi era: "Although the Nuba are black, not Aryan, Riefenstahl's portrait of them evokes some of the larger themes of Nazi ideology: the contrast between the clean and the impure, the incorruptible and the defiled, the physical and the mental, the joyful and the critical."[29] No one had expected this kind of attack, least of all Riefenstahl herself. The damage was done. No one who has read Sontag's text can look at Riefenstahl's Nuba photographs without thinking of *Triumph of the Will*.

CAMP

t had all been quite simple. Marlene Dietrich felt that her new career seemed to be taking off by itself, as she wrote in a positively giddy letter to her daughter in August 1953. She had been in Las Vegas, and "Tulla" (Tallulah Bankhead), who was performing at the trendy Sands Hotel, brought her onstage. Dietrich told her daughter, "I went out to see if I could get them to whistle."[1] She took the plunge without any rehearsals, or even nervousness, and performed as a nightclub singer. It worked; she still had it in her. So she signed a contract offered by the neighboring Sahara Hotel, which was not quite as chic as the Sands, but it was bigger. Besides, she would be earning ninety thousand dollars for three weeks— ten thousand more than what Bankhead was getting at the Sands. She proudly reported that no one had ever earned this much for performing in Vegas.[2]

Dietrich was well aware that her presentation would require careful planning. In movies she had not had direct contact with her audiences, but now she would. There would be no close-ups or retakes. Everything would take place in real time. Every inch of her had to be dazzling. Jean Louis, a costume designer at Columbia Pictures whose big coup had been the black satin dress that Rita Hayworth wore in *Gilda*, designed Dietrich's outfit. For her stage debut, he made a "see-through" style of dress, which draped her body in beaded lengths of diaphonous fabric that had been dyed the color of her skin and molded to a specially designed close-fitting foundation. Ten seamstresses spent three months of intense and tedious labor sewing each individual bead into place on the delicate fabric. The dress was tailor-made right on her body. She stood in the studio for up to ten hours a day while the seamstresses worked away at her six-thousand-dollar dress. Being the perfectionist that she was, she noticed any pearl that was not in its precise place.

It was worth all the effort that had gone into making this dress. The audience gasped when Dietrich proudly and confidently took the stage. After the first show, she invited the press into her dressing room for a glass of champagne. Media professional that she was, she let it be known that she was naked under the dress. When asked why she was wearing a dress like that, she replied: "This is Las Vegas. If you can't wear it here, you can't wear it anywhere."[3] She would not go onstage like this unless she was offered a similar fee, and she let it be known that she would not be staying long-term. The many yellowed newspaper clippings that describe her first performance focus on two things: her fee and her dress. Any mention of her singing was disparaging. Her performance was not regarded as an artistic success, let alone as the beginning of a new career. For Dietrich herself, the key issue was to be free of financial worries for a while and not to have to shoot one of those sappy movies. But not all was well with her in Las Vegas. Shortly before Christmas, she called up her friend Leo Lerman in New York and complained that a ninety-thousand-dollar job was also damned lonely. The soldier's daughter had gone off to battle alone. This was not so easy, especially because she was always being asked how old she was. Nearly every article called her "glamorous Granny" or "the movies' senior glamour queen." On her birthday, she was badgered by journalists to reveal her true age. Of course she kept to herself that she was already fifty-two and claimed that she had just turned forty-eight, even though for a woman over thirty, four years made no difference; either way, she was too old. Whenever she was asked what her next movie role would be—as she often was—she came up with some excuse. Charlie Feldman had the unpleasant duty of informing her that roles she had been promised had been cut out of the films or that the only roles on the table were for someone to play older women, which she categorically refused to do.

In this situation, Major Donald Neville-Willing, the manager of the London nightclub Café de Paris, offered Dietrich a set of performances. Her friend Noël Coward sent her a telegram urging her to accept the offer: DARLING CERTAINLY THINK YOU SHOULD APPEAR CAFE-DEPARIS STOP ROOM AND AMBIENCE PERFECT FOR YOU STOP YOU SHOULD GET ONE THOUSAND POUNDS A WEEK STOP MONTH OF JULY VERY GOOD AUGUST TOO LATE IN SEASON ALL LOVE NOEL.[4] In late March, she agreed to six performances a week for four weeks beginning on June 21, entertaining her audience for forty-five minutes after midnight. For the duration of her stay in London, she would be put up in a suite at The Dorchester. The airfare for Dietrich and her personal assistant would be covered. She insisted on booking seats in the last row, with a seat left empty beside her.

Every table at the Café de Paris was sold out for all four weeks. Each evening she was introduced by a different prominent guest. Coward was first, followed by Laurence Olivier, Robert Fleming, Richard Attenborough, and Alec Guiness. There was such a stampede in front of the café that the police had to contain the crowds. Inside, the illustrious guests enjoying pâté de foie gras and champagne while awaiting her performance included Deborah Kerr, David Niven, Douglas Fairbanks, Lord and Lady Norwich, and Jack Buchanan. Dietrich had not revealed what she would be wearing. To the audience's great delight, she came onstage in the famous translucent gown. As one critic wrote, you thought you were seeing everything underneath until you realized that you were actually seeing nothing. She knew her routine inside out. She sang a dozen of her most famous songs, including "The Boys in the Back Room," "Falling in Love Again," and "The Laziest Gal in Town." Dietrich sang in both English and German, knowing full well that she was the only one who could get away with introducing German songs. In contrast to her audiences in Las Vegas, these people had experienced the war firsthand. The German language was not music to the ears of the people in this city, which had been attacked by the German Luftwaffe, but Dietrich welcomed the challenge of showing that being a German and being a Nazi were not one and the same thing. She therefore made a point of including "Lili Marleen," the favorite song of the World War II soldiers, which earned her this caustic comment: "Rommel could have had no complaint about the enthusiasm with which she sang it."[5] Her interludes were short and pithy, and she retained a polite distance from her audiences. She did not do encores, no matter how thunderous the applause, even though she was said to have enjoyed playing recordings of the applause she received to friends and visitors—*only* the applause.

There was only one person in London she wanted to see: Kenneth Tynan. The young theater critic was the star of the London arts scene. Tynan was witty, knowledgeable, eloquent, highly gifted, melancholy, and flamboyant. He always stood out in a crowd, yet he was smartly dressed. After the performance, he generally went backstage, and she reached her hand out of the dressing room and pulled him in while snubbing her other fans. He watched her bathe and get her clothes on, then he took her out to dinner. It was from Tynan that the British learned that Dietrich listened to Beethoven's late string quartets and the early Stravinsky in her suite in the Dorchester until the early morning hours. Tynan and Dietrich related to each other as equals. She enjoyed his cultivated eccentricity, loved his witty malicious gossip, and admired his intellectual aggressiveness. He was fascinated by her androgynous nature and famously remarked: "She has sex but no particular gender."[6] His parties and high spirits were legendary, and his essays uni-

versally admired. Tynan numbered Tennessee Williams, Samuel
Beckett, and Lillian Hellman among his friends—and, now, Marlene Dietrich. In his eyes, she was the personification of the kind
of glamour that was anchored in the past.[7] Tynan, who was an
exhibitionist by design, knew the kind of energy it took to unfurl
this glamour evening after evening. Dietrich was twenty-five years
his senior; her history was intertwined with the heyday of Hollywood and went back to the fabled Berlin of Isherwood, Auden, and
Spender. With Tynan, she could relax into her actual age. He was
interested in her life experience, her professionalism, and her dalli-
ances. Tynan and Dietrich got along famously, and in the summer
of 1954, they became friends for life.

While one set of performances was still running, she had to be
thinking about the next one. Starting in mid-October, she would
be back in Las Vegas. In the intervening time, she had to play the
successful, urbane artist, and that role required a suitable wardrobe. She often flew to Paris for the weekend and spent her days
there with fittings at Balmain or Dior, meetings with Françoise
Sagan, and cooking for her friend Jean Marais. She would spend
rainy hours at Fouquet's, her thoughts on Jean Gabin. Rumor had
it that she would watch his new movies on the sly and bemoan
the love she had lost. Gabin had banished her from his life. All
the same, she remained loyal to France. On August 21 at six in the
evening, Dietrich strode down the Champs-Élysées side by side
with former front-line soldiers and members of the resistance to
commemorate the tenth anniversary of the liberation. She had on
a dark blue, high-necked raincoat, her honorary war medals, her
American Legion forage cap, and white gloves; the expression on
her face was proud and serious. This was the role of her life: standing up for a good cause in a uniform and flats. She would think
about Remarque, who always called the Arc de Triomphe a locus
of their love. Four years earlier, she had sent him a telegram on his
birthday and told him she wished he were with her in New York,

"this forsaken town." He wrote to her every once in a while, telling her about his drawers filled with pictures of Marlene and how nice it was to hear from her, the "floor-scrubbing Nike," in the middle of the night across the continents. She could not hide her jealousy of Boni's new girlfriend, the lovely Paulette Goddard, who was close to ten years younger than she. In contrast to Dietrich, Goddard had no financial problems. At the side of the wealthy Remarque, she could afford to live a life of luxury without needing to work. Dietrich conveniently forgot that she had been offered that place first. She missed the company of Hemingway, with whom she could indulge in malicious gossip about Remarque. Hemingway was living in Cuba with his wife Mary, whom he called "Papa's pocket Venus," and Dietrich and her friends adopted the epithet. At night he listened to Dietrich's recordings at his hacienda, and during the day he went fishing and swimming while longing for the camaraderie of the war. Hemingway understood and shared Dietrich's tormenting loneliness. He wrote to her in 1955: "You sound in worse shape than me. We'll have to pull ourselves to pieces and throw in the counter-attack. Any good kraut can mount a counter-attack from memory."[8] Although he was quite successful—his new book was selling "like the Bible or *Mein Kampf* in Germany"—and had been awarded the Nobel Prize in Literature the previous year, he could not find his footing in the postwar world.[9] Time and again, he invited Dietrich, "my great and bravest and wonderful Kraut," to Cuba, but just as she had never gone to Porto Ronco, she would never take Hemingway up on his invitation to visit his country home in Cuba.

Her second set of performances in Las Vegas began on October 15. The attraction was once again not her singing, but her dress. This time Dietrich showed her famous legs in a gown that fit tightly to the hip and was made of an almost transparent fabric. As an added effect, a wind machine set the wispy material in motion.

In 1955, her show was divided into a female and a male portion. She was able to shed her dress and slip into a classic tailcoat in under a minute.[10] To this day there is no other actress or female singer who can wear a tailcoat the way Dietrich could. Next to her, everyone else looks like an imitation.

She was still agonizing over Yul Brynner. Waiting for the phone to ring, hoping for signs of love, exhilarating nights of passion, and raging jealousy continued to define her daily life. She lay awake night after night, agonizing and entertaining thoughts of suicide as she pictured him in the arms of another woman. She wrote to him: "If you want to change your mind about us and end the love you called 'infinite' you must know that I will end my life. It cannot be that you want to do this without reason, to me who loves you so much since so long."[11] Nothing made sense without him. But where could she actually carry out her suicide—in Billy Wilder's summer house? She could not come up with a suitable spot, so she dropped the idea. No matter how angry or desperate she felt, she was defenseless when he turned up at her door. She described her jumble of emotions in a letter to Noël Coward:

> He came in smiling, bottle under his coat. He came into the bedroom and told me about Paris, the fog around the Eiffel Tower, the streets, the bridges and how he thought about me. I stood there thinking this is not a dream. He is really back and loves me. Then the hurricane broke over me for three hours and I fell asleep for the first time in two months to the day without torture and sleeping pills.[12]

When she was with Brynner, she made solemn promises that she would change and stop asking questions of him, yet the very next moment she would pester him about when they could get together again. It would appear that over the course of their years of enervating conflicts, he lost his respect for her. When he came to see her at night, he was usually drunk, and would wake up the next morning without remembering anything he had said. He was confident that she would stay with him, and she humiliated herself in the process. Her friends had to listen to her unburden herself for hours on end. The affair with Brynner dragged on until the end of the 1950s. She found moments of solace in affairs with other men, but they did not free her from the gnawing fear of being alone.

In 1956, Rudi Sieber suffered his first heart attack. He was still living on his chicken farm, Sunset Ranch. His diary entries had been frighteningly repetitive for years. On any given day, he was sure to provide updates on the number of eggs the hens had laid, his expenditures, the weather, his telephone calls, and any birthdays. He used a sharp pencil to record the minutest details of when he bathed or washed his hair, how often he took down the curtains, and on which day "Russian Easter" was celebrated. Sieber was leading a life that continually looked back to the past and kept old memories alive: "Kaiser Franz Josef's birthday!" was a typical comment. Apparently his rundown ranch in this California valley had become the perfect nostalgic setting for the homeland he had lost forever. His visitors were friends from Vienna (Josef von Sternberg, Friedrich Torberg) and from the Berlin of the 1920s (Grete Mosheim, Fritzi Massary, Max Kolpé). He would bring back the old times with them over Moselle wine, Salzburg dumplings, or Wiener schnitzel. He was well liked, entertained frequently, and enjoyed hosting parties. Dietrich sent him packages of bockwurst, salami, Berliner Weisse beer, cognac, and shirts. He needed her checks and was positively obsequious in his gratitude, although he did not write to her as often as she would have liked.

Tamara Matul stayed with him. Although this relationship made her ill and unhappy, she was unable to end it. She lived a rootless life in the shadow of Sieber, who in turn was dependent on Dietrich. Matul had hoped to start a family with Sieber and move on from her role as lover, but there was no escaping the family she had been drawn into. Dietrich called the shots, and she wanted Sieber to remain her husband. Dietrich made sure that each of Matul's pregnancies was aborted. A child born to Matul and Sieber would have posed a threat to their complicated arrangement, and was therefore out of the question as far as she was concerned. Each time Matul underwent an abortion—and there were several—a part of her died. Sieber's diaries contain lists of his consumption of alcohol and hers of pills. She could not get through the day without psychotropic drugs. She grew bloated from all those pills, and her eyes were red from all her crying. Rumors were swirling that she was mentally ill, but Dietrich and Sieber chose not to comment on them in public. After a visit to the ranch, Dietrich wrote to her daughter: "Tami is nuttier than ever and I was crying into my beard driving home from the ranch because it still affects me to see the crazy be stronger than the sane." Since Matul was unable to cook, the three of them had gone to their usual diner, "a lousy little joint with a loud jukebox. The food was so greasy that I ate some old cottage cheese instead and did not touch it." To her horror, Sieber ate up everything. On the way back, she offered to pre-cook a pot au feu in her apartment in Beverly Hills and bring it to the ranch. "When I arrived Tami yelled she could not keep it all, she would still have to wash the dishes even if she would only heat it, and I calmly packed everything together, washed the dishes after dinner and left too sad to say goodbye."[13]

Dietrich had to go out into the world and earn money. Finally she was offered a part in a new movie with Vittorio De Sica. *The Monte Carlo Story* was filmed in Rome and Monte Carlo. It was about a destitute count, naïve Americans, jewelry, pawnbrokers, and gambling. Dietrich played the Marquise de Crevecoeur, whose addiction to gambling turned her into a con artist. She looked ill. She was quite thin and had a glazed expression on her face. Her waist was down to twenty-one inches.[14] Clothing and jewelry seemed to be holding together both the role and the actress. She did not go out a single time during the filming, neither in Rome nor in Monte Carlo. The worst part was her insomnia. Although she generally got by on very little sleep and was famous for staying out until daybreak, the sleep she was now getting was too little even for her. Sleeping pills had no effect.

Since leaving Germany nearly thirty years earlier, she had been living out of a suitcase. She always carried lists of which items of clothing were in which location. In her case, location referred not only to a geographical place (Los Angeles, New York, or Paris), but also to which suitcase contained it. For her performances, she could not forget a single thing, and she had to have everything she needed to go onstage—shoes, dresses, wigs, makeup—with her, in duplicate if at all possible. Her daughter Maria, who was familiar with all the logistics, served as Dietrich's support system and personal help as she had for the past thirty years, even though Maria now had a family and had become a sought-after actress in various television series. In May 1957 she gave birth to her third son, Paul, in New York. Dietrich—or Massy, as she was called in the family—was at her side.

In the spring, Dietrich performed in Las Vegas and acted in a movie directed by, and starring, her friend Orson Welles. They knew each other since the 1940s, when they performed together for a group of draftees. She had been crazy for him back then, but he was married to Rita Hayworth and not interested in an affair. Both Welles and Dietrich were horrified by Hollywood, yet they had to keep on working there.[15] Welles had asked her to be in his new movie in no uncertain terms: REFUSE ATTEMPT TO IMAGINE PICTURE WITHOUT YOU. . . . ALL MY LOVE ORSON.[16] Her role was actually not in the original script; the idea was for her to show up during the filming and shoot her part within one day or night. There was no salary, and she would have to provide her own outfit. The blonde Dietrich had to be transformed into a dark-haired, fiery-eyed Gypsy woman, the type of woman that Welles preferred. When she arrived that evening, wearing a dark wig, at the appointed meeting place—a dilapidated bungalow in Venice—Welles embraced her and rejoiced. Dietrich played a cigar-smoking madam in a brothel with whom the drunken police captain, played by Welles, seeks refuge. The police captain is a "bad lieutenant": he is corrupt, fabricates evidence, and becomes a murderer. *Touch of Evil* is set in a Mexican border town, yet a lack of funds made it necessary to shoot it in Venice at night. But that is not evident to the viewer, who feels transported to this small town right from the start. Dietrich was the only easygoing character in the movie. She played Tana as a woman of the world who is nobody's fool. Besides, she is the only one who manages to like the fat, evil police captain. In this film, Dietrich proved what she was capable of when she worked with a good director. She proudly remarked: "I worked with him for only one long evening. But to hell with my modesty; I don't think I've ever performed as well as on that day."[17]

It took years for the outstanding quality of *Touch of Evil* to be recognized, but a great deal of attention was showered on her next movie, *Witness for the Prosecution*. Dietrich had seen the stage version of the Agatha Christie play on Broadway and agreed to play the female lead in a movie version if Billy Wilder directed it. She chose Edith Head, whom she knew from the days when Head had been Travis Banton's assistant, as the costume designer. Head knew whom she was dealing with: "Dietrich was not difficult; she was a perfectionist. She had incredible discipline and energy. She could work all day to the point of exhaustion, then catch a second breath and work all night just to get something right."[18] Head's costumes brought out the icy beauty of Christine Vole. The witness for the prosecution wears simple, figure-hugging suits, white blouses, and small hats. Vole is a German woman, and her outfits are her uniforms. The cast also featured Charles Laughton, Tyrone Power, and Elsa Lanchester. Dietrich got the impression that Wilder had not thought her capable of taking on this role. When he called to tell her that her acting had been superb, she remarked that this praise was meaningless to her because *Yul* had not said anything.

In November, *Witness for the Prosecution* was celebrated with a big party in New York. The guest list included Truman Capote, Rex Harrison, Irene Selznick, and Douglas Fairbanks, Jr. The box-office returns were quite impressive, and the movie was nominated for six Oscars, including Wilder for Best Director (for the sixth time), and Charles Laughton for Best Actor—his third nomination. Dietrich deserved a nomination, but just as in the case of *A Foreign Affair*, she was passed over.[19]

Although she did many radio broadcasts, there was no real money to be made in this medium, because radio had lost a good deal of its attractiveness with the advent of television.[20] Dietrich disdained television. She was proud of her daughter Maria, who often appeared on television, but she herself wanted nothing to do with it, apart from watching *Peter Pan* with her grandchildren in the afternoon. She decided to direct all her efforts at the stage. At long last, she would not have to hide behind imaginary characters but could decide on her own what she would bring to the audience— namely, her life. For her, the outside world—including her friends, foes, and benefactors—existed solely with respect to herself. Her countless love affairs intensified this singleminded concentration on herself. She had spent her whole life playing unhappy women who had suffered for love, and there was no reason not to remain true to this role. She was almost sixty years old when she decided to stand onstage in the spotlight and sing about love, desire, and sorrow. On the stage she was conceived of as ageless. Her show was a wistful reminiscence of a woman who seemed blessed with eternal youth. Dietrich remained tied to the cinema, but now she was directing the film of her life.

Three miracle workers stood by her side in this undertaking. The first was the aforementioned Jean Louis, head costume designer at Columbia Pictures, who kept coming up with bold new creations for her, such as the now-legendary swan coat in 1955 and the "tassel dress" three years later. The second was Joe Davis, who, according to Dietrich, "had the gift of turning even the barest and filthiest stage into a fairy tale world."[21] She bowed to his expertise even though she considered herself an inspired lighting artist. Davis was a steadfast worker who was always out to achieve the optimal solution and would not brook compromises. Dietrich liked this division of labor. On the stage, she was unsparingly exposed to the eyes of the audience. She had to hide her age while putting herself on display. In Davis's light, she felt protected and at the same time shown off to good advantage. The third miracle worker was Burt Bacharach, the man who put the soul in her songs. One fine day, Bacharach showed up at the door of her hotel room.[22] She asked him to come in, looked him over, and was instantly smitten: "He was young, very young and very good-looking and I had never seen such blue eyes."[23] This young god intuited what she wanted. Bacharach became Josef von Sternberg's successor. She described meeting him as the most profound change in her professional life. Dietrich had blind faith in him, and his praise and criticism became her standard from this point forth. But in contrast to her partnership with Jo, these two were not close to the same age; Bacharach was twenty-six years her junior. Although he was not a big name yet, everyone considered him a man with great promise. When he wrote how, shortly after they met, Dietrich went to his apartment without his knowledge and waited until he came back from playing tennis so she could serve him her famous consommé, it becomes evident that she thought of this as the prelude to an affair. While he washed off his sweat in the shower, she washed his tennis outfit. He does not reveal whether he responded to her advances. Her love for him was an open secret. "As a man, he embodies everything that a woman could want. He was considerate and tender, brave and valiant, strong and sincere, but above all he was admirable, enormously sensitive, and loving. And he was vulnerable."[24] He, in turn, valued her as an artist, respected her as a person, and at times perhaps loved her as a woman. "You are the sweetest of all possible angels. What a wonderful surprise."[25] His arrangements were adapted to the pitch of her voice; he took her preferences into consideration, concealing her weaknesses and bringing out her strengths. She now had an experienced and brilliant songwriter at her side. Bacharach drew his inspiration from many styles of music, including bebop, Maurice Ravel, avant-garde movements, and gospel. His elegant music gave Dietrich a connection to the buoyant modernity of the early 1960s. Bacharach dusted off her songs. Dietrich, who had never been able to take pleasure in the American promise of happiness, suddenly sounded much lighter. With this program, thoroughly tailored to her artistic style, she was poised to take the world by storm. In the preceding years she had usually performed in Las Vegas, and once in London, but she now expanded her radius. Bacharach traveled around the world with her. "When you went into a country with her, you went in as a conquering army."[26]

From July to August 1959, she went on tour through South America, giving rousing concerts in Rio de Janeiro, Santiago de Chile, São Paulo, Buenos Aires, and Montevideo. SNOWED UNDER ORCHIDS GOOD SHOW GREAT REVIEWS STOP FOUND HEAVENLY ARISTOCRATIC CREATURE LIKE COLETTE PLAY.[27] In São Paulo, she met a young man whose youth and naivete she found intriguing. The letter to Maria in which she describes this platonic affair, declaring that she will not try to seduce him despite being sorely tempted, is a letter of farewell to love.[28]

By now, Dietrich had to admit to herself that her affair with Yul Brynner was hopeless.

As far as love is concerned, I am still suffering from an old wound from the time before it even *was* one. It wouldn't be so hard if he would let me go, but he isn't doing that. From time to time, he shows up again and then I don't have the nerve to end it. I haven't seen anything new for years. All this is not good, I know. The children get all the love that remains, so all is not lost. *I* am lost, and that is a shame. Waste, waste, waste.[29]

Her grandchildren were a source of comfort to her. Her home was where the Rivas were, she wrote in one of her dejected letters to Maria. "Kiss Michael's knee, Peter's black eyes, Pauly's mouth and your heart and all that is in it."[30] The boys were aware that they had a very special grandmother, but she was quite easygoing with them. She took them to the movies, baked delicious jelly dough-nuts for Christmas, and made them scrambled eggs that turned their stomachs.

In November, she performed in Paris at the Théatre de L'Étoile near the Arc de Triomphe. Maria sent her a telegram to let her know she was thinking of her: GO GIRL AS THEY SAY IN THE OLD COUN-TRY MACHS GUT.[31] Dietrich wrapped the pampered Paris audience around her little finger. Her cosmopolitan spirit, charm, style, and beauty were a far cry from the popular perception Parisians had about dumpy German women. She celebrated her triumph at Maxim's nightclub, with a smiling Burt Bacharach to her left and a doleful Yves Saint Laurent to her right. During this fall season, she was seen at the side of Jean Cocteau, Noël Coward, Maurice Chevalier, and Alberto Giacometti, and sitting at dinner tables with Yves Montand, Sophia Loren, Alain Delon, and Romy Schneider. Rumor had it that Gabin was planning to show up with his wife. The photographers and Dietrich waited every evening, but Gabin did not come.

In March 1960, Dietrich's American promoter, Norman Granz, told the press that Dietrich's tour of Europe would start in Ger-many. Her first concert was planned for April 30 at the Titania

Palace Theater in Berlin. This announcement created quite a stir. Why was this artist, whose antipathy to Germany was well known, giving concerts in Germany? The short answer was: for the money. "Will Marlene Dietrich—as people have been saying—be getting 15,000 to 20,000 marks per performance during her tour? No— she will not be pulling in 15,000 or 20,000 marks every evening. As Norman Granz tells us: 'Marlene is getting much more!' The ticket prices will reflect this."[32] Dietrich's high fee, which commanded respect from Americans, was scorned by some members of the German press. There was an explosion of envy about an artist who had proved that one could preserve one's dignity as a German when confronted with Hitler as a Führer. A parochial mob ran riot in letters to the editor with the usual clichés about her being a traitor to her country, and there were demands that she stay away from Germany. But some journalists were mortified by these carryings-on, and understood that Dietrich's visit fifteen years after the end of the war represented a test of character for the Germans. The chief reporter at *Die Welt* traveled to New York for an interview. In Dietrich's Park Avenue apartment, he met "a lady full of reserve and culture."[33] She talked with him while smoking one cigarette after another, and made it clear that she was coming to Germany to sing, not to face the Nuremberg trials. She hated Hitler, but not her own people. She had no need for explanations; she had gone to Bergen-Belsen with the American troops when thousands of murder victims were still lying there. Asked how she felt about being a German, she replied, "If you're a Jew, it's easier to forgive, the way that you can more easily forgive something that is inflicted on you by others. But I feel the shared responsibility; I was part of the nation that caused all of it." Even so, Dietrich wanted her visit to Germany to be viewed as a statement that it was time "to stop making accusations and to bury the shadows of the grim past."[34]

There was no direct flight from Paris to Berlin. On April 30, after a stopover in Frankfurt, Dietrich flew on Air France and landed in Berlin's Tegel airport at 10:30 p.m. Hildegard Knef picked her up. The two of them are laughing in almost every photograph, but Dietrich's laughter looks forced. She had on a beige spring outfit under a three-quarter-length mink coat, and she wore a big hat. Her rooms were reserved at the Hilton, where her eagerly anticipated press conference would also take place the following day. The crowd was enormous. For over an hour, there was such a racket that people could not hear their own words. Dietrich was in black: a simple dress with a sophisticated cut. High-heeled shoes showed off her lovely legs, and her face was partly concealed behind the wide brim of her hat. The small French Legion of Honor ribbon was her only adornment. She endured the popping of flashbulbs in grim-faced silence. She wore white gloves and smoked one unfiltered cigarette after another, seemingly indifferent to her surroundings. *Der Tagesspiegel* published this lyrical description, "Eyes with a good deal of past, cool polished eroticism, a white pain in her composed face that does not allow for the expression of feelings and remains inscrutable. She has lovely, large, and patient movements. Something monkish about her; so severe. Lasciviousness, devil from head to toe? No."[35] Dietrich answered questions in a soft voice. No, she had not been to the Tiergarten section of town, and no, she had not visited her former apartment building on Bundesallee either. She had recognized the zoo, where she had played marbles as a child, from her hotel room. She did not have mixed feelings. You don't go to a city to be sad just because you had been a child there. She did not lapse into Berlin dialect, nor did she wax nostalgic. Instead, she displayed wit and intelligence. When she discovered that reporters were secretly holding microphones, she threatened to call off the press conference. She had explicitly asked that no microphones be used, because she had an exclusive contract with NBC. She had come to Berlin in order to work and to earn more money; that was all there was to it. The room-service receipts indicate that she ate in her room—veal steaks, green salad, and tea with lemon. She did not eat at the bar. Why go out? Where would she go, and with whom? The Silhouette was closed down, and Schwannecke and Mutzbacher had not been there for quite some time either.

On Tuesday, May 3, at 8 p.m., she gave her first concert. Sixty police officers were on hand in order to contain possible rioters, but this precaution proved unnecessary. Even though it has become customary to describe her reception in Berlin as hostile, there were no organized protests. The people who had declared their antipathy in anonymous letters or in letters to the editor were nowhere in evidence. There were only "two timid individuals waving cardboard signs saying 'Marlene go home' and 'Marlene get lost,' who were first quite proud of their efforts, but later felt rather stupid."[36] The attendees included the governing mayor of Berlin, Willy Brandt, with his wife, Rut; film producer Atze Brauner; Hildegard Knef in a skintight black sheath dress with her companion, David Cameron; and director Harry Meyen with his colleague Wilhelm Dieterle. Everyone who was anyone in Berlin showed up. There were many elderly married couples who were dressed festively but modestly. Dietrich made her audience wait while a French jazz group played a set. Finally she came onstage. Dietrich was visibly moved by the big applause. The concert began with "Allein in einer grossen Stadt" and ended with "Wer wird denn weinen." Her notes show that the banter she had jotted down to fill the time in between songs was in English. Dietrich's well-crafted lecture to the people of Berlin, which was insistent but never condescending, emphasized what they had lost by having Hitler as their Führer. Friedrich Luft compared her art of showmanship to Piaf and Montand. "She didn't have the tear in her eye that people were hoping to see. She did not bow to an inflamed public opinion, but instead remained consistently and courageously the person she was, and held firm to her stance."[37] After the concert, former emigrant Brandt rose from his seat and prompted the audience to give her a standing ovation.

In Bad Kissingen, the concert hall was only half filled. Afterward Dietrich had to leave through the back entrance; out front, a waiting throng of teenagers was cursing and booing her. This jeering crowd was not a group of former Nazis; these were young people who had come of age in the 1960s. A similar situation had occurred in Düsseldorf when a seventeen-year-old girl spit in her face and yelled "traitor" at her as she was leaving her hotel. Bacharach, who was standing next to her, was still horrified by this incident decades after the fact. He thought it was acid. Dietrich bore up, and her proud and lovely face was unscathed. She wrote in her memoirs that when she was spat upon and then had to go onstage, Bacharach's support and her own German obstinacy are what got her through. But the succeeding events make it plain that she was quite thrown. In Wiesbaden she fell off the stage. It was the first fall of her singing career—and another fall of this kind would bring her career to an end fifteen years later. But more bad news was to follow. Josef von Sternberg, her discoverer, was witness to her fall. He was sitting in the audience with his son, and they had planned to have dinner with her afterward. She had no intention of calling off the dinner, and she spent the evening with Jo. It was only when she returned to her room that she realized that something was terribly wrong. Maria urged her to have X-rays done at the American hospital, and it turned out that her collarbone was broken. Dietrich did not cancel any of her concerts. For the press conference in Munich, she lashed her broken shoulder to her raw silk dress with a Dior chiffon scarf. The roses on the scarf were the same shade of red as the tiny ribbon from the French Legion of Honor she had fastened to her dress. Her tour in Germany was a financial disaster, and she looked forward to leaving the country once again.

Two weeks later, she flew from Paris to Israel. When she arrived in Tel Aviv, one of the reporters advised her that she would not be allowed to sing in German. It was forbidden to speak German on the stage and in movies. Dietrich replied quite calmly: "No, I won't sing one song in German; I'll sing nine." Bacharach, who related this story, claimed that the man was shocked by her response. Her concert in Tel Aviv began with two English-language songs: "My Blue Heaven" and "Cream in My Coffee." Then she sang her first German song: "Mein blondes Baby" ("My Blonde Baby"), a mother's lullaby. According to Bacharach, this moment in the concert hall in Tel Aviv was one of the most emotional experiences of his life, "because it was sort of like the dam had broken, and people were crying. Nobody was upset in a negative way. It was like a catharsis that freed them."[38] Next came the Richard Tauber song "Frag nicht warum" ("Don't Ask Why"). She sang all nine German songs in a row, including "Lili Marleen," in response to a request from her audience. The Israeli author Ephraim Kishon thought the audience had lost its mind: "A stanza of Mahler, who was a Jew—they'd rather die. A Nazi song by a German singer—by popular request."[39] Dietrich donated the proceeds of her first concert to a rehabilition center for the Israeli army. She had agreed to this tour in Israel on the condition that she be able to meet Moshe Dayan and perform for the armed forces. Dietrich's estate contains handwritten letters she received from German Jews whose lives had been saved by heading to what was now Israel. They thanked her for having come and for her commitment to fighting Hitler, wrote about the suffering they had endured, and celebrated her as a great artist of the twentieth century. Dietrich had been invited to Yad Vashem, but she did not visit the Holocaust research center until her second tour through Israel in February 1966, when she was honored as one of the "righteous."

Dietrich had become a businesswoman. She spent her days writing letters, making telephone calls, sending telegrams to all parts of the globe, giving instructions, and rehearsing. Photographs had to be taken and sent out, lists drawn up and gone through, recordings arranged, and studios found. There was a constant hustle and bustle on matters concerning notes, dollars, and percentages. Even though she had her agency, a great many matters still fell to her in ensuring successful performances. She had to make arrangements for the musicians, hotel rooms, clothing, new songs, and finances. Although she was always working, she did not end up with much income. Her chaotic life, her thriving business, her financial worries, and, increasingly, her physical ailments also meant that she had no time left to focus on men.

Her sister Elisabeth was the only remaining member of her close family. There have been many speculations as to why she rarely mentioned Elisabeth. Was it because Elisabeth's husband had been a member of the Nazi party, or was it a simple question of vanity, a means of disguising her age? The letters that the sisters exchanged until Elisabeth's death in 1973 show that Dietrich wanted only to protect her. It was clear to her that Elisabeth would not be able to endure being hounded by the press. These two very different sisters had retained their childhood intimacy. Elisabeth called Marlene "pussycat," and Marlene called her "my sweetie." Elisabeth ungrudgingly acknowledged that her younger sister was the cleverer and more beautiful of the two. She described her physical appearance in self-deprecating terms: "I am fat, not dainty, and know that I look hideous."[40] When she made awkward attempts to show interest in her sister's life by talking about Paris or New York, she seemed to have no idea what she was saying. For her, Marlene lived only in the memories of the childhood and teenage years they had spent together in Berlin and as a film star on the screen, in photographs, and in magazines. She commented on the films and enjoyed the many pictures Dietrich gave her. She felt close to Boni, Étoile, and all the other famous lovers without ever having met them. Elisabeth was Marlene's tie to her childhood and adolescence. When she wrote her memoirs, she asked her sister what color the army postal service envelopes were or what area their father's side of the family was from. Elisabeth received a monthly check from her as well as the royalties from Deutsche Grammophon. Without this help, she would not have known how to get by. In addition, she got regular packages with dresses, stockings, instant mashed potatoes, records, and English-language newspapers. A whiff of the big wide world spread through Elisabeth's little apartment in Celle whenever a package arrived from Fauchon in Paris. Elisabeth felt that her sister Marlene brought "sparkle and shine" into her otherwise bleak life. She found it somewhat disconcerting to put on Marlene's luxurious coats, but she enjoyed being the sister of a woman who frequented Parisian fashion boutiques. To return the favor, she copied out page after page of poems by George, Hölderlin, Platen, Goethe, Heine, and Shakespeare for her sister; tracked down song lyrics for her; got her books by Joseph Roth; and at the pharmacy, large quantities of a drug called Geriatrea, which Rudi needed to take as well. Dietrich's shy, humbled sister may have been ingenuous and poor, but she had attained a reasonable level of education and decorum. Journalists kept ambushing her, hoping to take pictures of her in her apartment or get an exclusive story about how the sister of the antifascist Dietrich had been the wife of an SS man. Elisabeth assured her sister in 1965: "My dear pussycat, all I can say is that neither my husband nor my son worked in a concentration camp. . . . We spent five years showing movies to the Jews."[41]

Although she did not want to stir up her own family secrets, Dietrich was willing to play the cinematic role of a German who was convinced of the innocence of her people, a conviction she had never held in real life. In late January 1961, the shooting for Stanley Kramer's film *Judgment at Nuremberg* began in Los Angeles. This would be the last movie with a leading role envisaged for Dietrich. Her fellow cast members were Spencer Tracy, Burt Lancaster, Richard Widmark, Judy Garland, Montgomery Clift, and Maximilian Schell. Never did she play a more Prussian character than in *Judgment at Nuremberg.* In this movie, she is the standoffish widow of a Wehrmacht general who has been executed by the Americans because of his war crimes. Her antagonist, whom she hopes to convince of the innocence of the Germans, is Dan Haywood, an American judge played by Spencer Tracy. He comes to Nuremberg to mete out justice to judges who cooperated with the Nazis. Dan is fascinated by and drawn to the poise and beauty of the widow Bertholt. She introduces him to German Moselle wine and the German way of life. She proudly rebuffs his compassion for her plight. While making him real coffee that she had managed to save in the war, she explains to him:

> I'm not fragile, Judge Haywood. I'm a daughter of the military. You know what that means, don't you? . . . It means I was taught discipline. A very special kind of discipline. For instance, when I was a child . . . we used to go for long rides into the country in summertime. But I was never allowed to run to the lemonade stand with the others. I was told, 'Control your thirst. Control hunger. Control emotion.' It has served me well.

This widow of a general and daughter of an officer claimed to embody the better Germany: She emphasized her anti-Nazi stance and the necessity of forgetting. Still, the American stood firm. He sentenced all the defendants to life in prison, and Frau Bertholt condoned neither his action nor this American tendency to paint all Germans with the same brush. Maria reported how hard it was for her mother to play this role.[42] Even so, she was able to embody the role of the widow convincingly with her detached charm, self-discipline, and moral haughtiness. *Judgment at Nuremberg* was nominated for nine Oscars, and it received two.[43] Dietrich was not even nominated for her role as Frau Bertholt. However, *Black Fox*, a film in which she had no acting role but served as narrator, won an Oscar that same year as the best feature-length documentary. *Black Fox* was a film about Hitler inspired by Goethe's retelling of the folk tale "Reynard the Fox." The film posters read, "Marlene Dietrich tells the story of Adolf Hitler." For *Black Fox*, Dietrich contacted Remarque and asked him to translate the text. Remarque, who had married Paulette Goddard in 1958, was delighted to receive this letter. He had also collaborated on the German version of *Judgment at Nuremberg* and thought Dietrich was "beautiful and magnificent" in it.[44] But he could not help her now because he had to continue working on his new book, and he assumed that the translation would not pay well. Remarque was quite business-minded and not as generous as Dietrich.[45]

o   o   o

Gary Cooper died in May 1961. Dietrich attended the funeral service alone, looking stony-faced. In the summer of 1961, Ernest Hemingway committed suicide; the soldier and hunter had shot himself. Dietrich grieved for a great love of her life. She would most likely never be called "the Kraut" again.

In the same year that Hemingway took his own life, the young, charismatic John F. Kennedy was inaugurated as the thirty-fifth president of the United States. Dietrich had known him from the last carefree summer before the outbreak of World War II. This president initiated an American age of "poetry and power," as Robert Frost had prophesied. Kennedy was the youngest man ever to be elected president—a war veteran who appealed to Americans to work together for a better country. He was assassinated in Dallas on November 22, 1963. "The days go by, and there are always hundreds of things to do, although I get up early; once again I've been unable to sleep since the Kennedy thing. Maybe it's the loneliness," Dietrich wrote to Rudi on November 29. She enjoyed telling her friend Kenneth Tynan about her affairs—including the one with Kennedy. In 1962, she had performed in a nightclub in Washington. The president's brothers, Bobby and Ted, came to the performance, but a president cannot go to a nightclub—so he invited her to the White House for a drink. A bottle of German white wine had been chilled for her. The president started to talk about Lincoln, then asked her how much time she had. She replied that she had an appointment in half an hour. "'That—doesn't give us much time, does it?' said J.F.K., looking straight into her eyes. Marlene confessed that she liked powerful men and enjoyed hanging their scalps on her belt. So she looked right back at him and said: 'No, Jack, I guess it doesn't.'"[46] With that, he took her glass and led her into his bedroom.

In January 1964, Dietrich traveled to Warsaw with her musicians. They made a stopover at the Berlin-Schönefeld airport, "and there they were all with the flowers and the Russian champagne, which, by the way, is very good, and the tears and the love."[47] She was presented with a bouquet of red carnations and white chrysanthemums on behalf of Helene Weigel to honor her antifascist actions. She had never been received with as much eagerness, enthusiasm, and love as on that visit to Poland. The minister of culture made a toast in her honor, quoting from Proust and Descartes; she felt as though she was in Paris, not Warsaw. The Poles were polite, well educated, and cordial. The traces of war were still evident everywhere.

One Sunday, she placed a bouquet of white lilacs at the monument to commemorate the uprising in the Warsaw ghetto. "I went to the Ghetto site (all rebuilt now just the monument of marble Hitler had reserved for his own after the war stands there all alone in the middle of a huge square) and I cried again for the sins of my fatherland."[48]

In May and June, she gave guest performances in Moscow and Leningrad. Dietrich was the first American entertainer to perform behind the Iron Curtain. She enjoyed the Russians because they were never lukewarm—they either loved or hated. Dietrich felt that she herself had a Russian soul. Her concerts turned into a grand celebration of this spiritual affinity. Thirty minutes after the end of the concerts, no one in the audience had any intention of leaving.

Once these tours were over, she felt emotionally and physically drained. Her one-woman show was the summation of her life. Dietrich no longer wanted to take on any roles, but instead to portray what life had made of her: a nightclub singer with a rich past. That was the role she had been assigned in *The Blue Angel*, and it had become the role of her life. *The Blue Angel* had had two central settings: the stage and Lola Lola's dressing room. This is where Dietrich's career had begun, and that is where it would end. The dressing rooms and stages may have changed over the years, yet they remained the closest thing to a home for her. She always took what she needed with her. When she arrived, her suitcases were already there. Her clothing was hung up and inspected. Her swan coat hung over the screen like a trophy. (Hemingway, the big game hunter, would have approved of that.) Others might put up a cross to bless a room; Dietrich attached a photograph of Papa Hemingway to the wall. From the observation point above her mirror, he followed her transformation and waited for her to finish her performance. She piled up her congratulatory telegrams along the edge of the big mirror, so she could keep up with whoever was thinking about her while applying her makeup. The light on the mirror was very bright, and it took several seconds for her eyes to adjust to the blinding glow. Cigarettes, ashtrays, and a lighter always needed to be within reach. She smoked continuously, but never frantically. Even when she was upset, she retained her leisurely style of smoking. Her scissors and tweezers, laid out on her vanity, sparkled like surgical tools in an operating room; there was also an array of jars, bottles, lipsticks, brushes, and ointments, along with Kleenex, wigs, hand mirrors, cotton pads, and hairbands. A glass of champagne or scotch was always at hand. The alcohol alone was not enough to give her a sense of well-being, so wherever she went, she found Dr. Feelgoods to prescribe her amphetamines and sleeping pills. Many of her friends, including Kenneth Tynan, Romy Schneider, and Judy Garland, took these magic pills. She would quickly shake a few into her hand and wash them down with scotch. Then it was time for her medicine to treat her circulatory problems. As she had done so many times before, she successfully transformed herself into the woman the audience out there was awaiting. She needed help putting on her girdle and dress, and she was loath to slip off her silk kimono. As the skintight dress stretched over her body, she was overcome with panic that she had put on weight again. Then she would make a pledge to lay off the scotch starting the following day. She kept threaded needles and pearls handy so that if a pearl fell off, she would be able to sew in a new one on the spot. She squeezed her swollen feet into high-heeled, narrow Ferragamo shoes. She felt like screaming in pain for the first few steps, but slowly made her way to the stage. From the semi-darkness she was warned not to trip over the cables on the floor. Everyone wished her good luck, but she barely registered what they were saying. Finally she was standing alone in front of the curtain. It went up, and she took her first step into the glistening light. From this point on, everything proceeded according to plan. The position of the microphone stand had been precisely determined; before each performance, she checked to see whether the distance and height were set up correctly. Every movement of her head was rehearsed. Dietrich knew how to create great effects with minimal props. After she gave brief introductions to her songs, photographs portraying her life story were projected behind her back. The applause she received was a tribute to her life as a whole. In Berlin, in Jerusalem, in Warsaw, in Moscow, and in Paris, Dietrich was a World War II soldier onstage. Awarded the American Medal of Freedom and several medals by the French Legion of Honor, she kept alive the memory of a war that divided the century in two. Her strict Prussian upbringing taught her how to present herself in public. Her body, encased in seductive clothing, had known war. Dietrich was herself a piece of history. Only she was allowed to sing German songs in Israel. She proudly pointed out that she was a holdover from the Weimar Republic. After the musical tour through her life, which she carried out with a cool distance and a frozen look on her face, she received her applause. She took a bow in front of her audience with perfect posture. By the end of her career, she herself was paying for the bouquets of flowers that were tossed onto the stage. Once she was back in her dressing room, her transformation back into a woman of her age got underway. She was weary and knew that, once again, she would not be able to sleep. When the tour came to an end, her feelings of loneliness and desolation intensified. She had not been enjoying life in the United States for quite some time. She had never liked Los Angeles, and as she grew older, she was less and less content in New York. She felt "unkempt and far from home," as she wrote to Friedrich Torberg.[49]

In 1963, she rented an apartment in Paris on the elegant Avenue Montaigne, near the Champs-Élysées. Her friends Ginette and Paul-Émile Seidman lived around the corner. The furniture from Sieber's former Paris apartment was taken out of storage after nearly thirty years. Dietrich sent him photographs of her new apartment and of his furniture. He had left the decision to her on what ought to happen to it, thus signaling that he had no intention of returning to Europe. At least once a year, when she was setting up her show in Los Angeles, she would visit him on his farm. He had not been well for the past few years. He suffered from chest pains and found it difficult to endure being alone all the time. The phases that Tamara had to spend in the clinic grew longer and longer. All he had left were the chickens and television. Then Dietrich received a telegram from Tel Aviv with the news that her mother-in-law had died. Sieber did not go to Europe for the funeral; he sent wreaths. Dietrich was his link to the world. On one occasion, he spent forty minutes listening to her concert in Las Vegas by telephone, and on another, he was with von Sternberg at Dietrich's concert in the

Congo Room of Hotel Sahara. On occasions of this kind, he bought a drink at the hotel bar and entered the cost into his daily planner. She sent him the exact schedule of her performances, and in return he kept her up to date about their old friends. He criticized her nostalgic recording (the album was called "Berlin—The Smashing City") for featuring too many "ghosts": "Cannot imagine that this record would interest younger people; how is it selling?"[50] When Dietrich came to see him along with Jo and Jo's family, and cooked a meal for them all at the farm, Sieber cherished the memory of this evening. There was some tension between von Sternberg and Dietrich. His creation was enjoying triumph as a singer on the stages of the world, and he was jealous. Sieber wrote to her, "A new star was born! Never have I read reviews like those, and I cried so much and am so happy for you. . . . I'll write more soon, especially about Jo, who behaved horribly again—mean, hostile, surely envious of your success. He is dead to me—I will never call him up again."[51]

In June 1961, Dietrich and Sieber became grandparents for the fourth time. Dietrich was with Maria in New York when she brought her son David into the world. Conscientious as he was, Sieber wanted to be a good grandfather. Although he had to count every penny and did not see his grandchildren very often, he sent each of them five dollars for their birthdays and at Christmas. Tamara needed to be hospitalized, but he was out of money and could not pay a previous bill. "I could use some money urgently—if you can. Forgive me!"[52] The check arrived promptly, but this money was not enough for the expensive clinic. Dietrich paid, and insisted that he hire someone for the farm work. Tamara now needed electroshock therapy. In order to save money, Sieber wanted to take her home right after the treatment. After the first round, in March 1963, he wrote, "A sad sight when she came out into the waiting room. Red in the face, crying, staggering. In the car she kept on crying for a while, then she slept nearly the whole way. At home, she can't do anything, and if she tries, she does everything wrong."[53] Her speech was slurred, she was unwashed and unkempt, her teeth were unbrushed, and her face was smeared with lipstick. The beautiful young woman she had once been was gone for good.

Sieber assured Dietrich that no one in the clinic knew who he was. Every letter to his wife ended with a request for money. He urged Tamara to write to Dietrich, and she tried her best, but her memory had been impaired by the shock treatments. In early 1965 she was diagnosed with schizophrenia, and about a year before her death, Tamara seemed to lose her mind altogether. Sieber described the woman he had loved as "a living corpse." On March 26, 1965, his daily planner noted in bold letters, underlined in red, "Tamara has died." On March 31, she was buried in the Hollywood Memorial Cemetery. Dietrich didn't attend the funeral.

During her dazzling, stirring performances, Dietrich was wracked with pain in her legs. An obstruction in her aorta was blocking the blood flow, and her famous legs were giving out. She knew that in public she had to appear unchanged, otherwise she would be regarded as old, and that would spell the end of her career. The latest fashion worked in her favor, and she took to wearing slacks again. The now-famous series of photographs that Alexander Liberman took in her New York apartment shows her in slim-cut black leather pants and a black pullover; her lipstick is red and her hair is short. Marlene Dietrich looks astonishingly young and energetic.

In the mid-1960s, she began to be plagued by frequent bleeding and unexpected weight loss. Panic-stricken, she examined her daily habits for clues to what might be causing it. She noted what she was eating. Although she certainly liked being slim, she feared that an insidious illness was at the root of the weight loss. Just as she had spent many years frantically noting telephone calls and visits from Yul Brynner, she was now busily recording her bouts of bleeding. Kamillosan ointment and Tampax were her constant companions. For several days in a row, she restricted herself to water and avoided her beloved champagne. She could not decide whether the bleeding had originated from a physical or a mental condition.

Eventually, Maria persuaded her to see a Swiss specialist. Maria asked the doctor to tell her the diagnosis before talking to her mother. When he called her up to let her know that Dietrich had cervical cancer, she realized that it would be best not to reveal the unvarnished truth to her mother. The doctor recommended inserting radium inlays. He claimed that the success of this therapy was miraculous, and at the very minimum, it would postpone the need for surgery. Dietrich was told simply that this therapy would impede the development of cancer. Maria took her mother to the clinic. While Dietrich was being treated for cancer in a clinic in Geneva, Tamara Matul died in California.

In April, Dietrich was back on stage in Johannesburg; this concert was followed by many others in Great Britain, and in early October she headed to Australia. Before her departure, she spent an evening with Sieber at his farm. He brought her to the airport the following morning. The long, exhausting flight was followed by days full of rehearsals and sleepless nights, but the opening night on October 7 was a success. As long as she had something that needed to be done, she bore up. The lonely Sundays and nights were hard on her. She had no one to confide in down in Australia, so she typed a letter to Maria on a tattered piece of hotel stationery almost entirely in capital letters, which reinforced the sense of panic conveyed by the contents. She told her daughter about her first sexual encounter after the medical treatment in Switzerland and about her persistent bleeding. Between rehearsals, interviews, and going on stage in the evenings, she had to find a doctor to prescribe Proluton, a progestin drug. She wrote about the color, consistency, and frequency of her discharge in excruciating detail.

I am sick with worry as you can imagine. . . . I have nobody
to talk to. I am talking as I am writing. The damned logic.
Call me collect whenever you want to. . . . I am 9 hours later
than you. I go to the theater from 7.30 p.m. till 1 a.m. (latest) Thursday and Saturdays from 1.30 p.m. till 1 a.m.[54]

She still had four weeks and a great many performances ahead of
her, and she was not expected back in Los Angeles until November 14. She was now considering flying to her gynecologist in
Europe directly from Sydney. Maybe she could have a third round
of radium? She wrote out the new flight connections by hand. But
what would happen with Rudi, who had been looking forward to
her return? The first thing was to get this Australian tour behind
her. "Love joy and call me. I am lonely lonely lonely down under,"
she wrote at the bottom of the letter.

Dietrich survived the cancer. As planned, she landed in Los
Angeles on November 14 and visited Sieber on his farm. She cooked
scallopini for him, and they enjoyed a bottle of Pouilly Fumé.

Her year came to an unhappy conclusion when Bacharach
announced that he would be ending his partnership with her.
Bacharach embodied everything Dietrich sought in an artist and
a man. They had gone through quite a bit together. He had been
at her side when she was spat at in Düsseldorf; he had gone with
her to the hospital after her fall in Wiesbaden, celebrated with her
in Warsaw, was deeply moved along with her in Jerusalem, and
strolled through Moscow with her. Dietrich was aware that he was
more interested in younger women, but she never fully accepted
this. Bacharach was from a different generation. He admired her
long and glorious past, yet he also knew that the place at her side
offered no future for him. But Bacharach's solo career was successful; he was known as "this generation's Gershwin." He had everything to gain by parting ways with Dietrich, while she lost her
maestro. When von Sternberg and Dietrich had gone their separate

ways, she was still young enough to find new directors. Back then, she could rest assured that something new would come along after their split. This time was different. Dietrich was sixty-three years old, and she knew that she would no longer find anyone better than him. His departure made her painfully aware that she was anchored in the past.

From this point on she returned to the sites of her success, and she flourished. She spent an average of four months a year on tour. But once Bacharach left her, singing was no longer a pleasure. She was also missing love. Dietrich had always gotten any man she wanted, yet was never satisfied. She thought she had found the love of her life in Yul Brynner. He enjoyed her desire for him and she was enraptured by the sexual intensity of the relationship, but from the very start, this love affair had no future—which was probably the true basis of her attraction to him.

From time to time, she reignited old affairs, but the grand passions of her life were behind her. Her relationships with her friends were no easy matter either. Over the years, von Sternberg checked up on her every now and then, and at times their paths crossed: at Sieber's farm, at the memorable concert in Wiesbaden, or at film festivals in France. Now that von Sternberg had undergone psychoanalysis, entered into another marriage, and enjoyed fatherhood, he was able to ward off the shadows of the past. He sported a white beard and continued his eccentric ways. His ivory tower kept growing higher, he assured Dietrich. Photographs of the two of them in the 1960s seem to suggest that they belonged together. The same melancholy and shyness can be read in their eyes, and they still clung to each other. They responded to the impertinences of the world with elegance. In his letters, he would continue to strike the "Marlene tone." "Yesterday I came from Venice to Vienna by way of the North Pole. In Venice, our Spanish film was being shown to great success. Once again, you acted brilliantly. The people there were captivated by the twenty-year-old movie, which looked as though it had just been shot."[55] In 1966, the forthcoming publication of von Sternberg's memoirs was announced in the United States. Dietrich was beside herself: "Von Sternberg's book is coming out here and there is a lot of comment in the papers, but they like me better. The son of a bitch. When I read frontpage headline POOR MARLENE I could kill him."[56] Once she had read the book, she no longer wanted to see him. On December 22, 1969, von Sternberg died of a heart attack in Los Angeles. Sieber noted it in his daily planner, and also that Dietrich was on his farm at this time. Dietrich did not attend von Sternberg's funeral. It is unknown whether she shed a tear for her creator.

Noël Coward chronicled Dietrich's egocentric caprices in his diary. Dietrich claimed that Coward was the only homosexual she could trust, and he nicknamed her "Prussian Cow" and "Darling Achtung." The two of them got together in New York, Los Angeles, southern France, London, and Paris. Far more than Dietrich, Coward was part of the urbane, cultivated, European postwar upper crust. Coward took her out to dinner, to the theater, and to the movies. They went to garden parties in Hollywood and the opera in New York. Dietrich's mood could turn on a dime; she could be wonderful company or someone to get away from as quickly as possible. Most of the time she looked gorgeous, and appearing at her side was sure to create a sensation.

o   o   o

Her first book, *Marlene Dietrich's ABC*, was published by Doubleday in 1962. From *accordion* to *zipper*, she composed a set of reasonably interesting texts, but this was no substitute for an autobiography. Tynan suggested that they write her biography together. "You know how I hate biographies. Someone better than I said that one has to be without humility to collaborate on one or even write an autobiography. Not that I have humility; I just don't want to talk about myself."[57] She had already received an advance for a book in which she was to write about the two wars she had lived through, but she had yet to write a single line of it. Tynan invited her to spend the summer with him in Tuscany, but as usual, she turned down invitations that involved vacations or relaxation. She had just finished an exhausting tour through the United States and wanted to go to Paris. "I toured (for the first and last time) in America. . . . Unbelievable, this country. I am through with it. It's wrotten [*sic*]."

Tynan's successful musical *Oh! Calcutta!* was being performed in New York at this time. She had read all about it, but did not want to see it. "Nakedness and 'sex' in public world repulse me. Being German both of those things are very private, personal and not at all 'funny.' "[58] Dietrich had a critical and sometimes dismissive view of the sexual revolution in the late 1960s. This attitude was alien to her; she was part of a different generation. She shared this feeling with Leo Lerman, her friend in New York. Whereas Coward and Torberg responded to her egocentricity with humor, Reisch was almost paternal, and Tynan above all curious, Lerman was pessimistic like her. Their gloomy moods notwithstanding, the two of them got along famously. Dietrich and Lerman went to see the remake of *The Blue Angel* at an old movie theater in Times Square. The film was so bad that she insisted on leaving early. Lerman then took her to Café Geiger in Yorkville, where he ordered her coffee with whipped cream and cookies. The café orchestra played "Falling in Love Again," "Johnny," and "Peter." Lerman was captivated by her beauty and quick-wittedness.

> One evening we went to a party together. And she was done up with perfect simplicity. She always let her body speak for itself. There wasn't a woman in the room—and the room was filled with all sorts of beautiful women wonderfully dressed—who looked better than Marlene. And little Hope Hampton, a flurry of feathers, diamonds, crystal drop-

beads, came up to her and peered at her and said, looking up at her face, "Who did it?" And Marlene said, "God."[59]

In April 1967, Dietrich was in Los Angeles, sharing an apartment with a girlfriend who, unlike herself, had a love life. "I am still fat. Still feeling awful. Disliking myself."[60] She went to two parties, and that was quite enough for her. Some of the guests were even smoking marijuana. There was no one for her to talk to. She began to diet and decided to stop drinking alcohol, because her stage costumes revealed every extra ounce she was carrying. Her diary entries were chaotic; she noted down, in an assortment of colored inks, what she bought, what she was eating, whom she met, where her costumes were, departures and landings, and her expenditures for friends, family, and relatives. Bacharach suggested that they appear onstage together on Broadway. Her fear of Broadway audiences used to sophisticated performances proved unfounded. Bacharach prepared the concert perfectly and hired the best musicians. The tickets were sold out shortly after the event was announced. Large crowds gathered in front of the theater on Forty-Sixth Street. Photographs show a beaming Dietrich in the middle of a throng that was cheering her on; it resembled her greeting from the Americans after her return from the war. She invited her husband to the premiere on Broadway. Sieber flew to New York. Seated next to Dietrich, whose wig and makeup made her appear far younger, her "phantom hubby" (as the American press often called him) looked like an old man. With a somewhat dazed look on his face and wearing an old-fashioned suit, he accompanied his wife through the city in which he had lived for many years. After ten days he headed back to his farm.

With her success on Broadway, she had achieved everything a singer could achieve. After Bacharach left, she made very few changes to her show. From year to year, she came more and more to resemble the machine she had described herself as. Without Bacharach, the verve of youth was gone. Everything was mediocre, and she hated mediocrity. Almost ten years after they had parted ways, her feelings of loss had not changed in the slightest. "I still look for you every time I stand in the wings. I also look for you every time I finish the show. In other words: I look *for* you and *to* you and wish you were there to tell me what I did right and what I did wrong."[61] Dietrich was weary. She had been on the road, and around the world, for forty years. When she was in Los Angeles, she rented a small apartment. All she needed was two rooms and a refrigerator for her Dom Perignon and liverwurst. Her daily planner is full of notes about which suitcase is where, which dress has to be altered or cleaned, and when she needs to be at which fitting. In Paris, she frequented the fashion boutiques of Chanel, Balmain, Dior, and Balenciaga. Now that she was over sixty, she gravitated to the timeless ideal of the elegant lady. Her minimalism is evident in her Chanel suit and her fashionable Mao-style jacket. She knew how to wear haute couture in a way that made her body stand out rather than the fashion itself. She worried about being overweight, even though she still had a good figure without doing any sort of exercise or sports. Fashion was a means to keep the artist "Marlene Dietrich" alive. She picked out her clothes as though she were fighting a battle. She knew exactly how to outshine all the other women. Her visits to the boutiques of Paris were just as feared as her earlier shopping trips to Hollywood. She arrived early and did not say hello. Any attempt to chat with her was doomed to failure; she did not like small talk, nor could she be talked into trying on something she had not selected, because she knew how clothing was made and how it looked on her. Her search could take hours. She paid no attention whatsoever to lunch breaks and showed no signs of fatigue or hunger. Pale, beautiful, and unapproachable, Dietrich studied the fabrics with an unerring eye. And she spent the whole time on her feet, despite her aching legs and her high-heeled shoes.

She kept a cool head while making her selections. Other women might revel in the luxurious pastime of shopping for clothes, but for her it was the fulfillment of an obligation. Shoes, hat, gloves, stockings, handbag, and jewelry had to go with skirts, dresses, slacks, blouses, and overcoats. It was only when she was satisfied with her purchases that the desired effect could be achieved.

Her life revolved around flight schedules. For years, she had been traveling primarily in the triangle of Paris, Los Angeles, and New York, punctuated by visits to the rest of the world, such as Montreal, Melbourne, Moscow, and Connecticut. She made a lifestyle out of restlessness. "I don't know what world you're living in that makes Copenhagen 'far away.' It's 1½ hours from here. That's nothing at all. I was just in Japan and Australia. That is far. Zurich to Paris is 45 minutes. What does that mean?"[62] Dietrich did advertising for Pan Am. Her lack of a home base was regarded as cosmopolitanism. She visited Sieber for several days a year on his farm. In July 1969, they were sitting together in front of the television set watching the landing on the moon. Now that passions were behind her, she found contentment in their longstanding familiarity. At least with Rudi she could count on being the center of his life.

On September 12, 1970, Torberg asked her whether she had heard that Boni was quite ill. Remarque had suffered a stroke in 1963, which brought him his first brush with death. In the years that followed, he had a series of heart attacks and experienced ongoing pain and panic attacks. When Torberg wrote to Dietrich, Boni had been admitted to the clinic in Locarno again, and they were prepared for the worst. Dietrich received this letter after her return from Japan. Every day, she had flowers sent to Remarque at the clinic. On September 25, Remarque died in the Clinica Sant'Agnese in Locarno. "I feel the loss very much because I had always hoped that I might see him again."[63] In Dietrich's eyes, Paulette Goddard was at fault, because Goddard did not want Remarque to get together with her. Was she afraid he might give her one of his precious paintings? She could not picture Boni being happy with another woman. "Boni must have been very lonesome when he died. But then—he was always lonesome with his thoughts." She did not attend the funeral. In a letter to Maria on the day of Boni's burial, she wrote about a beautiful old Russian cemetery she had gone to, and conveniently included a sketch of how to get there. The cemetery was near Orly, fifteen miles from Paris and close to the town of Massy. This would have been an appropriate burial place for her, near the airport and near Paris. She had had to take two Valium pills the previous night to stave off troubling thoughts. Remarque's death made it apparent to her that she had lost him long ago. No matter how much she may have loved him, his wife was now in charge. In the eyes of the world, Goddard was Remarque's heiress and widow. Dietrich had not even been allowed to visit him. She wondered what would happen with Gabin if she outlived him. He had always been fair, but one never knew how a man's wife would react. Perhaps she ought to ask for the valuable paintings to be returned. "Maybe I am wrong. But when the people you have been so close to, much closer than one knows, die and you have no way to contact them before or his family after—then you start thinking more terrible thoughts."[64]

In the year that Remarque died, Dietrich made two trips to Montreux for live cell therapy treatments. Since the early 1960s, she had been a regular guest at the Clinique La Prairie, where she would be injected with fresh cells taken from fetal sheep, a procedure that was said to slow down the natural aging process. She spent an average of a week at the clinic. "On Thursday, the injections, and then five days of rest, and then back to Paris."[65]

When Coco Chanel died on January 10, 1971, Sieber entered that fact into his daily planner. Dietrich was with him, and they may have thought of Coco while dining on roast veal and Dom Perignon. She flew to Paris for Chanel's burial. Charles de Gaulle died in November 1970. Dietrich paid her last respects to the "capitaine." She felt as though everyone around her was dying, and she was receiving medals. The president of France, Georges Pompidou, awarded her the rank of officer in the Legion of Honor at the Élysée Palace. Dietrich was sure that there could not be so many existing medals to award, and that they were invented especially for her. She wrote to Orson Welles shortly before her seventieth birthday that she was faring badly both physically and mentally. And to make matters worse, she was convinced that she now looked like a toad: "Cannot drink because of that. So, have no, even momentary, lift. Too much flying too. Money-worries as always but cannot take advances on the contracts before not everything is in order. All in life is miserable at the moment. Not even sleeping-pills make me sleep which doesn't help the TOAD-LOOK."[66] She had had it all in life: love, money, beauty, and success. Now she had the feeling that she was losing it all.

On July 27, 1972, Dietrich signed a contract to tape a television show. It was the $125,000 fee that lured her; she hated television. She paid for her wardrobe, the orchestration, and the conductor, Burt Bacharach, out of pocket. When the preliminary work began in November, it was soon clear that she would not be her own boss the way she was used to. The rehearsal times were cut back drastically, and all the titles in German were taken out. The orchestra was supposed to play behind the stage. She ranted and raved, but the taping proceeded without undue difficulty. The interviews to which she was contractually obligated to submit were another matter. In conversation with the final journalist, she did not mince words, declaring that the taping had been amateurish. "The first thing you see is a curtain with my portrait, drawn by René Bouché. That is okay. Then I'm supposed to sing 'La Vie en Rose,' and the light turns orange. What's going on? Am I supposed to sing 'La Vie en Orange' now?"[67] The interview continued along these lines. When it appeared in print in the major British and American daily newspapers, her producer, Alexander Cohen, declared that he was finished with Dietrich. A five-year legal battle ensued about the pending fee. In 1977, she received a payment of sixty thousand dollars. In view of the costs she had already incurred and the immense expectations, this was a paltry sum of money.

A few days after the television broadcast of the show, there was a revue for Noël Coward in New York. The honoree appeared on the arm of his friend Marlene Dietrich. The two of them were in good form; they gossiped, joked, sang, and clung together. Two months later, Coward was dead. Then Dietrich's sister died in Celle. Only Elisabeth had known what it was like to be on Sedanstrasse or to skate on the Neuer See. Dietrich was glad that this news reached her while she was in London, where Maria lived. In the evening, she went to see Maria and made dinner for the children. She was in terrible shape; not even scotch helped. Now Rudi was the only one left to remember the time in Berlin with Dietrich. She did not want to eat for days, and she only drank tea. On May 14, the day her sister was buried in Hanover, Dietrich opened her show in Birmingham.

"I have to earn money as always" had become her mantra. Even close friends had to rely on the newspaper or television to find out where she was at any given time. It became harder and harder for her to manage everyday chores on her own. She wanted someone to talk to, to take care of her, to help her out. To take her mind off her unhappiness, she overate. "I look awfully fat in those amateur photos and now I am even fatter. I don't know how I will get down because I am hungry all the time and as I am at home I eat anything in sight except what is good for me. . . . It is now 5:30 p.m. and it is raining and windy. My six geraniums are falling over and I go and put them up. Some occupation!"[68] At a concert on November 7, 1973, in Washington, she suffered a fall. At the end of the concert, she reached her hand down to the orchestra pit to shake hands with her musical director, Stan Freeman, as she always did. He decided to stand on the piano bench to come closer, but the bench broke, and Freeman pulled her into the pit. She lay on her back like a helpless insect, unable to move. Her calls for help went unheard because "Falling in Love Again" was booming. She had not broken any bones, but half her leg had been sliced open. Still, a veteran of a world war was not about to head straight to the hospital; instead she gritted her teeth and called up her old friend Ted Kennedy, who discreetly sent a doctor to examine her. The upcoming concerts in Washington were canceled. As her friends and family had feared, she did not fly to New York to rest up, but decided to fulfill her concert obligations in Canada. Maria made all the preparations for her arrival in Montreal. Although the accident had been extremely painful and vexing for Dietrich, it posed a challenge that she was determined to rise to. She mobilized her strength and put on a fine performance. No one noticed that the ageless woman on the stage was seriously injured.

Before embarking on her tour through South America, she had to undergo heart surgery. Michael DeBakey, a renowned cardiac specialist, told her that she would lose her leg if her circulatory disorders were not remedied. In earlier years, she had used the name "Sieber" to book hotel rooms for her amorous escapades; now she was being admitted to the Methodist Medical Center in Houston as a patient under this name. DeBakey, who was only seven years her junior, had pioneered cardiac artery bypass surgery back in 1964. Dietrich and Lyndon B. Johnson were two of his famous patients. Once she left the intensive care unit, she focused on her leg. She no longer sent celebrity phtographs to her friends, but instead pictures of her leg, complete with skin grafts.

Soon after she left the hospital, with her legs still swollen and painful, she resumed her performances. Her life gathered momentum again, and she went back to focusing on the usual issues of contracts, rehearsals, flight schedules, and checks, with a hodge-podge of hotel reservations, departure times, proverbs, recommended medications, and notes about who had gotten how many dollars from her and on what date. These papers make it hard to fathom how she was able to keep up with her schedule and make it onstage.

On August 10, Dietrich fell in her bedroom in Paris and fractured her left hip. Because she had no faith in French doctors, she was flown to New York for a hip operation. Maria, who brought her to the hospital, had to come up with an elaborate scheme to keep the press from getting wind of what was going on. The operation was a success. One month after her hip surgery, Dietrich began her concerts in London. She came onstage without limping. Her doctors declared that she was in extraordinarily good shape for her age. "I certainly don't live a good life. I eat like a dog (whatever I find) and the only thing that I don't do is smoking. . . . Still poor as a church-mouse, but a young one All Love Marlene."[69]

In early December she flew to Japan, where she gave concerts until the end of 1974. Since returning from the conservatory in Weimar, Dietrich had earned her living with acting and singing. She had always worked hard and spent extravagant sums of money. She could not imagine a life without an audience, admiration, and spotlights. The older she grew, the more she lived for this one hour on the stage. She was not cut out to spend her time visiting friends at the Côte d'Azur, picking up the children from school, organizing charity balls, or sitting on a park bench holding hands with an aging lover. Her biggest concessions to old age were her apartments in New York and Paris, which were the sanctuaries she needed from the world.

She could not imagine any option but to carry on as she always had: living out of a suitcase, spending nights in hotel rooms, jotting down flight schedules, inspecting stages, taking bows, handing out checks, descending on fashion boutiques, and creating sensations. At the age of seventy, she had crossed a threshold that would make it harder for her to take hold of the future. Being young had become such a part of her that she could not let go of it. In addition to makeup, corsets, live cell therapy treatments, and vitamin pills, she now also availed herself of the services of cosmetic surgery. Her friend Kenneth Tynan, who got together with her for dinner in London in May 1972, noted, "Marlene has clearly undergone some facial renovation: cheeks and neck are smooth and unwrinkled."[70] But alcohol was most important. In the past, she had enjoyed drinking a glass of champagne before going onstage, but after all these years she had lost control of it. Champagne turned into scotch, and one glass turned into many. Because she could no longer overlook the fact that she was a lonely old woman, she needed the alcohol to revive the memory of her youth and erotic omnipotence. Was she still able to bring magic to the stage? Only if she herself believed in what she was singing, but she failed to realize that the alcohol only heightened her inertia. Alcohol made her indifferent even to her perfection. Every time she sang "Sentimental Journey," she had to cry. And when she listened to her Berlin record, she teared up. She had grown old and sentimental. Her famous swan coat was showing signs of wear, and her once breathtaking dresses had seen better days. If she was too drunk when she sat down at the dressing table, she smeared her lipstick, applied her makeup sloppily, and put on her wig askew. Without a masquerade, she could no longer appear in public. She no longer dreamed of enticing a man, who would, after all, see her swollen feet, the thinned-out hair on her head, and her many wrinkles. Now that she had problems with balance, she had to be brought to the stage curtain in a wheelchair. As long as no photographs of that got out, she enjoyed this little luxury, which made it less apparent that she was no longer so steady on her feet after a good helping of scotch. Alone in her hotel room after the show, she was unable to sleep. "No wonder I don't sleep other than drugged. (I take no more than one.) But I still wake up at 2 p.m. and then what?"[71] How much could she read? She had already devoured every book by her favorite author, Rex Stout, and sometimes, out of pure desperation, she resorted to reading a cookbook at night. Dietrich, whom the stage had finally freed from the necessity of portraying other women, had become "a prisoner of her own legend," as Coward cleverly put it. Only she could free herself from it.

She still had to take care of Sieber. In the 1970s, his handwriting looked like an old man's, and he began to repeat himself. The reader can almost feel him frantically grasping for something to say to Dietrich, but there was not much to report. On the final pages of his daily planner, he had entered the birth dates of his friends after their names. During the final years of his life, the dates of their deaths, marked with a cross, were added on. And there were more and more crosses. He held to his routine of noting every detail of his life. Gifts, expenses, telephone calls, Russian Easter, Dietrich's flight schedules and performances, food, drink, reading, hair washing, bathing, and bedtimes. At one point he asked Dietrich to go out with him, reminding her that he had the good suit he had bought for Tamara's funeral. She sent him packages with pear brandy; a type of vodka that could be found only in Paris; autobiographies of their friends; articles about his hometown, Aussig; records by Horowitz; medicines; and products to stimulate hair growth. He sometimes dreamed about his time in Berlin; he collected wine labels from back home, and looked forward to visits from his grandchildren, who were as big as giants. There is little information about Sieber's feelings. He recorded every last detail of how his life was slowly coming to an end. Dietrich was caught up with her own illnesses and did not have as much time for him as she had had in the past. When she sent him ten stamped and self-addressed envelopes, he asked huffily whether she wanted some from him as well.

Sieber's whole life had revolved around Dietrich, and she had assumed full responsibility for him. Not even Tamara could induce him to venture out on his own. Now it was too late to do so. Dietrich had never freed Sieber from his obligations to her, and he had never asked her to do so. The farm had become a refuge for her. No one there was interested in the star. There is a photograph of Dietrich at Sieber's farm, sitting in a wheelchair dressed in a denim outfit and smiling uncertainly at the camera.

At the beginning of 1975, she resolved to drink less. Alcohol was making her fat, and she no longer fit into her clothes. Before leaving on another tour in Australia in the fall, she had to get through almost two dozen performances in North America and Europe. Maria called her mother on August 11 with the news that Sieber had had a stroke and been brought to a clinic, where he was unresponsive. Mother and daughter were in constant contact by phone. In late August, Dietrich arrived in Los Angeles. She visited Sieber, then flew on to Sydney via Honolulu. The tour did not go well. Ticket sales were sluggish, and the producer was considering canceling the entire tour. He had not failed to notice that his star was rarely sober. At a concert in Sydney, she stumbled and fell over a cable that was lying around as she came onstage; she was quite likely drunk. The audience was sent home, and Dietrich was brought into her dressing room to be examined. The doctor diagnosed a fracture of the left femoral neck. Wrapped up like the finest porcelain, she was flown to Los Angeles. A photograph shows her on a stretcher at the airport covered up to her neck. Sieber suffered from paralysis after his stroke, and Dietrich was in a full body cast after her fall. Since she had no faith in Californian doctors either, she was brought to New York and then to Paris, where she lay in extension bandages until February 1976. Dietrich's life had come to a standstill.

THE
END
GAME

—

(1976–2003)

IN THE MATTRESS CRYPT

I n April 1976, when Dietrich's health had improved, she once again flew the familiar route from Paris to Los Angeles to be with her husband. She spent several days with Sieber and was relieved to find that all the money she had paid to the army of doctors, nurses, and therapists had been worth it. In early June she returned to Europe. Fourteen days later she got the news that Sieber had died.

It somehow typified the life they shared that he passed away in Los Angeles while she was furnishing her apartment in Paris. She did not want to fly to America again, and she tried to avoid going to funerals anyway, especially when everyone was just waiting to take pictures of her as the grieving and ailing widow. Maria would take care of everything.

On June 30, 1976, Rudolf Emilian Sieber was buried in Holly-wood Memorial Park Cemetery. His grave is near Tamara's and a stone's throw from Paramount Studios. The inscription on his gravestone reads: "Rudi 1897–1976." His last name was left off; he had spent his life being "Herr Dietrich."

On November 15, Dietrich's daily planner noted the death of Jean Gabin. Her last great love had died of heart failure. In the days to follow, sleep was out of the question. Billy Wilder called her up; perhaps he was thinking about the lonely old Dietrich mourning her ex-lover. Shortly before Christmas, she received a letter from Gabin's attorney, who told her that Gabin had bequeathed her photographs and a cigarette case. One day before New Year's Eve, these items were delivered to her, and a few months later, she put them on her auction list.[1] Since she no longer smoked, she had no need for the cigarette case, and she preferred money to sentimental keepsakes. Now that Gabin had died, all the men who had been truly important to her were gone. Jo was the first, then Boni, and now Rudi and Jean in the same year. Jo, Boni, and Jean had become nothing but memories over the years, but Rudi was still part of her daily life. In September, Dietrich wrote to her daughter Maria that since his death, nothing mattered to her anymore. "His handwriting in my telephone books, his notes that pop up everywhere keep me running back in my mind and torture me. 'Never more' is a horrible saying. From the things he liked from here to the magazines I used to send—I stop so many times and remind myself that all is over."[2] Since there were no longer performances or planes to catch or rendezvous, she had nothing to divert her from her pain about the past. The nights were the worst. She slept until two o'clock and then woke up. "Think Papi is sitting all alone in the livingroom and I get up to look. Stupid."[3]

On top of that, she now needed to write those silly memoirs, which meant dredging up old memories. Every completed chapter went straight to Maria. If Dietrich died before finishing the book, Maria would know how to carry on. She had to churn out pages in order to get the advance, but writing felt like torture. She did not really want to reflect about herself. Dietrich had no desire to divulge the details of her life and felt trapped. She told Kenneth Tynan, who had wanted to write a biography together with her some years back, that her accidents and Sieber's death had deeply depressed her. What could she do without Rudi? He always carried a postcard with him on which she had written the text of "Falling in Love": a true sign of abiding love.

She went back to Paris so as not to be a burden to Maria. "It bores me stiff. I guess I was always spoiled and had people who recharged my batteries. Now, there is nobody to talk to, to advise me."[4] She found the chapters about Hemingway and Remarque quite difficult, but the one about Coward was easy. "The Childhood Chapters are by far the best because I find it so much easier to write from a child's viewpoint." But she knew that this would not be enough. She did not want to compose a set of anecdotes, because she had hated anecdotes her whole life. Her readers would not be getting any bedtime stories from her.

She was particularly hard on her old friend and assistant Max Kolpé. He was part of the memoirs project right from the start because he would be doing the German translation. They had put their heads together to figure out which publisher would be likely to pay the highest advance. If Hildegard Knef had made millions with an uninteresting story of her life, this project ought to be a breeze for Dietrich. She was dissatisfied with Kolpé's translation and insinuated that he was translating into Bavarian rather than German. Finding his German sloppy, she pointed out that Sieber had always been a stickler for proper German grammar. She herself read, spoke, and wrote primarily in English, yet she found fault with friends who had forgotten standard German.

Dietrich noted which chapter was complete and who had been asked to look it over. Criticism was of course unwelcome. She had no idea how she would complete the project. The secretaries were incompetent, Kolpé was bungling his work, and there was too much noise in the house. "Mme. Miron gave me the weekly bath.

She is still the best. I am all scrubbed and clean. Otherwise there is nothing but a terrible vast emptiness that I know I have to fill and write about my—what? I ordered food from the restaurant because I could not face the cooking. God knows how I am going to pay for ALL of that."[5] She began to count up what she had written character by character. When would the advance be coming? And what in the world was a keystroke? If it were not for the money, she would not be writing a single line. Her recollections were nobody's business. "What an easy time when I worked on stage."

The filming of *Just a Gigolo* offered a change of pace. This movie, set in the Berlin of the Weimar Republic, was about Prussian officers, lost honor, cocottes, communists, and Nazis. The "Eden" bar that Boni liked so much was also in it. Dietrich, as the Baroness von Semering, her face hidden in the shadow of a large hat, sang the title song. She considered the story inane and did the movie just for the money. David Bowie, who played the leading role, reminded screenwriter Walter Reisch of the young Rudi Sieber. Perhaps Dietrich felt the same way, and she had one more reason to appear before the camera again. *Just a Gigolo* would be her final motion picture. The film was a box-office and critical flop. Under a film still showing her as the Baroness von Semering, she noted, "How ugly can you get?"[6]

On March 14, 1979, Dietrich received a telegram from her publisher, Bertelsmann, informing her that her book had been published. After considerable thought, she had chosen the title of a poem by Goethe, *Just Take My Life*, as the book's title. Kolpé asked not to be listed as the German translator, "so that people won't keep saying that you refuse to speak German."[7] She enjoyed reading the review in the *Frankfurter Allgemeine Zeitung*, which put her on par with Wolfgang Borchert and Heinrich Böll. Reviewers delighted at the way her words mirrored her world of artifice. After all, who would be expecting the truth? "The memoirs are as stylized as she herself is, and as true as the artful Dietrich when onstage in Las

Vegas."[8] The book did not become the bestseller she had hoped for. Dietrich refused to boost sales with readings, television appearances, or book signings. She did not need the aggravation.

She had decorated her parlor in Paris with photographs of her famous lovers and admirers. Ronald Reagan and Jacques Chirac had been added recently. She had the private telephone number of both politicians. Chirac sent her flowers, and she wrote him letters. She enjoyed telephone conversations with Nancy Reagan, who gave her a signed copy of her memoir. Dietrich had no intention of dreaming about the past once she retired; she took a lively interest in current events, yet her interest in movies, the theater, and fashion seemed to ebb once she had left the stage. She delighted in watching Frank Sinatra on television, but she was far more absorbed in the issues surrounding Watergate, the strikes in France, and the neo-Nazis in Germany. She kept up with an impressive number of newspapers and magazines, reading the London *Times*, the *Daily Telegraph*, the *New York Times, France-Soir, Le Figaro*, and *Die Welt* on a daily basis, and supplemented these with *Die Zeit, Bunte, Quick, Stern*, and *The New Yorker*. While she was still active in the world of performance, she had disparaged television, but in her later years she made her peace with it.

She had to attend to business on a near-constant basis. She continued to record her schedule on a calendar. Dietrich preferred British daily planners that came with a map of the London Underground and of England. As someone who had so often crossed the Atlantic, she made a point of noting the time difference between Paris and New York, and between Paris and Los Angeles, at the beginning of each new year. She wrote an average of four letters a day, which went out to destinations around the world. She had two typewriters and a copy machine in her apartment. "When I worked on the stage I had 6 different dresses, so, why not now when my only source of income is this bloody book, have 2 typewriters?"[9] In most cases, she gave Maria copies of the letters she received or sent.

When books about her were published, she requested a copy and carefully inspected what had been written about her and which photographs had been selected to accompany the text. She sent her famous chicken soup to sick friends by taxi. She spent whole days drawing up lists of things that could be sold. Requests for interviews interested her only if they came with the offer of a good fee. Most of the time, she pretended not to be at home, and said that she was in the United States or Switzerland.

When Maximilian Schell announced his arrival, she claimed to be elsewhere as well. He had taken a room at the Hotel George V and was waiting for her to call. Dietrich sent a message that she had an appointment in London. The two of them knew each other from the filming of *Judgment at Nuremberg*. He had garnered the Oscar for best actor for that movie, an honor to which she had felt entitled for so long. But eventually she did do a project with him. In the fall of 1982, they got together to shoot a film about Dietrich's life. She spent six days conversing with him for three-hour stints, one day in German and the next in English. Once again, she was doing this only for the money, and she was furious to learn that she was expected to speak the whole time. She stubbornly referred to her book, where all this could be read. She had figured that in the film he would show pictures or film clips and read from her book or from von Sternberg's. Instead, he tried to force her to reflect about herself on camera. She considered Schell good-looking, but timid and unimaginative. When the two of them had a look at scenes from her old movies, an activity she considered silly, Dietrich astonished her viewers. She still knew every image, recalled every shot. But overall, her performance in *Marlene*—as the film would be named—was proof positive of Remarque's playful observation: "You can't argue with Aunt Lena."[10] She constantly contradicted herself, but that did not bother her. At the age of eighty, she was witty and sharp, and a larger-than-life presence. Schell might as well have packed up and gone home. Only at the very end of the film did he try to prove to her that she was a sentimental person. When they recite Freiligrath's famous love poem together: "Oh, love as long as you can love! / Oh, love as long as you wish to love," there is a catch in Dietrich's voice. Her mother had loved this poem. It had been framed and displayed on the living room wall in Berlin. It might seem kitschy, but she could not recite these words without weeping.

Schell, in turn, could not get her to pose for the camera. Her reasoning was short and sweet—and smart: "I've been photographed to death my whole life. That's enough."[11] She did not want any camera to capture what old age had done to her face. It was nobody's business that she had lost the battle for youth. This was not vanity but an artistic stance. In this film, which is about her, she is never onscreen. She was declaring the official end of her lifelong romance with the camera. Von Sternberg would have liked that.

It was not only the public that was no longer permitted to see her; she was also shutting out her old friends, such as Romy Schneider and Hildegard Knef, who received a generous supply of prescription pills from Dietrich by mail. Dietrich did not appreciate the way Knef kept putting herself on a pedestal. When Knef asked her for a French fashion designer, Dietrich felt it was time to give her a piece of her mind and declared that a world-famous man like Yves Saint Laurent would not travel to Germany for some lady named Hildegard. Her own situation was, of course, a different matter. The couturiers worshipped her and considered themselves lucky if Dietrich wore their creations.

She wrote to Willi Forst, but he rebuffed her with the remark that you cannot warm things up again in old age. Her former lover Brian Aherne was different; he kept his word and stayed in touch with her from time to time. He was stung to realize that she barely mentioned him in her memoirs, but that did nothing to diminish his admiration. "You are one of the great ones of the world and God bless the memory of Josef von Sternberg who was the first to see that and to put you on the track."[12] She must have been delighted to read that. Her opinion of von Sternberg had mellowed, and she stayed in touch with his widow. Every letter from Walter Reisch expressed the hope that she would come to California again. He was horrified at how she had hidden herself away in Paris and was so isolated. What had happened to her vitality and her "affirmation of life"? Wasn't there anyone who loved her? In California, she could get together with people from the old clique: the Wilders, Preminger, Mia May, Eric Ambler and Joan Harrison, and Reisch himself. He kept her up to date about how things were in Hollywood after the war. The new producers wanted nothing to do with old-timers like himself, so he was now giving lectures and was pleased about the students' great interest in Lubitsch, May, and Lang.

Dietrich did not agree to see even Billy Wilder, with whom she could have indulged in some juicy Hollywood gossip.[13] Like Reisch, he called her up every time he was in Paris. Although she disguised her voice, he recognized her instantly. "Come on, for Christ's sake, Marlene, we know it's you! . . . Marlene, I'll come up, I want to see you. I'll blindfold myself, how about that?"[14] She agreed to call him the following day, but then demurred, claiming she had to go to Neuilly for an eye-doctor appointment. This went on for several more days, and he eventually flew back to Los Angeles without having seen Dietrich.

People could call her up or write her letters, but a face-to-face meeting was out of the question.[15] If one of her friends dared to say something about her, she sent offended and offensive letters. If they asked what she was doing, they would get answers along the lines of "I'm the same . . . in bed, with a book and a bottle."[16]

She maintained contact with the outside world by writing letters or making telephone calls. She called her telephone "my only extravagance." It was always within reach, and she availed herself of it whenever the mood struck her. And that was often, as we can see just by looking at it today. This white telephone is in pitiful shape. It is filthy, stained, and pasted together in many spots. Dietrich's telephone looks more like a scruffy, exhausted animal than a piece of technical equipment. Books and the telephone helped combat her loneliness. She spent Christmas, her birthday, New Year's Eve, Easter, Pentecost, and the long French summer vacations alone.

Apart from the big wide world in which she thought she still had a role, there was also the small world of the apartment in which she set the tone. Dietrich was intent on cleanliness, and noted when the curtains had been washed, the mattresses turned, and the linens changed. Throughout her life, she had been dissatisfied with the people who were inclined to spend their time with her. Her old age did nothing to change that, except that back then they had come out of love, and now she had to pay people to keep her company. Sooner or later, she quarreled with her secretaries, promoters, and maids. In her eyes, they were hysterical, neurotic, incompetent, alcoholic, ungrateful, or insolent. She really wanted Maria to be with her, and called her up several times a day. If Maria did not answer the phone, her mother was utterly distraught and feared that something had happened to her. Maria did not come very often, but when she did visit, she bathed her mother and cooked for her.

Once the prose of her life had been committed to paper, Dietrich began to write poems. One of them contains these lines: "If a surgeon / Would open my heart / He would see / A gigantic sea / Of love / For my only child. / He would be stunned / At the force of it / The violence / The fury of it / All entangled in / One human heart."[17] These poems may be the only things she did not try to turn into money. She never stopped thinking about how she could get her hands on money, which prompted her to dig out an old photograph from *The Blue Angel* to compare what Madonna might have copied from her costume. She offered her clothing for sale, wrote articles about Garbo's death, mulled over whether she ought to make commercials for beer, and approached her friend Karl Lagerfeld with the suggestion that he market a perfume named "Marlene."

Josef von Sternberg had made Dietrich's face an icon of the twentieth century. Old age had destroyed not Dietrich's beauty, but the work of art that her face had been. Dietrich's twentieth century came to an end when she announced that she would no longer be showing her face. She herself had turned off the spotlight. By retreating from the world, she could ensure that "Marlene Dietrich" would remain intact as a work of art. The myth of Marlene lived on, while the phantom, the mortal Marlene, stepped into the obscurity of solitude.

She had no more use for glamorous get-ups, haute couture clothing, tailor-made suits from famed haberdashers, and intricately detailed works of art by Italian shoemakers. Dietrich now dressed in bed jackets—not just any old ones, of course: they were by Dior. These bed jackets were gossamer works of art in blue, pink, and white wool. Under the knitted fabric, they were lined with chiffon in the same color scheme and gathered at the sleeves, with a ribbon at the neckline. Some of the bed jackets have big holes in the delicate weave. Someone who no longer had good vision had tried to patch up these spots. Under the jackets she wore plain cotton nightshirts or men's pajamas. Even though she was no longer in the public eye, she remained true to herself; her sleepwear was simple and elegant. Her pink and bright blue slippers appear to be unworn. It is impossible to picture Dietrich's famous legs in these woolen, pompom-topped shoes.

"The ranks are thinning out," Reisch had written her from Hollywood.[18] Just as Sieber had done, she now began to note a whole series of death dates in her daily planner: Orson Welles, Simone Signoret, Mischa Spoliansky, Lilli Palmer, the Duchess of Windsor, and Romy Schneider. She sent flowers for Michael Wilding's funeral, and when Axel Springer's son took his own life, she wrote to him that her thoughts were with him. Serge Gainsbourg died, and Dietrich sent her condolences to Jane Birkin in a letter that was delivered by taxi. The death of Kenneth Tynan weighed on her heavily, and she was shocked by the death of Ernst Sieber, Rudi's brother, probably because she realized he was the last of the Siebers to go.

She did not accept her relatives' invitations to Germany. The German language was no more than a memory for her, although there were things she could express only in German, such as *welt-fremd, Jugendzeit, Hopfen und Malz verloren, In der Not frisst der Teufel Fliegen, Schnitzel*, and *Langschläfer*.

When a pre-publication excerpt of Leni Riefenstahl's *Memoirs* appeared in print in the German magazine *Bunte*, Dietrich sent her maid to the Champs-Élysées to pick up a copy for her. She promptly called Max Kolpé to tell him about it. The two of them seemed to be in full agreement about their contempt for Riefenstahl. Kolpé wrote to her: "What can you say about this? Everything is a pack of lies! Did you expect anything else? Of course they happily go on printing these lies by 'the Reich's glacial crevasse,' as this fiery narcissus was called. . . . L.R.'s most unabashed lie of all is that she supposedly heard the name 'HITLER' for the first time in 1932."[19]

Avenue Montaigne was an upscale address situated near the Eiffel Tower, the Rue du Faubourg Saint-Honoré, and the Champs-Élysées. Here, Paris has the kind of dove-gray, silent elegance that is not found anywhere else in the world. Dietrich lived on the fifth floor of a large apartment building that connotes genteel anonymity. Soraya, the beautiful woman who was cast off by the Shah of Iran, also lived in this building. Paris, declared Franz Hessel, was the "home of the foreigner." Empresses without a country, wearing dark sunglasses to shield them from prying eyes, were at home on this broad, tree-lined avenue of high fashion and luxury hotels. Dietrich's apartment was a sanctuary and an archive. She would spend hours looking for a Chanel outfit and was vexed when she did not find it, then suspected that one of her helpers had taken it.

Sometimes she gave away or sold her belongings. Fashion was part of her former life, when she could still stand, sing, and fly. "Isn't it strange: / The legs / That made / My rise to glory / Easy, No? / Became / My Downfall / Into Misery! / Queasy, No?"[20]

She cleaned her medals and polished her rings. Then there were the many photographs, presents, and letters that she kept looking over, commenting on, and sorting through. Her estate includes large brown envelopes, in no apparent order, on which she noted names and dates with her elegant, straight-up-and-down penmanship. She was critical of her appearance on many photographs, and jotted down, "Is that me?"

Her walls were covered with photographs of people she loved and those who loved her. Everywhere there were piles of paper and books, and countless newspapers in English, French, and German—Dietrich's languages. Cartons, boxes, a television set, and a grand piano. The soaring elegance of the city was in evidence here as well. Mirrors, a cream-colored sofa, Louis Vuitton luggage, and silk pillows.

In 1979 she got a wheelchair, and it became part of the furnishings. In a wheelchair, she could wash herself and sit at the window and look up at the trees. Her future was the next day. When the telephone rang at night, she was taken aback. Her publicly announced retirement had made her fodder for the tabloids. When a photographer found his way into her apartment and took pictures of the defenseless old lady in her wheelchair, she threw a towel over her head—the only form of self-defense she had left.[21] From then on, she kept the heavy curtains closed as a safeguard. Her hair was cut short. She was in pain and on medication. Her blood and urine were monitored at regular intervals. Sleeping pills and books helped her make it through the long nights. In addition to her old favorite authors, namely Goethe, Heine, and Rilke, she immersed herself in books by John Updike, Heinrich Böll, Günter Grass, Virginia Woolf, Norman Mailer, and Marguerite Yourcenar. Her book collection, which is now stored in a warehouse in Berlin-Moabit, contains many English and German titles, but very few in French. These books range from volumes of photographs to Hans Fallada, Knut Hamsun, Peter Handke, Erich Kästner, Irmgard Keun, Thomas Mann, Marcel Proust, Alexander Pushkin, Johannes Mario Simmel, John Steinbeck, and Jakob Wassermann. She liked Michael Jackson, but she also listened to Brahms, Chopin, and Liszt.

There were days in Dietrich's "mattress crypt" that were so bleak that even her gallows humor did not help her to rise above them. She was tormented by isolation and hunger. Sundays and holidays were the worst. No one came to see her; no one called. No one went shopping for her, or cooked her a meal. There was no cheese or bread to be found in the kitchen. Luckily, she had a telephone and could order Chinese food. Three years before her death, she began to have food brought to her from the Maison d'Allemagne. Perhaps she was fighting off her vague feeling of homesickness with lentil stew, Teltow turnips, veal sausages, potato salad, and cut-up sweet pancakes with raisins.

Every year on the eighth of May, she thought about the end of the war and heard the parade on the nearby Champs-Élysées. She was deeply concerned about the crisis in Iraq and the outbreak of the war. She watched the television coverage of Mitterand's and Bush's politics. She was haunted by the fear of war. Where would she go if there was war? Back to the States?

In 1989, Dietrich was appointed Commandeur of the Légion d'Honneur and given an honorarium. Congratulations poured in from around the world. Her penmanship in her daily planner evened out, as though to say: *Look at me; I'm still worth something.* It was the last major event in her life.

One day the bailiff came to her door. Her rent was in arrears. Could the eighty-six-year-old Dietrich be put out on the street along with her letters from Jean Gabin and her medals for bravery? The city of Paris began to pay her rent, and Commandeur Dietrich could save face.

She felt she could no longer afford help in the house and she lived alone, typing her letters by herself and leaving the phone off the hook. She could have sold her apartment on Park Avenue in New York, but she was determined to leave a good inheritance for Maria and the grandchildren, as befitted a daughter of a Prussian officer, even if that daughter had been an American movie star. The doctors were making more frequent visits. Dietrich was in pain and no longer wanted to live. She could not commit suicide, because her life insurance would not pay out if she did. She spent her ninetieth birthday alone, as she had in the preceding years. To cheer herself up, she called Billy Wilder and Beate Klarsfeld. Her days were long, dark, and lonely. The German newspaper *Bild* reported that she lay dying. She continued to make entries in her daily planner in a shaky handwriting. The proud, modern haughtiness that had characterized her penmanship was no longer in evidence. After a second stroke, she could barely speak. She was down to three words: *yes, no,* and *Maria.* Her grandson Peter came to her side. He carried her from her bedroom into the parlor.[22] She had been washed and dressed in clean clothes for a visit with the doctor. She knew that death was imminent, but she remained calm and collected. Dietrich lay on the couch and looked at the photographs on the wall: her family, lovers, friends, and herself. The last important conversation of her life was a telephone call from Paris to New York, in which Maria told her she would be taking the next plane to see her.

It was springtime in Paris. Dietrich was alone when she died on May 6, 1992. The Cannes Film Festival would begin the following day. All of France was awash with posters advertising the festival and featuring Dietrich in all her glory as Shanghai Lily.

The image outlived her; art had prevailed.

AT THE
BOTTOM
OF
THE SEA

T he dream that had eluded her during Hitler's lifetime came true in the 1970s: Leni Riefenstahl was an internationally acclaimed artist, traveling to Paris, London, and New York. Now it was not old or new Nazis trying to claim her as one of their own, but rather the artists of pop culture.

In 1974, she got a surprising offer from the *Sunday Times* to photograph Mick Jagger and his wife Bianca. The couple was willing to pose for the camera only if Riefenstahl was the photographer. She flew to London and was charmed by these fans. There is a beautiful color photograph in which Jagger, wearing a partially unbuttoned shirt, has flung his arm around a smiling Riefenstahl and is casting a lascivious glance at her. Her beaming expression tells us that she was finally able to eclipse Hitler. Bianca Jagger published an article about her new German friend in Andy Warhol's *Interview*, which celebrates Riefenstahl as a brave, determined artist out to prove that a beautiful woman could also be intelligent and successful.[1]

o   o   o

The Telluride Film Festival proudly called itself the smallest of the big film festivals, and regarded its artistic mission as seeking out films whose interest was not purely market-driven. Thus the program was not published until the morning of the opening day of the festival, because they did not want participants to come on the basis of name appeal. Telluride brought together Hollywood stars and avant-garde theorists. One of the Festival's initiators was James Card, who worked closely with Henri Langlois from the Cinémathèque Française in Paris and Iris Barry of the Museum of Modern Art in New York. The cofounder was Tom Luddy of the Pacific Film Archive, which has officially belonged to the University of California, Berkeley since 1971. Luddy in particular was intent on preserving nonprofit avant-garde films. Card and Luddy invited Riefenstahl to Telluride. She was one of the first three artists to be honored there, along with silent-film diva Gloria Swanson and director Francis Ford Coppola, although Paul Kohner had tried to dissuade the latter two from attending the festival and meeting with Riefenstahl. Riefenstahl's *Olympia* film and *The Blue Light* were shown. From then on, she was mentioned in the same breath as internationally renowned film artists, and the 2012 festival featured several of her films:

> Since its inception in 1974, the Telluride Film Festival has paid tribute to numerous influential filmmakers and artists. Gloria Swanson, Francis Ford Coppola and Leni Riefenstahl were the first to be honored, and forty years later the prestigious list has grown to include Pedro Almovar, Claudia Cardinale, George Clooney, Penelope Cruz, Daniel Day-Lewis, Catherine Deneuve, Laura Linney, Clint Eastwood,

Colin Firth, Jodie Foster, Stephen Frears, Werner Herzog,
Isabelle Huppert, Jack Nicholson, Jean Simmons, Meryl
Streep, Tilda Swinton, Andrei Tarkovsky, and Agnès Varda,
to name a few.[2]

At about the same time that Riefenstahl was photographing the
Jaggers, an essay by the young American scholar Peggy Ann Wallace about *The Blue Light* was published in *Image*, the journal of the
George Eastman House in Rochester. The article was an excerpt
from her dissertation about Riefenstahl.[3] In reading it, we are
astounded at Riefenstahl's audacity, because we learn that Riefenstahl conjures up the very ghosts that she had shooed away during
her liaison with the Nazis. Her Jewish producer, Harry Sokal,
whom she had stopped mentioning in 1933, was now presented
as her former fiancé. The Jewish screenplay writer Carl Mayer was
suddenly part of her old circle of friends, and Béla Balász, communist and Jew, whose name had been deleted from the film poster for
The Blue Light in 1938, was now billed as someone who had been an
enormous help to her and who had written the dialogue. In 1973,
Riefenstahl was portraying *The Blue Light* just as she had back in
1933, in *Struggle in Snow and Ice*: as a joint production of young,
enthusiastic artists who did not want to bow to the laws of profit
and the strictures of the industry, but instead sought to implement
their artistic ideas freely and collectively and be their own bosses.
And that was not all: The artistic center and head of this troupe
was a beautiful woman who was intent on proving that women too
could direct films. Because Riefenstahl supposedly feared prejudices against women artists, she stated that the script was based on
a legend and did not mention that it had been her own idea. The
main impression a reader takes away from Wallace's essay is that
Riefenstahl was a self-confident, avant-garde artist who preferred
working in a collective. "The most important factor was the spirit"
is a phrase that reveals a great deal about Riefenstahl's ambitious

career strategy.[4] If the Goddess of Fortune offered no more than her coat tails, Riefenstahl clung to them tightly, in the 1970s as well as the 1930s. She had no artistic or personal loyalties because she was committed only to her own advancement, and had no qualms about tweaking the truth. In both 1933 and 1973, Riefenstahl was adept at adapting to the spirit of the times. In the 1970s, American feminists, proponents of collective work, and opponents of the film industry saw her as one of their own.

There were certainly protests in Telluride. She found them distressing, but not enlightening. She had no particular desire to deal with the accusations directed at her, and because she dreaded having to face demonstrators, she turned down a subsequent invitation to the "Women in Film" series at the Chicago Art Festival.[5] She was rewarded for this "disappointment" when she and Horst Kettner were strolling along Fifth Avenue and she saw the entire window display of a bookstore directly across the street from Tiffany's decorated with her Nuba book. Her publisher, Harper & Row, confirmed the great commercial success of her book. Exhilarating conversations with Mick and Bianca Jagger and Faye Dunaway at a fancy French restaurant in New York rounded out her trip. With great satisfaction, Riefenstahl smugly noted the interest being shown to her art in the United States, where people had dared to snub her in 1938. It seemed as though Susan Sontag's critical intervention had only heightened Riefenstahl's significance. Thanks to Jagger, Telluride, Sontag, and the Nubas, she had one foot in the door. Riefenstahl would not rest until she was firmly inside.

One year before her seventy-fifth birthday, she was a guest on a German talk show.[6] Riefenstahl looked astonishingly young and had lost none of her sexual attractiveness. Her hair was dyed blonde, her nails were polished, and she still had a remarkable figure. She provided a slick self-portrait, claiming that as a young woman, she had gone "against the entire industry" so she could fulfill her dream and make a movie, which was unheard of for a woman at that time. Moreover, this film had become a "worldwide success." She herself had been a "worldwide star" before 1933, with regular performances in Paris and London, and telegrams from Hollywood. She did not understand why people wanted to talk to her about Hitler, because she had shot only one film for the National Socialists: *Triumph of the Will*. No one on the talk show seems to have known that she had also made *Victory of Faith* and *Day of Freedom: Our Wehrmacht*. Riefenstahl stuck to this tactic in dealing with her past; as long as the opposite had not been proven, she stuck by her version of the truth.[7]

Her final grueling journeys to Africa had made her aware that there was nothing more for her to accomplish there.[8] *The People of Kau* could certainly build on the success of her earlier books, but she knew that this would be her final photographic foray. Riefenstahl had already discovered a new stamping ground. In 1973, she had taken a diving course near Mombasa. In order to pass the test, she had claimed to be twenty years younger, and was thus able to add a new superlative: Riefenstahl was now the oldest certified diver in the world. On her hundredth birthday, she proudly reported that she had completed more than two thousand dives. She was not going on these dives as a hobby or for relaxation; instead, she soon began to take photographs under water. In her mid-seventies, she was planning her next career move, and she eagerly immersed herself in the latest technology. She was as pleased as Punch with her new camera, which she had ordered in New York. As an underwater photographer, she not only had to be able to dive quite well, but also to master each technique perfectly. Every second counted. Riefenstahl was proving to the world that neither her age nor the perils of the sea would hold her back from capturing beautiful images. Because she sensed that her art would not be exhibited in any museums during her lifetime, she set about creating her own archive by building another house: not a Bavarian-style villa, but a majestic prefabricated building with a great deal of glass and wood, hidden behind trees. She moved from Schwabing in Munich to Pöcking at Lake Starnberg, which tended to attract wealthy people who sought peace and quiet. The heart of the house, the air-conditioned archive, was in the cellar. Enormous steel cabinets stored neatly sorted photographs of Junta, Goebbels, Nuba, SA men, pole vaulters, and sea creatures. In the basement of the wood-paneled house, she collected and archived films, photographs, certificates, prizes, trial documents, and the letters from her admirers. Riefenstahl would live in this house at Lake Starnberg with Horst Kettner until her death.

"I have been writing my memoirs here for two years—it is hard, almost desolate work," Riefenstahl wrote to Bernhard Minetti in January 1985, on the occasion of his eightieth birthday, with cordial wishes and recollections of the good old days when they worked on *Lowlands*.[9] The five years she spent writing the memoirs were punctuated with diving trips to the Bahamas, the Caribbean, Indonesia, the Maldives, and Papua New Guinea. Just as she had in her previous careers, Riefenstahl was quite adept at combining business with pleasure. At the age of eighty, she had become a frequent flyer who was at home in the most beautiful diving sites in the world. Photographs show her with a weather-beaten face and her scuba tank and technical equipment at dream beaches. Only illnesses and accidents could slow her down. There was not a bone in her body that she had not already broken, but she saw that as more of an incentive than an impediment. Riefenstahl freely confessed that she availed herself of medical intervention to preserve her vitality. She took regular trips to Lenggries for live cell therapy treatments. Professor Block, who oversaw her treatments, had been a student of Dr. Niehans from Switzerland. In the clinic, she was shielded from the world and could concentrate on her recuperation without interruption. After every round of treatments, she felt well rested and able to sleep again. She did not provide any information as to what memories, images, or worries had been robbing her of sleep.

The anguish involved in writing her memoirs stemmed from her recognition that her readers' interest would be focused not on her, but on Adolf Hitler. She worked her way around this balancing act by providing many insights into her close relationship with him, but at the same time making it clear that she had been somebody both before and after Hitler. Despite the awkward prose, skewed images, and grammatical gaffes in the memoir, the book sold well. A "worldwide exclusive" advance publication in *Bunte* magazine drew in readers and boosted sales.

In the run-up to the book's publication, a suit that Riefenstahl brought against the filmmaker Nina Gladitz drew even more attention to it. Gladitz had claimed in her film *Time of Silence and Darkness* that nearly all of the Gypsies who had appeared in Riefenstahl's *Lowlands* had been killed in Auschwitz. She brought forth and named witnesses for this claim. In addition, she explained that Maxglan was not, as Riefenstahl had maintained, a "public welfare and relief camp," but a concentration camp. Riefenstahl saw these accusations as an attack on her integrity, and in 1983 obtained an injunction against showing Gladitz's film on German television. Gladitz filed an appeal against this injunction, and after years of litigation, the court decided that Gladitz no longer had the right to claim that Riefenstahl had known about the looming deportation of the Sinti to Auschwitz. Riefenstahl played the emotionally charged diva in court. Anyone who had experienced the angry outbursts of this eighty-five-year-old woman could well imagine that she had already twice attacked other people and bitten their necks.[10] She insisted adamantly and vehemently on her version of the story, no matter how the witness statements read, and maintained that she had had nothing to do with Auschwitz, concentration camps, and death. Her purview had been art, beauty, and the Führer. Riefenstahl made no claim to have been a member of the resistance, and she had no desire to descend into anonymity. And she did not seek refuge with the neo-Nazis. She had never deigned to interact with the ordinary party members; her bond had been with Hitler. She portrayed herself as both an active framer of her life and a victim of her fate. She had rejected the career her father had envisioned for her and put all her energy into becoming an artist. She remained childless and rarely formed a lasting attachment to a man. The most important thing in her life was art, which also brought her to Hitler. Hitler was not a temporal power in her eyes; he was a miraculous, inexplicable phenomenon. The artist-ruler Hitler created a world for which Riefenstahl, as his court artist, provided the visual representation. Hitler stood above her. He was the creator of what she filmed. This did not change until his death and the downfall of his Reich. Riefenstahl lost her privileges, but she gained the exclusive power over her art. She no longer had to share her fame with him. The glory was all hers.

Riefenstahl was the only artist favored by the Nazis who did not suffer a loss of her fame (albeit of a tainted variety) in the postwar period. She never denied Hitler's charisma. She was keenly aware that her association with him shaped her postwar career. The reverberations of National Socialism worked to her benefit.

Academic studies of film have delved into the notional level and investigated the nature of National Socialism's powerful imagery. They looked at the specific capability for truth in the aesthetic realm and the identification of phantasms that point the way to the unconscious. Riefenstahl's art was predestined for these questions, yet she herself refused to provide the answers to them.

The artist dove down and sought her ideal world of beauty at the bottom of the sea. In 1978, she published her first underwater volume, *Coral Gardens*, which was followed by *Wonders under Water* in 1990. As always, her artistic work involved a high degree of physical exertion. The unending blackness began just a few yards under the surface of the water. Those who wanted to bring colorful pictures to the light of day could not be afraid of the horrors of the depths, the cold, and the pitch-black night. Riefenstahl went even farther and sought out proximity to sharks, the murderers of the sea. In her view, fear spurred growth.

Like the Nuba people, the peasants in the Sarntal valley in South Tyrol, or the SA men in her photographic and cinematic past, the fish, corals, and marine creatures could be had for free, and she could take as many photographs as she liked. The sheer abundance allowed for a fine selection. Riefenstahl felt hers was a noble cause, because the world underwater was also being threatened by civilization. She would have to move quickly so as to capture this endangered beauty for posterity.

o o o

In 1990, when Luis Trenker died at the age of ninety-seven, Riefenstahl was surely aware that her own days were numbered. Now that her memoirs had been written, the next gap to fill was a film about her life. For years she had rebuffed any attempts to make a film of this kind, but shortly before her ninetieth birthday, she took a different view. The search for a director turned out to be complicated; nobody wanted the assignment. It was known that people would have to dance to her tune, but a film that reflected only her view would be more vexing than intriguing. Moreover, no director of note wanted to be associated with her. But the documentary filmmaker Ray Müller was willing to take the gamble. They agreed to make a ninety-minute film; in the end, though, it swelled to three hours in order to accommodate portrayals of all her careers. Riefenstahl speaks at great length and gets to play herself in a constantly changing set of costumes. Her recollections are reeled off as though from a tape recorder, and whenever Müller dares to contradict her, she loses her train of thought and chides him. At these moments, the viewer senses that Riefenstahl has scripted her life like a movie role. Of course she toyed with the idea of calling off the project on the second day of filming and felt as though she was in a denazification trial. But her lust for renown won out, and she kept on with it. The greatest experiment in the documentary film *The Wonderful, Horrible Life of Leni Riefenstahl* (the original title of which, *Die Macht der Bilder [The Power of Images]: Leni Riefenstahl*, is far less giddy) is the leading lady herself.

Even though she would soon be reaching the age of one hundred, she could not imagine life as a retiree. When she was not traveling, she was sitting in her cutting room in Pöcking, which was equipped with state-of-the-art technology, and working on photographs of the Nuba or fish. For the first time, there were exhibitions about her in Japan, Finland, Italy, Spain, and Germany. She carefully monitored how her work was received and tried to prevent her films from being shown if she did not approve of the context; only the exhibition organizers whose approach was compatible with her ideas were rewarded with exhibits. Each of her exhibitions was sure to be accompanied by critical articles, but these did nothing to harm sales. Her pictures of the Olympic Games of 1936, of the Nuba people, and of the corals were in brisk demand. Riefenstahl was not interested in artistic inquiry or in experiments; she was "on the quest for the unusual and marvelous, and for the mysteries of life."[11] But this kind of art had now grown uninteresting and inconsequential. The attraction of her pictures derived from their context. The symbolic effect of her name was greater than the aesthetic effect of her images. The tactical skill that her friend Albert Speer had shown in dealing with his past eluded her. Riefenstahl was a jumble of contradictions and emotions. She did not deny the fascination that Hitler had exerted on her, but she showed some degree of dismay about having been so deluded by him. She viewed herself as a victim of Hitler; it was *his* fault that she was no longer an international star.

As she grew older, the Germans seemed to grow less and less eager to ignore her. Riefenstahl was now part of the political culture of the Federal Republic of Germany. Susan Sontag's essay as well as the high regard in which she was held in America made her a worthy object of interest in the intellectual and academic realm. She was the darling of German cultural reporting each time she reached a milestone birthday; every five years brought a spate of clever articles about the incredibly vigorous old lady from Lake Starnberg. She enjoyed serving as evidence of the covert continuity of National Socialism. She did not disappoint her enemies, who could count on her intransigence. She did not pander to them, and insisted on her version of the past.[12]

Riefenstahl was one of the last living connections to Hitler. She loved him, as so many other Germans had, even without having been a party member. For many Germans, she stood for a sad and loving memory of the Führer. She was the subject of countless interviews, illustrated books, and biographies. In the tabloid gossip columns she was pictured with her friends, including American lion tamers, Leo Kirch, Uschi Glas, and Reinhold Messner. When *Time* magazine celebrated its seventy-fifth birthday in 1998, she and Claudia Schiffer were the only German guests of honor.[13] Riefenstahl was flattered by the invitation to join Henry Kissinger, Tom Cruise, and Sophia Loren at the event in New York, and she happily accepted.

In 2000, Kettner went with her to Sudan for the last time. Her desire to see old friends again served as a pretext. Müller would be shooting a film about this journey; Riefenstahl wanted to play the big star one more time. She risked her life for her final appearance in front of the camera. Despite explicit warnings about the politically unstable and unsafe situation in Sudan, there was no holding her back. Wearing a fashionable safari outfit, a big pair of sunglasses, and smeared lipstick, she set off for a country that had been plagued by civil war for the past seventeen years. With temperatures soaring to more than one hundred degrees, she hurtled through the desert in an old jeep, her iron will almost visibly triumphing over her physical frailty. Riefenstahl wanted to savor the memory of the time she had spent with the people of Nuba thirty years earlier. People rejoicing at the sight of her made her forget the strain of the journey. Even though her friends were now old and no longer naked, they still worshipped her. While she was settling into her role, reality caught up with her. The civil war thwarted the grand entrance she had planned. Just as she was getting ready to show the Nuba the old photographs she had brought along, a shot rang out. She was quickly—and forcibly—brought to a helicopter. This helicopter was supposed to bring her and her companions to safety, but it crashed and flipped over. She wound up in the hospital in Khartoum with two broken ribs, a damaged lung, and multiple contusions, and was flown to Munich. In her view, the worst part was not the pain, but the fact that the cameraman (who was himself severely injured) did not film her when she was brought out of the helicopter. Magnificent pictures had been irretrievably lost in the process. Riefenstahl wanted to reenact the scene in Germany in order to incorporate it into the film later on. Most likely she would even have been willing to repeat the crash for the sake of these images. But who would want to see a hundred-year-old woman survive a helicopter crash? Her egocentricity knew no bounds, and she circulated photographs that showed her lying utterly exhausted in a hospital bed in El Obeid with blood-smeared scratches on her face. The most memorable aspect of this film is that Riefenstahl had not changed—she would do literally anything for a good picture.

Cold showers, work, and morphine got her to the age of one hundred. She was cared for by her family, which consisted of Kettner and her secretary. Both remained loyal to her and kept her away from anything unpleasant. She lived according to a highly disciplined schedule and had no patience for anything she deemed nonessential. Her house was antiseptically clean, and her strict love of order was legendary. Her penmanship was thin and sharp, and her hair was still dyed blonde. Tobacco and alcohol were taboo. Her weight had not changed in eighty years, and her ramrod posture

still revealed the dancer in her. She never appeared in public without makeup. Spinal surgery, pneumonia, and plane crashes did not
rob her of her vitality. At the age of ninety-seven, she was still being
photographed in swimsuits, and she cut a fine figure. She came to
interviews in top form and enjoyed showing off her legs, as Helmut
Newton knew when he photographed her for *Vanity Fair* in 2000.
He had seen all her films as a schoolboy in Berlin and admired her
artistry. Even so, he did not shy away from calling her an old Nazi.
She, in turn, was flattered that the infamous Jewish photographer
of glamorous women was interested in her, and the two of them
hit it off. For the photo shoot, he asked her to change into a skirt
because he knew of her proud claim that she had better legs than
Marlene Dietrich. "Well, the pants came off in a jiffy and she was in
the shortest skirt. As they say, 'The legs are the last to go.'"[14] Vanity
and egocentrism had kept Riefenstahl young.

When she turned one hundred, she completed her first film in
forty-eight years. *Impressions of the Deep* is a colorful, psychedelic
film in which fish dance to synthesizer music composed by Luis
Trenker's nephew, Giorgio Moroder. With this film she wanted to
show the beauty that mankind stood to lose if nothing was done to
stop the pollution of the oceans, and to make a political declaration:
"I was never in the Nazi party, and do not feel an attachment to Nazi
ideology. The only organization I belong to is Greenpeace."[15] When
a judicial inquiry was initiated against her once more on charges
of sedition and denigrating the memory of the dead, she was too
tired to go to court again. For the first time, she was acknowledging
that she had become more placid and forbearing in her old age.
She submitted a declaration of intent to cease and desist, pledging
to stop claiming that she had later seen all the people from the
camp she had used as extras alive again. The fight had gone out of
her. More and more frequently, she spoke of her longing for death.
On the occasion of her hundredth birthday in August 2002, she

gathered up all her strength and, surrounded by her friends, she held court in a shimmering dress with high slits up the sides and a plunging neckline.

In March 2003, Riefenstahl went diving with Kettner in the Maldives and Kenya. After another difficult operation in May, she retired to Lake Starnberg. She spent most of her days in bed, but when it came time for interviews, she primped for the occasion. On August 22, she turned 101. Fourteen days later, she died in her house in Pöcking. Kettner was with Riefenstahl on September 8, 2003, when her heart simply stopped beating.

Death had released her from art.

ACKNOWLEDGMENTS

Without Jan Philipp Reemtsma, this book would not have been written. Over the course of five years, he supported my work through his Hamburg Foundation to Promote Scholarship and the Arts and spurred me on as the first reader of this text. I am so grateful to him.

Thank you to Tobias Heyl, my editor at Carl Hanser Verlag, for pruning a manuscript that contained at least three additional books. I would also like to give special thanks to Friederike Barakat for establishing the transatlantic contact.

John Borneman, of Princeton University, is my "American friend" whose hermeneutic distance sheds fresh perspectives on my own country time and again and makes me admire the dauntless nature of Americans.

I am grateful to Bob Weil, editor in chief and publishing director at Liveright, for so quickly recognizing that the dissonance between the two women in this book goes to the heart of twentieth-century history, and to my Liveright editor, Katie Adams, whose enthusiasm and professional dedication have encouraged and supported me. Thanks to Cordelia Calvert for her meticulous attention to detail.

My greatest thanks go to my translator, Shelley Frisch, for providing a fresh reading of my book. It was a fascinating experience to watch her transform the book into a new one. Working with Shelley was a great intellectual and personal pleasure, and I have come to realize that translation is far more than transferring a text from one language to another; it is a process of creation.

NOTES

List of Abbreviations

AdK	Akademie der Künste, Berlin
BA	Bundesarchiv Berlin
BDC	Berlin Document Center
BFAB	Bundesarchiv—Filmarchiv Berlin
DTK	Deutsches Tanzarchiv Köln
DLA	Deutsches Literaturarchiv Marbach
MDCB	Filmmuseum Berlin—Marlene Dietrich Collection
SAdK	StiftungArchiv Akademie der Künste, Berlin
SdK	Stiftung Deutsche Kinemathek Berlin
SdK NLA	Stiftung Deutsche Kinemathek Nachlassarchiv
SdK SGA	Stiftung Deutsche Kinemathek Schriftgutarchiv

I Youth (1901–1923)

The Streets of Berlin

1 Hildegard Knef, *The Gift Horse*, trans. David Anthony Palastanga (New York: McGraw-Hill, 1971), p. 1.

2 The gray composition books in which Elisabeth Will kept her notes are housed in the MDCB.

3 Peter Bahl, "Marlene Dietrich—Herkunft und Verwandtschaft, Teil 1," in *Herold-Jahrbuch*, new series, vol. 6 (2001): 9–94.

4 Marlene Dietrich, quoted in Maria Riva, *Marlene Dietrich* (New York: Knopf, 1992), p. 785.

5 Leni Riefenstahl, *Memoiren* (Munich: Albrecht Knaus, 1987), p. 21.

6 Ibid., p. 15.

Body, Art, and War

1 Joseph Roth, "Literarischer Wedding" in *Freie Deutsche Buehne*, March 3, 1921; reprinted in Reinhardt Tgahrt, *Dichter lesen*, vol. 3 (Stuttgart: Klett-Cotta, 1995), p. 248ff.

2 Leni Riefenstahl, *Memoiren* (Munich: Albrecht Knaus, 1987), p. 23.

3 Ibid., p. 27.

4 In the Cologne dance archives, there are playbills for performances by the Helen-Grimm-Reiter-Schule. For promotional purposes, the names of well-known pupils were also listed here. Leni Riefenstahl's name is not on any of the playbills.

5 Theodor Fontane portrayed a Berlin society lady seeking rest and relaxation in the Harz Mountains in his novel *Cécile*, which was published in 1884.

6 Peter von Matt, *Verkommene Söhne, missratene Töchter. Familiendesaster in der Literatur* (Munich: dtv, 1995), p. 69.

7 Prominent *Wandervogel* members included Martin Heidegger, Walter Benjamin, Ernst Jünger, Hermann Hesse, Gottfried Benn, and Martin Buber.

8 Robert Musil, *The Man Without Qualities*. Vol. 1: *A Sort of Introduction the Like of It Now Happens*, trans. Eithne Wilkins and Ernst Kaiser (New York: Capricorn Books, 1965), p. 60.

9 "In Berlin, an outdated tradition succumbed to the necessary process of destruction in order to open up the possibility of the birth of a new age. This was a new feeling, one that I had not known before." Maria Ley Piscator, *Der Tanz im Spiegel. Mein Leben mit Erwin Piscator* (Reinbek: Rowohlt, 1989), p. 77f.

10 Isadora Duncan was born in San Francisco in 1878. In the 1910s, she became world famous, danced in Paris, and choreographed in Bayreuth. This barefoot dancer from the New World soon grew too old and too heavy. By the 1920s, her art was passé. In September 1927, she died in Nice during a joyride with one of her gigolos when her scarf got caught in the open-spoked wheels of the Bugatti and broke her neck.

11 Mary Wigman, "The Dance and the Modern Woman," n.d., SAdK, Berlin, estate of Mary Wigman.

12 Heinz-Gerhard Haupt, Die radikale Mitte. Lebensweise und Politik von Handwerkern und Kleinhändlern in Deutschland seit 1848 (Munich: dtv, 1985), p. 110.

13 Riefenstahl, *Memoiren*, p. 43.

14 "The French author of one article, entitled 'Berlin Amuses Itself,' noted with disbelief that even the invitation to a memorial service for the murdered Sparticist leader Karl Liebknecht stated that there would be dancing ['On dansera']." Wolfgang Schivelbusch, *The Culture of Defeat: On National Trauma, Mourning, and Recovery*, trans. Jefferson Chase (New York: Metropolitan Books, 2003), p. 167.

15 Thomas Nipperdey, *Wie das Bürgertum die Moderne erfand* (Berlin: Siedler Verlag, 1988), p. 84.

16 Mary Wigman, *Rudolf von Labans Lehre vom Tanz*. Manuscript written in the summer of 1920. SAdK, Berlin, Estate of Mary Wigman.

17 When the school first opened on September 1, 1920, there were seven girls enrolled; seven years later, the number had swelled to three hundred sixty.

18 Mary Wigman was the lover of the psychiatrist Hans Prinzhorn, who amassed the famous Prinzhorn collection in Heidelberg, and of the psychiatrist Herbert Binswanger, whose uncle, the psychiatrist Otto Binswanger, had treated Friedrich Nietzsche in Jena.

19 Vicki Baum, *Es war alles ganz anders. Erinnerungen* (Stuttgart: Deutscher Bücherbund, 1987), p. 320.

20 Riefenstahl, *Memoiren*, p. 59.

21 Ibid., p. 60.

22 Fred Hildebrandt, *Die Tänzerin Valeska Gert* (Stuttgart: Hädecke, 1928), p. 99.

23 Sebastian Haffner, *Defying Hitler: A Memoir*, trans. Oliver Pretzel (New York: Farrar, Straus & Giroux, 2002), pp. 52, 56.

24 Robert Musil called Froitzheim "a genius of boredom" in his essay, "Randglossen zu Tennisplätzen," in Robert Musil, *Tagebücher, Aphorismen, Essays und Reden* (Hamburg: Rowohlt, 1955), pp. 828–30; this passage appears on p. 828.

25 Riefenstahl, *Memoiren*, p. 50.

26 Harry R. Sokal "Lebt wohl, Leidenschaften! Erinnerungen eines Filmproduzenten." Unpublished manuscript, p. 43. SdK NLA, Berlin.

27 Ibid, p. 52.

28 Marlene Dietrich, *Ich bin, Gott sei Dank, Berlinerin* (Frankfurt: Ullstein, 1987), p. 31.

29 Ibid., p. 26.

30 Ibid., p. 34.

31 Ibid., p. 15.

32 See Klaus Saul, "Jugend im Schatten des Krieges," in *Militärgeschichtliche Mitteilungen* 34, no. 2 (1983): 91–184, esp. 112.

33 Dietrich, *Ich bin, Gott sei Dank, Berlinerin*, p. 20.

34 Detlev Peukert, *The Weimar Republic: The Crisis of Classical Modernity*, trans. Richard Deveson (New York: New York: Hill & Wang, 1992), pp. 14–18.

35 Haffner, *Defying Hitler*, p. 12.

36 Dietrich, *Ich bin, Gott sei Dank, Berlinerin*, p. 25.

37 Ibid., p. 38.

38 Ibid., p. 31.

39 Ibid., p. 28.

40 Ibid., p. 40.

41 Ibid., p. 35.

42 Ibid., p. 29.

43 Ibid., p. 27.

44 Ibid., p. 20.

45 Ibid., p. 41.

46 Maria Riva, *Marlene Dietrich* (New York: Knopf, 1992), p. 33.

47 Dietrich, *Ich bin, Gott sei Dank, Berlinerin*, p. 40.

48 "Surprising as it may seem, I took my father's place—against my mother's will." Ibid., p. 59.

49 Riva, *Marlene Dietrich*, p. 36.

50 Robert Musil, *Precision and Soul: Essays and Addresses*, trans. Burton Pike and David S. Luft (Chicago, IL: University of Chicago Press, 1995), p. 213.

51 Dietrich, *Ich bin, Gott sei Dank, Berlinerin*, p. 53.

52 Ibid., p. 53.

53 Ibid., p. 56.

54 Julius Levin's papers are housed in the DLA Marbach.

II Carving Out a Career (1923–1932)

Early Sorrow

1 Sebastian Haffner, *Defying Hitler: A Memoir*, trans. Oliver Pretzel (New York: Farrar, Straus & Giroux, 2002), p. 61.

2 Elias Canetti, *Crowds and Power*, trans. Carol Stewart (New York: Farrar, Straus and Giroux, 1984), p. 187.

3 Thomas Mann, "Disorder and Early Sorrow," in *Stories of Three Decades*, trans. H. T. Lowe-Porter (New York, Alfred A. Knopf, 1936), p. 502.

4 Stefan Zweig, *The World of Yesterday*, trans. Anthea Bell (Lincoln: Univ. of Nebraska, 2013), p. 313.

5 Marlene Dietrich, *Ich bin, Gott sei Dank, Berlinerin* (Frankfurt: Ullstein, 1987), p. 59.

6 The following remarks owe a great debt to the work of Professor Dr. Gerhard Ebert, who wrote up a chronicle of the acting school (now known as the Schauspielschule Ernst Busch) on the occasion of its hundredth anniversary: www.Berliner-schauspielschule.de.

7 Dietrich, *Ich bin, Gott sei Dank, Berlinerin*, p. 66.

8 Ibid., p. 61

9 Ibid., p. 62.

10 Ibid., p. 66.

11 Bernhard Minetti, in Klaus Völker, *Bernhard Minetti. "Meine Existenz ist mein Theaterleben"* (Berlin: Propyläen Verlag, 2004), p. 34.

12 Gusti Adler, . . . *aber vergessen Sie nicht die chinesischen Nachtigallen. Erinnerungen an Max Reinhardt* (Munich: Langen Müller Verlag, 1980), p. 87.

13 Kurt Pinthus, quoted in Otto Schneidereit, *Fritzi Massary. Versuch eines Porträts* (Berlin: VEB Lied der Zeit, 1970), p. 82.

14 Herbert Ihering, "Publikum und Bühnenwirkung" in *Der Kampf ums Theater und andere Streitschriften 1918 bis 1933* (Berlin: Henschelverlag Kunst und Gesellschaft, 1974), pp. 220–24.

15 Dietrich, p. 67.

16 Ibid.

17 Ibid., p. 68.

18 See Guido Thielscher, *Erinnerungen eines alten Komödianten* (Berlin: Landsmann Verlag, 1938).

19 Joseph Roth, "Die 'Girls,'" in *Frankfurter Zeitung*, April 28, 1925; reprinted in Joseph Roth, *Werke 2, Das journalistische Werk 1924–1928*, ed. Klaus Westermann (Frankfurt: Kiepenheuer & Witsch, 1989), pp. 393–94; this passage is on p. 393.

20 Hubert von Meyerinck, *Meine berühmten Freundinnen. Erinnerungen* (Düsseldorf: Econ-Verlag, 1967), p. 218f.

21 Dietrich, *Ich bin, Gott sei Dank, Berlinerin*, p. 62.

22 Rudolf Sieber in a letter to the regional authorities in Prague dated November 30, 1933, MDCB.

23 I am grateful to Silke Ronneburg at the MDCB for this information.

24 Dietrich, *Ich bin, Gott sei Dank, Berlinerin*, p. 69.

25 Emil Orlik (1870–1932), a painter and graphic artist, was a professor at the Staatliche Lehranstalt des Kunstgewerbemuseums in Berlin.

26 Bodo Niemann, "Orlik als Fotograf" in Emil Orlik and Eugen Otto, *Emil Orlik. Leben und Werk 1870–1932. Prag. Wien. Berlin* (Vienna: Brandstätter, 1997), pp. 59–64.

27 Peter Panter (aka Kurt Tucholsky), "Tragödie der Liebe," *Weltbühne*, no. 43, Oct. 25, 1923.

28 "The flood of historical films that swamped the German cinema from 1919 to 1923–24—usually designated, rather significantly, by the term *Kostümfilme*—was an expression of the escapism of a poverty-stricken, disappointed nation which, moreover, had always been fond of the glitter of parades." Lotte H. Eisner, *The Haunted Screen*, trans. Roger Greaves (Berkeley: University of California Press, 1973), p. 75.

29 Newspaper clipping, no publication details, MDCB.

30 The second Korda movie in which Dietrich acted was *A Modern Dubarry;* she played a cocotte alongside Maria Corda and Hans Albers.

31 *Lichtbild-Bühne*, Dec. 15, 1926, SdK SGA, Berlin.

32 Louise Brooks, *Lulu in Hollywood* (Minneapolis: University of Minnesota Press, 2000), p. 96.

33 Maria Riva, *Marlene Dietrich* (New York: Knopf, 1992), p. 54.

34 Felix Salten in *Neue Freie Presse Wien*, November 26, 1927, MDCB.

35 The letters from Willi Forst to Marlene Dietrich are housed at the MDCB.

36 Margo Lion, born in 1899 in Constantinople to French parents, enjoyed success as a cabarettist in Berlin in the 1920s. In 1933 she went to Paris and made a name for herself as a Brecht performer. She died in Paris in 1989.

37 For a good overview of the world of Schiffer and his fellow artists, see Viktor

Rotthaler, ed., *Marcellus Schiffer: Heute nacht oder nie. Tagebücher, Erzählungen, Gedichte, Zeichnungen* (Bonn: Weidle Verlag, 2003).

38 "In the German-speaking world the *imago* of the twenties is probably not so strongly marked by the intellectual movements of the period. Expressionism and the new music at the time probably found far less resonance than do the radical aesthetic tendencies of today. It was rather an imagistic world of erotic fantasy, and was nourished by theatrical works that at the time stood for the spirit of the age and that today still easily pass for the same, even though their composition does not have anything especially avant-garde about it. The *Song-spiele* that Brecht and Weill composed together, *The Threepenny Opera* and *Mahagonny*, and Ernst Krenek's *Jonny* are representative of this sphere. The subsequent discontent with civilization's progressive desexualizing of the world, which at the same time paradoxically keeps pace with the lifting of taboos, transfers onto the twenties romantic desires for sexual anarchy, the *red light district* and the *wide open city*. There is something immeasurably mendacious in all this." Theodor W. Adorno, "Those Twenties," in *Critical Models: Interventions and Catchwords*, trans. Henry W. Pickford (New York: Columbia University Press, 2005), pp. 41–48; this passage is on p. 42.

39 *Film-Kurier*, May 19, 1928, Berlin, SAdK, Berlin, Nachlass Marcellus Schiffer.

40 Oscar Bie, "Es liegt in der Luft," in *Berliner Börsen-Courier*, May 16, 1928.

41 Hubert von Meyerinck, *Meine berühmten Freundinnen. Erinnerungen* (Düsseldorf: Econ-Verlag, 1967), p. 109.

42 Erich Kästner, "Das Rendezvous der Künstler," in *Neue Leipziger Zeitung*, April 26, 1928.

43 Tamara Matul was born in Moscow on September 30, 1905. She evidently came to Berlin with her parents and brother while she was still a child, and worked as a dancer and stage extra.

44 Roth explained: "There is something fragmentary about its history. Its frequently interrupted, still more frequently diverted or averted development has been checked and advanced, and by unconscious mistakes as well as by bad intentions; the many obstacles in its path have, it would seem, helped it to grow. The wickedness, sheer cluelessness, and avarice of its rulers, builders, and protectors draw up the plans, muddle them up again, and confusedly put them into practice." Joseph Roth, "Stone Berlin," in *What I Saw: Reports from Berlin 1920–1933*, trans. Michael Hofmann (New York: W. W. Norton, 2003), entry dated July 5, pp. 125–28; this passage is on p. 125.

45 Riva, *Marlene Dietrich*, p. 56.

46 See, for example, *Illustrierte Film-Zeitung*, February 28, 1929, MDCB.

47 Leni Riefenstahl, *Kampf in Schnee und Eis* (Leipzig: Hesse & Becker, 1933), p. 9.

48 Information from Hans Rübesame, archivist at the Deutsches Theater, Berlin.

49 "What the public, and particularly the revivalist vogue, nowadays thinks

belonged to the nineteen-twenties was in fact already fading at that time, by 1924 at the latest. The heroic age of the new art was actually around 1910: synthetic cubism, early German expressionism, the free atonalism of Schönberg and his school. . . . It was not, as is usually assumed, the pressure exerted by the National Socialist terror that brought regression, neutralization, and a funereal silence to the arts, for these phenomena had already taken shape in the Weimar Republic, and in liberal continental European society generally." Adorno, "Those Twenties," in *Critical Models*, p. 41.

50 "A social revolution has roared into the land of the poets and thinkers, and has rendered poetry and thinking needless luxuries." J. M. Bonn, "Die wahre Weltrevolution" in *Die neue Rundschau*, 34, no. 1 (1923): 394.

51 For a discussion of the difference between art that stems from a cause and art that aims at effect, see Clement Greenberg's essay "Avant-Garde and Kitsch" in *Partisan Review* 6, no. 5 (1939): 34–49.

52 "Tanzmatinee im Lobetheater" in *Breslauer Neueste Nachrichten*, April 7, 1924.

53 *Züricher Kämpfer*, February 24, 1924.

54 Eugenia Eduardowa was born in St. Petersburg in 1882 and died in New York in 1960. She gave up her large and successful ballet school in Berlin in 1938 and followed her husband, Joseph Lewitan, whom the Nazis dismissed from his position as the editor of the magazine *Der Tanz*, to Paris.

55 Klamt's school brochure was designed by De Stijl artist Cesar Domela. "The design created a bold sense of dance and dance study as a radically abstract conflict between elemental geometric forces, between line and curve, between relative powers seeking to penetrate the closed, inner, circular zone of connection." Karl Eric Toepfer, *Empire of Ecstasy: Nudity and Movement in German Body Culture, 1910–1935* (Berkeley: University of California Press, 1997), p. 256.

56 "Dance was freedom because it made the body into a symbol of those innately healthy emotions that narrative logic suppresses by compelling the body to read the self in the life of another person." Ibid.

57 Ulrich Linse, "Mazdaznan—die Rassenreligion vom arischen Friedensreich" in Stefanie von Schnurbein and Justus H. Ulbricht, eds., *Völkische Religion und Krisen der Moderne. Entwürfe 'arteigener' Glaubenssysteme seit der Jahrhundertwende* (Würzburg: Königshausen u. Neumann, 2001), pp. 268–91.

58 Like Adolf Hitler, Klamt was a confirmed vegetarian. She claimed that she had been adhering to a vegetarian diet since 1911. In the 1950s, she published essays on this topic in the magazine *Vegetarisches Universum. Zeitschrift für die gesamte Lebensreform und verwandte Bestrebungen*, and proudly asserted that she had been living meat-free for forty years. According to Mazdaznan, God does not reveal himself in an unclean body; it is regarded as the loftiest mission of the Aryan to regain his purity of body, which includes eating no meat.

59 Jutta Klamt, *Vom Erleben zum Gestalten* (Berlin: Dorn-Verlag, 1938), p. 104.

60 Leni Riefenstahl, *Memoiren* (Munich: Albrecht Knaus, 1987), p. 68.

61 "Wie Vogue die Mode sieht: Unsere Zeit ist von einem starken Willen zur Schönheit beseelt" in *Vogue* (German edition), October 10, 1928, p. 7.

62 Marion Beckers and Elisabeth Moortgat learned this from photographer Elisabeth Röttgers. See Beckers and Moortgat, *Atelier Lotte Jacobi Berlin New York* (Berlin: Nicolai Verlag, 1997), p. 35.

63 This photograph was printed in *Scherl's Magazin* 6, no. 2 (February 1930): 201.

64 Riefenstahl, *Memoiren*, p. 74.

65 Ibid., p. 69.

66 Ibid., p. 70.

67 Ibid., p. 71.

68 In the first version of the story, which Riefenstahl published in 1933, she did not mention a travel companion or a letter sent to Trenker. She met Trenker in the hotel, and he tried to dissuade her from her plan. "Even if Trenker had explained to me a hundred times, and mobilized every last bit of his male logic to prove that the prospects of acting in a movie by Dr. Fanck were virtually nil, that wouldn't have made the slightest impression on me. That is how firmly convinced I was that my wish had not arisen from mere impulse or accident. I would have tried anything, no matter how obsessive, to reach my goal." She wrote that as soon as she was back in Berlin, she got in touch with Fanck. Riefenstahl, *Kampf in Schnee und Eis*, p. 12.

69 Harry R. Sokal, "Lebt wohl, Leidenschaften! Erinnerungen eines Filmproduzenten." Unpublished manuscript, p. 53, SdK NLA, Berlin.

70 Luis Trenker, *Alles gut gegangen. Geschichten aus meinem Leben* (Hamburg: Mosaik-Verlag, 1965), p. 207f.

71 See Christian Rapp, *Höhenrausch. Der deutsche Bergfilm* (Vienna: Sonderzahl, 1997).

72 Siegfried Kracauer, *From Caligari to Hitler: A Psychological History of the German Film* (Princeton, NJ: Princeton University Press, 1947), p. 112. Eric Rentschler has argued, however, that Kracauer's attitude toward Fanck's films is ambivalent: "Kracauer—for all his ideological misgivings—could not fully deny the haptic frisson of the mountain film." Eric Rentschler, "Mountains and Modernity: Relocating the *Bergfilm*," in *New German Critique*, no. 51 (1990): 137–61; this passage is on p. 145.

73 In 2003, the theme of an exhibition at the Museum of Modern and Contemporary Art of Trento and Rovereto was the fascination with mountains. The captivating catalogue for this exhibition features a great many images that display the mystery and splendor of the mountains. Gabriella Belli, Paolo Giacomoni, and Anna Ottani Cavina, eds., *Montagna. Arte, scienza, mito da Dürer a Warhol* (Milan: Skira, 2003).

74 New mechanical devices such as carabiners made it possible to venture out onto mountain faces that had been considered impregnable.

75 Riefenstahl, *Kampf in Schnee und Eis*, p. 12.

76 Ibid., p. 13.

77 Riefenstahl, *Memoiren*, p. 73.

78 Arnold Fanck, *Er führte Regie mit Gletschern, Stürmen und Lawinen. Ein Filmpionier Erzählt* (Munich: Nymphenburger Verlag, 1973), p. 9.

79 A remake of the film was found in Allgeier's estate, and the Cinématheque Suisse Lausanne has a nitrate copy.

80 "Berg, Film und Seele" in *Der Berg. Monatsschrift für Bergsteiger*, September 1924, vol. 9, Munich Film Museum, Nachlass Arnold Fanck.

81 "I made an agreement with Fanck to function . . . as a sports adviser. More importantly, however, I had to use my South Tyrolean connections to provide financing for him. There was inflation in Germany at that time, and so we needed to raise a portion of the foreign funding for our film, which I was able to do." Luis Trenker, *Alles gut gegangen! Geschichten aus meinem Leben* (Gütersloh: Bertelsmann, 1972), p. 201.

82 Arnold Fanck, "Wie der heilige Berg entstand" [newspaper clipping], Stadtarchiv Freiburg K 1/25, folder 35, no. 1a. This passage is noteworthy because Fanck does not mention his first encounter with Riefenstahl in his autobiography.

83 *Berliner Morgenpost*, December 19, 1926. Axel Eggebrecht praised the film's technology, but could barely tolerate its message. "*The Holy Mountain* turned out to be quite a mundane heap of triteness and malicious misunderstandings. It is difficult to determine how much of that is Ufa's fault. In any case . . . the intrusive propaganda for the cult of the superior blond species of man comes as a surprise." *Die Weltbühne*, January 11, 1927.

84 "Henry Jaworsky, Cameraman for Leni Riefenstahl, interviewed by Gordon Hitchens, Kirk Bond, and John Hanhardt" in *Film Culture* 56/57 (Spring 1973): 122–61; this quotation is on p. 136.

85 Riefenstahl, *Memoiren*, p. 77.

86 Ibid., p. 78.

87 Luis Trenker, *Alles gut gegangen. Geschichten aus meinem Leben* (Gütersloh: Bertelsmann, 1972), p. 213.

88 Sokal, "Lebt wohl Leidenschaften! Erinnerungen eines Filmproduzenten," p. 54.

89 L. Andrew Mannheim, "Leni," in *Modern Photography*, February 1974, p. 113.

90 Riefenstahl, *Kampf in Schnee und Eis*, p. 25.

91 "There is also quite a bit of sadism in this farce; Trenker in particular is shamelessly mistreated by Fanck here, that is, all the men in the film are positively emasculated." Jan-Christopher Horak, "Dr. Arnold Fanck: Träume vom Wolkenmeer und einer guten Stube," in Horak, ed., *Berge, Licht und Traum. Dr. Arnold Fanck und der deutsche Bergfilm* (Munich: GeraNova Bruckmann, 1997), pp. 14–67; this passage is on p. 36.

92 Riefensthal, *Kampf in Schnee und Eis*, p. 39.

93 Riefenstahl, *Memoiren*, p. 98.

94 One exception was a minor role in the movie *Das Schicksal derer von Habsburg—Die Tragödie eines Kaiserreiches* (1928), directed by Rudolf Raffé, in which she played Baroness Vetsera, the lover of the crown prince of Austria. Her fellow cast member, Carmen Cartellieri, a Hungarian-Austrian silent film star, had been making mountain films since the early 1920s, and in 1921 she and Cornelius Hintner, the man who discovered her, had founded Cartellieri Film Productions. I would like to thank Helma Türk in Bad Reichenhall for this information.

95 Riefenstahl, *Kampf in Schnee und Eis*, p. 39f.

96 Harry Sokal, "Lebt wohl, Leidenschaften! Erinnerungen eines Filmproduzenten," p. 71a. In a questionnaire issued by the *Frankfurter Allgemeine Zeitung*, which Riefenstahl filled out on March 25, 1994, she indicated that her greatest flaw was "a lack of humor."

97 "To me, she was 'kitsch' personified and the only good film she ever made I think was *Piz Palü*, where she was in the hands of a very fine director, who wouldn't stand for any sentimental nonsense." Interview with Paul Falkenberg, "Six Talks on G. W. Pabst," *cinemages* 3 (1955): 41–52; this quotation appears on p. 47.

98 Interview with Marc Sorkin, in "Six Talks on G. W. Pabst," *cinemages* 3 (1955): 23–40; this quotation is on p. 36.

99 Fanck was continually accused of having faked individual scenes. He was incensed by these charges. His literary estate contains long letters that refute each accusation in detail. Like Riefenstahl, he could not stand to be criticized. However, he was never able to allay the many suspicions that the filming was not quite as perilous as he described it.

100 Riefenstahl, *Memoiren*, p. 112.

101 *The Wonderful, Horrible Life of Leni Riefenstahl* (1993), directed by Ray Müller. See http://www.amazon.com/Wonderful-Horrible-Life-Leni-Riefenstahl/dp/B00000INUB.

102 Dr. Mühsam in *B. Z. am Mittag*, November 16, 1929; *8 Uhr Abendblatt,* November 16, 1929, Munich Film Museum, Nachlass Arnold Fanck.

103 *Berliner Morgenpost*, November 17, 1929, Munich Film Museum, Nachlass Arnold Fanck.

104 Douglas Fairbanks to Arnold Fanck, in *Lichtbild-Bühne Berlin* 4 (1930), Munich Film Museum, Nachlass Arnold Fanck.

105 Christopher Hitchens, "Leni Riefenstahl interviewed by Gordon Hitchens," in *Film Culture* 56/57 (Spring 1973): 94–121; this passage is on p. 119.

106 Riefenstahl, *Memoiren*, p.117.

107 Ibid., p, 120.

108 Ibid., p. 121f.

109 Ibid., p. 124.

110 Ibid., p. 125.

111 *Bunte*, June 20, 1987; Dietrich's letter to the editor.

112 Josef von Sternberg, *Fun in a Chinese Laundry* (San Francisco: Mercury House, 1965), p. 144.

113 Steven Bach based this information on an interview he conducted with Hans Feld on May 25, 1990; see Steven Bach, *Marlene Dietrich: Life and Legend* (New York: William Morrow, 1992), p. 110.

114 *Berliner Börsen-Zeitung*, February 3, 1931.

115 Hans Feld, "Der Fanck-film der Aafa. Stürme über dem Mont Blanc," in *Film-Kurier*, January 3, 1931.

116 "Das Mikrophon als Erzieher—Stimmbandtraining für den Sprechfilm" in *Scherl's Magazin* 6, no. 5 (1930): 506–7.

117 Leni Riefenstahl, "Zwei Wochen Filmen auf dem Mont Blanc," 1930; typed manuscript, Munich Film Museum, Nachlass Arnold Fanck.

118 Riefenstahl, *Memoiren*, p. 132.

119 Henry Hoek, *Skiheil, Kamerad! Skikurs für eine Freundin* (Hamburg: Gebrüder Enoch, 1934). The cover features a cheery picture of Riefenstahl on the ski trail.

120 In Bolzano people say that Paula Wiesinger sometime filled in for Riefenstahl in hazardous scenes. Paula Wiesinger (1907–2001) climbed the most difficult routes of the Dolomites, and was one of the few women who could achieve the sixth degree of climbing, which was then the highest level on the difficulty scale. She also won many ski trophies. I would like to thank Helma Türk of Bad-Reichenhall for this information.

121 Marta Feuchtwanger, *Nur eine Frau. Jahre—Tage—Stunden* (Munich: Knaur, 1983), p. 204ff.

122 The co-organizer was the German National Association of Visual Artists; all artists living in Germany were invited to participate. Three hundred sixty-five artists submitted their work, and twenty-six were selected, including Spiro with his portrait of Leni Riefenstahl. The prize came with a generous ten thousand reichsmarks, and the contest was promoted with a publicity campaign and numerous articles in the daily newspapers and art journals. Willy Jaeckel was awarded first prize.

123 Susanne Meyer-Büser, "Das schönste deutsche Frauenporträt," *Tendenzen der Bildnismalerei in der Weimarer Republik* (Berlin: Reimer, 1994).

124 Sepp Allgeier, *Die Jagd nach dem Bild. 18 Jahre Kameramann in Arktis und Hochgebirge* (Stuttgart: J. Engelhorns Nachfahren, 1931), p. 44.

125 Luis Trenker, *Kampf in den Bergen. Das unvergängliche Denkmal der Alpenfront* (Berlin: Neufeld & Henius, 1931). It was the illustrated edition of his novel *Mountains in Flames*.

126 Hans Schneeberger, *Der berstende Berg. Vom Heldenkampf der Kaiserjäger und Alpini* (Berlin: G. Stalling, 1941); this book was the model for Trenker's *Berge in Flammen*.

127 Harry Sokal, "Lebt wohl, Leidenschaften! Erinnerungen eines Filmproduzenten."

128 Ernst Jünger, "Über die Gefahr," in *Der gefährliche Augenblick. Eine Sammlung von Bildern und Berichten*, ed. Ferdinand Bucholtz (Berlin: Junker und Dünnhaupt Verlag, 1931), pp. 11–16; this passage is on p. 14.

Blue

1 Leni Riefenstahl, *Kampf in Schnee und Eis* (Leipzig: Hesse & Becker, 1933), p. 67.

2 Leni Riefenstahl, *Memoiren* (Munich: Albrecht Knaus, 1987), p. 140.

3 Klaus Mann, *Tagebücher 1931–1933* (Munich: edition spangenberg, 1989), p. 29.

4 Harry Sokal, "Lebt wohl, Leidenschaften! Erinnerungen eines Filmproduzenten." Unpublished manuscript, p. 80, SdK NLA, Berlin.

5 Riefenstahl, *Memoiren*, p. 150.

6 Leni Riefenstahl to Béla Balázs, February 21, 1932 in Balázs-Nachlass, MTA (Magyar Tudományos Akadémia), Ms. 5021/320; quoted in Hanno Loewy, *Béla Balázs—Märchen, Ritual und Film* (Berlin: Verlag Vorwerk 8, 2003), p. 362.

7 In her book dedicated to Fanck, all these difficulties went unmentioned. "I never want to leave my cutting room at all; if I could, I would sleep there. And the many thousands of snippets gradually became a real film, more visible by the week, until at long last, the legend of the 'Blue Light,' which just a year earlier had been a mere dream, lay finished before me." Riefenstahl, *Kampf in Schnee und Eis*, p. 78.

8 Heinz von Jaworsky, born in Berlin in 1912, was a cameraman for Riefenstahl's films about the Olympic Games in 1936. A specialist in aerial shots, he served with the Luftwaffe during the war. In 1952, he moved to the United States and went by the name Henry V. Javorsky. He died in 1999.

9 Riefenstahl is quoted according to the documentary film by Ray Müller, *The Wonderful, Horrible Life of Leni Riefenstahl* (1993). See http://www.amazon.com/Wonderful-Horrible-Life-Leni-Riefenstahl/dp/B00000INUB.

10 Leni Riefenstahl to Jürgen Kasten, February 9, 1994, quoted in Jürgen Kasten, *Carl Mayer: Filmpoet. Ein Drehbuchautor schreibt Filmgeschichte* (Berlin: Vistas, 1994), p. 38.

11 Carl Mayer was born in 1894 in Graz, and in 1917, he came to Berlin to try his luck in acting on various stages. Between 1919 and 1927, he wrote the screenplays for eighteen films. Mayer, who was Jewish, left Germany in 1933, first for Prague, and then for London. He died ailing and impoverished in June 1944. See Brigitte Mayr, "Aufbruch ins Ungewisse. Carl Mayer: Ein Leben im Exil. Graz, Wien, Berlin, Prag, London," in Michael Omasta et al., *Carl Mayer: Scenar(t)ist* (Vienna: Synema Gesellschaft für Film und Medien, 2003), pp. 9–52.

12 Fanck's *Stürme über dem Mont Blanc. Ein Filmbildbuch* (Basel: Concordia Verlag, 1931) was the only text in which he mentioned Mayer's work on the film, giving credit to a "Karl Maier" for "participation in the staging."

13 Joseph Roth, "Der letzte Mann," in *Frankfurter Zeitung*, January 8, 1925; quoted in Hans Helmut Prinzler, ed., *Friedrich Wilhelm Murnau. Ein Melancholiker des Films* (Berlin: Bertz + Fischer Verlag, 2003), pp. 165–67; this quotation is on pp. 165–66.

14 Riefenstahl, *Memoiren*, p. 137f.

15 "From now on, I want only to be an artist, and nothing else. I have also decided to steer clear of any kind of revolutionary affiliation and do not wish to maintain contact with anyone." Balázs's diary entry in Vienna, dated December 4, 1919, in Èva Karádi and Erzsébet Vezér, *Georg Lukacs, Karl Mannheim und der Sonntagskreis* (Frankfurt: Sendler, 1985), p. 121f.

16 Béla Balázs to Emma Ritoók, fall 1919, quoted in Èva Karádi, "Introduction," in Karádi and Vezér, *Georg Lukacs, Karl Mannheim und der Sonntagskreis*, pp. 7–27; this passage is on p. 21.

17 His first monograph about film theory was published in March 1924: *Visible Man or the Culture of Film*; his second, *The Spirit of Film*, followed in 1930.

18 Letter from Heinz von Jaworsky to Joseph Zsuffa, dated December 9, 1976, quoted in Joseph Zsuffa, *Béla Balázs: The Man and the Artist* (Berkeley: University of California Press, 1987), p. 215.

19 See Massimo Locatelli: *Béla Balázs. Die Physiognomik des Films* (Berlin: Vistas, 1999), p. 32.

20 Riefenstahl, *Kampf in Schnee und Eis*, p. 69.

21 Riefenstahl, *Memoiren*, p. 144

22 Ibid., p. 141.

23 Ibid., p. 151.

24 *Film-Kurier* 14, no. 73 (March 26, 1932).

25 Hermann Sinsheimer, "Zwei Legenden. Das blaue Licht im Ufapalast am Zoo," in *Berliner Tagblatt*, March 26, 1932, SdK SGA, Berlin.

26 In 1932, all the advertisements read: "A joint effort by Leni Riefenstahl, Béla Balázs, Hans Schneeberger; production: LR Studio of H. R. Sokal-Film Inc. in Aafa Special Distribution."

27 "Italy's highest authorities gave their approval to what would rightly be considered the first international event of this type. The 1932 festival was held on the terrace of the Hotel Excelsior on the Venice Lido, and while at that stage it was not a competitive event, it included foremost films which became classics in the history of cinema: *It Happened One Night* by Frank Capra, *Grand Hotel* by Edmund Goulding, *The Champ* by King Vidor, *Frankenstein* by James Whale, *Zemlya* [Earth] by Aleksandr Dovzhenko, *Gli uomini, che mascalzoni* [What Scoundrels Men Are!] by Mario Camerini, and *À Nous la Liberté* by René Clair." www.labiennale.org/en/cinema/history/en/4791.html.

28 "Something unexpected to everyone involved in the movie occurred at the premiere in Berlin. A good many newspapers in Berlin found the film's romanticism phony and ran negative reviews. The most prominent of these critics were

Jews. This was in early 1932. Riefenstahl had just read Hitler's *Mein Kampf*. Inspired by his theories, and a perennial sore loser, she now took the negative statements about her film as a reason to become a passionate anti-Semite overnight." Sokal, "Lebt wohl, Leidenschaften! Erinnerungen eines Filmproduzenten," p. 99.

29 Riefenstahl, *Kampf in Schnee und Eis*, p. 6.

30 Arnold Fanck, *Er führte Regie mit Gletschern, Stürmen und Lawinen. Ein Filmpionier erzählt* (Munich: Nymphenburger Verlag, 1973), p. 253.

31 Ibid., p. 254.

32 *Film-Kurier*, no. 108 (May 10, 1926).

33 For a general overview, see Hans-Michael Bock, Wolfgang Jacobsen, Jörg Schöning, and Erika Wottrich, eds., *Deutsche Universal. Transatlantische Verleih- und Produktionsstrategien eins Hollywood-Studios in den 20er und 30er Jahren* (Hamburg: edition text + kritik, 2001).

34 "One of the jobs he certainly did was to fit out the expedition to shoot the film *S.O.S. Eisberg*, a polar adventure with Luis Trenker [and] Ernst Udet." Eric Hobsbawm, *Interesting Times: A Twentieth-Century Life* (New York: Pantheon, 2003), p. 51.

35 "A cost estimate projected film expenses of Mk 7,000,000. The four airplanes were estimated at Mk 60,000, including fuel and oil; 600,000 m of film stock, developed and copied, also estimated at Mk 60,000; fees for the director Mk 95,000, for the lead actors Leni Riefenstahl and Ernst Udet Mk 35,000 each, Sepp Rist Mk 12,000, for the cameramen Hans Schneeberger and Richard Angst Mk 1000 and Mk 800 per month." Werner Klipfel, *Vom Feldberg zur weissen Hölle von Piz Palü. Die Freiburger Bergfilmpioniere Dr. Arnold Fanck und Sepp Allgeier* (Freiburg: Schillinger Verlag, 1999), p. 37.

36 Riefenstahl, *Memoiren*, p. 166.

37 Hans Ertl in the movie *Der Gratwanderer. Die Lehren des Filmpioniers Hans Ertl*, by Hannes Zell (1995).

38 Ernst Sorge, *With 'Plane, Boat, & Camera in Greenland: An Account of the Universal Dr. Fanck Greenland Expedition* (New York: D. Appleton-Century Co., Inc., 1936), pp. 77–78.

39 Fanck, *Er führte Regie mit Gletschern, Stürmen und Lawinen. Ein Filmpionier Erzählt*, p. 266.

40 Riefenstahl, *Memoiren*, p. 152.

41 Ibid., p. 154f.

42 Ibid., p. 157.

43 Ibid., p. 158.

44 Ibid.

45 Ian Kershaw's biography of Hitler concludes, unsurprisingly, that Hitler did not in fact appreciate people who contradicted him or posed awkward questions;

he would note their names and, sooner or later, they fell from favor. Ian Kershaw, *Hitler: 1889–1936* (New York: W. W. Norton, 1999), p. 342.

46 Riefenstahl, *Memoiren*, p. 159.

47 Ibid.

48 Ibid., p. 160.

49 Ian Kershaw writes, "In the giant state of Prussia, embracing two-thirds of Reich territory, the NSDAP's vote of 36.3 per cent made it easily the largest party, now far ahead of the SPD which had been the dominant party since 1919. Since the previous election, in 1928, the Nazis had held six seats in the Prussian Landtag. Now they had 162 seats. In Bavaria, with 32.5 per cent, they came to within 0.1 per cent of the ruling BVP. In Württemberg, they rose from 1.8 per cent in 1928, to 26.4 per cent. In Hamburg, they attained 31.2 per cent. And in Anhalt, with 40.9 per cent, they could nominate the first Nazi Minister President of a German state." Kershaw, *Hitler: 1889–1936*, p. 364.

50 Sorge, *With 'Plane, Boat, & Camera in Greenland*, pp. 202–3.

51 "As one looked into Hitler's face and tried to think of some social group which looked approximately like that, there came to mind the dubious peddlers of dubious postcards as carriers of similar faces, those peddlers of a certain type who climb up and down the stairs of city apartment houses." Max Picard, *Hitler in Our Selves*, trans. Heinrich Hauser (Washington, D.C.: H. Regnery Co., 1947), p. 80.

52 Riefenstahl, *Memoiren*, p. 181.

53 Ernst Hanfstaengl, *Hitler: The Missing Years*, trans. John Toland (New York: Arcade Publishing, 1994), p. 193.

54 Ibid.

55 *Film-Kurier*, August 17, 1929.

56 Josef von Sternberg, *Fun in a Chinese Laundry* (San Francisco, CA: Mercury House, 1965), p. 228.

57 See Werner Sudendorf, "Produktionsgeschichte" in Sudendorf, ed., *Marlene Dietrich, Dokumente, Essays, Filme* (Munich: Hanser, 1977), pp. 65–76.

58 Von Sternberg, *Fun in a Chinese Laundry*, p. 137.

59 Heinrich Mann, *Ein Zeitalter wird besichtigt* (Berlin: Aufbau, 1973), p. 345.

60 See Luise Dirscherl and Gunther Nickel, eds., *Der blaue Engel. Die Drehbuchentwürfe* (St. Ingbert: Röhrig Universitätsverlag, 2000).

61 Von Sternberg, *Fun in a Chinese Laundry*, p. 231.

62 There are many versions of how, why, and where Sternberg discovered Marlene Dietrich. Nearly everyone involved claimed to have been the one to have led him to her. The discussion that follows draws primarily on von Sternberg's own account.

63 From the 1984 documentary film *Marlene*, directed by Maximilian Schell.

64 Von Sternberg, *Fun in a Chinese Laundry*, p. 235.

65　Friedrich Hollaender, *Von Kopf bis Fuss. Mein Leben mit Text und Musik* (Bonn: Henschelverlag, 1996), p. 219.

66　Marlene Dietrich, in a conversation with Maximilian Schell in the 1984 documentary film *Marlene*, directed by Schell.

67　Von Sternberg, *Fun in a Chinese Laundry*, p. 237.

68　Dietrich, in a conversation with Schell in *Marlene* (1984).

69　Sebastian Haffner, *Defying Hitler: A Memoir*, trans. Oliver Pretzel (New York: Farrar, Straus & Giroux, 2002), p. 84.

70　See "Das Kollektiv der Dichter. Jannings' erstes Tonfilmwerk," in *Film-Kurier*, October 26, 1929.

71　The National Socialists drove the musicians in this outstanding band out of Germany. One of them, Franz Wachsmann, became an important film composer in Hollywood; another, Martin Roman, was sent to Theresienstadt and there founded the Ghetto Swingers. Roman survived both Theresienstadt and Auschwitz, and died in 1996.

72　Von Sternberg, *Fun in a Chinese Laundry*, p. 145.

73　Ibid., p. 146.

74　"The other actors in *The Blue Angel* cast were not exactly sociable. Yet that was nothing compared to Emil Jannings, who hated all of creation, himself included. Sometimes we had to wait two full hours in our dressing rooms until Jannings was at last 'ready to work,' and during these two hours, von Sternberg would put to use all of his inexhaustible imagination to lure this psychopathic stellar performer onto the set." Marlene Dietrich, *Ich bin, Gott sei Dank, Berlinerin* (Frankfurt: Ullstein, 1987), p. 81.

75　Ibid., p. 82.

76　Ibid., p. 84.

77　Theodor Fontane, "Berliner Ton" in Heinz Knobloch, *Der Berliner zweifelt immer. Seine Stadt in Feuilletons von damals* (Berlin: Verlag der Morgen, 1977), pp. 172–79.

78　*Film-Kurier*, December 21, 1929.

79　Von Sternberg, *Fun in a Chinese Laundry*, p. 226.

80　Letter from Josef von Sternberg to Frieda Grafe, August 31, 1969, in Frieda Grafe, *Aus dem Off. Zum Kino in den Sechzigern* (Berlin: Brinkmann U. Bose, 2003), p. 196.

81　Riza von Sternberg (née Royce) was two years younger than Marlene, and also an actress. She and von Sternberg had married in 1926.

82　Von Sternberg, *Fun in a Chinese Laundry*, p. 225.

83　Maria Riva, *Marlene Dietrich* (New York: Knopf, 1992), p. 63.

84　"Marlene Dietrich geht nach Hollywood," in *Tempo*, no. 37 (February 13, 1930).

85　*Film-Kurier*, February 14, 1930.

86　Von Sternberg, *Fun in a Chinese Laundry*, p. 242.

87　"Every object seen in *The Blue Angel* is there because the director wanted it there; nothing comes before the camera accidentally. Sternberg abominated what he called 'dead space' between the camera eye and the actors, and he filled this with a profusion of props. At the same time, however, he wanted to stimulate the imagination by concealing parts of his set: through objects looming into the frame from above or below, or double framing it with stove-pipes or screens or pillars, or draping gauze over part of it." S. S. Prawer, *The Blue Angel* (New York: Palgrave Macmillan, 2002), p. 33f.

88 Haffner, *Defying Hitler*, p. 87.

89 Riva, *Marlene Dietrich*, p. 66.

90 *Die Filmwoche*, April 9, 1930.

III Success (1932–1939)

Hollywood

1 *Bremen* Passenger List Archive of the Handelskammer Bremen Archive Ident. No. AIII15-April 2, 1930 N. There were 1,208 passengers on board.

2 *Reichsfilmblatt*, May 17, 1930.

3 *Berliner Börsen-Courier* 62, no. 156 (April 2, 1930).

4 Raoul Ploquin, "Ein Gespräch mit Heinrich Mann," in *Revue du Cinéma* 2, no. 17 (December 1, 1930); quoted in Werner Sudendorf, *Marlene Dietrich, Dokumente, Essays, Filme* (Munich: Hanser, 1977), p. 92.

5 Josef von Sternberg, *Fun in a Chinese Laundry* (San Francisco: Mercury House, 1965), pp. 243–44.

6 Ibid., p. 245.

7 Ibid.

8 "I had on what any German wore when traveling—a gray flannel suit and a slouch hat, very manly, and gloves. All the Americans had black dresses and pearls and mink coats and the orchids, ropes of orchids." Marlene Dietrich, quoted by Leo Lerman in a journal entry dated August 19, 1971, in Leo Lerman, *The Grand Surprise: The Journals of Leo Lerman* (New York: Knopf, 2007), p. 351.

9 Marlene Dietrich, *Ich bin, Gott sei Dank, Berlinerin* (Frankfurt: Ullstein, 1987), p. 106.

10 Ibid., p. 107.

11 Salka Viertel, *The Kindness of Strangers* (New York: Holt, Rinehart, and Winston, 1969); p. 183.

12 Dietrich, *Ich bin, Gott sei Dank, Berlinerin*, p. 108.

13 Von Sternberg, *Fun in a Chinese Laundry*, pp. 158–59.

14 Adolphe Menjou was paid $20,000 for this movie, and Gary Cooper $6,750. Dietrich brought up the rear with $5,625.

15 Dietrich, *Ich bin, Gott sei Dank, Berlinerin*, p. 112f.

16 Drake Stutesman uses the example of the hats in *Morocco* to show the sub-

tlety of von Sternberg's cinematic subtexts. See Drake Stutesman, "Storytelling: Marlene Dietrich's Face and John Frederics' Hats" in Rachel Moseley, ed., *Fashioning Film Stars: Dress, Culture, Identity* (London: British Film Institute, 2005), pp. 27–38.

17 This scene has been analyzed in detail in queer and lesbian studies. See especially Andrea Weiss, *Vampires and Violets: Lesbians in Film* (New York: Penguin, 1993); Andrea Weiss, "A Queer Feeling When I Look at You: Hollywood Stars and Lesbian Spectatorship in the 1930s," in Christine Gledhill, ed., *Stardom: Industry of Desire* (London: Routledge, 1991), pp. 283–99; Patricia White, *Uninvited: Classical Hollywood Cinema and Lesbian Representability* (Bloomington: Indiana University Press, 1999).

18 See Sybil DelGaudio, "Stylization as Distance: Morocco and the Devil is a Woman" in DelGaudio, *Dressing the Part: Sternberg, Dietrich, and Costume* (Madison, NJ: Fairleigh Dickinson University Press, 1993), pp. 99–126.

19 Quoted in Herman G. Weinberg, *Josef von Sternberg: A Critical Study* (New York: Dutton, 1967), p. 56.

20 Roland Barthes, "The Face of Garbo," in Barthes, *Mythologies*, trans. Annette Lavers (New York: Farrar, Straus and Giroux, 1972), pp. 56–57; this passage is on p. 56.

21 Dietrich, *Ich bin, Gott sei Dank, Berlinerin*, p. 109.

22 Quoted in Peter Bogdanovich, *Who the Hell's In It? Portraits and Conversations* (New York, Alfred Knopf, 2004), p. 378–79.

23 Carlo Ginzburg, "Geschichte und Geschichten. Über Archive, Marlene Dietrich und die Lust an der Geschichte. Carlo Ginzburg im Gespräch mit Adriano Sofri" in Ginzburg, *Spurensicherungen. Über verborgene Geschichte, Kunst und soziales Gedächtnis* (Munich: Klaus Wagenbach, 1988), pp. 7–29; this quotation is on p. 20.

24 Franz Hessel, "Marlene als Mutter, Marlene als Kind" in Hessel, *Sämtliche Werke*, vol. 3, *Städte und Porträts* (Oldenburg: Igel Verlag, 1999), pp. 223–32; this passage is on p. 231.

25 Maria Riva, *Marlene Dietrich* (New York: Knopf, 1992), p. 94.

26 Ibid., p. 102.

27 Stephen Spender, *World Within World: The Autobiography of Stephen Spender* (Berkeley: University of California Press, 1966), p. 130.

28 Dietrich, *Ich bin, Gott sei Dank, Berlinerin*, p. 118.

29 Quoted in Diane Johnson, *Dashiell Hammett: A Life* (New York: Random House, 1983), p. 100.

30 Marlene Dietrich to Rudi Sieber, n.d., MDCB.

31 A letter from European Paramount dated June 30, 1932, states that Monsieur Sieber, "qui parle le francais, l'anglais et l'allemand s'occupera specialement de la mise en scène de nos productions tournées dans ces langues." The contract was for a term of one year. MDCB.

32 She added that she had seen a miracle of this sort only one other time, when Luchino Visconti was making a film with his lover, Helmut Berger. Dietrich, *Ich bin, Gott sei Dank, Berlinerin*, p. 114.

33 Von Sternberg, *Fun in a Chinese Laundry*, p. 225.

34 Dietrich, *Ich bin, Gott sei Dank, Berlinerin*, p. 115.

35 He added, "I then put her into the crucible of my conception, blended her image to correspond with mine, and, pouring lights on her until the alchemy was complete, proceeded with the test." Von Sternberg, *Fun in a Chinese Laundry*, p. 237.

36 Josef von Sternberg to Marlene Sieber, May 11, 1933, MCDB.

37 Riva, *Marlene Dietrich*, p. 172.

38 Ibid., p. 173. This account is a blend of Riva's and Dietrich's descriptions. The passages about the preparations for shooting represent a rare instance of congruent descriptions by the two women.

39 Ibid., p. 174.

40 He worked with his trusted staff: Jules Furthman wrote the script, Lee Garmes did the camera work, and Hans Dreier, a German, designed the sets.

41 Walter Wanger had discovered Travis Banton in the 1920s in New York and hired him for Paramount. He quickly rose to the position of head designer and was one of the most prominent set designers in the movie industry. Banton worked for Mae West, Carole Lombard, and Claudette Colbert in addition to Dietrich.

42 The Motion Picture Production Code known as the Hays Code was adopted by the Motion Picture Producers and Distributors of America in 1930 on a voluntary basis, and made mandatory in 1934. The Hays Code was abandoned in 1968.

43 Marlene Dietrich to Rudi Sieber, June 19, 1931, MDCB.

44 Marlene Dietrich to Rudi Sieber, June 1931, MDCB.

45 Marlene Dietrich to Rudi Sieber, June 4, 1931; quoted in J. David Riva and Guy Stern, eds., *A Woman at War: Marlene Dietrich Remembered* (Detroit: Wayne State University Press, 2006), p. 19.

46 Marlene Dietrich to Rudi Sieber, December 10, 1931, MDCB.

47 Walter Reisch to Marlene Dietrich, November 1, 1931, MDCB.

48 Walter Reisch, who was born in 1903 in Vienna, worked for Ufa in Berlin. His screenplay credits included *F.P. 1 Is Not Responding* with Hans Albers. In 1933, he returned to Vienna and worked with Willi Forst. In 1937, he immigrated to Hollywood, where he worked on *Ninotchka* with Greta Garbo and *Niagara* with Marilyn Monroe. In 1954, he was awarded an Oscar for his *Titanic* screenplay. Like Wilder and Kolpé, he was one of Dietrich's oldest friends. Reisch died in Los Angeles in 1983.

49 Marlene Dietrich to Rudi Sieber, December 20, 1931, MDCB.

50 Tamara Matul to Rudi Sieber, July 21, 1931, MDCB.

51 Von Sternberg's silent film *The Case of Lena Smith* (1929) was also based on a story of maternal love. See Alexander Hortwart and Michael Omasta, eds., *Josef von Sternberg: The Case of Lena Smith* (Vienna: Österreichisches Filmmuseum, 2007).

52 Telegram from B. P. Schulberg to Emanuel Cohen; quoted in Peter Baxter, *Just Watch!: Sternberg, Paramount, and America* (London: British Film Institute, 1993), p. 49.

53 Von Sternberg, *Fun in a Chinese Laundry*, p. 264.

54 Walter Reisch to Marlene Dietrich, January 9, 1932, MDCB.

55 Riva, *Marlene Dietrich*, p. 135.

56 Maurice Chevalier to Marlene Dietrich, September 23, 1932, MDCB.

57 Rudi Sieber to Marlene Dietrich, July 17, 1932, MDCB.

58 Rudi Sieber to Marlene Dietrich, September 16, 1932, MDCB.

59 Dwight MacDonald, *Dwight MacDonald on Movies* (Englewood Cliffs, NJ: Prentice-Hall, Inc., 1969), p. 97.

60 Rudi Sieber to Marlene Dietrich, November 22, 1932, MDCB.

61 Marlene Dietrich to Rudi Sieber, December 5, 1932, MDCB.

62 Josef von Sternberg to Marlene Dietrich, January 21, 1933, MDCB.

63 Joseph Goebbels, diary entry dated January 31, 1933, in Elke Fröhlich, ed., *Die Tagebücher von Joseph Goebbels*, vol. 2, October 1932–March 1934 (Munich: De Gruyter Saur, 2006).

64 Rudi Sieber to Marlene Dietrich, March 31, 1933, MDCB.

65 Marlene Dietrich to Rudi Sieber, March 2, 1933, MDCB.

66 Josefine von Losch to Marlene Dietrich, March 13, 1933.

67 Willi Forst to Marlene Dietrich, April 23, 1932, MDCB.

68 Rudi Sieber to Marlene Dietrich, May 8, 1933, MDCB.

69 Marlene Dietrich, "Warum ich Männerkleidung trage," in *Mein Film* no. 381 (1933): 13–14; this passage is on p. 14. She explained why: "[T]hese clothes give you perfect freedom and comfort, which is more than I can say for women's dresses and skirts. And women's clothing requires so much time; it is so draining to buy it. You need hats, shoes, handbags, scarves, coats and all kinds of accessories that have to match. That takes a lot of thought and picking out just the right things, and I really have neither the time nor the interest for that. And the fashion changes every minute, and you have to start all over again."

70 Riva, *Marlene Dietrich*, p. 216.

71 Janet Flanner, *Paris Was Yesterday, 1925–1939* (New York: Viking, 1972), p. 97.

72 Josef von Sternberg to Marlene Dietrich, May 10, 1933, MDCB; Josef von Sternberg to Marlene Dietrich, May 17, 1933, MDCB.

73 "We went into the studio during the filming of *Morocco* [USA, 1930], with Marlene Dietrich and Gary Cooper. There was a deathly silence. A crowd scene: a packed Moroccan cabaret and not a sound. A platform in the middle of the

studio. He was on that platform, in a black velvet jacket. A hand supported his head. He was thinking. Everyone was silent, holding their breath. Ten minutes . . . fifteen. It didn't work. He was not accepted into the higher circle of Hollywood society. He tried to humble 'this Hollywood' by a Europeanism." S. M. Eisenstein, *Selected Works*, vol. 4: *Beyond the Stars: The Memoirs of Sergei Eisenstein*, trans. William Powell, ed. Richard Taylor (London: BFI Publishing, 1995), p. 322.

74 Riva, *Marlene Dietrich*, pp. 293–94.

75 Dietrich, *Ich bin, Gott sei Dank, Berlinerin*, p. 116.

76 In *Time* magazine, their relationship was described as "the strangest director–star relationship of U.S. cinema"; *Time*, November 30, 1936.

77 Josef von Sternberg to Marlene Dietrich, June 4, 1933, MDCB.

78 Andrew Sarris, *The Films of Josef von Sternberg* (New York: Museum of Modern Art, 1966), p. 5.

79 Marlene Dietrich to Rudi Sieber, November 7, 1933, MDCB.

80 See Hugo Vickers, *Loving Garbo: The Story of Greta Garbo, Cecil Beaton, and Mercedes de Acosta* (New York: Random House, 1994), pp. 55–60.

81 Mercedes de Acosta to Marlene Dietrich, n.d. 1932, MDCB.

82 Sam Green, a friend of Greta Garbo's, remarked to Garbo biographer Karen Swenson: "Everyone had to be a lesbian in the thirties, even if they didn't want to be. They certainly dressed up and went to lesbian bars—it was the thing to do." Karen Swenson, *Greta Garbo: A Life Apart* (New York: Scribner, 1997), p. 250.

83 Marlene Dietrich to Mercedes de Acosta, n.d., MDCB. For a brief time, the actor Hans Heinrich von Twardowski and his friend Martin Kosleck were in Dietrich's circle of friends. Twardowski had a minor role in *The Scarlet Empress*.

84 Brian Aherne to Marlene Dietrich, n.d., MDCB.

85 Brian Aherne to Marlene Dietrich, September 21, 1933, MDCB.

86 Marlene Dietrich to Rudi Sieber, November 21, 1933, MDCB.

87 According to Silke Ronneburg, Sieber applied for Czech citizenship for himself and his wife in order to avoid paying back taxes in Germany.

88 Rudi Sieber to Marlene Dietrich, December 7, 1933, MDCB.

89 Von Sternberg, *Fun in a Chinese Laundry*, p. 268.

90 Dietrich, *Ich bin, Gott sei Dank, Berlinerin*, p. 142.

91 Marlene Dietrich to Max Kolpé, April 2, 1934, MDCB.

92 See Peter Bogdanovich, "Marlene Dietrich," in Bogdanovich, *Who the Hell's In It?*, pp. 375–91.

93 Dietrich, *Ich bin, Gott sei Dank, Berlinerin*, p. 115.

94 Riva, *Marlene Dietrich*, p. 159.

95 Marlene Dietrich in *Daily Sketch*, December 24, 1936; quoted in Alexander Walker, *Dietrich* (New York: Harper & Row, 1984), p. 125f.

96   "Dearest . . . how strange that you, too, have to drink—in order to be able to sleep—I am finding the very same thing! I must say, though, that I am distressed by the thought that it could do damage to your face—the drinking!" Letter from Willi Forst to Marlene Dietrich, January 15, 1935, MDCB.

97   "[T]he essence of Los Angeles lies in the fact that it hardly has a center. It is, if one can say this, a fluid, a 'moving' city, not only a city that moves itself—but also a city in which movement, freedom of movement, is a strong premise of life." Cees Nooteboom, "Autopia," in Charles G. Salas and Michael S. Roth, eds., *Looking for Los Angeles: Architecture, Film, Photography, and the Urban Landscape* (Los Angeles, CA: Getty Research Institute, 2001), pp. 13–21; this passage is on p. 15.

98   Information from Cornelius Schnauber, Los Angeles.

99   Neal Gabler, *An Empire of Their Own: How the Jews Invented Hollywood* (New York: Crown Publishers, 1988), p. 340.

100 Josefine von Losch to Marlene Dietrich, May 21, 1931, MDCB.

101 Josefine von Losch to Marlene Dietrich, March 24, 1934, MDCB.

102 Josefine von Losch to Marlene Dietrich, August 3, 1935, MDCB.

103 Elisabeth Bergner to Marlene Dietrich, April 16, 1935, MDCB. Silke Ronneburg reports that it took a long time to figure out who this "Lisl" might be. On the basis of Rudi Sieber's telegram bills—he kept an account of his wife's expenditures—the inescapable conclusion was that "Lisl" was Elisabeth Bergner.

104 Riva, *Marlene Dietrich*, p. 392.

105 *Graham Greene on Film: Collected Film Criticism 1935–1940*, ed. John Russell Taylor (New York: Simon and Schuster, 1972), p. 126.

106 See Hans Dieter Schäfer, Das gespaltene Bewusstsein. Deutsche Kultur und Lebenswirklichkeit 1933–1945 (Munich: Carl Hanser, 1981).

107 Joseph Goebbels, diary entry dated December 21, 1933, in Elke Fröhlich, ed., *Die Tagebücher von Joseph Goebbels*, vol. 2, October 1932–March 1934 (Munich: De Gruyter Saur, 2006), p. 341.

108 "*Desire* with Marlene Dietrich and Cooper, who are both great actors. Especially Dietrich, whom we unfortunately no longer have in Germany." Joseph Goebbels, diary entry dated April 2, 1936, in Fröhlich, ed., *Die Tagebücher von Joseph Goebbels*.

109 Reichsministerium für Volksaufklärung und Propaganda to Alexander von der Heyde, December 12, 1936, MDCB.

110 Richard Neutra and Josef von Sternberg were too egocentric to get along. Neutra never visited von Sternberg in his house, and von Sternberg sold it before 1939—to Ayn Rand. In 1971 it went to an investor, who converted it into condominiums.

111 Josef von Sternberg to Marlene Dietrich, Fall 1936, MDCB.

112 Erich Maria Remarque to Marlene Dietrich, after December 24, 1937, MDCB.

113 Erich Maria Remarque to Marlene Dietrich, April 3, 1938, MDCB.

114 Erich Maria Remarque to Marlene Dietrich, December 14, 1938, MDCB.

115 Dietrich, *Ich bin, Gott sei Dank, Berlinerin*, p. 210.

116 Quoted in Werner Fuld's introduction, in Werner Fuld and Thomas F. Schneider, eds., *"Sag mir, dass Du mich liebst." Erich Maria Remarque—Marlene Dietrich, Zeugnisse einer Leidenschaft* (Cologne: Kiepenheuer & Witsch, 2001), pp. 13–19; this passage is on p. 15.

117 He sent her a postcard from Ascona showing the lake framed by the mountains and several houses on the banks. He proudly noted on the card: "That is my house!" MDCB.

118 Erich Maria Remarque to Marlene Dietrich, n.d., MDCB.

119 Harry Edington to Marlene Dietrich, August 9, 1937, MDCB.

120 Joseph Goebbels, diary entry dated November 7, 1937, in Fröhlich, ed., *Die Tagebücher von Joseph Goebbels*.

121 Joseph Goebbels, diary entry dated November 12, 1937, in Fröhlich, ed., *Die Tagebücher von Joseph Goebbels*.

122 "Telegram Klement. Film of the book sold to Metro. Can't really believe it yet. Would be marvelous. Perhaps a Cézanne in it." Erich Maria Remarque, diary entry dated July 17, 1937; quoted in Wilhelm von Sternburg, *"Als wäre alles das letzte Mal." Erich Maria Remarque. Eine Biographie* (Cologne: Kiepenheuer & Witsch, 1998), p. 267.

123 Erich Maria Remarque to Marlene Dietrich, February 24, 1938, MDCB.

124 Erich Maria Remarque met Ilse Jutta Zambona, a dancer and actress, in 1923, and they were married in Berlin in 1925. Their unhappy, turbulent marriage ended in divorce in 1930. They remarried in St. Moritz in 1938.

125 Erich Maria Remarque to Marlene Dietrich, n.d., MDCB.

126 Erich Maria Remarque to Marlene Dietrich, n.d., MDCB.

127 Erich Maria Remarque to Marlene Dietrich, February 24, 1938, MDCB.

128 Erich Maria Remarque to Marlene Dietrich, n.d., MDCB.

129 Erich Maria Remarque, diary entry dated February 21, 1938, in Erich Maria Remarque, *Das unbekannte Werk*, vol. 5: *Briefe und Tagebücher* (Cologne: Kiepenheuer & Witsch, 1998), p. 280.

130 Erich Maria Remarque to Marlene Dietrich, n.d., MDCB.

131 Erich Maria Remarque, diary entry dated June 21, 1938, in Remarque, *Das unbekannte Werk*, vol. 5, p. 284.

132 Erich Maria Remarque, diary entry dated September 4, 1938, in ibid., p. 289.

133 Erich Maria Remarque, diary entry dated July 9, 1938, in ibid., p. 285.

134 Erich Maria Remarque, diary entry dated July 20, 1938, in ibid., p. 286.

135 Erich Maria Remarque, diary entry dated September 14, 1938, in ibid., p. 290.

136 Erich Maria Remarque, diary entry dated September 23, 1938, in ibid., p. 292.

137 Erich Maria Remarque, diary entry dated November 1, 1938, in ibid., p. 295.

138 Erich Maria Remarque, diary entry dated March 23, 1939, in ibid., p. 299.

139 Erich Maria Remarque, diary entry dated March 27, 1939, in ibid., p. 302.

140 Erich Maria Remarque, diary entry dated March 30, 1939, in ibid., p. 303.

141 Erich Maria Remarque, diary entry dated April 7, 1939, in ibid., p. 303.

142 Thomas Mann, *Tagebücher 1937–1939*, ed. Peter de Mendelssohn (Frankfurt: S. Fischer, 1980), p. 378.

143 Erich Maria Remarque to Marlene Dietrich, n.d., MDCB.

144 Remarque reports that they initially asked for $120,000, then raised the required sum to $240,000. Diary entry dated June 22, 1939, in Remarque, *Das unbekannte Werk,* vol. 5, p. 306.

145 Dietrich, *Ich bin, Gott sei Dank, Berlinerin*, p. 250.

Berlin

1 Leni Riefenstahl, *Memoiren* (Munich: Albrecht Knaus, 1987), p. 193.

2 For a detailed discussion of this terminology, see Norbert Frei, "Machtergreifung. Anmerkungen zu einem historischen Begriff," *VfZ* 31 (1983): 136–45.

3 Riefenstahl, *Memoiren*, p. 194.

4 Ibid., pp. 194, 195.

5 Ibid., p. 196.

6 Joseph Goebbels, diary entry dated May 17, 1933, in Fröhlich, ed., *Die Tagebücher von Joseph Goebbels*, vol. 2, October 1932–March 1934 (Munich: De Gruyter Saur, 2006).

7 In 1992, in the former "Special Archive" in Moscow, the historian Elke Fröhlich discovered the contemporary glass-plate copies of the entire set that had been produced from the original diary entries on Goebbels's orders.

8 Joseph Goebbels, diary entry dated November 3, 1932, in Fröhlich, ed., *Die Tagebücher von Joseph Goebbels*, vol. 2.

9 Joseph Goebbels, diary entry dated November 22, 1932, in Fröhlich, ed., *Die Tagebücher von Joseph Goebbels*, vol. 2.

10 Joseph Goebbels, diary entry dated December 6, 1932, in Fröhlich, ed., *Die Tagebücher von Joseph Goebbels*, vol. 2.

11 In a newspaper interview near the end of her life, Riefenstahl claimed, "I did not gain Hitler's trust and rarely got together with him. I had only one telephone conversation with him in all those years." "'Zum 100. Mein neuer Film.' Ihr Werk, ihr Verhältnis zu Hitler, ihr Tauchprojekt. Leni Riefenstahl mit Hilmar Hoffmann," in *Die Welt*, January 7, 2002.

12 Sebastian Haffner, *Defying Hitler: A Memoir*, trans. Oliver Pretzel (New York: Farrar, Straus & Giroux, 2002), p. 194.

13 Two years earlier, Marlene Dietrich had played the spy X-27 and Greta Garbo, Mata Hari.

14 Joseph Goebbels, diary entry dated December 1, 1929, in Fröhlich, ed., *Die Tagebücher von Joseph Goebbels*, vol. 2/1, December 1929–May 1931 (Munich: De Gruyter Saur, 2005).

15 Joseph Goebbels, diary entry dated June 12, 1933, in Fröhlich, ed., *Die Tagebücher von Joseph Goebbels*, vol. 2.

16 Joseph Goebbels, diary entry dated July 19, 1933, in Fröhlich, ed., *Die Tagebücher von Joseph Goebbels*, vol. 2.

17 Joseph Goebbels, diary entry dated August 16, 1933, in Fröhlich, ed., *Die Tagebücher von Joseph Goebbels*, vol. 2.

18 *Film-Kurier*, no. 199 (August 25, 1933). The first official announcement for party members is contained in National Socialist correspondence dated August 23, 1933, BFAB.

19 Confidential memo from Lange to von Allwörden, dated August 28, 1933, BDC.

20 Arnold Raether to Hans Hinkel, September 8, 1933, BDC.

21 Albert Speer, *Inside the Third Reich*, trans. Richard and Clara Winston (New York: Simon & Schuster, 1997), p. 61.

22 Gitta Sereny, *Albert Speer: His Battle with Truth* (New York: Vintage, 1996), p. 129.

23 "While the rallies of the 1920s had been comparatively isolated party affairs, this year, for the first time, the Party Day became a major national project. All the mass media of Germany were employed to drown the nations in propaganda. . . . Six hundred reporters were given special permission to attend; all the remainder were German journalists. An additional 3,000 reporters were registered to attend the Party Day, but they had no access to the indoor meetings." Hamilton T. Burden, *The Nuremberg Party Rallies: 1923–39* (New York: Frederick A. Praeger, 1967), p. 66f.

24 "'Der Sieg des Glaubens.' Wie der Reichsparteitag-Film entstand: Eine Unterredung mit Leni Riefenstahl," *Film-Journal* (November 19, 1933), BFAB.

25 "Imposante Wochenschauberichte. Vorschau auf den Film vom Parteitag. Leni Riefenstahl erzählt," *Lichtbild-Bühne* (September 6, 1933), BFAB.

26 *Film-Kurier*, no. 277 (November 25, 1933), BFAB.

27 "Der Sieg des Glaubens," *Die Filmwoche* 50 (1933): 1602–3; this passage is on p. 1603.

28 "Leni Riefenstahl oder die DuBarry des III. Reiches," *Paris Soir*, September 13, 1936. Translated newspaper article from the literary estate of Paul Kohner, SdK NLA, Berlin.

29 Wolfgang Ertel-Breithaupt in *Berliner Tagblatt*, August 31, 1933.

30 Joseph Goebbels, diary entry dated September 5, 1933, in Fröhlich, ed., *Die Tagebücher von Joseph Goebbels*, vol. 2.

31 All quotations from "*Der Sieg des Glaubens*," *Lichtbild-Bühne*, December 2, 1933, BFAB.

32 "In Wannsee with L. Riefenst. Advised about the Nuremberg film. She will

certainly achieve something." Joseph Goebbels, diary entry dated September 11, 1933, in Fröhlich, ed., *Die Tagebücher von Joseph Goebbels*, vol. 2.

33 Joseph Goebbels, diary entry dated November 29, 1933, in Fröhlich, ed., *Die Tagebücher von Joseph Goebbels*, vol. 2.

34 *The Wonderful, Horrible Life of Leni Riefenstahl* (1993), directed by Ray Müller. See http://www.amazon.com/Wonderful-Horrible-Life-Leni-Riefenstahl/dp/B0 0000INUB.

35 Joseph Goebbels directed the party's local group leaders not to schedule any other events for the day that the film would be shown "in order to give the party members and people at large the opportunity to attend en masse and thus to make the showing of the party convention film a powerful rally." "Dr. Goebbels ruft auf!" *Lichtbild-Bühne*, no. 284 (1933), BFAB.

36 "Imposante Wochenschauberichte. Vorschau auf den Film vom Parteitag. Leni Riefenstahl erzählt," *Lichtbild-Bühne*, December 6, 1933, BFAB.

37 Note by Leni Riefenstahl, December 11, 1933, BDC.

38 "Joseph Zsuffa assumes that in January 1933, Balázs was in Germany again and must have met with Riefenstahl as well, but he does not supply any sources. We don't know whether and when Balázs may have begun to pursue his claims in court." Hanno Loewy, *Béla Balázs—Märchen, Ritual und Film* (Berlin: Vorwerk 8, 2003), p. 366.

39 Her course of action seems especially disturbing when read against her depiction of her return to National Socialist Germany in her memoirs: "There was also a letter from Moscow, from Béla Balázs, with whom I had a friendly relationship. An ardent Communist, he wanted to remain in Russia for the time being, he told me, then return to his native Hungary. I wept as I held these letters in my hands." Riefenstahl, *Memoiren*, p. 194.

40 By the spring of 1934, Ian Kershaw writes, "The position of the German economy—chronically lacking raw materials, with falling exports, soaring imports, and a hemorrhage of hard currency fast approaching disaster level— had become highly precarious." Ian Kershaw, *Hitler: 1889–1936* (New York: W. W. Norton, 1999), p. 507.

41 "Failure on Hitler's part to solve the problem of the SA could conceivably lead to army leaders favoring an alternative as Head of State on Hindenburg's death— perhaps resulting in a restoration of the monarchy, and a *de facto* military dictatorship. Such a development would have met with favor among sections, not just of the military old guard, but of some national-conservative groups, which had favored an authoritarian, anti-democratic form of state but had become appalled by the Hitler regime." Kershaw, *Hitler*, p. 500.

42 BFAB Berlin R 109I/1929b, sheet 28.

43 Quoted in Jeanpaul Goergen, "Walter Ruttmann—Ein Porträt" in Jeanpaul Goergen, *Walter Ruttmann. Eine Dokumentation* (Berlin: Freunde der deutschen Kinamethek, 1989), pp. 17–56; this quotation is on p. 41.

44 Riefenstahl, *Memoiren*, p. 221.

45 "Cahiers: Certain people have said that you were aided, in both your documentary films, by Walter Ruttmann. – Riefenstahl: I have never had either an artistic collaborator or a directorial collaborator. It has been said, in effect, and you have heard, that Mr. Walter Ruttmann, who made *Berlin*, collaborated on *Triumph of the Will* as well as *Olympia*. To that I answer that I know—or rather knew—Mr. Ruttmann well, but he didn't shoot a single meter of my films *Triumph of the Will* and *Olympia*. During the shooting of these films, quite simply, he wasn't there." "Leni and the Wolf. Interview with Leni Riefenstahl by Michael Delahaye," *Cahiers Du Cinéma* 5 (1966): 49–55; this passage is on p. 53.

46 The timetable Leni Riefenstahl laid out cannot be correct. In October, newspapers were still reporting about Ruttmann's work on the party congress film. "Until late October, the party congress film was depicted as 'collaborative work in the best sense.' Afterwards, however, Ruttmann stopped being mentioned in connection with *Triumph of the Will*. The elaborately constructed framework is not used in the finished product." Jeanpaul Goergen, "Walter Ruttmann—Ein Porträt," in Goergen, *Walter Ruttmann. Eine Dokumentation* (Berlin: Freunde der deutschen Kinamethek, 1989), pp. 17–56; this quotation is on p. 41.

47 "I did not write a single word of it; unfortunately I did not even have a chance to read it or else it would have been written in a different style." "Hermann Weigel: Interview mit Leni Riefenstahl," *Filmkritik* 16, no. 8 (August 1, 1972): 395–410.

48 "Der *Triumph des Willens*—ein deutsches Meisterwerk. Eine notwendige Vorbereitung für den Reichsparteitag-Film 1934," BFAB.

49 Leni Riefenstahl, *Hinter den Kulissen des Reichsparteitag-Films* (Munich: Zentralverlag der NSDAP, 1935), p. 13f.

50 See Martin Loiperdinger, "Riefenstahls Parteitagsfilme zwischen Bergfilm und Kriegswochenschau" *Filmblatt* 8, no. 21 (Winter/Spring 2003): 12–28.

51 "Regiesitzung mit Leni Riefenstahl. Kameradschaftsarbeit der besten Filmoperateure Deutschlands," in Presseabteilung der Universum-Film Aktiengesellschaft, ed., *Feuilletons für* Triumph des Willens, BFAB.

52 See Siegfried Zelnhefer, *Die Reichsparteitage der NSDAP in Nürnberg* (Nuremberg: Nürnberger Presse Druckhaus, 2002).

53 Hamilton T. Burden, *The Nuremberg Party Rallies: 1923–39* (New York: Frederick A. Praeger, 1967), p. 79.

54 A seat for the military exercises cost ten reichsmarks; a spot in the standing area during the roll call of the Reich labor service was only thirty pfennigs.

55 Albert Speer, *Inside the Third Reich*, trans. Richard and Clara Winston (New York: Simon & Schuster, 1997), p. 61. Speer recalled, "Given this background, it is understandable that the Nuremberg Opera House was almost empty in 1933 when Hitler entered the central box to hear *Die Meistersinger*. He reacted with intense vexation. Nothing, he said, was so insulting and so difficult for an artist as playing to an empty house. He ordered patrols sent out to bring the

high party functionaries from their quarters, beer halls, and cafés to the opera house; but even so the seats could not be filled." Ibid., p. 60.

56 "Regiesitzung mit Leni Riefenstahl. Kameradschaftsarbeit der besten Film-operateure Deutschlands," in Feuilletons für Triumph des Willens, Bundes-archiv Filmarchiv Berlin, BFAB 17345.

57 William L. Shirer, Berlin Diary: The Journal of a Foreign Correspondent, 1934–1941 (Baltimore: Johns Hopkins University Press, 2002), p. 20: "Standing there in the early morning sunlight which sparkled on their shiny spades, fifty thou-sand of them, with the first thousand bared above the waist, suddenly made the German spectators go mad with joy when, without warning, they broke into a perfect goose-step. . . . Spontaneously they jumped up and shouted their applause. There was a ritual even for the Labour Service boys. They formed an immense Sprechchor—a chanting chorus—and with one voice intoned such words as these: 'We want one leader! Nothing for us! Everything for Germany! Heil Hitler!'"

58 Martin Loiperdinger, "Riefenstahls Parteitagsfilme zwischen Bergfilm und Kriegswochenschau," Filmblatt 8, no. 21 (Winter/Spring 2003): 12–28; this quotation is on p. 16.

59 For further details, see Yvonne Karow, Deutsches Opfer. Kultische Selbstauslö-schung auf den Reichsparteitagen der NSDAP (Berlin: Akademie Verlag, 1994).

60 Christa Schroeder, Er war mein Chef. Aus dem Nachlass der Sekretärin von Adolf Hitler, ed. Anton Joachimsthaler (Munich: Langen Müller. 1985), p. 73.

61 Steven Bach, Leni: The Life and Work of Leni Riefenstahl (New York: Knopf, 2007), p. 137.

62 Riefenstahl, Memoiren, p. 231.

63 Newspaper clipping, n.d., BFAB.

64 Carl Zuckmayer, Geheimreport, ed. Gunther Nickel and Johanna Schrön (Göt-tingen: Wallstein Verlag, 2002), pp. 93–94; this passage is on p. 93.

65 Telegram, Leni Riefenstahl to Adolf Hitler, May 1, 1935, BArch, R 43 II/388, sheet 151.

66 Stefanie Grote has traced the origins of this film and concludes that Riefen-stahl was assigned the job of filming the entire party rally in order to enhance the party rally archives. Stefanie Grote, "'Objekt' Mensch. Körper als Ikon und Ideologem in den cineastischen Werken Leni Riefenstahls. Ästhetisierter Despotismus oder die Reziprozität von Auftragskunst und Politik im Dritten Reich." Ph.D. dissertation, Viadrina European University, 2004.

67 The Steel Animal was planned as an advertisement for the Deutsche Bahn. However, jolly conductors and happy passengers are not the focus of the film; instead, it centers on hissing steam locomotives and glistening tracks. The film was rejected by the head office of the Deutsche Reichsbahn and was not used for advertising purposes.

68 Hans Ertl, Meine wilden dreissiger Jahre. Bergsteiger, Filmpionier, Welten-
   bummler (Munich: Herbig Verlag, 1982), p. 198.

69 Ibid., p. 205.

70 See David Culbert and Martin Loiperdinger, "Leni Riefenstahl's *Tag der Einheit*,
   the 1935 Nazi Party Rally film," in *Historical Journal of Film, Radio and Television*
   12, no. 1 (1992): 3–40.

71 *Völkischer Beobachter*, no. 1, January 1, 1936.

72 William E. Dodd, *Ambassador Dodd's Diary: 1933–1938*, ed. William E. Dodd,
   Jr., and Martha Dodd (New York: Harcourt, Brace and Company, 1941), p. 296;
   entry dated January 9, 1936.

73 Konrad Heiden, Adolf Hitler. Das Zeitalter der Verantwortungslosigkeit. Eine
   Biographie (Zurich: Europa Verlag, 1936), p. 357.

74 "At Garmisch-Partenkirchen last week, much too occupied to engage in her
   customary practice of skiing up and down the hill in a bathing suit to acquire
   a tan, she was even busier than usual, keeping an expert Nazi eye on winter
   sports for Führer Hitler and giving visitors to Germany a startling picture of
   what he thinks German girls should be." "Sport: Games at Garmisch," cover
   story in *Time* magazine, February 17, 1936, pp. 38–39.

75 British and American IOC members campaigned for a boycott of the Games in
   Berlin; see Reinhard Rürup, ed, *1936. Die Olympischen Spiele und der National-
   sozialismus. Eine Dokumentation* (Berlin: Argon Verlag, 1996).

76 Joseph Goebbels, diary entry dated August 17, 1935, in Fröhlich, ed., *Die Tagebücher von Joseph Goebbels*, vol. 3/1, April 1934–February 1936 (Munich: De
   Gruyter Saur, 2005).

77 Joseph Goebbels, diary entry dated August 21, 1935, in Fröhlich, ed., *Die Tagebücher von Joseph Goebbels*, vol. 3/1.

78 Joseph Goebbels, diary entry dated October 5, 1935, in Fröhlich, ed., *Die Tagebücher von Joseph Goebbels*, vol. 3/1.

79 Joseph Goebbels, diary entry dated October 13, 1935, in Fröhlich, ed., *Die
   Tagebücher von Joseph Goebbels*, vol. 3/1.

80 "An example of Riefenstahl's elaborate preparations is her selection of what
   kind of film to use. She experimented with every major film on the market,
   and after extensive tests, discovered that each had a characteristic quality that
   the others didn't have. Agfa, she discovered, was best with people and faces;
   and the newly marketed Perutz film was best with outdoor shots and nature
   scenes. Rather than make any sacrifice to quality, Riefenstahl decided to use all
   three in Olympia." David B. Hinton, *The Films of Leni Riefenstahl* (Metuchen, NJ:
   Scarecrow Press, 1978), p. 68.

81 Leni Riefenstahl, "Der Olympia-Film" in *Filmwelt*, July 19, 1938, BFAB.

82 Quoted in Bach, *Leni*, p. 155; this article appeared in the *New York Times* on
   August 14, 1936.

83 Hans-Walther Betz, "Das Fest der Völker. Sachliche Betrachtung zum ersten Olympia-Film," in *Der Film*, April 23, 1938, BFAB.

84 Riefenstahl, *Memoiren*, p. 272.

85 Thomas Wolfe, *You Can't Go Home Again* (New York: Scribner, 2011), pp. 530–31.

86 Riefenstahl's production company carved out short films from the outtakes, and these were usually shown before the main feature. Their titles included *Strength and Momentum* (1940), *The Leap* (1940), *White Water* (1942), and *The Greatest Earthly Joy on Horseback* (1943).

87 All of these letters are in Paul Kohner's estate, SdK NLA, Berlin.

88 "Leni and the Wolf. Interview with Leni Riefenstahl by Michel Delahaye," in *Cahiers du Cinéma* 5 (1966): 49–55; this quotation is on p. 54.

89 Joseph Goebbels, diary entry dated November 6, 1936, in Fröhlich, ed., *Die Tagebücher von Joseph Goebbels*, vol. 4, March–November 1937 (Munich: De Gruyter Saur, 2000).

90 Dr. Paul Laven, "Neue Sprechkunst beim Olympia-Film. Der Sprecher als 'Star,'" in *Presseheft zum Olympia-Film*, BFAB.

91 Joseph Goebbels, diary entry dated July 1, 1937, in Fröhlich, ed., *Die Tagebücher von Joseph Goebbels*, vol. 4.

92 Erich Maria Remarque, *Das unbekannte Werk*, vol. 5: *Briefe und Tagebücher* (Cologne: Kiepenheuer & Witsch, 1998), p. 276.

93 This information draws on the following articles in the April 21, 1938, evening edition of the *Berliner Illustrierte*: "Der Führer bei der festlichen Welturaufführung des Olympia-Films im UFA-Palast am Zoo"; "Das Heldenlied vom Sportkampf der Völker"; "Von Tschammer und Osten ausgezeichnet—Adolf Hitler dankt Leni Riefenstahl—Empfang bei Dr. Goebbels"; and on a report in *Film-Kurier* on April 21, 1938: "In Anwesenheit des Führers. Begeisterte Aufnahme des Olympia-Films. Zwei gewaltige Filmwerke vermitteln der ganzen Welt das Erlebnis der Olympischen Spiele 1936."

94 Underwater shots of the kind Hans Ertl made for the *Olympia* film were unusual at that time. Ertl constructed his underwater camera on his own and tested it out in his bathtub at home. At the competitions, Guzzi Lantschner stood with his handheld camera on the high board and Ertl waited in the swimming pool. When the diver lifted off from the edge of the board, Ertl's camera filmed him from the waterline. As the diver entered the water, Ertl's camera did the same until the diver resurfaced right in front of the lens. In order not to be lifted above the surface, he wore sandals with lead soles and a belt with lead weights.

95 "Paris vom Olympiafilm begeistert," in *Lichtbild-Bühne*, July 7, 1938, BFAB.

96 "Aus den Filmkunstwochen in Venedig. Beifallsstürme um den Olympiafilm," in *Völkischer Beobachter*, August 28, 1938, BFAB.

97 Issue 1748 of the *Illustrierter Film-Kurier*, which was published in 1932, carried this listing for the film: "*The Blue Light*: A collaborative effort of Leni Riefenstahl, Béla Balász, Hans Schneeberger; producer: Leni Riefenstahl Studio of

H. R. Sokal Film, Inc." By issue 2797, published in 1938, the listing looked quite different: "Degeto is showing a Leni Riefenstahl Studio film, *The Blue Light*: A mountain legend written and filmed by LENI Riefenstahl; camera: Hans Schneeberger." BFAB.

98 Quoted in Thomas Doherty, *Hollywood and Hitler 1933–1939* (New York: Columbia University Press, 2013), p. 306.

99 Riefenstahl, *Memoiren*, p. 345.

IV War (1939–1945)

The Amazon

1 Adolf Hitler quoted in Max Domarus, *Hitler. Reden und Proklamationen 1932–1945* (Würzburg: R. Löwit, 1962), p. 1312f.

2 Nicolaus von Below, Hitler's Luftwaffe adjutant, wrote: "The Poles were not equipped for modern war. They had 36 infantry and two mountain divisions and one mountain, one motorized, and eleven cavalry brigades, but lacked armor and artillery. Against them the German Army ranged more than 50 divisions, including six panzer and four motorized—a clear superiority. The Polish Air Force was not an independent arm and its 900 aircraft, roughly half modern and half obsolescent, were distributed amongst Army units. The military leadership was good, and some groups fought on doggedly in ignorance of the overall situation." Nicolaus von Below, *At Hitler's Side: The Memoirs of Hitler's Luftwaffe Adjutant*, trans. Geoffrey Brooks (London: Greenhill Books, 2001), p. 35.

3 BA-Militärchiv, Berlin, RW 4/185, sheets 1 and 2.

4 "Reichsministerium für Volksaufklärung und Propaganda, September 10, 1939, Betrifft: Film-Sondertrupp Riefenstahl," Bundesarchiv-Militärarchiv RW 4/185, sheets 1 and 2; this passage is on sheet 2.

5 Erich von Manstein, *Verlorene Siege* (Munich: Bernhard und Graefe, 1976), p. 43ff.

6 Ibid., p. 43.

7 Ilse Collignon described her sister-in-law's appearance in very similar terms. Although her notes are generally quite unreliable, they seem accurate when recounting a visit she and her husband made to Leni Riefenstahl. "I suddenly noticed that she had disappeared, but by then she was already coming down the stairs, wearing a uniform, trousers, and boots, a leather belt around her slender waist, a narrow sash diagonally across her shoulder and torso. 'Well?' she said, and beamed at her brother. 'What do you think of the Führer's war correspondent for Poland?' Heinz regarded her with a mixture of embarrassment and admiration. 'And where are you toting your weapon?' She laughed shrilly. 'You dummy, I've got the camera; that's my weapon!'" Ilse Collignon, *"Liebe Leni. . . . " Eine Riefenstahl erinnert sich* (Munich: Langen Müller, 2003), p. 96.

8 Von Below, *At Hitler's Side*, p. 36.

9 BA-Militärarchiv, Berlin, RH 20-10/ 2, AoK I, appendix to the war diary of General von Rundstedt, August 23–October 2, 1939.

10 Leni Riefenstahl, *Memoiren* (Munich: Albrecht Knaus, 1987), p. 350.

11 Ibid., p. 351.

12 Ibid.

13 Ibid.

14 Alexander B. Rossino, "Destructive Impulses: German Soldiers and the Conquest of Poland," in *Holocaust and Genocide Studies* 11, no. 3 (Winter 1997): 351–64.

15 Von Manstein, *Verlorene Siege*, p. 44.

16 Gerald Reitlinger, *The Final Solution: The Attempt to Exterminate the Jews of Europe, 1939–1945* (London: Vallentine, Mitchell, 1968), p. 36.

17 Riefenstahl, *Memoiren*, p. 352.

18 Joseph Goebbels, diary entry dated June 21, 1939, in Fröhlich, ed., *Die Tagebücher von Joseph Goebbels*.

19 Riefenstahl, *Memoiren*, p. 215.

20 Leni Riefenstahl, "Why I Am Filming *Penthesilea*," *Film Culture* 56/57 (Spring 1973): 194–215; this quotation is on p. 203.

21 Hermann Weigel, "Interview mit Leni Riefenstahl" in *Filmkritik*, no. 8 (August 1, 1972): 395–411; this quotation is on p. 407.

22 Leni Riefenstahl to Professor Doctor Minde-Pouet, August 4, 1939; quoted in *Was für ein Kerl! Heinrich von Kleist im "Dritten Reich*, Exhibition catalogue (Neuhardenberg: Stiftung Schloss Neuhardenberg, 2008), p. 63.

23 Leni Riefenstahl to Professor Doctor Minde-Pouet, August 7, 1939, quoted in ibid.

24 Riefenstahl, "Why I Am Filming *Penthesilea*," p. 195.

25 Telegram from Leni Riefenstahl to Führer Headquarters, BDC.

26 Joseph Goebbels, diary entry dated December 16, 1942, in Fröhlich, ed., *Die Tagebücher von Joseph Goebbels*.

27 Albert Speer, *Inside the Third Reich*, trans. Richard and Clara Winston (New York: Simon & Schuster, 1997), p. 87.

28 Bernhard Minetti, *Erinnerungen eines Schauspielers*, ed. Günther Rühle (Stuttgart: Deutsche Verlags-Anstalt, 1985), p. 151.

29 BA, Berlin, R 43/II 810b, sheets 81–83.

30 BA, Berlin, R 43/810b, sheet 93.

31 For example, in a 1966 interview she claimed: "For this romantic and harmless opera of the highlands, I was absolutely denied the support that would willingly have been granted me for the other films. In any case, everything went for the war." "Leni and the Wolf. Interview with Leni Riefenstahl by Michel Delahaye," in *Cahiers du Cinéma* 5 (1966): 49–55; this passage is on p. 54.

32 Joseph Goebbels, diary entry dated December 16, 1942, in Fröhlich, ed., *Die Tagebücher von Joseph Goebbels*.

33 Riefenstahl, *Memoiren*, p. 391.

34. "The Führer and Reich Chancellor wishes to have a film made about the new Reich chancellery, and Frau Leni Riefenstahl will be commissioned to make it. The overall production costs are now estimated to amount to 700,000 reichsmarks." Memorandum from the inspector general for the construction of the Reich capital to the Reich minister and director of the Reich chancellery, dated May 11, 1940, BA, Berlin, R 43/389, sheet 13.

35. "I also had to make a film about the Reich chancellery, inside and out, and also to film the entire Atlantic Wall. All these films were photographically fine, as always, but nothing special from a cinematic standpoint. I had neither the talent nor the interest for these kinds of cultural films with lifeless objects." Arnold Fanck, *Er führte Regie mit Gletschern, Stürmen und Lawinen. Ein Filmpionier erzählt* (Munich: Nymphenburger Verlag, 1973), p. 376.

36 Reimar Gilsenbach and Otto Rosenberg, "Riefenstahls Liste. Zum Gedenken an die ermordeten Komparsen" in *Berliner Zeitung*, February 17–18, 2001.

37 Riefenstahl, *Memoiren*, p. 361.

38 Ibid., p. 364.

39 Ilse Zielke to Albrecht Knaus, April 18, 1988. Filmarchiv Potsdam/Nachlass Willy Zielke.

40 His estate, which was saved by chance by a staff member of the Potsdam Film Archive, contains a green membership card of the Association of Victims of Euthanasia and Forced Sterilization Association, Detmold. As compensation for all claims relating to his sterilization, which took place in 1937, he received a lump sum of five thousand marks from the Federal Republic of Germany.

41 "Willy Zielke is not the only person I helped and who eventually disappointed me bitterly. But at least for Zielke, whose abilities have always fascinated me, whose *Steel Animal* I fought for with Goebbels, and whom I got out of the mental hospital by assuming personal responsibility for him, there is an excuse: his pitiful lot in life." Riefenstahl, *Memoiren*, p. 283.

42 Ilse Zielke to Albrecht Knaus, April 18, 1988. Filmarchiv Potsdam/Nachlass Willy Zielke.

43 Ibid.

44 Helma Sanders-Brahms's conjecture that Riefenstahl's *Lowlands* represented a plea for tyrannicide is feminist hyperbole. She speculated that Riefenstahl was hoping for the end of the Nazi era and may have wanted to bring it about with this film. Helma Sanders-Brahms, "Tyrannenmord: Tiefland von Leni Riefenstahl," in Norbert Grob, ed., *Das Dunkle zwischen den Bildern: Essays, Porträts, Kritiken* (Frankfurt: Verlag der Autoren, 1992), pp. 245–51).

45 Leni Riefenstahl to Albert Speer, January 11, 1944, BDC.

46 The list of the company's commissions includes a camp for foreigners known as Priesterweg (approx. 250,000 reichsmarks), a camp at Wilhelmshagen

(450,000 reichsmarks), a Russian camp (3,500 reichsmarks), the Reich chancellery (approx. 12,000 reichsmarks), and various bunkers (approx. 30,000).

47   Letter from Leni Riefenstahl to Albert Speer, May 12, 1944, BDC.

The Soldier

1   Franklin D. Roosevelt quoted in David Fromkin, *In the Time of the Americans: FDR, Truman, Eisenhower, Marshall, MacArthur: The Generation That Changed America's Role in the World* (New York: Knopf, 1995), p. 383.

2   Josefine von Losch to Marlene Dietrich, March 4, 1940, MDCB.

3   Unidentified newspaper clipping, "Marlene Dietrich Is Star Who Has Beauty and Brains," MDCB.

4   Red Cross, civilian message from Maria Magdalena Sieber to Josefine von Losch, March 30, 1943, MDCB.

5   Diary entry dated October 9, 1942, Beverly Hills, in Erich Maria Remarque, *Das unbekannte Werk*, vol. 5: *Briefe und Tagebücher* (Cologne: Kiepenheuer & Witsch, 1998), p. 372.

6   Remarque wrote in his diary, "October 31, 1939. Los Angeles. At noon telephone Klement, who said that Levy, the lawyer in New York we hired for our immigration, found out there was a complication in getting Peter [nickname for Jutta Zambona] out, because the puma had worked against it at a department in Washington. Levy confirmed this news explicitly only as having come from an official at the department. I think it's impossible, but haven't seen the puma yet." Remarque, *Das unbekannte Werk*, vol. 5, p. 316.

7   Erich Maria Remarque, diary entry dated July 11, 1940, New York, in ibid., p. 330.

8   Erich Maria Remarque, diary entry dated November 3, 1940, in ibid., p. 333f.

9   Erich Maria Remarque, diary entry dated April 3, 1941, in ibid., p. 349f.

10   Marlene Dietrich, *Ich bin, Gott sei Dank, Berlinerin* (Frankfurt: Ullstein, 1987), p. 188.

11   Marlene Dietrich to Rudi Sieber, February 16, 1942, MDCB.

12   Quoted in Claude Gauteur and Ginette Vincendeau, *Jean Gabin. Anatomie d'un Mythe* (Paris: Nouveau Monde Editions, 1993), p. 130.

13   Marlene Dietrich to Jean Gabin, March 15, 1942, MDCB.

14   Marlene Dietrich to Rudi Sieber, March 17, 1942, MDCB.

15   Marlene Dietrich to Rudi Sieber, September 3, 1943, MDCB.

16   Marlene Dietrich to Rudi Sieber, February 16, 1942, MDCB.

17   Marlene Dietrich to Rudi Sieber, March 17, 1942, MDCB.

18   Letter dated April 16, 1943, from Nat Wolff, Deputy Chief Domestic Radio Bureau Office of War Information, Washington, to Marlene Dietrich, MDCB.

19   Abe Lastfogel to Marlene Dietrich, June 29, 1944.

20   Dietrich, *Ich bin, Gott sei Dank, Berlinerin*, p. 269.

21 Her USO identification card states, "In event of capture by the enemy is entitled to be treated as a prisoner of war, and . . . s/he will be given the treatment and afforded privileges as an officer in the Army of the United States with the grade of captain." MDCB.

22 Maria Manton to Marlene Dietrich, May 8, 1944, MDCB.

23 Interview with Marlene Dietrich in the *New York Herald Tribune*, August 13, 1944, MDCB.

24 "Marlene Comes Back from Italy," *Picture News* magazine, July 2, 1944.

25 Jean Gabin to Marlene Dietrich, July 15, 1944, MDCB.

26 Leo Lerman, "Welcome, Marlene," *Vogue*, August 15, 1944, pp. 154–55 and 188–91; this passage is on p. 154.

27 Ibid., pp. 154–55.

28 Ibid., p. 191.

29 Ibid.

30 Patton wrote to his wife that Dietrich's show was "very low comedy, almost an insult to human intelligence." General Patton to Beatrice Ayer Patton, November 7, 1944; quoted in Stanley P. Hirshson, *General Patton: A Soldier's Life* (New York: Harper, 2002), p. 554.

31 Rudi Sieber to Marlene Dietrich, September 11, 1944, MDCB.

32 Charlie Trezona to Marlene Dietrich, February 16, 1945, MDCB.

33 Walter Reisch to Marlene Dietrich, December 13, 1944, MDCB.

34 From 1942–1943, Dietrich was suspected of being a German spy, and the FBI was assigned her case. She had been denounced. Her family and her lovers were subjected to a thorough investigation. When the suspicion proved to be unfounded, the investigation was called to a halt. See Werner Sudendorf, "Marlene, Hitler und das FBI. War die Dietrich eine Spionin? Über Wahn und Unsinn eines Verdachts," in *Süddeutsche Zeitung*, no. 233 (October 10/11, 1998).

35 Hans Leip, a soldier from Hamburg, wrote the lyrics of this song in 1915. The song came to be known with a melody by Norbert Schultze, a Berlin composer, in 1938. Schultze was a Nazi party member whose other compositions including "Bombs on England" and "Tanks Roll into Africa."

36 Ernest Hemingway, "A Tribute to Mamma from Papa Hemingway," *Life*, August 18, 1952, p. 92.

37 Mary Welsh Hemingway, *How It Was* (New York: Knopf, 1976), pp. 128–29.

38 Ernest Hemingway to Marlene Dietrich, July 13, 1950; John F. Kennedy Presidential Library and Museum / Ernest Hemingway Collecton, Boston.

39 Welsh Hemingway, *How It Was*, p. 127.

40 Ibid.

41 Lee Miller, "Players in Paris," in *Lee Miller's War: Photographer and Correspondent with the Allies in Europe 1944–1945* (Boston: Bulfinch Press, 1992), pp. 94–97; this quotation is on p. 97.

42 Dietrich, *Ich bin, Gott sei Dank, Berlinerin*, p. 275.

43 After the invasion of Normandy, he noted in his diary, "Have been wearing my shoulder holster . . . so as to get myself into the spirit of the part." General George S. Patton, quoted in Paul Fussell, *Uniforms: Why We Are What We Wear* (Boston: Houghton Mifflin, 2002), p. 38.

44 Dietrich, *Ich bin, Gott sei Dank, Berlinerin*, p. 289.

45 Ibid., p. 293.

V *Prosecution (1945–1954)*

The Witness

1 Marlene Dietrich to Jean Gabin, August 31, 1945, MDCB.

2 Marlene Dietrich to Rudi Sieber, September 16, 1945, MDCB.

3 Marlene Dietrich to Rudi Sieber, September 27, 1945, MDCB.

4 "He is the pioneer of the paratroopers, started with a handful of men in 41 against all odds. Went through Sicily, Anzio Campaign, Normandy, Holland. Only division which has 4 Combat Jumps. The red things on his shoulders are the Belgian and Dutch Fouragères—maybe they will have the French by the time they get home. But for that they would need one more shoulder. He is born 1907. I am 9 months older than he, see?" Marlene Dietrich to Rudi Sieber, December 5, 1945, MDCB.

5 "Had a pleasant visit with your mother she is fine the 82nd is looking forward to seeing you soon general gavin" August 30, 1945, MDCB.

6 Colonel Barry Oldfield, in J. David Riva and Guy Stern, eds., *A Woman at War: Marlene Dietrich Remembered* (Detroit: Wayne State University Press, 2006), pp. 49–75.

7 Marlene Dietrich to Maria Manton [stage name of Maria Riva], Thanksgiving Day, 1945, MDCB.

8 Marlene Dietrich to Rudi Sieber, late 1945, MDCB.

9 Marlene Dietrich to Rudi Sieber, January 6, 1946, MDCB.

10 Marlene Dietrich to Rudi Sieber, December 5, 1945, MDCB.

11 Marlene Dietrich to Maria Manton, February 10, 1946, MDCB.

12 Ibid.

13 Marlene Dietrich to Rudi Sieber, December 23, 1945, MDCB.

14 Marlene Dietrich to Maria Manton, February 10, 1946, MDCB.

15 Marlene Dietrich to Rudi Sieber, February 9, 1946, MDCB.

16 Marlene Dietrich to Rudi Sieber, June 21, 1946, MDCB.

17 Marlene Dietrich to Charlie Feldman, May 10, 1946, MDCB.

18 Marlene Dietrich to Maria Manton, May 12, 1946, MDCB.

19 Marlene Dietrich to Erich Maria Remarque, December 1, 1945, MDCB.

20 Erich Maria Remarque to Marlene Dietrich, early 1946, MDCB.

21 Appleton-Century, the New York publisher of *Arch of Triumph*, sold more than a million copies within one year.

22 Marlene Dietrich to Rudi Sieber, April 8, 1946, MDCB.

23 Helmuth Karasek, *Billy Wilder. Eine Nahaufnahme* (Hamburg: Hoffmann und Campe, 1992), pp. 309–10.

24 Ibid., p. 319.

25 Cameron Crowe, *Conversations with Wilder* (New York: Knopf, 1999), p. 80. In the same interview, Wilder describes his original intention to make Pringle Jewish. "What I wanted to do was not only is Captain Pringle in the American army, he also was Jewish. *That* is going to really *cement* it, you know. The American lieutenant with whom Dietrich is having the affair, and is going to marry, is Jewish. 'What? She's going to marry a . . . !' That picture I would have loved to make. But then we chickened out." Ibid., p. 75.

26 "Marlene Dietrich and Major Gen. Maxwell D. Taylor, superintendent of the U.S. Military Academy at West Point, stand at attention as Col. Robert Nourse reads citation accompanying Medal of Freedom awarded Marlene for her work in entertaining troops overseas during the war. Following the citation Gen. Taylor pins the medal on the curvaceous screen star." "Medal for Marlene," in *Daily News*, November 19, 1947, MDCB.

27 Marlene Dietrich to Rudi Sieber, November 22, 1947, MDCB.

28 Jean Gabin to Marlene Dietrich, November 13, 1947, MDCB.

29 "Trois machines à écrire tapaient le texte à un rythme infernal, en français, en allemande et en italien. Une des trois dactylos n'était autre que Marlene Dietrich, qui s'était à vouée a cette besogne ingrate pour aider Rossellini à faire vite. Sans maquillage, ses blondes cheveux en désordre, un tas de mégots dans le cendrier, Marlène, durant deux jours pleins, de neuf heures du matin à dix heures du soir, a traduit en effet dans SA langue d'origine les dialogues du film, sans donner le moindre signe de fatigue." *Cinemarche,* September 9, 1947, MDCB.

30 Marlene Dietrich to Maria Riva, June 6, 1945, MDCB.

31 Marlene Dietrich to Erich Maria Remarque, September 12, 1948, MDCB.

32 Erich Maria Remarque, *Liebe Deinen Nächsten* (Cologne: Kiepenheuer & Witsch, 2001), p. 3.

33 "Richard had a very special place in his heart for you Marlene dear which no one has ever taken and you have it still." Diana Tauber to Marlene Dietrich, January 9, 1948, MDCB. Tauber had kept in touch every now and then by telegram: "Dearest Marlene thanks for message so real friendship still exists thanks my thoughts and love follow yours ever Richard." Richard Tauber to Marlene Dietrich, October 21, 1947.

34 Charlie Feldman to Marlene Dietrich, April 13, 1951, MDCB.

35 Quoted in Patrick McGilligan, *Alfred Hitchcock: A Life in Darkness and Light* (New York: Harper, 2003), p. 433.

36 François Truffaut, *Hitchcock by Truffaut* (New York: Simon and Schuster, 1983), p. 190.

37 Alexander Liberman, *Marlene: An Intimate Photographic Memoir* (New York: Random House, 1992).

38 Billy Wilder to Marlene Dietrich, October 14, 1950, MDCB.

39 Marlene Dietrich to Friedrich Torberg, November 11, 1950, in Marcel Atze, ed. *Schreib. Nein, schreib nicht. Marlene Dietrich/Friedrich Torberg Briefwechsel 1946–1979* (Vienna: SYNEMA Gesellschaft für Film und Medien, 2008), p. 32.

40 Ibid.

41 Rock Brynner, *Yul: The Man Who Would Be King* (New York: Simon & Schuster, 1989), p. 103.

42 Marlene Dietrich to Maria Riva, n.d., MDCB.

43 Erich Maria Remarque, diary entry dated December 9, 1952, New York, in Erich Maria Remarque, *Das unbekannte Werk*, vol. 5: *Briefe und Tagebücher* (Cologne: Kiepenheuer & Witsch, 1998), p. 480.

44 Dietrich, *Ich bin, Gott sei Dank, Berlinerin*, p. 253.

45 Ibid.

46 Ibid., p. 255.

47 Peter Bogdanovich, *Fritz Lang in America* (New York: Praeger, 1967), p. 77.

48 Cornelius Schnauber, an expert on Fritz Lang who lives in Los Angeles, replied to my question about the relationship between Lang and Dietrich as follows: "Unfortunately I did not discuss Marlene Dietrich much with Fritz Lang, or at least I can't recall doing so. I only know that he felt she made things difficult for him in the *Rancho Notorious* movie—starting with the title. But I didn't notice what had gone on before and after. Still, I do know that Lang's wife, Lily Latté, claimed until the time of her death that her own relationship with Marlene Dietrich remained quite close." E-mail dated June 23, 2009.

49 Ernest Hemingway to Marlene Dietrich, July 13, 1950. John F. Kennedy Presidential Library and Museum / Ernest Hemingway Collection, Boston.

50 Ernest Hemingway to Marlene Dietrich, June 27, 1950. John F. Kennedy Presidential Library and Museum / Ernest Hemingway Collection, Boston.

51 Ernest Hemingway, *Life* magazine, August 18, 1952, p. 92.

52 Hildegard Knef, *The Gift Horse*, trans. David Anthony Palastanga (New York: McGraw-Hill, 1971), p. 192.

53 Ibid., p. 191.

The Accused

1 The whereabouts of the boxes are unknown.

2 Leni Riefenstahl, *Memoiren* (Munich: Albrecht Knaus, 1987), p. 408.

3 In a conversation with the *Süddeutsche Zeitung* on the occasion of her hundredth birthday, she declared that the initial postwar period had been an "entry into hell." Joachim Käppner, "Die Frau, die mit dem Bösen paktierte," *Süddeutsche Zeitung*, August 20, 2002.

4 German Intelligence Section / Special Interrogation Series no. 3; This report is published in cooperation with Seventh Army Interrogation Center, Captain Hans Wallenberg and Captain Ernst Langendorf, May 3, 1945, Institut für Zeitgeschichte, Munich, F 135/3.

5 Ibid.

6 The Temporary Nationality Act of July 10, 1945, stipulated that the only people who could retain their Austrian citizenship were those who had been Austrian prior to March 13, 1938, or could have attained it since then in accordance with Austrian law.

7 Budd Schulberg, "Nazi Pin-Up Girl," in *Saturday Evening Post*, March 30, 1946, pp. 11, 36, 39, 41.

8 Ibid.

9 Christopher Hitchens, "Leni Riefenstahl Interviewed by Gordon Hitchens," *Film Culture* 56/57 (Spring 1973): 94–121; this passage is on p. 96.

10 Janet Flanner, *Janet Flanner's World: Uncollected Writings, 1932–1975* (New York: Harcourt Brace Jovanovich, 1979), p. 98.

11 Riefenstahl, *Memoiren*, p. 447.

12 The trustee of Leni Riefenstahl's possessions, appointed by the Austrian government, was Hans Schneeberger.

13 See Klaus Eisterer, *Französische Besatzungspolitik. Tirol und Vorarlberg 1945/46* (Innsbruck: Haymon, 1990), p. 115.

14 Riefenstahl, *Memoiren*, p. 436.

15 "Tatbestand und Entscheidungsgründe." Report issued on November 9, 1948 by the Baden State Commission for Political Purgation. Denazification file for Leni Riefenstahl, Staatsarchiv Freiburg D 180/2 no. 228.165.

16 These disputes are discussed on pp. 443–47 of Riefenstahl, *Memoiren*.

17 Amtsgericht München, Aktenzeichen 7 Bs 692–693.

18 Alfred Polgar, "Leni Riefenstahl," in Polgar, *Kleine Schriften*, vol. 1: *Musterung*, ed. Marcel Reich-Ranicki with Ulrich Weinzierl (Reinbek bei Hamburg: Rowohlt, 1982), pp. 245–48.

19 *Süddeutsche Zeitung*, November 24, 1949.

20 "I noticed that Leni Riefenstahl was occupying an adjoining table with a group of friends. She had obviously been cleared by the denazification board of the U.S. military government in 1946 and was a free citizen once again, which did not altogether surprise me, as she had been a Nazi sympathizer and not an active war criminal." Peter Viertel, *Dangerous Friends: At Large with Huston and Hemingway in the Fifties* (New York: Nan A. Talese/Doubleday, 1992), p. 109.

21 Riefenstahl, *Memoiren*, p. 489.

22 Ibid., p. 525.

VI *New Chapter of Fame (1954–1976)*

The Icon

1   "The 'Haus' appears to be developing into a meeting place for prominent NS figures. Besides Leni Riefenstahl, who lives in the 'Savoy,' Emmi Goering who lives nearby and former 'Reichsleiter' Max Amann frequent the place. It appears strange even to circles of former 'old warriors' that Amann should be getting so much leave from the labor camp in Eichstätt." Institut für Zeitgeschichte München F 135/3.

2. "It was a very large village and out of it came running long-legged, brown, smooth-moving men who all seemed to be of the same age and who wore their hair in a heavy, club-like queue. . . . They were all tall, their teeth were white and good, and their hair was stained a red brown and arranged in a looped fringe on their foreheads." Ernest Hemingway, *Green Hills of Africa* (New York: Scribner, 1998), p. 219.

3   Leni Riefenstahl, *Memoiren* (Munich: Albrecht Knaus, 1987), p. 550.

4   Leni Riefenstahl, *Die Nuba. Menschen wie von einem anderen Stern* (Munich: List Verlag, 1973), p. 9.

5   Hemingway, *Green Hills of Africa*, p. 219.

6   Riefenstahl, *Memoiren*, p. 557.

7   For details on the rights situation of the films she made during the National Socialist rule, see Rainer Rother, *Leni Riefenstahl: The Seduction of Genius*, trans. Martin H. Bott (New York: Continuum, 2002), pp. 148–59.

8   Leni Riefenstahl, "Wie ich die Nuba fand," in Riefenstahl, *Die Nuba. Menschen wie von einem anderen Stern*, pp. 9–11; this passage is on p. 9.

9   *Le Village des Noubas* appeared in the "Huit" series (Paris: Rupert Delpire, 1955) and was later published in English as *Village of the Nubas* (London: Phaidon Press, Ltd., 1995). The text in *National Geographic* was by Robin Strachan, a young British colonial officer who was working in Kordofan for the British foreign ministry He indirectly gainsaid Riefenstahl's cliché about the noble savages. George Rodger and Robin Strachan, "With the Nuba Hillmen of Kordofan," in *National Geographic* 99, no. 2 (February 1951): 249–78.

10 George Rodger to Leni Riefenstahl, n.d. [Spring 1951], Smarden Archive; quoted in Carole Naggar, *George Rodger: An Adventure in Photography, 1980–1995* (Syracuse, NY: Syracuse University Press, 2003), p. 190. Naggar writes that Rodger felt ambivalent toward Riefenstahl. "He kept her books (with her written dedications to him) on the shelves of his library in Smarden, along with his other books on Africa. Publicly, however, he always disparaged her. When later in his life he became a fierce advocate of the Nuba cause and was asked if he knew whether Riefenstahl was aware of what was happening to them, he growled: " 'I don't really know. But if she did I doubt she would care' " (pp. 191–92). Naggar

surmises that he had a guilty conscience, since it was his photographs that had made Riefenstahl aware of the Nuba. In the 1980s, Riefenstahl and Rodger got together for lunch in London.

11 See Oskar Luz, "Proud Primitives, the Nuba People," in *National Geographic* 130, no. 5 (November 1966): 673–99.

12 Riefenstahl, *Memoiren*, p. 634.

13 Ibid., p. 635.

14 "Actually, the photos were not so important to me. I went there to get to know people, and I took a few pictures there, the way I always do when I travel. . . . I photographed without ever expecting that I might publish the pictures." Leni Riefenstahl in the Ray Müller film *The Wonderful, Horrible Life of Leni Riefenstahl*.

15 Handwritten letter from Leni Riefenstahl in Uganda to Theo von Hörmann, March 5, 1963, personal archive of Theo von Hörmann.

16 Riefenstahl, *Memoiren*, p. 656.

17 Ibid., p. 740.

18 Ibid., p. 755.

19 Ibid., p. 757.

20 Ibid., p. 753.

21 Ibid., p. 800.

22 This followed on the heels of the publication of several of her photographs in the Time-Life volume *African Kingdom* and in the *Sunday Times Magazine*, London 1967.

23 Rolf Gillhausen brought Bert Stern's "Marilyn's Last Sitting," fashion photography by Irving Penn, and Helmut Newton's erotic photography into *Stern*.

24 "Es geht rauf, es geht runter," *Spiegel* interview with Leni Riefenstahl about the visual aspect of the Olympic Games, in *Der Spiegel*, no. 36 (August 28, 1972): 33.

25 Riefenstahl, *Memoiren*, p. 830.

26 *Stern*, no. 41 (1975).

27 See, for example, Wilhelm Bittorf, "Blut und Hoden," in *Der Spiegel*, no. 36 (October 25, 1976), and James C. Faris, "Leni Riefenstahl and the Nuba Peoples of Kordofan Province, Sudan," in *Historical Journal of Film, Radio, and Television* 13, no. 1 (1993): 95–97.

28 For the 1973 New York Film Festival, Niki de Saint Phalle designed a poster announcing "Agnes Leni Shirley." According to Susan Sontag, this phrase "accurately reflected the contribution made by feminist consciousness at a certain level to whitewashing Riefenstahl." "Feminism and Fascism: An Exchange" (Adrienne Rich, with a reply by Susan Sontag in response to February 6, 1975 issue), *New York Review of Books* 22, no. 4 (March 20, 1975).

29 Susan Sontag, "Fascinating Fascism," published in *New York Review of Books*, February 6, 1975; reprinted in Susan Sontag, *Under the Sign of Saturn* (New York: Farrar, Straus & Giroux, 1980), pp. 73–105; this quotation is on p. 88.

Camp

1 Marlene Dietrich to Maria Riva, August 13, 1953, MDCB.

2 Maria Riva, *Marlene Dietrich* (New York: Knopf, 1992), p. 634.

3 *Sunday Chronicle*, n.d., MDCB; Marlene Dietrich quoted in *Daily News*, December 22, 1953.

4 Noël Coward to Marlene Dietrich, February 17, 1954, MDCB.

5 Milton Shulman, "In came Marlene like a glacier glinting in the sunlight," *Evening Standard*, June 22, 1954.

6 Kenneth Tynan, *Profiles* (London: Nick Hern Books/Walker, 1989), p. 216.

7 On April 22, 1954, he had written a letter to her when he found out from Major Neville-Willing that she would be coming: "This is simply to tell you that I await the encounter with ill-concealed hysteria, and to reassure you of my continued devotion between now and then." Kenneth Tynan to Marlene Dietrich, MDCB.

8 Ernest Hemingway to Marlene Dietrich, March 24, 1955, John F. Kennedy Presidential Library and Museum, Ernest Hemingway Collection, Boston.

9 494 Ernest Hemingway, April 9, 1953.

10 "First I rush upstairs and into my dressing-room. Then I throw off my shoes and then I throw off my gown. I take off my earrings and rings, dry my lips and grab two brushes full of brilliantine and put down my hair. Then I put on socks, my shirt, pants, suspenders and zip up my pants. The girl gives me my coat, I ring the buzzer for the orchestra, jump into shoes, put on my hat, and I'm ready. The whole thing takes a minute. It has to be fast to be effective. I'm not even out of breath when I come on." Art Buchwald, "Night Out With Marlene," in *Sunday Chronicle*, July 17, 1955. By her own account, her record was thirty-two seconds.

11 Marlene Dietrich to Yul Brynner, n.d., MDCB.

12 Marlene Dietrich to Noël Coward, n.d., MDCB.

13 Marlene Dietrich to Maria Riva, August 13, 1953, MDCB.

14 Information from Barbara Schröter, MDCB.

15 See, for example, the letter he sent her on February 9, 1945: "Dearest, Dearest Marlene . . . I read that you don't expect to come back to Hollywood, and I send you here my heartiest congratulations. I wish I could leave, too. Let's hope we can do a picture together in Paris next year. All my love, Orson." MDCB.

16 Portion of a telegram from Orson Welles to Marlene Dietrich, April 16, 1954, MDCB.

17 Marlene Dietrich, *Ich bin, Gott sei Dank, Berlinerin* (Frankfurt: Ullstein, 1987), p. 169.

18 Edith Head and Paddy Calistro, *Edith Head's Hollywood* (New York: Dutton, 1983), p. 28.

19 "Fully expecting Academy laurels, she had already arranged for the recorded introduction to her Las Vegas nightclub act to include a reference to her Oscar bid." Kevin Lally, *Wilder Times: The Life of Billy Wilder* (New York: Henry Holt & Co., 1996), p. 273. Dietrich did receive a nomination for a Golden Globe from the Foreign Press Association in Hollywood.

20 "By 1947, 34.8 million of the 38.5 million households in the country had at least one radio receiver; there were 8.5 million in use in automobiles; and another 21.6 million in stores, hotels and institutions. . . . Radio reigned as America's sole 'national' means of communication. With listening patterns enhanced by the war, people got into the habit of switching on news on broadcasts and forgetting to turn off the radio when they ended." Joseph C. Goulden, *The Best Years 1945–1950* (New York: Atheneum, 1976), p. 148.

21 Dietrich, *Ich bin, Gott sei dank, Berlinerin*, p. 245.

22 "I was on my way to California to try to learn something about film scoring and maybe get a chance to score a movie. And I got a call from Peter Matz, a friend who conducted both Dietrich and Noël Coward. Matz was in a bind and asked whether I would consider, like, working with her. I said, shoot, yes, that would be great! I went to see her the next day at the Beverly Hills hotel in one of the villas. She was intimidating." Burt Bacharach, quoted in Michael Brocken, *Bacharach: Maestro! The Life of a Pop Genius* (New Malden, UK: Chrome Dreams, 2003), p. 66.

23 Dietrich, *Ich bin, Gott sei Dank, Berlinerin*, p. 314.

24 Ibid., p. 320.

25 Burt Bacharach to Marlene Dietrich, n.d., MDCB.

26 Brocken, *Bachrach*, p. 70.

27 Marlene Dietrich to Maria Riva, 1959, MDCB.

28 "But, God, how he looks at me. It makes your teeth rattle." Marlene Dietrich to Maria Riva, August 5, 1959, MDCB.

29 Marlene Dietrich to Friedrich Torberg, November 3, 1959, in Marcel Atze, ed., *Schreib. Nein schreib nicht, Marlene Dietrich/Friedrich Torberg Briefwechsel 1946–1979* (Vienna: SYNEMA Gesellschaft für Film und Medien, 2008), p. 63.

30 Marlene Dietrich to Maria Riva, August 5, 1959, MDCB.

31 Maria Riva to Marlene Dietrich, n.d., MDCB.

32 "Marlene kommt. Mehr als 20 000 DM Abendgage!" in *Nacht-Depesche*, February 13, 1960, MDCB.

33 Joachim Besser "Haben wir wirklich nichts gelernt? Bewährungsprobe für uns: Marlene Dietrichs Besuch," *Die Welt* 6 (April 1960).

34 Joachim Besser, "Heben wir wirklich nichts gelernt? Bewährungsprobe für uns: Marlene Dietrichs Besuch," *Die Welt*, April 6, 1960.

35 Karena Niehoff, "Zwei Beine, die die Welt erschütterten. Gerührtes und anstrengendes Wiedersehen mit Marlene Dietrich," *Der Tagesspiegel*, May 4, 1960.

36 Sabine Lietzmann, "Majestät im Schwanenpelz," *FAZ*, May 5, 1960.

37 RIAS (Radio in the American Sector) Berlin, "Stimme der Kritik" (radio broadcast by the well-known theater critic Friedrich Luft), May 8, 1960.

38 From the documentary film *Marlene Dietrich: Her Own Song* (2002), directed by David Riva.

39 Quoted in Christian Burkhard, "Von Kopf bis Fuss auf Zion engestellt. Marlene Dietrich und Israel—eine Liebeseschichte," *Jüdische Allgemeine*, no. 25 (June 19, 2008), MDCB.

40 Elisabeth Will to Marlene Dietrich, 1963, MDCB.

41 Elisabeth Will to Marlene Dietrich, 1965, MDCB.

42 Riva, *Marlene Dietrich* (film).

43 The other Oscar for this movie went to Abby Mann for Best Screenplay. *Judgment at Nuremberg* also won two Golden Globe awards, one for Stanley Kramer as the Best Motion Picture Director, and the other for Maximilian Schell as Best Motion Picture Actor in a Drama.

44 Erich Maria Remarque, March 23, 1962, MDCB.

45 In 1953, Marlene Dietrich had been paid twenty thousand dollars for a four-thousand-line article in the *Ladies' Home Journal*. She wrote her daughter about a quarrel that ensued with Remarque: "Remarque was furious at the price. It did not help that I pointed out that crap is better paid than good stuff, he was burning up." Marlene Dietrich to Maria Riva, August 13, 1953, MDCB.

46 Marlene Dietrich, quoted in John Lahr, ed., *The Diaries of Kenneth Tynan* (New York: Bloomsbury, 2001), pp. 38–39.

47 Marlene Dietrich to Maria Riva, January 23, 1964, MDCB.

48 Ibid.

49 Marlene Dietrich to Friedrich Torberg, November 3, 1958, in Atze, ed., *Schreib. Nein, schreib nicht*, pp. 62–64; this phrase is on p. 64.

50 Rudi Sieber to Marlene Dietrich, August 14, 1964, MDCB.

51 Rudi Sieber to Marlene Dietrich, September 9, 1964, MDCB.

52 Ibid.

53 Rudi Sieber to Marlene Dietrich, March 16, 1963, MDCB.

54 Marlene Dietrich to Maria Riva, October 12, 1965, MDCB.

55 Josef von Sternberg to Marlene Dietrich, September 14, 1959, MDCB.

56 Marlene Dietrich to Leo Lerman, February 3, 1966, MDCB.

57 Marlene Dietrich to Kenneth Tynan, March 17, 1967, MDCB.

58 Marlene Dietrich to Kenneth Tynan, September 5, 1969, MDCB.

59 Leo Lerman, *The Grand Surprise: The Journals of Leo Lerman* (New York: Knopf, 2007), p. 615.

60 Marlene Dietrich to Maria Riva, n.d., MDCB.

61 Marlene Dietrich to Burt Bacharach, June 17, 1972, MDCB.

62 Marlene Dietrich to Friedrich Torberg, in Atze, ed, *Schreib. Nein, schreib nicht*, p. 100.

63 Marlene Dietrich to Maria Riva, September 28, 1970, MDCB.

64 Ibid.

65 Marlene Dietrich to Margo Lion, August 2, 1970, MDCB.

66 Marlene Dietrich to Orson Welles, November 10, 1971, MDCB.

67 Quoted in Werner Sudendorf, "Die wütende Venus. Marlene Dietrich und das Fernsehen," *Filmgeschichte*, no. 20 (December 2005). This article contains an extensive description of the events surrounding Dietrich's television show. Excerpts from the interview with Rex Reed can be read in newsletter no. 63, dated April 30, 2004.

68 Marlene Dietrich to Maria Riva, July 21, 1973, MDCB.

69 Marlene Dietrich to Brian Aherne, September 23, 1974, MDCB.

70 Kenneth Tynan, May 25, 1972, in Lahr, ed., *The Diaries of Kenneth Tynan*, p. 96.

71 Marlene Dietrich to Maria Riva, July 21, 1973, MDCB.

VII The End Game (1976–2003)

In the Mattress Crypt

1 At the auction of the contents of her New York apartment at Sotheby's in Los Angeles in November 1997, the gifts from her lovers held a magic attraction for the buyers. A gold money clip that Gabin had returned to her, for example, brought in more than six thousand dollars.

2 Marlene Dietrich to Maria Riva, September 7, 1976, MDCB.

3 Marlene Dietrich to Maria Riva, October 24, 1976, MDCB.

4 Marlene Dietrich to Kenneth Tynan, June 19, 1977, MDCB.

5 Marlene Dietrich to Maria Riva, October 25, 1976, MDCB.

6 MDCB.

7 Max Kolpé to Marlene Dietrich, January 14, 1979, MDCB.

8 Klaus Jerziorkowski, "Die schönen Beine erinnern sich. Marlene Dietrichs Reflexionen 'Nehmt nur mein Leben,'" in *Frankfurter Allgemeine Zeitung*, May 4, 1979.

9 Marlene Dietrich to Maria Riva, April 22, 1977, MDCB.

10 Erich Maria Remarque to Marlene Dietrich, 1948, MDCB.

11 From the documentary film *Marlene* (1984), directed by Maximilian Schell.

12 Brian Aherne to Marlene Dietrich, October 19, 1984, MDCB.

13 Billy Wilder had sent her the screenplay of *Fedora*, but she sent it back to him by return mail, with the remark: "How could you possibly think!" She did not want to play an aging actress.

14 Kevin Lally, *Wilder Times: The Life of Billy Wilder* (New York: Henry Holt and Company, 1996).

15 In 1989, when the German premiere of *A Foreign Affair* was being planned for what was then the Quartier Latin in Berlin, Dietrich was invited to attend. Messengers who came with deliveries to Avenue Montaigne 12 were told that Dietrich did not live there. After the premiere enjoyed great success, the orga-

nizers received a light blue, hand-addressed envelope from Dietrich, thanking them for the invitation and apologizing that she would not be able to attend a premiere that would take place forty years hence. The odd thing about the letter was that it had been posted in Bel Air, Los Angeles. Dietrich had sent it to Billy Wilder from Paris, and he then brought the letter to the post office in Bel Air to send it to Berlin.

16 Entry dated July 22, 1981, Leo Lerman, *The Grand Surprise: The Journals of Leo Lerman* (New York: Knopf, 2007), p. 471.

17 Marlene Dietrich, *Nachtgedanken* (München, 2005), p. 105.

18 Walter Reisch to Marlene Dietrich, October 9, 1976, MDCB

19 Max Kolpé to Marlene Dietrich, June 19, 1987, MDCB.

20 Marlene Dietrich, April 9, 1985, MDCB; reprinted in *Marlene Dietrich: Photographs and Memories*, compiled by Jean-Jacques Naud and captioned by Maria Riva (New York: Random House, 2001), p. 207.

21 The magazine *Bunte* bought these photographs. Josef Wagner, who was the editor in chief at the time, did not publish the pictures, but gave the set to Maria Riva, who brought them to her mother. She burned them and thanked Wagner for his tact.

22 This information stems from the description Peter Riva provided for the May 2004 MDCB newsletter 64. His purpose in writing this was to counter the claim by Dietrich's former secretary, Norma Bosquet, that Dietrich had taken her own life.

At the Bottom of the Sea

1 Bianca Jagger, "Leni's Back and Bianca's Got Her," *Interview* 5 (January 1975): 35–37.

2 http://telluridefilmfestival.org/news/2013-8.

3 Peggy Ann Wallace, "An Historical Study of the Career of Leni Riefenstahl from 1923 to 1933," Ph.D. dissertation, University of Southern California, 1975.

4 From Riefenstahl's cameraman Henry von Javorsky, in Peggy A. Wallace, "The Most Important Factor Was the Spirit: Leni Riefenstahl During the Filming of *The Blue Light*," *Image* 17, no. 1 (1974): 17–29.

5 "In the Art Institute of Chicago, Leni Riefenstahl's *The Blue Light*, made in 1932, was the first film to be shown in a series featuring women directors, and also highlighted the work of Mai Zetterlin, Agnès Varda, and Susan Sontag. The three showings of the film were sold out." Henry Marx, "Wenn Eisenstein, dann auch Riefenstahl. Amerika entdeckt die Werke der 'ersten Filmemacherin überhaupt'—Ehrungen und Diskussionen," *Die Welt*, January 31, 1975.

6 The program, "Je später der Abend," with Hans-Jürgen Rosenbauer, was broadcast on October 30, 1976. In addition to Riefenstahl, the songwriter Knut Kiesewetter and the unionist Elfriede Kretschmer were invited.

7   All quotes in this paragraph from the talk show *Je später der Abend*, October 30, 1976.

8   After spending several months in Africa in 1974 and 1975, she traveled to southeast Nuba once again in 1977 for an assignment with *Geo* magazine. During this trip, she was awarded a medal by Sudan's president, Jaafar Mohammed an-Numeiri. She had been granted Sudanese citizenship several years earlier.

9   Leni Riefenstahl to Bernhard Minetti, January 23, 1985, AdK Berlin, estate of Bernhard Minetti.

10 She provides a description in her memoirs; Leni Riefenstahl, *Memoiren* (Munich: Albrecht Knaus, 1987), p. 437.

11 *Je später der Abend*, October 30, 1976.

12 A few weeks before her death, André Müller conducted an interview with her and asked her to react to Helma Sanders-Brahms's claim that *Lowlands* contained a masked indictment of the National Socialist regime. She spurned this chance to be seen as one of the good ones after all: "Yes, but there was nothing behind it. People have read so much into my work. I actually viewed this movie as no more than a stopgap so that I would not have to make a propaganda film. It is silly to presume that there was something critical in it." André Müller, "Gespräch mit Riefenstahl," *Weltwoche*, August 15, 2002.

13 Anyone who had appeared on the cover of *Time* magazine was a guest of honor. Her photograph had been featured on the cover of the February 17, 1936, edition. A photograph by Martin Munkacsi shows her skiing in a bathing suit. The caption read: "Hitler's Leni Riefenstahl."

14 Helmut Newton, *Autobiography* (London: Gerald Duckworth & Co. Ltd., 2003), p. 275. When he was asked about her after her death, he told the *Süddeutsche Zeitung*: "Leni and I had an interesting relationship. I admired her as a director and photographer, although I didn't like her political views." *Süddeutsche Zeitung*, September 10, 2003.

15 Leni Riefenstahl, "Ich habe einen Traum," *Zeit-Magazin* 35 (2002).

SUGGESTIONS FOR
FURTHER READING

Aichinger, Ilse. *Film und Verhängnis*. *Blitzlichter auf ein Leben*. Frankfurt: Fischer, 2001.

Arnheim, Rudolf. *Die Seele in der Silberschicht. Medientheoretische Texte Photographie—Film—Rundfunk*. Frankfurt: Suhrkamp Verlag, 2004.

Blumenberg, Hans. *Geistesgeschichte der Technik*. Frankfurt: Suhrkamp Verlag, 2009.

———. *Lebenszeit und Weltzeit*. Frankfurt: Suhrkamp Verlag, 1986.

Costantino, Maria. *Fashions of a Decade: The 1930s*. London: Batsford, 1991.

Douglas, Ann. *Terrible Honesty: Mongrel Manhattan in the 1920s*. New York: Farrar, Straus and Giroux, 1995.

Ehrlicher, Hanno. *Die Kunst der Zerstörung: Gewaltphantasien und Manifestationspraktiken europäischer Avantgarden*. Berlin: Akademie Verlag, 2001.

Feilchenfeldt-Breslauer. *Bilder meines Lebens: Erinnerungen*. Wädenswil: NIMBUS, 2009.

Gadamer, Hans-Georg. *Philosophische Lehrjahre*. Frankfurt: Vittorio Klostermann, 1995.

Hambourg, Maria Morris, and Christopher Phillips. *The New Vision: Photography Between the World Wars. The Ford Motor Company Collection at the Metropolitan Museum of Art*. New York: Harry N. Abrams, Inc., 1994.

Hecht, Ben. *Revolution im Wasserglas: Geschichten aus Deutschland 1919*. Berlin: Berenberg Verlag, 2006.

Hollander, Anne. *Sex and Suits*. New York: Knopf, 1994.

Lepsius, Rainer M. *Demokratie in Deutschland: Soziologisch-historische Konstellationsanalysen*. Göttingen: Vandenhoeck & Ruprecht, 1993.

Lukacs, Georg. *Die Seele und die Formen*. Berlin: Luchterhand, 1971.

Nicolson, Harold. *Diaries and Letters 1930–1939*. London: Collins, 1966.

Nostitz, Helene von. *Aus dem alten Europa*. Frankfurt: Insel, 1978

Roseman, Mark. *Generations in Conflict: Youth Revolt and Generation Formation in Germany 1770–1968*. Cambridge, UK: Cambridge University Press, 1995.

Spackman, Barbara. *Fascist Virilities: Rhetoric, Ideology, and Social Fantasy in Italy*. Minneapolis: University of Minnesota Press, 1996.

CREDITS

Pages viii and ix: Marianne Raschig, *Hand und Persönlichkeit: Einführung in das System der Handlehre* (Hamburg: Gebrüder Enoch Verlag, 1931), p. 109 (top) and 121 (top).

Insert photographs:

Rolls Press / Popperfoto / Contributor / Getty Images.

Harvard Art Museums / Busch-Reisinger Museum, Gift of Lufthansa German Airlines.

Harvard Art Museums / Busch-Reisinger Museum, Gift of Lufthansa German Airlines.

bpk, Berlin / Art Resource, NY.

Associated Press.

bpk, Berlin / Art Resource, NY.

© Martin Munkacsi / Howard Greenberg Gallery / Art Resource.

bpk, Berlin / Art Resource, NY.

HIP / Art Resource, NY.

© Laszlo Willinger / Art Resource, NY.

Hulton Archive / Stringer / Getty Images.

Associated Press.

bpk, Berlin / Art Resource, NY.

Keystone-France / Gamma-Keystone via Getty Images.

INDEX

Acosta, Mercedes de, 223–24
Adalbert, Prince, 77
Adler, Gusti, 59
Adorno, Theodor W., 35, 532n38
Adventures of a Ten-Mark Note (film), 130
Africa:
  Kau people in, 444, 515
  Nuba people of, 436–44, 446–47, 514, 520, 521–22
  tourists in, 445
AGFA, 134, 555n80
Aherne, Brian, 224–25, 503
Albers, Hans, 157, 263
Albu, Ruth, 250
Allgeier, Sepp:
  and Fanck, 103, 109, 442
  Leni's relationship with, 267
  and mountain films, 91, 94, 115, 281, 442
  and Nazi party films, 267, 268, 279, 280, 281, 321, 327, 442
  as skier, 94, 103, 120, 281
  and Trenker, 120, 267
  and World War I, 120
Allianz-Verleih, 428
All Quiet on the Western Front (film), 148

Amann, Max, 431, 432, 566n1
Ambler, Eric, 504
Angel (film), 243
Angst, Richard, 109, 111, 115, 119, 122, 123
"Annie Doesn't Live Here Anymore" (song), 364
an-Numeiri, Jaafar Mohammed, 573n8
Anti-Nazi League, 314
Archipenko, Alexander, 242
Arch of Triumph (film), 389
Arendt, Hannah, 235
Arnoldi, Frau, 47–48
Arthur, Jean, 391
Attenborough, Richard, 450
Attolico, Bernardo, 296
Auden, W. H., 452
August Wilhelm, Prince, 261
Auschwitz concentration camp, 338–39, 391, 517
Austria:
  Allied occupation of, 414–15
  German invasion of, 308
  Leni's deportation from, 419
  liberation of, 411
  Seebichl House in, 412–13, 415, 416

Avalanche (film), 114–20, 127, 128, 162, 435

Bach, Steven, 287
Bacharach, Burt, 460–61, 462, 466, 467, 479–80, 483–84, 487
Baker, Josephine, 62
Balázs, Béla:
 and *The Blue Light,* 126, 127–28, 129, 130–31, 136, 137, 312, 513, 556–57n97
 early years of, 129–30
 and Leni's changing memories, 312, 552n39, 556–57n97
 and Leni's power of attorney, 275
 Leni's use of, 278
 and *Madame Doesn't Want Children,* 68
 "The Revolutionary Film" by, 68
Balbo, Italo, 261, 327–28
Balmain, 452
Bankhead, Tallulah, 448
Banton, Travis, 200, 220, 458, 545n42
Bardot, Brigitte, 432
Barry, Iris, 512
Battleship Potemkin (film), 263
Bauer, Herbert (Balász), 129
Baum, Vicki, 24, 233
Beckett, Samuel, 452
Beinhorn, Elly, 139
Bel Ami (film), 70
Belling, Rudolf, 242

Below, Nicolaus von, 323, 557n2
Bendow, Wilhelm, 62
Benitz, Albert, 122
Berber, Anita, 14–15, 18
Bergen-Belsen concentration camp, 463
Berger, Helmut, 545n32
Bergman, Ingrid, 246, 389
Bergner, Elisabeth, 57, 75, 128, 238, 259
Berlin:
 beauty ideal in, 85
 boxing in, 59, 60, 85
 Brandenburg Gate, 22
 dance in, 18–20, 23, 26
 death squads in, 277
 Deutsches Theater, 56–59, 80, 163, 246–47
 Dietrich home in, 3, 76
 film ball (1955), 432
 as film setting, 391, 394
 food rationing in, 316
 immigrants in, 7
 industry and technology in, 8, 12, 13
 instability in, 191, 203–4, 208, 262
 Kaiser Wilhelm Memorial Church, 75, 153
 Komödie Theater, 71
 lack of tradition in, 23–24, 76–77
 Marlene's films shown in, 207, 210, 213, 240, 351
 Marlene's stage performances in, 462–66
 Nazi party in, 211, 213
 nightlife in, 74–75, 79

Olympic Games (1936) in, 294, 295, 296, 297–98
post-World War I in, 22–24, 45–46, 53–54, 59–60, 76–77
post–World War II in, 380–81
pre–World War II politics in, 203–4, 208
Reinhardt theaters in, 56, 62, 71, 80, 162
revolution in, 45, 59, 60
Schauspielschule Ernst Busch, 530n6
Schwannecke wine bar in, 74–75, 79, 113
sexual ambiguities in, 62, 63, 72–73, 74, 86, 154
theater in, 56, 57
Thielscher Girls in, 61–62
Tiller Girls in, 61
Titania Palace Theater, 462–63
trendy, 84–85
World War I in, 11, 22, 38, 41–43
World War II in, 339, 353
Berlin: Symphony of a Great City (film), 278
Berlin Symphony Orchestra, 306
Bernhardt, Kurt, 77, 263
Bertelsmann, publisher, 500
Binswanger, Herbert, 529n18
Birkin, Jane, 507
Black Cargo (film), 434–35
Black Fox (film), 470–71
"Black Market" (song), 392
Black Thursday, 160

Blonde Venus (film), 204–7, 208, 210
Blue Angel, The (film), 162–73, 183, 211
    authors of, 155–56, 162, 169, 170
    Jannings as star in, 155, 156, 158, 163–64, 166–68, 169, 172
    Marlene created by von Sternberg in, 159, 165, 167, 172, 476
    Marlene in, 155, 163–73, 349, 370, 385, 473
    Marlene's casting in, 112–13, 157–59
    Marlene's triumph in, 169, 172–73, 178–79
    music for, 163, 168, 191
    preliminaries for, 152–59
    premiere of, 171–72
    remakes of, 383, 394, 482, 505
    set of, 542–43n87
    as sound film, 162, 166, 171
    story of, 169–71
    U.S. version of, 169
Blue Light, The (film), 126–29, 130–38
    awards and honors for, 137, 307, 572n5
    and Balázs, 126, 127–28, 130–31, 136, 137, 139, 312, 556–57n97
    cast and crew for, 127–29, 130, 513, 556–57n97
    comparisons with, 135, 333
    critical reception of, 137–38

Blue Light, The (film) (*continued*)
  and Fanck, 126–27, 136
  filming of, 131, 134–35
  and Hitler, 145, 148, 150–51
  Leni's acting in, 135, 136, 137
  Leni's directorial debut with,
    126–27, 136, 137, 278
  premiere of, 136–37, 148
  revival of, 275, 312, 313, 436,
    512
  screenplay for, 126, 129, 131,
    136
  story of, 131–33, 135–36
  success of, 259
  tour with, 143
Blumenthal, Mr., 180–81
Bogdanovich, Peter, 230
Bois, Curt, 62
Böll, Heinrich, 500
Borchert, Wolfgang, 500
Bormann, Martin, 334, 335,
    341, 413, 422
Borzage, Frank, 231
Bouché, René, 487
Boursier, Marcel, 214
Bowie, David, 500
"Boys in the Back Room, The"
    (song), 348, 349, 364, 451
Brancusi, Constantin, 242
Brandt, Willy, 465
Braun, Eva, 334, 423
Braun, Lily, 34
Braun, Otto, 34
Brauner, Atze, 465
Brecht, Bertolt, 59, 60, 75, 384
  Drums in the Night, 54
Brecht, Bertolt, and Kurt Weill:
  Mahagonny, 532n38

Songspiele, 532n38
  The Threepenny Opera, 86, 153,
    532n38
Bronnen, Arnolt, *Parricide,* 54
Brooks, Louise, 68–69
Brückner, Wilhelm, 145, 149
Bruhn, Ada, 19
Brundage, Avery, 314
Brüning, Heinrich, 147, 149,
    171, 203
Brynner, Yul, 403–5, 454–55,
    459, 461–62, 477, 480
Buchanan, Jack, 450
By Divine Right (film), 196

Cabinet of Doctor Caligari, The
    (film), 128, 297
Café de Paris, London, 450–52
Café Electric (film), 69, 70
Cagney, James, 137
Cameron, David, 465
Cannes Film Festival, 510
Capote, Truman, 459
Card, James, 512
Carmen (film), 45
Carné, Marcel, 357, 383
Carpenter, Ken, 302
Carstairs, Marion Barbara "Joe,"
    251–52
Cartellieri, Carmen, 536n94
Casablanca (film), 130
Catherine the Great (film), 238
Cerrutti, Vittorio, 260
Chanel, Coco, 486
Charell, Erik, 62–63
Chekhova, Olga, 137
Chevalier, Maurice, 208, 209,
    213, 224, 462

Chicago Art Festival, 514
Chirac, Jacques, 501
Chopin, Frédéric, 80
Christie, Agatha, 89
  Witness for the Prosecution, 458
Churchill, Winston, 89, 350
Ciano, Countess Edda Mus-
  solini, 296
Cinémathèque Française, 512
Clair, René, 278, 351
Clift, Montgomery, 469
Cobalt 60 (film), 432
Cocteau, Jean, 462
Cohen, Alexander, 487
Cohen, Emanuel, 205
Collignon, Ilse, 557n7
Columbia Pictures, 460
Cooper, Gary, 183, 184, 188,
  471
Coppola, Francis Ford, 446, 512
Correll, Ernst Hugo, 161
Coward, Noël, 403, 450, 454,
  462, 481, 482, 488, 492,
  499
Crawford, Joan, 137, 240, 247
Cruise, Tom, 521
Curtiz, Michael (Mihály
  Kertész), 130
Czechoslovakia, German threats
  against, 313, 315
Czinner, Paul, 128

Dagover, Lil, 77
d'Albert, Eugen, 330
dance:
  abstraction of, 83
  ballroom, 23
  body as temple of, 18–19

classical ballet, 21, 23
  expression through the body
    in, 22, 23, 46, 82, 83
  and gymnastics, 18, 23, 46,
    83, 85
  harmony of mind and body,
    19
  Mazdaznan movement, 83
  méthode rhythmique, 19
  modern, 18–20, 21, 24–26, 80
  physical elasticity achieved
    via, 85
  as rhythmic thinking, 82
  women in, 20, 23, 26–27
Das Schicksal derer von Habsburg
  (film), 536n94
Davis, Joe, 460
Dayan, Moshe, 467
Day of Freedom—Our Wehr-
  macht—Nuremberg 1935
  (film), 290, 291–92, 323,
  415, 416–17, 515
DeBakey, Michael, 489
de Gaulle, Charles, 361, 368,
  486–87
Dehmel, Richard, 34
Delahaye, Michel, 305
Delon, Alain, 462
De Sica, Vittorio, 426, 432, 456
Desire (film), 231–32, 240
Dessau, Paul, 115
De Stijl movement, 533n55
Destry Rides Again (film), 347–
  49, 354, 406
Deutsche Grammophon, 468
Devil Is a Woman, The (film),
  227–28, 240
Devil's General, The (film), 106

Diaghilev, Serge, 19

Diem, Carl, 294

Diessl, Gustav, 108, 121

Dieterle, William, 362, 465

Dietrich, Elisabeth Ottilie (sister):
  birth of, 5
  childhood of, 6–7
  death of, 468, 488
  discipline instilled in, 6–7, 66
  and family background, 3–7
  financial support from Marlene, 468–69
  letters to and from Marlene, 468
  post–World War II, 399, 468–69
  as teacher, 53
  teen years of, 30, 31, 38, 43

Dietrich, Hermann (uncle), 65–66

Dietrich, Josefine (Wilhelmina Elisabeth Josefine Felsing) (mother):
  in Berlin, 194, 202–3, 212, 225, 351, 352, 363, 380, 381, 503
  death of, 381, 382, 385
  and family life, 31–32, 37–39, 44, 66
  first husband of, 5, 6
  hopes resting on her children, 38–39, 66
  Marlene in U.S., 171, 194, 208, 236–38, 351
  Marlene's financial support of, 208
  and Marlene's marriage, 64

and Marlene's schooling, 46–49

and Prussian pride, 31

punctuality and discipline enforced by, 6–7, 30, 31, 37, 39, 44, 55, 66, 78

second husband of, 30–31, 37–38

social status as concern of, 31, 43, 56, 61, 64, 76

and World War I, 37–38, 46

Dietrich, Louis Erich Otto (father), 3–6, 43

Dietrich, Marie Magdalene, see Dietrich, Marlene

Dietrich, Marlene:
  and acting career, 55–56, 57–61, 71, 78–79, 230
  affairs of, 70–71, 75, 167–68, 196, 209, 222–25, 240–41, 243–45, 251, 353–59, 364–65, 368, 371, 379–80, 381, 385, 401, 403–5, 454–55, 457, 460–62, 479, 480; see also specific names
  and agents, 231, 247, 255, 387, 399–400, 402, 406, 450
  and aging, 222, 229, 230, 350, 360, 375, 383, 387–88, 402, 403, 404, 405, 407, 410, 449–50, 452, 459, 468, 475, 477, 480, 483–84, 486, 490–93, 497–510
  ambition of, 58, 61, 66, 77, 79, 164
  awards and honors to, 395, 452, 464, 466, 467, 474, 487, 509, 563n26

birth and background of, 3–7
book collection of, 509
boxing lessons taken by, 59
as businesswoman, 467–68,
    489–90, 501–2
charity work of, 402
childhood of, 6–7, 36, 363,
    499
citizenship of, 65, 246–47,
    255, 256, 349, 351, 352
in commercials, 485
and cosmetic surgery, 491
critical reviews of, 68, 69, 73,
    350, 361, 451, 500
death of, 510, 572n22
descriptions of, 59, 79, 408–9,
    464, 484
diary and dreams of, 30,
    32–34, 36, 38, 39–41, 42,
    44, 55, 69, 79
discipline instilled in, 6–7,
    30, 31, 37, 39, 78, 230, 374,
    406, 489
entertaining U.S. troops, 70,
    362–67, 370–71, 373–76,
    463
estate of, 508–10
fading popularity of, 246, 247,
    254, 350–51, 355, 383, 385,
    387, 388, 399, 402
falls from the stage, 466, 479,
    488–89, 493, 499
and fame, 72, 75, 186, 190,
    192, 232–33, 255
and family ideal, 32, 39, 40,
    43, 167, 193, 250, 257,
    401–2
and Fanck, 139

fears of, 374, 384, 385, 387,
    397, 405, 509
financial support of others,
    71, 76, 79, 208, 215, 222,
    223, 251, 255, 359, 369,
    371, 396–97, 399, 455–56,
    468–69, 477, 492–93
friends of, 408–9, 480, 482,
    503, 504
as grandmother, 395–96, 397,
    398, 401, 403, 459, 462, 476
health issues of, 387, 388, 474,
    477–79, 486, 489, 490, 491,
    493, 508, 510
and her daughter, 66; see also
    Riva, Maria
and her grandmother, 32–33,
    36, 43, 53, 59, 60, 401
and her mother, see Dietrich,
    Josefine
home movies of, 241, 256,
    358
homesick and unhappy in
    U.S., 181–82, 183, 190, 193,
    194, 208, 212, 215, 225,
    233–34, 390
income and finances of, 56,
    60, 187, 192, 208, 209, 238,
    251, 255, 256, 351, 359,
    360, 369, 371–72, 379, 387,
    391, 396–97, 399, 449, 456,
    463, 464, 467–68, 487, 488,
    500, 505, 509–10, 570n45
isolation of, 178, 382, 388–90,
    449, 471, 475, 478, 479,
    504–10
Just Take My Life, 481–82,
    498–99, 500–501, 503, 505

Dietrich, Marlene (*continued*)
  legs of, 61, 63, 364, 370, 398,
    409, 453, 464, 477, 489,
    506, 508
  letters to and from lovers, 70,
    209, 211, 224–25, 238, 255,
    364–65, 368–69, 401, 405;
    see also specific names
  lifestyle of, 58–59, 71, 74–75,
    79, 193–94, 215, 232–34,
    236, 249, 457
  loss of virginity, 49
  Marlene Dietrich's ABC, 481–82
  and *Marlene* film, 502–3
  marriage of, 63–67; *see also*
    Sieber, Rudolf Emilian
  medications of, 473–74
  memorabilia of, 363, 396, 467,
    508, 571n1
  monocle worn by, 61, 65, 67,
    78
  move to Hollywood, 168–69,
    171–73, 177–82, 187, 200
  movie roles of, 67–71, 77–78,
    179–87, 188–90, 197–200,
    204–5, 212, 216–17, 219–
    21, 227–28, 231, 238–40,
    308, 347–51, 359–61, 370,
    386–87, 391, 392, 400, 401,
    402, 406, 458, 470, 471,
    500; *see also Blue Angel, The;*
    other titles
  movies as escape for, 39–40,
    41, 44
  musical saw of, 70, 196, 364
  musical talents of, 78
  music and dance lessons of,
    46, 49, 55, 69

  new name for herself, 34
  as nightclub singer, 410,
    448–54, 459–61, 465–68,
    472–75, 477, 478, 479, 480,
    485, 489–90
  in Paris, 213–15, 249–50,
    379–80, 381, 383–84, 388,
    397–98, 452, 462, 475, 484,
    497, 499, 501, 504–10
  physical appearance of, 59,
    66, 68, 73, 408
  poems written by, 505, 508
  post–World War I, 53–79, 383
  post–World War II, 383–84,
    385, 388–90, 396, 398
  as prisoner of her own legend,
    492
  professional contacts of, 67,
    71, 76–77
  Prussian pride of, 43, 79, 466,
    474
  public image of, 187, 233,
    238, 248–49, 358, 370
  quest for adventure, 39
  radio broadcasts of, 372–73,
    402, 459
  return trips to Berlin, 190–92,
    380–81, 462–66
  and schooling, 33–34, 35, 40,
    46–49
  and sexual ambiguities, 73
  in show business, 61–63,
    65, 71–73, 156, 448–49,
    483–85
  songs of, 77, 179, 184, 191–92,
    212, 347, 348, 349, 364,
    373, 392, 393, 400, 451,
    461, 467, 474–75, 500

and sound films, 162
suspected of being a German
    spy, 561n34
teen years of, 30–49
and television, 459, 487, 501,
    509, 571n67
transformation for her roles,
    196–97, 199–200, 245–46,
    459–60, 473–75, 568n10
in U.S., 171, 180–90, 192–
    257, 351
and USO, 362–67, 370–71,
    373–76
wardrobe of, 68, 69, 79, 165–
    66, 172, 180, 192, 198, 214,
    220, 232, 363, 367, 368,
    369, 374–75, 393, 400–401,
    448–49, 452, 454, 458, 464,
    482, 484–85, 505, 506
wheelchair of, 508
work ethic of, 58, 78, 458
and World War I, 30, 34–38,
    41–43, 48
and World War II, 351–52,
    361, 362–76, 382–83, 474
Dietrich, Otto, 149
Dietrich, Sepp, 149
Dior, Christian, 400–401, 402,
    423, 452, 506
Dirksen, Viktoria von, 261
Dishonored (film), 188–90
Disney, Walt, 315
Dix, Otto, 14
Döblin, Alfred, Berlin Alexander-
    platz, 161
Docks of New York, The (film),
    112
Dr. Mabuse, the Gambler (film), 54

Dodd, William E., 292
Dolly Sisters, 73
Domela, Cesar, 533n55
Dos Passos, John, 227–28
Douglas, Louis, 62
Dreier, Hans, 545n40
Dresden:
    Riefenstahl's move to, 20
    Wigman's school of dance in,
        24–26
Dunaway, Faye, 514
Duncan, Isadora, 18, 528n10
Duse, Eleonora, 57

Edington, Harry, 231, 246, 247,
    255
Eduardowa, Eugenia, 82,
    533n54
Eggebrecht, Axel, 535n83
Eisenstein, Sergei, 187, 209, 263,
    278
Eisner, Lotte, 59, 407
Eitel Friedrich, Prince, 77
Elisabeth, Empress, 89
Emil and the Detectives (film), 128
Ertl, Hans, 122, 142, 290–91,
    297, 299, 327, 442, 556n94
Esser, Hermann, 431
Europe, Nazi takeovers in, 70,
    249, 257, 294, 308, 331
Express-Film Company, 94
Eysoldt, Gertrud, 57

Fairbanks, Douglas, Jr., 240–41,
    242, 450, 459
Fairbanks, Douglas, Sr., 111,
    183
Falkenberg, Paul, 108

"Falling in Love Again" (song), 77, 179, 451, 482, 489, 499

Fanck, Arnold, 88–106, 132, 134, 297

and *Avalanche,* 114–17, 162

birth and background of, 93

and *Blue Light,* 126–27, 136

in counterintelligence, 120

and *Great Leap,* 103–6

and *Holy Mountain,* 90–99, 101

and Leni, 88, 90–106, 110, 114, 117, 119–20, 122, 125, 136, 139–40, 262, 267, 304, 419, 442

and *Lowlands,* 335

and *Miracle of the Snowshoe,* 94, 103

and *Mountain of Destiny,* 88, 90, 94

as NSDAP member, 337

obsession with mountains, 94, 122–23

and *Piz Palü,* 108–11, 116, 120

and Reich chancellery film, 337

sadism of, 109, 125, 535n91

and *S.O.S. Iceberg,* 138–43, 152

war veterans in films of, 122

and *White Frenzy,* 119, 124–25, 140

Fangauf, Eberhard, 264, 266–67

Fashion Side of Hollywood, The (film), 232

Faust (film), 154

FBI, 561n34

Fedora (film), 571n13

Feilchenfeldt, Walter, 256

Feld, Hans, 114, 117

Feldman, Charles, 387, 399–400, 402, 406, 450

Fellini, Federico, 428

Felsing, Albert, 5, 32

Felsing, Elisabeth, 32–33, 36, 43, 53, 59, 60, 401

Felsing, Hasso Conrad, 30, 77, 192

Felsing, Jolly, 76, 77, 117, 237

Felsing, Willibald, 32, 36, 76, 77

Felsing family, 5, 32

social and professional contacts in, 77

and the theater, 55

and Wilhelmine Germany, 41, 53, 61

feminist film festivals, 446

Feuchtwanger, Lion, 75, 119

Feuchtwanger, Marta, 119

Film-Kurier, 264

Fitzgerald, F. Scott, 247

Flame of New Orleans, The (film), 351

Flanner, Janet, 215, 419

Flaubert, Gustave, 197

Fleckhaus, Willy, 443

Fleming, Robert, 450

Flesch, Carl, 49

Flickenschildt, Elisabeth, 328

Foreign Affair, A (film), 390–95, 399, 459, 571–72n15

Forst, Willi, 69, 70–71, 171, 209, 233, 503

Forster-Larrinaga, Robert, 156

4628 Meter High on Skis: Climbing Monte Rosa (film), 94
Fournier, Dominique, 397
Fraenkel, Ernst, 258
France:
    Austria occupied by, 414–15
    German occupation of, 331, 357
    Marlene with USO in, 373–74
    Paris retaken by Allies, 340
    prelude to World War II, 250–51, 252, 256, 257
    "Train Bleu," 373
    war declared by, 353
Franco, Francisco, 331
Franco-Prussian War, 53
Frankfurt Book Fair, 445
Fräulein Else (film), 128
Frederick the Great, 3
Free French Forces, 361–62
Freeman, Stan, 488–89
Freiligrath, Ferdinand, "O lieb, so lang du lieben kannst," 503
Frentz, Walter, 122, 267, 268, 280, 297, 327
Freud, Sigmund, 21
Freund, Karl, 128
Frick, Wilhelm, 273
Friedrich, Caspar David, 94
Friedrich, Kaiser, 33
Froitzheim, Otto, 28, 29, 84, 87
Frost, Robert, 471
Führer Builds His Reich Capital, The (filmstrip), 336–37
Funk, Walter, 335
Furthman, Jules, 545n40
Furtwängler, Wilhelm, 426

Gabin, Jean, 356–59
    death of, 498
    end of affair with, 384, 385, 389, 396–97, 398, 399, 452
    and film roles, 357, 383, 385–87
    and Free French Forces, 361–62
    letters to and from Marlene, 364–65, 368, 379–80
    Marlene's affair with, 356, 357–59, 361–62, 364–65, 368–69, 371, 379, 382, 383, 384, 486
    marriage to Fournier, 397, 405, 462
Gable, Clark, 137
Gainsbourg, Serge, 506
Gance, Abel, 278
Garbo, Greta, 106, 137, 187, 223, 231, 263, 349, 356, 505
Garden of Allah (film), 238–39
Garland, Judy, 469, 473
Garmes, Lee, 184, 545n40
Gavin, James M., 381, 382, 384–85, 407, 562n4
George, Heinrich, 75, 279
George Eastman House, Rochester, 513
Georgi, Yvonne, 24–25
Geriatrea, 469
German Nansen Society, 437
German National Association of Visual Arts, 537n122
Germany:
    anti-Semitism in, 314
    and Battle of Stalingrad, 336

Germany (*continued*)
  beaten-down men in, 22
  compulsory military service
    in, 290, 295
  currency reform in, 425
  delusions of grandeur in, 45
  exiles in U.S. from, 233–35,
    259
  expressionism in, 532n38
  extraordinary year (1923), 27
  Federal Republic, 425
  industry and technology in,
    13, 60
  inflation in, 26–27, 54, 60, 63,
    73, 81
  instability in, 63, 160, 191,
    203, 208
  Kostümfilme in, 531n28
  Kristallnacht in, 314
  Marlene's assets in, 208, 209,
    225
  Marlene's films accepted in,
    240
  Marlene's stage performances
    in, 462–67
  military films in, 291–92
  mountain films in, 88–101,
    102–11, 115–23, 129, 273,
    287, 413, 434, 534n72
  Munich Agreement (1938), 313
  Nazi Party in, *see* National
    Socialism
  New Woman in, 22–24, 45,
    57, 60, 68, 85–86, 115
  Night of the Long Knives in,
    277
  1920s in, 27, 73, 532n38,
    533n49
  and Olympic Games (1936),
    294, 295, 296, 297–98, 444
  postwar films in, 426
  post–World War I, 22, 53–54,
    59–60, 85–86, 122
  post–World War II, 411–12,
    419
  prelude to World War II in,
    249, 287–88
  Reichstag dissolved, 149
  revolution of 1918 in, 10, 43,
    45, 53, 59, 60
  Sedan Day in, 53
  Siegfried Line in, 330
  stock market crash and world
    economic crisis (1929), 160,
    208
  Third Reich, 258, 421, 446
  upward mobility sought in, 83
  war-crimes trials in, 415–16,
    419
  Weimar Republic, 20, 22, 57,
    61, 69, 79, 83, 147, 161, 171,
    258, 475
  World War I in, 11, 22,
    34–38, 41–43
  World War II in, *see* World
    War II
Gerron, Kurt, 163
Gershwin, George, 62, 73
Gert, Valeska, 26
Giacometti, Alberto, 462
Gilda (film), 448
Gillhausen, Rolf, 443, 445
Ginzburg, Carlo, 190
Gladitz, Nina, 517
Glas, Uschi, 521
Goddard, Paulette, 453, 485–86

Goebbels, Joseph:
  and approved films, 263, 267
  and banned films, 148
  and banned songs, 373
  death of, 412
  diaries of, 422
  and Leni's films, 260–61,
    263–64, 273, 274, 279, 280,
    287, 288, 290, 292, 295,
    296, 300, 303, 304, 305–6,
    309, 328, 330, 332, 336,
    341, 413, 421, 424
  and Marlene, 240, 246–47
  and Ministry of Propaganda,
    262–63, 266, 305, 309, 321,
    322, 328, 413
  and Nazi rize to power, 21
  socializing with Leni, 150–51,
    260–62, 263–64, 307, 315,
    334, 422
Goebbels, Magda, 150, 151, 260,
  261
Goethe, Johann Wolfgang von:
  "Just Take My Life," 500
  "Reynard the Fox," 470
Goetz, Ben, 303
Golden Earrings (film), 387
Gone With the Wind (film), 349
Goodman, Dean, 359, 382
Göring, Emmy, 431, 566n1
Göring, Hermann, 151, 261,
  277, 292, 431
Gotthart, Bernhard, 94
Göttler, Fritz, 426
Goulding, Edmund, 263
Grant, Cary, 206
Granz, Norman, 462, 463
Great Depression, 204, 232, 235

Greatest Earthly Joy on Horseback,
  The (short film), 556n86
Great Leap, The (film), 103–6,
  127
Great War, see World War I
Greenland, film shooting in,
  138–43, 293, 335
Grimm-Reiter, Helene, 13–14
Grosskopf, Walter, 316
Grosz, George, 99
Guiness, Alec, 450
Guitry, Sasha, 311
Gulbranssen, Trygve, Beyond
  Sing the Woods, 331

Haas, Willy, 39
Habsburg Empire, 63
Haffner, Sebastian, 27, 35, 53,
  160, 171, 262
Hameister, Willy, 297
Hammett, Dashiell, 193
Hampton, Hope, 482
Hanfstaengl, Ernst, 150, 151,
  261–62
Harrison, Joan, 504
Harrison, Rex, 459
Hassell, Ulrich von, 296
Hauser, Arnold, 130
Hays Code, 201, 545n42
Hayworth, Rita, 352, 457
Head, Edith, 458
Heiden, Konrad, 293
"Heidenröslein" (song), 212
Heimatfilm (sentimental film in
  rural setting), 92
Hellman, Lillian, 452
Hemingway, Ernest, 473
  death of, 471

Hemingway, Ernest (*continued*)
  Green Hills of Africa, 433–35,
    436
  and Leni, 432–34
  and Marlene, 373–74, 406,
    407–8, 453, 499
Hemingway, Mary Welsh, 373,
  374, 453
Henning, Hanna, 137
Hepburn, Audrey, 402
Hepburn, Katharine, 247
Hermès accessories, 200
Hess, Rudolf, 268, 271, 273,
  284, 334, 415
Hessel, Franz, 190, 507
Heuser, Kurt, 434
Hilpert, Heinz, 246–47
Himmler, Heinrich, 35, 286
Hindenburg, Paul von, 42, 77,
  147–48, 276, 277
Hinkel, Hans, 265–67, 341
Hintner, Cornelius, 536n94
Hinze, Ingetraud, 396
Hitchcock, Alfred, 400
Hitchens, Gordon, 419
Hitler, Adolf:
  attempted assassination of, 343
  charisma of, 144, 268, 269,
    271, 518
  death of, 412, 413
  and Leni, 28, 144–47, 149–52,
    258–65, 267–69, 277–79,
    283–84, 289–91, 292–93,
    305–9, 331, 340, 421, 423,
    518
  and Leni's films, 136, 148,
    260, 261, 267, 271–72, 273–
    75, 277–78, 283–90, 291,
    292–93, 295, 300, 305–7,
    311–12, 321–23, 328, 329,
    337, 424, 518
  lifestyle of, 150
  losing self-control, 313
  loss of power, 343, 367
  and Marlene's films, 240
  and Marlene's postwar stage
    performances, 463, 467
  Mein Kampf, 149, 151, 293,
    331, 431
  movies about, 470–71
  and Night of the Long Knives,
    277
  at the opera, 553–54n55
  and party members, 276–77
  postwar investigations about,
    416
  rise to power, 143–52, 203,
    211, 213, 259, 264, 267, 431
  takeovers in Europe, 70, 249,
    257, 315
  and the *Volk,* 268, 269, 288, 427
  Wilder's triumph over,
    393–94
  and World War II, 257, 313,
    315, 319–23, 326–27, 331,
    334, 335, 336, 367
Hitler Over Germany (film), 266
Hitler Youth, 285–86
Hitler Youth in the Mountains
  (film), 266
Hobsbawm, Eric, 141
Hobsbawm, Sidney, 141
Hoffmann, Erna, 19
Hoffmann, Heinrich, 150, 261
Hohenzollern dynasty, 43
Hölderlin, Friedrich, 99

Hollaender, Friedrich, 62, 158–59, 163, 168, 191, 233, 347, 393

Hollywood:
"box office poison" in, 247, 257
and Depression, 204, 232
exiles from Germany in, 233–35
film industry in, 236
Hays Code in, 201, 545n42
Leni boycotted in, 313–15, 415, 418, 514
Marlene's life in, 193–94, 215, 232–34, 236, 249, 358, 389, 457
Marlene's move to, 168–69, 171–73, 177–82, 187, 200
postwar, 504
scandals in, 201
in wartime, 351–52, 354, 372, 394

Hollywood Canteen, 352

Hollywood Victory Committee, 351–52

Holy Mountain, The (film), 90–99, 100–103, 145, 535n83

Homecoming (propaganda film), 70

Hörmann, Gheo von, 439

Horst Wessel Song, 272, 273, 289

Hugenberg, Alfred, 65, 77, 211

Huston, John, 351

Ickes, Paul, 138

Ihering, Herbert, 60

I Kiss Your Hand, Madame (film), 69, 399

"Illusions" (song), 393

Image, 513

Impressions of the Deep (film), 523

Internal Revenue Service, 256

International Exposition (1937), Paris, 307

International Olympics Committee, 294

Interview, 511–12

Isherwood, Christopher, 452

Israel, Marlene's stage performances in, 466–67, 479

Italy:
Leni's visit to, 426–27
postwar filmmaking in, 426, 427, 428

It's in the Air (musical revue), 71–73, 75, 156

Jabs, Waldemar, 162

Jacob, Peter, 340, 416, 417, 418, 420, 432

Jacobi, Lotte, photographs of Leni by, 86–87, 118

Jacobi, Mia, 86

Jäger, Ernst, 280, 313, 413

Jagger, Bianca, 511, 514

Jagger, Mick, 446, 511, 514

Jannings, Emil:
and The Blue Angel, 155, 156, 158, 163–64, 166–68, 169, 172
in Pandora's Box, 57
and Paramount, 209
socializing, 77

Jannings, Emil (*continued*)
  and sound films, 162
  in *Tragedy of Love,* 67
  and von Sternberg, 152–55,
    163–64
Janowitz, Hans, 128
Jaques-Dalcroze, Émile, 19
Jaworsky, Heinz von, 99, 127,
    131, 538n8
Jazz Singer, The (film), 161
Jigsaw (film), 399
"Johnny wenn du Geburtstag
    hast" (song), 191, 212, 482
Johnson, Lyndon B., 489
Joyce, James, 278
Judgment at Nuremberg (film),
    469–70, 502, 570n43
Jung, Edgar, 277
Jünger, Ernst, 121–22
Just a Gigolo (film), 500

Kafka, Franz, 19
Karajan, Herbert von, 345
Karlweis, Oskar, 72, 73
Kasten, Jürgen, 128
Kästner, Erich, 75, 385
Kau people of Nuba tribe, 444,
    515
Kennedy, Edward M. "Ted," 471,
    489
Kennedy, John F., 256, 471–72
Kennedy, Robert F., 471
Kent, Sidney, 168
Kerr, Deborah, 450
Kettelhut, Erich, 67
Kettner, Horst, 441–42, 444,
    514, 516, 521, 522, 524
Kiesewetter, Knut, 572n6

Kindler, Helmut, 423–25
Kirch, Leo, 521
Kisch, Egon Erwin, 86
Kishon, Ephraim, 467
Kismet (film), 362, 370
Kissinger, Henry A., 521
Klamt, Hermann, 80, 81
Klamt, Jutta, 82–84, 533n58
Klarsfeld, Beate, 510
Klausener, Erich, 277
Kleist, Heinrich von, *Penthesilea,*
    328–29
Klimt, Gustav, 69
Klingenberg, Werner, 313
Knef, Hildegard, 408–9, 464,
    465, 499, 503
Knight Without Armour (film),
    239–40, 246
Koebner, F. W., 27–28
Kohner, Paul, 140, 302–4, 512
Kokoschka, Oskar, 242
Kolbe, Georg, 242
Kollwitz, Käthe, 99
Kolpé, Max, 228, 250, 384, 390,
    409, 455, 499, 500, 507
Koppenhöfer, Maria, 328, 330
Korda, Alexander (Sander), 68,
    130
Kortner, Fritz, 77–78
Kosleck, Martin, 547n83
Koster, Henry, 402–3
Kracauer, Siegfried, 92
Kramer, Stanley, 469, 570n43
Krauss, Werner, 57
Krenek, Ernst, *Jonny,* 532
Kretschmer, Elfriede, 572n6
Kreuder, Peter, 191, 291
Kreutzberg, Harald, 222–23

Kuchenbuch, Herbert, 117–18
Kunzmann, Theresia, 177

Lacombe, Georges, 386
Ladies' Home Journal, 570n45
Lady Is Willing, The (film), 360
Laemmle, Carl, 139, 140, 141
Lagerfeld, Karl, 506
LaGuardia, Fiorello, 368
Lamarr, Hedy, 246
Lamprecht, Gerhard, 128
Lancaster, Burt, 469
Lanchester, Elsa, 458
Lang, Fritz, 504
   and *Dr. Mabuse,* 54
   and *M,* 147
   and Marlene, 238, 405–7
   and *Metropolis,* 112
   and *Nibelungs,* 162, 263
   and *Rancho Notorious,* 405–7
   and *Woman in the Moon,* 111
Langendorf, Captain, 413
Langhaeuser, Rudolf, 325
Langlois, Henri, 512
Lantin, Rolf, 299
Lantschner, Guzzi and Otto,
   280, 321, 327, 556n94
Lasker-Schüler, Else, 158
Last Command, The (film), 154
Lastfogel, Abe, 362
Last Laugh, The (film), 128, 154
La Strada (film), 428
Las Vegas, Marlene's stage
   appearances in, 448–49,
   451, 452–54, 457, 461
Laughton, Charles, 458, 459
"La Vie en Rose" (song), 400,
   487

"Laziest Gal in Town, The"
   (song), 400, 451
League of Nations, 287, 295
Leap, The (short film), 556n86
"Leben ohne Liebe kannst du
   nicht" (song), 191
Lebensreformer (back to nature
   advocates), 18
Le Corbusier, 19
Lehnich, Oswald, 296
Leip, Hans, 561n35
Leisen, Mitchell, 387
Leni, Paul, 67
Leni Riefenstahl Film Inc., 316,
   335, 336–37
Lenya, Lotte, 86
Lerman, Leo, 369, 404, 449,
   482
Leuwerik, Ruth, 432
Levin, Julius, 48
Lewitan, Joseph, 533n54
Liberman, Alexander, 401–2,
   477
Liberman, Tatjana, 402
Liebknecht, Karl, 528n14
Life, 408, 437
"Lili Marleen" (song), 373, 451,
   467
Lindbergh, Charles, 208
Lion, Margo, 72, 73, 74–75, 130,
   210, 384, 531n36
Little Napoleon, The (film), 67
Locarno Pact, 294
Loesser, Frank, 347
Lollobrigida, Gina, 427
London, Marlene's stage perfor-
   mances in, 450–52, 461
Loren, Sophia, 462, 521

Lorre, Peter, 233
Los Angeles, *see* Hollywood
Losch, Eduard von, 30–31, 37–38
Losch, Josefine von, *see* Dietrich,
    Josefine
Louis, Jean, 448, 459–60
Louys, Pierre, *The Woman and
    the Puppet,* 227
Love (film), 263
Lowlands (film), 330–34
    based on opera by d'Albert,
        330
    cast and crew of, 279, 330,
        337–39, 341, 342, 423–24,
        517
    comparisons with, 333
    failure of, 343, 414, 428
    filming of, 331–32, 516
    lawsuits related to, 423–24
    Leni as director of, 330, 333,
        341–43
    Leni's acting in, 135, 330, 333,
        343
    Leni's changing claims about,
        330, 333–34, 413, 573n12
    Leni's continued work on, 411,
        414, 421, 426, 427
    meaning sought in, 559n44,
        573n12
    story of, 332–33
L. R. Studio Films, Inc., 126
Lubitsch, Ernst, 45, 105, 154,
    209, 231, 243, 398, 504
Luddy, Tom, 512
Ludendorff, Erich, 45
Ludwig, Emil, 244
Luft, Friedrich, 465
Lukács, Georg, 130

Lund, John, 392
Lutze, Viktor, 285, 286
Luz, Oskar, 437

M (film), 147
Madam Doctor (film), 262
Madame Doesn't Want Children
    (film), 68, 130, 390
Mademoiselle Docteur (film), 421
Madonna, 505
Magnani, Anna, 396, 432
Magnum Photos, 436
Mahir, Sabri, 85
Mahler, Gustav, 355, 467
Maillol, Aristide, 242
Mainz, Friedrich, 425
Maltese Falcon, The (film), 351
Mamoulian, Rouben, 211, 212,
    223
Man by the Roadside (film), 362
Mann, Abby, 570n43
Mann, Erika, 86, 307
Mann, Heinrich:
    and *The Blue Angel,* 155–56,
        179
    Professor Unrat, 155, 169, 170
Mann, Klaus, 86, 125
Mann, Thomas, 54, 160–61,
    233, 254
Mannheim, Karl, 130
Mannheim, Lucie, 158–59
Manon Lescaut (film), 67–68
Manpower (film), 359–60
Manstein, Erich von, 322–23,
    325
Manton, Maria, 359
Marais, Jean, 432, 452
Marlene (film), 502–3

Marzahn concentration camp, 338–39, 423, 517
Massary, Fritzi, 455
Matul, Tamara, 204, 241, 532n43
abortions of, 456
death of, 477, 478
health issues of, 256, 409, 476–77
as Maria's nanny, 75
and Marlene's money, 396–97, 409
in New York, 353
other lovers of, 353
in Paris, 214, 226, 251
passport of, 226–27, 353
as Sieber's lover, 75–76, 157, 190–91, 194, 238, 256–57, 353, 409, 410, 455–56
Matz, Peter, 569n22
Maxglan camp, 338, 424, 517
May, Joe, 67
May, Karl, 89
May, Mia, 504
Mayer, Carl, 127–29, 133, 279, 312, 513, 538n11
May-Film, 63, 64
Mazdaznan movement, 83
McLaglen, Victor, 188
Meadows, Earle, 302
Medal of Freedom, 395
"Mein blondes Baby" ("My Blonde Baby") (song), 467
Menjou, Adolphe, 183, 184
Messner, Reinhold, 521
Messter, Oskar, 76
Metro-Goldwyn-Mayer, 247, 302–4, 362

Metropolis (film), 112
Meyen, Harry, 465
Meyerinck, Hubert von, 63, 72
Mies van der Rohe, Ludwig, 19
Milestone, Lewis, 148, 389
Miller, Lee, 374
Minde-Pouet, Georg, 329
Minetti, Bernhard, 59, 330, 332, 334, 337, 341, 342, 343, 516
Miracle of the Snowshoe: A System for Skiing Correctly, The (film), 94, 103
Mitchell, Margaret, Gone With the Wind, 331
Modern Dubarry, A (film), 531n30
Moissi, Alexander, 34
Mollinger, Dolly, 256
Monroe, Marilyn, 402
Montand, Yves, 462, 465
Monte Carlo Story (film), 456–57
Morocco (film), 179–87
Academy Award nominations for, 208
comparisons with, 190, 197
filming of, 546–47n73
premiere of, 203
story of, 183–87, 350
vocal numbers from, 191
Moroder, Giorgio, 523
Morris, Glenn, 301, 302, 315
Mosheim, Grete, 57, 64, 455
Mountain of Destiny (film), 88–90, 94–95
Müller, André, 573n12
Müller, Hermann, 171
Müller, Ray, 110, 274, 521
The Wonderful, Horrible Life of Leni Riefenstahl, 127, 519–20

Munich Agreement (1938), 313
Munkacsi, Martin, 119
Murnau, Friedrich Wilhelm,
    128, 133–34, 154
Musil, Robert, 45
    The Man Without Qualities, 17
Mussolini, Benito, 131, 137, 286,
    295, 330, 331, 365
Muthesius, Eckart, 344

Nannen, Henri, 443
Nansen passports, 226–27, 353
National Film Archives, 417
National Geographic, 437
National Socialism (Nazi party):
    anti-Semitism of, 259, 296,
        314, 336
    and the arts, 83, 290
    covert continuity of, 521
    and cultural revolt (1968), 443
    and *Day of Freedom,* 515
    exiles in U.S. from, 233–34
    factions within, 276–77
    failed 1923 putsch, 286
    fanatical pathos of, 288, 296
    forced laborers used by,
        343–44
    Germany ruled by, 258
    Horst Wessel Song, 272, 273,
        289
    ideology of, 447
    and Leni, 130, 136, 147,
        264–68, 273, 275, 315, 413,
        422, 442–43, 518, 523
    and Leni's films, 261, 264,
        270–75, 279, 288, 296–97,
        299–300, 321, 330, 333,
        417, 420–21, 425, 435, 446

nations liberated from, 411
and Night of the Long Knives,
    277
and Olympic Games, 296,
    301–2, 304, 440
party rallies, 268, 269–72,
    275, 277, 278, 279, 282–87,
    290, 412, 417, 422, 440
post–World War II, 413–15,
    419
public disenchantment with,
    276
and Remarque, 248
rise to power, 21, 147–50, 211,
    213, 215, 259, 280, 431
and *Triumph of the Will,* 515
and *Victory of Faith,* 270–75,
    515
Nazi party, *see* National
    Socialism
NBC, 464
Negri, Pola, 28, 45
Neurath, Konstantin von, 273
Neutra, Richard, 242, 548n110
Neville-Willing, Donald, 450
New Look, 423
New Objectivity, 278
Newton, Helmut, 523
New Woman, 22–24, 45, 57, 60,
    68, 85–86, 115, 446
Nibelungs, The (film), 162, 263
Nietzsche, Friedrich, 18, 99
Night of the Long Knives, 277
Niven, David, 450
No Highway in the Sky (film),
    402–3
Normandy, Allied landings in,
    340, 367

Norwich, Lord and Lady, 450
Nosferatu (film), 133
Nuba people, 436–44, 446–47,
    514, 520, 521–22
Nuremberg:
    Judgment at Nuremberg (film),
        469–70, 502, 570n43
    war-crimes trials in, 415–16,
        419

Office of Strategic Services
    (OSS), 372–73
Olivier, Laurence, 450
Olympia (film), 290, 294–312
    Festival of Beauty (Part II),
        310–11
    Festival of Nations (Part I),
        309–10
    filming of, 297–301, 342, 440,
        556n94
    as fine sports film, 309
    honors and awards to, 311
    international versions of, 309,
        311–12, 313, 315, 321
    premiere of, 308–9
    reissue of (1960s), 444
    at Telluride Film Festival, 512
Olympia Film Inc., 295, 303
Olympiaverlag, publisher, 423
Olympic Games (1932), 296
Olympic Games (1936), 294,
    295, 296, 297–302, 313,
    440, 444, 520
Olympic Games (1940), 313
Olympic Games (1972), 444
Opel, Margot von, 307, 329
Orla, Ressel, 66
Orlik, Emil, 66

OSS (Office of Strategic Ser-
    vices), 372–73
Owens, Jesse, 302

Pabst, G. W., 69, 106, 108–9,
    121, 335
Pacific Film Archive, 512
Palmer, Lilli, 506
Palucca, Gret, 24, 25
Pan Am, Marlene's ads for, 485
Pandora's Box (drama), 57, 58, 69
Papen, Franz von, 149, 273, 277
Paramount Pictures, 169,
    180–81, 182, 187, 192, 202,
    214, 226, 236, 415
Paramount Studios, 204–5, 209,
    211, 247, 249, 387
Pasternak, Joe, 168, 257,
    347–49
Patcevitch, Iva, 403
Patton, George S., 375, 376
Pavlova, Anna, 84
Pawlinin, Helge, 434
Penthesilea (proposed film), 316,
    320, 327–30, 340, 445
"Peter" (song), 191, 482
Peters, Erna, 272
Petersen, Ernst, 96, 111
Peukert, Detlev, 35
Piaf, Edith, 400, 465
Picasso, Pablo, *La Gameuse,* 242
Pickford, Mary, 111
Pinthus, Kurt, 60
Piscator, Erwin, 113
Pittsburgh (film), 360–61
*Piz Palü, see White Hell of Piz
    Palü, The*
Poelzig, Hans, 19, 56

Poland:
  German invasion of, 319, 321,
    325, 326
  Leni's attempt to film in,
    320–25
  Marlene's travel to, 472
  Warsaw ghetto uprising, 472
Polgar, Alfred, 424
Pommer, Erich, 157, 162, 179,
  259
Pompidou, Georges, 487
Porten, Henny, 39–40
Porter, Cole, 400
Power, Tyrone, 458
Prager, Walter, 152, 275, 280
Prager, Willy, 72
Preminger, Otto, 504
Prévert, Jacques, 383
Prinzhorn, Hans, 19, 529n18
Putti, Lya de, 67

"Quand l'amour meurt" (song),
  184
Queen Christine (film), 223

Rabenalt, Arthur Maria, 335
Raether, Arnold, 264, 265–67,
  268, 274
Raffé, Rudolf, 536n94
Raft, George, 359
Rancho Notorious (film), 405–7,
  564n48
Rasmussen, Knud, 139
Rathenau, Walter, 160
Raubal, Geli, 151
Ravel, Maurice, 461
Reagan, Nancy, 501
Reagan, Ronald, 501

Rebel, The (film), 263, 267
Red Devils, The (film), 432
Reichenau, Walther von, 323,
  324
Reich Film Chamber, 296, 299
Reinhardt, Max, 56, 59, 62, 71,
  75, 80, 162, 246, 259, 328
Reinl, Harald, 330
Reisch, Walter, 203, 372, 390,
  409, 482, 500, 504, 506,
  545n48
Reitz, Robert, 48–49
Remarque, Erich Maria "Boni,"
  243–57
  affair with Marlene, 245–46,
    251–56, 353–56, 358, 359,
    499
  All Quiet on the Western Front,
    244
  Arch of Triumph "Ravic novel,"
    248, 253, 254, 356, 389
  art collection of, 256
  and Black Fox, 471
  citizenship of, 252, 354, 355
  death of, 485–86, 498
  and end of affair, 243, 251,
    353–54, 355, 356, 357
  Flotsam, 253
  health issues of, 398, 485
  and Judgment at Nuremberg,
    471
  and Leni, 105, 114, 148, 307
  messages to and from Mar-
    lene, 243, 247–49, 253, 254,
    352, 388–89, 398, 452–53
  moods and drinking of,
    256–57, 356
  in New York, 253–54

in Paris, 249–51

personal traits of, 244, 248, 251

post–World War II, 398

and preludes to World War II, 249

remarriage to ex-wife, 248, 250

socializing, 257, 307, 353, 397–98, 500

Three Comrades, 247

and World War II, 352–53, 356, 361

Renoir, Jean, 357

Revue, 423–24

Rhineland, German takeover of, 294

Ribbentrop, Joachim von, 422

Richard, Frida, 330

Richee, Eugene, 232

Riefenstahl, Alfred Theodor Paul (father), 7–9, 12–16

aspiring to wealth, 12, 23

attempts to control his daughter, 9, 10, 11, 13–14, 15–16, 20–21, 22, 25, 83, 127

business of, 12, 13, 17, 344

death of, 343, 346

and his son, 12–13, 16

and Leni's career, 29, 80, 308

Riefenstahl, Bertha Ida Scherlach (mother), 7–8

aspiring to wealth, 12, 13, 23

and the cinema, 14

and her husband's strictness, 10

and Leni's artistic ambitions, 14, 80

and Leni's career, 308

and Leni's early years, 10, 13

post–World War II, 411, 419–20

Riefenstahl, Heinz (brother):

artistic interests of, 12

childhood of, 9

death of, 346

father's plans for, 12–13, 16

and his father's business, 344–46

and Leni's ambition, 89

and Leni's work, 295, 306, 308, 557n7

and Nazi party, 344–45

and Olympia Film Inc., 295

Riefenstahl, Helene Amalia Bertha, *see* Riefenstahl, Leni

Riefenstahl, Inge (Heinz's wife), 306

Riefenstahl, Leni, 10–29, 79–152, 319–46, 431–47, 511–24

and Africa, 433–35, 436–47, 515

and aging, 442, 444, 446, 514, 516, 519, 520–24

ambition of, 11, 16, 21, 27–29, 82, 84–85, 87, 89, 105–6, 110, 125, 127, 128, 129, 147, 149, 261–62, 269, 275, 278, 287, 296, 513–14, 519–20

arrests and escapes of, 412

art, beauty, and strength as core of, 83, 105, 517

artistic rise of, 81–83, 128, 136

as artist with nothing to learn, 25, 82

Riefenstahl, Leni (*continued*)
assets confiscated, 419,
    421–23, 435
attention sought by, 11,
    142–43, 419, 423, 432
*Behind the Scenes of the Reich
    Party Rally Film,* 280
birth and family background
    of, 7–8, 265
boxing lessons taken by, 85
car accident of, 433–34, 436
career advancement of, 80,
    124–27, 136, 147, 261, 264,
    287, 291, 314, 320, 427, 514,
    518
childhood of, 8–9, 122
as "child of nature," 9, 10, 95,
    96, 123
as cinema fan, 14, 112
comeback of, 446–47
competition avoided by, 26,
    119
Coral Gardens, 518, 520
as dancer, 14–16, 18–19,
    20–21, 22, 25, 27, 29,
    79–81, 84, 92, 93, 96–97,
    104, 105, 117, 124, 145, 440,
    523
"Dances of Eros" performed
    by, 29
dealings with men, 11, 27–28,
    29, 80, 84, 87, 90–92,
    99–102, 105, 110–11,
    113–14, 123, 125–27, 131,
    140, 142, 147, 148–49, 151,
    261, 293, 301, 330, 340,
    341–42, 442
death of, 524

and deep-sea diving, 515, 516,
    518–19, 520, 524
denazification hearings of,
    420–22, 425
deported from Austria, 419
disregarding her father's
    wishes, 9, 10, 11, 13–14,
    15–16, 20–21, 22, 25, 127
divorce of, 420, 432
"Dream Blossom" choreo-
    graphed by, 96
fading influence of, 313, 314,
    326, 330, 340, 436
and fame, 293, 313, 314, 444,
    511, 518, 520
as film actress, 15, 95, 97, 99,
    103–5, 108, 111, 116–17,
    124, 125, 135, 136, 137,
    273, 312, 330, 333, 343,
    426, 428; *see also* Riefen-
    stahl, Leni, films acted in
film apprenticeship of, 123,
    126; *see also* Riefenstahl,
    Leni, films directed by
financing sought by, 27–29,
    81, 259, 423, 425, 426, 432,
    436, 535n81
first sexual experience, 28
flights from reality, 114, 342–
    43, 411, 436, 438, 440–41,
    513–15
and Goebbels, 150–51,
    260–64, 274, 295, 300,
    305–6
health problems of, 335–36,
    339–40, 343, 420, 516–17,
    522, 524
in helicopter accident, 522

history rewritten by, 80, 90,
128, 136–37, 261, 263–64,
274, 280, 312, 326, 330,
412, 413, 417–19, 421–23,
507, 513–15, 517–18, 521
and Hitler, 144–47, 149–52,
258–65, 267–69, 273–75,
277–79, 283–84, 289–91,
292–93, 305–9, 331, 337,
412, 417–18, 421, 423, 424,
440, 515, 517–18, 520
honors and awards to, 137,
289–90, 295–96, 311, 417
houses built by, 306–7, 515–16
income of, 95, 105, 124, 292,
295, 336–37, 413, 421, 423,
439
international travel of, 293–
94, 307, 313–15
interrogations of, 413–16, 418
judicial inquiry initiated
against, 523
knee injury of, 84, 87, 88, 89,
93
The Last of the Nuba, 444, 514,
520
lawsuits initiated by, 423–25,
517
and Marlene, 112–14
marriage of, 340
memoirs of, 25, 114, 128,
326, 426, 507, 516–17, 519,
552n39
and modeling, 86–87
and mountain films, 88–101,
102–11, 115–23, 129, 261,
267, 269, 273, 278, 287,
292, 413, 433, 434, 440, 442

Müller's film about: *The Wonderful, Horrible Life of Leni
Riefenstahl,* 127, 519–20
and Mussolini, 295
and Nazi party, 130, 136, 263,
264–68, 273, 275, 280, 290,
293, 315, 330, 333, 413,
420–22, 425, 435, 518, 523
in New York, 514
and Nuba people, 436–44,
446–47, 514, 519, 520,
521–22
outsider status of, 25, 440
peasants and Gypsies used for
filming by, 337–39, 423–25,
434, 439, 517, 519, 523
People of Kau, 445, 515
photographs by, 438–47, 511,
515, 516, 518–19, 520
physical appearance of, 86,
120, 446, 514
piano lessons of, 13
and politics, 143–44, 147,
148, 259, 308, 313, 314–15,
413–14, 426
post–World War II, 411–28,
431
production company of, 126
professional contacts of, 85,
297, 299–300, 321, 421, 427,
441–42
public image of, 292, 293, 313,
520–21
reputation of, 136
on the run, 411
Schulberg's visit to, 416–19
self-confidence of, 29, 91, 95,
99

Riefenstahl, Leni (*continued*)
  self-image of, 102–3, 105,
    329–30, 333, 412, 413, 414,
    419–20, 522, 523
  self-promotion of, 82, 89, 91,
    106, 114, 118, 127, 131, 144,
    145–48, 151, 292, 314
  Special Film Unit of, 321–23
  speech lessons for, 117–18
  sports played by, 9, 10, 16, 22
  Struggle in Snow and Ice, 110,
    127, 138, 513
  studio lot built for, 315–16
  success achieved by, 258–59,
    274, 289–90, 302, 309,
    311–12, 321, 327
  teen years of, 10–23
  at Telluride Film Festival,
    512–13, 514
  training her body, 9, 85, 93,
    103, 316
  triumph over her father, 29,
    83
  as typist in her father's office,
    15–16, 83
  and war, 316, 319–27, 330–31,
    334–35, 346
  Wonders under Water, 518
  work ethic of, 292–93, 299–
    301, 305
  working through her pain,
    14, 82, 84, 104, 108–10,
    433–34, 518–19
Riefenstahl, Leni, films acted in:
  Avalanche, 115–20, 127, 162,
    435
  The Great Leap, 103–4, 106,
    127

  The Holy Mountain, 93–99,
    100–103, 145, 535n83
  Piz Palü, 107–11, 116, 120,
    139, 263
  S.O.S. Iceberg, 138–43, 145, 273
  White Frenzy, 119, 124–25,
    127, 131, 140
Riefenstahl, Leni, films directed
    by:
  archive of, 435–36, 515–16
  Black Cargo, 434–35
  *The Blue Light, see Blue Light,
    The*
  critical reviews of, 137, 138
  *Day of Freedom—Our Wehr-
    macht—Nuremberg 1935,*
    290, 291–92, 323, 415,
    416–17, 515
  dreams as sources for, 129,
    136, 268, 333, 418, 427
  Lowlands, see Lowlands
  military precision in planning
    of, 269–70, 280–83, 297–
    98, 300–301, 305, 306
  money squandered on, 332,
    335
  Olympia, 290, 294–312, 315,
    321, 342, 440, 512
  and postwar hearings, 420–22
  postwar projects, 432–33
  remakes of, 436
  technical innovations in,
    134–35, 287, 311, 555n80
  *Triumph of the Will, see Triumph
    of the Will*
  Victory of Faith, 152, 264,
    270–75, 276, 415, 416–17,
    515

Riefenstahl film Inc., 316, 335, 336–39

Rilke, Rainer Maria, 19, 57, 243, 385

Riml, Walter, 127, 131, 137, 142, 280

Rist, Sepp, 115, 121, 142, 279

Rittau, Günter, 112, 162

Riva, John Michael, 401

Riva, Maria Elisabeth:
  as actress, 219, 459
  birth of, 63
  childhood of, 66–67, 75, 76, 77, 238
  children of, 395–96, 398, 399, 401, 457, 462, 476
  citizenship of, 65
  and her father, 202, 214, 366, 382, 493
  and her mother, 66, 190–91, 192, 193–94, 381–82, 403, 461, 462, 466, 478, 486, 488, 510
  as "Maria Manton," 359
  Marlene in U.S., 171
  Marlene's attachment to, 196, 382, 505
  on Marlene's life, 49, 77, 167
  and Marlene's memoirs, 498–99
  and Marlene's work, 199–200, 217, 230, 239, 366, 462
  marriage to Goodman, 359, 382
  marriage to Riva, 390
  as teenager, 257
  travel to Europe, 213, 215

Riva, Paul, 457

Riva, Peter, 395–96, 397, 398, 401, 510, 572n22

Riva, William, 390

Robison, Arthur, 67

Rodger, George, 436–37, 438, 566–67n10

Le Village des Noubas, 437

Rodin, Auguste, 242

Röhm, Ernst, 271, 273, 276–77, 285

Roman, Martin, 542n71

Rome:
  Allied conquest of, 367
  Leni's visit to, 426–27

Rommel, Erwin, 327

Room Upstairs, The (Martin Roumagnac) (film), 386–87

Roosevelt, Franklin D., 204, 235–36, 350

Rops, Félicien, 165

Rossellini, Roberto, 396, 426, 427

Rossino, Alexander B., 325

Roth, Joseph, 11, 61–62, 76, 128, 469

Rundstedt, Gerd von, 323

Ruttmann, Walter, 105, 278–80, 553n45, 553n46

Sagan, Françoise, 452

Sagan, Leontine, 137

Saint Laurent, Yves, 462, 503

Salonom, Erich, 288

Salvador, Henri, 400

Salvation Hunters (film), 196

Sanders-Brahms, Helma, 559n44, 573n12

Sarris, Andrew, 221

Scarlet Empress, The (film), 216–17, 218–21, 223, 228, 238, 240

Schaub, Julius, 341, 411

Schaub, Wilma, 411–12

Scheib, Hans, 297

Schell, Maximilian, 158, 469, 502–3, 570n43

Schiaparelli, Elsa, 374

Schiele, Egon, 242

Schiffer, Claudia, 521

Schiffer, Marcellus, 71–73, 210

Schirach, Baldur von, 285–86

Schlageter, Albert Leo, 279

Schleicher, Kurt von, 277

Schmidt-Rottluff, Karl, 242

Schnauber, Cornelius, 564n48

Schneeberger, Gisela, 280

Schneeberger, Hans:
  and *The Blue Angel,* 112, 162
  and *The Blue Light,* 127, 137, 556n97
  The Exploding Mountain by, 121
  Leni's relationship with, 101, 103–5, 109, 110, 111–12, 113, 124, 127, 420
  and *Lowlands,* 279
  and mountain films, 91, 101, 103–5, 109, 115, 127, 137, 162
  and professional contacts, 112, 114, 121
  as trustee of Leni's possessions, 565n12
  war experiences of, 121

Schneider, Hannes, 103, 119, 121

Schneider, Romy, 432, 462, 473, 503, 506

Schönberg, Arnold, 233, 533n49

Schubert, Franz, 80

Schulberg, B. P., 205, 415

Schulberg, Budd, 415–19

Schultze, Norbert, 561n35

Schwarzenbach, Annemarie, 307

Seidman, Ginette and Paul-Émile, 475

Selznick, Irene, 459

Senso (film), 428

Seven Sinners (film), 349–50

Shanghai Express (film), 197–200, 213, 240, 351

Shaw, George Bernard, *Misalliance,* 246

Shirer, William, 285

Sieber, Anton, 64

Sieber, Ernst, 507

Sieber, Rudolf Emilian "Rudi":
  aging, 469, 492–93
  birth certificate of, 63
  chicken farm of, 410, 455, 475, 478, 479, 480, 485
  citizenship of, 226
  death of, 497–98, 499
  diaries of, 455, 456, 506
  family background of, 64
  film connections of, 64, 67
  film work of, 68, 69, 71, 194, 202, 214, 226, 353
  as grandfather, 396, 401, 476
  health problems of, 455–56, 475, 493
  and Maria (daughter), 202, 214, 366, 382, 493

Marlene in U.S., 171, 201, 208, 211, 212
and Marlene's assets in Germany, 208, 209, 225
and Marlene's lovers, 202, 209, 211, 222, 251, 252, 253, 353, 357, 365, 371, 389, 404, 455, 475, 480
marriage to Marlene, 63–67, 157, 193, 257, 379
messages to and from Marlene, 192, 201, 202–4, 209–10, 211–13, 221–22, 225–27, 253, 359, 360, 380, 382, 388, 395, 471
money from Marlene, 76, 202–3, 209, 215, 222, 371, 409–10, 455–56, 477, 492–93
in Paris, 194, 202, 209, 211, 213–14, 221, 226, 238, 251, 395
separate life of, 67, 75, 157, 194, 410, 488
Tamara as lover of, 75–76, 157, 190–91, 194, 227, 238, 256–57, 353, 409, 410, 455–56
U.S., family visits of, 201–2, 208, 238, 241, 353, 409
Signoret, Simone, 506
Silk Stockings (musical), 408
Simmel, Johannes Mario, 244
Sinatra, Frank, 367, 501
skiing, Arlberg technique, 103
Skoronel, Vera, 25
Slezak, Walter, 261

Sokal, Harry, 28–29
affair with Leni, 29, 101–2, 125–26
departure from Germany, 259
as film producer, 91, 101, 106, 119, 125, 126, 127, 426, 513, 556n97
financial support to Leni from, 28, 29, 82, 90–91, 312
gifts from, 90
war experience of, 121
wealth of, 81
Sol y Sombra (film), 432
Song of Songs (film), 212, 214, 223, 224
Sontag, Susan, "Fascinating Fascism," 446–47, 514, 520
Sorge, Ernst, 142, 149
Sorkin, Marc, 108
S.O.S. Iceberg (film), 138–43, 145, 152, 273
Soupault, Philippe, 278
Southern California, American dream in, 234–35
Soviet Union:
German invasion of, 336
Marlene's stage performances in, 472–73, 479
Spanish Civil War, 331
Sparkuhl, Theodor, 67
Speer, Albert, 305, 520
and International Pavilion, Paris (1937), 307
and Leni, 267–68, 343
and Leni's family, 344, 345, 411
and Leni's films, 267–68, 315, 412

Speer, Albert (*continued*)
  memoirs of, 267–68, 334
  and party congresses, 267,
    282–83
Spender, Stephen, 191, 452
Spiro, Eugen, 119–20
Spitz, René, 130
Spoilers, The (film), 360
Spoliansky, Mischa, 62, 71, 156,
    191, 506
Springer, Axel, 506
Stage Fright (film), 400–401, 402
Stauffenberg, Claus Schenck
    Graf von, 343
Steel Animal, The (film), 290, 291,
    342, 435, 554n67, 559n41
Stern, 442–43, 445
Sternberg, Josef von "Jo," 152–59
  affair with Marlene, 167–68,
    172, 182, 190, 192–93,
    197, 208, 210, 215–18, 227,
    229–30, 241, 355, 460
  art collection of, 241–42
  in Berlin, 211
  and *Blonde Venus,* 204–6, 210
  and *Blue Angel,* 112–13,
    157–59, 162–73
  death of, 481, 498
  and *The Devil Is a Woman,*
    227–28
  as director, 216, 217, 218, 349
  and *Dishonored,* 188–90
  early years of, 195–96
  and end of the affair, 221,
    229–30, 233, 237, 238,
    242–43, 256, 479–80
  fading influence of, 229
  and financial matters, 203

  and Jannings, 152–55,
    163–64
  and Leni, 113–14, 413
  Marlene created by, 159, 165,
    167, 172, 196–97, 216–18,
    227, 229–30, 395, 476, 506
  Marlene discovered by, 503–4,
    541n62
  and Marlene's film roles, 164,
    166–69, 179–87, 197–200,
    212, 215, 217, 227, 230,
    231–32, 350, 406, 503
  memoirs of, 481
  messages to and from Mar-
    lene, 210, 211, 215–16, 218,
    242–43, 405
  and *Morocco,* 179–87, 197
  move to Hollywood, 168–69,
    179, 233
  name change of, 196
  and *The Scarlet Empress,*
    216–17, 218–21, 228
  and *Shanghai Express,* 197–200
  and Sieber, 202, 209, 211,
    222, 455, 480
  socializing with, 238, 256,
    257, 356, 405, 466, 468,
    480–81
  travels of, 242–43
  and war, 257
Sternberg, Riza von, 167, 182,
    192, 200–201, 202
Stern Film, Inc., 434
Stewart, James, 347, 348, 354,
    402
Stolze, SS-Hauptsturmbann-
    führer, 321, 424
Storr, Hermann, 321

Stout, Rex, 491
Strachan, Robin, 566n9
Strasser, Gregor, 277
Stravinsky, Igor, 355
Streicher, Julius, 275
Strength and Momentum (short film), 556n86
Stresemann, Gustav, 160
Sudan, civil war in, 522
Sudermann, Hermann, *Song of Songs,* 211
Sudetenland, Hitler's threats against, 313
Sullavan, Margaret, 248
Swanson, Gloria, 512
Sym, Igo, 70

"Taking a Chance on Love" (song), 364
Taming of the Shrew, The (Shakespeare), 57
Tauber, Richard, 76, 77, 399, 467
Taylor, Elizabeth, 401, 402
Taylor, Maxwel D., 563n26
Technicolor, 238
Tel Aviv, Marlene's stage appearances in, 466–67
Telluride Film Festival, 512–13, 514
Temporary Nationality Act (1945), 565n6
Thale boarding school, 15
Théatre de L'Étoile, Paris, 462
Thielscher, Guido, 61
Thielscher Girls, 61–62
Thomas, Danny, 362, 363, 366
Threepenny Opera, The (film), 86

Three Stars on the Cloak of the Madonna (film), 432
Time, 521
Time of Silence and Darkness (film), 517
Tobis Cinema, 240, 334, 425
Toller, Ernst, 75
Torberg, Friedrich, 455, 475, 485
Touch of Evil (film), 457–58
Toulouse-Lautrec, Henri de, 165
Towns, Forrest, 302
Tracy, Spencer, 469, 470
Tragedy of Love (film), 64, 67, 164
Traut, Walter, 316, 321, 434, 435
Trenker, Luis, 423
    death of, 519
    and *Great Leap,* 103
    and *Holy Mountain,* 91, 95, 96
    and Leni, 89–92, 95, 100–101, 102, 103, 105
    marriage of, 105
    and *Mountain of Destiny,* 89–90, 94–95
    and *The Rebel,* 263, 267
    Struggle in the Mountains by, 120–21
Trezona, Charlie, 371–72, 396–97
Triumph of the Will (film), 92, 275–91
    Behind the Scenes of the Reich Party Rally Film, 280
    cast and crew for, 278–82
    filming of, 279–80, 284, 290, 305
    and Hitler, 277–79, 283–90

Triumph of the Will (film)
  (*continued*)
  honors and awards for,
    289–90, 295–96, 307
  impact of, 288, 447
  Leni as director of, 277–85,
    287, 288–90
  Leni's changing claims about,
    287, 417, 515
  and party rallies, 275–76,
    278–80, 282–87
  postwar distribution of, 435
  premiere of, 288–89
  preparations for, 280–81, 283
  and war-crimes trials, 415–16
Trümpy, Berthe, 25
Tucholsky, Kurt, 67
  Gripsholm Castle, 147
Twardowski, Hans Heinrich
  von, 547n83
Two Neckties (revue), 156, 157
Tynan, Kenneth, 451–52, 471,
  473, 481–82, 491, 499, 507

Ucicky, Gustav, 69, 70
Udet, Ernst:
  and *Avalanche,* 115, 117
  and Fanck, 140, 142
  and Leni, 111–12, 326–27
  and Marlene's Aunt Jolly (Fels-
    ing), 117, 237
  and *Piz Palü,* 106
  and *S.O.S. Iceberg,* 142, 143
  and World War I, 121, 151
Ufa Film Company, 112
  and *The Blue Angel,* 153, 154,
    155
  and *The Great Leap,* 106

and *The Holy Mountain,* 95
and *Manon Lescaut,* 67–68
ownership of, 65
and postwar films, 426
and sound film, 154, 161–62
and *Triumph of the Will,* 277–78
Uhlans (cavalry regiment), 4
Ultraphon studio, 191
United States:
  Anti-Nazi League in, 314
  censorship in, 362
  economy of, 204, 232, 235
  entry into World War II, 336,
    350, 360
  propaganda films, 360–61
  radio in, 569n20
Universal Pictures, 138–40, 145,
  148, 168, 353
USO (United Service Organizations), 362–67, 370–71,
  373–76

Vajda, Ladislav, 106, 130
Valentino, Rudolph, 183
Valetti, Rosa, 75, 157
van Gogh, Vincent, 242
Vanity Fair, 523
Veidt, Conrad, 75, 76, 77
Venice Biennale, 137
Victory of Faith (film), 152, 264,
  270–75, 276, 415, 416–17,
  515
Viertel, Berthold, 130
Viertel, Peter, 425
Viertel, Salka, 233, 425
Vigny, Benno, *Amy Jolly,* 180
Visconti, Luchino, 426, 427,
  428, 545n32

Vogel, Ady, 425
Vollmoeller, Karl, 27–28, 80, 155
von der Hyde, Horst Alexander, 240
von Losch family, 31, 38, 41, 42
Von Mund zu Mund ("From Mouth to Mouth") (musical production), 62

Wachsmann, Franz, 233, 542n71
Wagner, Josef, 572n21
Wagner, Winifred, 150
Waldoff, Claire, 62, 77
Wallace, Peggy Ann, 513
Wallburg, Otto, 72
Wallenberg, Captain, 413
Wandervogel movement, 17
Wanger, Walter, 181, 545n41
Warhol, Andy, 511
Wäscher, Aribert, 330
Wassman, Hans, 62
Wayne, John, 349
Way of All Flesh, The (film), 154
Wedekind, Frank, *Pandora's Box*, 58
Weigel, Helene, 472
Weihmayr, Franz, 267, 268, 280
Weill, Kurt, 532n38
Weimar Republic, 20, 22, 57, 61, 69, 79, 83, 147, 161, 171, 258, 475
Weintraub Syncopators, 163
Weissmuller, Johnny, 315
Welles, Orson, 457, 487, 506
Welsh, Mary, *see* Hemingway, Mary Welsh,
Werfel, Franz, 355

West, Mae, 247
Westfront (film), 121
West Wall (film), 330
White Frenzy, The (film), 119, 124–25, 127, 131, 140
White Hell of Piz Palü, The (film), 106–11, 113, 116, 120, 130, 139, 263
White Water (short film), 556n86
Widmark, Richard, 469
Wieman, Mathias, 115, 127, 335
Wiesinger, Paula, 537n120
Wigman, Mary, 19, 23–26, 80, 529n18
Wilder, Billy, 390–95, 398, 409, 454–55, 498, 504, 510
Wilding, Michael, 401, 506
Wilhelm I, Kaiser, 33
Wilhelm II, Kaiser, 12, 22, 33, 36, 42, 45
Will, Elisabeth, 399, 468–69
    death of, 488
    see also Dietrich, Elisabeth Ottilie
Williams, Tennessee, 452
Windsor, Duchess of, 506
Windt, Herbert, 306, 328
Winterstein, Eduard von, 162–63
With the Berlin SA to Nuremberg (film), 262
Witness for the Prosecution (film), 458–60
Wolfe, Thomas, *You Can't Go Home Again*, 301–2
Woman in the Moon (film), 111
Woman One Longs For, The (film), 77–78, 297

Wonderful, Horrible Life of Leni Riefenstahl, The (film), 127, 519–20

World War I:
  "aristocracy of the trenches," 286
  in Berlin, 11, 22, 34–38, 41–43
  combat pilots, 283–84
  high spirits in, 34–35
  and Marlene, 30, 34–38, 41–43, 48
  and postwar period, 22–24, 45–46, 53–54, 59–60, 76–77, 86–87, 122
  social changes in, 45
  U.S. entry into, 235
  veterans in film industry, 120–22

World War II, 319–27
  Allied victories in, 340–41, 367, 370, 419
  Battle of the Bulge, 375
  in Berlin, 339, 353
  censorship in, 362
  and Hitler, 257, 313, 315, 319–23, 326–27, 331, 334, 335, 336, 367
  and Marlene, 351–52, 361, 362–76, 382–83, 474
  onset of, 257

Pearl Harbor bombing, 336, 350
  postwar period, 380–81
  prelude to, 249–51, 252, 256, 257
  U.S. entry into, 336, 350, 360
  U.S. radio broadcasts in, 372–73
  war films in, 291, 320–25

Wüst, Ida, 72
Wyman, Jane, 400

"You Do Something to Me" (song), 364
"You Go to My Head" (song), 364
Youth Movement, 17–18

Zambona, Jutta, 248, 250, 354, 560n6
Ziegfeld, Florenz, 62
Zielke, Ilse, 342
Zielke, Willy, 290, 291, 341–42, 435, 559n40, 559n41
Zille, Heinrich, 99
Zuckmayer, Carl, 75, 106, 155–56, 289, 354
Zukor, Adolph, 236
Zweig, Stefan, *The World of Yesterday,* 54–55